South University Library
Richmond Campus
2151 Old Brick Road
Glen Allen, Va 23060

D1776716

SEP 2 8 2012

Life and Labor in the New New South

Working in the Americas

UNIVERSITY PRESS OF FLORIDA

Florida A&M University, Tallahassee
Florida Atlantic University, Boca Raton
Florida Gulf Coast University, Ft. Myers
Florida International University, Miami
Florida State University, Tallahassee
New College of Florida, Sarasota
University of Central Florida, Orlando
University of Florida, Gainesville
University of North Florida, Jacksonville
University of South Florida, Tampa
University of West Florida, Pensacola

Life and Labor in the New New South

Edited by Robert H. Zieger

Foreword by Richard Greenwald and Timothy J. Minchin

University Press of Florida
Gainesville · Tallahassee · Tampa · Boca Raton
Pensacola · Orlando · Miami · Jacksonville · Ft. Myers · Sarasota

Copyright 2012 by Robert H. Zieger
All rights reserved
Printed in the United States of America. This book is printed on Glatfelter Natures Book, a paper certified under the standards of the Forestry Stewardship Council (FSC). It is a recycled stock that contains 30 percent post-consumer waste and is acid-free.

17 16 15 14 13 12   6 5 4 3 2 1

Library of Congress Cataloging-in-Publication Data
Life and labor in the new New South / edited by Robert H. Zieger ; foreword by Richard Greenwald and Timothy J. Minchin.
p. cm.— (Working in the Americas)
Includes bibliographical references and index.
ISBN 978-0-8130-3795-0 (alk. paper)
1. Labor—Southern States—History. 2. Labor movement—Southern States—History. 3. Southern States—Social conditions. 4. Southern States—Economic conditions.
I. Zieger, Robert H.
HD8083.S9L54 2012
331.0975—dc23
2011037500

The University Press of Florida is the scholarly publishing agency for the State University System of Florida, comprising Florida A&M University, Florida Atlantic University, Florida Gulf Coast University, Florida International University, Florida State University, New College of Florida, University of Central Florida, University of Florida, University of North Florida, University of South Florida, and University of West Florida.

University Press of Florida
15 Northwest 15th Street
Gainesville, FL 32611-2079
http://www.upf.com

Contents

List of Illustrations / vii
Foreword / ix
Acknowledgments / xi

Introduction: Southern Workers in a Changing Economy / 1
Robert H. Zieger

1. "How Can Greenville Get New Industry to Come Here If We Get the Label of a C.I.O. Town?": Capital Migration and the Limits of Unionism in the Postwar South / 16
   Tami J. Friedman

2. John McClellan, the Teamsters, and Biracial Labor Politics in Arkansas, 1947–1959 / 45
   Michael Pierce

3. "A Lot Closer to What It Ought to Be": Black Women and Public-Sector Employment in Baltimore, 1950–1975 / 76
   Jane Berger

4. Worker-Citizens at the Community Bargaining Table: The St. Louis Teamsters' Community Stewards Program in the 1950s / 101
   Robert Bussel

5. Chicano Labor and Multiracial Politics in Post–World War II Texas: Two Case Studies / 133
   Max Krochmal

6. "Slaves of the State" Revolt: Southern Prison Labor and a Prison-Made Civil Rights Movement, 1945–1980 / 177
   Robert T. Chase

7. Obreros in the Peach State: The Growth of Georgia's Working-Class Mexican Immigrant Communities from a Transnational Perspective / 214
   Michael K. Bess

8. Race and Labor in Memphis since the King Assassination / 236
   Michael K. Honey and David H. Ciscel

9. Shutdowns in the Sun Belt: The Decline of the Textile and Apparel Industry and Deindustrialization in the South / 258
   Timothy J. Minchin

10. A Different Kind of Union: SEIU Healthcare Florida from the Mid-1990s through 2009 / 289
    Bruce Nissen

11. The Movement for Economic Democracy in the South: The Virginia Organizing Project, 1995–2004 / 314
    Michael Dennis

List of Contributors / 347
Index / 349

Illustrations

Figures

1.1. A page from "Welcome to Greenville Mills, Inc." company brochure / 17

2.1. Arkansas governor Sidney McMath / 46

3.1. Protest at headquarters of the Social Security Administration / 77

4.1. A community stewards meeting in St. Louis's second ward / 103

5.1. "Pancho" Medrano at the strike headquarters of the United Farm Workers Organizing Committee, Rio Grande City, Texas / 134

6.1. Inmates picking cotton at the Ramsey Prison, Rosharon, Texas / 178

7.1. Migrant farmworkers harvesting onions in Lyons, Georgia / 215

8.1. Thousands demonstrating in support of Memphis sanitation workers / 237

9.1. Virginians who took to the picket lines to protest federal trade policies in the 1980s / 259

10.1. Workers from Hillcrest nursing home in Hollywood, Florida, picketing for a fair contract / 290

11.1. Living-wage rally, University of Virginia, Charlottesville / 315

Tables

8.1. Distribution of jobs by industry: Memphis MSA 1996 and Shelby County 2007   243

8.2. Occupational participation rates by race in manufacturing in the Memphis MSA: 1966 and 2007   247

8.3. Occupational participation rates by race in medical services and logistics in the Memphis MSA 2007: Black participation rates by occupation   248

Foreword

The publication of *Life and Labor in the New New South* marks a significant milestone for the Working in the Americas series, which was established with the aim of capturing exciting research in labor history and working-class studies. Drawing on the contribution of both established and emerging scholars, the essays presented here provide an excellent illustration of the work that is helping to energize southern labor history and southern historiography more generally. As editor Robert H. Zieger notes in his introduction, these wide-ranging essays "provide a sampling of the dynamic scholarship characterizing this field."

Life and Labor in the New New South builds on earlier volumes of essays that Zieger edited in 1991 and 1997.[1] Traditional topics that featured heavily in those volumes, particularly union organizing efforts and labor's political battles, are also represented well here. At the same time, however, this new volume better reflects the rapid pace of social and economic change in the contemporary South, changes that Zieger summarizes well in his excellent introduction. As a result, this volume gives exclusive focus to the period after 1950, granting much greater emphasis to major recent developments such as the growth of the Latino population, the rise of the service-sector economy, and deindustrialization. Several of the essays also link growing economic inequality in the South to the steady decline of unions, another development that has accelerated lately. As Michael K. Honey and David H. Ciscel observe in their examination of race and labor in post-1968 Memphis, the contemporary South is a "society marked by economic inequality, the opposite of what Dr. King had envisioned."

Overall, the essays are held together by their engagement with the dual themes of "exceptionalism and congruence" as they probe the relationship between the South and the rest of the United States. Many of the essays focus explicitly on the rapidly evolving contemporary workplace, giving us valuable insights into the social transformations taking place across the region. While they aptly illustrate the fast pace of change, however, in places these essays also remind us of earlier developments. The social networks that recent Latino migrants to Georgia have relied on to survive in a hostile environment, for example, are reminiscent of how earlier generations of European immigrants also forged new lives in the industrial cities of the North.

Overall, these broad-ranging and well-researched essays explore the vibrant history of both the post–World War II "New South" and the more recent "New New South," as Leon Fink has termed it.

Richard A. Greenwald
Timothy J. Minchin
Series Editors

Notes

1. Robert H. Zieger, ed., *Organized Labor in the Twentieth-Century South* (Knoxville: University of Tennessee Press, 1991) and *Southern Labor in Transition, 1940–1995* (Knoxville: University of Tennessee Press, 1997).

Acknowledgments

Editing a collection featuring the work of an outstanding group of scholars has been a genuine pleasure. I am deeply appreciative for the enthusiasm, professionalism, and commitment the contributors have exhibited. Tim Minchin merits special mention, combining as he has done his role as contributor with that of series coeditor.

Meredith Babb, director of the University Press of Florida, played a key role in launching and nurturing this project. Heather Thompson also provided support and encouragement in the critical initial stages. The press's readers, Alex Lichtenstein and David Zonderman, offered challenging critiques. The introduction has benefited from thoughtful readings by Bill Link and LeRoy Ashby, while Andrew Battista directed me to important work by political scientists and to key electoral data. Jonathan Lawrence's copy-editing was exemplary. My ongoing association with the women and men of the North Central Florida Central Labor Council and with my colleagues in the United Faculty of Florida has enriched my understanding of southern labor.

As always, Gay Pitman Zieger has combined insightful commentary with nurturing companionship. I'm deeply grateful for her love and support.

Introduction

Southern Workers in a Changing Economy

ROBERT H. ZIEGER

In 1997, I published a collection of essays titled *Southern Labor in Transition, 1940–1995*.[1] Now I wish I had saved that title for this collection. Since 1950 the demographic and employment profile of southern workers has changed dramatically, with the pace of change accelerating since 1990. The first phase of postwar southern economic and social transformation was analyzed in several outstanding books published in the mid-1980s and early 1990s. Thus, James Cobb, Bruce Schulman, Gilbert Fite, Gavin Wright, and Numan Bartley examined the rapid transformation of the South's economy and its employment structure.[2] During the subsequent two decades, the pace of change quickened. Indeed, in terms of patterns of economic activity, employment profile, and demographic composition, the South of 2010 is as different from the South of the 1970s as was the latter from the classic South of C. Vann Woodward, William Faulkner, and W. J. Cash.[3]

The Southern Economy, 1945–1985: Progress and Poverty

In the four decades after the end of World War II, southern workers made significant gains both in absolute terms and in relation to workers in other U.S. regions. Writing in 1984, economist Robert Newman observed that in the 1960s and 1970s "the relative earnings position of male workers in the South improved dramatically."[4] The positive impact of civil rights legislation in expanding job opportunities for African Americans is responsible for some of this gain, especially during the 1970s. In addition, the departure of low-wage agricultural workers, tenants, and small farmers from the agricultural sector and the simultaneous large-scale expansion of employment in manufacturing, urban services, and construction boosted wage profiles. Thus, between 1950 and 1975, both the number of southern farms and the proportion of them worked by tenants fell precipitously.[5]

Meanwhile, from the late 1950s to the late 1970s the South gained more than 1.7 million workers in manufacturing, with an expanding textile sector growing by almost 10 percent and the apparel sector almost doubling. In the same period, southern employment in relatively high-wage electrical and transportation equipment manufacture grew from less than 360,000 to more than 850,000. Reflecting the infrastructural expansion of southern industry and commerce, employment in contract construction more than doubled. In all these relatively high-wage sectors, the southern share of national employment grew dramatically. By 1980, per capita income in the South had climbed to 88 percent of the national average, a sharp improvement over 1940's 60 percent.[6] As early as 1953, journalist William Polk declared of his beloved traditional South, "Now it is becoming urban, industrial, hard-working, comparatively prosperous and relatively standardized." In 1958 C. Vann Woodward wrote of the "Bulldozer Revolution" that was transforming the South.[7]

Despite these positive developments, however, most southern states continued to fall below national norms in key socioeconomic indicators. Newman's assessment of "southern" economic performance, for example, rested in part on a definition of the South that included Maryland and the District of Columbia, both high-wage jurisdictions buoyed by large-scale federal employment.[8] Writing in 1984, historian James Cobb, while duly noting economic advance, stressed the South's ongoing problems. Of all southern states, only Texas stood above the national average for per capita income. More than 40 percent of the nation's poor people lived in the South, which, in his view, "remained the nation's number one economic problem." Indeed, Cobb noted, much of the region's growth was confined to the seaboard periphery; between 1960 and 1980, six southern states, including North Carolina and Georgia, lagged behind growth in terms of the national average for per capita income. Rising standards largely bypassed the Appalachian South. The sharecroppers, tenant farmers, rural laborers, and smallholders driven off the land were rarely able to compete for high-tech jobs or housing in expanding metropolitan areas such as Charlotte, Atlanta, Houston, and other booming cities. Urban poverty and crime rates soared. Despite incessant celebration of the emerging "Sun Belt" as the nation's new engine of progress, the South continued to trail the rest of the country in educational attainment, health care, and income. Southern elites in their "desperate hunger for more growth," trumpeted the region's low wages, low taxes, and anti-unionism in continuing efforts to attract industry.[9]

The New New South

Since the 1980s, change has accelerated. The textile and garment industries, which in 1990 employed more than a million southern workers, shed jobs in massive numbers through the first decade of the new century. Agricultural employment has shrunk to about 1 percent of the region's workers, while mining and other extractive industries register ongoing job losses. Whole new industries such as poultry raising and processing have emerged, employing thousands, many of them recent Central American migrants. Southern employers, among them Walmart and FedEx, have pioneered in developing new employment and industrial relations paradigms, establishing patterns of labor use and management practices widely emulated elsewhere. Urban hubs such as Houston, Charlotte, Atlanta, and northern Virginia have continued to grow as centers of information- and research-based white-collar and professional employment. But, as one Research Triangle think tank notes, the "rise in high-end jobs comes accompanied by a surge in low-skill employment." Workers with good jobs "in offices, labs, schools, hospitals, and a variety of creative pursuits . . . increase the demand for shopping, restaurants, and services," sectors dependent on low-wage workers, most of them black or Hispanic and/or female. Indeed, for all the vaunted modernization of the southern economy, it is low-wage retail and service sector work that has been expanding most dramatically.[10]

To be sure, continuity has accompanied rapid change. Despite recent high-tech progress in the high-tech area, southern states continue to occupy the lower rungs of most socioeconomic ratings. In particular, the interior states of the Old South lag behind both their coastal cousins and non-southern states. In the words of a leading southern economic development consortium, "Poverty remains a characteristic blot upon the face of the South, a region with large swaths of rural destitution."[11]

The frequently invoked trope of "southern exceptionalism" both illuminates and obscures our understanding of the South's trajectory.[12] The region's ongoing lag in per capita income, personal wealth, school leaving rates, and poverty levels carries on its reputation as an area apart. However, other significant indices point toward convergence with other parts of the country. Thus its employment mix over the past generation has become more like national profiles than at any other time in U.S. history. Once marked as a pariah region on account of racist and segregationist public policies and social practices, the South now leads the nation in the numbers of black elected officials. Its public schools, while hardly paragons of biracialism, are less segregated than their northern counterparts. Southern universities and high-profile employers eagerly recruit African Americans. In metropolitan areas at least, shopping malls, restaurants, and other public venues exhibit a degree of racial integration inconceivable fifty years ago. The outflow of African Americans from the region has stopped, and during the 1990s almost 600,000 African Americans relocated to the South, a trend that has continued into the twenty-first century.[13]

Ethnic diversity, if not the fabled melting pot, has also come to the contemporary South, mainly in the form of the large-scale migration of workers from Mexico and Central America. Florida and Texas continue to host the largest concentrations of Hispanic workers, but in the 1990s the Latino population expanded everywhere, especially in Georgia and North Carolina, which together added 300,000 Hispanics. In that decade, the Latino population doubled and more in six southern states. "Even outside of Texas, Latinos are the south's fastest growing population among young adults and children," notes one recent report. In 1980, 2.5 percent of the South's population was Hispanic; by 2005 the figure had climbed to over 8 percent. As historian Leon Fink remarks, the country's "latest immigrant wave . . . speaks with a Spanish accent . . . and nowhere more dramatically than among the formerly ethnically insular southeastern states."[14]

Moreover, recent historical scholarship has blurred the traditionally stark contrast between southern racial injustice and putative northern enlightenment. For example, historians have been laying bare the discriminatory racial policies of the northern-based trade union movement.[15] Political scientist Anthony S. Chen documents the fierce resistance of northern politicians and other citizens to equal employment legislation, while Thomas Sugrue analyzes the tenacity of housing, employment, and educational segregation in northern states and cities.[16] Sugrue, Arnold Hirsch, Robert Self, and other scholars have amply documented the potency of northern racism in postwar housing, employment, and education patterns.[17] Meanwhile, historians such as Robert Korstad, Patricia Sullivan, and Michael Honey have celebrated the existence of genuine interracial activism in the postwar South, while lamenting its all too rapid decline.[18]

Politics

Nowhere is the theme of "southern exceptionalism" more contested than in the political realm. The region's post–World War II transformation into a Republican-leaning two-party system reinforces the theme of sectional convergence. A number of scholarly studies have documented this shift, the most authoritative of them stressing the role of suburban white voters in propelling GOP advance in the South, just as suburban voters undergird the Republican

Party elsewhere.[19] To be sure, through the first six decades of the twentieth century, single-party rule characterized Dixie, making it "exceptional" in an otherwise two-party nation. During and immediately after the heyday of the civil rights movement (ca. 1955–75), racial polarization characterized the southern electorate, with massive defection from the once unchallenged Democratic Party occurring, independent of voters' class standing. Indeed, this abrupt transformation in the behavior of the southern electorate was the mirror image of its previous allegiance to the segregationist Democratic organizations that characterized the pre-1965 South. As the national party came to identify ever more closely with the black freedom struggle, a development culminating in the passage of the Civil Rights and Voting Rights Acts of 1964 and 1965, white southerners turned against the party's presidential candidates. This trend peaked in the election of 1968, when party standard-bearer Hubert Humphrey could win only 12 percent of the votes of white southerners.[20]

Political observers, however, have charted a recovery of Democratic fortunes among white voters through the later 1970s and into the 1990s. Between 1976 and 1996, when southern governors Jimmy Carter (1976, 1980) and Bill Clinton (1992, 1996) headed the ticket, white defection from the Democratic Party began a mild reversal, bringing party identification and voting preference statistics closer to those of other regions. Moreover, while white working-class support for Democratic candidates in the South lagged behind that evident in more heavily unionized northern states, blue-collar workers, white and black, were consistently more Democratic than were middle- and upper-income suburban whites. Throughout the 1980s and 1990s, the South was distinctive in that white voters there, regardless of class position, were more likely to vote Republican and to identify themselves as "conservative" than their counterparts in the Northeast and Midwest and on the West Coast. But in the South, as elsewhere, the white working class showed higher levels of support for Democratic candidates than was exhibited by middle- and upper-income whites.[21]

Polling data and election returns from the 2008 presidential election provide evidence of both exceptionalism and congruence in the contemporary South. On the one hand, in a pattern mirroring the region's uneven economic development, Deep South states such as Alabama, Louisiana, and Mississippi—states that have continued to lag in income, educational attainment, and economic growth—exhibited an apparent return to race-influenced voting behavior. Thus, for example, exit polls in November 2008 showed that Republican presidential candidate John McCain gained the votes of about 87 percent of Alabama's white voters. Similar findings were reported for

Mississippi and Louisiana. (By way of comparison, white voters in Wisconsin gave McCain's opponent, African American Barack Obama, about 54 percent of their votes.)

The white South's emphatic preference for the Republican candidate was apparent in other states, but by substantially smaller margins (75 percent in Georgia; 67 percent in Arkansas). Moreover, several of the Atlantic seaboard southern states, notably Virginia, North Carolina, and Florida, bucked the trend and exhibited voting patterns closer to national norms. Thus, McCain captured only about 60 percent of the white vote in Virginia and did only marginally better in Florida. Meanwhile, in another trend edging some southern states closer to the national experience, Hispanic/Latino voters weighed in heavily in these immigrant-attracting states. Indeed, in Florida Hispanics accounted for a larger portion of the electorate than did African Americans (13 percent to 12 percent), while in Virginia they accounted for about 5 percent. In these states, as in northern and western states with large Hispanic populations, Obama was supported by wide margins (57 percent in Florida, 65 percent in Virginia).[22]

Broadly speaking, then, the emergence of a competitive two-party political process in the South reinforces the theme of southern congruence with national patterns. On the other hand, there is the divergence between the economically more dynamic and culturally diverse seaboard South and the less vibrant and demographically less diverse interior South. Politically, southern exceptionalism, once stark and unambiguous, remains, but now as a counterpoint to a southern electorate that otherwise tracks national patterns.[23]

Deindustrialization

Patterns of deindustrialization reinforce the theme of convergence. Southern states have joined their northern and midwestern counterparts in feeling the impact of plant shutdowns and relocations. For generations, southern boosters, entrepreneurs, and politicians have sought to address the region's chronic impoverishment by luring northern manufacturers to Dixie, stressing the region's low wages, low taxes, and successful union avoidance. Since at least 1990, however, southern promoters have felt the sharp reverse edge of the relocation sword. Globalization, national trade policies, and stock-market-driven corporate strategies have made towns in Tennessee and Alabama as vulnerable as their counterparts in Ohio and Connecticut to the quest for ever cheaper labor and ever laxer labor and environmental standards. In the 1990s, manufacturing employment in the South dropped by 7.7 percent even as total employment grew by almost 5 percent. Between 2001 and 2004 more than 20 percent of the national decline in manufacturing jobs occurred in the South.

During this period, virtually every southern state suffered a double-digit decline in industrial employment. Alabama, among the most industrialized of the southern states, lost one-eighth of its manufacturing jobs in the first two years of the new millennium as even once-depression-proof industries such as paper making, a leading southern employer, slashed payrolls in the face of international competition. Clearly, remarks historian Timothy Minchin, "deindustrialization cannot be dismissed as a regional phenomenon."[24]

The Rise of the Service Sector

Just as in the older industrial regions, the decline in relatively well-paid industrial work in the South has been accompanied by a surge in service and retail work. Since 1990 the proportion of southern workers in services, trade, professional, and managerial employment has expanded remarkably. By some calculations, at least 70 percent of wage earners in the South are now properly classified as service, retail, and white-collar workers. In part, this trend reflects the growing importance of education and research-oriented activity, bringing highly credentialed and well-paying jobs to southern university towns and metropolitan centers. Thus in the period 1998–2003 IRS tax returns from the southern states showed a dramatic increase in the number of taxpayers in the upper brackets. At the same time, however, the vast majority of the service-sector jobs being created were at the lower end of the wage curve. Just as in Michigan and Ohio, downsized and displaced factory workers have found it difficult to find jobs that match the wage and benefit levels of industrial employment. As in the country overall, since the mid-1990s the disparity in income separating affluent workers from low-end wage earners in the South has widened. Those concentrated in the low-wage sectors were hugely disproportionately black, Latino, and/or female. In the words of one authoritative report, "Low-slung brick plants were abandoned, while glassy suburban office buildings [have] sprouted." But the office parks "sprouted" primarily in the expanding metropolitan centers, while the "brick plants" that once produced cloth, garments, and furniture stand idle in the old manufacturing belt. Meanwhile, the enjoyment by affluent professionals, knowledge-based, and managerial workers of the entertainment and cultural amenities of burgeoning metropolitan areas rests critically on the ill-paid work of service, retail, and custodial workers.[25]

Labor Relations

The South's expanding service, retail, health care, and entertainment sector, employing as it does over a million low-wage workers, would seem to be an inviting target for hungry labor organizers. After all, while an electronics plant or a textile mill can be relocated to Honduras or Bangladesh, a shopping mall, restaurant district, or health-care facility must remain *in situ*. Despite some promising initiatives—such as the one described in Bruce Nissen's contribution to this volume—however, organized labor has been unable to exploit the putative potential for growth represented by these low-wage workers.

In part, of course, unions today, as historically has been the case, face southern political and economic elites determined to fight worker organization. Ten of the thirteen states with the lowest proportion of union membership are in the Confederate South; all eleven "Old South" states have constitutional or statutory provisions that bar union security arrangements ("right-to-work" provisions). Even otherwise liberal economic development institutions, while decrying income disparities and lamenting the low wages that keep the black, female, and Hispanic workers who toil in the expanding service sector from sharing adequately in the South's economic progress, ignore organized labor as a potential force for wage enhancement.[26]

Indeed, southerners have pioneered the establishment of what might be called an anti–New Deal labor relations regime. Even during the heyday of organized labor's national strength, the 1950s and 1960s, the unions' inability to organize substantial numbers of workers in the South's signature industry, textiles, set the region apart from the labor relations regime associated with the New Deal order. Many observers perceived the South's exception to the relatively union-friendly postwar order as a throwback to an earlier era of labor-management confrontation. By the 1980s, however, with organized labor's ranks diminishing virtually everywhere, the southern pattern began to seem prototypical rather than exceptional, as once-unionized northern industrial giants slashed payrolls, hired replacements for striking union members, and embarked on systematic campaigns of union diminishment and avoidance.[27] The southern "exception," it turned out, was becoming the new national norm.

Nowhere was the "southernization" of the U.S. labor relations regime more graphically illustrated than in the rise of Walmart. From its beginnings as a handful of general merchandise outlets in rural Arkansas, Sam Walton's empire has grown to mammoth proportions and global significance. Thus, observes historian Bethany Moreton, it is "the American periphery—Wal-Mart Country—[that has] won the economic commanding heights in the second half of the century." Walton and his carefully selected managers virtually reinvented the logistical and organizational aspects of retailing, first in the United States and eventually throughout the world. Using its enormous market power, the firm has imposed a low-wage, cost-cutting production regime on its increasingly dependent suppliers, both at home and abroad. Exuding contempt for the regulatory regime associated with the New Deal order, Walmart has repeatedly ignored or violated minimum wage, fair labor practices, and health and safety regulations. At the same time, it has inculcated a culture of loyalty and even self-sacrifice among store-level managers, who in turn have been highly successful in transmitting these qualities to ordinary employees.[28]

As his business began to expand in the 1950s and 1960s, Walton and his managers saw the men and women of the rural, upcountry South as an ideal source of labor. With low wage expectations and few other employment opportunities, rural and small-town women were particularly important to Walton's success. They not only provided the bulk of the sales force but also brought with them notions of Christian service and a commitment to a particular version of "family values" that Walmart's executives recognized as valuable in the advancement of its corporate agenda.[29]

Walton recruited his managers, most of them men, from nearby state colleges and religious institutions, men (and a few women) eager to join an enterprise that promoted the notion of the firm-as-family and identified closely with the regional version of Christian values. Basing his competitive advantage on obsessive attention to cost-cutting and on minimizing the wage bill, Walton tied incentives for managers to their success in extracting maximum effort from underlings. Store and department managers typically work long hours off the clock to meet corporate-imposed labor-cost goals. Hourly workers—termed "associates"—in many cases illegally put in unpaid overtime hours as a way of helping their managerial team leaders reach the company's exacting standards. All the while, Walton and his corporate associates have used pep sessions, focus groups, one-on-one meetings, and other forms of in-store social control to inculcate disdain for "outside" parties such as union organizers and government inspectors while promoting loyalty to the company and affection for Mr. Sam and his epigones.

When faced with evidences of employee dissent and dissatisfaction, Walmart's managers have not been slow to resort to traditional methods of intimidation. Employing the tactics—and eventually the person—of pioneer union-busting attorney John Tate, a North Carolina native, Sam Walton took full advantage of the expanding scope that an increasingly conservative National Labor Relations Board has permitted to "employer free speech." With NLRB approval, Walmart has perfected the practice of relentless exposure of employees ("associates") to anti-union presentations, in group meetings, in one-on-one settings with supervisors, and in propagandistic videos. Managers endlessly remind associates that in the event of dissatisfaction, their doors were "always open," that alien, outside parties (read: unions) are little more than dues-collection agencies, and that independent organizing would undermine the wholesome family spirit of the Walmart Way.

In important respects, Walmart has reversed the Fordist paradigm of labor use and reward that characterized the U.S. industrial relations system through much of the past century.[30] Walmart has accepted that its often arbitrary scheduling and disciplinary practices lead to a high degree of turnover. Indeed, Walmart managers rely on a quasi-casual approach to labor recruitment and retention as a means of weeding out potential troublemakers and of limiting access to the company's modest profit-sharing and benefits packages. The classic Fordist regime sought to reduce the instability of large-scale turnover by offering relatively high wages. It encouraged consumerism among workers and used corporate welfare and benefit programs to undergird a stable labor force committed to long-range career identification with the company and the industry.[31] In time, the industrial union movement challenged the private Fordist paradigm, but eventually the new unions both reformed and adapted to it, adding through collective bargaining and public social security measures a high degree of security and continuity to blue-collar workers. Walton's way, however, has been the reverse of the high-wage, stable industrial labor regime, "targeting the bottom half of the population for both employees and customers," in Nelson Lichtenstein's apt formulation.[32]

The Walmart paradigm is not limited to labor and employment relations in the new big-box stores. As the Bentonville behemoth has moved aggressively into vending groceries, it has challenged the bland, get-along industrial relations regime that has characterized the supermarket sector, where at its peak in the early 1990s more than half of the workers were represented by unions. Walmart's aggressive cost- and price-cutting has undermined the stable collective-bargaining arrangements that have characterized such chains as Safeway, Kroger, and Albertsons in non-southern states. Along with non-union southern employers such as Publix markets and FedEx, Walmart has developed a new paradigm, relying on temporary, part-time, short-tenure workers whose lack of skills, education, and alternative sources of employment undergird the anti-Fordist workplace order.

This is not to say that Walmart and other southern employers have acted alone. Convergence is evident in workplace regimes even as it is in employment mix and demographic profile. Employers everywhere have targeted the New Deal era's security- and continuity-based system of collective bargaining and labor relations, citing global competitive imperatives. "The most important development in recent southern history," declares historian Michael Dennis, "is the ascent of the marketplace as the regulating institution of public life" and "the unprecedented cultural authority of business." Nowhere is this phenomenon more evident than in a South that has for generations boasted of its workers' limited expectations and willingness to accept low wages. For generations, a combination of "minimal government and a docile working class" lay at the heart of the efforts of Virginia and other southern states to attract industry. Grafting onto the South's low-wage heritage the heightened work norms and job insecurity that has characterized the "quality management movement" that took root toward the end of the twentieth century, employers have cited a newly globalizing labor market as requiring the abandonment of the stable, high-wage Fordist system. As Dennis remarks, by the 1990s "the Virginia creed had become the national creed . . . ; the South was now becoming a frontier for the quality management movement."[33]

The Organization of This Volume

The essays in this collection reflect the overlapping series of changes that has characterized both the post–World War II "New" South and the more recent "New New South."[34] Those by Tami J. Friedman and Michael Pierce bring us back to the 1950s and early 1960s, focusing as they do, respectively, on the post–World War II efforts of Mississippi elites to attract northern-based industry and the Arkansas-specific subtext of the famous McClellan Committee hearings on labor union corruption. Robert Bussel and Jane Berger examine the workplace-related energies released by the successes of the civil rights movements of the 1950s and 1960s in key cities with strong southern ties. Max Krochmal and Robert T. Chase turn attention to Texas, with the former casting new light on the political activism of the "middle generation" of Mexican American workers and the latter linking race, ethnicity, and worker activism in the harsh world of the Lone Star State's work farms and prison complex.

Several of the contributions examine deindustrialization and changing workplace regimes. Timothy J. Minchin explores the human impact of industrial decline in the South's textile heartland in the 1980s and 1990s. Michael K. Honey and David H. Ciscel examine the impact of globalization and new industrial relations paradigms on Memphis's black working class in the decades since the storied sanitation workers' strike of 1968.

Essays by Michael K. Bess, Michael Dennis, and Bruce Nissen focus on demographic change and social activism in the rapidly changing southern workplace of the past two decades. Bess explores the scope and impact of the remarkable growth of Georgia's Latino population, stressing both the push and pull factors that have been transforming the cultural dynamics of Georgia communities. Dennis and Nissen stress the tenacity of worker activism during an era of ethnic change and globalization. Nissen calls attention to new forms of labor organization and to the successful efforts of service workers to form effective unions in the hostile environment of the nation's pioneer "right-to-work" state, Florida. Dennis's essay closes the volume with an account of a vigorous labor-citizen coalition whose efforts to assert the claims of moral economy into public dialogue have had an impact well beyond the borders of Virginia.

Just as "labor" and "the South" have no neat, universally understood definitions, the essays in this collection do not pretend to explore systematically the entire scope of southern labor over the past two generations. They do, it is hoped, provide a sampling of the dynamic scholarship characterizing this field. The product of both established and emerging scholars, the collection examines both traditional topics and those that have risen to importance over the past several decades. Union organizing, industrial relocation, and labor's political activities are well represented. At the same time, themes of the new ethnicity, prison labor, globalization, and the "retail revolution" have a contemporary ring. It is the hope of the editor that readers will agree that *Life and Labor in the New New South* makes an important contribution to the emerging stream of writing on the recent history of southern workers that has helped to invigorate southern historiography more generally.[35]

Notes

1. *Southern Labor in Transition, 1940–1995*, ed. Robert H. Zieger (Knoxville: University of Tennessee Press, 1997). See also *Organized Labor in the Twentieth-Century South*, ed. Robert H. Zieger (Knoxville: University of Tennessee Press, 1991).

2. James C. Cobb, *Industrialization and Southern Society, 1877–1984* (Lexington: University Press of Kentucky, 1984); Bruce J. Schulman, *From Cotton Belt to Sunbelt: Federal Policy, Economic Development, and the Transformation of the South, 1938–1980* (New York: Oxford University Press, 1991); Gilbert C. Fite, *Cotton Fields No More: Southern Agriculture, 1865–1980* (Lexington: University Press of Kentucky, 1984); Gavin Wright, *Old South, New South: Revolutions in the Southern Economy since the Civil War* (New York: Basic Books, 1986); and Numan V. Bartley, *The New South, 1945–1980* (Baton Rouge: Louisiana State University Press, 1995).

3. C. Vann Woodward, *Origins of the New South, 1877–1913* (1951; Baton Rouge: Louisiana State University Press, 1970); Joel Williamson, *William Faulkner and Southern History* (New York: Oxford University Press, 1993), 133–34, 330–31, 362–63; W. J. Cash, *The Mind of the South* (New York: Knopf, 1941).

4. Robert Newman, *Growth in the American South: Changing Regional Employment and Wage Patterns in the 1960s and 1970s* (New York: New York University Press, 1984), 152.

5. See Timothy J. Minchin, *Hiring the Black Worker: The Racial Integration of the Southern Textile Industry, 1960–1980* (Chapel Hill: University of North Carolina Press, 1999); and Timothy J. Minchin, *The Color of Work: The Struggle for Civil Rights in the Southern Paper Industry, 1945–1980* (Chapel Hill: University of North Carolina Press, 2001); Newman, *Growth in the American South*, 5–6, 143–60; Fite, *Cotton Fields No More*, 180–209.

6. Schulman, *From Cotton Belt to Sunbelt*, 173.

7. Polk quoted in Bartley, *New South*, 105; Woodward in Matthew D. Lassiter and Joseph

Crespino, "Introduction: The End of Southern History," in *The Myth of Southern Exceptionalism*, ed. Lassiter and Crespino (New York: Oxford University Press, 2010), 13.

8. Newman, *Growth in the American South*, 15.

9. Cobb, *Industrialization and Southern Society*, 137–41.

10. MDC, *The State of the South, 2004: Fifty Years after Brown v. Board of Education* (Chapel Hill: MDC, Inc., 2004), 8–9, at http://www.mdcinc.org/docs/sos_04.pdf; Todd Lewan, "Has Economic Twilight Come to the Sun Belt?" May 31, 2009, at msnbc.msn.com/id/31016073.

11. MDC, *The State of the South, 2007: Philanthropy as the South's "Passing Gear"* (Chapel Hill: MDC, Inc., 2007), 16–18, at http://www.mdcinc.org/contact/form.aspx.

12. Lassiter and Crespino, "Introduction," 3–22.

13. Gavin Wright, "Persisting Dixie: The South as an Economic Region," in *The American South in the Twentieth Century*, ed. Craig S. Pascoe, Karen Trahan Leathem, and Andy Ambrose (Athens: University of Georgia Press, 2005), 88–90.

14. MDC, *The State of the South, 2004*, 13–14; MDC, *The State of the South, 2007*, 14; John D. Studstill and Laura Nieto-Studstill, "Hospitality and Hostility: Latin Immigrants in Southern Georgia," in *Latino Workers in the Contemporary South*, ed. Arthur D. Murphy, Colleen Blanchard, and Jennifer A. Hill (Athens: University of Georgia Press, 2001), 68–81; Leon Fink, *The Maya of Morganton: Work and Community in the Nuevo New South* (Chapel Hill: University of North Carolina Press, 2003), 10.

15. See Robert H. Zieger, *For Jobs and Freedom: Race and Labor in America since 1865* (Lexington: University Press of Kentucky, 2007), 164–72, 223–28; Paul D. Moreno, *Black Americans and Organized Labor: A New History* (Baton Rouge: Louisiana State University Press, 2006), 220–88.

16. Anthony S. Chen, *The Fifth Freedom: Jobs, Politics, and Civil Rights in the United States, 1941–1972* (Princeton: Princeton University Press, 2009); Thomas J. Sugrue, *Sweet Land of Liberty: The Forgotten Struggle for Civil Rights in the North* (New York: Random House, 2008). See also Matthew D. Lassiter, "De Jure/De Facto Segregation: The Long Shadow of a National Myth," in Lassiter and Crespino, *Myth of Southern Exceptionalism*, 3–48.

17. Thomas J. Sugrue, *The Origins of the Urban Crisis: Race and Inequality in Postwar Detroit* (Princeton: Princeton University Press, 1996); Arnold R. Hirsch, *Making the Second Ghetto: Race and Housing in Chicago, 1940–1960* (Cambridge: Cambridge University Press, 1983); Robert O. Self, *American Babylon: Race and the Struggle for Postwar Oakland* (Princeton: Princeton University Press, 2003).

18. Robert Rodgers Korstad, *Civil Rights Unionism: Tobacco Workers and the Struggle for Democracy in the Mid-Twentieth Century South* (Chapel Hill: University of North Carolina Press, 2003); Patricia Sullivan, *Days of Hope: Race and Democracy in the New Deal Era* (Chapel Hill: University of North Carolina Press, 1996); Michael K. Honey, *Southern Labor and Black Civil Rights: Organizing Memphis Workers* (Urbana: University of Illinois Press, 1993).

19. Important recent studies include Joseph Crespino, *In Search of Another Country: Mississippi and the Conservative Counterrevolution* (Princeton: Princeton University Press, 2007); Matthew D. Lassiter, *The Silent Majority: Suburban Politics in the Sunbelt South* (Princeton: Princeton University Press, 2006); Joseph E. Lowndes, *From the New Deal to*

the New Right: Race and the Southern Origins of Modern Conservatism (New Haven: Yale University Press, 2008); Byron E. Shafer and Richard Johnston, *The End of Southern Exceptionalism: Class, Race, and Partisan Change in the Postwar South* (Cambridge: Harvard University Press, 2009); Kevin M. Kruse, *White Flight: Atlanta and the Making of Modern Conservatism* (Princeton: Princeton University Press, 2005); Earl Black and Merle Black, *The Rise of Southern Republicans* (Cambridge: Harvard/Belknap, 2002); Richard K. Scher, *Politics in the New South: Republicanism, Race and Leadership in the Twentieth Century*, 2nd ed. (Armonk, N.Y.: M. E. Sharpe, 1997); Earl Black and Merle Black, *Politics and Society in the South* (Cambridge: Harvard University Press, 1987); and Jeffrey M. Stonecash, *Class and Party in American Politics* (Boulder: Westview Press, 2000). Alan Draper's *Conflict of Interests: Organized Labor and the Civil Rights Movement in the South, 1954–1968* (Ithaca: ILR Press, 1994) is a cogent account of organized labor's efforts to bridge the racial divide in the 1960s and 1970s. See especially 109–21.

20. Jason Sokol, *There Goes My Everything: White Southerners in the Age of Civil Rights, 1945–1975* (New York: Knopf, 2006), 275.

21. Larry M. Bartels, *Unequal Democracy: The Political Economy of the New Gilded Age* (Princeton: Princeton University Press [Russell Sage Foundation], 2008), 76–78.

22. Exit poll data found at http://www.cnn.com/ELECTION/2008/results/polls/#ALP00p1.

23. See Shafer and Johnston, *End of Southern Exceptionalism*, 128–33, for a discussion of what the authors term the "peripheral" and the "deep" South.

24. MDC, *The State of the South, 2004*, http://www.mdcinc.org/docs/sos_04.pdf; MDC, *The State of the South, 2007*; Timothy J. Minchin, "'Just Like a Death': The Closing of the International Paper Company Mill in Mobile, Alabama, and the Deindustrialization of the South, 2000–2005," *Alabama Review* 59, no. 1 (2006): 46–48, 75. See also Peter Coclanis, "Down Highway 52: Globalization, Higher Education, and the Economic Future of the American South," *Journal of the Historical Society* 5 (Fall 2005): 333–34, 336–39; and Jefferson Cowie, *Capital Moves: RCA's Seventy-Year Quest for Cheap Labor* (Ithaca: Cornell University Press, 1999).

25. MDC, *State of the South, 2007*, 11, 15–16.

26. National Right to Work Legal Defense Foundation, Inc., "Employees in Right to Work States," n.d., at http://www.nrtw.org/d/rtwempl.htm; "Union Members by State," at http://www.aflcio/joinaunon/why/uniondifference/uniondiffl6.cfm (From U.S. Bureau of Labor Statistics, *Union Members in 2008*, January 28, 2009). The informative reports of MDC, Inc., a North Carolina economic research consortium, which express enlightened concern about the widening disparities in income and the troubled plight of black, Latino, and female workers in the service sector, for example, completely ignore union membership as a possible force for narrowing wage differentials (see the biannual reports at http://www.mdcinc.org/knowledge).

27. Robert H. Zieger and Gilbert Gall, *American Workers, American Unions*, 3rd ed. (Baltimore: Johns Hopkins University Press, 2002), 257–58; Marc Linder, *Wars of Attrition: Vietnam, the Business Roundtable, and the Decline of Construction Unions* (Iowa City, Iowa: Fanpihua Press, 1999), 182–230; Robert H. Zieger, "Textile Workers and Historians," in Zieger, *Organized Labor in the Twentieth-Century South*, 35, 52–53.

28. This and the next four paragraphs are based on Nelson Lichtenstein, *The Retail Revolution: How Wal-Mart Created a Brave New World of Business* (New York: Metropolitan

Books/Henry Holt, 2009), especially 53–148. See also Bethany Moreton, *To Serve God and Wal-Mart: The Making of Christian Free Enterprise* (Cambridge: Harvard University Press, 2009); Shane Hamilton, *Trucking Country: The Road to America's Wal-Mart Economy* (Princeton: Princeton University Press, 2008); and Thomas Jessen Adams, "Walmart and the Making of 'Postindustrial Society,'" *Labor: Studies in Working-Class History of the Americas* 8 no. 1 (2011): 117–25. The quote is from Moreton, *To Serve God and Wal-Mart*, 8.

29. Moreton, *To Serve God and Wal-Mart*, is a brilliant account of this phenomenon. See especially 100–124.

30. For a succinct discussion of Fordism as a concept and as a historical phenomenon, see Fred Thompson, "Fordism, Post-Fordism and the Flexible System of Production," http://www.willamette.edu/~fthompso/MgmtCon/Fordism_&_Postfordism.html.

31. On the five-dollar day and the quest for labor stability, see Stephen Meyer III, *The Five Dollar Day: Labor Management and Social Control in the Ford Motor Company, 1908–1921* (Albany: State University of New York Press, 1981), 67–94; and Richard J. Jensen, "The Causes and Cures of Unemployment in the Great Depression," *Journal of Interdisciplinary History* 19, no. 4 (1989): 553–83.

32. Lichtenstein, *Retail Revolution*, 62.

33. Michael Dennis, *The New Economy and the Modern South* (Gainesville: University Press of Florida, 2009), 19–47.

34. I borrow this phrase from the subtitle of Leon Fink's splendid book on North Carolina poultry-processing workers, *The Maya of Morganton*. As to the problem of defining "the South," the sources cited in this introduction have used a variety of definitional strategies. Economist Robert Newman, for example, relies on U.S. Census Bureau regional groupings in developing his analysis of "southern" employment and wage patterns. Thus, the "South Atlantic" category includes Delaware, Maryland, and the District of Columbia, while Missouri is excluded from both the "East South Central" and "West South Central" categories (Oklahoma is included in the latter). Some authorities exclude Texas and Florida as being "atypical" of "the South," while others confine their analysis to either the former Confederate states or states that practiced slavery at the time of the outbreak of the Civil War. MDC, a prestigious North Carolina NGO specializing in economic and social policy issues, employs variations of several of these categorization schemes in presenting its useful and revealing statistical analyses of recent developments (see http://www.mdcinc.org/about and the links to biannual reports). In this essay I have used a broad understanding of the meaning of "the South" while attempting to call attention to subregional distinctions. In recruiting and selecting the contributions to this volume I have also used an expansive view of what constitutes "the South," which regards both St. Louis and Baltimore as being "southern" for the purposes of this collection.

35. See Timothy J. Minchin, *Fighting against the Odds: A History of Southern Labor since World War II* (Gainesville: University Press of Florida, 2005); Timothy J. Minchin, *"Don't Sleep with Stevens": The J. P. Stevens Campaign and the Struggle to Organize the South, 1963–1980* (Gainesville: University Press of Florida, 2005); and Robert Cassanello and Colin J. Davis, eds., *Migration and the Transformation of the Southern Workplace since 1945* (Gainesville: University Press of Florida, 2009). The notes to this introduction, along with the endnotes accompanying each of this volume's essays, constitute an up-to-date bibliography of recent southern labor history scholarship.

1

"How Can Greenville Get New Industry to Come Here If We Get the Label of a C.I.O. Town?"

Capital Migration and the Limits of Unionism in the Postwar South

TAMI J. FRIEDMAN

For generations, scholars and labor organizers have grappled with the question, "Why has it been so difficult to organize the South?" One way to understand the limits of southern unionism, particularly since World War II, is to explore the impact of industry relocation from the North to the South. From the mid-1940s through at least the late 1970s, northern manufacturers often turned southward in hopes of escaping and perhaps eliminating labor's power. Their actions, coupled with those of southerners who—despite divergent views about the desirability of unionization—agreed on the need for industrial development in their region, created conditions that helped keep unions at bay.[1]

Efforts to explain the relative weakness of southern unions have often relied on the notion of "southern distinctiveness." Early observers, focusing on the southern textile industry before World War II, argued that cultural characteristics such as paternalism, individualism, and independence produced particularly intransigent mill owners and a particularly docile and degraded labor force. More recent scholarship has emphasized southern workers' militant activism in the prewar period as well as how factors such as anti-communism and racial division, among others, undermined postwar southern campaigns. These later accounts have not significantly altered the prevailing picture of the South as uniquely resistant to unionism, however. Nor has this portrayal been revised by the astute observation by some scholars that southern-style anti-unionism has become the national norm. Thus the region remains, in the

Employees take a break from work in one of several smoking areas set up throughout the plant.

Greenville Mills baseball team poses on plant recreation field before playing.

Plant nurse is available each day in well-equipped and efficient First Aid room.

Figure 1.1. A page from "Welcome to Greenville Mills, Inc.," a company brochure for plant visitors touting benefits available to its (non-union) employees. The brochure was probably prepared for "Greenville Mills Day," an open house held on September 30, 1954, that drew thousands of area residents. (Wisconsin Historical Society, Textile Workers Union of America Records, image number WHi-74224.)

Employee picnics provide fun and fellowship for employees and their families.

eyes of many, an exceptional place with an exceptional history of hostility to the union cause.[2]

The study of capital migration helps clarify the ways in which presumably southern responses to unionism reflected particular historical trends. The postwar shift in capital investment from northern to southern communities was a process in which many southerners—including business and political leaders, ordinary workers, and unions themselves—took part. This process decisively shaped the evolution of the southern economy for much of the twentieth century and, especially in the postwar era, was pivotal in solidifying the South's reputation as decidedly anti-union (if not always non-union) terrain. Importantly, capital flight reflected the shared agenda of southern pro-business boosters and non-southern historical actors, particularly industrialists, whose joint efforts to preserve the South's favorable (read: union-free) business climate turned a seemingly southern story into a national tale.

Capital flight, of course, was not the sole catalyst for southern anti-unionism. Indigenous southern industry existed prior to the infusion of northern investment dollars, as the histories of coal mining, iron and steel production, cotton and tobacco processing, lumbering, and textiles in the region attest. Employers' opposition to and workers' lack of interest in unions long predated northerners' arrival. At the same time, in certain sectors of the southern economy—including coal (in West Virginia), steel (in Alabama), and longshoring (along the Gulf Coast and in Mississippi River ports)—unions achieved significant gains. Nor was southward migration new in the postwar period: the first northern textile manufacturers to establish southern plants did so in the 1810s, while the exodus of New England textiles to the South, taking place nearly a century later, was well under way long before World War II. Finally, the movement of industry was not a uniquely southern phenomenon, for some northeastern manufacturers ventured westward as well.[3]

The postwar period, however, offers rich opportunities to consider how capital migration helped limit the prospects for unionism in the South. By the late 1940s and early 1950s, about one-third of U.S. nonagricultural workers belonged to unions. Anxious to curb labor's growing influence, U.S. businessmen launched a nationwide offensive to reestablish their authority in both the workplace and society at large. Union power was not evenly distributed across the country, however; while organized labor had made substantial gains in northern industrial strongholds, it remained far weaker in the South. Not surprisingly, some employers chose to flee from one region to the other in hopes of escaping labor troubles and reasserting corporate control. While labor was not the only factor stimulating migration—manufacturers also cited access to markets and natural resources, for example—it played a major role in propelling industry toward the South.[4]

In scouting out new locations, northern industrialists made it clear that labor was a central concern. Probably around 1950, Harold C. Zulauf, vice-president of operations and industrial relations at Alexander Smith, Inc., a ninety-five-year-old carpet firm based in Yonkers, New York, visited Puerto Rico on several occasions to assess its potential as an industrial site. Although delighted with the island's surplus of dedicated, low-wage workers (male workers were "a dime a dozen," he noted, while the women were "taught by the nuns"), he argued that the powerful National Maritime Union would interfere with the shipment of goods "unless you give way to their demands." Smith executives subsequently contracted with the Fantus Factory Locating Service to investigate possible sites of operation. In one report to company officials, Fantus staff urged the firm to steer clear of Chilhowie, a small Virginia community, in large part because more desirable employers—including a hosiery mill and a chemical plant—were operating nearby. Smith would have difficulty attracting an adequate workforce, both because anticipated plant expansions at existing facilities promised to place "future strain" on the labor supply and because workers already "familiar with clean work and high wage scales" would be reluctant to "have to take 'second best.'" Union organizers—including those associated with the United Mine Workers of America—were active in the area as well.[5]

Other communities appeared far more likely to offer the cheap, pliant, and plentiful labor for which northern employers yearned. In contrast with their assessment of Chilhowie, Fantus personnel sang the praises of Greenville, Mississippi, located in the heart of the Yazoo-Mississippi Delta. Wages in the Greenville area were so low and unemployment so high—as the result of mechanization of cotton production and federal restrictions on the amount of acreage planted—that Smith would have no trouble attracting employees. According to C. L. Morris, manager of the local Mississippi State Employment Service office, "an average wage of $1.10 per hour would be extremely generous for men and women." In calculating potential labor cost savings, Fantus staff compared this rate to an average hourly wage of $1.50 at the Yonkers mill. Noting that Mississippi was "one of the few non-union strongholds" in the nation, Fantus staff advised Smith official William F. C. "Bill" Ewing, "There is every indication that with proper management you could operate a non-union plant."[6]

Northerners' efforts to relocate production received ample assistance from southerners themselves. During the 1930s, New Deal agricultural policies enabled southern planters to reduce their reliance on farm labor. During World War II, moreover, more than 1.6 million southerners quit the region in search of superior industrial opportunities elsewhere. In response to the sharp drop in the agricultural workforce—as well as growing leverage among those who remained in the South—planters turned increasingly to mechanization and diversification, further shrinking demand for an exploitable (and usually black) farm labor supply. In the postwar period, then, southern leaders were faced with the dire prospect of long-term depopulation and economic decline. By the late 1940s they were avidly pursuing northern investment in hopes that increased industrialization would reverse these trends. At the same time, white southerners came under pressure from African American activists, the national Democratic Party, and some federal politicians to abandon racial segregation and discrimination in favor of civil rights. As they scrambled to defend Jim Crow practices, white southerners resurrected long-standing complaints that their region constituted an internal U.S. colony supplying raw materials and labor to the industrialized North. Some hoped that, by achieving greater economic sovereignty in the region, they could stave off federal control. That they pursued southern independence by appealing to northern investors made clear that their perceived enemy was federal authorities, not "the North."[7]

As with capital migration, the impulse to industrialize the South with Yankee dollars was particularly pronounced in the postwar years. Industrial development was not unique to that period, as the "New South" movement of the late nineteenth century—which helped launch a distinctly southern textile industry—makes clear. Moreover, numerous southern businesses were already northern-owned. Northern timber and mining interests acquired millions of acres of southern territory in the late nineteenth century (lending credence to claims about the South's colonial status), while in 1907 U.S. Steel bought up one of the region's leading iron and steel firms, the Birmingham-based Tennessee Coal and Iron Company. The first major southern initiative to promote industrialization through public subsidies was a product of the prewar era; in the mid-1930s, the state of Mississippi launched Balance Agriculture with Industry (BAWI), a program that enabled communities to issue industrial revenue bonds to help northern employers build southern plants. While the program enjoyed only limited success during the Great Depression, it proved a useful model for postwar economic planning; Mississippians revived BAWI a decade after its inception, and other southern states adopted similar plans.[8]

Already adept at resisting organized labor's incursions, southern boosters placed anti-unionism at the center of their postwar industrialization campaigns. While offering a variety of perquisites, such as tax abatements and low utility rates, they were particularly anxious to meet northern employers' labor needs. Mississippi's BAWI program required participating communities to guarantee the presence of a labor surplus: at least one and one-half available employees within a twenty-five-mile radius of the factory for each operative position that a new industry promised to create. To facilitate industrial promotion and recruitment, the state established the Agricultural and Industrial (A&I) Board when renewing BAWI in 1944. Advertising in such national publications as the *New York Times* and the *Wall Street Journal*, the board promised industrialists "intelligent, skilled, adaptable labor" and touted the state's population of "friendly, native-born citizens [who] believe as their forefathers believed, that an honest day's pay deserves an honest day's work."[9]

At the community level, local pro-industry advocates hawked labor's virtues as well. In the summer of 1949, Greenville, Mississippi, Chamber of Commerce leader N. E. Wingate, hoping to lure the Selby Shoe Company from Portsmouth, Ohio, told company president Gordon Carson not only that Greenville had "no labor trouble" but also that area citizens were "of strictly the conservative view, and 100% for the free enterprise system and the American way of life." A year later, when meeting with Fantus representatives who were surveying Greenville on behalf of Alexander Smith, the Chicago Mill and Lumber Company's plant manager, a Mr. McCormick, stressed that his firm's 450 employees, most of them male, earned a mere $0.93 per hour on average, which included ten hours of overtime per week. Despite belonging to a union—segregated locals of the United Brotherhood of Carpenters and Joiners—the workers received "no pension, insurance, accident, shift differential or any other fringe benefits" except for three paid holidays and "the usual vacation plan." Sam Smith, general manager of the U.S. Gypsum Company's Greenville facility, reported to Fantus that his 450 male workers ("50% colored") engaged in heavy labor that entailed "considerable hazard" for a base hourly rate of $0.965 and had no history of work stoppages or strikes.[10]

The looming prospect of unionization, however, threatened to undermine the status quo. Textile unions in particular had already been hard hit by southward migration in the prewar period, and labor leaders in a host of industries understood that the continued movement of factories to low-wage regions in the postwar era would put their members' wartime gains at risk. As a result, after the war the nation's leading labor federations launched major southern organizing campaigns. In the spring of 1946, Philip Murray, president of the Congress of Industrial Organizations (CIO), announced his organization's plan to unionize at least a million southern workers by 1947. Shortly thereafter, American Federation of Labor (AFL) chief William Green declared his group's intention to sign up a million southern employees as well. The CIO's drive, soon dubbed Operation Dixie, started out with 250 organizers and about $1 million committed by both the CIO and member unions. The principal aim of both campaigns, observers noted, was to narrow or eliminate the North-South wage differential, thus improving southern living standards while also helping unionized workers in the North and West to "resist wage-cutting and open-shop movements" in future periods of economic strain. By targeting such industries as textiles, rubber, furniture, and lumber, unionists hoped to reduce interregional differentials ranging from 15 to 40 percent.[11]

The failure of these efforts is a story often told. Within six months Operation Dixie was faltering badly; the CIO had already spent close to $800,000, and the drive was reeling from substantial budget and staffing cuts. In 1948 and 1949 the campaign dropped four states from its southern roster: Alabama, Louisiana, Mississippi, and Texas. As historian Barbara S. Griffith has observed, although it officially persisted until 1953, "as a large-scale organizing campaign Operation Dixie died in December 1946." Similarly, the AFL drive ended within a year. While the AFL effort has received little scholarly attention, students of Operation Dixie have highlighted a range of factors—including anti-communism, racial conflict, employers' intransigence, and unworkable organizing strategies—to explain the CIO campaign's demise. What remains unclear, however, is why the obstacles to labor organizing seemed so powerful in the southern context. Were southern employers more resistant to unions than were their northern counterparts? Did anti-unionism carry more weight among workers in the South than elsewhere? And if indeed anti-union feeling was particularly southern, why was this so?[12]

These questions can be addressed, in part, by considering how the impulse to promote capital migration from the North to the South intersected with southern union campaigns. In 1939 only 6.5 percent of nonagricultural workers in Mississippi belonged to unions; of thirteen thousand union members, only one hundred were members of the CIO. Impressively, between mid-1946 and early 1949 the CIO won fifty-seven out of eighty-two union elections held in the state. (In another eight cases, the CIO withdrew its petitions to hold elections.) The thirst for new industry, however, intensified boosters' desire to prevent unionism from taking hold. Early in Operation Dixie, for example, CIO organizers targeted Grenada Industries, an Indianapolis-based hosiery mill established in 1937 in Grenada, Mississippi, under the auspices of BAWI. Business and civic leaders, aided by the local media, responded with a vicious anti-union campaign. A front-page editorial in the local newspaper, the *Daily Sentinel-Star*, pitted potentially pro-union workers—whom it called "ingrates" and accused of "picking peas, or cockleburrs, or both, on a two bit basis" before the plant opened—against area citizens and taxpayers who had supported the BAWI bond issue precisely for the benefit of those coming from "the more drudging work of surrounding farms." A union election amounted to "taxation without representation," the editors argued, since those who had "agreed to tax themselves and mortgaged their homes and other real estate to launch an industry" were ineligible to vote.[13]

Concerns about Grenada's ability to lure northern business helped fuel the anti-union assault. Labor agitation threatened to diminish the gains brought by new industry, since the BAWI agreement with Grenada Industries not only stipulated that the city "so far as possible prevent any interference from outside sources which may cause or result in labor disputes or trouble" but also promised that, "during the period of any labor disturbance caused by outside interference," the firm would be released from its payroll guarantee. Union activity might also undermine the community's future economic progress; the *Grenada County Weekly* editorialized, "None of the prospective industries dickering with Grenada will come here at all if Grenada is dominated by the CIO." The hosiery workers rejected the union by a vote of 297 to 122. Thus boosters successfully invoked the quest for manufacturing in their effort to crush union drives. That the CIO later abandoned Mississippi as a site of postwar organizing represented a triumph not only for Mississippi's champions of industry but also for northern manufacturers considering a move to the Magnolia State.[14]

Alongside efforts to quash union activity in the workplace, southerners raised the banner of industry recruitment in order to block labor's progress in the political realm. The Taft-Hartley Act, passed by Congress in 1947, allowed individual states to adopt so-called right-to-work laws, which would make illegal any labor agreement that contained a "union shop" clause requiring employees to join a union as a condition of work. Southerners were pivotal in ensuring the act's passage; more than 80 percent of southern Democrats in Congress supported the measure, while 90 percent of those in the House and over 77 percent of those in the Senate voted to override President Harry S. Truman's veto of the bill. While a few states had already authorized right-to-work restrictions—voters in Arkansas and Florida approved right-to-work amendments to their state constitutions in 1944—Taft-Hartley infused new energy into campaigns to impede unionism in the South and West. In 1947 alone, six southern states (and five western and midwestern states) adopted right-to-work laws.[15]

In seeking to exploit Taft-Hartley's advantages, southern boosters were driven in part by the desire to attract and retain northern firms. In the late 1940s and early 1950s, Mississippi's powerful agricultural leaders—long fearful of union influence among farm laborers—were among their state's most avid promoters of right-to-work as well as bans on mass picketing, secondary boycotts, and jurisdictional strikes. Testifying on behalf of several anti-union measures in 1950, C. D. "Charlie" Maddox, a leader of the Mississippi Farm Bureau Federation, warned, "We are on the threshold of unprecedented and almost unlimited industrial opportunity.... The industrial eyes of the nation are upon the South, Mississippi in particular." Thus the state needed "laws to control improper use of union strength," he argued, "in order that public welfare may best be served." Dairyman W. A. Evans added that the bills would serve as a "'posted' sign to agitators . . . who would break up relationships between the small industries that we have scoured the country to bring in to Mississippi." Former Mississippi Federation of Labor president and national AFL representative Holt E. Ross countered that the state's own promotional materials (produced by the A&I Board) touted Mississippi's "complete harmony between labor and industry"; there was no reason, he insisted, to impose constraints on "friendly, native born Americans" who, according to boosters themselves, were already "meeting industry more than half way." The early efforts to pass right-to-work floundered, probably because Mississippi lawmakers—perhaps influenced by the state's fledgling labor movement—saw such measures as unnecessary in their largely agricultural state.[16]

By 1954, however, Mississippians' heightened commitment to industrial development and growing success in attracting manufacturing had shifted the terms of debate. The A&I Board's budget rose from $200,000 in 1946–48 to about $350,000 in 1948–50, and the allocation reached $450,000 in 1952–54. In part as a result of expanded promotional efforts, the number of new BAWI-financed factories in Mississippi increased from forty-six in 1950 to ninety-three in 1954. (Many other firms were established in the state during that period with non-BAWI forms of support.) Starting in late 1953, boosters revived calls for right-to-work legislation on the grounds that it would make their state more competitive in the quest for industry—a claim perhaps bolstered by evidence that, despite its industrial successes, Mississippi was lagging behind other southern states.[17]

This time organized labor tried to challenge boosters' premises more directly, but to no avail. The CIO-affiliated Mississippi State Industrial Union Council (IUC) agreed that "the thought back of the BAWI program is excellent" but asked, "What price new industry?" If northern manufacturers were lured by tax breaks and low-cost labor, and if workers were prevented from organizing unions to increase payrolls, the IUC argued, then "we are assuring ourselves that only minimum wages will be paid." "If we in Mississippi are going to permit greedy northern industrialists to stampede us into adopting laws to 'curb' labor," the council concluded, "we can forget our BAWI program and abandon all hope of bringing any degree of prosperity to our fair state." Perhaps because unionists deployed the rhetoric of resistance to Yankee exploitation, the point did not go unheeded; fifty-six legislators supported an amendment that would have required any new employer to pay Mississippians the same wages earned by its employees in other states. The amendment failed, however, and right-to-work passed by a vote of 92–42 in the House and 34–11 in the Senate. Its passage, in turn, gave fresh ammunition to local booster organizations such as the Greenville Chamber of Commerce, which highlighted the new policy in promotional materials designed to lure new firms.[18]

Unionists, increasingly constrained by hostile action at the local and state levels, appealed to the federal government for aid. During the Korean War (1950–53) the federal government offered manufacturers a host of financial advantages—such as loan guarantees and accelerated tax write-offs—if they expanded productive capacity or established new factories in order to produce military goods. At the same time, federal authorities held the power to determine whether to allocate scarce materials, such as steel, to build new plants. By blocking manufacturers' access to federal benefits, union leaders hoped to curtail capital flight. In late 1951, for example, Textile Workers Union of America (TWUA) official John W. Edelman alerted U.S. senator Herbert Lehman (Democrat–New York) that Utica and Mohawk Cotton Mills, Inc., was moving from Utica, New York, to South Carolina, throwing more than eight hundred people out of work. Aside from the "purely humanitarian aspects of this removal," Edelman noted that new plants required "quantities of scarce materials and skilled construction labor." "It is dangerously wasteful and economically stupid," he went on, to build new textile mills when existing facilities and trained workers were already on hand. In another instance involving the closure of a Nashua, New Hampshire, textile mill by Textron, Inc., a firm notorious for shifting northern-based production southward in the postwar period, state TWUA director Michael Botelho stressed the efficiency of northern workers and argued that they earned more than their southern counterparts "because of their greater skill." In these and other cases, unionists urged federal officials to deny certificates of necessity to migratory firms.[19]

In response to these actions, northern employers and southern boosters adopted a strategy of mutual defense. Kenneth Cook, president of the Rhode Island Textile Association, suggested that heading southward was a logical response to a lack of cooperation by northern workers. While agreeing that tax and utility costs played some role in relocation, he argued that "the real issue is that Southern mills can manufacture goods at a labor cost of 40 cents to 47 cents per hour less than we can." Lester Martin, president of the Whittenton Manufacturing Company, deemphasized wages and stressed instead the importance of "efficiency and workloads." Martin, who operated three southern factories, reported that his Taunton, Massachusetts, plant—idled in early 1952 for lack of business—"would stay closed indefinitely until such time as New England workers are willing to make it competitive with the South." Governor James F. Byrnes of South Carolina, enraged by what he saw as organized labor's attempt to undermine his region's industrial development efforts, agreed that northern businessmen were turning to the South not for lower wages but because they "know that the workers in the plants . . . are interested in how much work they can do instead of how little." Given the forces arrayed against them, northern-based unionists—weakened by the very process of capital migration that they sought to curtail—made little headway in convincing federal officials to address their concerns.[20]

The very process of establishing southern facilities offered additional opportunities for collaboration across the North-South divide. In December 1950, Alexander Smith officials and Greenville authorities agreed on a $4.75 million BAWI bond issue to finance a new carpet mill. Since such issues were subject to local referenda, the deal set in motion a flurry of activity designed to produce a vote that, as Greenville booster Hodding Carter Jr. assured Smith's Bill Ewing, would be "as topheavy as it possibly could be." Carter, a Pulitzer Prize–winning journalist and the editor of Greenville's daily newspaper, the *Delta Democrat-Times*, launched a month-long publicity blitz, much of it fueled by materials from Smith's public relations staff. On January 15, 1951, the city's eligible voters turned out in record numbers to give the bond issue near-unanimous support. After the election, the Greenville City Council became immersed in preparations—ranging from advertising and selling the bonds to hiring and compensating numerous building contractors—that required regular consultation with Smith representatives as well as contractors themselves. In the summer of 1951, when Korean War–era restrictions on materials threatened to delay construction, Greenville mayor George F. Archer appealed to federal officials on the grounds that the factory could be used to produce military goods. The southerners' efforts were not unrequited; on the eve of the bond election, Bill Ewing promised Hodding Carter that "we want to join up with you and your way of living and doing things." In the fall of 1954, at an "open house" that drew thousands of visitors to the Greenville facility, Ewing and other Smith executives were on hand—along with such luminaries as Mississippi governor Hugh L. White—to celebrate the joint venture between the southern community and the northern firm (see fig. 1.1).[21]

The interregional alliance was further solidified by the southward movement of northern businessmen themselves. When northern firms opened southern factories, they searched for executives and supervisors to oversee their new plants. In some cases, companies lured managers away from competing firms already operating in southern settings, choosing either native southerners or former northerners with experience living and working in the South. Alexander Smith recruited several highly ranked superintendents from the James Lees and Sons Company, a Philadelphia-based carpet firm that had operated a mill in Glasgow, Virginia, for many years. When recruiting from within, Smith officials tried to identify those who seemed most likely to welcome a transfer. New Yorker Herbert J. "Jack" Potts, for example, the first manager of Smith's Mississippi facility, was delighted to leave Yonkers, for he had lived in the South previously and longed to return. As Potts and other managerial personnel arrived in southern venues, they and their families were feted by area business and civic leaders and quickly became integrated into their new communities' local elites. Jack Potts not only was elected to the board of the Greenville Chamber of Commerce but became active in the Labor-Management Relations Committee of the Mississippi Manufacturers Association as well. The ranks of southern boosters, then, were swelled by northern corporate leaders who became, in essence, southern boosters themselves.[22]

Bound by complementary cross-regional loyalties, northern businessmen strengthened efforts already well under way to preserve industrial harmony in southern sites. Jack Potts, "constantly" concerned about the need to combat the union menace, worked closely with other manufacturers to establish noncompetitive wage scales and met regularly with new employees to tell them, "very frankly, 'We don't want a union in this plant.'" In so doing, he invoked the threat of industrial losses. In the summer of 1954, soon after Smith executives decided to close their Yonkers plant in the midst of a strike, Potts wrote a lengthy, detailed letter to Greenville Mills employees. In it, he blamed the TWUA for forcing the shutdown and urged workers not to allow the union, which would undoubtedly send organizers to Greenville, "to create another Yonkers situation" in the South. A union drive in Greenville "would be . . . harmful to the future of our company," he warned. For years thereafter, Potts routinely distributed the letter to new personnel.[23]

As competition for industry escalated across the nation, so did the intensity of southern anti-union campaigns. In 1954 the CIO-affiliated International Woodworkers Association (IWA) launched an organizing drive at U.S. Gypsum's Greenville plant. Although the union had won an election in 1948, it faced ongoing company resistance; indeed, manager Sam Smith had vowed to relocate the operation if the union triumphed, and he repeated that challenge when the union sought to bargain with the firm. The 1954 campaign, launched when the National Labor Relations Board finally ordered a new election, unleashed similar threats. While not directed at an industrial newcomer (U.S. Gypsum had operated in Greenville since 1930 after acquiring a fiberboard plant from Chicago Mill, whose own origins dated to the late nineteenth century), the 1954 effort generated intense resistance from boosters who insisted that, if the IWA proved victorious, Greenville would fail to recruit additional firms. The *Delta Democrat-Times* provided almost no coverage of the organizing activity. However, it did run several advertisements by a "Greenville Citizens Committee," warning ominously that "if a Laurel type strike is ordered"—a reference to bitter IWA-led walkouts at a Masonite Corporation plant in southeastern Mississippi—workers with "good, steady jobs" would be unable to feed and clothe their families or pay their rent. To drive home the message, the committee demanded: "HOW CAN GREENVILLE GET NEW INDUSTRY TO COME HERE IF WE GET THE LABEL OF A C.I.O. TOWN?" That manager Smith had recently been elected to the city council no doubt strengthened the anti-union campaign.[24]

As a result of such resistance, even union victories were short-lived. Remarkably, in the summer of 1954 Gypsum employees voted in favor of union representation by a margin of two to one. The company refused to negotiate a contract, however, and in the spring of 1957 the IWA local was decertified for, according to observers from within the labor movement, "lack of service" to Gypsum employees. To a great extent the union's weakness was conditioned by local and state action, including passage of right-to-work, which made it extraordinarily difficult to achieve tangible gains for members and establish a solid base of support.[25]

As the Gypsum campaign suggested, southern boosters, while hostile toward unions in general, were particularly worried about the CIO. During Operation Dixie, CIO leaders had vowed to enact sweeping changes in the South not only by organizing southern workers but also by challenging racist, anti-labor political structures that harmed black and white workers alike. CIO head Philip Murray had promised to conduct "almost a holy crusade" to "deliver to [southern workers] their political and economic emancipation." The CIO Political Action Committee, moreover, targeted several virulently racist, anti-labor southern politicians—including Senator Theodore Bilbo and Representative John Rankin, both of Mississippi—for removal from their congressional seats.[26]

At the same time, CIO representatives directly challenged boosters' claims that unionism impeded industrial progress in the South. In 1949, for example, Robert W. "Bob" Starnes, CIO director for Mississippi and Louisiana, stressed that unionization, by dramatically raising workers' wages, not only enabled workers themselves to live more comfortably but also benefited the community as a whole. More money in workers' pockets, he asserted, meant more money for merchants, professional men, small shopkeepers, even utility owners and tax collectors—"in short, to all those who share in the economic welfare of a thriving community." By stimulating residential and commercial expansion, moreover, the higher wages won by unions made more resources available for improved recreation, education, and other features of a healthy community life. Unionization, Starnes suggested, was a catalyst for southern economic progress rather than an obstacle to achieving economic gains. Southern boosters found such claims deeply disturbing, for they threatened to undermine the very conditions—in particular, low wages and hostility toward unions—that southern advocates of industry believed made their region so appealing to northern firms.[27]

AFL unions, by contrast, tended to be far more cautious and conservative and thus were somewhat more acceptable to the southern (and northern) business elite. In the spring of 1952, for example, building trades unionists in Greenville threw up picket lines at the construction site of the new Alexander Smith carpet factory on the grounds that some contractors were offering substandard wages and working conditions. After a group of prominent citizens pleaded with the tradesmen to desist in the interest of the "greatest good to the greatest number," union leaders backed away. Harold E. Cox, who headed both the plumbers union and the local Building and Construction Trades Council, made the point that low-paid workers could not make substantial contributions to the community at large. Still, agreeing to "do what is best for the most people not only now but for the future," Cox called off the picketing without a single concession in hand. AFL affiliation also brought few benefits to workers at Greenville's Chicago Mill facility, represented by the United Brotherhood of Carpenters and Joiners since World War II, as the plant manager indicated when highlighting for Fantus representatives the company's low wages and poor benefit plan.[28]

Also unlike CIO unionists, many of whom were committed to interracial organizing, AFL representatives were closely allied with the state's white supremacist elite. In 1949 several Mississippi unionists proudly reported to Governor Fielding Wright (who had served as the vice-presidential candidate on the segregationist States' Rights Democratic Party, or Dixiecrat, slate the previous year) that they had blocked support for a Fair Employment Practices Committee (FEPC) and other civil rights initiatives at a labor conference where they had served as delegates at the governor's request. In another expression of racial solidarity, Mississippi AFL leader Holt Ross attacked right-to-work in 1950 as an FEPC-type program, on the grounds that it would bar an employer from hiring only union members just as the FEPC would bar him from hiring only whites. When right-to-work did pass in 1954, Mississippi's railroad unions won exemption from the law, apparently on the grounds that, according to J. L. Pierce of the Brotherhood of Railroad Trainmen, application of the measure would result in "Negroes competing with whites for jobs" in the railroad trades.[29]

The national AFL-CIO merger in late 1955 and the subsequent mergers of the two bodies at the state level in no way diminished employers' and boosters' antipathy toward unionism, as efforts to organize in southern textiles made clear. By the late 1950s nearly two-thirds of textile employment was based in southern factories. While in 1956 there were still more than a million textile workers in the United States, the TWUA represented fewer than 20 percent of them nationally and a mere 9 percent of those in the South. The union's leaders vowed to tackle the carpet industry, a heavily organized branch of textiles that was rapidly becoming non-union as major firms headed southward.[30] Textile organizers encountered fierce resistance at southern mills. Walter Wolfe, for example, trying to build union support among workers at the New Jersey–based A. & M. Karagheusian plant in Albany, Georgia, in the fall of 1958, found his car "completely splattered with acid, inside and out." The following summer, the city of Albany adopted an ordinance requiring "professional organizers" to pay a licensing and registration fee, provided that they demonstrated good moral character, had no criminal record, and were free of Communist taint. For failing to register, Wolfe was arrested, fined $125, and sentenced to ten days in jail. Despite having signed up nearly two-thirds of the plant's workforce by early 1961, the TWUA suspended the campaign "due to our inability to move around freely" in town. TWUA carpet director William DuChessi, reporting anti-union abuses to Karagheusian official Walter J. Corno, wondered what had happened to the firm's once-fair approach to labor relations. The answer was clear: while anti-union activities in Albany may have seemed typical of "southern" resistance, they were driven by the interests of two powerful groups—northern executives and their southern allies—both of whom were deeply committed to protecting the favorable business climate of the South.[31]

As labor organizers continued to push southward, southern boosters devised new strategies to combat the union threat. By 1960 Mississippi boosters were praising right-to-work as a major stimulus to the state's economy; indeed, Delta Council president Sidney Levingston claimed that it was responsible for the state's rapid increases in manufacturing jobs and wage rates between 1954 and 1958, relative to the nation as a whole. Mississippi's industrial promoters apparently agreed, however, that additional steps were needed in order to preserve their state's competitive edge. As a result, they launched a campaign to incorporate right-to-work into the state constitution.[32]

In hopes of beating back the constitutional amendment, union leaders sharply contested boosters' claims regarding the state's economic growth. "The people of Mississippi have more than enough sweat shops in the State," the Mississippi State AFL-CIO asserted. "If Manufacturers in the East and the North can pay a decent wage there, they can surely pay the same wage here in Mississippi." According to Mississippi Labor Council president Claude Ramsay, even some boosters were insisting that industrialists no longer sought communities that were "bound and gagged." Labor's case was bolstered by support from newspapers in Mississippi's few union strongholds; the *Pascagoula Star and Moss Point Advertiser*, for example, emphasized the role of unions in protecting livelihoods, claimed that states without right-to-work had "moved far ahead of us in new industry," and accused "black belt and Delta politicians" of "trying to nail our state's boots to the 50th rung on the nation's economic ladder." Since organized labor was very weak in most areas of Mississippi, however, it was not surprising that, in a June 1960 referendum, the amendment passed in all but four of the state's eighty-two counties. With support from nearly 70 percent of voters, Mississippi became the first southern state to insert right-to-work into its constitution since World War II. That most black Mississippians were denied the right to vote may have played a key role in the outcome, since high turnout among black voters helped defeat similar measures in other states.[33]

While northern employers and southern boosters led the charge against organized labor, southern workers' own lack of interest or outright antipathy also played a key role in limiting union gains. Faced with declining economic opportunities in the postwar period, many white workers were enthusiastic about the arrival of new manufacturing plants. Northern-based firms typically offered southerners much lower wages than in the North while requiring longer hours and heavier workloads. In the early 1950s the starting wage for many operatives at Alexander Smith's Greenville plant ranged from about $1.05 to $1.20 per hour, at least 16 to 44 percent below the rates their Yonkers counterparts received. The Greenville employees also worked without a lunch break in the early years. Weavers in Greenville were required to tend two (and later, three) looms, moreover, while in Yonkers they operated only one. Such conditions compared favorably with the alternatives available to white southerners, however, such as sharecropping or, for some women, work in cafeterias or coffee shops. Since northern employers often used existing or former union contracts as a guide for establishing benefit programs, many southern workers earned their first paid vacations and time off for holidays in northern-owned mills. Smith's Greenville staff also enjoyed such perquisites as company picnics, Christmas parties, and the pleasures of working in an air-conditioned plant. White men were able to advance into highly skilled positions (such as loom fixer) or supervisory positions. White women in Greenville, whose employment options were severely limited, had the chance to apply their needlework talents and help others learn new skills.[34]

The lack of union feeling among white southern workers in northern-based factories reflected, in part, their superior treatment in comparison to that experienced by northern employees. Most northern manufacturers did not enact a literal "runaway shop" scenario in which the opening of southern factories was accompanied immediately by the shutdown of northern plants. Rather, company executives often eased into southern operations and then gradually shifted northern production to southern sites. Thus, a typical corporate migrant might operate plants simultaneously in both regions for quite some time. However, employers committed to southern locations tended to invest more heavily in those new operations while failing to dedicate resources to northern plants. Alexander Smith's Yonkers facility, for example, was not air-conditioned, and much of the newer equipment was shipped down to Greenville for southern workers' use. In the spring of 1954, Smith officials—while proposing to reduce pay rates in Yonkers—granted wage increases to Greenville employees and announced that those not yet eligible for paid vacations would receive them as a special bonus, just for that year.[35]

While black southern workers benefited far less from new industry than did their white counterparts, they too stood to gain from northern employers' largesse. In the early 1950s, Greenville's African American leaders agreed to support the Alexander Smith bond issue in exchange for promises that, once the carpet mill was up and running, black workers would receive good jobs. (Greenville was one of the few communities in Mississippi where black residents could vote.) Black leaders praised Smith for providing new employment opportunities and exhorted black workers to show loyalty to the firm. At Greenville Mills' first "colored" picnic in the summer of 1953, for example, Rev. H. H. Humes, editor of an accommodationist African American newspaper, the *Delta Leader*, told his audience that they were "pioneers in a new day, in a new age," and cautioned that whether other black people followed them into the carpet factory "will be left up to you and how well you do your job." While the plant did hire a large number of black male workers, they were relegated to menial posts. Black women were excluded altogether, since company officials presumably did not wish to interfere with their availability as domestic servants. According to plant manager Jack Potts, since white employees would "hire blacks to look after their family while they were working," the firm was "giving employment to blacks in a roundabout way." In the mid-1960s black community residents challenged these discriminatory practices, and their actions—to the great dismay of local boosters—threatened Greenville's reputation as welcoming to migratory firms. Once granted more and better job opportunities, however, black employees—according to union organizers—could not be counted upon to support the union cause.[36]

Certainly southern workers were not always content or grateful, but the circumstances by which their jobs were acquired could keep them from embracing unionism. In the summer of 1953, union organizer Dan Starnes traveled to Greenville to investigate conditions at the carpet factory for the TWUA. Starnes reported that "there seems to be little interest in any union and most everyone is very pleased to have this nice new mill come to town"; indeed, the "greatest obstacle" to organizing was the "feeling that Greenville should be very thankful for [the] new mill and nothing should interfere" with the company's success. Those who worked in facilities owned by northern companies were often well aware that their employers, in many cases, had fled southward to escape the union menace. They understood that those employers, if unhappy in their new locations, might decide to move again. Under Mississippi's postwar BAWI program, in which communities typically owned factory buildings for the life of a twenty- or twenty-five-year contract and rented space to employers for the annual cost of paying off the bond principal and interest, companies could relocate with relative ease. Dora Belue joined Greenville Mills as a production worker in 1954 and stayed on for nearly thirty-eight years. "They was under union up there, and they moved here," she remembered, "and we felt like . . . if [the union] was voted in here . . . [the company] would move someplace else, 'cause they didn't own the building out there. I believe that belongs to the city, and it wouldn't keep them from moving someplace else."[37]

Even when southern workers did support unions, they were stymied by the favorable business climate that northern employers and southern boosters worked so hard to maintain. As southern workers grew accustomed to the rhythms of industrial employment, some embraced collective action as a way to improve wages and conditions on the job. Greenville, for example, attracted five new manufacturing plants in the late 1950s and early 1960s, all of them relocating from midwestern states. Unions that were stronger and more resource-rich than the TWUA, such as the United Steelworkers of America (USWA), enjoyed greater success in organizing these migratory plants. Manufacturers not only mounted fierce resistance in the workplace but also worked with civic leaders to mobilize the community on industry's behalf. In the spring of 1962, just as the USWA was petitioning for an election at the Atkins Saw plant (a division of Borg-Warner Corporation formerly located in Indianapolis) and accusing the company of unfair labor practices, Mayor

Archer proclaimed "Industrial Progress Week" as an opportunity to laud local industries for creating "for all our citizens higher standards of living and more productive lives." The citywide celebration was marked by plant tours, product displays in banks and retail outlets, presentations to civic groups, and a flurry of stories in the *Delta Democrat-Times* featuring the accomplishments of individual firms. The election at Atkins—referred to by the newspaper as the city's "newest 'good citizens'"—was close and contested, but the USWA lost.[38]

Even when unions triumphed, they made only limited gains. With the union shop outlawed in Mississippi, many workers in Greenville's organized factories—in some cases a majority—did not carry union cards. Transplanted Chicago employer William A. "Bill" Mosow, whose Greenville screw factory was organized by the USWA in the early 1960s, reported that, under right-to-work conditions, unionization "turned out to be a bonanza for me." He found that the union offered several advantages. For example, collective bargaining enabled him to avoid engaging in separate wage negotiations with numerous individual employees. Moreover, workers active in the union demonstrated leadership abilities that made them strong candidates for supervisory positions; indeed, in two cases Mosow promoted union presidents, who "made excellent foremen" and "were much tougher on the employees than somebody who had not had the experience with the union." At the same time, the absence of union security provisions kept the local weak and divided, thus enabling Mosow to preserve workplace control. "Anybody that's in a right-to-work state really does not have to be apprehensive of a union," he observed.[39]

While most southern business and civic leaders viewed unionization as a loathsome prospect, there were a few dissenters among their ranks. Although Hodding Carter was deeply committed to southern industrial development, he castigated not only the Yankee exploiters of southern land and labor but also the southern industrial promoters who lured them with promises of "the willingness, the abundance, and the good behavior—the 100 per cent Americanism—of Southern workers." "We have more to offer the cruising industrialist," Carter insisted in 1949, "than docility, cheapness, and a blank check." Carter understood that higher earnings increased purchasing power, which in turn benefited southern communities; thus, during the 1952 dispute at the Greenville Mills construction site over compensation for building tradesmen, he editorialized that "no enduring prosperity was ever built upon a system of low wages for the many and big profits for the few." A decade later, the USWA spearheaded a drive to distribute cards to Greenville merchants, indicating that purchases were made possible by the union membership of those who patronized local stores. The area chamber of commerce's anxious warning to its members that workers' purchasing power resulted from payrolls that were "continually growing" due to the voluntary action of employers—who "above anyone else recognize that a good day's work justifies a good day's pay"—suggested that some local business owners had proved susceptible to the union campaign. By the mid-1960s, some business leaders seemed resigned to the presence of unions; during a series of chamber-sponsored meetings in the spring of 1966 to assess Greenville's economic prospects, one participant noted that northern industrialists, most of whom were fleeing from unions, expected no more than "5 years of trouble free operation" in the South. "Once [the unions] beat you, you live with them," he observed.[40]

Anti-union attitudes and action, however, were far more typical and remained a dominant feature of southern industrial development campaigns. Hodding Carter's thoughtful stance on southern labor was unusual among the region's boosters; indeed, as suggested by his failure to cover the 1954 conflict at U.S. Gypsum, he proved reluctant to promote workers' interests once new plants were in operation or union campaigns were under way. Outright opponents of unionism were often more proactive; in the early 1960s, communities across the South, eager to lure manufacturing, regularly employed local ordinances and police powers to keep union organizers at bay. In Greenville, local boosters persisted in efforts to stymie union activity. In the late 1960s, for example, the National Maritime Union launched a campaign to organize the city's towing industry, thriving as the result of Greenville's strategic location on the Mississippi River and boosters' efforts to promote the availability of water transport for newly arriving firms. During the union drive, the local chamber not only warned employees of "the possibility of strife" and loss of "personal contact with your employer" in the event of unionization but also urged local business owners to talk with workers they knew personally "about the hazards of belonging to a union." (The chamber provided workers' names and addresses to facilitate fulfillment of the request.) By the late 1970s, southern boosters were resisting overtures from northern employers who intended to establish southern plants with unions and high wage scales, on the grounds that such conditions were incompatible with the region's industrial development needs. Among them was Harry Vickery, a leading industrial promoter in Greenville, who asserted that area boosters were "being very selective" in order to keep out unionized firms.[41]

The establishment of northern-based industry on southern soil, then, played a pivotal role in hindering unionization in the South. The infusion of northern capital into the region, particularly in the postwar period, was premised on the presence of non-union—or at least anti-union—conditions that both northern employers and their southern supporters were eager to preserve. The desire to fashion a favorable investment climate produced forms of anti-union resistance that, rather than representing peculiarly "southern" traits or traditions, reflected the shared interests of business and civic leaders—both northern and southern—who avidly sought to bridge the regional divide. At the same time, the very economic conditions that impelled southern boosters to pursue industry also led many southerners—including workers and even union leaders—to adopt a compliant posture toward migratory firms. The benefits of new industry, of course, were not evenly distributed among those who lived and labored in the South. That so many reaped rewards from capital migration, however—or could not afford to contest its exploitative tendencies—helps explain not only why the impulse to prevent southern unionism was so strong in the postwar period but also why efforts to limit union power in the region so often met with success.

Notes

1. Elsewhere I have explored how industry relocation from the North to the South helped to both weaken the U.S. labor movement and strengthen political conservatism nationwide. See Tami J. Friedman, "Exploiting the North-South Differential: Corporate Power, Southern Politics, and the Decline of Organized Labor after World War II," *Journal of American History* 95 (September 2008): 323–48. In this essay I focus more closely on how capital flight undermined unionism in the South.

2. For cultural explanations of southern resistance to unionism, see George Sinclair Mitchell, *Textile Unionism in the South* (Chapel Hill: University of North Carolina Press, 1931), vi, 84; Herbert Lahne, *The Cotton Mill Worker* (New York: Farrar & Rinehart, 1944), 41, 64, 67, 122; and Irving Bernstein, *The Lean Years: A History of the American Worker, 1920–1933* (Boston: Houghton Mifflin, 1960), 6–7, 40–41. For studies that focus on workers' militancy, see James A. Hodges, *New Deal Labor Policy and the Southern Cotton Textile Industry, 1933–1941* (Knoxville: University of Tennessee Press, 1986); Jacquelyn Dowd Hall et al., *Like a Family: The Making of a Southern Cotton Mill World* (New York: Norton, 1987); Barbara S. Griffith, *The Crisis of American Labor: Operation Dixie and the Defeat of the CIO* (Philadelphia: Temple University Press, 1988); and Douglas Flamming, *Creating the Modern South: Millhands and Managers in Dalton, Georgia, 1884–1984* (Chapel Hill: University of North Carolina Press, 1992). See also the essays in Robert H. Zieger, ed., *Organized Labor in the Twentieth-Century South* (Knoxville: University of Tennessee Press, 1991); and Robert H. Zieger, ed., *Southern Labor in Transition, 1940–1995* (Knoxville: University of Tennessee Press, 1997). Griffith refers to the South's "distinct heritage . . . heightened by generations of poverty and provincialism" and its "culture of dependence," while Timothy J. Minchin calls the postwar weakness of southern unionism a "distinctive southern trait." Griffith, *Crisis of American Labor*, 16, 17; Minchin, *Fighting against the Odds: A History of Southern Labor since World War II* (Gainesville: University Press of Florida, 2005), 7. For anti-communism and racial division, see Griffith, *Crisis of American Labor*, 62–87, 139–60; Michael K. Honey, *Southern Labor and Black Civil Rights: Organizing Memphis Workers* (Urbana: University of Illinois Press, 1993), 214–77; and Michael K. Honey, "Operation Dixie, the Red Scare, and the Defeat of Southern Labor Organizing," in *American Labor and the Cold War: Grassroots*

Politics and Postwar Political Culture, ed. Robert W. Cherny, William Issel, and Kieran Walsh Taylor (New Brunswick: Rutgers University Press, 2004), 216–44. For the South as a national model, see Zieger's introduction to *Organized Labor in the Twentieth-Century South*, 5–6; and James C. Cobb, *The Selling of the South: The Southern Crusade for Industrial Development, 1936–1990* (Urbana: University of Illinois Press, 1993), 281.

3. For indigenous southern industry, see Gavin Wright, *Old South, New South: Revolutions in the Southern Economy since the Civil War* (New York: Basic Books, 1986), 47, 129–37; C. Vann Woodward, *Origins of the New South, 1877–1913* (1951; Baton Rouge: Louisiana State University Press, 1990), 126–35; and William P. Jones, *The Tribe of Black Ulysses: African American Lumber Workers in the Jim Crow South* (Urbana: University of Illinois Press, 2005), 17–20. For prewar southern union gains in coal, steel, and longshoring, see F. Ray Marshall, *Labor in the South* (Cambridge: Harvard University Press, 1967), 139–40, 147, 186–88, 211; and Michael Honey, "Industrial Unionism and Racial Justice in Memphis," in Zieger, *Organized Labor in the Twentieth-Century South*, 138–39. By 1939 the United Mine Workers of America claimed 89,200 southern members, who constituted 14 percent of all southern unionists. Between 1939 and 1953 the number of southerners belonging to the United Steelworkers of America rose by 850 percent (from 9,800 to 83,200). Marshall, *Labor in the South*, 267–68, table 4. For textile migration in the 1810s, see Aviva Chomsky, *Linked Labor Histories: New England, Colombia, and the Making of a Global Working Class* (Durham, N.C.: Duke University Press, 2008), 98. For westward migration, see Jefferson Cowie, *Capital Moves: RCA's 70-Year Quest for Cheap Labor* (Ithaca: Cornell University Press, 1999), 33–34; and Thomas J. Sugrue, *The Origins of the Urban Crisis: Race and Inequality in Postwar Detroit* (Princeton: Princeton University Press, 1996), 128–29.

4. For early postwar union membership data, see Michael Goldfield, *The Decline of Organized Labor in the United States* (Chicago: University of Chicago Press, 1987), 10, table 1; and Leo Troy, "The Rise and Fall of American Trade Unions: The Labor Movement from FDR to RR," in *Unions in Transition: Entering the Second Century*, ed. Seymour Martin Lipset (San Francisco: Institute for Contemporary Studies, 1986), 81, table 2. For the postwar managerial offensive, see Howell John Harris, *The Right to Manage: Industrial Relations Policies of American Business in the 1940s* (Madison: University of Wisconsin Press, 1982); Sanford M. Jacoby, *Modern Manors: Welfare Capitalism since the New Deal* (Princeton: Princeton University Press, 1997); Elizabeth Fones-Wolf, *Selling Free Enterprise: The Business Assault on Labor and Liberalism, 1945–60* (Urbana: University of Illinois Press, 1994); David Brody, *Workers in Industrial America: Essays on the Twentieth Century Struggle* (New York: Oxford University Press, 1980); 173–214; and Nelson Lichtenstein, *State of the Union: A Century of American Labor* (Princeton: Princeton University Press, 2002), 98–140. In 1953, 26.1 percent of workers in the mid-Atlantic states of New Jersey, New York, and Pennsylvania were union members, compared with just 6.9 percent in the south Atlantic states of Delaware, Florida, Georgia, Maryland, North Carolina, South Carolina, Virginia, and West Virginia, and the District of Columbia. Leo Troy, *Distribution of Union Membership among the States, 1939 and 1953* (New York: National Bureau of Economic Research Inc., 1957), 8, table 2. For labor as a factor stimulating migration, see Cobb, *Selling of the South*, 209–28.

5. Harold C. Zulauf interview by Rosalie Flynn, April 20, 1983, draft transcript, 6, "Alex Smith & Sons Carpet Co./H. Zulauf Oral History 1983" folder, Alexander Smith Company

Archives, Hudson River Museum, Yonkers, New York; Chilhowie, Virginia, survey, attached to Leonard C. Yaseen to Harold C. Zulauf, January 5, 1951 (copy in author's possession, courtesy Deloitte, Chicago). For labor supply, see ibid.

6. Leonard Yaseen to William F. C. Ewing, August 2, 1950, esp. 5, attached to Greenville, Mississippi, survey (copy in author's possession, courtesy Deloitte); Leonard C. Yaseen to William F. C. Ewing, June 22, 1950, esp. 1–2, attached to Mississippi survey, ibid.; "Conclusion," attached to ibid.

7. For migration data, see Pete Daniel, *Standing at the Crossroads: Southern Life in the Twentieth Century* (New York: Hill & Wang, 1986), 137. For planters' economic strategies, see Gilbert C. Fite, *Cotton Fields No More: Southern Agriculture, 1865–1980* (Lexington: University Press of Kentucky, 1984), 168–70, 185–87; Robert Daryl Lewis, "Delta Council: Transformer of an Agrarian Mind" (M.Ed. thesis, Delta State University, 1984), 37–43; and James C. Cobb, *The Most Southern Place on Earth: The Mississippi Delta and the Roots of Regional Identity* (New York: Oxford University Press, 1992), 205–8. For civil rights challenges, see Charles Erwin Wilson, *To Secure These Rights: The Report of the President's Committee on Civil Rights* (New York: Simon & Schuster, 1947), 139–73; "The Text of President Truman's Message on Civil Rights," *New York Times*, February 3, 1948, 22; and Ann Waldron, *Hodding Carter: The Reconstruction of a Racist* (Chapel Hill: Algonquin Books of Chapel Hill, 1993), 215. For the South's "colonial" status, see Hodding Carter, "Southern Towns and Northern Industry," *Atlantic Monthly*, November 1949, 49, box 55, Hodding and Betty Werlein Carter Papers, Special Collections Department, Mitchell Memorial Library, Mississippi State University, Starkville; Daniel, *Standing at the Crossroads*, 48–49, 150; and Hugh White, "Address of Governor Hugh White at the Daytona Beach, Florida, Chamber of Commerce on January 29, 1953," "Speeches, 1953" folder, series 960, Governors Records, RG 27, State Records, Mississippi Department of Archives and History [hereafter MDAH], Jackson. For economic sovereignty, see *BAWI Bulletin*, June 1948, 5; and remarks of Edmund Taylor in Delta Council Executive Committee minutes, July 7, 1948, 2, "Correspondence and Papers (9)" folder, Mississippi Economic Council Papers [hereafter MEC Papers], 1948–1949, MDAH.

8. For northern investment in southern lumber, mining, iron, and steel, see Woodward, *Origins of the New South*, 115–18, 126–29, 299–302. For BAWI and subsequent southern initiatives, see Ernest J. Hopkins, *Mississippi's BAWI Plan: Balance Agriculture with Industry: An Experiment in Industrial Subsidization* (Atlanta: Federal Reserve Bank of Atlanta, 1944); and Cobb, *Selling of the South*, 5–63.

9. State of Mississippi, *Balance Agriculture with Industry: Mississippi 1944 Law, House Bill 176* (Jackson: Mississippi A&I Board, 1944), 6; David Markstein, "Advertising Helps to Balance State's Agriculture with Its Industry," *Printers Ink*, March 1, 1946, 78, 80; Mississippi A&I Board, "There're Folks in Mississippi, Not Census Figures," advertisement, *New York Times*, February 5, 1947, 38; Mississippi A&I Board, "A Sixth Flag Over Mississippi," advertisement, *New York Times*, August 6, 1947, 37.

10. N. E. Wingate to Gordon Carson, August 22, 1949, "Selby Shoe Company" folder, Greenville Area Chamber of Commerce Records [hereafter GACOC Records], Greenville Area Chamber of Commerce, Greenville, Mississippi; McCormick and Sam Smith quoted in Yaseen to Ewing, August 2, 1950, 5 and 4, attached to Greenville survey.

11. Kendrick Lee, "Labor Organization in the South," *Editorial Research Reports*, May

29, 1946, 375–78, esp. 376, "Southern Legacy: 'Economic Dominion'" folder, box 47, Carter Papers; Griffith, *Crisis of American Labor*, 26.

12. Griffith, *Crisis of American Labor*, 42–43, 161–62, esp. 162; Marshall, *Labor in the South*, 252. For anti-communism and racism as factors explaining the collapse of Operation Dixie, see note 2. For employer resistance, see Griffith, *Crisis of American Labor*, 88–105; and Minchin, *Fighting against the Odds*, 40–46, 60, 65–66. For union limitations, see Michael Goldfield, "The Failure of Operation Dixie: A Critical Turning Point in American Political Development?" in *Race, Class, and Community in Southern Labor History*, ed. Gary M. Fink and Merl E. Reed (Tuscaloosa: University of Alabama Press, 1994), 180–82, 186–88.

13. Troy, *Distribution of Union Membership among the States*, 18–19, table 4, and 4–5, table 1; Eugene Albert Roper Jr., "The CIO Organizing Committee in Mississippi: June, 1946–January, 1949" (M.A. thesis, University of Mississippi, 1949), 10, 64–80, esp. 66–67; Hopkins, *Mississippi's BAWI Plan*, 39, table 3.

14. Hopkins, *Mississippi's BAWI Plan*, esp. 40–41; Roper, "CIO Organizing Committee in Mississippi," esp. 70, 80.

15. The calculations of southern Democrats' support for the Taft-Hartley Act draw on data in "House Vote on Labor Bill," *New York Times*, April 18, 1947, 6, and "Senate Vote on Passage of Labor Control Bill," *New York Times*, May 14, 1947, 3. The calculations of southern Democrats' support for overriding Truman's veto draw on data in Congressional Quarterly, *Congress and the Nation, 1945–1964: A Review of Government and Politics in the Postwar Years* (Washington, D.C., 1965), 46a–47a, chart 1, and 44a, chart 1; "State 'Right to Work' Laws," *Congressional Quarterly Almanac* 21 (1965), 819.

16. Delta Council, *Annual Report, 1947–1948*, 7; "House Bill No. 5," *Mississippi Legislature, Second Extraordinary Session, 1947*, "Legislature 1947" folder, Subject Files, MDAH; "House Bill No. 6," ibid.; "Testimony at a Hearing for Proponents of HB's 792, 793, and 794 Transcribed . . . through Courtesy of the Mississippi Economic Council," 3–4, esp. 2 and 6 (remarks of C. D. Maddox) and 8 (remarks of W. A. Evans), "Correspondence & Papers (7)" folder, MEC Papers; "Why Labor Opposes House Bills 792, 793 & 794: An Address Delivered by Holt Ross before the House Labor Committee," *Mississippi Labor Federationist*, March 17, 1950, esp. 1, Oversize Newspapers, Holt E. Ross Papers, Special Collections Department, Mitchell Memorial Library; "Judiciary Committee Kills Anti-Labor Bills," *Mississippi Labor Federationist*, April 2, 1950, 1–2, ibid.; remarks of Edmund Taylor, James Hand Jr., and Billy Wynn in Delta Council Executive Committee minutes, 1, 14–15, "Correspondence and Papers (9)" folder, MEC Papers, 1948–1949, MDAH; Mississippi State Federation of Labor, *Proceedings of the Twenty-ninth Annual Session . . .* , September 15–17, 1947, 3, 41, MDAH; Mississippi State Federation of Labor, *Proceedings of the Thirtieth Annual Session . . .* , September 27–29, 1948, 2, ibid.

17. For A&I Board budget data, see attachment to W. E. Barksdale to Hodding Carter, December 20, 1950, "Greenville: Cert. No. 104, 9/26/50 (Greenville Mills)" folder, Mississippi Department of Economic and Community Development [hereafter MDECD], Jackson; and Jack Edward Prince, "History and Development of the Mississippi Balance Agriculture with Industry Program, 1936–1958" (Ph.D. diss., Ohio State University, 1961), 134, table 3. For BAWI plant data, see "Summary of Mississippi BAWI Plants," 1–12, attached to Mickey Farmer to Kleo Hughes, November 26, 1962, "BAWI Contracts in State" folder, GACOC Records. For right-to-work and Mississippi's limited industrial successes,

see "Mississippi Solons Study 'Right to Work' Bill," *Delta Democrat-Times*, October 25, 1953, 1; John M. Peterson, "Is Mississippi Realizing Its Industrial Potential?" *Mississippi's Business*, February 1955, 1–7.

18. Mississippi State Industrial Union Council, "What Is Your Stake in Labor Laws?" leaflet, [1954], "Right to Work Laws, 1951–1959" folder, box 2220, "Subject Files, 1947–1986" series, Mississippi AFL-CIO Records, 1947–1986, Southern Labor Archives, Special Collections and Archives, Georgia State University, Atlanta; "Right to Work Measure Approved by House, 92–42," *Jackson Clarion-Ledger*, February 18, 1954, ibid.; and "Governor Signs 'Right to Work' Bill Outlawing Closed and Union Shops," *Jackson Daily News*, February 24, 1954, ibid.; "Industrial Survey of Greenville, Mississippi, 1960," 19–21, GACOC Records.

19. "Defense Production Act of 1950," *Congressional Quarterly Almanac* 6 (1950), 624; "Revenue Act of 1950," ibid., 573–75; "CIO Writes Lehman in Mill Move Protest," *Utica Press*, October 18, 1951, "Steel Allocations for Textile Mills, 1951" folder, box 21, file 10A, MSS 129A, Textile Workers Union of America Records [hereafter TWUA Records], Wisconsin Historical Society, Madison; Walter Murtagh, "Textron South Mills Project Strikes Snag," *Manchester Sunday News*, November 25, 1951, 1, esp. 5, ibid.

20. "New England Wages War on the South," *Mississippi Magic: The BAWI Bulletin* 7 (January 1952), MDAH; Murtagh, "Textron South Mills Project Strikes Snag," esp. 5.

21. "$8 Million Plant Coming to Greenville," *Delta Democrat-Times*, December 18, 1950, 1950–1953 Scrapbook, George F. Archer Papers, William Alexander Percy Memorial Library, Greenville, Mississippi; "Officials Exuberant at Overwhelming Vote Given to Bond Issue," *Delta Democrat-Times*, January 16, 1951, 1, ibid.; "City Engages Architect for Mill's Plans," *Delta Democrat-Times* [early 1950s], ibid.; "Carpet Firm Officers Fly In to Discuss Plans for Plant," ibid.; George F. Archer to Manly Fleischmann, June 21, 1951, "Greenville: Cert. No. 104, 9/26/50 (Greenville Mills)" folder, MDECD. For Carter's and Ewing's comments, see Hodding Carter to William F. C. Ewing, December 19, 1950, "HC: Correspondence: 1950: Personal (Oct.–Dec.)" folder, Carter Papers; and William F. C. Ewing to Dear Hodding, December 14, 1950, ibid. For publicity, see Richard de Luna to Hodding Carter, January 2, [1951], "HC: Correspondence: 1951: Personal (January–March)" folder, ibid.; and "White Begins Open House at Greenville Mills This Morning," *Delta Democrat-Times*, October 1, 1954, 1953–1954 Scrapbook, Archer Papers.

22. "Greenville (Miss.) Mills—Delta Civic Achievement," *America's Textile Reporter*, September 30, 1954, 10–11, 12, 44, "Alexander Smith, Inc., Greenville, Miss." folder, box 343, MSS 396, TWUA Records; Herbert J. Potts interview by author, Fairhope, Alabama, March 2, 1996, audiotape (in author's possession), side 2; "Mr. and Mrs. H. J. Potts Give Informal Party at Local Country Club," *Delta Democrat-Times*, April 15, 1953, 5; "Miss Jackie Potts Is Honoree at Country Club Luncheon on Tuesday," *Delta Democrat-Times*, August 27, 1953, 3; "Greenville Mills Group Have Luncheon Tuesday at Local Country Club," *Delta Democrat-Times*, May 13, 1954, 3; "Top Ten to be Elected C of C Directors from 20," *Delta Democrat-Times*, November 15, 1953, 1; "Seven Washington Countians on MEC Committees to Meet," *Delta Democrat-Times*, May 12, 1954, 16.

23. Potts interview, March 3, 1996, tape 1, side 2; Herbert J. Potts to Dear Fellow Employee, June 30, 1954, esp. 3 and 2, attached to Ken Kramer to Ken Fiester, memo, July 15, 1954, "Local 122" folder, box 609, MSS 396, TWUA Records; Boyd E. Payton to William

DuChessi, November 19, 1957, 1, "Payton, Boyd E." folder, box 489, ibid.; Herbert J. Potts to Dear Fellow Employee, [n.d.], attached to ibid.

24. "Gypsum Plant Wins Partial Victory," *Delta Democrat-Times*, January 2, 1952, 5; J. B. Hanna to All U.S. Gypsum Employees, March 22, 1954, "General Files, Miss. State IUC, 1955" folder, box 263, "General Files, 1948–1959" series, International Woodworkers of America, District 4 Records, Southern Labor Archives; John R. Shipley, "The Story of Chicago Mill and Lumber Company," in Washington County Historical Society, *Programs of 1980* (Greenville, Miss.: Washington County Historical Society, 1981), 70, 63 (Percy Library); *United States Gypsum Company and International Woodworkers of America*, 94 NLRB 112, 113–14 (1951); Greenville Citizens Committee, advertisement, "IF the CIO-IWA Comes to Greenville?" *Delta Democrat-Times*, July 29, 1954, esp. 2; "Sam Smith Wins over Ingram for City Council," *Delta Democrat-Times*, October 6, 1953, 1.

25. "Gypsum Employees OK Union, 2 to 1," *Delta Democrat-Times*, August 1, 1954, 2. For post-election problems and decertification, see "Summary of NLRB Industrial Elections at Greenville," attached to C. E. Landrum to Edgar Fain, February 19, 1962, "Edgar Fain" folder, GACOC Records; and William DuChessi to Harold Daoust, memo, February 11, 1958, esp. 3, "William DuChessi" folder, box 489, MSS 396, TWUA Records.

26. Lee, "Labor Organization in the South," esp. 376 and 385.

27. Robert W. Starnes, "Mississippi Gets a Boost from the CIO," *Southern Labor* 1 (February 1949): 14–15, esp. 14, "CIO, Atlanta, GA" folder, box 41, MSS 346, TWUA Records.

28. "Single Picket Marching by Greenville Mills," *Delta Democrat-Times*, March 25, 1952, 1; "More Workmen Stay Off Jobs at Greenville Plant," *Delta Democrat-Times*, March 27, 1952, 1; "Greenville Citizens Appeal to Strikers," *Delta Democrat-Times*, May 19, 1952, esp. 1; "Union Calls Off Carpet Mill Pickets," *Delta Democrat-Times*, May 20, 1952, esp. 1; notes, Chicago Mill and Lumber, Case File III-6458D, Region IV, Records of the National War Labor Board, RG 202, National Archives, Atlanta; Yaseen to Ewing, August 2, 1950, 5 (attached to Greenville survey).

29. Harmon McGee to Fielding Wright, December 9, 1949, "Conferences" folder, "A-I" box, series 940, RG 27, MDAH; Fielding Wright to Harmon McGee, December 12, 1949, ibid.; miscellaneous correspondence, ibid.; "Why Labor Opposes House Bills 792, 793 & 794," esp. 1; "Labor Committee Approves Bill to Restrict Unions," *Jackson Daily News*, February 10, 1954, "Right to Work Laws, 1951–1959" folder, box 2220, "Subject Files, 1947–1986" series, Mississippi AFL-CIO Records.

30. For textile employment data, see Barry E. Truchil, *Capital-Labor Relations in the U.S. Textile Industry* (New York: Praeger, 1988), 66, table 3.11. For TWUA membership data, see TWUA Research Department, "*Confidential*: Textile Workers Covered by TWUA Agreements and Total Production Worker Employment, by State, February 1956," April 24, 1956, attached to Solomon Barkin to William Pollock, memo, April 24, 1956, "Membership Figures (TWUA) 1956" folder, box 611, MSS 396, TWUA Records; and "Quarter-Million Mill Workers Goal of AFL-CIO South Drive," *America's Textile Reporter*, March 8, 1956, 14, "Research—1956" folder, box 14, ibid.

31. William DuChessi to Walter J. Corno, September 29, 1958, "William DuChessi Carpet Director—1958" folder, box 600, MSS 396, TWUA Records; "An Ordinance . . . Requiring the Registration and Licensing of Professional Organizers, and for Other Purposes,"

"Botelho-Southeastern Region Organizing-1961" folder, box 622, ibid.; M. Michael Botelho to William Pollock, April 5, 1960, 3, "Michael Botelho 1960/Southeastern Ga." folder, box 7, file 6A, MSS 129A, ibid.; M. Michael Botelho to William Pollock, March 6, 1961, esp. 2, "Michael Botelho, Southeastern, 1961" folder, box 629, MSS 396, ibid.

32. "Council President Stress Importance of Right to Work," news clipping, [Greenwood, Miss.?], May 26, 1960, "Right to Work Laws, 1951–1959" folder, box 2220, "Subject Files, 1947–1986" series, Mississippi AFL-CIO Records.

33. Sample letter to editor, [1960], "Right to Work Laws, June 1–8, 1960" folder, box 2220, "Subject Files, 1947–1986" series, Mississippi AFL-CIO Records; "Statement by Claude Ramsay, President, Mississippi Labor Council AFL-CIO . . . ," news release, May 25, 1960, esp. 10, "Right to Work Laws, 1951–1959," ibid.; editorial, "Right-to-Work is No Industry Lure," *Pascagoula Star and Moss Point Advertiser*, June 3, 1960, "Right to Work Laws, June 1–8, 1960" folder, ibid.; "State of Mississippi, Special Election, June 7, 1960, Constitutional Amendment, House Concurrent Resolution, No. 43," vote tally by county, attached to Thomas Knight to All Local Unions, June 23, 1960, "Miscellaneous 1960" folder, box 2142, "Affiliated Unions, 1957–1983" series, ibid.; "State 'Right to Work' Laws," 819. In 1964 just 6.7 percent of eligible black Mississippians were registered to vote; they composed 5 percent of all registered voters in the state. In 1958, high turnout among Ohio's black electorate helped defeat a right-to-work referendum in that state. Frank R. Parker, *Black Votes Count: Political Empowerment in Mississippi after 1965* (Chapel Hill: University of North Carolina Press, 1990), 32, table 1.3; Gilbert J. Gall, *The Politics of Right to Work: The Labor Federations as Special Interests, 1943–1979* (New York: Greenwood Press, 1988), 142–44.

34. Smith production workers' wages are difficult to compare across plants because, while TWUA records show hourly rates for Greenville jobs, they report actual average hourly earnings (which reflected incentive pay on top of base hourly rates) for most Yonkers jobs. However, comparable hourly data do exist for some occupations (and are supplemented here by the recollections of Greenville interviewees). For Greenville data, see TWUA Research Department, "Wage Schedule May 26, 1952: Company: Greenville Mills, Inc.," September 29, 1952, attached to memo, Solomon Barkin to Charles Hughes et al., August 29, 1952, "Alex Smith, Greenville, MS" folder, box 343, MSS 396, TWUA Records; and memo, Solomon Barkin to Charles Hughes, June 24, 1954, "Alexander Smith, Yonkers, NY, Labor V, 1954–" folder, ibid. For Yonkers wages, see TWUA Research Department, "Survey of Key Jobs in Carpet & Rug Industry . . . December 1951," March 11, 1952, 4, "Carpet Industry Negotiations 1952" folder, box 139, M86-019, ibid.; TWUA Research Department, "Table II: Yarn Processing Rates in Woolen and Carpet Mills, April 1952," April 14, 1952, "Research Dept. (Reports Only) 1952–53" folder, box 408, MSS 396, ibid.; and TWUA Research Department, "Present and Proposed Base or Hourly Rates and Average Hourly Earnings for those Jobs at Alexander Smith, Inc., Where a Wage Reduction is Proposed . . . ," June 23, 1954, 2, attached to memo, Solomon Barkin to Charles Hughes, June 24, 1954, "Local #122/Alexander Smith, Inc., Yonkers, NY" folder, box 609, ibid. Albert and Gladys Shirley interview by author, Greenville, Mississippi, January 24, 1996, audiotape (in author's possession), side 1, tape 1; Kenneth Radigan interview by author, Greenville, January 22, 1996, audiotape (in author's possession), sides 1 and 2; Willard Street interview by author, Greenville, February 10, 1996, audiotape (in author's possession), side 1; Dora Belue interview by author, Greenville, December 13, 1995, audiotape (in author's possession), sides 1

and 2; Potts interview, March 3, 1996, side 1, tape 1; Tom Karsell, "Carpet Mill Officers Visit Local Branch," *Delta Democrat-Times*, July 26, 1953, 10; Tom Karsell, "Greenville Mills Has First Annual Picnic," *Delta Democrat-Times*, June 28, 1953, 2; "2000 Attend Christmas Parties—Prize Winners Named," *Greenville Mills Woolgatherer*, January 1956, 2–3 (copy in author's possession, courtesy Martha Carlton); "Greenville Mills Is Cooled by Biggest System in Mississippi," *Delta Democrat-Times*, September 1, 1953, 3; William J. McQueen interview by author, Greenville, December 28, 1995, audiotape (in author's possession), side 1; "Mrs. Sanders Used Her Needle as a Burler," *Delta Democrat-Times*, September 29, 1954, 6B; "First Instructors at Greenville Mills Complete On-Job Training," *Delta Democrat-Times*, August 16, 1953, 24.

35. For corporate behavior, see, for example, William F. Hartford, *Where Is Our Responsibility? Unions and Economic Change in the New England Textile Industry, 1870–1960* (Amherst: University of Massachusetts Press, 1996), 122–24, 132, 140–41, 156–57; and Clete Daniel, *Culture of Misfortune: An Interpretive History of Textile Unionism in the United States* (Ithaca: ILR Press, 2001), 262. For superior conditions in Greenville, see Radigan interview, side 1; Potts interview, March 3, 1996, side 1, tape 1; "Greenville Mills, Inc., *Exhibit 'A,'*" attached to "Application for Exemption from Ad Valorem Taxes by Greenville Mills, Inc.," December 10, 1953, in *Application for Tax Exemption: State and County Ad Valorem, Washington County*, book 1, 95–96, Washington County Board of Supervisors, Greenville, Mississippi; "Average 4 Per Cent Increase," *Delta Democrat-Times*, April 25, 1954, 1; and "Most Greenville Mills Employees to Get Paid Vacations," *Delta Democrat-Times*, April 25, 1954, 20.

36. Betty Werlein Carter interview by author, New Orleans, March 4, 1996, audiotape (in author's possession); "Rounds Favors Plant," *Delta Democrat-Times*, December 31, 1950, 1; "Colored Folk Help on Bond Expenses," *Delta Democrat-Times*, January 14, 1951, 1; "Greenville Mills Has Picnic for Negro Employees," *Delta Democrat-Times*, July 16, 1953, 11; list of plant occupations by race and sex, February 13, 1965, attached to "Interrogatories to Defendants Greenville Mills Inc. and Mohasco Industries, Inc.," January 18, 1966, *Jane Chandler et al. v. Greenville Mills, Inc., Mohasco Industries, Inc., City of Greenville, Mississippi*, Civil Case File 65-24, Northern District of Mississippi, Greenville Division, Records of District Courts of the United States, RG 21, National Archives, Atlanta; Potts interview, March 3, 1996, side 2, tape 1; "21 Negroes File Rights Suit on Greenville Carpet Plant," *Memphis Commercial-Appeal*, May 14, 1965, "DM-COFO-Greenville" folder, box II-A, Eugene A. Cox Collection, Special Collections Department, Mitchell Memorial Library; Bill Dyndur to Paul [Swaity], November 19, 1966, "Wm. Dyndur" folder, box 54, M86-019, TWUA Records.

37. Boyd Payton to Emil Rieve, July 9, 1953, "Virginia State Director, Boyd Payton 1953, then So. Org. Director" folder, box 17, file 2A, MSS 129A, TWUA Records; Boyd E. Payton to William Pollock, July 14, 1953, "Alexander Smith, Yonkers, NY, Labor #IV, 1951–53" folder, box 343, MSS 396, ibid.; Belue interview, side 1.

38. William T. Edwards, advertisement, "Comes Now the Anti-Labor Attorney," *Delta Democrat-Times*, April 8, 1962, "Industry Appreciation Week Clippings" folder, GACOC Records; George F. Archer to the Citizens of Greenville, "Proclamation," [April 1962], "Industry Appreciation Week" folder, ibid.; "Special Week to Mark City Industrial Growth," *Delta Democrat Times*, 1962–1963 Scrapbook, Archer Papers; "Industry Role Stressed

at Kiwanis Club," *Delta Democrat-Times*, April 18, 1962, "Industry Appreciation Week" folder, GACOC Records; "Mosow Screw Makes 10,000 Products and Still Growing," *Delta Democrat-Times*, April 8, 1962, ibid.; "Atkins Saw Co. City's Newest 'Good Citizens,'" *Delta Democrat-Times*, April 13, 1962, ibid.; Joe Franko, "Disputed Votes Hold Key to Atkins Saw Election," *Delta Democrat-Times*, June 3, 1962, attached to Mary Thompson to Claude [Ramsay], June 10, 1962, "Greenville CLU, 1958–1978" folder, box 2161, "CIO and AFL-CIO, 1952–1985" series, Mississippi AFL-CIO Records; *Atkins Saw Division, Borg-Warner Corporation and United Steelworkers of America, AFL-CIO*, 148 NLRB 949, 951 (1964).

39. Calculations of union membership rates at several Greenville plants ranging from 44 to 52 percent draw on data in "Mississippi AFL-CIO Quarterly Standing of Affiliates, Sept. 30, 1968," "Miscellaneous, 1968" folder, box 2143, "Affiliated Unions, 1957–1983" series, Mississippi AFL-CIO Records; and "Greenville Industries," [1969?], "Industrial Plants" folder, GACOC Records. For Mosow's experience, see William A. Mosow interview by author, Greenville, Mississippi, December 23, 1995, audiotape (in author's possession), side 2, tape 1.

40. Carter, "Southern Towns and Northern Industry," 48–51, esp. 50 and 51; Hodding Carter to Lucy Randolph Mason, March 13, 1950, "HC: Correspondence: 1950: M (March–April)" folder, box 5, Carter Papers; editorial, "For the Greatest Good," *Delta Democrat-Times*, May 21, 1952, esp. 1; "Dear Chamber Member," [1961–1962], "Industrial Relations Program" folder, GACOC Records; remarks of Dick Hoffman in "3:15 p.m. Wednesday, April 27, 1966, Frank England—Ray Smith," untitled conference notes, April 25–29, 1966, "1962 Chamber Program" folder, ibid.

41. William E. Blundell, "Dixie vs. the Unions," *Wall Street Journal*, July 12, 1962, 1, 6, "Union File" folder, GACOC Records; Greenville Chamber of Commerce to All Workers in the Towboat Industries in Greenville, July 15, 1967, untitled folder, ibid.; Anse Dees to Claude Ayler, July 10, 1967, ibid.; Douglas Sease, "Yankee Go Home?: Many Northern Firms Seeking Sites in South Get Chilly Reception," *Wall Street Journal*, February 10, 1978, 1, esp. 17, attached to Claude Ramsay to E. M. Grantham, February 20, 1978, "Greenville CLU, 1958–1978" folder, box 2161, "CIO and AFL-CIO, 1952–1985" series, Mississippi AFL-CIO Records.

2

John McClellan, the Teamsters, and Biracial Labor Politics in Arkansas, 1947–1959

MICHAEL PIERCE

In late January 1957, Senator John L. McClellan of Arkansas gaveled the start of the Senate Select Committee on Improper Practices in the Labor or Management Field hearings on corruption and racketeering in the International Brotherhood of Teamsters. By the time the investigations of the McClellan Committee and subsequent congressional panels were over, the nation's labor movement had suffered a gruesome blow. Two Teamsters presidents had been imprisoned, the American Federation of Labor–Congress of Industrial Organizations (AFL-CIO) had expelled its largest and most powerful affiliate, Congress had passed the Landrum-Griffin Act (further restricting union activities), the AFL-CIO had prohibited Teamsters officials from holding positions of authority in local and state labor federations even if they carried a card from another union, and the nation's labor movement had become associated with extortion, racketeering, and organized crime.[1] The decline of the labor movement that has continued into the twenty-first century had begun.

While acknowledging that real corruption existed within the Teamsters and other unions investigated by the McClellan Committee, historians have argued that McClellan and other members of the committee had an anti-union agenda. According to David Witwer, "the McClellan Committee depicted the problem of union corruption as intrinsically bound up in the phenomenon of union power, and it pursued a political agenda intended to win new restraints on that power."[2] What these historians have not realized, though, is that McClellan's efforts to restrain union power were motivated by state and local political concerns as well as national ones. Although the McClellan Committee heard no evidence of any Teamster wrongdoing in Arkansas, McClellan's attack on the Teamsters helped put an end to the efforts of a biracial coalition

Figure 2.1. Arkansas governor Sidney McMath, one of the few southern politicians willing to be associated with Harry Truman after the president supported a civil rights program in 1948, emerged as the labor movement's favorite southern governor during Truman's second term. (Courtesy Special Collections, University of Arkansas Libraries, Fayetteville.)

of working-class Arkansans that sought to transform the state by eliminating the poll tax, increasing economic and political opportunities for blacks and whites alike, expanding New Deal programs, reforming a regressive tax code, and removing a "right-to-work" measure from the statute books. Led by former governor Sidney S. McMath, who served as chief legal counsel for the Arkansas State Federated Labor Council (more commonly known as the Arkansas AFL-CIO), and Odell Smith, a Teamsters official who served as president of the Arkansas AFL-CIO, this biracial coalition had battled McClellan and his conservative allies for nearly a decade before the start of the Teamsters hearings.[3]

Although McClellan had voted in 1935 for the National Labor Relations Act while a member of the House of Representatives and had promised his "unequivocal support of organized labor" when first elected to the Senate in 1942, by the end of the senator's first term his relationship with the nation's labor movement had soured. Believing the labor movement to be a threat to the businessmen and planters who were his biggest supporters and guardians of the South's racial status quo, he had allied himself with conservative southern Democrats in voting for the Smith-Connally Act in 1943, the Taft-Hartley Act in 1947, and an unsuccessful measure to repeal the Norris-LaGuardia Act. He also opposed much of labor's agenda, which featured civil rights protections, Fair Employment Practices legislation, increases in the minimum wage and Social Security benefits, and progressive changes in tax policy.[4]

As early as 1947, McClellan had identified labor unions, especially those associated with the CIO, as the biggest threat to his political survival, telling one supporter, "the Labor bosses will try to get someone to run against me [in 1948]. If they do, it is reasonably certain that the national labor organizations, or rather some of them, will spend a lot of money trying to defeat me." He and Arkansas conservatives had also identified Sidney McMath, then a handsome, young, liberal war hero who as a prosecuting attorney had successfully taken on the corrupt political machine that protected illegal gambling in Hot Springs, as the man labor would most likely tap to challenge for the Democratic nomination for the Senate.[5]

But instead of running for McClellan's Senate seat in 1948, McMath decided to seek the governor's office, which was being vacated after two terms by Benjamin Travis Laney Jr., a friend, business partner, and close political ally of McClellan's. The state's labor movement loathed Laney as much as it did McClellan, blaming him for passage of a 1947 measure that gave teeth to Arkansas's otherwise impotent right-to-work law. Laney was also especially close to the Arkansas Free Enterprise Association, a stridently anti-labor coalition of eastern Arkansas cotton planters and southern Arkansas businessmen that had pushed through the state's original right-to-work law in 1944 and resisted federal efforts to improve the status of African Americans.[6]

The 1948 campaign for the Democratic nomination for Arkansas governor—like most campaigns in the South that year—centered on President Harry Truman's civil rights program. McMath's main opponent, former attorney general Jack Holt, based his campaign almost entirely on his opposition to Truman's program and support for segregation, boasting, "The civil rights issue is my baby, and I can't talk enough about it." McMath never explicitly endorsed the specific measures included in Truman's program, though. As Arkansas journalist Harry S. Ashmore explained, "McMath could no more support the program and survive in Arkansas than Adam Clayton Powell could oppose it and survive in Harlem." But McMath made his support for the civil rights movement's overall goals clear, calling for Arkansas and other southern states to take action to eradicate discriminatory practices. This, he told voters, would forestall federal action and avoid confrontations over states' rights. McMath pledged to increase aid to schools of both black and white children, encourage black voting, ensure that African Americans be treated fairly before the law, and support a state anti-lynching measure. He also criticized Holt and other "cheap politicians" who used the black man "as a whipping boy" to get votes.[7]

In his campaign for governor, McMath put together a biracial coalition of the poor and working people. He called for the state government to take a more active role in promoting the welfare of all of its citizens, not just the cotton planters, bankers, and utility magnates who had traditionally controlled Arkansas politics. Like many other southern liberals of his generation, McMath thought that disfranchisement and Jim Crow were simply tools that elites used to keep poor people divided and powerless. Not only did he castigate "cheap politicians" like Holt for pitting whites against blacks, but he also told a black journalist that Arkansas's poll tax "is not a weapon in the war between whites and blacks, but rather is a hammer employed by the upper classes against the lower classes." McMath later described the segregationist movement that was energized by the *Brown* decision as a "Trojan Horse" whose real purpose was the "destruction" of the southern labor movement, the only institution capable of bringing working-class whites and blacks together to challenge the prerogatives of the southern elite. Thus McMath saw efforts to curtail the civil rights of African Americans and efforts to undermine the power of the labor movement as two sides of the same coin.[8]

During the gubernatorial campaign, McClellan remained publicly neutral, but his opposition to McMath was unmistakable. The senator agreed with Harry Ashmore that McMath's unwillingness to endorse Truman's civil rights program was tactical rather than a reflection of his true feelings and told his network of supporters across the state that he could never support a candidate who "espoused President Truman's civil liberties program." McClellan also used his friend and political ally Ben Laney as surrogate to talk about state political issues. This strategy allowed McClellan to avoid taking positions that might create trouble with his fellow Democrats in the nation's capital while still letting the voters of Arkansas know where he stood.[9]

Like many other southern Democrats in 1948, McClellan was more interested in national politics, especially the party's choice of a presidential nominee, than in state concerns. He did not want to see President Truman renominated. Sentiment against Truman had been running high in Arkansas and the rest of the South, especially after the introduction of the president's civil rights program in early 1948. Governor Laney had taken the lead in opposing the program, serving as permanent chairman of the States' Rights Democrats, the southern governors' organization that was formed to prevent Truman's renomination. Heading into the Democratic National Convention in Philadelphia in July that year, conservative southern Democrats had settled upon Laney as the man to challenge Truman for the party's nomination. No one expected Laney to get the nomination, but conservative southerners wanted to send a message to the national party. McClellan agreed to officially nominate Laney, even pre-releasing his speech to the press. In it, McClellan asserted, "We are striving for a choice in this convention of a leader in our party as the next President of the United States—not a man who favors this civil rights program, but one who will oppose its enactment." At the last moment, Laney called off his challenge to Truman, and McClellan never delivered his speech.[10]

In wake of the Philadelphia convention, conservative southern Democrats began planning the nomination of one of their own for president, and many in the press predicted that Laney would be that person. Laney even traveled to the Dixiecrat convention in Birmingham to accept the nomination, but, just as in Philadelphia, he had a last-minute change of heart and withdrew his name from consideration. Instead, the nomination went to South Carolina governor Strom Thurmond with Mississippi governor Fielding Wright in the second slot. Laney, though, quickly went to work to ensure that Arkansas's nine electoral votes went to Thurmond and Wright.[11]

After defeating Holt in the August Democratic primary, which in one-party Arkansas was the only election that really mattered, McMath entered the fray between Truman and those Arkansans supporting Thurmond and Wright. McMath traveled the state, promising jobs and roads to those local officials who pledged their support to the president's reelection. The showdown between McMath and the Dixiecrats came in late September when the Arkansas State Democratic Party met to choose electors for the presidential ballot. Led by Governor Laney and Arkansas Free Enterprise Association executive director John L. Daggett, the Dixiecrats proposed that the Democratic Party refuse to name any electors at all, a move that would force both the Dixiecrats and Truman's supporters to file petitions to have their candidates and slates of electors placed on the ballot. Passage of the proposal would have given the Dixiecrats, who had already secured the needed petitions to put Thurmond on the state ballot, a tremendous advantage over Truman Democrats, who would have had to scramble to secure signatures before the approaching deadline. McClellan arrived in Little Rock as the convention was getting under way, announcing his support for the Dixiecrat position and blaming Truman for destroying the unity of the Democratic Party. With the support of the state's senior senator, Laney and Daggett entered the convention confident of success but were soon astonished to find that McMath had already lined up the votes to defeat their efforts and to ensure that Truman's name alone appeared on the ballot as the party's nominee. Laney, though, did not concede defeat graciously, delivering a blistering attack on Truman: "A strong political party has been wrecked by a man . . . [whose] civil rights proposals are Communistic in principle." The results of the convention, though, signaled that Arkansas would not be joining neighboring Mississippi and Louisiana in the Dixiecrat column. In the November election, Thurmond and Wright won but 16.5 percent of the vote in the state, far behind Truman's 61.7 percent.[12]

After the elections of 1948, Arkansas's new governor became one of Truman's favorites, intensifying the rivalry between McMath and the state's senior senator. The president disliked both McClellan and Arkansas's junior senator, J. William Fulbright, whom he considered arrogant, so he had McMath dispense much of the federal patronage throughout the state. Truman's actions strengthened McMath's organization at McClellan's expense.[13] There were also rumors that Truman would appoint McClellan to a federal judgeship in order to open up his Senate seat for McMath, who would support the president's efforts to repeal the Taft-Hartley Act and push through civil rights legislation. The state's leading conservatives wrote McClellan, warning him that McMath's support of civil rights and labor legislation would make him a dangerous senator. As George Benson, the president of Harding College and an increasingly influential voice in the nation's conservative movement, explained, "The United States Senate needs you a lot more than it needs Sid McMath or anyone else pledged to back these socialist schemes."[14]

Governor McMath's state policies grew out of his conviction that "a well-paid working man benefits the whole community economically." To that end, as governor he vetoed several anti-labor measures and supported legislation that doubled the annual budget of the Labor Department, increased the state's minimum wage, strengthened mine regulations, and promoted vigorous enforcement of long-ignored workplace safety measures. He also intervened in several labor disputes, helping forge compromises and winning the praise of union leaders who were used to politicians serving the interests of management and owners. For instance, when the Brotherhood of Locomotive Engineers (BLE) struck the Missouri-Pacific Railroad, McMath traveled to St. Louis to mediate the dispute, which threatened commerce in much of Arkansas. McMath and his chief adviser, Henry Woods, framed the proposal that ended the walkout, earning the gratitude of a BLE representative: "The governor was not only interested in terminating the strike but was also interested in the [positive] reaction of the men to the kind of settlement made." McMath also pardoned three black union members who had been convicted of violating the state's anti–labor violence law and sentenced to prison. The three had been picketing the Southern Cotton Oil Mill when a replacement worker pulled a gun during a scuffle and killed a striker. Although the three had not been involved in the violence, the law held all picketers (but not company guards or scabs) responsible for any violence that occurred during a strike.[15]

McMath proved an important ally of the national labor movement as well. In 1949, northern Democrats on behalf of the Truman administration introduced a labor reform bill that would have essentially repealed the Taft-Hartley Act. But before it could come to a vote, Representative John Wood of Georgia offered a substitute that CIO president Phil Murray considered more "drastic" than Taft-Hartley. Caught flat-footed, the leaders of the AFL and the CIO feared that Republicans and southern Democrats had the votes to pass Wood's measure. McMath, according to labor columnist Victor Riesel, sprang into action: "As [the labor chiefs] bickered among themselves and hammered Congressmen with dizzying demands for hopelessly different stratagems, they were saved by midnight calls from a southern governor most of the labor leaders didn't even know. This long-distance phone calling was done by the youngish pal of President Truman, the ex-prosecutor, Arkansas's traveling governor, Sidney McMath." McMath convinced three Arkansas representatives to change their votes, providing the margin that defeated the most significant anti-labor bill of Truman's second term and transforming McMath into the national labor movement's favorite southern governor.[16]

McMath's first term in office—his friendship with Truman, his successful efforts to bring blacks into the state's Democratic Party, his support for organized labor, his advocacy of rural electrical cooperatives and public power—so angered the state's conservatives that they broke with the Arkansas tradition that usually accorded governors a second two-year term without serious opposition. In early 1950, Ben Laney announced that he would seek a return to the governor's office, and McClellan threw his political organization behind Laney's candidacy, with the senator's brother, W. H. "Pete" McClellan, serving as a top Laney campaign official. As the *El Dorado Daily News* declared, the election would be a "showdown" between the state's two largest political factions—the supporters of McMath against those who favored McClellan and Laney.[17]

Laney centered much of his campaign on his conservative record as governor—especially when it came to taxation and state spending—and his opposition to the fair employment practices legislation supported by the president. He argued that passage of a fair employment practices measure would give government officials "the authority to dictate private . . . affairs" and result in the "total destruction of American democracy." McMath insisted that he had never endorsed the fair employment measure and that it was federal legislation that had little to do with the issues that the next governor would face. Instead he focused on his road-building program, efforts to lure industry to the state, plan to increase rural electrification, and measures to improve education. McMath's avoidance of civil rights issues, his solid record during his first two years, and the state's tradition of giving governors a second two-year term all conspired to give McMath an easy victory, defeating Laney (and McClellan) by a margin of two to one.[18]

Not surprisingly, McMath's campaign funds in 1950 came mostly from organized labor, with black political groups and liquor dealers chipping in the rest. Indeed, CIO Political Action Committee (CIO PAC) director Jack Kroll took credit for Laney's defeat, telling McMath that his win was "the greatest of our victories in the South this year." The CIO's financial contribution, though, probably paled in comparison to that of Arkansas Labor's League for Political Education, since the AFL had between two and three times as many dues-paying members in the state.[19]

During his second term, McMath decided to seek a third, mostly for political reasons. As one of his sons later recalled, "Dad's idea was to get a third term as governor [in 1952], then beat John McClellan in '54, then run for president."[20] McMath's ambitions were no secret in the state, and Arkansas's senior senator decided that stopping (or at least damaging) McMath in 1952 would make his own reelection in 1954 easier. McClellan's opposition was not McMath's only obstacle to a third term: Arkansas tradition held that two terms were enough for any governor. Moreover, political opponents had accused McMath's Highway Commission of crooked practices, resulting in a high-profile investigation; and McMath was closely associated with an increasingly unpopular president.[21]

Several formidable candidates announced their plans to challenge McMath that year. They included Ike Murphy, the sitting attorney general; Jack Holt, the former attorney general who had lost to McMath in 1948; Congressman Boyd Tackett; and Francis Cherry, a respected but relatively unknown judge from Jonesboro. Anticipating that with so many strong candidates in the field no one would receive the majority needed to win during the initial round of voting, McClellan stayed quiet during the early stages of the campaign and waited for the runoff between the two top finishers. To most observers' surprise, Cherry emerged from the field as McMath's opponent for the runoff, and the senator promptly became the biggest Cherry backer in the state, providing advice, a political organization with experienced activists in every county, and, most importantly, money. McClellan also helped Cherry secure the endorsements of the eliminated candidates; rumors circulated that each was paid thirty thousand dollars. Cherry's main tactic during the runoff was to associate McMath with the increasingly unpopular president, calling him "Truman's boy," a denigration with not very subtle racial overtones.[22]

The labor movement rallied to McMath's side. Both Arkansas Labor's League for Political Education and the state's chapter of CIO PAC convened special meetings to boost the governor, and local labor councils did likewise. Both of the national labor federations sent political operatives into the state to advise the McMath campaign and rally trade unionists. The labor people's main strategy was to link Cherry to McClellan, telling members that since so little was known about Cherry, he had to be judged by the friends that he kept and that Cherry's best friends were the "true 'Dixiecrat'" McClellan and his "Eastern Arkansas clique of anti-union, anti-republic, unreconstructed rebels."[23]

Labor's efforts were for naught, however, as Cherry soundly defeated McMath. In announcing the election results, the *Arkansas Gazette* ran a large front-page photo of the state's senior senator embracing Cherry with the headline "McClellan Also Claims Victory." The paper suggested that the defeat had so badly damaged McMath's political career that McClellan's reelection in 1954 was almost assured.[24]

Although losing to Cherry had put a crimp in his ambitions, McMath decided to go ahead and run for the Senate in 1954. As Henry Woods, McMath's top political adviser, explained, "Sid had made up his mind that he was going to run against McClellan come hell or high water because McClellan had played a big part in Cherry's campaign. He had gone all out. So Sid—if nothing else—he was going to settle the score."[25] Woods, though, never agreed that McClellan had been responsible for McMath's defeat in 1952. He later explained that the most important factor in McMath's defeat was the governor's close association with President Truman, whose approval ratings hovered just above 20 percent and who would be two years removed from office when McMath challenged McClellan in 1954.[26]

McMath faced problems of a personal sort after leaving the governor's office. He was encumbered by debt and had a wife and five children to support. But working full time would have made it difficult to campaign and put together his political operation. McMath and Woods came up with a simple solution; they would open a law firm and solicit work from their political allies—especially trade unions and rural electrical cooperatives. The Arkansas State Federation of Labor promptly named McMath and Woods their chief legal counsels, and the Arkansas Industrial Union Council and several large international unions, including some that did not have much of a presence in the state, such as the United Auto Workers, put McMath and Woods on retainer. The unions expected to receive legal services for their money, but they were far more interested in sustaining McMath's political career.[27]

Preparing for his Senate bid, McMath forged a friendship and political alliance with Odell Smith, who had become the state's most powerful labor leader. The two men became so close that one of McMath's sons recalled, "Odell became like a godfather to me."[28] Together McMath, Woods, and Smith formed the core of the state's liberal community for the next decade, working to keep intact an alliance of working-class whites and blacks as conflict over civil rights roiled the state. Head of Arkansas Labor's League for Political Education, a trustee of the Teamster's Central States Pension Fund, and former president of the Little Rock labor council, Smith by the early 1950s had almost single-handedly organized two thousand truck drivers, warehouse workers, and hotel and restaurant employees into Teamsters Local 878, the state's largest and most powerful local. Called "unlettered and uneducated" by Woods, Smith nonetheless had the intellect and leadership qualities that made him a valuable friend and a dangerous opponent. During Little Rock's Central High crisis, Smith's fellow integrationists often stood in awe at his ability to sway opinion. Vivion Brewer, who led the 1959 campaign to reopen Little Rock's high schools after segregationists had closed them to avoid integration, watched Smith preside over a meeting of trade unionists discussing the viability of the state's public school system: "Mr. Smith was chairman nonpareil. Despite noticeable opposition, he maneuvered the discussion and the voting as a magician pulls a rabbit out of a hat, and before I could follow or apprehend his methods, he had triumphantly secured passage of a resolution to maintain the public schools. I was amused, amazed, and admiring."[29]

In the early 1950s, Smith was the one person capable of uniting the state's disparate trade unionists into a movement. Although an official in an AFL affiliate, Smith was, according to longtime Arkansas labor journalist Victor Ray, a "CIO-type of guy." Not only did he head a large industrial union local, but Smith was also politically liberal, believing in public power, public education, an expansion of the welfare state, and African American civil rights. Still, Smith commanded the respect of those in the building trades and more craft-oriented AFL unions. Like many Teamsters leaders, he had negotiated contracts that would allow his local to get around the Taft-Hartley Act's prohibition of secondary boycotts by including explicit language that drivers did not have to cross picket lines. This gave Teamsters Local 878 and Smith tremendous power that they could bring to bear to help trade unionists around the state. If a building trade local or factory workers went on strike, no supplies would be delivered to the job site. As a trustee of the Central States Pension Fund, Smith used his access to Teamster money to increase his influence.

He steered union funds into local banks and construction projects, winning allies in both the business community and among the building trades. The Teamsters also supplied loans for the construction of union halls around the state, held the largest block of stock in Little Rock's union-owned bus company, and provided capital for the expansion of the state's labor newspaper. By the early 1950s, Smith had built an Arkansas labor empire that wielded the type of power that would concern the McClellan Committee much more than the simple racketeering and corruption that the committee did so much to uncover.[30]

McMath began his senatorial bid almost immediately upon leaving the governor's mansion with visits to the nation's most prominent labor leaders—AFL president George Meany, CIO president Walter Reuther, CIO PAC director Jack Kroll, and the heads of the railroad brotherhoods. He asked the labor chiefs for the money and organizers needed to launch an unprecedented campaign to convince not only trade unionists but also African Americans and members of rural electrical cooperatives to pay their poll taxes before the October 1, 1953, deadline to be eligible for the 1954 election. McMath reasoned that his, and organized labor's, only hope of defeating McClellan was to dramatically expand the number of voters in the state.[31]

The labor federations responded positively to McMath's plan to send McClellan into early retirement, dispatching organizers and funds into the state to aid the poll-tax effort. The two big labor federations created special accounts—controlled by their state affiliates—to pay for the campaign. The effort began with a two-day meeting on May 18 and 19, 1953, at which officials from both the Arkansas State Federation of Labor and the Arkansas Industrial Union Council met with leaders of several African American political groups. Presided over by Henry Woods and Odell Smith, the meeting mapped out a two-pronged strategy: local labor leaders, most of whom were white, would work in their own communities to increase the number of poor and working-class voters, and African American activists would launch a coordinated effort designed to reach every potential black voter in the state.[32]

The CIO PAC—largely because of its ties to the state's black leadership and its reputation in Arkansas's African American communities—took the lead in helping black activists organize their part of the campaign, sending Philip Weightman, the organization's chief African American political organizer, to the state.[33] Weightman facilitated the creation of the Citizens' Committee, bringing together a who's who of Arkansas's African American leadership: Jeffrey Hawkins of Little Rock's East Side Civic League; I. S. McClinton of the Arkansas Democratic Voters Association; Ozell Sutton of the *Arkansas Democrat*; Harry Bass of the Urban League; Charles Bussey of Little Rock's

Veterans for Good Government; O. A. Sherman of the North Little Rock Civic League; J. R. Booker, Little Rock's most prominent civil rights attorney; J. M. Robinson, who had led the fight to allow African Americans to participate in the Democratic Party; and C. H. Jones of the *Southern Mediator Journal*, one of Little Rock's two black newspapers. These activists shared the labor movement's desire to empower blacks in Arkansas. For their part, laborites recognized that black voters were critical to liberal hopes in the state.[34]

Weightman stayed mostly behind the scenes, creating the impression that Citizens' Committee was a purely Arkansas creation, but he oversaw much of the committee's activity. He improvised its structure, showed activists the neighborhood-canvassing methods the CIO had perfected in the urban North, and provided fliers and other registration materials. Two young black attorneys, Wiley Branton and Jackie Shropshire, both recent graduates of the University of Arkansas School of Law, worked closely with the campaign, setting up county committees throughout Arkansas's black belt and mediating between Weightman and the state's older and often more conservative African American leadership.[35]

The climax of the poll-tax campaign among African Americans came on September 11, 1953, when the Citizens' Committee held a "massive poll tax meeting" at Little Rock's Dunbar High School. Weightman arranged for African American Chicago congressman William Dawson to serve as the main speaker, and more than a thousand people showed up for what was reportedly the largest African American political rally in Arkansas since the onset of Jim Crow in the early 1890s. Dawson told those assembled that "Negroes can solve all of their problems at the ballot box," and those who did not vote would only have themselves to blame for their race's second-class status. Dawson and other speakers never mentioned the upcoming Senate race or the role of organized labor in the poll-tax effort, but Sid McMath was on hand to welcome Dawson to the state and greet potential voters.[36]

The Arkansas Industrial Union Council and the Arkansas State Federation of Labor worked closely in the campaign to convince white trade unionists and their poor and working-class neighbors to become eligible to vote in the 1954 election. In a few sections of the state, labor already had extensive programs to ensure that members became eligible to vote each election cycle. In Fort Smith, for example, beer and liquor distributors gave the local labor federations six thousand dollars each year to pay the poll taxes of members. But in 1953 the state's labor movement redoubled its efforts, trying to reach every corner of the state with rallies, literature, and phone calls. The labor movement's strategy was to associate failure to vote to the state's regressive tax structure: "Only 37.8% of the people old enough to vote in Arkansas bothered to cast a ballot in 1952. If you were a politician, who would you tax—the wealthy who vote—or the working people who don't."[37]

The success of the poll-tax effort, especially among African Americans, had a collateral affect that pleased labor officials—it spurred other liberals to seek office.[38] One of those was Orval Eugene Faubus, a McMath protégé who told Henry Woods that he was preparing to challenge Francis Cherry in the 1954 gubernatorial race. McMath and Woods were not happy, believing that Faubus stood little chance of actually winning and fearing that his candidacy would mobilize Cherry supporters who would also cast ballots for McClellan. Nonetheless, after Faubus formally entered the race and the campaign began, McMath and the political organization that he had put together worked closely with the Faubus campaign.[39]

The other prominent liberal appearing on the 1954 statewide ballot was Attorney General Tom Gentry, who was seeking reelection. Arkansas had a long tradition of attorney generals' maintaining private legal practices while in office, and Gentry had continued that tradition. But instead of taking money from Arkansas Power and Light or banking interests, as his predecessors had done, Gentry was on retainer to Teamsters Local 878 and was especially close to Odell Smith. Gentry's main challenger, Jim Johnson, a state senator from southeast Arkansas who later became Arkansas's most influential segregationist, built his election campaign mostly on charges that Gentry was too close to the Teamsters to be impartial and that his work for Local 878 was taking too much time away from his official duties.[40]

In the winter and spring of 1954, before the campaign season got under way, McMath and Odell Smith made the rounds to union meetings around the state. In places such as Texarkana, Fort Smith, Pine Bluff, and Hot Springs, Smith would begin by trumpeting McMath's labor record. The former governor would then tear into McClellan for his Dixiecrat ways, arguing that the hidden agenda of those screaming for states' rights was to allow states to nullify the National Labor Relations Act and the Fair Labor Standards Act. Without the protections of these federal laws, McMath concluded, Arkansas's labor movement would founder and the wages of all of the state's workers would drop. These meetings culminated in McMath's appearance at the annual conference of the Arkansas State Federation of Labor, a meeting that featured one verbal attack after another aimed at "the Enemy of the People," John McClellan.[41]

During the summer campaign season, McMath continued to court the labor and black vote by disparaging McClellan. To labor groups, McMath emphasized McClellan's support for the Taft-Hartley Act and other measures designed to restrain the labor movement. To African American audiences, he talked about McClellan's opposition to a Senate motion against seating Theodore Bilbo, the demagogue elected to represent Mississippi who had been accused of inciting racial violence. To both groups he played up McClellan's opposition to increases in the minimum wage and Social Security benefits. McMath was in constant contact with national labor officials, seeking advice regarding television advertisements, keeping the labor chiefs informed about the campaign, requesting that political organizers be sent to the state, and asking for more money to buy newspaper advertisements and television and radio time. The labor movement was generous in its support for McMath's campaign, with Arkansas Labor's League for Political Education contributing $15,500, CIO PAC giving $5,000, the Machinists' Non-partisan Political League chipping in $2,000, and the United Steelworkers of America adding another $2,000. All told, more than 75 percent of the cash spent on McMath's campaign came from labor, in addition to contributions to the poll-tax campaign, the salaries of organizers working on the campaign, other forms of in-kind aid, and the legal fees that allowed McMath and Woods to support their families.[42]

The state's African American leadership, with two notable exceptions, got behind the McMath campaign. To help mobilize black voters, the International Woodworkers of America–CIO, whose membership included African American lumber mill and timber workers from the southeastern part of the state, assigned black staff members to work full-time on behalf of McMath and the other liberal candidates. Among the staff members were Will Boston, who was also the leader of the NAACP in Ashley County, and A. C. Hudson, who operated in Little Rock and central Arkansas. Although most of their work was behind the scenes, Boston did take the lead in publicly denouncing those black leaders—C. H. Jones of the *Southern Mediator Journal* and Pine Bluff attorney W. H. Flowers—who endorsed McClellan. He told the readers of the *Arkansas State Press* that Jones and Flowers "have the very audacity to ask Negroes in Arkansas to endorse six more years of the same treatment. . . . [McClellan] has endorsed the Bilbos, the Ben Laneys, and their Dixiecrat philosophies throughout his public career." Boston also reminded the state's black voters that McClellan had claimed that Truman's civil rights proposals "contravene and viciously violate both the letter and spirit of the constitution of the United States."[43]

McClellan mobilized his powerful organization for the reelection bid. With supporters throughout the state, strong financial backing, a states' rights agenda that was increasingly popular in the wake of the *Brown* decision, the power of incumbency, and a name that had often been in the news owing to his belated yet popular opposition to Joseph McCarthy's investigation into Communist infiltration of the United States Army, McClellan was a formidable candidate, and he used his influence to help like-minded politicians running that year. By the end of the campaign, something that many observers had suspected all along had become clear—McClellan, Cherry, and Johnson were coordinating their electoral efforts, running as an unofficial conservative slate. On the last night of the campaign, the three candidates appeared together at a large rally in Little Rock's MacArthur Park, with the speeches being relayed to television and radio stations across the state.[44]

When the votes were counted, McClellan barely won the majority needed to avoid a runoff with McMath and keep his Senate seat. The other candidates supported by McClellan were not so lucky. Tom Gentry prevailed over Jim Johnson in the attorney general's race, and Governor Francis Cherry found himself in a runoff with Orval Faubus. With McMath beaten, the coalition put together by McMath and the labor movement devoted itself to Faubus's gubernatorial effort. As Woods later recalled, "Our whole political organization, which was still fairly potent, swung in behind him, because Sid had been eliminated and here was a chance to come out with a winning gubernatorial candidate." Arkansas Industrial Union Council officials used almost the same language to describe their activity, asserting that they "swung behind Orval Faubus following McMath's defeat."[45]

During the runoff, Cherry pulled a surprise that he hoped would knock out Faubus. The governor attacked Faubus for having attended Commonwealth College, a socialist, labor institution in southwest Arkansas near the Oklahoma border, circulating an eight-page newspaper detailing a young Faubus's activities at the school, which the state had shut down in 1940 for subversive activity. Most of Cherry's charges were in fact true. Faubus had been born into a socialist household deep in the Ozark Mountains, his father giving him the middle name Eugene to honor Eugene V. Debs, and he had attended the college. Faubus's initial denial of Cherry's charges was awkward and unconvincing, and it appeared that Faubus's chances had been sunk. But several McMath supporters—Harry Ashmore, Edwin Dunaway of Little Rock's Urban League, and most importantly Henry Woods—sprang to Faubus's aid, writing an eloquent, albeit disingenuous, speech for Faubus to rebut the charges, securing money to broadcast the speech statewide, and portraying Cherry as a red-baiter in the mold of Joseph McCarthy. The speech did the trick, and Faubus went on to defeat Cherry by a narrow margin.[46]

The 1954 Democratic primary elections in Arkansas ended with McClellan holding onto his Senate seat but the two other men he and his organization had supported going down to defeat, Francis Cherry to a candidate with a socialist past and Jim Johnson to a Teamsters attorney. McClellan had good reason to fear that his political situation would become increasingly tenuous. The number of African American voters in Arkansas was increasing, and the anticipated merger of the American Federation of Labor and the Congress of Industrial Organizations promised to increase the power of those working the hardest to unseat him and his allies. For the next two years, McClellan watched as McMath, Woods, Smith, and the state's labor movement resumed their ambitious program to empower the white and black members of the poor and working classes.

At the heart of labor's program was the elimination of the state's poll tax, which had been on the books since 1892.[47] The poll tax served the interest of the Arkansas planters and businessmen who traditionally controlled state politics and supported McClellan in two ways. First, it discouraged poor people—both black and white—from voting. It was not so much the cost of the poll tax—one dollar per year—that kept people away from the polls as it was the fact that voters had to pay the tax so far in advance, had to follow overly complicated procedures, and had to keep their receipts secure for several months. Second, poll-tax receipts could be manipulated in ways that gave planters extra votes. The most common method of manipulation was for a landowner to purchase poll-tax receipts for his tenants and sharecroppers and then either vote for them or tell them how to vote. Although the old plantation system was in decline by 1954, Arkansas liberals believed that planters had stolen the Senate election by voting for their tenants. As Woods explained, "I can show you township after township in this state where a plantation owner goes down and buys six or 700 poll taxes and those six or 700 are voted on election day. . . . You also know that they used that very system to steal the senate election from us and to steal other elections from liberal candidates in the state." Woods boasted that when the poll tax was eliminated, the labor movement would "take political power," elect liberal politicians, and get rid of the state's right-to-work law, the anti-labor violence statute, and an array of anti-labor regulations enacted by municipalities in eastern Arkansas.[48]

As the first step toward repealing the poll tax, in the late summer of 1954 the leaders of the Arkansas Labor's League for Political Education and the state's CIO PAC, building on their cooperation during the McMath-McClellan race, met to form Labor's Joint Educational Committee, with Odell Smith serving as chairman. Both Woods and McMath were present as legal representatives for the State Federation of Labor. Labor's Joint Educational Committee decided that it would first try to convince the state legislature, which would meet in

January 1955, to put an amendment on the 1956 ballot repealing that portion of the Arkansas Constitution requiring the poll tax. If the General Assembly refused to act, labor would place the amendment on the ballot through the initiative process.[49]

Governor-elect Faubus pledged to support the Joint Educational Committee's efforts to repeal the poll tax, meeting with the group throughout the late summer and fall of 1954 to map out strategy. Faubus also took steps to remake the Arkansas Democratic Party along more liberal lines and to free it from the domination of planter and business interests. He added six seats (one for each of the state's congressional districts) to the party's Central Committee to be filled by African Americans. Faubus gave Labor's Joint Educational Committee the task of selecting the individuals for three of the slots. Arkansas thus became the first southern state with African Americans serving on state Democratic Central Committee, which determined the rules by which party nominees were selected and chose some of the state's delegates to national party conventions.[50]

On January 15, 1955, four days after his inauguration, Governor Faubus appeared before the Arkansas Industrial Union Council's annual conference, publicly crediting the labor movement for its role for his victory and pledging support for the elimination of the poll tax and the creation of a simple registration system. "You made the difference in my victory," he told the audience of black and white trade unionists assembled at the Joseph T. Robinson Auditorium in Little Rock. Faubus insisted that no one should have to pay for the right to vote.[51]

Around this time, the nationally syndicated columnist Westbrook Pegler attacked the new governor and his "chief henchman," Sidney McMath, calling them "violent political radicals." Pegler did not discuss their programs or policies; instead he attacked them personally, rehashing the Commonwealth College charges and an even older scandal involving the killing of McMath's father by his wife, a "pistol packing mama." He concluded that McMath and Faubus may appear to be "paltry and ephemeral clowns in a commonwealth of acorn-eaters," but he warned that they may "be men of giant significance," more dangerous than Harry Bridges, Alger Hiss, or any of New York City's "first string Reds."[52] It is unclear why a columnist of Pegler's stature would take an interest in the politics of such a small state so far away from the nation's political center, but his relationship with McClellan might provide a clue. Pegler, who pioneered the use of corruption and racketeering charges to undermine the effectiveness of the labor movement, had worked closely with Joseph McCarthy's Senate Permanent Investigations Committee when McClellan was the committee's ranking minority member. With the Democrats taking control of the Senate in 1955, Pegler needed to ingratiate himself with the new committee chairman.[53]

In 1955, Labor's Joint Educational Committee made little headway convincing the General Assembly to put an amendment to repeal the poll tax on the ballot, but it did flex its political muscle in a way that had to worry conservatives like McClellan. In the midst of two headline-grabbing strikes in Little Rock—the Teamsters' strike against Terry Dairy and the bus drivers' strike against the Capitol Transit Company—Labor's Joint Education Committee decided that it had to get rid of the city's anti-union mayor, Republican Pratt Remmel, and replace him with someone more sympathetic to organized labor. To that end, labor officials recruited Woodrow Wilson Mann, a handsome, young insurance executive, to challenge Remmel and employed the canvassing methods developed by the CIO in the urban North for the first time, putting the name of every person who had paid the poll tax on a note card, organizing the note cards into shoeboxes by blocks and wards, having ward organizers and block captains visit or call each potential voter, and making sure that those in favor of labor's candidate made it to the polls. Henry Woods would boast that labor's canvassing method had allowed Arkansas's labor movement to transform "a rank amateur in politics" into Little Rock's mayor and predicted that such methods would help elect liberals in the future.[54]

In 1955, Labor's Joint Educational Committee also began taking steps to repeal the state's poll tax through an initiated act that would appear on the ballot the following year. That March, Smith, Woods, and Faubus met with the CIO PAC's Jack Kroll to plot strategy and ask that Phil Weightman coordinate another effort to convince African Americans to pay the poll taxes to become eligible to vote.[55] When Weightman returned to Arkansas, he traveled the eastern part of the state, reconnecting with black activists and distributing poll-tax materials. Weightman was particularly active in Jefferson County, which, after Little Rock's Pulaski County, had the state's second-largest number of black residents. There he worked closely with the Jefferson County Voters Association, which was headed by a CIO member. Telling black residents that "Christians have a responsibility for civic and political action," the Jefferson County Voters Association distributed poll-tax forms supplied by the CIO to residents throughout the county. Kroll also convinced the International Woodworkers of America–CIO to again send black organizers to help out with the endeavor.[56]

The poll-tax effort among trade unionists and members of the white working class was just as robust. Labor's Joint Educational Committee organized a Citizenship Training Conference in each of the state's six congressional districts at which local union leaders learned how to collect poll-tax forms and file them with county officials. The committee also distributed a series of "Bulletins" across the state, keeping union members informed about the poll-tax effort and the larger campaign to repeal the poll tax.[57]

To facilitate the passage of the poll-tax amendment, the Arkansas State Federation of Labor and the Arkansas Industrial Union Council officially merged in March 1956, becoming the first unified state federation in the wake of the national AFL-CIO merger. In most states, jealousy and bickering among leaders over who would assume control of the new organization delayed unification, but Arkansas never had such a problem. Both the state's CIO unions and its AFL affiliates recognized Smith as the best person to lead the Arkansas State Federated Labor Council (more commonly Arkansas AFL-CIO)—he had the political connections to both Arkansas liberals and the state's African American community, his union was well positioned to help trade unionists throughout the state, and he had the forcefulness of personality to lead the effort to eliminate the poll tax.

The merger convention became a big pep rally for the effort to repeal the poll tax, with attacks on McClellan thrown in for good measure. The state's liberal politicians lined up to voice their support for labor's effort. Attorney General Tom Gentry assured African Americans that the poll tax could not legally be replaced by a more discriminatory registration system. Governor Faubus again endorsed the elimination of the poll tax, recalling that "people back home were so poor that they did not have the money at the right time to pay their poll tax and were left disfranchised." McMath warned that McClellan and states' rights politicians would use race hatred to try to prevent repeal of the poll tax. He said that the real objective of McClellan and his allies was the destruction of the labor movement—race hatred would keep white workers from joining unions with their black counterparts, and those supporting nullification and interposition would go after the Wagner Act and the Fair Labor Standards Act first.[58]

The timing of Arkansas labor's effort to repeal the poll tax could not have been worse, as it became bound up in the conflict over school integration that was roiling the state. The first stirrings of massive resistance in Arkansas had begun in the summer of 1955, when the Hoxie school district, on the edge of the Arkansas delta, peacefully integrated. After seeing a *Life* magazine piece detailing events in Hoxie, complete with pictures of little black girls and little white girls happily walking arm-in-arm, segregationist forces—led by Amis Guthridge, a Little Rock attorney associated with both the Arkansas Free Enterprise Association and the Dixiecrat movement, and Jim Johnson, who had run for secretary of state with McClellan's support—went to Hoxie intent on disrupting the process. They had some success until the Hoxie school board secured a federal court order enjoining the pair and the local affiliate of the White Citizens' Council they had formed from interfering with the lawful operation of the schools.[59]

By late spring 1956, Arkansas's massive resistance movement was in full swing. The ambitious Johnson was using school desegregation and the events in Hoxie as a springboard to challenge Faubus for the governorship later that year. Accompanied by McClellan's closest political ally, Ben Laney, Johnson traveled the state, complaining that Faubus had done nothing to stop school integration at Hoxie and other public schools in the state, that he had allowed the state's undergraduate institutions to desegregate, and that he had put "six niggers on the state Democratic Committee." The tour ended with a highly orchestrated event—presided over by Laney—in Little Rock at which the state's leading segregationists spontaneously "drafted" Johnson to challenge Faubus. To boost his campaign, Johnson and the state's conservatives used the initiative process to place an "interposition" amendment to the state's constitution on the 1956 ballot, a measure intended to give Arkansas the power to nullify any federal legislation or court order that threatened state sovereignty.[60]

In response to Johnson's challenge and the groundswell of segregationist sentiment, Faubus embraced a more moderate segregationist path, one without strident racist rhetoric, one that did not dwell on miscegenation. Faubus insisted that Arkansas school districts should not be forced by the federal courts to integrate and that he would use his power as governor to try to prevent that from happening. But he left open the possibility that local school boards could voluntarily integrate. Taking a cue from his rival, Faubus worked to place two measures on the 1956 ballot—a milder interposition proposal and a pupil placement law that would give school boards broad discretion over the assignment of students within an integrated district. As one historian puts it, Faubus "successfully co-opted the segregationist doctrine and superimposed it on his own moderate image."[61]

The labor movement—having already worked hard to make sure that trade unionists and African Americans were eligible to vote in 1956—invested heavily in Faubus's election despite his embrace of some segregationist positions. The way labor leaders saw it, Faubus was doing what he needed to do to get reelected. Arkansas's Committee on Political Education (COPE), the political arm of the Arkansas AFL-CIO, worked hard on Faubus's behalf, not only funneling money into the campaign but also warning union members not to be "blinded by racial hatred," insisting that Johnson's real purpose was to destroy Arkansas's labor movement. As a COPE broadside explained, "Johnson knows if he can get White and Negro workers and Union members hating and fighting each other that soon it will wreck the Union." Reminding voters that "under the Faubus administration the working people have had the highest wages and best working conditions in the history of Arkansas," COPE literature concluded, "Governor Orval Faubus Is Your Friend! Jim Johnson Is Your Enemy."[62]

Faubus won the Democratic primary, as did the other three candidates for statewide office supported by Arkansas COPE that summer, giving Odell Smith reason to believe that the state's labor movement had never been in better shape: its endorsed candidates controlled the top state offices; the mayor of the state's largest city owed his election to labor; several union members were serving in the General Assembly; the two branches of labor were united; the radical segregationist gubernatorial candidate had been defeated; and more Arkansans, nearly seventy-five thousand of them, belonged to trade unions than ever before. Predicting that the poll tax would soon be abolished, Smith declared in August 1956 that Arkansas labor's political power "has never been greater."[63]

Just as the Teamster at the head of the Arkansas AFL-CIO was boasting of his organization's political prowess, investigators for McClellan's Senate Permanent Subcommittee on Investigations began looking into the unlawful activities of the International Brotherhood of Teamsters, preparing for the hearings that would begin in January of the following year.[64] Critics suggested that behind the hearings was McClellan's desire to bolster his own election chances and those of his fellow states' rights candidates in the state and that his real targets were Sid McMath and Odell Smith rather than Dave Beck or Jimmy Hoffa. McClellan, of course, never acknowledged such motives. It is clear, however, that McClellan had to look no farther than his home state to see how Teamster power threatened the conservative southern Democratic ideals that he held dear. Arkansas's liberal coalition—put together by McMath, Woods, and Smith and sustained by money from the national labor federation—empowered African Americans, threatened the prerogatives of traditional elites, and called for an expansion of state and federal power.

The January 1957 start of public hearings into Teamster corruption and racketeering clearly weakened Smith, Arkansas's labor movement, and politicians like McMath. By April 1957, Smith was feeling pressure to step down as president of the Arkansas AFL-CIO. He insisted on staying at the helm, though, reassuring the board that "if there comes a time that I think that I am embarrassing the Labor Movement, insofar as my being the head of the labor movement in Arkansas, you won't have to tell Odell Smith to get out. He will be big enough to get out himself." As momentum built to expel the Teamsters from the AFL-CIO, Smith took out a card from Hodcarriers' Local 490 in Hot Springs, hoping that his membership in another AFL-CIO affiliate would allow him to keep his job if expulsion became a reality. At the executive board meeting in January 1958, Smith offered his resignation, but the board passed a resolution asking him to continue.[65]

McClellan kept pressuring on the AFL-CIO to expel the Teamsters. Testifying before a Senate subcommittee on labor in May 1958, the Arkansas senator praised the AFL-CIO's "commendable steps to clean its own house" but stressed that those efforts were not enough. He reminded the subcommittee, "the ultimate power of the AFL-CIO is expulsion" and that the "AFL-CIO can expel them."[66] The AFL-CIO bowed to McClellan's pressure, officially kicking the 1.5 million Teamsters out of the federation. Smith, with his card from the Hodcarriers, tried to stay on as head of the Arkansas AFL-CIO, but word soon came down from AFL-CIO national headquarters that Teamsters officials such as Smith were ineligible to serve as officers in a state labor federation even if they held a card from another union.[67]

At the same time that McClellan's investigations were weakening the standing of Odell Smith and the Arkansas AFL-CIO, another threat to the state's labor movement emerged from its erstwhile ally Orval Faubus. In the summer of 1956, Smith had received assurances that Faubus, having safely made it through the party's primary, would come out forcefully for the repeal of the poll tax. Specifically, the governor's chief of staff had promised that Faubus's Labor Day address would contain such an endorsement. But the governor's speech made no mention of the poll-tax measure and implied that organized labor had not lived up to its civic obligations. Ten days later, the Faubus-controlled state Democratic convention refused to endorse the repeal of the poll tax, a move that spelled the measure's defeat. Arkansas labor felt betrayed—Faubus had supported the resolution on interposition, but he did not lift a finger to help the poll-tax repeal as it went down to defeat.[68]

The breach between Faubus and the Arkansas AFL-CIO became an unbridgeable chasm in September 1957 when the governor deployed the Arkansas National Guard to prevent nine African American students from attending previously all-white Little Rock Central High School. When Faubus sought a third term in 1958, the Arkansas AFL-CIO emerged as his most important opposition. The federation passed a resolution accusing the governor of betraying the trust of the state's working people. Faubus responded by casting himself as the true leader of the state's white working class and attacking those who had been his most stalwart supporters. Evoking images from McClellan's ongoing hearings, Faubus portrayed Smith, Woods, and McMath as stooges of corrupt union leaders from Detroit, New York, and Washington, forging a type of anti-union populism that would take root in parts of the state. Faubus would use this populism to stay in office through 1966.[69]

Arkansas's labor-led, biracial working-class political alliance survived the cold war hysteria of the late 1940s and the early 1950s, the race-baiting of Dixiecrats, and the red-baiting of powerful conservatives such as Westbrook Pegler and George Benson. But what had probably been the South's most politically powerful labor movement could not survive the one-two punch of John McClellan and Orval Faubus. As Arkansas labor journalist Victor Ray explained, "Smith . . . might have repaired the cracks wrought by Faubus, but he was soon to be removed from power by . . . the expulsion of the Teamsters from the AFL-CIO."[70]

Never again would the labor movement be such an influential factor in Arkansas politics. This became clear when McClellan was up for reelection in 1960. Arkansas's labor movement tried to recruit an opponent, but there were no takers. Arkansas liberalism was all but dead; its practitioners had no hope of getting elected. Arkansas AFL-CIO officials became so desperate that they met with segregationist Jim Johnson in hopes of convincing him to challenge McClellan. These officials did not want to see Johnson in the Senate, but they hoped that his presence in the race would cause McClellan to die from heart failure. In the end, though, the labor leaders were unwilling to cough up the $200,000 that Johnson demanded to enter the race. They did, however, suggest to Johnson that Jimmy Hoffa might be willing to make a substantial campaign contribution.[71]

John McClellan always justified his committee's investigations into the illegal activities of the International Brotherhood of Teamsters as motivated by his simple desire to help common citizens by fighting crime and corruption.[72] While acknowledging that corruption existed within the Teamsters and other unions examined during the McClellan hearings, historians have never wholly bought McClellan's self-serving explanation. They have rightly seen the investigation within a national political context—part of broader effort of Republican and conservative Democratic members of Congress to roll back the gains that organized labor made during the New Deal.[73] But McClellan's motivations must also be understood within the context of Arkansas politics. Odell Smith and Teamsters Local 878 stood at the center of an effort to remake Arkansas politics along liberal lines—empowering black and white workers, expanding the New Deal, revising the tax code, and making it easier for unions to organize workers. These reforms not only threatened the political careers of conservatives like McClellan but also challenged the very things that traditional southern elites cherished most—unquestioned political control and white supremacy. Examining McClellan's investigations of the Teamsters through the lens of Arkansas politics makes it clear that the investigations into labor racketeering were part of the larger reaction of southern conservatives to what historian Jacquelyn Dowd Hall calls "the long civil rights movement."[74]

Notes

1. John L. McClellan, *Crime without Punishment* (New York: Duell, Sloan, & Pearce, 1962); Robert F. Kennedy, *The Enemy Within* (New York: Harper & Row, 1960).

2. David Witwer, *Corruption and Reform in the Teamsters Union* (Urbana: University of Illinois Press, 2003), 183–84. Also see Thaddeus Russell, *Out of the Jungle: Jimmy Hoffa and the Remaking of the American Working Class* (New York: Knopf, 2001); and David L. Stebenne, *Arthur J. Goldberg: New Deal Liberal* (Oxford: Oxford University Press, 1996), 157–75.

3. Most historians argue that such biracial working-class coalitions had foundered amid the cold war hysteria of the late 1940s and early 1950s. See, e.g., Robert Rodgers Korstad, *Civil Rights Unionism: Tobacco Workers and the Struggle for Democracy in the Mid-Twentieth Century South* (Chapel Hill: University of North Carolina Press, 2003); Patricia Sullivan, *Days of Hope: Race and Democracy in the New Deal Era* (Chapel Hill: University of North Carolina Press, 1996).

4. "A Direct Statement from John McClellan to Organized Labor in Arkansas," broadside found in box 1, folder 2, Benjamin Travis Laney, Jr. Papers, Special Collections, Torreyson Library, University of Central Arkansas, Conway. For McClellan's record, see "Voting Record of John McClellan, 1943–1952" in Arkansas State Industrial Union Council–CIO, "Arkansas Legislative Manual, 1953," box 1, folder 9, CIO PAC Papers, Walter Reuther Library, Wayne State University, Detroit; Arkansas State Industrial Union Council, "Voting Record of Senator John McClellan," box 1, folder 10, ibid.; "Statement of James L. McDevitt, National Director, Labor's League for Political Education, on Voting Record of John L. McClellan," box 5, folder 9, Sidney S. McMath Papers, Special Collections, University of Arkansas Libraries, Fayetteville; CIO PAC, "Report Comparing John L. McClellan to Robert Taft," box 5, folder 10, ibid.; "Has John L. McClellan Represented the People of Arkansas in the Senate? Let His Record Speak for Itself, 1943–1953" (Little Rock: Arkansas State Industrial Union Council, 1954).

5. John L. McClellan to D. Leonard Lingo, June 28, 1947, Lingo to McClellan, June 25, 1947, and John H. Caldwell to McClellan, June 3, 1947, box 160, unnumbered folder, John L. McClellan Papers, Riley Hickingbotham Library, Ouachita Baptist University, Arkadelphia, Arkansas.

6. Joe E. Covington, "'Freedom to Work' Act," *Arkansas Law Review and Bar Association Journal* 1 (Fall 1947): 204–9; Arkansas State Industrial Union Council–CIO, "Arkansas Legislative Manual, 1953"; Tom Forgey, "Benjamin Travis Laney Jr.," in *The Governors of Arkansas: Essays in Political Biography*, ed. Timothy P. Donovan, Willard B. Gatewood, and Jeannie M. Whayne, 2nd ed. (Fayetteville: University of Arkansas Press, 1995), 203–9; Gilbert J. Gall, "Southern Industrial Workers and Anti-Union Sentiment: Arkansas and Florida in 1944," in *Organized Labor in the Twentieth-Century South*, ed. Robert H. Zieger (Knoxville: University of Tennessee Press, 1991), 223–49.

7. Caleb Osborne, "*Regnat Populus*: The Influence of Progressive Politicians on Arkansas Politics" (B.A. honors' thesis, University of Arkansas, 2007), 21–37; Harry S. Ashmore, "McMath Enlarges His Beachhead," *Reporter*, April 25, 1950, 22–24; Jim Lester, *A Man for Arkansas: Sid McMath and the Southern Reform Tradition* (Little Rock: Rose Publishing, 1976), 98–99; Sidney S. McMath, *Promises Kept: A Memoir* (Fayetteville: University of Arkansas Press, 2003), 191–212.

8. C. C. Dejoie Jr., "Comments Here and There," *Louisiana Weekly*, December 31, 1949, clipping in box 161, unnumbered folder, McClellan Papers; Wilma Dykeman and James Stokely, *Neither Black nor White* (New York: Rinehart, 1957), 328; "Sidney S. McMath's Speech, [Arkansas] AFL-CIO Merger Convention, March 20, 1956," in *Merger Convention of the Arkansas State Federated Labor Council, AFL-CIO* (Little Rock: Arkansas State Federated Labor Council, 1956), 51–56.

9. John L. McClellan to D. Leonard Lingo, May 10, 1948, box 160, unnumbered folder, McClellan Papers. Also see other letters in folder.

10. Laney's activities at the Philadelphia convention can be followed in *New York Times*, July 10–16, 1948; McClellan's Speech Nominating Ben Laney, box 5, folder 8, McMath Papers. McClellan always couched his criticism of Truman's civil rights program in the language of states' rights, making it sound like a principled constitutional stand rather than Negrophobia or political opportunism. But no one committed to the ideology of states' rights would have launched such a massive congressional investigation into the criminal activities of Teamsters and other unions, activities that had traditionally been the concern of local and state governments.

11. Kari Frederickson, *The Dixiecrat Revolt and the End of the Solid South, 1932–1968* (Chapel Hill: University of North Carolina Press, 2001), 135, 137–38; *New York Times*, October 31, 1948.

12. *Arkansas Gazette*, September 20–25, 1948; *Arkansas Democrat*, September 20–25, 1948; *New York Times*, September 24, 1948; Ashmore, "McMath Enlarges His Beachhead," 22–24; McMath, *Promises Kept*, 200–205.

13. Lester, *Man for Arkansas*, 110; Ashmore, "McMath Enlarges His Beachhead," 22–24; McMath, *Promises Kept*, 200–205. On the Fulbright-Truman acrimony and allegations that Truman had made unkind remarks about Fulbright's mother, see Randall Bennett Woods, *Fulbright: A Biography* (Cambridge: Cambridge University Press, 1995), 293–94. Ironically the Truman-Fulbright rapprochement came when the two united in an unsuccessful effort to convince McMath to challenge Orval Faubus for Arkansas's governorship in 1960; ibid.

14. Benson to McClellan, June 7, 1949, box 160, unnumbered folder, McClellan Papers. For more on Benson and his role in the emergence of the nation's conservative movement, see L. Edward Hicks, *"Sometimes in the Wrong, but Never in Doubt": George S. Benson and the Education of the New Religious Right* (Knoxville: University of Tennessee Press, 1994); Bethany Moreton, *To Serve God and Wal-Mart: The Making of Christian Free Enterprise* (Cambridge: Harvard University Press, 2009), 164–68. For more on Benson's racialist theology and opposition to school integration, see Barclay Key, "On the Periphery of the Civil Rights Movement: Race and Religion at Harding College, 1945–1969," *Arkansas Historical Quarterly* 68 (Autumn 2009): 283–311.

15. Lester, *Man for Arkansas*, 223–25; *Hope Star*, July 6, 1950; Sidney S. McMath, Speech before Seventieth Annual Convention of the American Federation of Labor, San Francisco,

California, September 19, 1951, box 10, folder 1, McMath Papers; *Arkansas Gazette*, undated clipping in box 13, folder 8, ibid.; McMath, *Promises Kept*, 234–36. For more on Arkansas's anti-labor violence measure and the arrest of the three strikers, see Daisy Bates, *The Long Shadow of Little Rock* (1962; reprint, Fayetteville: University of Arkansas Press, 1986), 40–43. On the origins of the law, see Andrew E. Kersten, *Labor's Home Front: The American Federation of Labor during World War II* (New York: New York University Press, 2007), 59–62. On the U.S. Supreme Court's upholding of the law as constitutional, see *Cole et al. v. Arkansas* (1948) 333 U.S. 196 and *Cole et al. v. Arkansas* (1949) 338 U.S. 345.

16. Riesel wrote his "Inside Labor" column for the *New York Daily Mirror*, and it was syndicated to about 350 newspapers nationwide. See, e.g., *Chester (Pa.) Times*, May 9, 1949. For more on the Wood Bill, see Benjamin Aaron, "Amending the Taft-Hartley Act: A Decade of Frustration," *Industrial and Labor Relations Review* 11 (April 1958): 229–30; Gerald M. Pomper, "Labor and Congress: The Repeal of Taft-Hartley," *Labor History* 2 (Fall 1961): 323–44.

17. *Hot Springs Sentinel Record*, July 9, 1950, clipping in scrapbook 17, Laney Papers; *El Dorado Daily News*, April 8, 1950, and unidentified and undated clipping, ibid.; *Camden News*, July 9, 1950; Lester, *Man for Arkansas*, 218.

18. *Camden News*, June 25, 29, 1950; Lester, *Man for Arkansas*, 121–24.

19. James Woods, *The Era of Sid McMath, Arkansas Political Leader, 1946–1954: A Look at an Arkansas Progressive in the Light of the Political Tradition of the New South* (n.p., 1975), 55; Jack Kroll to Sid McMath, August 4, 1950, box 1, folder 14, CIO PAC Papers.

20. Phillip McMath quoted in John Brummett, "Sid McMath Lives On!" *Talk Business Quarterly* 1, no. 3 (2008): 46–53.

21. Henry Woods to editor of *Arkansas Gazette*, May 31, 1975, box 3, folder 2, Henry Woods Papers, Special Collections, University of Arkansas Libraries, Fayetteville.

22. *Arkansas Democrat*, August 2, 3, 5, 1952; *Arkansas Gazette*, August 1, 2, 4, 5, 7, 1952; *Northwest Arkansas Times* (Fayetteville), August 2, 1952; *Blytheville Courier News*, August 2, 7, 1952.

23. *Arkansas Gazette*, August 6, 7, 9, 1952; *Northwest Arkansas Times*, August 4, 1952; Arkansas Labor's League for Political Education circular dated August 4, 1952, reprinted in *Arkansas Gazette*, August 11, 1952; Tom Bowlin to Jack Kroll, August 8, 1952, box 1, folder 15, CIO PAC Papers.

24. *Arkansas Gazette*, August 13, 1952; also see *Blytheville Courier News*, August 13, 1952.

25. Henry Woods, interview by T. Harri Baker, December 8, 1972, 15, Eisenhower Administration Project, Oral History Research Office, Columbia University, New York.

26. Woods to editor of *Arkansas Gazette*, May 31, 1975.

27. McMath, *Promises Kept*, 1; Tilford E. Dudley to Roy Reuther, November 15, 1955, box 1, folder 9, CIO PAC Papers; Daniel Powell to James L. McDevitt, November 11, 1959, box 2, folder 29, Daniel Augustus Powell Papers, Southern Historical Collection, University of North Carolina, Chapel Hill.

28. Sandy McMath, telephone conversation with author, November 29, 2009.

29. *Union Labor Bulletin*, October 25, 1957; Vivion Lenon Brewer, *The Embattled Ladies of Little Rock, 1958–1963: The Struggle to Save Public Education at Central High* (Fort Bragg, Calif.: Lost Coast Press, 1999), 184–85; Sara Alderman Murphy, *Breaking the Silence: Little Rock's Women's Emergency Committee to Open Our Schools, 1958–1963* (Fayetteville:

University of Arkansas Press, 1997), 189–90; Irene Samuel and Pat House, interview by Sara Murphy, June 4, 1992, box 7, tape 42, Sara Alderman Murphy Papers, Special Collections, University of Arkansas Libraries, Fayetteville; Henry Woods, interview by Murphy, August 30, 1992, box 6, tape 60, ibid.

30. Victor Ray, interview with author, July 13, 2007, Little Rock; Wayne Glenn, interview with author, September 1, 2007, Franklin, Tennessee.

31. Don Ellinger to Jack Kroll, March 19, April 22, 1953, box 1, folder 10, CIO PAC Papers; Tilford E. Dudley to Phil Weightman, March 12, 1953, box 1, folder 5, Philip Weightman Papers, Tamiment Library, New York University. Historians Tony Badger and John Kirk have faulted McMath for failing to advance African American civil rights, suggesting that he was all talk and no action, but they have ignored his efforts to empower black Arkansans through poll-tax campaigns and the subsequent effort to repeal the poll tax. Anthony J. Badger, "'Closet Moderates': Why White Liberals Failed, 1940–1970," in *New Deal/ New South: An Anthony Badger Reader* (Fayetteville: University of Arkansas Press, 2007), 102–26; John A. Kirk, *Redefining the Color Line: Black Activism in Little Rock, Arkansas, 1940–1970* (Gainesville: University Press of Florida, 2002), esp. 54.

32. Phil Weightman to Jack Kroll, May 13, 1953, box 1, folder 10, and Sid McMath to Jack Kroll, May 19, 1953, box 1, folder 9, CIO PAC Papers.

33. Dudley to Weightman, March 12, 1953; Ellinger to Kroll, April 22, 1953, and Charles Catton to Kroll, May 21, 1953, box 1, folder 10, ibid.; Catton to Kroll, January 4, 1954, and Catton to Weightman, January 4, 1954, box 1, folder 6, Weightman Papers.

34. Wiley A. Branton to Phil Weightman, May 27, 1953, Jackie Shropshire to Weightman, May 26, 1953, Shropshire to Weightman, May 28, 1953, and I. S. McClinton to Weightman, September 20, 1953, box 1, folder 4, Weightman Papers; "Minutes of Meeting of Poll Tax Campaign Committee, June 2, 1953," ibid.; "Committee to Improve the Number of Qualified Voters in Pulaski County," *Arkansas Democrat*, September 12, 1953. On the prominence of these men to the civil rights movement in postwar Arkansas, see Kirk, *Redefining the Color Line*, 54–85; John A. Kirk, "'A Study in Second Class Citizenship: Race, Urban Development, and Little Rock's Gillam Park, 1934–2004," *Arkansas Historical Quarterly* 64 (Autumn 2005): 262–86. Daisy and L. C. Bates, leaders in the state branch of the NAACP, were the most prominent African American activists not associated with the poll-tax campaign, and their newspaper, the *Arkansas State Press*, barely mentioned it. Although the Bateses supported efforts to mobilize black voters and supported the labor movement, especially the CIO, throughout the postwar period, they were not on good terms with several of the other African American leaders, especially McClinton, Jones, and Booker. The antagonism was mutual, with one NAACP official noting that Booker "will have nothing to do with anything in which the Bateses are involved." Daisy Bates, though, would work closely with Phil Weightman in the 1960s, running AFL-CIO Committee on Political Education voter-registration drives in black communities in the industrial Midwest. See Grif Stockley, *Daisy Bates: Civil Rights Crusader from Arkansas* (Jackson: University Press of Mississippi, 2005), 57, 251.

35. Branton to Weightman, May 27, 1953, Shropshire to Weightman, May 26, 1953, Shropshire to Weightman, May 28, 1953, and McClinton to Weightman, September 20, 1953, box 1, folder 4, Weightman Papers. For more on Branton and Shropshire, especially their roles in integrating the University of Arkansas, see Judith Kilpatrick, "Desegregating

the University of Arkansas School of Law: L. Clifford Davis and the Six Pioneers," *Arkansas Historical Quarterly* 68 (Summer 2009): 123–56; Judith Kilpatrick, *There When We Needed Him: Wiley Austin Branton, Civil Rights Warrior* (Fayetteville: University of Arkansas Press, 2007).

36. *Arkansas Democrat*, September 12, 1953; *Southern Mediator Journal*, undated clippings in box 1, folder 5, Weightman Papers; Weightman to William Dawson, telegram, August 31, 1953, box 1, folder 4, ibid.

37. Samples of the literature can be found in box 1, folder 4, Weightman Papers; George Ellison to James L. McDevitt, October 30, 1959, box 2, folder 29, Powell Papers.

38. Charles Catton to Jack Kroll, May 21, 1953, box 1, folder 10, CIO PAC Papers; Catton to Kroll, January 4, 1954, box 1, folder 6, Weightman Papers; Catton to Weightman, January 4, 1954, ibid.; [CIO PAC], "Interim Report on 1954 Elections, February 15, 1954," box 2, folder 22, ibid.; Weightman and James E. Turner, "Report on Minority Group Vote, 1954 Elections," box 8, folder 11, ibid.

39. Woods, interview by Baker, 6–9; Sidney McMath, interview by John Luter, December 30, 1970, ibid., 4–6, Eisenhower Administration Project; Woods, *Era of Sidney McMath*, 66; Truman Baker to Orval Faubus, July 6, 1953, Clay C. Sizemore to Faubus, February 4, 1954, and Faubus to Sizemore, August 7, 1954, box 44, folder 4, Orval Eugene Faubus Papers, Special Collections, University of Arkansas Libraries, Fayetteville; Roy Reed, *Faubus: The Life and Times of an American Prodigal* (Fayetteville: University of Arkansas Press, 1997), 83–85.

40. *Arkansas Gazette*, July 18, 22, 1954; Glenn interview. Although Johnson was ideologically committed to states' rights, close to several infamous anti-labor politicians including McClellan and James Eastland, and an avowed racist, he had been a strong supporter of organized labor when in the Arkansas General Assembly. One Arkansas labor leader summed him up: "Fairly good on economics; bad on race." J. Bill Becker, interview by Jack Bass and Walter De Vries, June 13, 1974, 15, Southern Oral History Collection, University of North Carolina, Chapel Hill.

41. *Blytheville Courier News*, May 25, 1954; *Union Labor Bulletin*, February 7, April 2, 9, 23, May 28, 1954; *El Dorado Daily News*, June 4, 1954, clipping in box 160, unnumbered folder, McClellan Papers; *Hot Springs New Era*, undated clipping in box 161, ibid.; *Pine Bluff Commercial*, February 24, 1954, and *Texarkana Labor News*, March 12, 1954, clippings in ibid.; Don Ellinger to Jack Kroll, January 21, 1954, box 1, folder 9, CIO PAC Papers. Also see photos of McMath and Smith at Arkansas State Council of Machinists meeting, February 7, 1954, box 15, folder 5, McMath Papers.

42. "Arkansas," *Congressional Quarterly News*, July 16, 1954, clipping in box 1, folder 12, CIO PAC Papers; Don Ellinger to Jack Kroll, July 13, 1954, box 1, folder 11, ibid.; McMath to Kroll, June 12, 1954, June 25, 1954, July 9, 1954, ibid.; Arkansas Labor's League for Political Education circular, dated April 20, 1955, in Arkansas AFL-CIO files, Arkansas AFL-CIO Headquarters, Little Rock; Lester, *Man for Arkansas*, 268.

43. J. L. Baughman to Lee Tucker, June 25, 1954, and William C. Demers to Jack Kroll, June 11, 1954, box 1, folder 12, CIO PAC Papers; "Activity Program of the N.A.A.C.P. of Crossett, Arkansas, June 14, 1953," box 1, folder 4, Weightman Papers; *Arkansas State Press*, July 23, 1954. The McClellan quote is from McClellan's Speech Nominating Ben Laney.

44. *Arkansas Gazette*, August 7, 1954.

45. Woods, interview by Baker, 10; Report of the Arkansas Industrial Union Council Legislative and PAC Committee, January 15–16, 1955, box 1, folder 9, CIO PAC Papers.

46. Reed, *Faubus*, 91–124; Woods, interview by Baker, 7–14. For more on Commonwealth College and socialism in Arkansas, see James R. Green, *Grass-Roots Socialism: Radical Movements in the Southwest, 1895–1943* (Baton Rogue: Louisiana State University Press, 1978), esp. 396–438; William H. Cobb, *Radical Education in the Rural South: Commonwealth College, 1922–1940* (Detroit: Wayne State University Press, 2000).

47. On the origins of Arkansas's poll tax and other efforts to disfranchise poor Arkansans in the 1890s, see Kenneth C. Barnes, *Who Killed John Clayton? Political Violence and the Emergence of the New South, 1861–1893* (Durham, N.C.: Duke University Press, 1998), esp. 94–116; J. Morgan Kousser, *The Shaping of Southern Politics: Suffrage restriction and the Establishment of the One-party South, 1890–1910* (New Haven: Yale University Press, 1974); Michael Perman, *Struggle for Mastery: Disfranchisement in the South, 1888–1908* (Chapel Hill: University of North Carolina Press, 2001), 48–69.

48. *Merger Convention of Arkansas State Federated Labor Council, AFL-CIO,* 84; *Union Labor Bulletin,* October 29, 1954.

49. Don Ellinger to Jack Kroll, January 19, 1955, box 1, folder 9, CIO PAC Papers; "Report of the Arkansas Industrial Union Council Legislative and PAC Committee, January 15–16, 1955," ibid.; "Phases of CIO PAC Activity in Arkansas, January 1955," ibid.; Arkansas Labor's League for Political Education minutes, November 11, 1954, Arkansas AFL-CIO files.

50. Charles Catton to Jack Kroll, October 15, 1954, and Don Ellinger to Kroll, October 14, 1954, box 1, folder 9, CIO PAC Papers.

51. *Arkansas Democrat,* January 15, 1955, 1, January 16, 1955; Don Ellinger to Jack Kroll, January 19, 1955, box 1, folder 9, CIO PAC Papers; Minutes of Arkansas Labor's League for Political Education meeting, January 29, 1956, Arkansas AFL-CIO files. In the early 1950s, Arkansas labor federations led the way in integrating Little Rock's hotels and other public facilities, including Robinson Auditorium. The Arkansas Industrial Union Council even held an integrated dance at one downtown hotel. In the wake of the Central High crisis, nearly all of these facilities reinstituted the color line, prohibiting black patronage. Henry Woods interview report, September 25, 1957 (file LR44-341), Federal Bureau of Investigation, Little Rock, copy in box 5, folder 14, Murphy Papers; Daniel Powell to James L. McDevitt, November 11, 1959, box 2, folder 29, Powell Papers; L. C. Bates to Duke Ellington, August 30, 1961, box 2, folder 6, Daisy Gatson Bates Papers, State Historical Society of Wisconsin, Madison.

52. Pegler's syndicated column appeared in hundreds of papers, and he attacked McMath and Faubus on two separate occasions. For the first, see, e.g., *Logansport (Ind.) Press,* January 4, 1955; *San Antonio Light,* January 4, 1955. The second column appeared in *Lebanon (Pa.) Daily News,* January 18, 1955. McMath considered suing Pegler for libel, but national labor officials counseled him to let the matter die; Victor G. Reuther to Sidney McMath, February 3, 1955, and Thomas E. Harris to Victor Reuther, January 28, 1955, box 1, folder 9, CIO PAC Papers.

53. David Witwer, *Shadow of the Racketeer: Scandal in Organized Labor* (Urbana: University of Illinois Press, 2009).

54. Henry Woods to Jack Kroll, November 10, 1955, box 1, folder 9, CIO PAC Papers; *Officers' Report of the Arkansas State Federated Labor Council, March 19, 1956* (North Little Rock: Times Publishing, 1956), 7; William Jordan Patty, "'Victory Based on Violence Is Undesirable': The Little Rock Bus Strike of 1955–1956," *Arkansas Historical Quarterly* 61 (Autumn 2002): 233–54. The Republican Remmel had been planning to run for the U.S. Senate in 1954 if the Democratic nomination had gone to McMath, reasoning that most of the state's conservative Democrats were ideologically closer to Taft Republicans than to McMath Democrats. But the Republicans had no hope of (or interest in) unseating McClellan, so Remmel ran against Faubus in the general election for governor, receiving about 38 percent of the vote; Billy Burton Hathorn, "Pratt Cates Remmel: A Thrust toward Republicanism in Arkansas, 1951–1955," *Arkansas Historical Quarterly* 43 (Winter 1984): 304–23. After Mann and several pro-labor councilmen took office, the bus company surrendered its franchise and the city gave Division 704 of the Amalgamated Association of Street, Electric Railway, and Motor Coach Employees of America the authority to operate the bus line. Patty, "Victory Based on Violence."

55. Don Ellinger to Jack Kroll, March 30, 1955, and Kroll to Orval E. Faubus, March 30, 1955, box 1, folder 9, CIO PAC Papers.

56. Ethel B. Dawson to Phillip Weightman, March 3, 1955, Weightman to Dawson, June 6, 1956, and Dawson to Weightman, June 8, 1955, box 1, folder 4, Weightman Papers; "Pay Your Poll Tax Now, before Oct. 1, 1955," broadside in ibid.; Jack Kroll to A. F. Hartung, September 12, 1955, box 1, folder 9, CIO PAC Papers.

57. Charles Catton to T. E. Dudley, April 25, 1955, and Don Ellinger to Jack Kroll, May 26, 1955, box 1, folder 9, CIO PAC Papers; Ellinger to Kroll September 23, 1955, box 1, folder 7, ibid.; copies of Labor's Joint Educational Committee "Bulletins" can be found in box 1, folder 9, ibid.

58. *Merger Convention of the Arkansas State Federated Labor Council, AFL-CIO*, 5–15, 34–37, 40–42, 51–56.

59. "A Morally Right Decision," *Life*, July 25, 1955, 29–31; Elizabeth Jacoway, *Turn Away Thy Son: Little Rock, The Crisis That Shocked the Nation* (New York: Free Press, 2007), 28–45; Reed, *Faubus*, 172–74.

60. Jacoway, *Turn Away Thy Son*, 28–45; Reed, *Faubus*, 169–81; Johnson undated speech at Walnut Ridge, Arkansas, in box 34, file 354, Arkansas Human Relations Council Papers, Special Collections, University of Arkansas Libraries, Fayetteville.

61. Quoted in Jacoway, *Turn Away Thy Son*, 42.

62. "Don't Be Fooled! Know the Facts!" broadside in box 3, folder 42, Powell Papers; Arkansas State Federated Labor Council Executive Board Meeting Minutes, August 25, 1956, Arkansas AFL-CIO files. Leaders in the state's African American community supported Faubus for many of the same reasons that labor did; *Arkansas State Press*, July 27, August 10, 1956.

63. Arkansas State Federated Labor Council Executive Board Meeting Minutes, August 25, 1956.

64. On the timing of the investigation, see Kennedy, *Enemy Within*, 7.

65. Arkansas AFL-CIO executive board minutes, April 14, 1957, January 18, 1958, Arkansas AFL-CIO files.

66. "Statement of John McClellan (D. Ark.) before Subcommittee on Labor of the Committee on Labor and Public Welfare, May 5, 1958," box 189, unnumbered folder, McClellan Papers.

67. The effects on the Teamsters' expulsion on Smith and the Arkansas labor movement's stance toward school integration are documented in Donald Slaiman, "Summary Report on Arkansas, November 25, 1958," box 322, folder 63, Jewish Labor Committee Records, Tamiment Library.

68. Dan Powell to Jack Kroll and James McDevitt, September 10, 1956, box 3, folder 42, Powell Papers; Arkansas State Federated Labor Council Executive Board Meeting Minutes, August 25, October 27, 1956. Compounding Faubus's flip-flop, there was little support for poll-tax repeal from the African American community. The *Arkansas State Press*, edited by Daisy and L. C. Bates, did not even mention the measure in the run-up to election day. Likewise, the state's largest black political organization—the Arkansas Democratic Voters Association—failed to endorse the amendment in its open letter to African American voters. McMath would later explain that in the racially charged atmosphere of 1956, "the Negroes opposed repealing [the poll tax], fearing that . . . the legislature would pass more restrictive voting requirements." *Arkansas State Press*, November 2, 1956; Arkansas State Federated Labor Council executive board minutes, October 27, 1956; Sidney S. McMath to James A. Dombrowski, January 27, 1958, box 3, folder 2, McMath Papers.

69. Anti-Faubus resolution in box 3, folder 42, Powell Papers; David Franke and Douglas Caddy, "An Interview with Orval Faubus," *American Opinion,* November 1959, 12; Orval Faubus, campaign speech, undated, 1958, box 54, folder 9, Faubus Papers; *Arkansas Gazette,* July 3, 13, 25, 27, 1958; *New York Times,* September 3, 1958. Faubus's turn against the labor movement is more fully explored in Michael Pierce, "Orval Faubus and the Rise of Anti-Labor Populism in Northwest Arkansas," in *The Right and Labor in America: Politics, Ideology, Imagination,* ed. Nelson Liechtenstein and Elizabeth Shermer (Philadelphia: University of Pennsylvania Press, forthcoming).

70. Victor K. Ray, "The Role of the Labor Union," in *Arkansas: Colony and State,* ed. Leland DuVall (Little Rock: Rose Publishing, 1973), 103. Ray worked closely with Smith and McMath during the Little Rock crisis, especially the 1959 vote that recalled segregationist school board members and allowed the city's high schools to reopen. See, e.g., George Ellison to James L. McDevitt, June 4, 1959, box 2, folder 29, Powell Papers.

71. Daniel Powell to L. James McDevitt, May 23, 1959, box 3, folder 42, Powell Papers; George Ellison to McDevitt, September 1, 1959, Powell to Ellison, September 7, 1959, Powell to Henry Zon, September 7, 1959, Ellison to McDevitt, October 1, 1959, and Ellison to McDevitt, October 15, 1959, box 2, folder 29, ibid.

72. McClellan, *Crime without Punishment.*

73. Witwer, *Corruption and Reform*; Russell, *Out of the Jungle*; Stebenne, *Arthur J. Goldberg,* 157–75; Melvyn Dubofsky, *The State and Labor in Modern America* (Chapel Hill: University of North Carolina Press, 1994), 217–19.

74. Jacquelyn Dowd Hall, "The Long Civil Rights Movement and the Political Uses of the Past," *Journal of American History* 91 (March 2005): 1233–62.

3

"A Lot Closer to What It Ought to Be"

Black Women and Public-Sector Employment in Baltimore, 1950–1975

JANE BERGER

In January 1960 the editors of Baltimore's preeminent black newspaper, the *Afro-American*, sent an investigative reporter to the offices of the Baltimore City Municipal Building and City Hall. Since 1956, when the City Council passed a local fair employment practices ordinance, municipal officials had repeatedly promised that the new law would be used to root out discrimination in local government agencies. Most recently, the newly elected president of Baltimore's City Council had told a group of African Americans, "I am convinced that there is discrimination practiced in the city government. ... I believe [the Equal Employment Opportunity Commission] should start with the city government."[1] Having endorsed the same "good starting point" three years earlier, editors at the *Afro-American* had become increasingly impatient with the lack of results. This time they decided to take matters into their own hands by conducting an informal head count of African American city government workers. Peering into offices in the Municipal Building and City Hall, the journalist sought black faces in the sea of white. The Municipal Building investigation yielded only fourteen African Americans as compared to five hundred Caucasians, while the search to find black workers in City Hall proved almost fruitless. Only the presence of a lone "colored messenger boy" prevented the paper from having to report it could find no African Americans at all. The paper's editors were outraged by the results of their study. "When you have 32 percent of the population and no personnel employed in City Hall, you are in a bad way—and this is the situation facing the colored citizens of Baltimore," an *Afro-American* editorial argued. "Not even the rosiest of rose-colored glasses can hide the fact that City Hall is shot through with racial discrimination and when it comes to jobs it is as if the colored citizens of Baltimore do not even exist."[2]

Figure 3.1. During the 1960s, civil rights advocates in Baltimore worked hard to open public-sector employment to African American workers. In 1964, activists and workers staged a protest demanding equal opportunity at the headquarters of the Social Security Administration, located just outside the city. (Used with the permission of the Afro-American Newspapers Archives.)

But change came quickly. By the mid-1970s more than half the city's workforce was black. African American women had made particularly impressive gains, not just in the city government but throughout the public sector. By 1976 nearly a third of employed black women who lived in the city worked in local offices of the federal, state, or municipal government.[3] During the two previous decades, African American women had tripled their representation on government payrolls in a city in which, for decades, they largely had been confined to domestic work. To be sure, black women were concentrated at the bottom of public-sector hierarchies, but government workers often received health insurance, pensions, and other employment benefits. Unionization, which many public-sector workers won during the 1960s, increased the value of government work. Great Society programs and federal investment in cities produced many of the jobs African Americans filled. Community-participation mandates, which required recipients of some federal funding to include poor people in decision making, along with national civil rights legislation, put the weight of the federal government behind local efforts to open employment opportunities to African Americans. But black women were hardly the inevitable beneficiaries of new public-sector jobs. Ongoing civil rights battles in Baltimore proved critical to securing government work for African Americans. Public-sector employment, in turn, proved crucial to the economic well-being of black communities. Indeed, in a city undergoing deindustrialization, unionized public-sector jobs helped many families weather the storm and, in some cases, move up the economic ladder.

Understanding the dramatic job gains black women in Baltimore won in the public sector during the 1960s challenges standard accounts of recent urban African American and southern labor history in four important ways. First, it complicates scholarship that describes the War on Poverty as unsuccessful, charges that rest largely on the grounds that the federal government failed to respond to structural male unemployment with job creation and full-employment guarantees. By assessing 1960s liberalism using a gendered lens, it becomes clear that Great Society and federal urban initiatives were themselves a critical, albeit unintended, source of employment—in the public sector and especially, although not exclusively, for black women.[4] Second, a focus on government job gains by African Americans contributes to recent, innovative work in civil rights history. Within the last several decades, scholars have produced excellent studies which demonstrate that activists in the nation's "long civil rights movement" fought against employment discrimination and economic injustice in addition to segregation, disenfranchisement, and other manifestations of southern apartheid. Much of the focus of the newest scholarship in this field has been on battles that took place outside the South. As many scholars involved in the work caution, however, we should avoid drawing too sharp a distinction between the issues that ignited northern and southern activism. Understanding the fight for fair employment in Baltimore, an industrialized but also a Jim Crow city, counters the unintended implication that battles north of the Mason-Dixon Line explicitly addressed economic issues while those in the South did not.[5] Third, a focus on African American public-sector employment introduces a wrinkle into southern labor historiography. Many studies of the South accurately identify the state as a repressive force critical in repelling labor organizing and class-based interracial solidarity during the twentieth century.[6] In Baltimore during the 1960s, however, civil rights activists had more success opening public-sector jobs than private-sector jobs to black workers, and, ironically, the state became a critical source of employment. And finally, acknowledging the magnitude and importance of public-sector job gains for black women and men during the 1960s disentangles African American urban history from a strict alignment with the narrative of American industrial decline. In so doing, it exposes as flawed the conflation of the "urban crisis" with the economic history of African Americans during the 1960s.[7]

In January 1951, the *New York Times* predicted "Boom Times" for the Baltimore region. The business community had already identified 1950 as its best year since World War II, and corporate executives in several industries planned to expand production to meet demand for defense orders, making the new year even better. Unemployment in Maryland was at its lowest level since the war's end, and industrial employers expected to have to search out of state to fill a projected ten thousand positions for skilled workers.[8] But not everyone in Baltimore benefited equally from the region's boom times. In 1950, Baltimore was a Jim Crow city with a population of close to a million. Nearly a quarter of the city's residents were African American, and black in-migration continued through the decade even as white flight shrank the city's Caucasian population.[9] Unemployment was far more prevalent among African Americans than among whites. Yet racism on the part of employers, unions, and white workers largely barred black men from the thousands of skilled jobs available or soon to be available in the city. Throughout the 1950s, although they made important gains in the operative, or semi-skilled, industrial job category, black men were otherwise excluded from all but the lowest-paid and least-stable jobs in the city's factories, and most worked on the periphery of the industrial economy. By the end of the decade, with the process of deindustrialization clearly under way, African Americans made up nearly 70 percent of the city's unskilled workers while whites accounted for an astounding 92 percent of skilled workers. Black women, meanwhile, remained concentrated in domestic employment, despite modest gains in other parts of the city's low-wage service sector.[10]

Although its industrial economy won Baltimore the moniker of the nation's southernmost northern city, those who knew the city appreciated as well its status as the northernmost southern city. "In actual practice, Baltimore is a southern city and has adopted practices in race relations that far exceed in severity the practices of other large communities in the Deep South, as well as the border areas," noted researchers from the National Urban League in 1949.[11] Viciously policed segregation and entrenched white supremacy made industrialized Baltimore a city that native son and civil rights luminary Thurgood Marshall described as "Up South."[12] Despite multiple efforts early in twentieth century, however, white officials had never successfully disenfranchised African Americans in Maryland. During the Great Depression, deprived of the tool most white southerners used to eliminate black political participation, Baltimore's elected officials innovated new means. They gerrymandered black citizens out of representation by creating wards that prevented African Americans from joining forces as a voting bloc. Until the mid-1950s, African Americans were unable to win even a single seat on the City Council.[13]

Given the northern and southern dimensions of Baltimore's character, there were few civil rights issues the city's black leaders did not have to confront. During the postwar years, the National Association for the Advancement of

Colored People (NAACP) and the Baltimore Urban League (BUL) were the city's most active civil rights organizations. Lillie Mae Jackson and her daughter Juanita Jackson Mitchell were the force behind the city's and state's NAACP organizations. Jackson served as the president of the Baltimore NAACP between 1935 and 1970 with unrelenting dedication, if, at times, an autocrat's zeal. Her daughter, who in 1950 became the first African American woman to graduate from the University of Maryland's law school, pursued the city's civil rights battles in the courts as she also served in leadership positions in the Maryland NAACP. In 1938 she married Clarence Mitchell, who later became the national NAACP's chief lobbyist in Washington, D.C. The union strengthened the links between the Baltimore and national NAACP organizations.[14]

The Baltimore Urban League joined the NAACP at the forefront of Baltimore's civil rights movement. Known as a moderate organization with significant white leadership, the BUL was committed to the almost exclusive use of moral suasion to achieve its goals. Its leaders generally eschewed the picket lines and lawsuits that were the hallmarks of the Baltimore NAACP. In addition to the NAACP and the BUL, Baltimore boasted a critically important black-owned newspaper, the *Afro-American*, run by Carl Murphy, and a host of politically active churches and smaller activist, labor, and civic associations committed to civil rights.[15]

The fight for jobs was an ongoing component of civil rights activism in Baltimore. Following unrelenting efforts to open wartime work to African Americans, Baltimore residents actively sought the passage of a permanent national fair employment practices law. Black Baltimore barraged elected officials with letters and repeatedly sent delegations to lobby the U.S. Congress on behalf of the measure. Although not as aggressively pursued, legislation committing the federal government to ensuring full employment also won considerable support among black city residents. Ultimately, activists won neither federally mandated fair nor full employment. Baltimore residents did herald, however, the national NAACP's successful campaign to ban segregation in the federal workforce, a battle led by Clarence Mitchell. Harry Truman's executive orders in 1948 that ended segregation both in the military and in the federal government produced important job gains in Baltimore. The city housed the national headquarters of the Social Security Administration, branch offices of other federal agencies, and a large corps of postal workers. Desegregation opened new opportunities to black workers, and in 1949 the BUL noted with enthusiasm "a marked increase in the colored employment in Federal agencies."[16] In that year, African Americans made up 16 percent of local Social Security employees and over a quarter of Baltimore's U.S. postal service workers. In the one realm in which civil rights activists had won a fair-employment provision, the measure seemed to be helping.[17]

During the 1950s, new strategies in pursuit of fair employment built on the momentum of earlier campaigns. By mid-decade, activists had begun to pressure Baltimore's City Council for a local fair employment practices ordinance. By then, twelve states and twenty-nine cities had passed fair-employment legislation as an antidote to the failed federal effort. Baltimore activists hoped to make their city the first below the Mason-Dixon Line with a similar measure. In 1954 a large coalition of civic, labor, religious, and welfare organizations formed to support the adoption of a local Fair Employment Practices Commission (FEPC). Throughout the campaign, the BUL, historically the most active in efforts to open employment, played a leading role. The NAACP also backed the measure, which the *Afro-American* strongly endorsed. The proposal also had the support of the Baltimore Federation of Labor and the Congress of Industrial Organizations (CIO), both of which advocated on its behalf. The bill was modeled on similar legislation passed in Philadelphia in 1948 that prohibited employers, employment agencies, and unions from inquiring into the race, color, religion, ancestry, or national origin of a job applicant. It also created an Equal Employment Opportunity Commission (EEOC) empowered to investigate claims of discrimination. The Baltimore proposal was stronger than the Philadelphia law in one important aspect, however: the Baltimore bill would invest the EEOC with the authority to seek court action in cases in which disputes could not be resolved through mediation. In Philadelphia and most cities and states with similar measures, equal employment commissioners' enforcement powers enabled them only to conduct public hearings.[18]

Supporters faced a daunting task as they tried to convince a majority of the all-white City Council to support the creation of the FEPC. In March 1954, four relatively sympathetic members introduced the bill that would ban discrimination based on race and religion. Hundreds of African Americans immediately wrote to the council to urge passage. Two months later, at a hearing on behalf of the bill, more than two hundred supporters crowded into the council chambers as thirty speakers presented their case. Lillie Mae Jackson spoke in favor of the measure, as did BUL president William Passano, who forcefully informed the council that *all* of the businesses and industries in the city discriminated against African Americans.[19]

Public opponents of the baby FEPC included the city's two major white newspapers, several local residents, and a small group of members of the Brotherhood of Railroad Trainmen. The newspapers' editors cautioned that Baltimore had already made many advances in race relations and that passage of the bill would only antagonize whites and hamper further progress. Members of the union argued that the measure was communist-inspired and would impinge on the freedom of both individuals and businesses. Ultimately, the bill's opponents won the day. As the measure's supporters bemoaned their loss, Fred Nichols of the BUL pledged, "We are going to begin work immediately for the reintroduction of the bill before the full council in the fall. We shall let no grass grow under our feet."[20]

Ultimately, two summers' worth of grass grew before activists won an FEPC. By 1956, Baltimore finally had a black City Council member. The movement of whites out of the city, the continuing growth in the African American population, and ongoing voter-registration drives by civil rights groups finally overwhelmed white efforts to exclude black politicians from municipal office. Thus in late 1955, Walter Dixon won a seat in the City Council. The following spring he reintroduced the FEPC ordinance. This time the bill passed, but only after the City Council robbed it of enforcement power, stripping the language that invested the EEOC with the power to seek legal redress against employers it found guilty of discrimination. As a result, although the bill did create an EEOC, the commissioners could combat discrimination only by holding open hearings. The *Afro-American*'s editorial board described the new FEPC as "another step forward" but could not fully contain their skepticism. "If discrimination in employment can be cured by persuading employers and unions then it should be done that way. This is an effort to see if this method can be successful," the editors reflected.[21]

It quickly became apparent that many Baltimoreans had no intention of even putting the persuasion method to the test. At the FEPC signing ceremony, Mayor Thomas D'Alesandro Jr., a product of the city's Democratic machine, revealed his tepid commitment to equal opportunity: "The [EEOC] . . . will require intelligence, diplomacy and a recognition of the conditions which exist in our community," he intoned. "I shall give every thought to the selection of a Commission which will effectuate the purposes of this ordinance without disruption or unnecessary interference in the economic and business life of our community."[22] Six months later, the mayor followed through on his thinly veiled determination to minimize the law's enforcement when he announced his appointments to the commission. Although several of his appointees had been supportive of civil rights efforts, only one of the nine was an African American. Two months later, D'Alesandro appointed Francis Valle, a political crony who soon admitted to being prejudiced, to the directorship of the EEOC.[23] Although the appointment was eventually overturned, the mayor's lack of commitment undermined much of the utility of the fair-employment law. By 1957, the *Afro-American* noted with chagrin, "IT WAS hoped" that the

EEOC would do something to improve employment opportunities for black workers.[24]

Although the EEOC initially failed to achieve the ends its advocates had envisioned in terms of fighting employment discrimination, it did make headway in desegregating the two municipal employee organizations in the city that limited membership to whites. The City of Baltimore did not officially bargain over the terms of employment. The Classified Municipal Employees Association (CMEA), however, informally represented non-laboring and non-per-diem city workers. In 1954, the year activists began pushing for the municipal FEPC, the organization's bylaws limited membership to "Any White classified employee of the City of Baltimore or other White employees paid in full or in part by the City of Baltimore, and any White employee of this Association subject to the approval of the Board of Governors."[25] In 1959 the EEOC charged the seventy-five-hundred-member CMEA with discrimination. The organization's leaders responded with the stunning defense that "at no time in the history of the C.M.E.A. has there ever been so much as a flicker of suspicion about any act that would point to discrimination."[26] The EEOC disagreed and prevailed. As a result, CMEA's newfound disdain for discrimination became the foundation of its revised membership policy.[27]

The Baltimore local of the International Association of Firefighters trumped the CMEA's audacity in responding to charges of discrimination by the EEOC. Hounded by the Baltimore Urban League, in 1953 the city's fire department finally hired its first African Americans. By 1960 the city employed two hundred black firefighters, but none had been admitted to the firefighters' union. In response to the EEOC's charges, the union agreed to open its membership—but with a caveat. Although African American firefighters new to the fire department could join the union along with their white peers by paying an initiation fee of two dollars, the Baltimore local demanded payment of twenty-five dollars in back dues from seasoned black firefighters. The BUL endorsed the "compromise," but most other civil rights leaders were outraged. "Why should firefighters be penalized for not joining a union when they were prevented from doing so by that union?" demanded Troy Brailey, president of the Negro American Labor Council and chair of the labor committee of the Baltimore NAACP.[28] The firefighters took their complaint to A. Philip Randolph, a vice-president of the American Federation of Labor–Congress of Industrial Organizations (AFL-CIO), and to the civil rights committee of the AFL-CIO and won support for their case. They did not, however, win the war. In May 1961 the firefighters and union reached an agreement. The union reduced the fee it would charge to ten dollars, and the veteran firefighters agreed to pay it.[29]

As the EEOC met with success, albeit less than optimal, in integrating the city's public-sector employee organizations, ongoing efforts to win jobs for African Americans in Baltimore received a boost from the federal government. Since the 1930s, when Franklin Roosevelt created the nation's first national urban programs, the flow of federal aid to cities had significantly influenced local policy-making options and power arrangements. Intergovernmental aid, like national welfare programs, was a form of wealth redistribution, and political parties distributed it in ways intended to bolster their constituencies. During the 1950s, the urban-renewal emphasis of Dwight Eisenhower's urban policies had provided cities with resources that enhanced business leaders' ability to push municipal planning in the direction of commercial redevelopment. In contrast, John Kennedy and especially Lyndon Johnson channeled to cities federal funds earmarked for antipoverty efforts. Between 1964 and 1967, Congress passed more progressive legislation than at any other time since the New Deal years. It enacted the Economic Opportunity Act (which funded the War on Poverty), created Medicare and Medicaid, made permanent the Food Stamps program, and established the Model Cities program, which was intended to stimulate urban community development. Congress also increased spending on rent support, urban mass transit, the arts and humanities, the environment, and education.[30]

New sources of federal revenue dramatically expanded the public sectors of troubled cities like Baltimore. In Baltimore, while the city government had added about 7,000 positions during the 1950s, it more than doubled that rate of growth during the 1960s. In 1960 the city employed about 22,000 people; by 1970 that workforce had grown to about 35,000. Between 1962 and 1967 alone, the city added nearly 8,000 jobs, almost 95 percent of which were full-time positions. Much of the job growth occurred in human services agencies and the Department of Education.[31] Because many of the new jobs were in "helping" fields and thus gendered as female, women were more likely than men to fill the new positions.

The liberals who championed the federal government's antipoverty initiatives hardly intended their efforts to be an engine of job creation for women. In fact, Democratic policy makers who created the antipoverty programming rejected the pleas of progressive activists to redress mounting black male unemployment with job creation and full employment guarantees. The activists argued that structural economic changes were transforming the nation's industrial landscape. Early symptoms of deindustrialization presaged the loss of entire categories of working-class jobs that had helped generations of men provide for their families. Nothing appeared on the horizon likely to provide new employment opportunities for men in rusting cities that were increasingly populated by African Americans. Democratic policy makers, however, seemingly convinced that black unemployment was a cultural rather than a structural problem, focused on job training and investment in education to boost employment. The efforts largely failed to reverse male unemployment trends, which were exacerbated by shifts in the global economy and increasing capital mobility. Although during the 1960s civil rights activists won black workers greater access to skilled factory jobs than they had ever had in the past, the gains came as the city's industrial sector was collapsing. Additional victories activists won in opening jobs in the private sector to black workers also failed to compensate for the structural changes under way. Black male unemployment remained a debilitating urban issue.[32]

Simultaneously, federal funds produced tens of thousands of jobs in Baltimore—in fields in which women predominated. Over the course of the 1960s, the federal government fundamentally transformed the local labor market in a manner that favored female workers. To be sure, the expansion of the public sector opened large numbers of jobs that men did fill, but it created far more opportunities for women. African American women, however, faced a daunting challenge as they vied for federally subsidized positions in a city in which many whites continued to ardently defend recently outlawed Jim Crow practices.

In some cases, federal law helped the effort to win African Americans government posts. The Civil Rights Act of 1964 banned employment discrimination as well as segregation in places of public accommodations. It also prohibited discrimination in the use of federal funds, a stipulation civil rights activists had been advocating for decades. Meanwhile, federal antipoverty legislation included community-participation mandates that required cities to give residents with low incomes a role in implementing War on Poverty initiatives. In Baltimore, however, these measures met with fierce resistance.[33] By the mid-1960s, African Americans made up about 40 percent of Baltimore's population, but the nineteen-member City Council included only two black members. A powerful majority of the white members of the council was largely unsympathetic to civil rights issues. They also understood federal antipoverty initiatives for the threat that they were to white hegemony in Baltimore. In response, the council did all that it could to maintain its own authority over the use of new funds and to limit community and African American influence.[34]

Baltimore's mayor, Theodore McKeldin, was more sympathetic to civil rights issues than members of the City Council and most white elected officials in Maryland. In 1943, and with crucial African American electoral support, the Rockefeller Republican had defeated the candidate of the city's Democratic machine and won the office of mayor. Following a term in the office, McKeldin served as Maryland's governor between 1951 and 1959. Then, in 1962, he was reelected as Baltimore's mayor. McKeldin appreciated the significant role black voters had played in his political career, but during the 1960s he was also sympathetic to the concerns of the nation's mayors, many of whom resented federal involvement in local affairs. Even before Baltimore fully launched its War on Poverty, McKeldin wrote a letter to Lyndon Johnson on behalf of the Board of Advisors of the U.S. Conference of Mayors expressing that organization's concern about community-participation mandates. He described an "almost unanimous feeling" among member of the conference that federal officials running antipoverty programs did "not understand the problems and operations of local governments." McKeldin urged the president to rein in the enthusiasts of community participation. And on the ground in Baltimore, he did his part to limit community involvement.[35]

Ultimately, however, the Baltimore EEOC, in combination with ongoing pressure from civil rights activists, proved critical in winning new public-sector jobs for black workers. Although it was largely ineffective during the late 1950s, during the 1960s the commission became more successful at battling discrimination—particularly in the public sector. To be sure, white dominance was pervasive in both the public and private sectors. Caucasians ruled the city government almost as exclusively as they controlled most private-sector employment. The EEOC, however, could more exhaustively monitor the employment practices of the city government than those of private employers, whose decision making occurred largely in secret. What's more, as white flight and black in-migration increased the strength of their voting power, African Americans could successfully use political pressure to force elected officials to address discrimination in the public sector.

In 1963, civil rights activists convinced the City Council to increase the staff of the EEOC. The following year, the EEOC was renamed the Community Relations Commission (CRC). During the rest of the decade, the CRC's staff, themselves municipal employees, grew increasingly independent and assertive. In 1964 they conducted a comprehensive survey of African American municipal employment and found that black workers made up a little over a quarter of the workforce. (Had they included employees of the Department of Education, the figure would have been somewhat higher.) They discovered as well that African American municipal employees were concentrated in only a handful of agencies. Ninety percent of the city's black classified employees—those in civil service rather than at-will laboring positions—worked in only five city departments: Education, City Hospitals, Health, Fire, and Parks and Recreation. In addition, 41 percent of the employees of the Department of Public Welfare were African American, as were majorities of the staffs of federally funded antipoverty agencies. Alternatively, sixty-two city departments, most notably those that controlled the city's finances and planning, had no or minimal numbers of African Americans on their staffs. Ongoing discrimination led the CRC to conclude that "while some progress had been made in some city agencies in the employment of Negroes, there was a dismal lack of progress and concern by other agencies, and/or those who run them."[36]

In view of their findings, the CRC demanded the authority to investigate all instances in which African Americans were passed over for promotions. Although city officials did not grant the request, the CRC closely monitored employment practices and pressured directors of agencies with poor records of minority hiring. In 1967 the CRC received important support from the employment subcommittee of the Mayor's Task Force on Equal Rights. McKeldin created the task force that year following the announcement of the Congress of Racial Equality (CORE) that it had chosen Baltimore as a "target city" because of the city's poor civil rights record. McKeldin invited many of Baltimore's civil rights leaders to serve on the task force, and eventually he invited some CORE members to serve as well. The employment subcommittee included some of the most outspoken critics of the city's minority-employment practices. Declaring their intention to make the city government a "model" employer in Baltimore, task force members joined the staff of the CRC in pressuring municipal agencies to increase minority representation.[37]

Ongoing efforts by civil rights activists outside the government were also crucial in the battle to win city jobs for black workers. Informed by CRC findings, activists picketed city agencies with poor hiring records, and in 1967, an election year, they made minority hiring a campaign issue. A coalition of groups publicly accused the members of Baltimore's Civil Service Commission (CSC), and particularly the city's white personnel director, of racism, arguing that the CSC prevented low-income residents from gaining public-sector jobs. Mayoral candidate Thomas D'Alesandro III, whose father had sabotaged the EEOC during the 1950s, promised to conduct "a top-to-bottom review and revision of the city's civil service system and personnel policies" if he was elected. And McKeldin immediately appointed an advisory committee on the civil service that included some of the CSC's toughest critics.[38] As Leon Sachs, a member of the advisory committee and a Jewish leader central to the 1950s campaign that won Baltimore's fair-employment law, explained, the municipal employment issue had become "a festering sore in race relations in our community" in need of "immediate therapy."[39]

Following the 1967 municipal election, black City Council member Robert L. Douglass won passage of a resolution that called for the city to revamp the CSC's procedures. Newly elected Mayor D'Alesandro followed through on his campaign promise to address civil service issues. Determined to make procedures accessible to "low-income, low-skilled persons," the mayor proposed revisions to the City Charter to change civil service procedures. He also attempted to secure administratively those reforms he could not get through the City Council. The CSC staff, in turn, adopted several affirmative action–type strategies to improve minority hiring. They scrutinized exams for bias and took steps to better align tests with the skills actually required for individual jobs. In some cases they substituted performance for written exams. However, activists were less successful during the 1960s at winning preferential hiring for city residents. Angry that white suburbanites held many of the city's highest-paying jobs, city activists pressed officials to limit eligibility for municipal employment to Baltimore residents, and in 1969 the City Council did pass a hiring-preference ordinance. The measure was legally challenged and repealed, however, and the issue remained a source of contention in the city throughout the 1970s.[40]

Ongoing efforts by the CRC and civil rights activists to improve Baltimore's record of minority hiring during the 1960s produced substantial increases in the number of African Americans employed by the city. By 1970 almost 40 percent of city employees—compared to about 25 percent six years earlier—were African American. Including the Department of Education in the calculation raised that figure to 50 percent. In a little over five years African Americans had made tremendous gains in one of the few sectors of Baltimore's economy that was experiencing growth. Black women won the biggest share of the jobs. By the end of the 1960s they were the largest demographic group in the city workforce, outnumbering not only black men but also white women and white men.[41]

Although black women outpaced black men in entering the public sector, few CRC officials or civil rights activists publicly noted the fact. Census figures reveal the movement of black women into government jobs. Until the early 1970s, however, the CRC did not calculate municipal employment statistics by sex. Civil rights activists, to the extent that they did address gender, fought particularly hard to open to black men positions in traditionally male-dominated city departments such as police, sanitation, and highways.[42] No doubt during the late-1960s accusations that "the black family" was characterized by matriarchy, a charge leveled most famously in the Moynihan Report, stung many male activists and fueled their efforts to win employment opportunities for men.[43] Efforts to bolster African American male economic power also made sense given the exigency of accelerating deindustrialization. But short of intentionally steering men into occupations traditionally dominated by women, there was little activists could have done to counter the feminization of the black employment structure that the federal government helped to produce.

Black women, for their part, had quickly seized the openings public-sector expansion and civil rights victories created. They established a job niche in the government workforce that proved crucial to the economic security of their families and communities. To be sure, the employment structure of most city agencies that were growing because of infusions of federal funds mirrored the gendered and racialized hierarchies of the larger labor market: white men or in some cases black men served in most leadership roles; white women filled many professional positions; and African American women (and men) predominated in the lowest-paid jobs.[44] Training programs during the 1960s reproduced gendered and racialized employment expectations. "When you're offered job training, it's always something with 'aide' behind it," African American welfare-rights activist Margaret McCarthy complained in 1969. "I suppose some kind of job beats nothing, but it tells you what people think of you when they only think of your being a nurse's aide when you could be a nurse or teacher's aide when you could be a teacher."[45] Yet low-wage positions in human services agencies could serve multiple productive roles. As historian Rhonda Williams notes, during the 1960s, African American women with low incomes were becoming increasingly assertive in the demands they made of the state. "[Antipoverty] jobs further validated poor black women's concerns and empowered them to speak; after all, they believed they had the federal government behind them," she explains.[46] African American women employed in human services agencies also often had hands-on control over the delivery of human services in a city in which, until only recently, "separate but equal" had justified grossly inferior services for black residents. What's more, even low-wage municipal employment provided working conditions usually preferable to those generally available to black women in the wider labor market.

Black women won leadership posts and professional positions in the municipal government as well. Many worked hard to move up the employment ladder. In 1963, Ivy Logan Harris became the only woman in Baltimore to run a public-housing project. In 1968, Marguerite Campbell became Mayor D'Alesandro's Community Relations specialist and the first African American woman to serve on a mayoral staff. The same year, F. Eulalian Ferguson was appointed the Social Service coordinator in the Public Housing division of the Department of Housing and Community Development. And shortly thereafter, Pearl Cole Brackett, earlier a teacher, became the assistant superintendent for school-community relations. In addition, African American women won a host of white-collar positions, including jobs as principals, vice-principals, teachers, nurses, and social workers. From their posts in human services agencies and departments in the formerly Jim Crow city, they took very seriously their responsibility to make the city's welfare state responsive to the needs of all residents—both black and white.[47]

Fights for jobs for African Americans played out in the state and federal governments as well with similar gendered outcomes. During the 1960s, intergovernmental aid contributed to the expansion of the state's public workforce. Between 1962 and 1967, Maryland's payroll grew by nearly 11,500 jobs, and state officials opened close to 18,000 positions over the next five years. While only a portion of the new jobs were in Baltimore, the state became an important local employer. Ultimately, black workers did not make as much headway into state employment as they did into the municipal workforce. African American political pressure did not produce on the state level the results it achieved in Baltimore. The Maryland Commission on Interracial Problems and Relations did monitor minority hiring, however, and activists maintained pressure on state officials. By 1970, African Americans made up close to 20 percent of state workers in Baltimore. As in the municipal government, most of the job gains were in a handful of agencies, largely in the human services, and were filled largely by women.[48]

Great Society and other federal programs also expanded the ranks of Baltimore's federal workforce. Much of the growth occurred at the Social Security Administration. Local and national civil rights activists closely monitored the federal government's employment practices, pressing for the enforcement of anti-discrimination and affirmative action measures, demanding investigations by the U.S. Civil Rights Commission on employment issues, and, in Baltimore, even picketing Social Security.[49] The pressure worked. In 1969 the *Afro-American* reported that 30 percent of the agency's local staff was African American, up from 16 percent two decades earlier.[50] Overall, by 1970, African Americans made up over 50 percent of the city's residents who were employed by the state and federal governments. State and federal workers accounted for almost 15 percent of employed African Americans in the city.[51]

The job gains African Americans made in the public sector during the 1960s were remarkable, particularly given the repressive role the state had played in the Jim Crow city historically. In 1970 more than a quarter of all employed African Americans in Baltimore worked in the public sector. For black women the figure was particularly dramatic: while one in five African American men worked for the government, one in three black women were employed in a public agency.[52] To be sure, discrimination persisted. African American women as a group were the most poorly compensated of all government workers. The low-wage health, education, and welfare jobs many black women won often paid less than low-wage positions filled by men in other agencies. Civil rights activists noted as well that leadership positions in human services agencies tended to pay less than administrative posts in other agencies.[53] And whites continued to all but exclude African Americans from positions in which they could exercise authority over anyone other than the disproportionately African American recipients of social services. Nevertheless, government jobs were generally full-time, lacking the insecurity of domestic work and the periodic layoffs associated with factory jobs. Government positions also provided employees with better workplace protections than were available to African Americans generally as well as access to fringe benefits including pension plans and health insurance.

Unionization also improved the conditions of public-sector employment during the 1960s. President Kennedy's Executive Order 10989, issued in 1962, recognized the right of federal workers to engage in collective bargaining. In Baltimore, the order helped to extend union protection to thousands of residents employed in local offices of federal agencies. It also set the stage for struggles over public-sector labor relations on the state and local levels. Until the 1990s, Maryland officials refused to grant bargaining rights to state workers. On the municipal level, the Baltimore Teachers Union and the American Federation of State, County and Municipal Employees (AFSCME) led efforts to win collective bargaining rights. The unions, both of which had local African American leadership, prodded the now integrated CMEA and other municipal public-sector organizations into action, and they met with success in 1968. During the decades that followed, African American women made inroads into some leadership positions in the city's public-sector unions, and AFSCME's leaders in particular worked hard to improve women's employment prospects in the government workforce. Meanwhile, unionization created a stark distinction between the city's government employees and most private-sector service workers. Although the private service sector also expanded during the decade and was an important source of employment for black women, fewer of its workers enjoyed union-backed security.[54]

The expansion and unionization of the public sector hardly solved all of Baltimore's problems. The growth of the government workforce occurred as the city continued to hemorrhage factory jobs. Between 1950 and 1960, the city lost over 600 manufacturing firms, and deindustrialization accelerated during the 1970s.[55] To be sure, the industrial sector had never been the reliable source of employment for black men that it had been for white men. Nevertheless, the city's pool of jobs historically filled by men shrank as its female job base grew. At the same time, Baltimore's African American population was expanding and its white population was declining. The structural changes had profound implications for the emerging economic and social order of the city and help to account for discrepancies between African American men and women in terms of employment, education and other economic indicators that persist today.

Despite deindustrialization, it is problematic to describe the 1960s as a period of exceptional crisis for African Americans. During the decade, black workers won unprecedented access to a wide range of private-sector jobs from which they earlier had been excluded, including well-paying positions in the city's factories. More importantly, activists' efforts to win government jobs for black workers in Baltimore met with considerable success. To be sure, new public-sector jobs were more likely to attract female than male applicants, and black women's wages lagged behind whites' and black men's. Nevertheless, black women, long largely confined to the most insecure and poorly paid jobs in the city, seized many of the openings. They then used their positions within the state to extend to black communities much-needed social services, helping to reduce the city's poverty rate. Meanwhile, black men made significant, though less dramatic, gains in public-sector employment as well. Largely unionized by the end of the decade, the government workforce became a vital source of employment that helped to sustain, or in some cases boost, the well-being of black working- and middle-class families as the economic fortunes of their city declined. To a considerable extent, unionized public-sector employment provided many African American families with a measure of the security that unionized industrial employment had provided an earlier generation of white families.

Many jobs in the city's expanded public sector, however, depended for their continued existence on consistent streams of federal funding. As public-sector workers and city residents began to appreciate by the end of the 1960s, intergovernmental aid was an unstable foundation on which to build a job base. Their dependence on federal funds made Baltimore's public-sector workers, and particularly African American women employed in human services agencies, vulnerable to both the shifting mood of an increasingly conservative national electorate and to the reassertion of elite power over federal policy making, which characterized much of the 1970s and 1980s.

Notes

1. "Goodman Wants EEOC to Start on City Jobs: Feels Some Bypass City Merit Lists," *Afro-American*, January 23, 1960, 32.

2. "A Good Starting Point," editorial, *Afro-American*, October 27, 1956, 4; "City Hall Job Slip Is Showing," *Afro-American*, February 6, 1960, 1, 5; "City Job Picture," editorial, *Afro-American*, February 6, 1960, 4.

3. Baltimore Community Relations Commission, *Survey of Employment in City Government* (Baltimore: Baltimore Community Relations Commission, 1977), 5-8; and Stephen McKerrow, "Some Agencies in City 'Resist' Hiring of Blacks," *Baltimore Evening Sun*, September 27, 1977, folder "Civil Service Discrimination," Vertical Files [hereafter VF], Legislative Reference, City Hall, Baltimore, Maryland [hereafter LRCH]. In their overview of U.S. history based on U.S. census records, Michael Katz and Mark Stern note that federal spending was a major source of employment for African American women and Latinas in both the public and private sectors. *One Nation Divisible: What America Was and What It Is Becoming* (New York: Russell Sage Foundation, 2006).

4. In using a gendered lens to study the War on Poverty and other Great Society initiatives, I am following the lead of scholars who have recently produced rich studies focusing on the activism of social services recipients. The work uncovers the many ways in which African American women and other women with low incomes seized the opportunities War on Poverty funding and community-participation mandates provided to improve conditions in their communities. See, for example, Felicia Kornbluh, *The Battle for Welfare Rights: Politics and Poverty in Modern America* (Philadelphia: University of Pennsylvania Press, 2007); Premilla Nadison, *Welfare Warriors: The Welfare Rights Movement in the United States* (New York: Routledge, 2004); Annelise Orleck, *Storming Caesar's Palace: How Black Women Fought Their Own War on Poverty* (Boston: Beacon Press, 2005); and Rhonda Williams, *The Politics of Public Housing: Black Women's Struggles against Urban Inequality* (Oxford: Oxford University Press, 2005). See also Nancy Naples, *Grassroots Warriors: Activist Mothering, Community Work, and the War on Poverty* (New York: Routledge, 1998).

5. For an overview of scholarship reshaping civil rights historiography see Jacquelyn Dowd Hall, "The Long Civil Rights Movement and the Political Uses of the Past," *Journal of American History* 91 (March 2005): 1233-63. For recent studies of the North, see, for example, Matthew J. Countryman, *Up South: Civil Rights and Black Power in Philadelphia* (Philadelphia: University of Pennsylvania Press, 2005) and Thomas Sugrue, *Sweet Land of Liberty: The Forgotten Struggle for Civil Rights in the North* (New York: Random House, 2008).

6. See, for example, many of the contributions in Robert Zieger, ed., *Organized Labor in the Twentieth-Century South* (Knoxville: University of Tennessee Press, 1991) and *Southern Labor in Transition, 1940-1995* (Knoxville: University of Tennessee Press, 1997).

7. Michael Katz, Mark Stern and Jamie Fader, "The New African American Inequality," *Journal of American History* 92 (June 2005): 75-108 and "Women and the Paradox of Economic Inequality in the Twentieth Century," *Journal of Social History* 39 (Autumn 2005): 65-88. Studies that link "the urban crisis" with deindustrialization and African American male unemployment include William Julius Wilson, *The Truly Disadvantaged: The Inner City, The Underclass, and Public Policy* (Chicago: University of Chicago Press, 1990) and Thomas Sugrue, *The Origins of the Urban Crisis: Race and Inequality in Postwar Detroit* (Princeton: Princeton University Press, 1998).

8. James P. Connolly, "Baltimore Area Looks to Boom Times in '51; Surplus Labor Already Sought outside State," *New York Times*, January 2, 1951, 66.

9. U.S. Department of Commerce, Bureau of the Census, *United States Census of Population: 1950, Census Tract Statistics: Baltimore, Maryland and Adjacent Area* (Washington, D.C.: Government Printing Office, 1952); and U.S. Department of Commerce, Bureau of

the Census, *U.S. Census of Population and Housing: 1960, Census Tracts: Baltimore, Md.* (Washington, D.C.: Government Printing Office, 1963).

10. During the 1950s, mechanization contributed to African American unemployment rates by eroding the number of unskilled positions in the city and stalling growth in semi-skilled positions. Hammer and Company Associates, "Economic Report on the Baltimore Region" (October 1964), 4–11, available at the Department of Legislative Reference, City Hall, Baltimore; Maryland Department of Employment Security, "The Story of the Labor Force, Baltimore Metropolitan Area, 1950–1965," May 1967, 5, folder "Labor and Laboring Classes-Baltimore Area," VF, Maryland Room [hereafter MR], Enoch Pratt Free Library, Baltimore, Maryland [hereafter EPFL]. For general information on Baltimore's labor market see Maryland Commission on Interracial Problems and Relations [hereafter MCIPR], *An American City in Transition: The Baltimore Community Self-Survey of Inter-Group Relations* ([Baltimore], 1955), 61–72; and Kenneth Durr, *Behind the Backlash: White Working-Class Politics in Baltimore, 1940–1980* (Chapel Hill: University of North Carolina Press, 2003), 80. On employment statistics see Department of Commerce, *Census of Population: 1950, Baltimore*; and Department of Commerce, *Census of Population: 1960, Baltimore*.

11. Warren M. Banner, *A Review of the Program and Activities of the Baltimore Urban League and A Brief Analysis of Conditions in the Community which it Serves* (New York: National Urban League, October–November 1949), 130. See also Ira De A. Reid, *The Negro Community of Baltimore: A Social Survey* (Baltimore: National Urban League, 1934), 11–14.

12. Quoted in George Callcott, *Maryland and America, 1940 to 1980* (Baltimore: Johns Hopkins University Press, 1985), 145. See also David Terry, "'Tramping for Justice': The Dismantling of Jim Crow in Baltimore, 1942–1954" (Ph.D. diss., Howard University, 2002), 46, 57–62, 308.

13. On gerrymandering see Jo Ann Argersinger, *Toward a New Deal in Baltimore* (Chapel Hill: University of North Carolina Press, 1988), 13–16; Callcott, *Maryland and America*, 149–50; Durr, *Behind the Backlash*, 13–15; Shirley Kyle, "FEPC Hearing Set for Tuesday, 1 p.m.," *Afro-American* [Late City Edition], April 24, 1954, 1, 7; Juanita Mitchell, "A Demand for Negro City Councilmen," *Baltimore Sun*, May 3, 1943, folder "Negroes–Baltimore–Civil Rights," VF, MR, EPFL; Terry, "'Tramping for Justice,'" 37; and Bruce Thompson, "The Civil Rights Vanguard: The NAACP and the Black Community in Baltimore, 1931–1942" (Ph.D. diss., University of Maryland, 1996), 33.

14. On Jackson see "Oral History Clarence M. Mitchell, Jr. by Leroy Graham," OH 8185, July 29 and August 3, 1976, Maryland Historical Society [hereafter MHS], Baltimore; Lillie M. Jackson to John Morsell, June 22, 1959, attachment "Biographical Sketch of Dr. Lillie M. Jackson," National Association for the Advancement of Colored People [hereafter NAACP] Branch Files, 1940–1955, folder "Baltimore, Maryland, July–Dec. 1959," Library of Congress, Washington, D.C. [hereafter LC]; Gloster Current to Lillie Jackson, January 6, 1948, NAACP Branch Files, 1940–1955, "Baltimore, Maryland, 1948," LC; and "Some of the Achievements of the Baltimore Branch of the NAACP," [1943], NAACP Branch Files, 1940–1955, "Baltimore, Maryland, 1943," LC. On Juanita Mitchell see Mary McLeod Bethune to Juanita Mitchell, January 15, 1943, National Council of Negro Women [hereafter NCNW], collection 5, folder 7, box 20, collection 5; "Biographical Record: Juanita Jackson Mitchell," [n.d.]. NCNW, folder 1, box 2, collection 7; Bradford Jacobs, "Mitchells of the Middle," *Baltimore Evening Sun*, September 1965, folder "Negroes–Civil Rights," VF, MR,

EPFL. See also Denton Watson, *Lion in the Lobby: Clarence Mitchell, Jr.'s Struggle for the Passage of Civil Rights Laws* (Lanham, Md.: University Press of America, 2002).

15. On the BUL see "Leader Dies While Honors Being Set," *Afro-American*, February 14, 1970, 1. On the *Afro-American* see Hayward Farrar, *The Baltimore Afro-American, 1892–1950* (Westport, Conn.: Greenwood Press, 1998).

16. The BUL also noted that African Americans were concentrated in the lowest four pay grades. Banner, *A Review*, 45, 150.

17. Dona Cooper Hamilton and Charles V. Hamilton, *The Dual Agenda: Race and Social Welfare Policies of Civil Right Organizations* (New York: Columbia University Press, 1997), 54–55; Lillie M. Jackson to Walter White, April 29, 1944, NAACP Branch Files, 1940–1955, "Baltimore, Maryland, 1944 January–June," LC; "NAACP Wires President, Urging Permanent FEPC," *Afro-American*, November 21, 1944; "Full Employment Possible," editorial, *Afro-American*, August 21, 1945, 4; "Employment Crisis Tops Reconversion Problems," *Afro-American*, August 28, 1945, 15; "Urban League Battles for Jobs," *Afro-American*, August 28, 1945, 15; "NAACP Carries FEPC Fight to Washington" and "6 Maryland Congressmen Seen by Associated Groups on FEPC," newspaper articles, n.d., NAACP Branch Files, 1940–1955, "Baltimore, Maryland, 1946," LC; "Plea Made for Crusade for FEPC Legislation," *Afro-American*, January 19, 1946, 1–2; "The Baltimore Branch . . . ," [January 21, 1946], NAACP Branch Files, 1940–1955, "Baltimore, Maryland, 1946," LC; and "Protest Md. Senator's Speech against FEPC Bill," *Afro-American*, January 29, 1946, 11.

18. Leon Sachs of the Baltimore Jewish Council was among the measure's fiercest proponents. "Bar Job Bias, Parley Asks City Council," *Baltimore Sun*, March 7, 1954, 34; "Council Chambers Packed at FEPC Hearings," *Afro-American* [Late City Edition], May 1, 1954, 28; "Equal Job Rights Bill Championed," *Baltimore Sun*, April 28, 1954; "Fair Hiring Plan Lacks Majority in Council," *Baltimore Evening Sun*, June 1, 1954, folder "1954–1959," box 80, group IV, Commission on Governmental Efficiency and Economy [hereafter CGEE], University of Baltimore Special Collection [hereafter UB]; Leon Sachs to Thomas D'Alesandro, December 22, 1955, folder 271, box 23, collection 9, Baltimore City Archives [hereafter BCA]; and Countryman, *Up South*.

19. J. C. Furnas, "FEPC: How It Works in Seven States," *Look*, October 21, 1952, box 7, collection 7, BCA; "FEPC for Baltimore," *Afro-American*, editorial, [Late City Edition], March 13, 1954, 17; Shirley Kyle, "FEPC Hearings Set for Tuesday, 1 p.m.," *Afro-American* [Late City Edition], April 24, 1954, 1, 7; "Negro Jobs Bars Here Called General," *Baltimore Evening Sun*, April 27, 1954, folder "Negroes," box 128, group IV, CGEE, UB; "Council Chambers Packed at FEPC Hearings," *Afro-American* [Late City Edition], May 1, 1954, 28; "Goodman Promises He'll Fight for FEPC," *Afro-American*, May 1, 1954, 5; "Fair Hiring Plan Lacks Majority in Council," *Baltimore Evening Sun*, June 1, 1954, folder "1954–1959," box 80, group IV, CGEE, UB; Leon Sachs to Thomas D'Alesandro, December 22, 1955, folder 271, box 23, collection 9, BCA.

20. "FEPC for Baltimore," editorial, *Afro-American*, March 13, 1954, 4; "Equal Jobs Bill Opponents Assail It as 'Red-Inspired,'" *Baltimore Sun*, May 4, 1954, 10; and "FEPC Bill Sponsors Charge Politicing [sic] in Council Vote," *Afro-American*, June 19, 1954, 29 (Nichols quote).

21. "Another Step Forward," editorial, *Afro-American*, April 7, 1956, 4. See also Shirley Kyle, "Predict FEPC Bill Will Become Law on Tuesday: Pros, Cons Say the Bill Will Work,"

Afro-American, April 7, 1956, 32; "Valle to Head Commission on Job Rights," *Baltimore Sun*, November 14, 1956, folder "1954–1959," box 80, group IV, CGEE, UB.

22. [Thomas D'Alesandro, Jr.], public statement on EEOC, April 18, 1956, box 271, group 23, collection 9, BCA. See also "Citizens Watch as Mayor Signs FEPC into Law," *Afro-American*, April 14, 1956, 32; and "Job-Equality Bill Signed," *Baltimore Evening Sun*, April 18, 1956, folder "1954–1959," box 80, group IV, CGEE, UB.

23. "Valle to Head Commission on Job Rights," *Baltimore Sun*, November 14, 1956, "Appointment of Valle Hit as Irregular," *Baltimore Sun*, December 26, 1956, "New Job Post Ruled under Merit System," *Baltimore Sun*, January 4, 1957, "Merit Setup Change on 2 Jobs Opposed," *Baltimore Sun*, January 29, 1957, and "Oral Tests Given Valle Denounced," *Baltimore Sun*, March 30, 1957, all in folder "1954–1959," box 80, group IV, CGEE, UB; "Statement by Mayor D'Alesandro," September 17, 1956, box 271, group 23, collection 9, BCA.

24. "Time for Action," editorial, *Afro-American*, May 18, 1957, 4.

25. "Revision of CMEA By-Laws," *The Hall Light*, September 1954, 1–2 [available at EPFL]. On CMEA history see also "City Employees—Know Your CMEA," *The Hall Light*, June 1961, 1; and "Kowzan Resents 'Outside' Union," *Baltimore Sun*, January 22, 1960, folder "1954–1963," box 139, group IV, CGEE, UB.

26. "Hearing of Importance to Membership," *The Hall Light*, April 1960, 1.

27. "City Must Mend Ways Says EEOC," *Afro-American*, April 25, 1959, 3; "CMEA to Continue as Service Organization," *The Hall Light*, April 1961, 1.

28. "Firemen Admitted to Union Protest Back-Dues Penalty," *Afro-American*, July 30, 1960, 1, 3; and "Urban Unit Backs Union Bid to Negro Firefighters," *Baltimore Morning Sun*, August 2, 1960, folder "1954–1963," box 139, group VI, CGEE, UB.

29. "Firemen's Union Seen as Biased," *Baltimore Sun*, May 31, 1960, folder "1954–1963," box 139, group VI, CGEE, UB; Frank P. L. Somerville, "Union Opened to Negroes," *Baltimore Sun*, July 28, 1960; "'We Won't Pay It': Firemen Reject $25 Penalty," *Afro-American*, August 6, 1960, 1–2; "It's Still Too Much," *Afro-American*, August 6, 1960, 4; "200 Firemen Call Big Public Rally," *Afro-American*, September 24, 1960, 32; Frank Somerville, "Negroes Vote 'No' on Union," *Baltimore Sun*, September 30, 1960, 27; "Firemen Vote 94 to 0 against $25 penalty," *Afro-American*, October 1, 1960, 2; Frank Somerville, "D.C. Parley Hears Charges of Bias in City Fire Union," *Baltimore Sun*, February 19, 1961, 20; Frank Somerville, "Firefighters in Agreement," *Baltimore Sun*, May 9, 1961, 38.

30. Kevin Boyle, *The UAW and the Heyday of American Liberalism* (Ithaca: Cornell University Press, 1995); Mark Gelfand, *Nation of Cities: The Federal Government and Urban America, 1933–1965* (New York: Oxford University Press, 1975), 348–79; Hamilton and Hamilton, *The Dual Agenda*, 155; Dennis Judd and Todd Swanstrom, *City Politics: The Political Economy of Urban America*, 4th ed. (New York: Pearson, 2004), 168–69.

31. U.S. Department of Commerce, Bureau of the Census, *Census of Governments, 1962, Vol. 3, No. 2, Compendium of Public Employment* (Washington, D.C.: Government Printing Office, 1963), 222; and U.S. Department of Commerce, Bureau of the Census, *Census of Governments, 1967, Vol. 3, No. 2, Compendium of Public Employment* (Washington, D.C.: Government Printing Office, 1969), 238. See also Commission on Governmental Efficiency and Economy, "Municipal Payroll Growth" (June 1965), folder "Officials and Employees–Baltimore–1960–," VF, MR, EPFL; and Kathy Kraus, "City Payroll up 1,000 Yearly: Adding New Employees as 3,000 Move Out," *The News American*, December 4, 1967, folder "Officials and Employees–Baltimore–1960–," MR, VF, EPFL.

32. Irving Bernstein, *Promises Kept: John F. Kennedy's New Frontier* (New York: Oxford University Press, 1991); Judd and Swanstrom, *City Politics*; Nancy MacLean, *Freedom Is Not Enough: The Opening of the American Workplace* (Cambridge: Harvard University Press, 2008); John Mollenkopf, *The Contested City* (Princeton: Princeton University Press, 1983); Judith Stein, *Running Steel, Running America: Race, Economic Policy and the Decline of Liberalism* (Chapel Hill: University of North Carolina Press, 1998); U.S. Department of Labor, *The Negro Family: The Case for National Action* (Washington, D.C.: Government Printing Office, 1965).

33. Ronnie Goldberg, "The Politics of Local Government in Baltimore," in *Power and Poverty: Theory and Practice*, ed. Peter Bachrach and Morton Baratz (London: Oxford University Press, 1970), 119.

34. Marion Orr, "The Struggle for Black Empowerment in Baltimore," in *Racial Politics in American Cities*, ed. Rufus P. Browning, Dale Rogers Marshall, and David H. Tabb (New York: Longman, 2003), 255–77; Goldberg, "Politics of Local Government," 109–16; "Baltimore Community Relations Commission Newsletter" (January 1965), folder "Baltimore Community Relations Commission (2)," box 363, group 25, collection 9, BCA; and Michael Stetz, "War Stories: A History of the Urban Services Agency," *The City Paper*, August 1, 1986, folder "(Dept) Urban Services Agency," box 940, group 27, collection 9, BCA.

35. Quoted in Allan Matusow, *The Unraveling of America: A History of Liberalism in the 1960s* (New York: Harper & Row, 1984), 246. On wartime voter-registration drives in Baltimore, see, for example, "Keep Interest in Voting High, Leaders Urged: NAACP Intensifies Victory Vote Drive for 2-Month Push," *Afro-American*, January 1, 1944, 10. On pressure on McKeldin see, for example, "Three Vacancies on the School Board This Year," editorial, *Afro-American*, January 8, 1944, 4.

36. "City Employment Practices—Some Recommendations," *Baltimore CRC Newsletter*, February–March 1967, 2, folder "McK BCRC (2)," box 363, group 25, collection 9, BCA; Baltimore Community Relations Commission, *Survey of Employment in City Government*, i.

37. "Equal Opportunity Commission in Sad State of Affairs," *Afro-American*, May 25, 1963, 1; "Minutes of the Mayor's Task Force for Equal Rights Employment Subcommittee Meeting, Programs to Achieve Equality in Employment," September 8, 1966, folder "387 Employment Committee, Mayor's Task Force on Equal Rights," box 502, group 26, collection 9, BCA; Mayor's Task Force for Equal Rights Employment Committee, "Minutes," April 28, 1967, and Mayors Task Force for Equal Rights Employment Committee, [Membership List], July 10, 1967, folder "1963–1967 Mayor McKeldin," box 16, group 4, collection 7, BCA.

38. Norman P. Ramsey, Henry Henkelmann Jr., and G. James Fleming to Theodore R. McKeldin, "Report on Allegations of Racial Discrimination in the Civil Service," October 25, 1967, 7, folder "590 Civil Service Commission (1)," box 528, group 26, collection 9, BCA; and Leon Sachs to Thomas D'Alesandro III, December 26, 1967, with "Recommendations Designed to Overcome Imbalance in Negro Municipal Employment," folder "449. Mayor's Advisory Committee on the CSC," box 512, group 26, collection 9, BCA.

39. Sachs to D'Alesandro, December 26, 1967. On civil rights activists' efforts to fight discrimination in city government employment, see, for example, Rev. Jentry E. McDonald to Theodore McKeldin, September 17, 1963, and Theodore McKeldin to Rev. Jentry E. McDonald, October 2, 1963, folder "EEOC," box 387, group 25, collection 9, BCA; "Negroes

Rap Police Pace," *Baltimore Sun*, September 25, 1963, folder "1963," category "Negroes," box 128, CGEE, UB; "City's Police Department Due Picketing," *Baltimore Sun*, September 25, 1963, folder "1963," "Negroes," box 128, CGEE, UB; "Schmidt Denies Department Bias," *Baltimore Sun*, April 20, 1968, folder "1968," category "Negroes," box 128, CGEE, UB; and Alan Lupo, "C.O.R.E. Asks Shift of White City Foremen," *Baltimore Evening Sun*, July 19, 1966, folder "1966," category "Negroes," box 128, CGEE, UB.

40. "Plan Head Count of City Workers," *Evening Sun* (1963), and Adam Spiegel, "City Study Lists Few Negroes in Top Jobs," *The News American*, n.d., folder "Officials and Employees–Baltimore, 1960–," VF, MR, EPFL. On battles over cultural bias in testing see "City Employment Practices—Some Recommendations," *Baltimore CRC Newsletter*, February–March 1967, 2, folder "McK BCRC (2)," box 363, group 25, collection 9, BCA. On "preferential" hiring see Thomas J. Murphy to George L. Russell Jr., November 26, December 6, 1968, folder "1965–1968 Law Department," box 14, group 4, collection 7, BCA. On the achievements of activists see Baltimore City Council, *Journal of Proceedings of City Council of Baltimore at the Session of 1967–1971, Second Councilmanic Year, December, 1968–December, 1969* (Baltimore, [n.d.]), 820. On efforts to limit municipal employment to city residents see "Low City-Job Rank of Negroes Cites," *Evening Sun*, February 14, 1968, folder "1968," box 80, group IV, CGEE, UB; Baltimore City Council, *Journal of Proceedings of City Council of Baltimore at the Session of 1967–1971, First Councilmanic Year, December, 1967–December, 1968* (Baltimore, [n.d.]) 299–300; "Minutes of the Civil Service Commission of Baltimore," September 28, 1967, box 9, group 3, Records of the Civil Service Commission (7), BCA; and KRH to Thomas D'Alesandro III, May 23, 1968, folder "590 CSC (1)," box 528, group 26, collection 9, BCA; "Julian Hits Dixon, Urges Heavy Vote," *Afro-American*, September 5, 1967, 16; City Council Office of Financial Review, "Table 1: Analysis of Baltimore Departmental Payrolls: City and Non-City Residents . . . ," September 9, 1970, folder "1965–1971 City Council Members, Correspondence," box 11, group 4, collection 7, BCA; City Council Office of Financial Review, "Table II: Average Salaries Paid City Residents and Non-City Residents . . . ," September 9, 1970, folder "1965–1971 City Council Members, Correspondence," box 11, group 4, collection 7, BCA; "Law and City Jobs," editorial, *Afro-American*, November 14, 1970) 4; and "Many City Workers Live Outside," *Sunday Sun*, March 14, 1971, "1965–1971 City Council Members, Correspondence," box 11, group 4, collection 7, BCA. On similar efforts in other cities see Robert Self, *American Babylon: Race and the Struggle for Postwar Oakland* (Princeton: Princeton University Press, 2003) and Roger Waldinger, *Still the Promised City? African Americans and New Immigrants in Postindustrial New York* (Cambridge: Harvard University Press, 1996).

41. Baltimore Community Relations Commission, *Survey of Employment in City Government*, i.

42. See note 38 above.

43. U.S. Department of Labor, *The Negro Family*.

44. Naples, *Grassroots Warriors*.

45. Lee Lassiter, "Welfare: Reform or Revolt—'Income, Dignity, Democracy,'" *The News American*, May 1, 1969, folder "Social Welfare," VF, MR, EPFL.

46. Williams, *Politics of Public Housing*, 164.

47. "BURHA Names 2 Project Managers," *Afro-American*, May 21, 1963, 20; "Mrs. Ferguson Named Service Coordinator," *Afro-American*, October 29, 1968, 7; Corinne E.

Hammett, "Community School Idea Steams Ahead," *The News American*, November 24, 1968, folder "Education-Baltimore 1955-1969," VF, MR, EPFL; David Ahearn, "Women Wield Little Power at City Hall," *The News American*, November 11, 1969, folder "Officials and Employees-Baltimore-1960-," VF, MR, EPFL; Marguerite Campbell to Maurice Harmon, May 26, 1971, folder "270 Department of Welfare (1)," box 486, group 26, collection 9, BCA; and James D. Dilts, "Guitar, Ping Pong, and a Dream: Baltimore's Community Schools are a Focal Point for a Better Life," *Baltimore Sun*, April 18, 1971, folder "Education-Baltimore 1955-1969," VF, MR, EPFL.

    48. U.S. Department of Commerce, Bureau of the Census, *Census of Governments, 1962, 1967, 1972, Vol. 3, No. 2, Compendium of Public Employment* (Washington, D.C.: Government Printing Office, 1963, 1969, 1974); MCIPR, "Survey of Non-White Employees, Summary Report on a Decade in Race Relations" (1964), Maryland State Archives; "Job Bias Seen Continuing," *Baltimore Sun*, May 29, 1967; and Jonathan Cottin, "Official Claims State Job Rise for Negroes," *Baltimore Evening Sun*, April 14, 1967, folder "1967," box 80, group IV, CGEE, UB; Cleveland A. Chandler and Mainstream Associates, "Study of Equal Employment Opportunity in the Baltimore Metropolitan Area, Interim Report I," [Report for the Baltimore Community Relations Commission and the Equal Employment Opportunity Commission], July 28, 1967, 4, is available at LRCH; "Governor's Proclamation Promulgating a Code of Fair Practices," December 18, 1967, folder "348 Civil Rights," box 495, group 26, collection 9, BCA; Paul D. Samuel, "Code of Fair Practices Issued by Governor," *Baltimore Sun*, December 19, 1967, and "Order Aims to Abolish Md. Bias," *Baltimore Evening Sun*, December 20, 1967, folder "1967," box 80, group IV, CGEE, UB; and "Griffin, City School Official, Named to State Racial Post," *Baltimore Sun*, March 23, 1968, and Paul D. Samuel, "Agnew Aide Is 'Virtually Powerless' to Act on Discrimination Charges," *Baltimore Evening Sun*, September 19, 1968, folder "1968," box 80, group IV, CGEE, UB.

    49. On efforts to improve employment opportunities for African Americans in the federal government's workforce, see "Few Top $$ For Tan PO Employees," *Afro-American*, May 21, 1963, 1-2 and "NAPE Charges Postal Service Employment Bias," *Afro-American*, August 29, 1967, 24. On efforts to win jobs for African Americans at the Social Security Administration's Baltimore headquarters, see Dr. Lillie Mae Jackson to Lyndon Johnson, August 20, 1963; Robert M. Ball to Lillie Mae Jackson, August 24, 1963; Ralph Matthews Jr., "Can Social Security Clean House in 90 Days?" *The News American*, September 1963; "Commissioner's Bulletin to All Baltimore Employees, Draft," September 13, 1963; "Comparison of 1962 and 1963 Minority Reports, Headquarters Office (OCO, DAO, DDO)"; "F. Z. Nichols, Jr. Named to Post," *Baltimore Sun*, September 5, 1963; "Meeting between Representatives of the NAACP and the SSA, with Representatives of the Baltimore Sun and the Afro-American . . ." August 26, 1963; "More Charge Discrimination in Social Security Agency," *Afro-American*, [September 1963]; "Social Security to Recruit Graduates in Colored Schools," *Afro-American*, October 12, 1963; "S S Meeting Averts Picket Line," *Afro-American* [n.d.]; and Roy E. Touchet to Robert M. Ball, September 6, 1963; "'Widespread' Bias Denied," *Baltimore Sun*, August 23, 1963, all in folder "PE-6-3-1 1963 Vc's . . . ," box 292, Reading Group [hereafter RG] 47, Social Security Papers [hereafter SSP], National Archives [hereafter NA]. On demonstrations at the Social Security Administration's headquarters, see "Social Security Protest Being Joined by CORE," *Afro-American*, May 23, 1964; Furman Templeton and Clarence Mitchell III, "An Open Letter to SSA Employees," *Afro-American*, May 23, 1964;

"100 Stage March on SS Building at Woodlawn," *Afro-American*, May 28, 1964; Marion Bascom to Director Social Security Admin, May 25, 1964; "Concluding Report of the Social Security Administration Advisory Committee on Personnel Practices in Baltimore to the Commissioner of Social Security," May 2, 1964; "Social Security Protest Being Joined by CORE," *Afro-American*, May 23, 1964; "Expect 2,000 in Woodlawn March," *The News American*, May 28, 1964, 2C; "Maryland Sizzle and Fizzle," *Baltimore News-Post*, May 31, 1964; "Protest Held at Woodlawn," *Baltimore Sun*, May 29, 1964, folder "PE-6-3-1 President's Committee on Equal Employment ...," box 292, RG 47, SSP, NA. See also Robert M. Ball to All Baltimore Employees, May 12, 1966, folder "OCREO," VF, History Department [hereafter HD], Social Security Administration, Baltimore [hereafter SSA]; and Robert M. Ball to All Baltimore Employees, January 16, 1967, folder "Buildings–Baltimore," VF, HD, SSA. A discussion of the protest at Social Security appears in Harry William Holt, "Charges Brought against a Federal Agency—The Second Time Around' (unpublished paper, George Washington University, Fall 1999). I am grateful to civil rights activist and former Social Security employee Harts Brown for his willingness to share his recollections of the protest.

50. "At Social Security: Bob Johnson Thrives on Helping People in Need," *Afro-American*, March 18, 1969, 5.

51. U.S. Department of Commerce, Bureau of the Census, *1970 Census of Population, Volume 1, Characteristics of the Population, Part 22: Maryland* (Washington, D.C.: Government Printing Office, 1973), 212 and 347.

52. Ibid.

53. MCIPR, "Survey of Non-White Employees," Maryland State Archives.

54. On the unionization of the federal workforce see Sar A. Levitan and Alexandra B. Noden, *Working for the Sovereign: Employee Relations in the Federal Government* (Baltimore: Johns Hopkins University Press, 1993), 13–43; William MacNeil, "A Union's Role in the Federal Government," *Oasis*, June 1960, 12; and Willem B. Vosloo, *Collective Bargaining in the United States Federal Civil Service* (Chicago: Public Personnel Association, 1966). On union organizing in Baltimore and Maryland see Kathy Kraus, "His Job: Grappling with City Labor Problems," *The News American*, July 11, 1968, folder "1968," box 139, group IV, CGEE, UB; "State Unionists Push Labor Law," *Baltimore Sun*, January 30, 1968, C6; Bentley Orrick, "Della Pushes for a Public Strike Right," *Baltimore Sun*, February 28, 1968, C22; Bentley Orrick, "Teacher Bill Nears Vote," *Baltimore Sun*, March 14, 1968; Kay Mills "Teachers Union Adds 1,000 Members," *Baltimore Sun*, October 11, 1968, folder "1968," box 139, group IV, CGEE, UB; Betty Miller, "Defeat in Maryland, Prelude to Victory," *The Public Employee*, February 1968, 11; and "Mayor Will Sign Labor Bill Today," *Baltimore Sun*, September 30, 1968, C20, C10. For an important treatment of the history of public-sector unions prior to the 1960s, see Joseph Slater, *Public Workers: Government Employees, the Law and the State, 1900–1962* (Ithaca: Cornell University Press, 2004); and on the history of AFSCME see Joseph Goulden, *Jerry Wurf: Labor's Last Angry Man* (New York: Atheneum, 1982). On successful organizing in Baltimore's low-wage private service sector see Gregg L. Michel, "'Union Power, Soul Power': Unionizing Johns Hopkins University Hospital, 1959–1974," *Labor History* 38, no. 1 (1996–97): 28–66.

55. U.S. Commission on Civil Rights, *Greater Baltimore Commitment: A Study of Urban Minority Economic Development* (Washington, D.C., April 1983), 13.

4

Worker-Citizens at the Community Bargaining Table

The St. Louis Teamsters' Community Stewards Program in the 1950s

ROBERT BUSSEL

The August 7, 1957, front page of the *St. Louis Post-Dispatch* featured an exultant Harold Gibbons, leader of Teamsters Local 688, and other members of his union celebrating the overwhelming defeat of proposed changes in the city charter favored by St. Louis's mayor, business elite, and news media. Along with the city's NAACP, which was headed by Local 688 staff member Ernest Calloway, the union had been instrumental in mobilizing community opposition to charter revisions that would have dramatically altered the structure of political representation in St. Louis. Speaking on behalf of the anti-charter-change coalition that Local 688 had spearheaded, Gibbons declared: "Any future attempt to create a new city charter must be based upon a free exchange of ideas between big business and all the other groups in the city." In response, St. Louis mayor Raymond Tucker complained that the defeat of the charter raised the question of "whether the citizens of St. Louis or the Teamsters would run the city." The charter's defeat also captured national attention, with a *Business Week* article observing that St. Louis business leaders would have to deal with the "Problem of Gibbons" and suggesting they seek a "civil rapprochement" with labor in order to advance their agenda for urban revitalization and political reform. These postmortems testified to the power of the community stewards program launched six years earlier by Local 688. This program, which had made the Teamsters a highly visible force in community affairs, enabled the union to mobilize effective opposition to the proposed charter change and thwart the plans of St. Louis's civic and business elite to recast St. Louis politics in its favor.[1]

The St. Louis Teamsters' community stewards program was a bold attempt to address several of the most significant challenges that faced the post–World War II union movement. Following the passage of the Taft-Hartley Act in 1947, the rise of McCarthyism, and dimming prospects for expanding the welfare state, labor's political approach grew more parochial and defensive. Instead of being seen as a social movement dedicated to upgrading the status of all workers, unions were often characterized, however unfairly, as an interest group content with negotiating their own private welfare states and using politics to maintain their preferential status. Labor's ability to translate economic power into political influence in the post–World War II city, where unions had established their strongest beachheads, was often undercut by municipal reforms that limited mayoral authority and discouraged efforts to form labor parties. The union movement's political efforts were also complicated by the persistence, in some cities, of machine politics that made ethnic or racial loyalty a compelling alternative to class-based appeals. Moreover, given the tangible rewards unions could obtain by acting as a well-organized interest group in an urban setting, they were often reluctant to upset established political norms or seek a larger civic role.[2]

The organizers of the community stewards program in St. Louis looked to redefine labor's political approach by creating what one Local 688 leader called the "community bargaining table," an arena in which the Teamsters would lead a progressive coalition to play an integral role in shaping urban policy. Applying their shop-floor expertise as workers' representatives to neighborhood and community issues, the community steward became the linchpin of the St. Louis Teamsters' efforts to enhance the quality of life for their members outside the workplace. Seeking to improve public transit, expand recreational opportunities for youth, increase access to higher education, and make housing more attractive and affordable, community stewards raised basic questions about the quality of life in St. Louis and the kinds of institutional supports needed, in Gibbons's words, to make the city "a really livable place for working people." In their quest to encourage Local 688 members to "broaden their horizon beyond the shop and into the community in which they live," Gibbons and other Teamsters leaders also aimed to revive notions of working-class citizenship that in earlier periods had fueled labor's ambitions to function as a transformational social force.[3]

After World War II, promising labor-led progressive coalitions in cities such as Memphis, Winston-Salem, Birmingham, Atlanta, and Miami reeled under the impact of race-baiting, indiscriminate anti-communism, and concerted

Figure 4.1. A community stewards meeting in St. Louis's second ward, 1951. The St. Louis Teamsters pioneered in building labor-citizen coalitions. (Missouri Teamsters Collection, Western Historical Manuscript Collection at University of Missouri–St. Louis.)

political attacks on unions.[4] In St. Louis, however, the Teamster-generated community stewards program demonstrated the possibilities of continued union-community collaboration. Its success occurred in the complex social environment of a border city, memorably described by one civil rights activist as a "northern city with a southern exposure," that was led by a self-conscious business and civic elite that sought to contain civil rights and labor militancy within well-defined parameters in order to sustain its hegemony.[5]

Community stewards also attempted to address one of labor's most enduring challenges, what historians have described as the "radical separation in people's consciousness . . . of the politics of work from the politics of community," and the tendency of those who were "good unionists on the job [to] quickly shed these principles once they walked outside the factory gate," especially in their approach to political issues and matters of racial justice. By focusing their efforts on what they called "the other sixteen hours" workers spent away from the shop floor, Local 688's community stewards attempted to bridge this historic divide by demonstrating that the split between the "politics of work" and the "politics of community" was neither inevitable nor intractable.[6]

Coal Miners' Sons: From the CIO to Teamsters Local 688

Three talented men whose political sensibilities had been shaped by their association with industrial unionism during the 1930s played instrumental roles in formulating Local 688's community stewards program. By 1950, Harold Gibbons, secretary-treasurer and principal leader of Teamsters Local 688, had compiled an admirable record of achievement in his fifteen years as a union activist. The youngest of twenty-three children in a Pennsylvania coal-mining family, Gibbons knew firsthand the stress of economic hardship, which was accentuated by his father's death when Harold was twelve. Gibbons sought improved opportunities by moving to Chicago but found his hopes of attending college dashed by the Depression. Instead, he plunged into the ferment of union organizing and left-wing politics, finding employment in a Works Progress Administration program that ultimately led him to a vice-presidency in the fledgling American Federation of Teachers and a visible presence in the local branch of the Committee on Industrial Organization.[7]

During the late 1930s, Gibbons worked for the Congress of Industrial Organizations' (CIO's) Textile Workers Organizing Committee in Kentucky and Missouri before becoming head of the United Retail, Wholesale, and Department Store Employees Association (URWDSEA) in St. Louis in 1941. He quickly moved to coordinate the activities of the union's disparate local chapters, expand its political involvement, and reinvigorate its organizing efforts. Dissatisfied with the national union's continuing ties to Communists (Gibbons retained his socialist loyalties but was a staunch anti-communist) and its failure to support more aggressive organizing, he engineered the St. Louis locals' disaffiliation from the URWDSEA in 1948 and a year later merged his union with Local 688 of the American Federation of Labor's (AFL) International Brotherhood of Teamsters.[8]

In 1950, Ernest Calloway, an African American from a coal-mining background in Kentucky whom Gibbons had known in Chicago, accepted the Teamster leader's request to join him in St. Louis. Educated at Brookwood Labor College, a pioneering institution that provided the early CIO with some of its most capable organizers, Calloway helped to found the redcaps union (later the United Transport Service Employees, or UTSE) and also became deeply involved in anti-machine politics in Chicago, where the UTSE was headquartered. Prior to coming to St. Louis, Calloway had studied at Ruskin College in England under a British Trades Union Congress scholarship. He provided

Gibbons with organizational, intellectual, and technical expertise in developing the community stewards program. Later, in his capacity as president of the St. Louis NAACP, Calloway collaborated closely with the Teamsters in opposing the proposed charter change in 1957.[9]

Sidney Zagri, a Harvard-trained lawyer who assumed direction of the community stewards program in 1954, led the initiative to some of its greatest successes. In the late 1930s, Zagri had worked as an investigator for the La Follette Committee's probe into corporate resistance to union organizing and held positions with both the National Labor Relations Board and the National War Labor Board. During a stint with the California Labor Federation, he served on a state mental health advisory board appointed by governor Earl Warren. An articulate, aggressive man who favored a vigorous social role for unions, Zagri became the most visible spokesperson for the community stewards program, frequently appearing before government agencies, writing opinion pieces in the local press, and overseeing Local 688's outreach to community organizations.[10]

At midcentury, Teamsters Local 688 was the largest local union in Missouri, with a membership of approximately ten thousand. Rooted in historically low-paying warehouse, distribution, and retail occupations, the union had a diverse membership that was approximately 20 percent African American and nearly 30 percent female, with more than 70 percent of its members residing within the city of St. Louis. Local 688 made impressive gains in raising its members' standard of living and in upgrading conditions throughout metropolitan St. Louis. Its Labor Health Institute was one of the largest and most highly regarded medical centers operated by an American union. Local 688's willingness to confront racial intolerance in a segregated city earned the union a well-deserved reputation as a leading practitioner of interracial unionism. Politicians in St. Louis coveted the union's support, and the Teamsters underscored their political clout in 1948 by running an insurgent campaign to elect one of their own members to the Missouri legislature. By all measures, Harold Gibbons and Ernest Calloway had traveled far from their hardscrabble coal-mining origins and the battlefields of industrial union organizing to build a vibrant local union that was a showcase for what well-organized workers and strong unions could accomplish.[11]

Nonetheless, Gibbons, Calloway, and other leaders in Local 688 feared that their achievements rested on fragile foundations. The political reversal of labor's fortunes, underscored by the passage of the Taft-Hartley Act, signified that unions, in Calloway's words, could no longer rely on "the apron strings of government a la FDR days." The prospect of an indifferent or even hostile administrative state led Calloway to ask, "If the time comes when [government] protection is not forthcoming, then where is the necessary vitality among workers' organizations to resist?"[12]

Gibbons and Local 688 also achieved pariah status among large segments of St. Louis's business and civic elite. The union's reputation for hard bargaining and militant strikes generated considerable anxiety about excessive union power at a time when St. Louis's economy was beginning to experience industrial flight and serious job losses. The union's aggressive forays in local politics upset the city's entrenched ward leaders, who felt threatened by Local 688's fierce political independence and its proven capacity to mobilize its members. Perhaps most importantly, Gibbons emerged as an enigmatic, even dangerous figure whose intentions became the subject of intense speculation. As union publicist and journalist Jake McCarthy later recalled, Gibbons was often portrayed as a "scary guy" by some St. Louis business and political leaders and "was . . . anathema to [the city's] power elite." During the 1950s these concerns intensified as Gibbons became closely aligned with the country's most notorious Teamster, Jimmy Hoffa, and Local 688 came under combined local and federal scrutiny well before Arkansas senator John McClellan launched his much-publicized investigation into union corruption in 1957.[13]

Having been socialized in the stark class relations of coal-mining towns and the crucible of industrial union organizing, Calloway and Gibbons fully appreciated the challenge of establishing labor's reputation at the community level. As they explained at a 1953 staff orientation, from "the early days of the American trade union movement [that] saw the entire community pitted against the union," with labor's new economic power, "many church, educational, and community leaders are seeing unions in a new light." The union movement was now poised, in Calloway's words, to take "its place as an integral part of the social and economic family" and to demonstrate its "real understanding of the fact that we are the community, and it's our community, too." Along with other Local 688 leaders, he and Gibbons began to envision a community-based effort that would offer a new conception of both unions and union membership. As one Teamster leader asserted, "unions must be more than dues collecting agencies or slot machines for wage increases. Members must be seen as total human beings and not as economic units only."[14]

Workers as Citizens: Launching the Community Stewards Program in St. Louis

In developing a community stewards program, Local 688 strategists also angled to exert greater influence in St. Louis politics. According to political scientist Lana Stein, the union faced a local political culture whose most salient characteristics were a "weak mayor, fragmented power, and ward factionalism." At the root of St. Louis's complicated politics was a post–Civil War "divorce" that separated the city of St. Louis from adjacent St. Louis County but left important elective city offices under state rather than city jurisdiction. In addition to creating positions with budgets and patronage opportunities that were not under the full authority of city officials, the divorce and St. Louis's adoption of home rule resulted in a decentralized governing structure that encouraged the exercise of political power at the ward level. After 1950 the Democratic Party dominated city politics, but serious divisions remained between the "mayor's group" (the business elite, the press, and the city's middle and upper middle class) and the "county group" (county officeholders, aldermen, African Americans, unions, the working class, and the poor). This conservative, parochial culture was the uninviting soil in which Local 688 sought to cultivate its community stewards program, and its strategy reflected a keen awareness of St. Louis's distinctive political history.[15]

In order to blunt the power of ward leaders, gain recognition as an independent political force, and play a larger role in shaping social and economic decision-making, Local 688 leaders aimed to convince the rank and file that effective political action encompassed activities beyond the election of labor-friendly candidates or lobbying for pro-worker legislation. Moreover, given the importance of the ward as the principal arena in which politics was practiced in St. Louis, the union's community program needed to establish itself at this most basic level. As Gibbons explained in a 1953 *New Republic* article titled "Labor's Task in the Precinct," "the natural habitat of political action is in the wards and precincts, not in the union hall. The development of ward organizations is perhaps the most important task we face during the next few years." For men such as Gibbons and Calloway, who abhorred the paternalistic relationships that characterized the city's ward politics, developing an alternative locus of power and authority at the ward level was a high strategic priority.[16]

Gibbons elaborated on the union's strategy in his 1953 *New Republic* piece. "At their present level of understanding," he observed, "most workers are much more concerned over the fact that their garbage is not collected in time rather than the pending Tidelands Oil giveaway. A worker's wife who will not even attempt to understand the complexities of American foreign policy may be well aware of the need for a stop sign near the school the child attends." Over time, Gibbons contended in an earlier *New Republic* article, "as politics are brought down to earth, [and] made a part of the everyday life of the individual union member, greater political consciousness is developed. It is only one short step in the political awareness of the member from lower bus fares to lower taxes, from better trash collection to better labor legislation, from more street lights to more civil rights."[17]

Local 688 strategists also sought to reduce the separation between work and community that existed in the minds of the union's members and discouraged the kind of political action they hoped to promote. In affirming the connection between the workers and their communities, Gibbons, Calloway, and Zagri argued that active civic engagement was required to preserve the enhanced security and social status that workers had gained during the industrial union upsurge and World War II. Elaborating on this connection, they explained in a 1955 training course for shop stewards: "Workers are citizens first. While they pledge loyalty to their union because it has improved conditions in the shop, they and their union must necessarily broaden their horizons beyond the shop and into the community in which they live. For while shop conditions affect their lives only a comparatively short segment of the day, they spend the remainder of their lives in their neighborhoods and their communities." This formulation echoed the aspirations, a generation earlier, of industrial democracy advocates, who saw the democratization of the shop floor as a fulcrum for inspiring greater democracy in the political sphere. And by focusing on the union member as a "total person," the community stewards would help workers overcome the social fragmentation and isolation prevalent in modern life by allowing them to apply their shop-floor skills and expertise in their neighborhoods and communities.[18]

In order to create worker-citizens, Local 688 leaders appropriated the familiar apparatus and practices of the shop floor, especially the role of the union steward, and transplanted them to the community sphere. Officially launched in November 1951, the new program established a community steward system in St. Louis's twenty-eight wards and in adjacent communities where Local 688 members lived. The plan called for every fifteen to twenty-five rank-and-file members in a ward or neighborhood to be represented by a community steward, who was appointed by the union's leadership. Most of the community stewards appear to have demonstrated leadership capabilities on the shop floor, thereby making them attractive candidates to help implement Local 688's new community-oriented program. At least once a year, union leaders suspended regular shop meetings and encouraged members to attend community meetings in their wards. At these gatherings, workers would discuss neighborhood and community issues and decide on priorities for the union to address. Although these meetings often involved city officials, community stewards directed members to avoid discussion of party politics and to focus instead on mobilizing to press for improvements in their neighborhood. This directive anticipated the possibility that ward leaders might seek to co-opt the new effort and attempt to contain it within the familiar parameters of patron-client relations.[19]

Adapting elements of the formal grievance procedure used in Local 688 shops (the union even distributed copies of a community grievance form), the community stewards initially approached the ward's alderman seeking action on a specific concern. If a satisfactory resolution was not reached within a specified time period, the steward could then take the grievance to the appropriate city department or agency for redress. Subsequent options included bringing the unresolved grievance to the mayoral level, going to court, publicizing the issue in the media, or attempting to mobilize public opinion if political leaders and city officials proved unresponsive. Underscoring the political dimensions of the program, the union offered one final step if the "grievance procedure" proved unavailing, declaring that the "ultimate recourse is the traditional weapon of democracy—our action at the polls." To reinforce this message of engagement and empowerment, Local 688 developed an eight-week training program covering issues such as leadership, politics, and advocacy skills in order to prepare community stewards for their new responsibilities as worker-citizens.[20]

Many of the issues Local 688 members brought to the attention of their community stewards dealt with matters of public safety and the quality of neighborhood life. By the mid-1950s the union claimed to have successfully processed more than 250 separate grievances with city agencies. These grievances involved dirty streets, cracked sidewalks, the lack of stop signs and traffic lights, and irregular trash collection. In these instances the community steward or program director simply contacted the appropriate city agency or department and requested that it undertake needed repairs or service improvements. Some observers noted that in conducting such intercessions, the Teamsters appeared to be challenging ward leaders by assuming their traditional roles. This perception heightened as the community stewards became increasingly visible and assertive at the ward level.[21]

Local 688 leaders also attempted to use these members' concerns as teachable moments. For example, in 1957, after the home of union member Betty Hill flooded during a rainstorm, Zagri called the St. Louis Department of Public Safety to address the immediate problem. However, he also convinced Hill to convene her neighbors to meet with a representative of the local sewer district and discuss the creation of a new subdistrict station to address persistent drainage problems. Whenever possible, the union conducted its meetings with city officials in private homes, reflecting Zagri's conviction that "neighbors develop a feeling of cohesion and intimacy in a living room." This approach represented an explicit attempt to inspire a new sense of citizen obligation and social solidarity among Local 688's members. As Zagri observed, "the blight of our cities is not only to be found in the physical conditions of our neighborhoods but in the blight of our indifference as city neighbors one to the other."[22]

These encounters created the sense of neighborly connection and common purpose that could help mobilize fellow citizens to pursue community grievances. "The man who wins a small bout with the city administration," Zagri explained, "uses this as an argument with his neighbors to get them involved in the political stream." Underscoring the program's political dimension, community stewards asked members presenting grievances if they were registered to vote, emphasizing that electoral involvement was integral to obtaining the attention of political leaders. Political and civic education, then, became an essential feature of the community stewards program, with voting portrayed as one—but certainly not the only—tool for exercising effective citizenship.[23]

The most powerful civic education for Local 688 members, however, resulted when community stewards launched specific campaigns that led to their direct engagement with the city's major social and political institutions. The union's first forays involved issues that crossed racial and class lines and dealt with the quality of community life at a most basic level: inadequate service provided by the city's transit and sewer systems. Attendees at the union's initial community meetings in 1951 and 1952, many of whom relied on buses and streetcars, complained of rising fares and poor service. In December 1951, twenty-two members of Local 688, including eight women, gave testimony before the city's Board of Aldermen. A passionate plea from Thelma Lee Stone, a staff member at the union's Labor Health Institute and a resident of St. Louis's twenty-fifth ward, climaxed their appearance. "We have had enough of absentee landlords, of higher fares, of poor service," she declared. "We suggest that the transit system should be used by St. Louisans—by all of us. We ask that the city make plans to take over ownership."[24]

Dissatisfied with the aldermen's tepid response, Local 688 members sought voters' approval to create a public transit district to provide more efficient operation and better customer service. The community stewards convinced nearly forty thousand people to sign petitions supporting this initiative and helped formulate plans for the new entity, refusing to cede this authority to elected officials or bureaucrats. At a citywide union meeting, Local 688 political action chair Robert Pentland presented signatures gathered by the community stewards to St. Louis mayor Joseph Darst. This public presentation illustrated the community stewards' growing political capabilities and affirmed Local 688's determination to bring popular concerns directly to elected officials, bypassing the backdoor relations that characterized ward politics in St. Louis. In January 1955, however, voters rejected the union's plan for a consolidated transit district amid fears that increased taxes might be needed to subsidize a new public entity. Nonetheless, Local 688 and the community stewards had introduced the argument that public oversight would serve popular needs more efficiently than private management and had demonstrated the union's commitment to grant citizens the opportunity to decide how public services could most effectively be administered.[25]

In the case of the sewer system, community stewards' activists called attention to the persistent flooding and drainage problems associated with St. Louis's weather patterns and riverine geography. The lack of an adequate sewer system posed an ongoing threat to public health, most dramatically in 1933 when the city had experienced an encephalitis epidemic. In part these problems existed because of the separation between the city and the county, which left nearly one hundred separate municipalities that often duplicated services and were unable to act cohesively. Driven by their distrust of unaccountable private power, Local 688 and the community stewards fought for public administration of this essential service. As Gibbons bluntly recalled in a subsequent interview: "When a private company fucked up the sewerage system in the county, we went out and got all the signatures necessary and got a metropolitan sewer district." In 1954 voters approved the proposed metropolitan sewer district, an important victory for the community stewards in their quest to surmount the structural political barriers impeding the provision of vital public services in St. Louis.[26]

Under Zagri's leadership, the community stewards also began to engage in a deeper form of civic participation that involved mobilizing members to investigate a grievance, develop a proposed solution, and create sufficient public pressure to compel city officials to act. Taking on a social problem that had become a national preoccupation during the 1950s, Local 688 formed a committee on juvenile delinquency. Although the extent of juvenile delinquency was subject to exaggeration and even social hysteria, upwardly mobile working-class members of Local 688 expressed concern about teenage misbehavior. They had struggled hard to gain economic security and social respect and did not want their children to succumb to antisocial activity that would detract from the expanded opportunities now available to them.[27]

Community stewards Robert Weber, Floyd Glisper, and Vera Vinyard led Local 688's committee that helped formulate union policy on juvenile delinquency. In order to provide youth with greater opportunities for structured activity, the committee recommended that municipalities expand recreational programs for teenagers and urged schools to make their facilities more available for after-hours activities. Many of the committee's recommendations were incorporated in a grand jury report on juvenile delinquency that had been commissioned by the St. Louis Circuit Court. Zagri presented Local 688's perspective before the grand jury, an aldermanic committee, and a U.S. Senate subcommittee on delinquency. At the Senate hearing, held in 1956, he chided the press for superficial coverage of the subject, denounced "get-tough" policies that emphasized "vengeance," and he criticized local political leaders for failing "to provide desirable outlets for the energy of youth."[28]

In a September 1955 letter to the editor of the *St. Louis Globe-Democrat*, community steward Robert Weber explained the union's involvement in language that clearly demonstrated an awareness of himself as a worker-citizen. Referring to concerns about teenage drug abuse, he declared: "I think this 'Goof Ball' rage is a serious community problem. I think we as good and decent citizens should unite and wipe it out." Subsequently, Weber questioned the priorities of city leaders, criticizing their inaction in explicit moral terms: "While our city is being beautified by new housing projects, our children are being left to decay." Weber and other community stewards went on to work with a citizens committee that sought to secure funds for a supervised drag strip where youth could safely pursue their interest in car racing. The juvenile delinquency committee also established "Teamster Teentown," a program that offered entertainment for youth within a supervised setting. The committee's actions drew support from a local Parent Teacher Association president, attesting to increasing social recognition of the community stewards' efforts.[29]

The community stewards program appears to have attracted a cross section of the union's membership as it established roots in many of St. Louis's neighborhoods. Although white migration to the suburbs was under way, Local 688 still had members of Irish, German, and Italian ancestry residing within St. Louis who became community stewards. Harold Gibbons recalled that the twenty-fourth ward, with a sizable Italian American population, was one of the most active sites for community steward activity. Housing issues seem to have involved African American community stewards most heavily, and they gained strong support from the union's white leadership in agitating for action on their concerns.[30]

Although Local 688's male leaders made no special outreach efforts to the union's female members, women came to play a visible role in the community stewards program. As one union leader noted after the initial round of community meetings, "another surprise was the way in which women members who have never spoken before in the meetings took the floor repeatedly." Historically, women tended to place work and family affairs on a continuum rather than regard them as separate social spheres. Within Local 688, a visible segment of the female members endorsed Gibbons's observation that "there is not much sense in winning higher wages and shorter hours unless the community is improved simultaneously so that workers [and their families] get fuller enjoyment out of higher wages and leisure."[31]

The experience of Vera Vinyard, a community steward in St. Louis's twenty-second ward, illustrates the power of this understanding and the opportunity the program offered for women in Local 688 to assume a more public role. Vinyard hosted the first home meeting of community stewards, appeared on television discussing the union's opposition to charter change, and became secretary of the community assembly that Local 688 later formed to coordinate the community stewards' activities. Her husband and two daughters also participated actively in community stewards iniatives. Their involvement reflected Vinyard's belief that her entire family had a stake in the union's efforts to make St. Louis a more "livable" city. By addressing issues of immediate interest to its members and showing how union power could be used to prompt change in the community, Local 688 helped a diverse segment of its members conceive of themselves as citizens who could speak with confidence and authority on matters affecting their lives outside the workplace.[32]

As their activities evolved, the community stewards began to articulate the belief that citizens had not only legal but also social rights that government was obligated to honor. This insistence that government fulfill its obligation to ensure citizens a basic level of security and protection manifested itself most visibly around housing issues.

"A Stake in Good Neighborhoods": Fighting for Decent Housing

One of St. Louis's largest challenges following World War II was the deterioration of its housing stock, which created conditions that even the city's planning commission conceded were unacceptable. In a city in which housing had been rigidly segregated and from which the 1948 U.S. Supreme Court case striking down restrictive covenants had emanated, St. Louis's African American population was especially affected by the lack of decent, affordable housing. From the outset of the community stewards program, black members of Local 688 voiced concerns about the inadequate housing and recreational facilities in their neighborhoods while also noting that poor conditions in their neighborhood schools denied their children a quality education. And as new public housing was erected in St. Louis during the 1950s, complaints emerged about selection policies that favored white applicants while relegating African Americans to waiting lists.[33]

Exemplifying Local 688's long-standing commitment to racial equality, the community stewards aggressively engaged the problems posed by Local 688's African American members. In 1955 they mobilized three hundred members to attend a ward meeting after a household fire killed four African American children, pressing for mandatory rather than discretionary enforcement of the city's housing code. The union responded to concerns expressed by 142 of its members residing in public housing by forming a council to address issues such as crime, lack of recreational opportunities, and recurring rent increases. When police refused to patrol the Pruitt-Igoe housing project on the grounds it was federal property, Local 688 obtained a ruling from the city requiring police to provide residents with protection. The union also convinced the city's superintendent of schools to provide hot lunches for those children residing in public housing whose nutritional needs were not being fully met at home.[34]

The union recognized urban deterioration and flight to the suburbs as urgent problems that demanded a timely and aggressive social response. As Zagri noted in a 1957 article titled "Labor's Stake in Good Neighborhoods," many of Local 688's members lived in "twilight" neighborhoods suspended between conservation and decay. He predicted accelerated suburban migration without an infusion of both public and private resources.[35]

The union's housing activists anticipated the problems that a decade later made Pruitt-Igoe and other public housing projects in St. Louis a vivid example of failed government policy. Local 688's housing committee proposed eliminating high-rise complexes and providing greater access to shopping, recreation, and social services, along with more strictly enforcing city housing ordinances and making low interest loans available to residents for home improvements. The committee also recommended building new public housing for city residents facing displacement by slum-clearance initiatives the city was planning to undertake. This agenda garnered support from other community groups, including the St. Louis Catholic Archdiocese and the Metropolitan Church Federation, an organization of Protestant churches. In November 1956 these groups joined the Public Housing Tenants Council to meet with staff from the St. Louis Housing Authority. By bringing area clergy into the discussion, the community stewards gained moral sanction for their arguments about housing and warned city officials that inaction on their part would provoke wider community scrutiny. The housing issue also helped introduce the community stewards' emerging conception of the "community bargaining table," whereby citizens under its leadership began to negotiate the terms of their social contract with St. Louis's public officials and other members of the city's civic elite.[36]

Along with ward leaders who warily eyed the community stewards' expanding activities, St. Louis mayor Raymond Tucker experienced a series of uncomfortable encounters with Local 688's band of worker-citizens. Formerly an engineering professor at Washington University and a city commissioner, Tucker was a consummate technocrat who relied on the advice of professional staff and resented the community stewards' intrusion into city decision making. In November 1955 he informed Zagri that "the method you have established constitutes a duplication of effort for the average citizen, yourselves, and city officials." The clash between Tucker's technocratic sensibilities and the union's determination to gain acceptance for the community bargaining table culminated in one of the community stewards' most visible and dramatic public campaigns: a protracted effort to induce the city to enforce its rat-control ordinance that applied to residential housing.[37]

Experts versus Citizens: Campaigning for a Rat-Control Ordinance

The context for this contentious dispute was the decaying housing stock in St. Louis's inner core, which civic and political leaders were planning to demolish in order to launch massive downtown redevelopment. With the prevalence of dilapidated housing and outdoor privies, rat infestation was a significant public health hazard. This issue evoked widespread community anger in February 1955 when two-month-old Reginald Harrington was hospitalized suffering from life-threatening injuries caused by rat bites. Community steward Floyd Glisper of the sixth ward brought the issue to Local 688's attention, and the union quickly formed a committee to investigate. Putting their shop-floor representational skills to use, a mostly African American group of community stewards and union members toured affected areas, photographed the conditions they observed, and interviewed residents and local officials. The committee found that in almost one-third of St. Louis's wards, the city had failed to enforce its rat-control ordinance, and it estimated that 150 residents had suffered rat bites during the past year.[38]

The city's deputy health commissioner privately confirmed the accuracy of the community stewards' claims and acknowledged that rats were causing extensive property damage in addition to injuring residents. Nonetheless, facing pressure from realtors and landlords not to enforce the ordinance and reluctant to invest resources in areas slated for demolition, city officials had taken minimal steps to control rat infestation. Also, in keeping with the mayor's technocratic sensibilities and his desire to retain decision-making control, the city contended that the mandatory inspection provisions of the rat-control ordinance inspired by public agitation usurped "discretion exercised by professionally trained public health personnel." Although the community stewards orchestrated a series of community meetings, testified at hearings before the Board of Aldermen, and gained sympathetic media coverage, the Tucker administration remained unmoved. With the union charging that there was a "gentlemen's agreement" not to enforce the rat-control ordinance, community stewards Rothchild Hall and Leoulie Adams filed a suit in March 1955 directing the city to meet its legal obligations. Several months later, a local judge concurred and issued an order directing the city to enforce the rat-control ordinance.[39]

An exchange of letters between Gibbons and Tucker after the judge's decision highlighted sharply contrasting views of the social contract between city government and the citizens of St. Louis. Gibbons proclaimed that the judge's decision represented a "victory for social responsibility, a frank recognition of the city's responsibility for a large segment of its population during a long transitional period from slums to land clearance and low-cost housing." Accusing Tucker of "social irresponsibility" in appealing the judge's decision, Gibbons noted that the Teamsters had supported a recent bond issue to fund redevelopment but now saw the city reneging on the social improvements it had promised would accompany urban renewal. "Your protestations for progress during the Bond Issue Campaign which we supported are mere empty phrases when the chips are down and the welfare of the people is at stake," Gibbons charged. "Your words are on the side of progress. Your acts are on the side of decay." In response, Tucker rejected the legitimacy of the community stewards–inspired protests and retorted that he would continue to be guided by the advice of his professional staff, declaring, "I attach great importance to the recommendations of disinterested experts in this or any other field." Convinced that the Teamsters were using the rat-control issue for political purposes, Tucker decided to defy the judge's ruling and took no action to enforce the ordinance.[40]

Early in 1957, after more than a year of foot dragging, the city launched a determined counteroffensive, proposing revisions to the ordinance aimed at weakening enforcement procedures. City health commissioner J. Earl Smith accused the Teamsters of exaggerating the issue's true public health significance, insisting that "rats are not now or ever have been a public health problem." Local 688 and the community stewards mobilized broad opposition to the city's proposal, with Gibbons informing Tucker that placing "discretionary powers in the hands of an unsympathetic administrator could have the same effect as no ordinance at all." This was also a case in which the rest of St. Louis's union movement, along with key community organizations such as the NAACP and the Metropolitan Church Federation, vocally supported Local 688's stance. Spotlighting the class implications and implicitly identifying the racial overtones embodied in the dispute, United Auto Workers regional director Russell Letner asserted that "the health of any person living in a slum area is as important as the health of any person fortunate enough to live in the most exclusive area." Letner also rebuked city health commissioner Smith for suggesting that unions had no business injecting themselves into the issue, which Letner described as one in which "community welfare" was at stake.[41]

In March 1957 the city's public effort to weaken the rat-control ordinance was defeated, with the Board of Aldermen unanimously approving a new arrangement ensuring that regular inspections would continue. While the health commissioner complained that "if they [Local 688] are going to run the city, we might as well stop having elections and let Dave Beck or one of his appointees take over," Local 688 leaders proclaimed that the union had achieved a "clear cut victory on the rat control fight with the cooperation of the entire labor movement." Beyond rallying union support, the rat-control controversy brought Local 688 and the community stewards enhanced prestige in St. Louis's African American community, as evidenced by extensive coverage in the black press that praised the Teamsters for pressing the city to protect some of its most vulnerable citizens. St. Louis's other major newspapers also followed events closely and hailed the community stewards' efforts. In a report to an assembly of community stewards, Local 688 leaders explained the broader implications of the union's work on rat control and public health: "Although city officials termed rat control in the slums 'impracticable,' our union believed that human rights and the basic protection of government belonged to ALL people, regardless of their economic position in the community." The rat-control campaign accomplished two vital objectives for the community stewards program: it educated participants about urban power relations and the development of appropriate tactics, and it mobilized popular opinion around an issue of public health that enabled Local 688 to emerge as an identifiable defender of the community's safety and well-being.[42]

Another major initiative championed by the community stewards illustrated their expansive view of what subjects were appropriate for the community bargaining table. Anticipating that a changing economy would increase the need for future generations of St. Louis residents to attain higher levels of education and reflecting the social aspirations of a more confident and ambitious working class, the community stewards explored the possibility of establishing a free, four-year city college. After a December 1954 survey of Local 688 members found widespread interest in the idea, community stewards moved to mobilize public support. Although the free city college attracted support from other unions and community groups, the initiative faltered when the city claimed it lacked authority to issue bonds to fund the project. Nonetheless, the campaign to establish the free city college advanced the community stewards' conception of the union member as a "total person" with important needs outside the workplace and affirmed the union's commitment to create a local version of the welfare state that encompassed a broad set of government responsibilities.[43]

Taking on Civic Progress: The Charter-Change Fight of 1957

The community stewards' most visible engagement that brought them into direct conflict with St. Louis's power elite arose in a bitter 1957 fight over proposed changes in the city charter. An informal redevelopment coalition led this effort, seeking to stem job and population losses that threatened the city's viability. Along with Mayor Tucker, the city's major newspapers, churches, community groups, longtime African American leaders, and most notably a recently formed organization of business leaders called Civic Progress coalesced to advance sweeping plans aimed at revitalizing the city's decaying urban core. Created in 1953 by the previous mayor to spur economic development and civic improvement, Civic Progress included the leaders of almost all of St. Louis's most influential businesses. Reflecting his commitment to transcend interest group politics, Mayor Tucker portrayed Civic Progress as a "civic conscience" and "benign father" that would function as an unselfish promoter of the public good, in contrast to interest groups which existed for "the sole purpose of representing one particular segment of our community."[44]

After gaining approval of a $110 million civic improvement bond issue in 1955 (Local 688 and other St. Louis unions had supported this undertaking), Mayor Tucker and Civic Progress leaders sought private capital to fund clearance of slums that were impeding their redevelopment plans. The determination to pursue this agenda had guided the city's stance during the rat-control dispute and made Tucker and his business allies particularly sensitive to public scrutiny of their activities. In their view, the power of local ward leaders and aldermen to stymie neighborhood development represented the most serious obstacle to urban renewal. Ernest Calloway and other critics also alleged that outside banking interests demanded structural political reform before they would commit to investing in St. Louis. To dilute the power of aldermen and ward leaders, Tucker, Civic Progress officials, and their supporters proposed to reduce the size of the Board of Aldermen by half while increasing the number of aldermen elected on an at-large basis rather than a ward basis. The mayor's office would also gain enhanced executive authority under the new charter. For middle-class supporters such as the St. Louis League of Women Voters who were eager to transcend the pettiness and parochialism of ward politics, charter reform represented "a last ditch fight for St. Louis" and was "absolutely necessary for the future of the city." The clear intention of these changes was, as Tucker explained, to break the power of aldermen "under the tight control of selfish political interests and the officers of the Teamsters

Union who seek control of city government without running for election." Clearly smarting from his earlier confrontations with Local 688 and the community stewards, Tucker portrayed the Teamsters as a special interest out for their own aggrandizement at the expense of civic betterment and the public good.[45]

With the community stewards playing an important role, Local 688 mobilized broad opposition to the changes proposed by the city's business, civic, and media elites. By reducing aldermanic representation and creating more at-large seats, opponents argued, charter change would result in greater business domination of city politics by making candidates more reliant on corporate resources to run successfully citywide. Along with the St. Louis NAACP, which was headed by Calloway, Local 688 recognized the racial implications of the new charter, which, in Calloway's words, sought "to contain the growing political influence of the Negro community by carving out a new political ghetto for the increasing Negro population." Opponents also regarded the charter's language on racial discrimination as unresponsive to rising African American demands for equal access to municipal employment. The Teamsters and the NAACP gained support from other unions, some city aldermen who resisted this frontal assault on their power, and small business owners who worried corporate interests would benefit at their expense. Anticipating higher taxes and fearing that the charter's support for slum clearance would prompt more African American settlement in their neighborhoods, working-class whites also embraced the anti-charter campaign. Although this coalition brought together strange bedfellows and was not ideologically cohesive, some of its members—the Teamsters, other unions, the NAACP—shared the view that the new charter threatened to rewrite the social contract in St. Louis on terms that would reduce their growing influence and grant the city's civic elite a free hand to make critical economic and social decisions at the community's expense.[46]

Advised by the respected Fleishman-Hillard public relations firm, Civic Progress and the mayor touted the civic and social benefits to be gained from charter reform. The local press took a harsher tone, directly attacking Local 688 and the NAACP in an effort to discredit the opposition. Claiming that the Teamsters and the NAACP feared creation of a new political system they would no longer be able to control, the *St. Louis Globe-Democrat* charged in a June 1957 article that "the NAACP was asked, and to their shame, acceded, to be a stalking horse for the Teamsters Union in their mad grab for power in St. Louis." The paper also drew on powerful racial and anti-communist imagery. Spotlighting Calloway's Teamsters connection and implying he was being manipulated by white handlers, the *Globe-Democrat* observed: "The president of the group [NAACP] is a paid employee of the Teamsters Union. He was flanked by two other officers of the Teamsters Union, neither of them colored." Moreover, while "the best thinking colored people support the charter," the NAACP stood "side by side with the Communist Party" in its opposition. Critics also cited corruption charges swirling around the Teamsters, the union's numerous brushes with the law during strikes in St. Louis, and Gibbons's indictment on misuse of union funds in 1954, even though the latter charge had subsequently been dismissed. Depicting the Teamsters as a corrupt special interest, a manipulator of the African American community, and a power-hungry institution bent on dominating St. Louis politics, charter proponents sought to undermine the good will and respect Local 688 had earned over the past five years through the activities of its community stewards.[47]

Local 688 vowed to match the pro-charter forces "dollar for dollar" and worked in conjunction with the NAACP, other unions, neighborhood associations, and small businesses in opposing charter change. Taking direct aim at Civic Progress and its agenda, Teamster leaders alleged that the charter would establish "Blue Ribbon Control," with "big business benefit[ing] at the expense of everyone else." In a hyperbolic but politically effective charge, Zagri asserted that the new executive powers granted under the charter would make the mayor a "king." One piece of campaign literature invoked earlier efforts by the community stewards and implored voters to remain vigilant in protecting community interests: "Do you want to turn the political future of your community over to downtown bankers, high-rent absentee landlords, and the big operators of rat-infested slums?" The NAACP supplemented these class appeals with direct invocations of racial solidarity and the spirit of the emerging civil rights movement. While "They Walked for Freedom in Montgomery," one leaflet asserted, "We Will Vote for Freedom in St. Louis." Along with the NAACP, the community stewards and Local 688 leaders helped mobilize other St. Louis unions and worked tirelessly at the ward and precinct levels to disseminate the anti-charter message.[48]

On August 6, 1957, the charter was defeated by a three-to-two margin that reflected sharp class and racial cleavages. Voters in only five of the city's twenty-eight wards, all encompassing middle- or upper-income areas of St. Louis, supported the measure. The city's African Americans followed the NAACP's lead in rejecting charter change by a margin of five to one. To be sure, the white working-class vote that opposed charter change was partially animated by anti-tax sentiment, racial fear, and continuing loyalty to the ward system, in contrast to Local 688's concerns that increased mayoral power and structural political changes threatened the union's attempt to establish the community bargaining table. Yet several students of efforts to reform St. Louis politics later noted that the city's civic elite and its media had been unable to mobilize public support for their agenda, largely because their arguments had avoided tough questions about the racial and class implications of their proposal regarding access to essential social and economic resources. Almost all observers recognized the vital role the community stewards had played in mobilizing the anti-charter forces and upsetting the plans of St. Louis's power elite. As Alfred Fleishman, the charter-change movement's chief public relations adviser observed at a December 1957 meeting of Civic Progress, Local 688 had developed a ward-level organization that, in addition to promoting civic action and improvement, "provide[d] the union with a useful political vehicle."[49]

In the aftermath of the charter vote, many St. Louis journalists and political observers concluded that the community stewards had embarrassed ward officials with their superior grassroots mobilization capabilities. Herbert Trask of the *Post-Dispatch* proclaimed that Local 688's success in mobilizing a broad coalition to defeat the charter represented a striking development in St. Louis politics, observing that "this combination of forces creates a new power in St. Louis which must be reckoned with." Having witnessed the close Teamsters-NAACP cooperation during the charter fight, Washington University political scientist Robert Salisbury noted that the "militant and volatile character of the Teamsters and the increasing numbers and self-consciousness of blacks make possible" a political realignment in St. Louis. Describing Local 688's plan to establish a "Metropolitan Community Stewards Assembly" that would develop a "giant get-out-the-vote setup," *Globe-Democrat* reporter John Hahn predicted that the union "could become the strongest pressure group in the city because they may well move into the position to deliver more votes on any given election day than anyone else."[50]

Following the charter-change victory, the community stewards appeared poised to capitalize on their enhanced visibility and power. Pronouncing that the union now had "new status at the community bargaining table," Zagri boasted that the "community steward supplanted the role of the precinct captain" during the charter fight, creating a new locus of power that the business community needed to recognize. Along with Gibbons, Zagri called on business to enter into a new social compact with labor in St. Louis. "How much more effective would the Business Community be in attracting new businesses into our dying downtown area," Zagri asked, "if the old bugaboo of high labor costs could be dispelled through a joint labor-management approach to the recruitment of industry?"[51]

In the months immediately following the charter fight, Local 688 flexed its enhanced political muscle on a variety of fronts. Gibbons demanded public hearings on city redevelopment plans to ensure that taxpayer dollars used to subsidize slum clearance would deliver genuine community benefits. The union denounced as a "new tax grab" a Civic Progress–sponsored effort to increase the city's earnings tax, protesting that the proposal provided insufficient protection for small property owners and failed to make ability to pay a core principle of St. Louis's tax policy. Civic Progress leaders closely monitored Local 688's expanding influence, lamenting that St. Louis aldermen were "only hearing from the Teamsters and not the business community" and bemoaning the "disintegration of the political parties" that was leaving a vacuum for the Teamsters and the NAACP to fill. Community stewards also began to extend their efforts into the suburbs of St. Louis County, where, one steward reported, "people are hopping mad at the real estate developers who give people out here a real trimming." They began a promising effort to mobilize city residents to seek abatement of pollution from soap and chemical plants that emitted noxious fumes and were affecting public health. And, by the summer of 1958, union leaders announced plans to create a "community assembly" that would enable community stewards to adopt a citywide approach in dealing with quality-of-life issues.[52]

Basking in the glow of media speculation regarding their potential political influence and reveling in Civic Progress's chastened attitude, Local 688 leaders ignored the underlying volatility of the coalition they had assembled to defeat charter change, especially the attitudes of white working-class homeowners animated by antipathy toward taxes and racial fear. Their actions following the anti-charter campaign suggested that Gibbons, Calloway, and Zagri hoped to deflect these sentiments by encouraging the community stewards to focus on matters of concern to white homeowners, thereby enabling them to protect their investment and reinforce their fragile sense of security. At the same time, Zagri argued in the *St. Louis Argus*, a local African American newspaper, that "our civic conscience should not be hemmed in by the prejudices of race or class" and called for proposed bond issue funds to be spent equally in white and black neighborhoods. Combining civil rights advocacy with attentiveness to quality-of-life issues relevant to the white working class, Local 688 leaders aimed to create a foundation for interracial cooperation by devoting equivalent attention to the basic needs and aspirations of both black and white workers.[53]

Yet as a direct result of Local 688's deepening involvement in national Teamster politics, the possibility that the community stewards might mobilize an even larger coalition, expand their activities into the suburbs, and gain further legitimacy for the community bargaining table failed to materialize. In 1958, Gibbons became a vice-president of the international union and began serving as a top aide to the Teamsters' president, Jimmy Hoffa. Although

Gibbons retained his leadership positions with Local 688 and Teamsters Joint Council 13, the regional unit he headed after a controversial election in 1958, his attention was increasingly diverted from St. Louis, especially as his own activities came under the scrutiny of the McClellan Committee. A year later, Gibbons persuaded Zagri to leave his position as community stewards director and come to Washington to coordinate the Teamsters' opposition to congressional passage of the proposed Landrum-Griffin Act. Subsequently, Hoffa tapped Zagri to develop the union's national legislative and political action program, making his departure from St. Louis permanent. In addition to losing key leaders, both Local 688 and the community stewards became preoccupied with defending the union against a drumbeat of corruption charges that emerged from the McClellan Committee's investigations. As a result, Local 688 amassed considerable legal fees and could no longer afford to subsidize the community stewards' efforts. In January 1959, Gibbons acknowledged the program's shift away from local organizing and the diminished resources it was receiving. "Our enemies have made this inevitable," Gibbons concluded, lamenting the community stewards' loss of momentum as a social force.[54]

Calloway, the other principal leader attached to the community stewards program, remained in St. Louis. Perhaps sensing that the program was losing its earlier élan with the diverted attention of Local 688's leadership, he began to focus his considerable talents in the civil rights arena, working with the NAACP on issues of employment discrimination and managing the campaigns of African American candidates seeking elective office. Celebrating the tenth anniversary of the community stewards program in 1961, leaders of Local 688 insisted that the effort remained relevant but of necessity had been compelled to shift its focus from local to national concerns. This shift toward playing political defense, however, meant that community stewards were no longer articulating the notions of working-class citizenship and the community bargaining table that had been so instrumental in inspiring and mobilizing Local 688's members.

Conclusion

In two important essays written in 1980, the historian David Brody reflected on what he called "the uses of power" by the post–World War II union movement in the arenas of collective bargaining and political action. Seen in this context, the community stewards' effort to legitimate the concept of a community bargaining table marked a bold attempt to establish yet another arena in which labor could exercise its newfound power. Indeed, many unions recognized the possibilities and the importance of creating a visible community presence in the 1950s. Under the aegis of the CIO, both individual unions and local industrial union councils formed community services committees, which in some cases, most notably the United Auto Workers in Chicago, pressed for neighborhood improvements as part of their social agenda. Many AFL unions also joined their CIO counterparts in developing community services programs. However, as Sidney Zagri pointed out in a May 1957 article, business interests generally paid the salaries of the AFL's community services representatives, thereby limiting their independence and inhibiting their ability to engage in aggressive social action. In both the sophistication of its analysis and the scope of its ambitions, the St. Louis Teamsters' community stewards program had few peers during its short but eventful existence.[55]

The union movement's ability to affect the broader trends influencing the deterioration of the post–World War II American city—deindustrialization, suburban flight, growing racial disparities—was modest, and during the course of the 1950s its public voice on such matters grew less audible. Still, the community stewards' efforts to create the identity of worker-citizen for Local 688 members and to establish the concept of the community bargaining table had a discernible impact on St. Louis's quality of life and demonstrated how unions might apply their workplace power and expertise in influencing community affairs. In addition to helping create the metropolitan sewer district, the community stewards' efforts led to the establishment of other important institutions that addressed the basic needs of St. Louis residents and affirmed their vision of the union member as a total person. Although initially rebuffed, their demands for a free city college were partially realized in the 1960s with the development of a community college system that gave the working class in St. Louis greater access to higher education. In the early 1960s, fifteen private companies merged to form a new public agency that created a bi-state transit system. Recalling this event two decades later, Harold Gibbons bragged to an interviewer that "we socialized the g—ddamn transit system." And the union's attention to housing issues enabled it to play an important role a decade later when public housing tenants struck in St. Louis. Gibbons and other Local 688 leaders intervened to help negotiate a settlement of the dispute, along with developing new approaches to public housing management that won national attention. In an insular political culture dominated by ward politics and the business-oriented agenda of Civic Progress, these efforts represented substantial achievements for which the community stewards could justifiably claim credit.[56]

The community stewards program also had pronounced limitations. Although building a broader community coalition had not been an explicit component of its strategy, Local 688 leaders recognized the need to work with other organizations—unions, churches, neighborhood associations, civil rights groups—if they were to persuade the city's elite to negotiate about critical social and economic decisions. The union did demonstrate its ability to establish relationships with community organizations in several of its campaigns, including housing, rat control, and juvenile delinquency, although some of its community allies opposed Local 688's stand on the charter fight. Its relations with the rest of the union movement, however, were often contentious. Although the community stewards collaborated with other unions on the rat-control fight and during the charter-change campaign, persistent suspicions about Gibbons's ambitions meant that, as one journalist observed, "in union affairs Gibbons and Local 688 often play a lone hand." The demise of the program left unanswered the question of what kind of broader coalition might have emerged in St. Louis had the effort continued. The community stewards did, however, begin to develop a web of relationships rooted in shared values and common purpose that enabled them, however briefly, to transcend the episodic, utilitarian approach that often characterized labor's attempts to forge closer relations with community allies.[57]

For Gibbons and Calloway, who had been raised in coal-mining communities where working-class aspirations were sharply circumscribed, helping workers realize their potential as "first-class citizens" was one of the most significant achievements of the community stewards program. As Gibbons noted in a September 1955 letter responding to a *St. Louis Post-Dispatch* reader's complaint that the community stewards were functioning as an unnecessary "intermediary" between citizens and government: "The working man, the average citizen, is apt to be bewildered by the many pressure groups, apt to feel helpless and ultimately to become complacent or cynical about his own role in a democracy." Far from being an "intermediary," Gibbons asserted, "the union's role is solely to encourage our working members to use their rights as citizens in a democracy."[58]

This abiding faith in working-class potential remained a central feature of the St. Louis Teamsters' continuing efforts to transcend the constraints of interest-group politics, establish the community bargaining table, and enable workers to function as first-class citizens. It resurfaced powerfully less than a decade later when Gibbons and Calloway launched a new effort in St. Louis to revitalize working-class citizenship, wage "a trade-union oriented war on the slums," align the union with the insurgent spirit of the 1960s, and reclaim Local 688's status as a leading community standard bearer for social justice.[59]

Notes

The author wishes to express his appreciation to Joe McCartin, Bruce Smith, and Robert Zieger for their thoughtful comments on this essay.

1. Herbert A. Trask, "New Charter Defeated by Margin of 35,000 in Big Setback for Tucker," August 7, 1957, and "Charter Foes Criticize Tucker for 'Misrepresentation' Charge," November 20, 1957, both in *St. Louis Post-Dispatch*; Civic Progress Minutes, December 26, 1957, Series 5, Box 1, Raymond R. Tucker Papers, Manuscripts Division, Olin Library, Washington University, St. Louis; "St. Louis Gets Experts' Blueprints for Areawide City-County Rule," *Business Week*, August 24, 1957, 68.

2. Michael K. Brown, *Race, Money, and the American Welfare State* (Ithaca: Cornell University Press,1999), 26, 131–65, 199; Nelson Lichtenstein, *State of the Union: A Century of American Labor* (Princeton: Princeton University Press, 2002), 126–28; Alan Draper, *A Rope of Sand: The AFL-CIO Committee on Political Education, 1955–1967* (New York: Praeger, 1989); Colin Gordon, "The Lost City of Solidarity: Metropolitan Unionism in Historical Perspective," *Politics and Society* 27, no. 4 (1999): 575–76; Joshua B. Freeman, *Working-Class New York: Life and Labor since World War II* (New York: New Press, 2000).

3. "Community Meetings Proved Popularity," *Midwest Labor World*, December 13, 1951; "New Shop Stewards Training Course: The Political and Community Action Program of Teamsters Local 688," May 4, 1955, Box 8, File 240, Ernest Calloway Papers, no. 540, Thomas Jefferson Library, Western Historical Manuscripts Collection, University of Missouri at St. Louis.

4. Robert H. Zieger, "Is Southern Labor History Exceptional?" and Alex Lichtenstein, "'Scientific Unionism' and the 'Negro Question': Communists and the Transport Workers Union in Miami, 1944–1949," in *Southern Labor in Transition, 1940–1995*, ed. Robert H. Zieger (Knoxville: University of Tennessee Press, 1997), 3–6, 58–77; Kenneth D. Durr, *Behind the Backlash: White Working-Class Politics in Baltimore, 1940–1980* (Chapel Hill: University of North Carolina Press, 2003); Robert Rodgers Korstad, *Civil Rights Unionism: Tobacco Workers and the Struggle for Democracy in the Mid-Twentieth-Century South* (Chapel Hill: University of North Carolina Press, 2003); and Michael K. Honey, *Southern Labor and Black Civil Rights: Organizing Memphis Workers* (Urbana: University of Illinois Press, 1993).

5. Annetta M. Dieckmann, "Report of the St. Louis Labor Education Project, 1948–1950," Box 5, File 53, Annetta M. Dieckmann Papers, Special Collections, University Library, University of Illinois at Chicago; Clarence Lang, *Grassroots at the Gateway: Class Politics and Black Freedom Struggle in St. Louis, 1936–75* (Ann Arbor: University of Michigan Press, 2009), 7–12.

6. "Political and Community Action Program." On the work-community divide, see Ira Katznelson, *City Trenches: Urban Politics and the Patterning of Class in the United States* (New York: Pantheon, 1981), 6–19; Becky Nicolaides, *My Blue Heaven: Life and Politics in the Working-Class Suburbs of Los Angeles, 1920–1965* (Chicago: University of Chicago Press, 2002), 254; John T. McGreevy, *Parish Boundaries: The Catholic Encounter with Race in the Twentieth-Century Urban North* (Chicago: University of Chicago Press, 1996), 4; and Thomas J. Sugrue, *The Origins of the Urban Crisis: Race and Inequality in Post-War Detroit* (Princeton: Princeton University Press, 1996), 84. On the work-community divide being less applicable to African Americans due to the pervasiveness of racism in both work and community settings, see Earl Lewis, *In Their Own Interests: Race, Class, and Power in Twentieth-Century Virginia* (Berkeley: University of California Press, 1991), 5–6, 128–31.

7. Jake McCarthy, "First Draft: Portrait of Gibbons," Box 1, File 16, Teamsters Joint

Council 13 Papers, Louisa H. Bowen University Archives and Special Collections, Lovejoy Library, Southern Illinois University at Edwardsville [hereafter Teamsters Joint Council 13 Papers]; Jerry Curry, "Gibbons, Hoffa's Stand-in a Solid Teamster," *Newark Star-Ledger*, August 9, 1964, Box 1, File 5, and John Keiser, "Harold Gibbons: Idealist as Realist," Box 1, File 7, John Keiser Papers, University of Illinois at Springfield; Testimony of Harold J. Gibbons, "Hearings before the Select Committee on Improper Activities in the Labor or Management Field," Eighty-fifth Congress, September 2, 1958, 14558–62; Steven Brill, *The Teamsters* (New York: Simon and Schuster, 1978), 354–55.

8. Testimony of Harold Gibbons, "Hearings before the Select Committee," 14563; McCarthy, "Portrait of Gibbons"; Brill, *The Teamsters*, 355.

9. "Ernest Calloway: Biographical Sketch," 1976, Box 50, File 31, Harold J. Gibbons Collection, Louisa H. Bowen University Archives and Special Collections, Lovejoy Library, Southern Illinois University at Edwardsville; and Ernest Calloway, "Unionizing the Nation's Red Caps in the 30's," Box 51, File 600, Calloway Papers, no. 540.

10. "Community Man," March 1, 1955, "Judge's Liver," January 1, 1957, "Hunger of Jobless Union Members Sparked Drive," March 15, 1958, and "Zagri Appointed as Director of Public Relations," June 1, 1958, all in *Midwest Labor World*.

11. Harold Gibbons talk, "The CIO in the South, July 27, 1945," Box 5, File 3, Gibbons Collection; "Toward Suburbs," *Midwest Labor World*, October 15, 1955; Jack Barbash, "Labor Education in Local 688," Box 4, File 40, Calloway Papers, no. 540; Edward C. Banfield, *Big City Politics* (New York: Random House, 1965), 128; Ernest Calloway, ed., "10 Years of Trade Union Democracy in Action, commemorating the 10th anniversary of the Warehouse and Distribution Workers Union, 1941–1951," Box 42, File 41, Gibbons Collection; and "Teamsters Local 688: Pioneers in Union Race Relations," *New Citizen*, September 1–14, 1961, Box 5, File 2, Teamsters Joint Council 13 Papers. The union was even the subject of a 1952 book by well-known sociologist Arnold Rose titled *Union Solidarity: The Internal Cohesion of a Labor Union* (Minneapolis: University of Minnesota Press, 1952).

12. Harry Vernon Ball Jr., "Case History of a Labor Union: The United Distribution Workers" (master's thesis, Washington University, June 1950), 455; "Union History," Box 40, File 11, Gibbons Collection; Sallie Heller to Ernest Calloway, June 7, 1954, Box 49, File 579, Calloway Papers, no. 540; Calloway, "Ten Years of Democracy in Action," 30–31.

13. Jake McCarthy, "Harold Gibbons, Idealist: A Reminiscence," *St. Louis Post-Dispatch*, November 21, 1982; Sally Bixby Defty, "Gibbons Kept Cool under Senate Fire," *St. Louis Post-Dispatch*, May 12, 1969.

14. Ernest Calloway, "The Goals of U.S. Unionism Today," Lecture Series Sponsored by the Workers' Educational Trade Union Committee of London, March 29, 1949, in "Ernest Calloway Writings," compiled by Kenn Thomas, Western Historical Manuscripts Collection, University of Missouri at St. Louis [hereafter WHMC]; "Unions in the Community," Local 688 Notes, Staff Orientation, 1953, Box 40, File 24, Gibbons Collection.

15. On St. Louis's political culture, see Lana Stein, *St. Louis Politics: The Triumph of Tradition* (St. Louis: Missouri Historical Press, 2002), xvii, xxi, 3–7; Colin Gordon, *Mapping Decline: St. Louis and the Fate of the American City* (Philadelphia: University of Pennsylvania Press, 2008), 40–41; Robert Salisbury, "St. Louis Politics: Relationships among Interests, Parties, and Governmental Structure," *Western Political Quarterly* 18 (1960): 329–32; Banfield, *Big City Politics*, 124; "The City-County Problem in St. Louis," Digest of Remarks

Made by Dr. Paul Steinbicker before the St. Louis Chapter, Public Relations Society of America, December 8, 1955, Series 1, Box 7, Tucker Papers; and especially E. Terrence Jones, *Fragmented by Design: Why St. Louis Has So Many Governments* (St. Louis: Palmerston & Reed, 2000), 4–14.

16. "Report of Senator Robert Pentland and a General Summary of Local 688's Political Education Program During 1951," Box 41, File 35, Gibbons Collection; Harold Gibbons, "Labor's Task in the Precinct," *New Republic*, January 5, 1953, 21; Ernest Calloway, "Requiem for a Free, Compassionate Spirit," *Missouri Teamster*, May 13, 1966. Calloway in particular knew the challenge that machine politics posed for labor's political independence, and while in Chicago he was involved in an insurgent attempt to unseat a machine-controlled black congressman. Calloway's wife, Deverne, became a Missouri state legislator in the 1960s and saw herself as an "independent force" in St. Louis politics who attempted to maintain her distance from ward politics. See Deverne Calloway interview with Irene Cortinovis, September 9, 1971, Oral History Program, WHMC.

17. Gibbons, "Labor's Task," 21–22; Gibbons quoted in Harry Conn, "A Union in St. Louis . . . ," *New Republic*, February 4, 1952, 9; "Transcript of Harold Gibbons Talk at Westminster," January 21, 1965, Box 1, File 5, Keiser Papers.

18. "Minutes, Community Meetings," November 1954, Box 40, File 23, Gibbons Collection; "Political and Community Action Program." The literature on social fragmentation and personal alienation in the immediate post–World War II period is extensive. For a good overview see Richard H. Pells, *The Liberal Mind in a Conservative Age: American Intellectuals in the 1940s and 1950s* (New York: Harper and Row, 1985), 182–97, 253–61.

19. "Gibbons Talk at Westminster"; McCarthy, "Portrait of Gibbons," 28; Report of the Committee on Continuing Education to the Teamster City-wide Educational Conference, Joint Council 13, January 31, 1954, Box 50, File 4, Gibbons Collection; Banfield, *Big City Politics*, 128.

20. "Community Action no. 8," September 30, 1954, and Teamsters Local 688, "The People Must Act: A Report to the Community Stewards Assembly," n.d., both in Box 41, File 36, Gibbons Collection; "Community Meetings: A New Approach to Political Action," Box 48, File 567, Calloway Papers, no. 540; "How 'Community Action' Succeeds in St. Louis," *International Teamster*, March 1956, 11. At the peak of the community stewards program, the union also offered several members internships in which they were released from their jobs and had the opportunity to learn firsthand about the program's operations and initiatives.

21. Sid Zagri to staff, n.d., Box 41, File 36, and "Committee Action Progress Report to Be Used in Community Meetings," Minutes, Community Meetings, November 1956, March 1957, Box 40, File 23, both in Gibbons Collection; Con Kelliher, "Meet Harold J. Gibbons," *St. Louis Globe-Democrat*, August 26, 1956.

22. "The Plaza Drive," June 15, 1956, and "Home Meeting Given Tryout," April 1, 1957, both in *Midwest Labor World*; Harry Wilensky, "Community Action Gives Teamsters Power in Fight against City Charter," *St. Louis Post-Dispatch*, June 23, 1957. Hill and her mother had been active in the initial drive to organize office workers in the trucking firm where they worked, and Hill later became a union steward prior to contacting Local 688 about her neighborhood concern.

23. Zagri quoted in Wilensky, "Community Action Gives Teamsters Power"; Sidney Lens, "Year 'Round Grass Roots Politics May Boost Labor," *Labor's Daily*, November 20, 1956.

24. "Community Meetings Are Popular—Bus Fares and Service Lead Complaints," November 14, 1951, and "Transportation Problem First Tackled By Local," December 12, 1951, both in *Midwest Labor World*.

25. "Community Action no. 8" and Discussion Guide for Staff Members, Staff Meetings, March 1952, Box 40, File 23, Gibbons Collection; "Up to the People," August 16, 1952, and "A St. Louis Union: Its Members and Its Community," March 8, 1954, both in *St. Louis Post-Dispatch*.

26. "County Chamber of Commerce Board Endorses Sewer Proposal," *St. Louis Post-Dispatch*, December 3, 1953; "How 'Community Action' Succeeds in St. Louis," 8–9; "Facts about the Metropolitan St. Louis Sewer District Plan," Series 1, Box 11, Tucker Papers; Brill, *The Teamsters*, 357; Gordon, *Mapping Decline*, 46–47; Henry J. Schandt, Paul G. Steinbicker, and George D. Wendel, *Metropolitan Reform in St. Louis: A Case Study* (New York: Holt, Rinehart, and Winston, 1961), 2–6; Steinbicker, "City-County Problem"; "Community Action," September 30, 1954, Box 41, File 36, Gibbons Collection; "A St. Louis Union: Its Members and Its Community"; James Neal Primm, *Lion of the Valley: St. Louis, Missouri*, 3rd ed. (St. Louis: Missouri Historical Society Press, 1998), 477.

27. James Gilbert, *A Cycle of Outrage: America's Reaction to the Juvenile Delinquent in the 1950s* (New York: Oxford University Press, 1986), 74–78.

28. Sid Zagri to staff; "Members Say Delinquency Big Problem," November 15, 1955, and "688 Spokesman Calls for Attack on Juvenile Crime Causes," July 15, 1956, both in *Midwest Labor World*.

29. Robert E. Weber Jr., letter to the editor, *St. Louis Globe-Democrat*, September 5, 1955; "October Stewards' Council Proceedings," November 1, 1955, "Goof Ball Letter Interests Parents," September 15, 1955, and "Back Youth Plans," September 15, 1956, all in *Midwest Labor World*.

30. Brill, *The Teamsters*, 357.

31. "Community Meetings Are Popular"; Conn, "A Union in St. Louis"; "The Taxi Drivers' Strike," *St. Louis Argus*, August 31, 1956. On women connecting workplace, family, and community, see Elizabeth Faue, *Community of Suffering and Struggle: Women, Men, and the Labor Movement in Minneapolis, 1915–1945* (Chapel Hill: University of North Carolina Press, 1991), 15–18, 108–25; and Colette A. Hyman, "Labor Organizing and Female Institution Building: The Chicago Women's Trade Union League," in *Women, Work, and Protest: A Century of US Women's Labor History*, ed. Ruth Milkman (Boston: Routledge and Kegan Paul, 1985), 22–38. For a contrary view, see Durr, *Behind the Backlash*, 77–78.

32. "Lifeline of the Union," December 1, 1954, "Baby-Sitters at Community Open House," May 1, 1955, "Home Meeting Given Tryout," April 1, 1957, and "Assembly Elects First Officers," October 1, 1958, all in *Midwest Labor World*; Kenneth E. Gray, *A Report on Politics in Saint Louis* (Cambridge: Center for Urban Studies, Harvard University, 1961), part 5, 10. Photographs of community stewards that appeared in the press and in Local 688 publications showed both black and white participants at meetings and program activities, with African Americans being most prominently featured during the rat-control campaign. During the program's heyday, each issue of Local 688's official publication, *Midwest Labor World*, featured several pages highlighting the community stewards' activities, often quoting their views on issues under consideration.

33. Primm, *Lion of the Valley*, 459; Gordon, *Mapping Decline*, 71–83; "Reports from Local 688's Neighborhood Meetings," *Midwest Labor World*, November 1, 1954.

34. "Additional Police Assigned to Igoe, Pruitt Housing Sites," August 10, 1955, "Obstacles Cited to Enforcing Housing Rules," November 2, 1955, and "Tenants Protest Higher Public Housing Rates," November 9, 1956, all in *St. Louis Globe-Democrat*.

35. Sidney Zagri, "Labor's Stake in Good Neighborhoods," *St. Louis Argus*, November 8, 1957.

36. Primm, *Lion of the Valley*, 460–63; "Additional Police Assigned to Igoe, Pruitt Housing Sites"; "Obstacles Cited to Enforcing Housing Rules"; "Tenants Protest Higher Public Housing Rates"; Sid Zagri to staff.

37. On Tucker see Primm, *Lion of the Valley*, 449; and Stein, *St. Louis Politics*, 89, 111–13. "Statement by Mayor Tucker," July 17, 1953, Box 5, Teamsters Joint Council 13 Papers; Robert E. Smith to Sidney Zagri, November 2, 1955 (a copy of this letter that described the community stewards' ward meetings as "unnecessary" and "duplicative" was sent to all members of Tucker's cabinet), Mayoral Files, Series 1, Box 15, Labor Organizations, Other Matters, Tucker Papers. During a protracted, bitter strike of Teamster concrete truck drivers in 1953, Tucker portrayed himself as a defender of the public interest, accusing both the employers and the Teamsters of acting "as if the society and community around them has no part in or interest in their struggle."

38. "The People Must Act"; "How 'Community Action' Succeeds in St. Louis," 7; "St. Louis Rat Probe Draws Fire," February 28, 1955, "Teamsters' Official Says City Still Does Nothing About Rats," June 15, 1955, and "Teamsters' Union Shows Vigorous Interest in Controlling City's Rats," n.d., 1955, all in *St. Louis Argus*; "Rat Control Report Is Scheduled Today," February 18, 1955, Box 6, File 3, Teamsters Joint Council 13 Papers.

39. C. M. Copley Jr. to J. Earl Smith, March 5, 1955, C. M. Copley Jr. to Honorable Raymond B. Tucker, August 11, 1955, Raymond Tucker to Jack Brune, April 5, 1956, Thomas J. Neenan and Charles J. Dolan to J. Edward Smith, May 22, 1956, and Raymond Tucker to Edward A. Pollack, August 30, 1956, all in Series 1, Box 27, Tucker Papers; "Action for Rat Control," March 15, 1955, and "Red Faces," May 1, 1955, both in *Midwest Labor World*.

40. Harold J. Gibbons to Raymond Tucker, August 10, 1955, and Mayor to Harold J. Gibbons, August 11, 1955, Series 1, Box 27, Tucker Papers.

41. J. Earl Smith to Mrs. Edward J. Brumgard (confidential), September 12, 1955; "The Health Division's Proposed New Rat Ordinance"; Statement, J. Earl Smith, January 23, 1957; "A Statement Made before the Public Welfare Committee of the Board of Aldermen on Board Bill #55" (Rat Control Ordinance), February 22, 1957; Harold J. Gibbons to Raymond Tucker, February 5, 1957; Mayor to Harold J. Gibbons, February 7, 1957; and Russell Letner to J. Earl Smith, February 15, 1957—all in Series 1, Box 27, Tucker Papers; "Rat Control Victory Won by Members Who Kept the Issue Alive," *Midwest Labor World*, March 15, 1957.

42. Teamsters Local 688 Agenda Guide," March 1957, Box 40, File 23, Gibbons Collection; "The People Must Act"; "Rat Control Victory Won by Members."

43. "Survey Made on Free City College Idea," December 15, 1954, and "Free College Plan Endorsed by AFL Trades," February 15, 1955, both in *Midwest Labor World*; "Bond Group to Consider 4-Year City College," March 29, 1955, and "Union Leaders Urge Free City College," April 9, 1955; both in *St. Louis Globe-Democrat*; "How 'Community Action' Succeeds in St. Louis," 11. As Joshua Freeman observes, union leaders in New York City supported open admissions policies for the city university system in the late 1960s. However, in

contrast to the St. Louis Teamsters, these initiatives followed rather than preceded the efforts of minority student activists to demand greater inclusion of blacks and Puerto Ricans in the student body. See Freeman, *Working-Class New York*, 228–33.

44. Joseph Heathcott and Maire Agnes Murphy, "Corridors of Flight, Zones of Renewal: Industry, Planning, and Policy in the Making of Metropolitan St. Louis, 1940–1980," *Journal of Urban History* 31, no. 2 (2005): 152–57; Clarence Lang, "Civil Rights versus 'Civic Progress': The St. Louis NAACP and the City Charter Fight, 1956–1957," *Journal of Urban History* 34, no. 4 (2008): 617–21; Gray, *Report on Politics in Saint Louis*, part 3, 11–12; Salisbury, "St. Louis Politics," 326. On Civic Progress, see Mayor to Powell B. McHaney, January 8, 1954, Harry B. Wilson to Raymond R. Tucker, May 23, 1958, and Harry B. Wilson to George J. Ringrose, November 27, 1959, all in Series 5, Box 1, Tucker Papers; Primm, *Lion of the Valley*, 465–66; and Stein, *St. Louis Politics*, 93.

45. Primm, *Lion of the Valley*, 467; Stein, *St. Louis Politics*, 98–99; Citizens Charter Committee Statement by Mayor Raymond B. Tucker, August 3, 1957, Series 1, Box 5, Tucker Papers; Lang, "Civil Rights versus 'Civic Progress,'" 619–21; Gray, *Report on Politics in Saint Louis*, part 3, 9–10; "League Reporter," May–June 1957, Box 70, File 889, League of Women Voters of St. Louis Papers, WHMC. Calloway went so far as to charge that the proposed charter change was "not so much a new constitution for the city as it was a 'treaty of surrender' for the Chase banking interests of New York who were demanding this as a condition in making extensive investments in the St. Louis area." See Ernest Calloway, "Unfinished Dialogue with a St. Louis Decision-Maker," *Missouri Teamster*, November 24, 1967, Box 6, File 171, Calloway Papers, no. 540; and "The Time of the St. Louis Black Renaissance, Part 2," *St. Louis American*, June 19, 1980.

46. "Why We Are in Opposition to the Proposed New City Charter," July 30, 1957, Box 1, File 4, Calloway Papers, no. 11; "NAACP Citizen Groups Formed in Nine Wards to Work against Charter," July 8, 1957, and "An Official Statement of the St. Louis NAACP in the Matter of the Composition and Structure of the Board of Aldermen as Proposed by the Board of Freeholders in the New City Charter," n.d., 1957, both in Group III, Box C77, St. Louis, Missouri, 1957, NAACP Papers, Library of Congress; "A Bad Charter," n.d., and "To Members of Civic Progress, Inc. from Fleishman-Hillard," September 25, 1957, both in Series 1, Box 4, Tucker Papers; Lang, "Civil Rights versus 'Civic Progress,'" 623–24.

47. Sidney Zagri, "'Slick' Public Relations Job Being Set Up on Charter," *North County Journal*, January 10, 1957; Frank Bick Jr., "Thoughts on the Charter," *Southside Journal*, July 24, 1957, Box 6, File 2, Teamsters Joint Council 13 Papers; *St. Louis Globe-Democrat*, June 24, 1957, 10A.

48. "Unionist Says New Charter Would Make Mayor a 'King,'" *St. Louis Post-Dispatch*, June 19, 1957. Leaflets opposing the charter change can be found in Group III, Box C77, NAACP Papers. See also "A Bad Charter."

49. Civic Progress Minutes, December 26, 1957, Series 5, Box 1, Tucker Papers; Schandt et al., *Metropolitan Reform in St. Louis*, 63–64; Gray, *Report on Politics in Saint Louis*, part 3, 9–17; Stein, *St. Louis Politics*, 98–99, 106–7; Lang, "Civil Rights versus 'Civic Progress,'" 629.

50. Kelliher, "Meet Harold J. Gibbons"; Trask, "New Charter Defeated"; Salisbury, "St. Louis Politics," 332; John R. Hahn, "Teamsters Plan Giant Get-out-Vote Setup," *St. Louis Globe-Democrat*, December 1, 1957; Jim Spreche, "St. Louis Teamsters Union Experiments in Grass Roots Approach to Government," November 10, 1957, and "AFL-CIO, Unlike

Teamsters' Setup, Concentrates on Welfare Field," November 24, 1957, both in *E. St. Louis Journal*.

51. "Landslide Defeat for Charter May Result in Real Civic Cooperation," October 1, 1957, and Sidney Zagri, "Charter Defeat Places Labor in a New Position," October 4, 1957, both in *Midwest Labor World*.

52. "News Release," January 9, 1958, Box 2, File 18, Teamsters Joint Council 13 Papers; "School Merger Would Create More Problems, Economist Says," June 13, 1958, and "Teamsters Will Open Community Action Program," April 28, 1958, both in *St. Louis Globe-Democrat*; "Petitions Filed in County for Freeholders," *St. Louis Post-Dispatch*, March 26, 1958; Civic Progress Minutes, February 27 and May 22, 1958, Series 5, Box 1, Tucker Papers; "Steward Council Proceedings," March 1, 1958, "'Groups of Seven' Organized as Grassroots for Assembly," March 1, 1958, "County Area 'Crawls with Grievances,'" April 1, 1958, "New Faces in Neighborhood Local Action Work," May 1, 1958, "History Made as Community Assembly Opens," June 15, 1958, "Odor Control," August 1, 1958, and "Area Wide Attack on Pollution Urged," October 16, 1958, all in *Midwest Labor World*.

53. Sidney Zagri, "Your Community and Mine," *St. Louis Argus*, August 2, 1957.

54. "Trainee Program Is Suspended," January 1, 1959, "Home Stewards' Responsibility Bigger," February 1959, "Stewards Council Proceedings," October 1959, and "It Started Here Ten Years Ago," November 1961, all in *Midwest Labor World*.

55. David Brody, "The Uses of Power I: Industrial Battleground" and "The Uses of Power II: Political Action," in his *Workers in Industrial America: Essays on the 20th Century Struggle* (New York: Oxford University Press, 1980), 173–75 and 214–16; Elizabeth A. Fones-Wolf, *Selling Free Enterprise: The Business Assault on Labor and Liberalism, 1945–60* (Urbana: University of Illinois Press, 1994), 143–47; Spreche, "AFL-CIO, Unlike Teamsters' Setup"; Sidney Zagri, "Your Community and Mine," *St. Louis Labor Tribune*, May 9, 1957, placed in the *Congressional Record* by Wayne Morse, May 23, 1957, 7551.

56. Gordon, *Mapping Decline*, 224; Nicolaides, *My Blue Heaven*, 225; Brill, *The Teamsters*, 357–58; Minutes, Local 688 Stewards Council, May 15, 1958, Box 41, File 17, Gibbons Collection; "Notes on St. Louis Mass Transit Developments," Series 3, Box 4, Tucker Papers; Primm, *Lion of the Valley*, 477; Gordon Burnside, "The Socialist Teamster," *St. Louis Weekly*, July 20–26, 1983.

57. "The Junior College District, St, Louis-St. Louis County," February 1965, Box 40, File 508, League of Women Voters of St. Louis Papers; Harry B. Wilson, "Between the Lines," *St. Louis Globe-Democrat*, October 23, 1951; Salisbury, "St. Louis Politics," 327; "Union Contact, Reported by Mrs. Marie Alger, with Oscar Ehrhardt," January 10, 1950, Box 34, File 28, American Labor Education Service Papers, Kheel Center for Labor Management Documentation and Archives, Martin P. Catherwood Library, Cornell University; Gray, *Report on Politics in St. Louis*, part 5, 10; Stein, *St. Louis Politics*, 79–80; Bill Clay, *A Political Voice at the Grassroots* (St. Louis: Missouri Historical Society Press, 2004), 163–64. Gibbons was quite dismissive of other labor leaders in St. Louis. Describing three of the city's top labor leaders in an August 1957 interview with *Business Week*, he concluded: "Together, they don't add up to zero."

58. Gibbons to editor, *St. Louis Post-Dispatch*, September 24, 1955.

59. On Local 688's community action program in the 1960s, see Robert Bussel, "'A Trade Union War on the Slums': Harold Gibbons, Ernest Calloway, and the St. Louis Teamsters in the 1960s," *Labor History* 44, no. 1 (2002): 51–69.

5

Chicano Labor and Multiracial Politics in Post–World War II Texas

Two Case Studies

MAX KROCHMAL

In late 1963 a group of Dallas political operatives left its campaign headquarters and staged a sit-in at El Fenix, the city's first Tex-Mex restaurant and the economic foundation of the influential Martinez family. The protesters in this case were not students, and the restaurant was owned by Mexican Americans. It was also a holdout in a city where virtually all downtown lunch counters had already desegregated their seating. The sit-in featured an alliance of white, black, and Chicano/Chicana trade unionists and working-class community activists who left their storefront office, walked to the restaurant, and sat down as a group at a large table. The manager, a member of the Martinez family, asked them to leave and then promptly closed down for the day.[1]

The sit-in at El Fenix bubbled up from a larger underground reservoir of multiracial, working-class political activism that took place beyond the gaze of most historians, journalists, and social scientists. In the two decades following World War II, African American and Chicano/Chicana working people across Texas quietly and tentatively approached one another as well as white laborers for support in their efforts to counter discrimination at work, in their unions, and in the cities in which they lived. By the mid-1960s such collaboration had gradually expanded from its origins in the barrios, ghettos, union halls, and shop floors to become a broad-based coalition in support of liberal politicians and an expansive civil rights agenda.[2]

Scholars of the post–World War II black and brown freedom struggles have traditionally privileged the middle-class, public leadership of the most visible civil rights organizations.[3] Yet working-class activists such as the protestors at El Fenix represented the lifeblood of the effort to democratize Texas. Their story remains particularly obscure in the case of Chicano/Chicana

Figure 5.1. "Pancho" Medrano at the strike headquarters of the United Farm Workers Organizing Committee, Rio Grande City, Texas, ca. 1967. For activists such as Medrano, labor rights and civil rights were inextricable. (Courtesy F. F. "Pancho" Medrano Collection, Special Collections, University of Texas at Arlington Library, AR55-2-6.)

historiography. Most accounts of the "Mexican American Generation" suggest that activists in the postwar period sought to improve their condition through court cases and quiet diplomacy alone, by disavowing confrontational tactics, and in some cases by embracing a white racial identity that separated them from black civil rights advocates.

Yet many ethnic Mexican working people in postwar Texas developed a political praxis that did not depend upon a white racial identity but instead encouraged fierce, constant resistance to Jim Crow in both the workplace and the community. They did so—critically—through constant conversation and collaboration with like-minded African Americans. In many cases, distinctions of class and political philosophy mattered at least as much as did ties of ethnicity. A detailed examination of the biographies of two working-class Chicano organizers reveals the central importance of shop-floor conflicts and trade unionism to the development of the larger ethnic Mexican civil rights struggle. Their life stories highlight the decisive role of coalition building across the color line and suggest a wide range of continuities that link the so-called Mexican American generation to the more familiar "Chicano movement" of the 1970s.[4]

The Survival of the Generational Model

The success of that movement in giving birth to the discipline of Chicano/Chicana Studies has, ironically, obscured a clear historical accounting of the movement's immediate antecedents. Although historians now know much more about the experiences of ethnic Mexicans in North America from the conquest through the present, many of the scholar-activists who emerged from the movement and began searching for its roots initially overlooked the first two decades following World War II.

Published in 1989, Mario T. García's *Mexican Americans: Leadership, Ideology, and Identity, 1930–1960* authoritatively filled this gap. In this foundational study, García joined other early Chicano/Chicana historians in proposing a generational approach to the field, a perspective that remains the dominant scholarly paradigm. It holds that most Mexicans emigrated to the United States during the late Porfiriato and Revolutionary periods (the decades before and after 1910). Like many other immigrants, these new arrivals formed social clubs based on their towns or states of origin and looked southward in order to celebrate *lo mexicano* (Mexicanness). But their children, who came of age during and after World War II, instead looked northward to Washington, seeking to fulfill the promise of their U.S. citizenship and participate fully in American society. This "Mexican American generation" is generally understood as composed of first-generation "ethnic" Americans who developed a hybrid identity and culture. They promoted patriotism and served in the U.S. military, but they continued to observe Mexican Independence Day and refashioned the Cinco de Mayo celebration for inclusion on the civic calendars of the Southwest. They were bilingual but desired assimilation into mainstream America. They advanced integration and in most cases supported the New Deal liberal impulse of expanding the role of government in order to ensure civil rights and social provision for all. They organized civic groups aimed at overturning the obstacles that stood in the way of exercising their rightful first-class citizenship. All of these characteristics distinguished them sharply from their own children, the so-called Chicano/Chicana generation of the 1960s and 1970s, who advocated militant tactics, developed a cultural nationalism that rejected whiteness, demanded recognition as a nonwhite racial (rather than ethnic) group, and abandoned Johnson-era liberalism for a range of radical alternatives.[5]

Most scholars of the Chicano experience, including García, debate the finer points of this portrait, but most agree that the political evolution of the ethnic Mexican community in the American Southwest developed in a linear, teleological fashion best described in generational terms. Nonetheless, many of the distinguishing features of this telos remain obscure, starting with the exact chronology. García originally proposed that the Mexican American generation spanned both sides of the war, from 1930 to 1960. Cynthia Orozco, in contrast, identified Mexican American activism occurring as early as the 1920s. George J. Sánchez detailed the emergence of a Mexican American community in Los Angeles before and during World War II, while an earlier wave of scholars, including Carlos Muñoz, posited that Mexicans became Mexican Americans only after 1945. Ignacio M. García, the author of several volumes on the group, posits a subtle transition between the activism of the prewar era and the more absolute demands of returning veterans during and after the war. Still, he argues that both groups made up a single generational predecessor that fell short of and gave way to the "militant ethos" of the Chicano movement.[6]

If the chronology is inexact, the defining political characteristics of this cohort are even less clear. Most studies support Ignacio García's 2009 conclusion that the leadership of the Mexican American civil rights movement passed from the hands of workers and radicals to the offices of the more tentative, middle-class leaders of the League of United Latin American Citizens (LULAC) and the American G.I. Forum, the two dominant civil rights organizations of the era. In Texas, men such as attorney Gus García, University of Texas education professor George I. Sánchez, and G.I. Forum leader and physician Hector García supposedly held the reins of the struggle until the rise of the Chicano student movement.[7]

A growing body of research suggests that this approach fails to account for myriad sharp and protracted intra-ethnic differences, disagreements that frequently divided ethnic Mexican political sentiments throughout the twentieth century even as other forces sought to create common ground. David Gutiérrez, for example, has shown that the great men of the movement advanced diverse opinions concerning ongoing immigration from Mexico into the United States.[8] Emma Pérez decenters those great men, arguing that paying attention to the experiences of working-class ethnic Mexican women "means to transfigure questions that have been assumed to be universal." She adds: "Statistically, the majority of women were not assimilating into the institutions of dominant culture; that would have been a luxury and a privilege. Instead, they were working in the factories of Houston or in the fields of the surrounding rural areas during the first decades of the twentieth century.... The voice of an emerging middle class was not the single voice of the community. Conflict coexisted. Contradictions arose. Race wars, gender wars, class wars—all were characteristic of diasporic communities in the early-twentieth-century United States."⁹

Pérez's assertion highlights the critical importance of broadening ethnic Mexican civil rights history, yet scholars still know surprisingly little about the lives of ordinary working people among the Mexican American generation. Zaragosa Vargas, Mario García, and others have outlined the rise and fall of radical—at times Communist—labor organizations in the 1930s and 1940s, but cold war repression stamped out even the last holdouts from this movement by the early 1950s.¹⁰ According to Cletus Daniel and Emilio Zamora, a broader, less partisan fight during World War II included thousands of ethnic Mexican workers who appealed to both the U.S. federal government and the Mexican consulate to gain access to employment in defense industries. In the process, Zamora adds, they forged cross-class alliances with Mexican American professionals who led LULAC and the G.I. Forum, groups that have long been considered too conservative to engage in such advocacy.¹¹ Irene Ledesma and Vicki Ruiz have drawn attention to several strikes waged by ethnic Mexican women workers in the postwar period, showing how their struggles both diverged from and were often misunderstood by their male counterparts. At the same time, their work highlights the existence of a wide range of civil rights activism that took place outside the bounds of LULAC and the G.I. Forum, not in the courtroom but on the job and in the community.¹²

Meanwhile, scholars' efforts to unpack the racial politics of the Mexican American generation have produced conflicting conclusions, with at times incendiary and in all cases revealing implications. Neil Foley, Thomas Guglielmo, and others have shown that Mexican American litigants for a decade before and after *Brown v. Board of Education* (1954) adopted a legal strategy which claimed that Mexican Americans were "other whites" who faced discrimination based on language and ethnicity but were legally white and therefore entitled to first-class citizenship, even within the confines of the Jim Crow South. Tying this legal maneuver to a handful of other local skirmishes led by LULACers and G.I. Forum activists, these historians further conclude that Mexican Americans self-identified as white and cast their lot with white supremacy in opposition to blackness.¹³ In contrast, Ariela Gross, Ignacio García, and others look at the same cases and contend that Mexican Americans used the "other white" or "class apart" argument only as an instrumentalist tool within the courtroom.¹⁴ Carlos Blanton delved deeply into the career of educator and Mexican American civil rights activist George I. Sánchez and discovered that even this respectable, seemingly middle-class race leader forged significant if tenuous ties with the black freedom struggle, from the 1940s until his death in 1972.¹⁵

These texts, in sum, produce a diverse picture of the Mexican American generation, a portrait that defies easy categorization in terms of political philosophy, leadership, and even chronology. The biographies of the two working-class ethnic Mexican activists presented in this essay reveal that they often advocated confrontational political tactics, coalition organizing with African Americans, and engagement with trade unionism and the fight against poverty. These workers' experiences on the job and in their unions belie the traditional scholarly depiction of a quiescent, assimilationist, Mexican American civil rights movement, while their ongoing commitment to multiracial organizing clearly shows that they did not positions themselves as "white" ethnics opposed to black civil rights. Their stories also add to the growing body of research that calls into question the generational model itself, suggesting that it may finally be the time to discard it.

Francisco F. "Pancho" Medrano

Francisco Franco Medrano, better known as "Pancho," already had four decades of experience in the barrio, shop floor, and black and brown civil rights movements when he helped instigate the sit-in at the El Fenix restaurant. Born in 1920, Medrano was raised in the Dallas barrio known as Little Mexico, where intense poverty and discrimination defined his childhood. He grew up without indoor plumbing and electricity and was urged to drop out of high school by his principal, who helped him find work. By sheer luck, Pancho ended up in a New Deal training program and landed a job at North American Aviation in nearby Grand Prairie in 1941. He dominated the company boxing league, gaining the respect of his white co-workers. An organizer from the United Auto Workers gave Medrano a pamphlet in which the union highlighted its commitment to non-discrimination, so he joined the drive to organize a local at the plant. The UAW won recognition and a contract, and Pancho served as shop steward while also working full-time and boxing professionally. After retiring from prizefighting, he became a delegate to the state and local labor councils and volunteered as an ad hoc organizer of both African American and Mexican American workers for myriad Dallas-area unions.[16]

In the early 1960s, Medrano jumped headlong into the black and brown civil rights movements in Dallas. He served as an officer for a chapter of the G.I. Forum, joined the NAACP, and aided the sit-in demonstrations of black students at downtown department stores. Such community organizing went hand in glove with mobilizing for electoral politics. Pancho alternated between collecting poll taxes for the Progressive Voters League, an African American organization, and organizing ethnic Mexicans into first a local Viva Kennedy club and then the Political Association of Spanish-Speaking Organizations (PASO).[17]

Two decades of labor, civil rights, and political organizing had already garnered Medrano a sizable reputation in activist circles, but nobody who knew him could have anticipated the opportunities and dramatic changes that lay ahead. In late 1963 or early 1964, UAW president Walter Reuther offered Pancho a full-time position working directly for the international union's Citizenship Department, a job that gave him carte blanche to travel the country assisting local civil rights struggles and political candidates "wherever it was needed."[18] He personally participated in and in many cases brought delegations of local activists to many of the iconic events of the 1960s. Medrano attended the "March for Jobs and Freedom" in Washington, D.C., in August 1963, the Selma-to-Montgomery voting rights march in March 1965, and the multiracial Poor People's Campaign encampment in May 1968. He joined Chicano/Chicana activists from across the country in walking out in protest from a hearing of the Equal Employment Opportunity Commission in Albuquerque in 1966 and then from a subsequent summit of the Inter-Agency Committee on Mexican American Affairs held in El Paso the following year. In June 1968 he stood a few feet from Senator Robert F. Kennedy when the latter was assassinated following his victory in the California presidential primary victory. He returned to Los Angeles in 1970 to march in the Chicano Moratorium demonstrations against the Vietnam War and then assisted local activists in denouncing the sheriff's deputy who murdered Chicano journalist Ruben Salazar during the protests.[19]

Pancho traveled far and wide for the UAW, but his presence at these many public demonstrations did not detract from his commitment to assisting local organizing efforts among black and ethnic Mexican workers. A closer look at his long and far-flung career makes plain the intimate relationships between labor, civil rights, and political activism; the black and brown freedom struggles; and Mexican American generation advocacy and the rise of the Chicano movement.

Medrano's expansive political vision and practice stemmed from and reflected the longtime aspirations of many black and brown workers: access to good jobs, an end to discrimination, and meaningful, independent political power for their communities. Pancho was intimately familiar with such goals. Life in the barrio and on the job had taught him both the depth of white supremacist resistance to civil rights and the central importance of economic justice issues. As a child, he ventured with his siblings and mother to white sections of Dallas, where the family was frequently refused access to restaurants, movie theaters, and public swimming pools and parks. When he got his first lucrative job, at North American Aviation, Pancho was one of only a half-dozen Mexican Americans among the tens of thousands of workers in the plant. Discrimination was rampant. Although he held the title of jig builder, a skilled trades position, Medrano had trouble acquiring tools from the "crib attendant" who readily supplied them to white workers. Many white workers saw him as racially inferior and initially refused to be paired with him for two-man jobs. Like all workers in the plant, Pancho also knew that African Americans remained strictly confined to janitorial service. He probably did not know that white union officials had depended upon black workers for help in organizing the union local—the highly mobile janitors distributed and collected union cards across the sprawling North American compound—but he could plainly see that they then ignored the UAW's non-discrimination policy and negotiated a contract with separate lines of seniority, cementing the company's preexisting practice of reserving the best jobs for whites.[20]

Thanks to his boxing prowess, Medrano managed to integrate himself into the white-dominated union, becoming a shop steward and later an international representative. Nonetheless, he still made common cause with the less-fortunate black and brown workers on the shop floor. Despite resistance from both the company and the local union, he helped both groups of workers achieve upward occupational mobility. In 1962, Vice-President Lyndon Johnson visited the plant as part of his duties as chair of the President's Committee on Equal Employment Opportunity, a predecessor to the EEOC that worked to curb racial employment practices by encouraging voluntary action on the part of government contractors. With no hope of achieving compliance with their own "voluntary" commitments, management asked a number of black janitors to put on mechanics' coveralls and stand by the machines as the vice-president toured the facilities. Several agreed to do it; others resisted participating in the deception. The trick worked, and Johnson believed what he saw and returned to Washington without incident. But when Pancho met LBJ for the first time shortly thereafter, he told him the truth, and Johnson was furious. The company soon abandoned its strategy of misleading federal authorities and instead began to take affirmative action to reverse the plant's long-standing employment discrimination practices.

After the passage of the Civil Rights Act in 1964, Pancho remained an ally of black and brown workers at the plant as they took advantage of Title VII to win skilled jobs for the first time. Shop foremen and white union officials continued to resist integration, so Medrano helped the African American workers organize independently of local union leadership in order to demand (and gain) access to skilled, mechanized jobs. At the same time, Pancho worked with the Texas Employment Commission to bring over more than five hundred ethnic Mexican skilled workers north from the Rio Grande Valley and into a new training program at the plant—finally desegregating it nearly twenty-five years after the wartime FEPC first promised to do so.[21]

The company cooperated with Medrano, but the president of UAW Local 848, Nova Howard, resisted his efforts. In a 1969 letter to UAW regional secretary H. A. Moon, Howard complained that "an unknown stranger has ridden into our town, spreading seed[s] of discontent, uneasiness and fear among my people." Medrano, with Reuther's blessing, "came into my local's hall . . . drew out portions of my membership," and held a "special meeting" for "minority groups," even conducting some business in Spanish. Howard felt that Pancho, an international representative, should be reprimanded for violating protocol and meddling in local union and company affairs. Yet Howard's protest ended up backfiring. Not only did Medrano in fact have Reuther's support, but he also made Howard's letter into a leaflet and distributed it on the floor of a UAW convention, embarrassing the local union chief and helping garner support for rival white union leaders who supported the cause of civil rights.[22]

As this story suggests, Medrano brought resources, clout, and technical expertise to the broader struggle for racial equality and economic opportunity. On the shop floor and in electoral politics, he formed coalitions between black and ethnic Mexican workers and then sought allies among a wide range of partners, from white workers and liberal politicians to African American and ethnic Mexican civil rights activists. Although he was a lifelong unionist, Medrano never shied from confronting injustice within the labor movement itself. He relentlessly tied his own fortunes to those of ordinary black and brown workers, generally outmaneuvering his opponents along the way.

Experiences in the barrio, at the aircraft plant, and in the union all proved pivotal to the development of Medrano's organizing praxis. His close ties to ordinary workers and decades of experimentation in multiracial coalition building tied black to brown and "Mexican American" civil rights to "Chicano" militancy. Born in 1920 and becoming active during World War II, Pancho followed a path from barrio to barnstormer that was a product of New Deal opportunities and the rising civil rights movement of the postwar Mexican American generation. He became an organizer in the labor movement, cut his political teeth in the Viva Kennedy clubs, and built close ties with local chapters of LULAC and the G.I. Forum.

As an international representative, Medrano strategically used his position to spread the gospel of community organizing. From rural New Mexico to small towns in West Texas, from the borderlands of the Rio Grande Valley to the piney woods black belt of East Texas, Medrano crisscrossed the countryside in a car filled with leaflets and a film projector. He made connections with local chapters of LULAC, the G.I. Forum, and the NAACP and joined the campaigns of countless senators, congressmen, and state legislators throughout the West. Even in towns where he had no local contacts, he found a white wall in a poor neighborhood and began projecting movies, often popular feature films with no political content. Once the crowd grew around him, Pancho introduced his audiences to the possibility of making change through electoral politics. At every stop on his journeys, he recruited local poll-tax deputies and precinct captains, talked up the benefits of trade unionism, and highlighted the critical links between labor, civil rights, and political activism.[23]

Yet these activities among the Mexican American generation did not preclude Pancho's early and protracted involvement in the rising Chicano movement that took root in the late 1960s and early 1970s. In fact, in some cases Medrano's organizing highlights the direct continuities between earlier activism and the supposedly new, separate, and youth-led Chicano movement. In 1963, on assignment from UAW headquarters in Detroit, Pancho traveled to Crystal City in South Texas to aid the campaign of Juan Cornejo and "los cinco candidatos," five working-class ethnic Mexican candidates for local office. In this landmark municipal election, a coalition of PASO, ethnic Mexican workers at the Teamster-organized Del Monte packing plant, and high school students led by José Ángel Gutiérrez combined to overthrow the all-white conservative government that had dominated for decades. Teamster representative Carlos Moore invited Pancho to stay and join the unprecedented effort. Medrano brought not only his organizing skills but the all-important seed money from the UAW, funds that allowed the town's ethnic Mexican working people to pay their poll taxes and vote. Cornejo and *los cinco* won the election. It was the opening salvo of the Chicano movement in Texas, the first time a majority-ethnic-Mexican jurisdiction had cast off the minority white government and replaced it with ordinary, uneducated Chicano workers. What came to be known as the "first Chicano revolt" at Crystal City served as a symbol and example of Chicano/Chicana empowerment that resonated nationwide, and the young Gutiérrez later became a principal spokesman of the larger movement. Yet Pancho's story points to the centrality of older activists like Medrano, Moore, and the leaders of PASO, all of whom drew upon years or decades of experience in the trenches of organized labor or electoral politics.[24]

Pancho also played a significant role in another enduring symbol of Chicano liberation, the effort to unionize farmworkers. Like the Crystal City revolt, the farmworker struggle did not represent a sharp break from the past but rather an outgrowth of prior Mexican American civil rights and labor activism. César Chávez's United Farm Workers Organizing Committee (UF-WOC)—itself the product of the Fred Ross's Community Services Organization of the 1950s—decided to send organizer Gene Nelson to Rio Grande City in South Texas in 1966. Melon pickers went on strike within a month of Nelson's arrival. The UAW's Walter Reuther, who was the first union or liberal leader to aid the farmworkers' efforts in California, sent Medrano to join the strike in the Rio Grande Valley. Pancho had visited Delano with Reuther the previous year, so it made sense that it was he who brought the money from the UAW to the Texas strike. As in California, the Texas walkout turned into a protracted civil rights battle, culminating in a five-hundred-mile, two-month-long march from the Valley to the state capitol in Austin. Meanwhile, a delegation of African Americans from East Texas, led by a local chapter of the Southern Christian Leadership Conference, staged its own march to the capitol. Labor activists from across the state joined both groups at the Austin rally on Labor Day, calling on the legislature to enact a $1.25 hourly minimum wage and demanding that Governor John Connally make good on his campaign pledge to support civil rights for all blacks and Chicanos/Chicanas.[25]

Medrano walked in many segments of the march and aided with daily campaign activities, serving as what one organizer called a "diplomat" between UFWOC organizers, the Texas labor movement, and the UAW's vast network of lawyers and political connections.[26] In May 1967, several months after the march, Pancho returned to the Valley to mount a picket line aimed at convincing unionized railroad workers to refuse to load produce that originated at the struck farms. Members of the Texas Rangers accosted and arrested him and a dozen other pickets, adding them to the long list of ethnic Mexican unionists and their allies who had suffered physical abuse and detention by the Rangers in the first year of the UFWOC campaign. Medrano used his position on the UAW staff to secure bail and the release of his compatriots before launching a multi-year lawsuit against the state police force. The U.S. Supreme Court eventually sided with the union in *Medrano v. Allee*, issuing a landmark ruling in 1974 that forced a complete overhaul of the agency and struck down Texas laws against mass picketing and free assembly. Pancho also joined a number of UFWOC activists who testified against the Rangers before a subcommittee hearing of the U.S. Senate Committee on Labor and Public Welfare held in Rio Grande City on June 29, 1967. Between witnesses, the audience of farmworkers cheered "Viva justicia" ("Long live justice") and "Viva Kennedy"—the latter phrase celebrating not only the political awakening spurred by the clubs carrying that name during the presidential campaign seven years earlier but also the presence of Senator Edward M. "Ted" Kennedy as an advocate for farmworkers on the Senate subcommittee panel.[27]

The UFWOC's Texas campaign captured the imagination of Chicanos and Chicanas across the state, serving as an example of militant self-empowerment. But it gained critical support from a coalition composed of the UAW, the Texas AFL-CIO, sympathetic elected officials, and black civil rights activists. Veteran organizers like Medrano mobilized their preexisting networks of labor activists and political connections for the farmworkers' cause. Such ties served as the invisible, multiracial, and intergenerational infrastructure behind the widely publicized Chicano uprising.

Medrano's community organizing within his hometown of Dallas further demonstrates the importance of interracial organizing while cementing the link between his "Mexican American" activism and the so-called Chicano generation. Pancho's work in Dallas politics began within his own family and neighborhood and ended with mass demonstrations and finally the acquisition of formal political power. After growing up in a barrio, Pancho moved to a nearby public housing project named, without irony, Little Mexico Village. In the early 1950s, Pancho's wages at the aircraft plant allowed him to buy a house in a previously all-white neighborhood a mile to the north, on the edge of Oak Lawn. White residents objected to the new arrivals and soon began moving away, while other upwardly mobile ethnic Mexican families gradually replaced them. The proximate barrios continued expanding over the next decade until the Medrano household was again sandwiched between the growing ethnic Mexican enclaves located just north of downtown and in West Dallas (immediately across the Trinity River).[28]

Pancho responded to this change by attempting to organize his new neighbors. Rather than flee the poverty enveloping him, Medrano helped his son Ricardo purchase a small neighborhood grocery store around the corner from their house. Along with Pancho's wife, Esperanza, Ricardo opened Kiko's grocery in 1964. The store sold some food and other conveniences, but its main business was performing the functions of a community center. Esperanza offered informal day-care services, and Kiko's bustled with children each day after school. The kids attracted the parents to the store, and Ricardo took advantage of their presence to provide them with political education materials. Kiko's became a social and political clearinghouse for the surrounding barrios. In 1967, when the Rangers arrested Pancho in Starr County, family friend and union printer Joe Landín helped Ricardo make a leaflet to raise money for the farmworker struggle. Ricardo spread the news and distributed information from the counter at Kiko's.[29]

The Medranos' other children also received a political education from their earliest childhood days. Pancho Jr., the eldest, followed his father into the aircraft industry and became a union steward. In the late 1950s and early 1960s he joined his father in helping African American and ethnic Mexican workers organize a local of the carpenters' union at Scotty's Aluminum and the William Cameron Company. The family's second son, Robert, was the first to attend college. After graduation he took a job in the War on Poverty and eventually advanced to the position of director at the West Dallas Community Center. Just as Ricardo used Kiko's as an informational clearinghouse, Robert made the provision of social services part of a broader project of political education and community organizing. Together, the two political hubs brought the Medrano family into direct contact with countless barrio residents.[30]

Over the course of the 1970s, this sustained contact transformed into mass mobilization. In late February 1971, Dallas city, county, and surrounding law enforcement agencies conducted a general reign of terror in the barrios, ostensibly seeking the murderers of three slain sheriff's deputies. They arrested ethnic Mexicans at will and physically abused those who dared to resist. In the early morning hours of February 19, a group of plainclothes police officers kicked down the door of the East Dallas home of Tomás and Berta Rodríguez and opened fire on the terrified couple sleeping inside. Tomás returned fire before being shot, beaten, chained to a hospital bed, and charged with assault and intent to murder. Berta, who was pregnant, was hospitalized with gunshot wounds, and one of their children was also injured in the melee. The policemen initially claimed that they had received a tip that their colleagues' slayers were inside, but they later tried to discredit Tomás by filing what turned out to be false drug charges against him.[31]

The assault on the Rodriguez family galvanized the city's growing Chicano movement and also heralded the emergence of a militant multiracial coalition for social justice. The Medranos stood at the center of this new citywide mobilization. Police brutality was also a chronic problem in the black neighborhoods of South Dallas, but common grievances did not automatically produce cooperation across ethnic lines. Rather, Pancho and his family drew upon decades of contact with black civil rights activists to begin organizing a partnership immediately after the Rodriguez assault and arrest. Pancho had served on the board of the local NAACP; his children grew up in the association's youth chapter led by renowned activist Juanita Craft. He had collected poll taxes and registered black Dallasites while serving on the board of the Texas Council of Voters, and he was now participating in the long-shot mayoral candidacy of black community organizer Al Lipscomb.[32]

Beginning at Kiko's and the West Dallas Community Center, the Medranos connected student leaders of all races to barrio residents and reached out to a wide range of established Mexican American, Chicano, and African American civil rights organizations. Robert and Ricardo proved critical to reaching out to Chicano youth. About a year earlier, Pancho had visited Los Angeles and brought home the idea of organizing a chapter of the Brown Berets, the stylish paramilitary Chicano counterpart to the Black Panthers. Ricardo had taken the lead in creating the Dallas unit and had become an outspoken, flamboyant, and well-known critic of the city's school board and city council. In contrast, Robert quietly spread the word of upcoming events through his contacts from the War on Poverty, using his position at the West Dallas Community Center to mobilize the service agency's clients. While his kids reached out to Chicano students and barrio residents, Pancho activated his networks in the labor movement and among elected officials to bring political pressure to bear upon the Dallas Police Department.[33]

All of this spadework remained outside the public view, causing most journalists to marvel at the depth of multiracial collaboration that seemed to emerge suddenly when the coalition finally took to the streets.[34] On March 6, 1971, Pancho led a small group of "Latins, Blacks," and "a few Anglos" in staging a vigil for Tomás Rodríguez at the Kennedy Memorial Plaza.[35] A week later, a multiracial group of more than 150 protesters attended another rally at the same site, featuring two principal speakers. Pancho spoke on "how we have been suffering from bad government in Dallas," while Fred L. Bell, an African American leader affiliated with the Student Nonviolent Coordinating Committee (SNCC), railed against police brutality meted out to blacks.[36] The next afternoon, on Sunday, March 14, some three thousand mostly ethnic Mexican people assembled in Reverchon Park for a benefit dinner designed to raise funds for the Rodríguez case. The nonconfrontational, private nature of the Mexican food picnic benefit likely brought many middle-class, respectable Mexican Americans into the campaign, allowing these activists to quietly show support and donate to the confrontational Chicano cause without taking to the streets in protest.[37] The next Saturday, March 20, a column of two to three hundred demonstrators—"blacks, whites, and Mexican-Americans," according to the hostile *Dallas Morning News*—tacked themselves onto the annual Shriners parade, taking advantage of the occasion to march down the already-blockaded streets with a police escort. The marchers chanted slogans and carried signs as they wound their way to a rally on the steps of City Hall, where Pancho addressed the assembled crowd. "The coalition between minorities became stronger," one paper reported, "as the chicanos [sic] expressed solidarity with the Rev. Peter Johnson, a black man, who was in the second week of a hunger strike to dramatize the plight of the city's poor" at the same location.[38] *El Sol de Texas* optimistically declared, "What countless injustices have not achieved, the Rodríguez case accomplished—it united Mexican Americans, Anglos, and Negroes." One photograph in the Spanish-language weekly shows Pancho standing side-by-side with black mayoral candidate Al Lipscomb and Ed Polk, Tomás's long-haired white defense attorney. The caption reads: "Three different skin colors in defense of a single cause . . . justice."[39]

By the end of March 1971, the black and Chicano/Chicana struggles were indeed becoming one, and African Americans' support for the Rodríguez cause was clearly reciprocated by Chicanos/Chicanas. Photographs of the rallies show ethnic Mexican protestors lifting placards reading "Lipscomb for Mayor" alongside posters of the UFWOC eagle.[40] According to *El Sol de Texas*, several Chicano/Chicana, black, and white organizations were planning a broad selective-buying campaign at downtown grocery stores that would be a "combined protest of the [United Farm Workers'] Lettuce Boycott, the Hunger Strike, and Police Brutality."[41] It appears that such plans were postponed, possibly inevitably—one week later the paper reported plans for yet another march and rally, this time with a twist. On March 27, Pancho led a delegation on foot from Fort Worth, some thirty miles west of Dallas. In the end, a diverse group of more than seven hundred protestors from throughout the region arrived at City Hall. The protests appear to have fizzled out soon after this demonstration, but at least some of the momentum was channeled into electoral politics. Organizers urged supporters of the Rodríguez case to not only vote for Lipscomb but to "Vote 'NO'" to all of the incumbents and their allies on the City Council.[42]

Many historians point to multiracial collaboration and militant protest tactics as innovative strategies first developed by the Chicano movement, a set of key departures that separated the younger activists from the more moderate advocacy of their parents. Yet the Rodríguez case in Dallas suggests that such seemingly new organizing actually grew out of the earlier networks established by more senior activists. To a remarkable degree, Pancho brought older Mexican American groups together with the new Chicano organizations, and he placed both in conversation with black activists (also elderly and young) and liberal white labor leaders, students, and politicians. Although the conclusion of the Rodríguez campaign remains murky, it is clear that these diverse activists achieved an unprecedented level of cooperation and public visibility in March 1971. At the same time, Pancho's pivotal role cautions that the coalition, though newly vibrant, was less a break from the past than a product of it.[43]

The Rodríguez case built on earlier organizing efforts, but it also raised the already-substantial profile of the Medrano family to new heights in the arena of electoral politics. After the protests subsided, the Medranos continued their work of building a local electoral machine based upon tireless advocacy for civil rights and the provision of basic services for the ethnic Mexican residents of Dallas. Both Kiko's and the West Dallas Community Center performed these functions. If the Madranos' clients needed help with their power bill, their plumbing, a streetlight, or a school principal, they came to Kiko's and got help from Esperanza and Ricardo. If they needed a job or food stamps, they went to visit Robert in West Dallas. In this way, the family gained what Ricardo called "political clout."[44]

Many of the Medrano children, who had been at Pancho's side in various campaigns throughout the 1950s and 1960s, became local leaders in their own right. In 1974, Robert ran for and won a seat on the Dallas Independent School District board, a post he held until 1988. The Citizens' Charter Association, a conservative nominating body led by white businessmen, had long dominated the city's at-large municipal elections, and only one ethnic Mexican (and no African Americans) had ever won a City Council seat without the group's support. But in 1975 the door swung open when the courts sided with a suit filed by former mayoral candidate Al Lipscomb, ordering the city to create district elections in compliance with the Voting Rights Act of 1965. Ricardo gained a spot on the Dallas City Council from 1980 to 1984.[45] Lipscomb joined the council as a representative for a South Dallas district in 1984, and he remained an ally of the Medranos both on the council and in the community.[46] For nearly two decades, the ethnic Mexican precincts of downtown and West Dallas were in permanent campaign mode, always littered with yard signs, posters, and bumper stickers that read simply "Medrano"—first names were omitted to keep the ads current. Before Little Mexico's destruction owing to urban renewal, local journalists gave it a new nickname: Medranoville.[47] As late as 2010, Pancho's daughter Pauline served as the city's deputy mayor pro tem, while Adam, Pancho's grandson, chaired the school board.[48]

When Pancho Medrano led the sit-in at El Fenix in 1962, he probably had few clues that his daily civil rights and labor activism would eventually result in a political dynasty. Yet many of the puzzle pieces were already in place. When Pancho first visited the restaurant as a young man soon after World War II, "Papa Martinez," the founder, recognized him from news reports of his prizefighting and invited him in with open arms. Meanwhile, the owners forced other ethnic Mexican workers to eat in a hallway and flatly excluded all African Americans. By the early 1960s, Medrano frequently made common cause with black and white laborers and liberals, and they combined to stage a bold protest that nonetheless was immediately forgotten by all but the participants. After the sit-in, Pancho and his fellow campaign staffers continued to work in obscurity, registering and mobilizing voters outside the public eye until a seemingly new multiracial, militant coalition exploded onto the streets and into the newspapers during the Rodríguez affair of 1971. They demanded that the city take action to curb police brutality, but the City Council defended the officers' actions. Among the council's ranks was Anita Martinez, the daughter-in-law of the restaurant's founder, elected on a conservative ticket in 1969. Many Chicanos and African Americans in the flowering coalition to her political left denounced her, setting the stage for the transition to independent representation embodied in the electoral victories of the Medrano children.[49]

Pancho Medrano's life and legacy points to the need to finally cast away the generational terminology that dominates the historiography of the Chicano/Chicana experience in the postwar period. Although middle-class leaders of the so-called Mexican American generation have dominated scholarly treatments of the era, ethnic Mexican workers waged their own distinctive struggles for both racial and economic justice. At the same time, working-class organizers like Pancho connected and blurred together the two groups, as working people helped animate a wide range of the more familiar, mainstream "Mexican American" activism. Medrano's activism also linked the older cohort with the young Chicano/Chicana militants of the 1960s and 1970s. He played a pivotal role in founding a G.I. Forum chapter and a Viva Kennedy club in Dallas and participated in PASO and other electoral campaigns and community organizations across the Southwest. Yet he also contributed significantly to several "Chicano" struggles, including Crystal City, the United Farm Workers, the Rodríguez campaign, and independent electoral politics.[50]

Medrano's career began at the work site and centered upon organizing all working people—black, brown, and white. These two traits proved central to his success. They also open up an entirely new perspective on ethnic Mexican political history in the three decades after World War II. By beginning the story at work and focusing relentlessly on multiracial coalitions rather than strictly monoracial activism, his narrative suggests the need to replace the generational model with a new interpretation that is more sensitive to the nuances of class and political philosophy. Medrano's work site and multiracial organizing also clearly demonstrate the limits of "whiteness" as an explanation of ethnic Mexicans' racial positioning, highlighting instead the importance of studying not simply rhetoric but the nuts and bolts of on-the-ground community activism.

Arnold Flores

Medrano's case may at first appear extraordinary, but Pancho was just one of many working-class civil rights activists throughout postwar Texas. In San Antonio, nearly three hundred miles south of Dallas, an otherwise ordinary veteran turned civilian base worker followed a remarkably similar trajectory.

Born in the Rio Grande Valley in 1936, Arnold Flores grew up in relatively comfortable conditions within San Antonio's ethnic Mexican Westside enclave. His father's success as a small businessman did not shield Arnold from the rampant racial discrimination that dominated the city in the years after World War II. Flores attended Lanier High, an all-ethnic-Mexican school, until he dropped out to join the air force in 1954. He served at bases in Texas and Germany but decided not to reenlist after an officer called him "a greaser." Flores returned to civilian life in 1959 and quickly developed an interest in electoral politics and civil rights, serving as a block walker for the Viva Kennedy effort and local campaigns beginning in 1960.[51]

For the next several years Arnold continued to support and participate as a foot soldier in the flowering Mexican American civil rights struggle, yet he probably would have remained in historical obscurity had he not agreed to spearhead a fight against employment discrimination at Kelly Air Force Base. San Antonio's several military installations offered some of the best civilian jobs available to ethnic Mexican and African American workers in the area, but nonwhites rarely advanced beyond menial positions. Flores did not initially plan to rock the boat when he was hired into a permanent position at Kelly Field in 1964. Yet in 1967 he grew fed up with widespread, routine ethnic favoritism at the hands of the base's German American supervisors, and he filed a complaint denouncing a wide range of discriminatory working conditions, from the assignment of overtime and daily tasks to compensation and promotion practices.

Arnold's complaint transformed him into a leader among ethnic Mexican workers at the base and then catapulted him into the center of the civil rights movement and a career in organized labor and politics. His experiences on the shop floor at Kelly Field served as ammunition for the most militant activists among the so-called Mexican American generation, while his own participation helped link that older group to the emerging Chicano/Chicana youth movement. In 1969, after winning his case at Kelly, Flores accepted an offer to serve as an organizer of the Service Employees International Union, a position that for the better part of the next decade allowed him to fuse shop-floor activism with the civil rights struggle.

Like Medrano, Flores searched for and found allies both within and outside his ethnic group. He drew strength from other activists—black, brown, and white—who shared his expansive vision of combating both racial discrimination and economic exclusion. Flores's story, like Medrano's, illuminates the critical importance of both workplace activism and multiracial collaboration in the development of ethnic Mexicans' civil rights struggle. It underscores the continuities between the historiographically separate activism of the Mexican American and Chicano generations and further questions the salience of "whiteness" among ethnic Mexican working people.

Looking back at his early activism fifty years later, Flores cannot remember exactly why he became involved in electoral politics. He likely followed the same path as thousands of other ethnic Mexicans in Texas who first participated during the 1960 presidential campaign of John F. Kennedy. In Texas, one of the state chairmen of the Viva Kennedy clubs was Albert A. Peña Jr., the firebrand San Antonio civil rights attorney who first won election to the Bexar County Commissioners Court in 1956. Peña served as the leader of a loose "liberal" faction among ethnic Mexican activists from the mid-1950s through the late 1960s. Stymied by the business-friendly Good Government League and the at-large electoral system in municipal politics, Peña helped organize a coalition of white, black, and ethnic Mexican liberals who slowly won control of the Bexar County Democratic Party (the Republican Party was barely beginning to organize in Texas at this time, and it was often led by conservative registered Democrats). Flores began working for Peña around 1960 and eventually became the commissioner's "unofficial assistant." A passion for politics also cemented Flores's marriage to his wife, Gloria, that same year, and the young couple attended countless civil rights seminars together throughout the early 1960s. Evening workshops and all-day meetings on weekends became routine for the pair. "That was our social life," Flores later remembered.[52]

Yet unlike Peña and most of the professionals who led early ethnic Mexican civil rights organizations, Arnold and Gloria also had to find and hold down jobs. Gloria got a clerical position at Kelly, but Arnold struggled to find a trade. He drove a mixing truck for a concrete company, where he helped his fellow drivers unionize by putting them in contact with the Teamsters—a connection doubtlessly forged thanks to the Teamsters' periodic support for liberal politicians like Peña. The work at the concrete company was seasonal, so Flores also worked at odd jobs and found time to attend political rallies and to coach a local boxing team—like Pancho, Arnold had been a prizefighter in his youth. Flores worked briefly for an insurance company, where he again attempted to organize a union among the agents. Then in 1964, after years of unsuccessful attempts, he finally gained admission to a training program for a permanent position at Kelly Field, and he quickly joined Gloria at the base.[53]

Arnold was doubtlessly aware of the discrimination that dominated work at Kelly, but the base still offered the best blue-collar work available. He looked forward to stable employment by the federal government and hoped that he could rise up through the ranks and enjoy some degree of upward economic mobility. The couple bought a house and began to settle down. They likely planned to continue to their political activism in the community while slowly advancing into the ethnic Mexican middle class at work.

But the daily indignities of ethnic favoritism, a series of conflicts with supervisors, and the realization that he was working a dead-end job with no possibility of promotion set Arnold on a collision course with base management. He had begun his work at Kelly along with a training class of twenty-four new hires. They entered a rotation in which trainees could in theory sample work in several posts before receiving their permanent assignments, but in practice the schedule did not rotate all of the trainees equally. Ethnic Mexicans never worked upstairs in warehouse offices, nor did they have opportunities to work directly on the aircraft. Instead, they worked as "gofers" with no possibility of advancement. Flores became a "parts expediter," a job that required taking parts from one plane to another. Meanwhile, supervisors placed white workers in positions that would prepare them for promotion. Networks of kin often combined with ethnic favoritism, as German American managers elevated their distant cousins to serve as foremen, regardless of qualifications.[54]

Flores did not initially protest, preferring instead to keep his head down and do his work. But as Christmas approached in 1965, he noticed that white managers routinely gave weekend overtime hours and thus the opportunity to earn extra income to two white workers whom they favored most. Arnold chafed at this unequal assignment of overtime work, but he might have still stayed quiet had he not directly observed the resulting inequity. One Saturday he visited a downtown department store and encountered one of his white co-workers. Flores initially thought nothing unusual about the encounter, but he learned a week later that the man, Andrew Wharram, had been given credit for working overtime the previous weekend. Flores discovered that Wharram was on the clock and drawing pay. He had slipped away from work at the base to go shopping—using money he hadn't earned during an extra overtime shift won through favoritism![55]

Arnold had had enough. In early 1966 he approached his manager and reported seeing Wharram downtown. The manager initially threatened Flores, reminding him that he was making a serious charge and that propagating unfounded rumors would be met with severe punishment. But when Wharram joined Flores in the manager's office and admitted going absent without a leave (AWOL), the boss did not punish his favorite employee. Instead, he transferred Flores to another department. Facing discrimination at Kelly Field had been a bad enough indignity, Arnold later explained, but this blatant stealing and favoritism contradicted his belief, honed in civil rights seminars, that the federal government and especially the armed services should treat all people fairly.⁵⁶

Flores's work environment continued to deteriorate until it resulted in a formal discrimination complaint. Arnold and his new manager, John Cronk, immediately differed over his job description. Nearly a year after the AWOL incident, Cronk assigned a foreman to follow Flores around the base as he worked. Arnold interpreted this as an act of harassment and in December 1966 filed a grievance through his union, the International Association of Machinists. The case eventually failed when union officials missed a deadline for appeal.⁵⁷ In July 1967, Arnold approached another foreman and discreetly asked for permission to see the base's equal employment opportunity (EEO) officer, hoping the latter would help him close the ever-widening rift with his new boss. The foreman promised to quietly forward Arnold's request to the EEO department but then promptly took it to Cronk instead.⁵⁸

Arnold decided it was time to take matters into his own hands, and he quickly called upon his colleagues in the civil rights movement for support. In 1965, a group of ethnic Mexican professionals had formed the Federation for the Advancement of Mexican Americans (FAMA), a civil rights group that aimed to quietly contribute funding and other support to the more militant activists who were engaged in public confrontations with conservative whites. The group's logo featured a pair of roosters and the slogan "FAMA is not for chickens." Through FAMA, a wide range of ethnic Mexican professionals could pool their resources to support the student-activists at local universities, who in turn pushed the elders to support an ever broader array of causes. In 1966 FAMA organized a series of caravans to bring food and other aid to the UFWOC campaign in the Rio Grande Valley. Erasmo Andrade, a language interpreter at Kelly Air Force Base, chaired the Valley Workers Assistance Committee before serving as FAMA's sole staff member. Arnold Flores never formally joined the group—FAMA's ten-dollar monthly membership fee proved far too expensive for even the relatively well-off workers at Kelly—but he traded service in lieu of dues. Virtually every Saturday, Flores arrived early and stayed late at the FAMA office, preparing and cleaning up the conference room before and after the group's day-long weekly meetings. As a result, he gained informal membership in FAMA and became a regular participant, bringing him into contact with a wider range of leaders in San Antonio's large ethnic Mexican community. Meanwhile, the FAMA offices Flores maintained gradually became a gathering place for countless ethnic Mexican civil rights organizations. Arnold befriended Joe J. Bernal, a World War II veteran and teacher who became a state representative in 1964 and a state senator in 1966;

Matt García, a wealthy attorney with a growing concern for civil rights; Father Henry Casso, a local Catholic priest and activist; and countless leaders of the city's LULAC and G.I. Forum chapters.[59]

In the summer of 1967, coinciding with Arnold's attempt to see the EEO officer, FAMA leaders began to discuss the problem of employment discrimination against ethnic Mexicans, and the problems at Kelly put the base at the top of their list of potential targets. Most FAMA members were lawyers who wanted to build a well-documented case in order to take a polite but pointed appeal to Kelly management. They needed to gather concrete data, and Flores, the group's only blue-collar employee at the base, emerged as the obvious choice to coordinate the effort. Arnold began to talk with other ethnic Mexican workers at the base about their own experiences of discrimination, and more than twenty came to him with complaints. In coordination with FAMA, these workers began to file complaints with the base EEO office as part of a collective attempt to gauge and document the department's lack of responsiveness to problems. The workers' testimony provided vital information to FAMA's aspiring civil rights activists, and Arnold served as a de facto diplomat who connected the professionals with a constituency among blue-collar workers at Kelly Field.[60]

In August 1967, Flores filed a formal discrimination complaint. After his own boss refused to allow him to visit the EEO office, Flores called state senator Bernal, who in turn called Kelly management and demanded that Arnold be allowed to submit his complaint. The next morning the EEO officer summoned Flores and interrogated him for more than five hours.[61] His case detailed the numerous ways in which ethnic Mexicans faced discrimination in the area of promotion, but his main complaint centered on the capricious disciplinary actions and harassment he faced in the wake of reporting the AWOL incident. He did not demand a raise but called for punishment for his supervisors and a wholesale rooting out of discrimination at Kelly. He hoped to end the practice of assigning ethnic Mexicans to dead-end jobs while simultaneously improving daily working conditions. Mostly he wanted respect.[62]

At the same time, Senator Bernal asked the Texas State Advisory Committee to the U.S. Commission on Civil Rights to investigate employment practices at the base. Ernesto Cortés, who later gained renown as the Texas head of Saul Alinsky's Industrial Areas Foundation, served on the committee's staff and interviewed Flores as part of its preliminary investigation. In November 1967 the committee held widely publicized hearings on discrimination at the base. Forty people testified, with Flores emerging as the spokesman for the ethnic Mexican workers. The state committee published its report in June 1968 and forwarded its findings to the federal Commission on Civil Rights. It charged that widespread, systemic discrimination prevailed at the base, that nonwhite employees had no faith in the EEO procedures, and that base management had failed to address the inequities despite being made aware of them.[63]

Even before these findings were made public, Kelly officials responded to Arnold's complaint, the broader FAMA campaign, and the committee hearings with a mixture of harassment, intimidation, and bribery on the shop floor. Flores was relegated to sweeping a warehouse, stolen property was placed in his car in order to frame him, and even Gloria became an object of constant surveillance. Other complainants received discipline or transfers and dropped their cases, while still others were offered promotions in exchange for renouncing the cause and its proponents. Meanwhile, Kelly officials investigated Arnold's complaint. In December, a month after the Advisory Committee hearings, the commanding general at Kelly wrote to Flores to inform him that his complaint lacked merit and would be dismissed.[64]

Arnold appealed the verdict and won a hearing beginning in February 1968. Three FAMA members served as his representatives: Senator Bernal, Father Casso (who also served as vice-chairman of the state Advisory Committee), and attorney Matt Garcia, who led the effort despite having no experience with civil rights litigation. Working pro bono, Garcia dominated the six-week-long hearing, while the presence of Bernal and Casso kept the case newsworthy. Management continued to harass and intimidate Flores, but Arnold documented each instance and brought it to Garcia, who then used the evidence of retaliation to further embarrass base officials. Garcia discredited management's key witness by showing that he had stolen scrap materials from the base. Then, Arnold remembers, "Their whole case broke down." The commanding general personally offered Flores a promotion to end the case, but Arnold saw it through its resolution. Numerous ethnic Mexican complainants won promotions as a result of the case, and several managers faced reprimand, quit, or retired under pressure.[65]

Still, the case's successful conclusion did little to change Arnold's immediate working conditions. He faced ongoing harassment, and Kelly management continued to drag its feet with regard to ending discrimination at the base. A second Texas State Advisory Committee report, published in 1970, noted "some improvement" in promotion procedures and results over the previous two years but added that there remained "much room for improvement in equal employment opportunities at all levels at Kelly AFB."[66]

Already a seasoned civil rights activist and a leader among ethnic Mexican workers at the base, in 1969 Arnold jumped at the opportunity to leave Kelly to work full-time for a local labor union. The organizing department of the Service Employees International Union (SEIU) hoped to revive San Antonio's

Local 84, which had been created in 1937 but by 1968 was nearly dormant. Composed of about thirty members, all head janitors for the San Antonio Independent School District, the union had devolved into what Flores called a "*compadre* club" that also ran a credit union and remained cozy with management (*compadre* can refer to a godfather or tie of fictive kinship, or to a close friend). The union members doubled as officers in the credit union, and they all enjoyed supervisory positions and harmonious relations with the school district as long as they ignored the grievances of rank-and-file employees. The credit union safe sat in a district office, and the leaders refused to lend money to workers who rocked the boat. Membership was stagnant, and monthly meetings were dominated by drinking.[67]

In early 1969 Arnold took the job and began reorganizing the union. Earning a small stipend from the international union, he formed a committee of about ten entry-level janitors whom he paid to recruit new members. Several months later, he presented the union's board meeting with 130 mostly young ethnic Mexican workers ready to be sworn in to the local. The longtime leaders chafed at the influx of new members, but Arnold pointed to his assignment from the international union, and the workers were added to the rolls. At the next annual membership meeting, a group of new, younger members formed a slate to oppose the head janitors of the *compadre* club. The current president, Joe Estrada, called on an old friend, Congressman Henry B. Gonzalez, for support. Gonzalez had proven himself a stalwart supporter of both labor and civil rights, but he advocated gradual change and above all civility. He had disapproved of Flores's discrimination case at Kelly and had feuded with Arnold's mentor, Albert Peña. In front of the membership, Gonzalez branded Flores a "Communist-trained" organizer who had "infiltrated the labor movement." Flores recalls that these tactics proved effective and turned some of the new members against both him and the other insurgent candidates for union office. When the ballots were cast, the members did elect the new leaders, but they also offered Estrada the ceremonial post of "chairman emeritus."[68]

The election validated Flores's approach to both union organizing and electoral politics. Under the new leadership, the union quickly grew to nearly five hundred members. It expanded beyond the San Antonio schools to include the Harlandale and Edgewood districts and added cafeteria workers and bus drivers to its traditional base among janitors. In addition to his local duties, Flores traveled the state organizing new SEIU locals. At the University of Texas at Austin, he won recognition for a bus drivers union led by long-haired white student activists, including a former chairman of the Young Communist League. In Houston, Arnold aided a strike of white and black steelworkers at the Hughes Tool Company. Students at the historically black Texas Southern

University, including local SNCC leaders and an ethnic Mexican law school student from San Antonio, helped Flores persuade the janitors to honor the steelworkers' picket line. Once they got their new contract, the blue-collar workers threatened to strike again in order to support the janitors' bid for recognition of their new SEIU local.[69]

Multiracial collaboration represented a critical component of Flores's labor activism. Throughout the 1960s and 1970s, union organizing brought Arnold into sustained contact with the African American civil rights movement. As early as the late 1940s, Rev. Claude Black Jr. of Mt. Zion First Baptist Church, funeral home director G. J. Sutton, and photographer and publisher Eugene Coleman had led African American residents of San Antonio's Eastside in a sustained offensive against Jim Crow. Like Bernal, Peña, and Flores, these activists demanded immediate social change and did not shy away from engaging in sit-ins, rallies, and other contentious tactics. They too faced opposition from within their own racial group, as many other African American leaders preferred to work for inclusion through cooperation with the conservative Good Government League rather than the liberal Bexar County Democratic Coalition. In 1948 Sutton and company had formed temporary coalitions with the more militant ethnic Mexican civil rights activists, and by the mid-1960s leaders of both groups depended upon one another for support. In 1967, for example, Sutton joined Flores on a picket line outside the Kelly Air Force Base Anniversary Ball. The duo carried signs denouncing "50 Years of Discrimination" at the base. Coleman's *SNAP News* publicized Sutton and Black's civil rights activism directly alongside a front-page column written by Albert Peña. Flores joined all of these men and a wide range of white liberal activists at informal monthly meetings of the "lunch bunch," sessions of planning and coordination that began in the mid-1960s and continued into the twenty-first century.[70]

Arnold drew upon his relationship with African American leaders to build multiracial solidarity within his union. Although ethnic Mexicans constituted the vast majority of the union's membership, Flores had been working with Rev. Black to bring African American workers into the local as well. School district supervisors at times attempted to play the racial groups off of one another, telling ethnic Mexican men that the black janitors wanted to seduce their wives, or vice versa. In other cases, black or brown workers would complain about working under the supervision of a member of the other race. Flores invited Rev. Black to come to monthly membership meetings to urge interracial cooperation, and Black's oratory proved effective at helping the two groups better understand one another as well as their common cause in the union. For example, the newly elected officers of the local initially resisted when Arnold suggested that they create new posts on the board of directors in order to include an African American and a woman. Though they had recently rejected the old *compadre* club, Flores feared, the new officers now stood in danger of replacing it with an equally unrepresentative monocultural clique. Arnold noted that he had no formal power to make demands on the board, but he threatened to resign publicly and denounce the union's bigotry if they did not comply. Rev. Black spoke in support of the measure, and the two then left the meeting. Soon after Flores returned to his house, the new chairman called him and said that they had elected as directors both a black janitor and a white woman cafeteria worker. Arnold continued to work for the union. The San Antonio chapter of the NAACP, of which Rev. Black was an officer, later honored Flores for taking this stand in support of racial inclusion.[71]

Flores sought to create a local that closely resembled a social movement organization like FAMA rather than emulating the heavily bureaucratic and generally unresponsive unions that had surrounded him at Kelly Air Force Base. Local 84's monthly membership meetings represented the critical tool for fostering an activist culture within the union. While most contemporary unions had little rank-and-file participation except in times of strikes, contract negotiations, and other crises, Flores drew upon the community-based organizing of the United Farm Workers, a group he had personally encountered through FAMA beginning in 1966. Using the service centers established by United Farm Workers leaders in California and South Texas as a model, Arnold created classes and recreational programs for women and children. Thus, even if a man did not want to come to the union meeting, his wife and kids would still want to go to their respective activities and would drag the man along with them. The meetings themselves included a diverse set of speakers who reported on the black and Chicano/Chicana civil rights movements as well as political developments and union activities. In addition to Rev. Black, Commissioner Peña, attorney Matt Garcia, Senator Bernal, G. J. Sutton, and other black, white, and ethnic Mexican "lunch bunch" activists would rotate through the agenda. In a given month, Rev. Black might attend to encourage black members to seek common cause with their ethnic Mexican counterparts. Peña would then appear at the following meeting to ask the latter group to support their black co-workers and the larger civil rights struggle. The monthly meetings concluded with tamales, a keg of beer, and a fiesta for the entire family.[72]

Such spadework paid dividends for the union. In December 1970, Flores organized a mass march protesting the school district's decision to end the automatic payroll deduction of dues for union members. The predominantly white San Antonio Central Labor Council rented Flores a small office, but the council rebuffed Local 84 members from assembling in the building's parking lot prior to the demonstration. Flores and the mostly ethnic Mexican union membership instead gathered at a park in the historic King William neighborhood, where Rev. Black, G. J. Sutton, and a group of black schoolchildren joined them. The group marched through downtown and rallied at City Hall. Peña and young Chicano movement activists also attended the march, as did Father Sherrill Smith, a Catholic priest who had formerly coordinated the social justice activities for the San Antonio archdiocese.[73]

While Flores worked to foster multiracial collaboration and social movement style dynamism within Local 84, he also used his post as a staff organizer to offer the union's support for a wide range of ethnic Mexican civil rights activism. He did so by using the personal ties he had forged with movement activists during the previous decade of work in electoral politics and through his complaint at Kelly Air Force Base. In 1968, even before he began working at SEIU, Flores attended the first meeting of the Mexican American Unity Council, a body that coordinated numerous activist efforts in San Antonio. In March 1969, Flores participated in a march of more than three thousand Chicanos/Chicanas in nearby Del Rio in support of the Mexican American Youth Organization (MAYO). Protestors nailed a list of grievances to the Val Verde County courthouse door. The document later became known as the "Del Rio Manifesto," a Chicano/Chicana declaration of independence that reverberated across the country. In late 1969 and early 1970 he traveled to Crystal City to help José Ángel Gutiérrez and MAYO members organize a school boycott and voter mobilization effort. The campaign completed the South Texas agricultural town's transition from all-white political dominance to representation by the majority ethnic Mexican population—a process that Gutiérrez had begun in 1963 with assistance from the Teamsters, PASO, Peña, and Pancho Madrano. Flores later served on the board of the Southwest (now National) Council of La Raza and, in 1974, co-founded the Southwest Voter Registration and Education Project.[74]

Through the union, the "lunch bunch," and this constellation of ethnic Mexican organizations, Arnold helped bridge the gap between his early days in Viva Kennedy and FAMA—the Mexican American generation—and the rising Chicano movement. Such connections ranged from his support for MAYO, the most militant of Chicano/Chicana groups in Texas, to his mentoring and friendship of Willie Velásquez, another young Chicano and MAYO member who directed the staff of first the Unity Council and then Southwest Voter.[75] These multigenerational and multiracial ties are particularly clear in the case of the crisis created when Chicano/Chicana activists staged a series of protests against San Antonio mayor William McAllister. When McAllister questioned the ambition of ethnic Mexicans in a nationally televised interview in June 1970, young Chicano/Chicana organizers called a boycott of the San Antonio Savings Association, a community bank owned by the mayor. At one particularly contentious rally during the conflict, police detained dozens and arrested some thirty pickets, including not only Velásquez and other "young Turks" but also older activists such as Peña, Flores, and their "lunch bunch" collaborator G. J. Sutton, an African American leader. Robert de León, a Texas Southern University law student who had helped Arnold organize janitors at Hughes Tool in Houston, was also arrested.[76]

The city's Chicano movement and Chicano-led unions increasingly overlapped. The first Crystal City coalition in 1963, the farmworkers struggle beginning in 1966, and the demonstrations of 1969 and 1970 all highlighted the growing union between the movement and organized labor. The fusion found its apogee in San Antonio Chicano Organizers (SACO), a body founded by Flores around 1970. SACO created a network of union organizers that allowed members to ask one another for help, whether that meant seeking technical expertise with negotiations or getting assistance with turning out workers to support a particular picket action or rally. It also doubled as a Chicano caucus within the white-dominated San Antonio Central Labor Council. The combined membership of the unions that SACO activists represented—the Service Employees, Amalgamated Meat Cutters, International Union of Electrical Workers (IUE), Amalgamated Clothing Workers, and United Auto Workers—never gave the group an absolute majority of votes at labor council meetings, but their combined numbers did give them sufficient clout to block the two-thirds supermajority vote needed to endorse political candidates. In 1972, Arnold and company wielded this power when SACO threatened to prolong a labor council meeting all night in order to force it to support Peña's bid for reelection. Their tenacity forced the all-white building trade unions to endorse the firebrand Peña, while SACO agreed to the endorsement of a slate of white candidates. By the mid-1970s, SACO served as the key bridge between organized labor and the often youthful leaders of the Chicano movement. If a particular voter registration campaign or protest demonstration needed money or picket signs, Velásquez, Gutiérrez, or other community activists asked a SACO member, who in turn took the request to his fellow union organizers for fulfillment. SACO members also helped advance African American causes both in unions and the community. In 1967, for example, IUE organizer Paul Javior, a SACO activist, recruited Clarence "C. J." Littlefield to serve as the city's first black union president, while in 1975 Franklin García of the Meat

Cutters spoke at rallies with local SNCC activists in the national campaign to free political prisoner Angela Davis.[77]

In 1977, Flores resigned from the union and moved away from San Antonio, temporarily leaving behind the multiracial, working-class activist civil rights struggle that he had helped lead for nearly two decades. Local 84 had grown from 30 to 1,800 members. The "lunch bunch" coalition had elected Rev. Black to the City Council and G. J. Sutton to the post of state representative, although Peña and Bernal both lost their reelection bids in 1972. For his part, Arnold went to Washington, D.C., to join the Carter administration as a special assistant to the commissioner of the U.S. Immigration and Naturalization Service, Leonel Castillo of Houston.[78]

Like Pancho Medrano, Arnold Flores followed an unusual path from the barrio to political prominence. A child of immigrants, Flores sought upward mobility through government service, working in the military and then at Kelly Air Force Base. He developed an interest in politics that eventually led him to challenge the base's systemic employment discrimination. He built ties across occupational and ethnic lines and helped connect FAMA to ethnic Mexican workers and the latter to the labor, Chicano/Chicana, and African American civil rights movements. Like Medrano, Flores aligned himself with community organizers and elected officials that encouraged street protests and other unruly tactics in the name of sweeping social change. He faced opposition from members of his own ethnic group and drew upon a durable coalition with black activists—a collaboration that far exceeded its counterpart in Dallas in terms of size, longevity, and political power.

Arnold's story, like Pancho's, suggests the need to rethink the defining characteristics and cleavages of ethnic Mexican political history. Multiracial alliances, distinctively working-class experiences and grievances, trade unionism, a commitment to confrontational politics and direct action—all of these mattered far more to Flores than did simple generational divides. Instead of making a "Faustian pact with whiteness," Flores helped forge a multiracial coalition that dovetailed seamlessly with all of his activities at the workplace, in organized labor, in electoral politics, and in the Chicano movement. His activism connected several struggles long understood as separate. It brought trade unionism together with the older "Mexican American" campaign for equal rights, the younger "Chicano/Chicana" struggle, and the "long" African American civil rights movement. And he was not alone, either within or beyond his ethnic group. Rather, he joined Albert Peña, Joe Bernal, Rev. Black, G. J. Sutton, and countless others to demand a complete, immediate end to racial discrimination, a complete opening of future economic opportunities, and a significant share of independent political power.

Conclusion

The lives of Pancho Medrano and Arnold Flores may appear exceptional, but their expansive visions and dedication to social change clearly struck a chord among ethnic Mexican workers in Dallas and San Antonio. Leaders like Medrano and Flores by definition had followers. Unfortunately, very few primary sources illuminate the lives of ordinary ethnic Mexican workers during this period. Most surviving union records overlook the rank and file of all races, and workers of color appear only sporadically in the archives—usually on a single piece of correspondence related to a grievance and at time in letters and press coverage during a rare strike. The best available documentary evidence on the day-to-day work of ordinary ethnic Mexican workers centers on the small handful among them who managed to rise up the ranks of their respective unions and eventually land staff jobs as union organizers. While their careers are not statistically representative of the masses they organized, the lives of these workers-turned-organizers offer the clearest—if still not transparent—window into the political perspectives and tendencies of the people they quite literally represented.

By examining the lives of organizers over a protracted period, scholars can at least glimpse the world of the organized. One quickly discovers that Medrano and Flores represent but the most visible tip of a much larger iceberg. Other working-class ethnic Mexican organizers similarly combined labor and civil rights advocacy and worked to build coalitions of black and brown workers across postwar Texas. Many more supported their efforts. And they had their counterparts in the black and white communities. Franklin "Tortillas" García, Mary Salinas, Jaime Martinez, Moses and Erma LeRoy, George and Latane Lambert, and dozens of other ethnic Mexican, African American, and white unionists built multiracial coalitions that similarly blended labor, political, and civil rights activism—as did the many community-based organizers and elected officials who collaborated with them.[79]

If the careers of Medrano and Flores offer any indication, future research into the lives of such organizers will likely uncover a radically different picture of ethnic Mexican activism in the postwar period, one that replaces familiar assumptions of generational teleology and white racial positioning with detailed accounts of the on-the-ground organizing at work and in the community. This more representative group of activists draws attention away from the courtroom and from traditional "Mexican American" leaders and instead focuses it squarely on the barrios, shop floors, union halls, political clubs, and even across the tracks into black working-class communities. After all, these were the places where the vast majority of brown and black people lived, worked, and raised hell—the sites at the very center of the civil rights movements. On-the-ground organizers like Medrano and Flores bridged the gap between "Mexican American" and "Chicano," black and brown, and workplace and community-based activism. In so doing, they connected the so-called race leaders to the people they aspired to represent.

Notes

The author thanks Dr. José Ángel Gutiérrez for his guidance during several informal talks in Arlington, Texas, in the fall of 2008, which included his encouraging me to track down the Medrano family and introducing me to Arnold Flores. Thanks also to Lorena Oropeza, Pedro Castillo, and the audiences at the conferences of the Organization of American Historians in Seattle and Southwest Labor Studies Association in Santa Cruz, who commented on drafts of portions of this chapter. Thanks to my mentors Bill Chafe, Sally Deutsch, Larry Goodwyn, Bob Korstad, Paul Ortiz, and Dana Frank; to my editor, Bob Zieger; and to two new friends who read and critiqued earlier drafts of this essay, Zaragosa Vargas and Carlos Blanton. Thanks to the Graduate School at Duke University for supporting this research, and to my fellow graduate students Gordon Mantler, Jacob Remes, Orion Teal, and Anne-Marie Angelo for their help and support. Thanks to George N. Green for creating the Texas Labor Archives, and to Claire Galloway and all the staff at the Special Collections library at the University of Texas at Arlington for helping me work my way through countless boxes. Thanks also to the archives staff at the Institute of Texan Cultures, University of Texas at San Antonio Libraries Special Collections and the Benson Latin American Collection at the University of Texas, Austin. And thanks especially to the Medranos, Arnold Flores, and other folks in Dallas and San Antonio who sat down and shared their stories with me.

    1. José Ángel Gutiérrez, Oral History Interview with Francisco Medrano, CMAS 37, Special Collections, University of Texas at Arlington Libraries, *Tejano Voices* collection [hereinafter Medrano, interview with Gutiérrez, CMAS 37, TV-UTA], (Dallas, June 27, 1996), 56–58; author's typed field notes on conversation with Ricardo Medrano, Dallas, November 2, 2008; author's interview with Robert Medrano, Dallas, September 24, 2009 (audio recording). On the middle-class Mexican American leadership that included the Martinez family, see Carolyn Barta, "New Brown Leaders Emerge," *Dallas Morning News*, August 19, 1972; and Gilbert Bailon, "Quiet Effort Opened Doors for Hispanics," *Dallas Morning News*, September 15, 1987.

    2. This paragraph draws on my Ph.D. dissertation, "Labor, Civil Rights, and the Struggle for Democracy in Texas, 1935–1975" (Duke University, 2011).

    3. For a summary of the "master narrative" of the black civil rights movement, see the new introduction in Charles M. Payne, *I've Got the Light of Freedom: The Organizing Tradition and the Mississippi Freedom Struggle*, rev. ed. (Berkeley: University of California Press, 2007). Many scholars, including Payne, have since added "local people" to this narrative, often decentering the church-based, middle-class leaders of older studies. For an antiquated overview of the movement, see Aldon D. Morris, *The Origins of the Civil Rights Movement: Black Communities Organizing for Change* (New York: Free Press, 1984). For a new interpretive framework, see Jacquelyn Dowd Hall, "The Long Civil Rights Movement and the Political Uses of the Past," *Journal of American History* 91, no. 4 (2005): 1233–63.

Hall's depiction of the "classical phase," roughly 1954 to 1965, points toward the presence of working-class activists in the "short" civil rights movement, but much research remains to be done.

4. I use "Chicano/Chicana" and "Mexican American" to refer to subgroups of the umbrella "ethnic Mexicans," separating them on the basis of their political philosophies rather than age alone: "Chicano/Chicana" describes those who advocate militant, confrontational politics, while "Mexican American" refers to those who adhere to traditional assumptions of that so-called generation, including tendencies toward assimilation, patriotism, white racial identity, and a rejection of radicalism. I use "black" and "African American" interchangeably, and "white" instead of "Anglo" in all cases (except quotations). I use "Chicano/Chicana" and the plural "Chicanos/Chicanas" to denote the presence of both men and women among this activist cohort. I use the phrase "Chicano movement" without quotation marks only in reference to the scholarly labeling of that particular phase of the struggle, while understanding that the phrase's emphasis on youth and male leaders obscured the contributions of women activists of all ages.

5. Mario T. García, *Mexican Americans: Leadership, Ideology, and Identity, 1930–1960* (New Haven: Yale University Press, 1989). The metaphors of looking southward and northward and the reference to Cinco de Mayo paraphrase the observations of Emma Pérez, *The Decolonial Imaginary: Writing Chicanas into History* (Bloomington: Indiana University Press, 1999), 80. For additional works from the traditional scholarly perspective, see Rodolfo F. Acuña, *Occupied America: A History of Chicanos*, 6th ed. (New York: Longman, 2006); Carlos Muñoz, *Youth, Identity, Power: The Chicano Movement* (London: Verso, 1989); David Montejano, *Anglos and Mexicans in the Making of Texas, 1836–1986* (Austin: University of Texas Press, 1987); Guadalupe San Miguel Jr., *"Let All of Them Take Heed": Mexican Americans and the Campaign for Educational Equality in Texas, 1910–1981* (College Station: Texas A&M University Press, 1987); Guadalupe San Miguel Jr., *Brown, Not White: School Integration and the Chicano Movement in Houston* (College Station: Texas A&M University Press, 2001); and Arnoldo De León, *Ethnicity in the Sunbelt:Mexican Americans in Houston* (College Station: Texas A&M University Press, 2001).

6. M. T. García, *Mexican Americans*; Cynthia Orozco, *No Mexicans, Women, or Dogs Allowed: the Rise of the Mexican American Civil Rights Movement* (Austin: University of Texas Press, 2009); George J. Sánchez, *Becoming Mexican American: Ethnicity, Culture, and Identity in Chicano Los Angeles, 1900–1945* (New York: Oxford University Press, 1993); Muñoz, *Youth, Identity, Power*; Ignacio M. García, *Hector P. García: In Relentless Pursuit of Justice* (Houston: Arte Público Press, 2002); Ignacio M. García, *United We Win: The Rise and Fall of La Raza Unida Party* (Tucson: MASRC, the University of Arizona, 1989); Ignacio M. García, *Chicanismo: The Forging of a Militant Ethos among Mexican Americans* (Tucson: University of Arizona Press, 1997); Ignacio M. García, *Viva Kennedy: Mexican Americans in Search of Camelot* (College Station: Texas A&M University Press, 2000); Ignacio M. García, *White But Not Equal: Mexican Americans, Jury Discrimination, and the Supreme Court* (Tucson: University of Arizona Press, 2009).

7. In addition to the sources cited above, see Benjamin Marquez, *LULAC: The Evolution of a Mexican American Political Organization* (Austin: University of Texas Press, 1993); Craig Allan Kaplowitz, *LULAC, Mexican Americans, and National Policy* (College Station: Texas A&M University Press, 2005); Henry Ramos, *The American GI Forum: In Pursuit of*

the Dream, 1948–1983 (Houston: Arte Público Press, 1998); and Patrick James Carroll, *Felix Longoria's Wake: Bereavement, Racism, and the Rise of Mexican American Activism* (Austin: University of Texas Press, 2003).

8. David Gutiérrez, *Walls and Mirrors: Mexican Americans, Mexican Immigrants, and the Politics of Ethnicity* (Berkeley: University of California Press, 1995).

9. Pérez, *Decolonial Imaginary*, 82. Stephen J. Pitti has also rehabilitated the broad activism of the "Mexican American generation" in and around San Jose, California. Pitti, *The Devil in Silicon Valley: Northern California, Race, and Mexican Americans* (Princeton: Princeton University Press, 2003).

10. Zaragosa Vargas, *Labor Rights Are Civil Rights: Mexican American Workers in Twentieth-Century America* (Princeton: Princeton University Press, 2005); M. T. García, *Mexican Americans*; Sanchez, *Becoming Mexican American*.

11. Cletus E. Daniel, *Chicano Workers and the Politics of Fairness: The FEPC in the Southwest, 1941–1945* (Austin: University of Texas Press, 1991); Emilio Zamora, *Claiming Rights and Righting Wrongs in Texas: Mexican Workers and Job Politics During World War II* (College Station: Texas A&M University Press, 2009).

12. Irene Ledesma, "Unlikely Strikers: Mexican-American Women in Strike Activity in Texas, 1919–1974" (Ph.D. diss., Ohio State University, 1992); Vicki Ruíz, *From Out of the Shadows: Mexican Women in Twentieth-century America* (New York: Oxford University Press, 1998). Also see Mario T. García, *Memories of Chicano History: The Life and Narrative of Bert Corona* (Berkeley: University of California, 1994); Pitti, *Devil in Silicon Valley*.

13. Neil Foley, "Becoming Hispanic: Mexican Americans and the Faustian Pact with Whiteness," in *Reflexiones 1997: New Directions in Mexican American Studies*, ed. Foley (Austin: University of Texas, 1998); Neil Foley, "Straddling the Color Line: The Legal Construction of Hispanic Identity in Texas," in *Not Just Black and White: Historical and Contemporary Perspectives on Immigration, Race, and Ethnicity in the United States*, ed. Nancy Foner and George M. Fredrickson (New York: Russell Sage Foundation, 2004); Neil Foley, "Partly Colored or Other White?: Mexican Americans and Their Problem with the Color Line," in *Beyond Black & White: Race, Ethnicity, and Gender in the U.S. South and Southwest*, ed. Stephanie Cole and Alison M. Parker (College Station: Published for the University of Texas at Arlington by Texas A&M University Press, 2004); Thomas A. Guglielmo, "Fighting for Caucasian Rights: Mexicans, Mexican Americans, and the Transnational Struggle for Civil Rights in World War II Texas," *Journal of American History* 92, no. 4 (2006): 1212–37. See also Brian D. Behnken, "Fighting Their Own Battles: Blacks, Mexican Americans, and Civil Rights in Texas" (Ph.D. diss., University of California, Davis, 2007); Brian D. Behnken, "Elusive Unity: African Americans, Mexican Americans, and Civil Rights in Houston," in *Seeking Inalienable Rights: Texans and Their Quests for Justice*, ed. Debra A. Reid (College Station: Texas A&M University Press, 2009), 123–45.

14. Ariela J. Gross, "'The Caucasian Cloak': Mexican Americans and the Politics of Whiteness in the Twentieth Century Southwest," *Georgetown Law Journal* 95 (2007): 337–92; Ariela J. Gross, "Comment: Texas Mexicans and the Politics of Whiteness," *Law and History Review* 21, no. 1 (2003): 195–205; Steven H. Wilson, "Brown over 'Other White': Mexican Americans' Legal Arguments and Litigation Strategy in School Desegregation Lawsuits," *Law and History Review* 21, no. 1 (2003): 145–94; Ignacio M. García, *White But Not Equal*. Also see Lisa Y. Ramos, "A Class Apart: Mexican Americans, Race, and Civil Rights in Texas" (Ph.D. diss., Columbia University, 2008).

15. Carlos K. Blanton, "George I. Sánchez, Ideology, and Whiteness in the Making of the Mexican American Civil Rights Movement, 1930-1960," *Journal of Southern History* 72, no. 3 (2006): 569-604.

16. An extended version of this biographical sketch can be found in my unpublished conference paper "'A Faustian Pact?': Mexican American Workers and Civil Rights in post-World War II Texas," presented at the Organization of American Historians, Seattle, March 27, 2009. This sketch draws on a wide range of printed sources as well as two principal oral history interviews: George N. Green and Carr Winn, Oral History Interview with Pancho Medrano, Dallas, August 4, 1971, Texas Labor Archives, University of Texas, Arlington [hereinafter TLA-UTA]; and Medrano, interview with Gutiérrez, CMAS 37, TV-UTA. Many of the written sources are housed in the Pancho Medrano Papers, 1946-1971, AR55, TLA-UTA [hereinafter Medrano Papers].

On Pancho's childhood, boxing, and early work history, see Medrano, interview with Green and Winn, TLA-UTA, pp. 1-21; Medrano, interview with Gutiérrez, CMAS 37, TV-UTA, pp. 1-44, 52-53; Tony Castro, "The Medranos: Family of Activists," *Dallas Times Herald*, November 22, 1970, copy in Medrano Papers, Box 1, Folder 8; "Unionists' Reunion—25 Years Ago They Were Barefoot Buddies in Texas," unidentified newspaper, ca. 1968, in Medrano Papers, Box 1, Folder 8; Barta, "New Brown Leaders Emerge"; Sharon Cobler, "Unidad: Family Fights Inside Establishment," *Dallas Morning News*, July 11, 1976; Carol Trujillo, "Dallas' First Barrio-Hispanics Started Out, Struggled in Little Mexico," *Dallas Morning News*, September 13, 1987; Ellen Sweets, "'Everyone Was Scared to Death—and Anyone Who Says They Weren't Is Lying,'" *Dallas Morning News*, March 25, 1990; Rosanna Ruiz, "A Lifetime Struggle for Rights—Champion of Many Causes Was Shaped by Unjust Times," *Fort Worth Star-Telegram*, October 27, 1995; Nora Lopez, "Board Delays Historic Status for Pike Park—Resident Says Racist Past Should be Acknowledged," *Dallas Morning News*, September 8, 1999; Nora Lopez, "Panel to Back Landmark for Pike Park—Questions Answered about Segregated Past," *Dallas Morning News*, September 10, 1999; Joe Simnacher, "Francisco Medrano Sr.: 1920-2002—Political Patriarch Mourned," *Dallas Morning News*, April 5, 2002; *Francisco 'Pancho' Medrano Post Office Building*, HR 4561, 109th Cong., *Congressional Record* 152 (April 5, 2006): H1493-4; "Pancho Walked and Talked Union," *Texas Aerospacer* (United Aerospace Workers Local 848: May, 2002) [in author's possession, courtesy Ricardo Medrano]; Bill Deener, "Hispanic Leaders Debate Ways of Solidifying Power," *Dallas Morning News*, September 17, 1986; Gene Lantz, "Milestones in UAW Local 848 History," *Labor History from Texas*, http://www.labordallas.org/hist/848miles.htm; Gene Lantz, "Dallas, and I, Remember Pancho Medrano," *News for Activists*, http://www.labordallas.org/panch.htm; Gene Lantz, "Pancho Medrano Honored Again," *News for Activists*, http://www.labordallas.org/medr9.htm; "Union Body Names Chief," *Dallas Morning News*, May 17, 1957; list of delegates to Texas AFL-CIO convention proceedings (year unknown), photocopy, in UAW Local 848 Records, 1941-1989 (includes Local 893), unprocessed collection, Accession 91-42, Box 1, TLA-UTA. Also see various campaign posters and leaflets for Pancho's union elections in the Pancho Medrano Papers, Box 1, Folder 3, TLA-UTA.

17. Medrano, interview with Gutiérrez, CMAS 37, TV-UTA, pp. 55, 63-65, 75-76, 81-85, 90-92; author's field notes on Ricardo Medrano, November 2, 2008; Clarence A. Laws, regional director (NAACP), to Glover Pettes of Las Cruces, New Mexico, July 22, 1964,

Medrano Papers, Box 1, Folder 2; Roy Reuther to Ted Hawks, September 24, 1964 (citing a Roy Wilkins letter that vouches for Pancho), Medrano Papers, Box 1, Folder 2; Gillespie C. Wilson, President of Texas Conference of NAACP Branches, to Medrano, April 10, 1969, Medrano Papers, Box 1, Folder 2; "Interest Mounts in Effort to Abolish Poll Tax on November 9th," October 12, 1963, *Dallas Express*, copy inMedrano Papers, Box 1, Folder 8. The article lists "Pancho Medrano, U.A.W. Staff member, and organizer, Labor P.A.S.O." alongside a group of leaders of the predominantly black Texas Council of Voters, including Dallasites A. Maceo Smith and W. J. Durham of the NAACP. Also see Simnacher, "Francisco Medrano Sr."; Bob Ray Sanders, "Activist's Life Was a Fight for Justice," *Fort Worth Star-Telegram*, April 10, 2002; "Medrano Was Force in Dallas—He Was Political, Civil Rights Leader," *San Antonio Express-News* (Associated Press), April 6, 2002; "Congresswoman Johnson to Unveil the Francisco 'Pancho' Medrano Post Office," *Congresswoman Eddie Bernice Johnson (TX 30) Press Release*, http://www.house.gov/list/press/tx30_johnson/102606a.html; *Medrano Post Office Building*, H1493; Castro, "The Medranos"; American G.I. Forum National Convention program (San Diego, 1966), Medrano Papers, Box 1, Folder 1; "Excerpt from a Bulletin Sent Out by the New Mexico Chapter of the American GI Forum," 1965, Medrano Papers, Box 1, Folder 1; "Pancho's Qualifications," Medrano Papers, Box 1, Folder 3. Also see scattered invitations for G.I. Forum and LULAC meetings in Medrano Papers, Box 1, Folder 8; and Michael Phillips, *White Metropolis: Race, Ethnicity, and Religion in Dallas, 1841–2001* (Austin: University of Texas Press, 2006), 129–30; "Trujillo Heads Kennedy Group," *Dallas Morning News*, October 11, 1960.

For general background, see Michael Lowery Gillette, "The NAACP in Texas, 1937–1957" (Ph.D. diss, University of Texas at Austin, 1984); W. Marvin Dulaney, "Whatever Happened to the Civil Rights Movement in Dallas, Texas?" in *Essays on the American Civil Rights Movement*, ed. W. Marvin Dulaney and Kathleen Underwood (College Station: Texas A&M University Press), 66–95; and I. M. García, *Viva Kennedy*.

18. Medrano, interview with Green and Winn, TLA-UTA, pp. 28–29, 31; Medrano, interview with Gutiérrez, CMAS 37, TV-UTA, pp. 48–49; Castro, "The Medranos"; author's field notes on Ricardo Medrano, November 6, 2008. The exact date of Reuther's hiring of Pancho remains unclear. Writing in 1970, Castro states that Pancho joined the international staff in 1962, while in his 1971 interview with Green and Winn, Pancho seems fuzzy on the year of his hiring, switching back and forth between 1963 and 1964. The flyer "Pancho's Qualifications" lists his work as a shop steward and volunteer organizer as late as April 1963. Pancho's participation in the first Crystal City revolt suggests that he began working for Reuther later that month, though it is probable that he initially did so on an ad hoc basis before becoming a permanent staffer. Medrano also served as a Public Information Officer for the state AFL-CIO during the 1963 poll-tax campaign, though it is also unclear whether or not this was a full-time position. See F. F. Pancho Medrano file, Texas AFL-CIO Records, Mexican American Affairs Committee, AR110-7, Box 2, Folder 3, TLA-UTA.

19. Medrano served as an ad hoc organizer prior to his permanent appointment to the UAW staff; he was probably classified as temporary at the time of the March on Washington. Medrano, interview with Green and Winn, TLA-UTA, pp. 29, 38; Medrano, interview with Gutiérrez, CMAS 37, TV-UTA, pp. 67, 69, 71–75, 87–88, 95–96, 121–29, 138; Douglas Domeier, "Torrent of Sympathy Pours Out Here for Dr. King," *Dallas Morning News*, April 6, 1968; "Dallasite among Rights Marchers," n.d.; "Waiting," n.d., both unknown newspaper

clippings, Medrano Papers, Box 1, Folder 8; Sweets, "'Everyone Was Scared to Death'"; "Pancho Walked and Talked Union"; "Congresswoman Johnson to Unveil . . ."; Sanders, "Activist's Life Was a Fight for Justice"; Jim Lane, "Civil Rights Legend Pancho Medrano Honored," *People's Weekly World*, http://www.pww.org/article/articleprint/10139; Thalia I. Longoria, "Escuela lleva nombre de activista hispano—Nombran escuela del DISD en honor a latino que luchó junto a César Chávez y Martin Luther King Jr.," *El Día*, December 8, 2008; "UAW Representative Medrano Deplores Violent Tactics of Los Angeles County Sheriff," press release from UAW-CAP, September 2, 1970, Medrano Papers, Box 1, Folder 8; photographs and clippings in Medrano Papers, Box 2, Folders 4 and 6; Castro, "The Medranos." On the Moratorium and Salazar, see Lorena Oropeza, *"Raza Si! Guerra No!": Chicano Protest and Patriotism during the Viet Nam War Era* (Berkeley: University of California Press, 2005).

20. See note 16 on Pancho's childhood and experiences of discrimination on the shop floor. On the experience of African American workers at North American Aviation (later renamed Temco, then LTV, and now Chance-Vought), see author's typed field notes on UAW 848 Black Retirees, Grand Prairie, November 13, 2008; and Davis West, Clarence Barrett, Larond Daniels, Roosevelt Love, Douglas Smith, oral history group interview with author and Joseph Abel, Dallas, November 20, 2008 (audio recording); "Transcript of Tape on 'History of Local 645' Made by Jack Anderson in 1994," collected and transcribed by Gene Lantz, UAW Local 848 Records, 1937–1994 (includes Locals 645 and 390), unprocessed collection, Accession 95-66, Box 1, TLA-UTA; e-mail from Gene Lantz to author, November 2, 2008; Lantz, "Milestones in UAW Local 848 History"; author's typed field notes on conversation with Gene Lantz, Dallas, November 12, 2008; and *Medrano Post Office Building*, H1493.

21. Author's typed field notes on conversation with Ricardo Medrano, Dallas, November 2, 2008; author's typed field notes on UAW 848 Black Retirees, November 13, 2008; West et al., oral history group interview with author and Abel; e-mail from Gene Lantz to author, November 2, 2008; author's notes on conversation with Gene Lantz, November 12, 2008; "Vice President Johnson Lauds Employees," *LTV News*, December 21, 1962, copy in UAW Local 848 (893) Records, 91-42, Box 1 (features a photograph of black worker Fulton Plouche meeting LBJ); G. L. Bearden to George F. Dull, July 24, 1964, UAW Local 848 (893) Records, 91-42, Box 1 (cites grievance concerning black shop steward M. C. Shelton); Texas State Advisory Committee to the U.S. Commission on Civil Rights, *Civil Rights in Texas* (Washington, D.C.: Government Printing Office, 1970), 30–31.

22. Nova Howard to H. A. Moon, February 7, 1969, UAW Local 848 (893) Records, 91-42, Box 6. This letter is unusual in that nothing like it survives in this collection. This copy likely exists because Pancho turned the letter into a pamphlet and distributed it on the floor of a UAW convention. Author's notes on conversation with Lantz, November 12, 2008.

23. Medrano, interview with Gutiérrez, CMAS 37, TV-UTA, pp. 92–93; Medrano, interview with Green and Winn, TLA-UTA, p. 33. Carlos Conde, "Poll Tax Campaign Launched," *Dallas Morning News*, December 21, 1964; *Medrano Post Office Building*, H1493. Governor Anne Richards gained some of her earliest political experience in 1958 stuffing envelopes for the Young Democrats at Dallas NAACP headquarters, along with her friend Pancho Medrano. Wayne Slater, "'Let Me Tell You about Mama,'" *Dallas Morning News*, November 5, 1989. On Pancho's role in the Progressive Voters League, see Emmet Whitman

to Whom It May Concern, January 4, 1964, Medrano Papers, Box 1, Folder 2. On Ralph Yarborough's senatorial campaign, see William D. Bonilla, National President of LULAC, to Walter Reuther, September 16, 1964, Medrano Papers, Box 1, Folder 2. See also untitled clipping from *El Sol de Texas*, December 12, 1970, Medrano Papers, Box 1, Folder 8. On New Mexico, see U.S. Senator Joe Montoya to Medrano, November 17, 1965, Medrano Papers, Box 1, Folder 2; "Excerpt from a Bulletin"; and Laws to Pettes, July 22, 1964.

24. Medrano, interview with Green and Winn, TLA-UTA, pp. 32, 34–35; Medrano, interview with Gutiérrez, CMAS 37, TV-UTA, pp. 74, 100–102, 139; Cobler, "Unidad"; Lawrence Goodwyn, "Los Cinco Candidatos," *Texas Observer*, April 18, 1963, 3–9. See also John S. Shockley, *Chicano Revolt in a Texas Town* (South Bend, Ind.: University of Notre Dame Press, 1974); Armando Navarro, *Mexican American Youth Organization: Avant-garde of the Chicano Movement in Texas* (Austin: University of Texas Press, 1995); José Ángel Gutiérrez, *The Making of a Chicano Militant: Lessons from Cristal* (Madison: University of Wisconsin Press, 1998); Armando Navarro, *The Cristal Experiment: A Chicano Struggle for Community Control* (Madison: University of Wisconsin Press, 1998).

25. Medrano, interview with Gutiérrez, CMAS 37, TV-UTA, pp. 67–68, 102–21; Medrano, interview with Green and Winn, TLA-UTA, pp. 37–44, 49–51, 62–99; "Mexican-American Farm Workers in Texas March for Minimum Wage," *Region 5 UAW News*, September 1966, p. 1, Medrano Papers, Box 1, Folder 1; Paul Schrade to Medrano in Rio Grande City, telegram, June 2 [1967], Medrano Papers, Box 1, Folder 2; "Sons of Zapata," leaflet, 1967, Medrano Papers, Box 2, Folder 2; "The Union Fights On in Texas," *El Malcriado*, June 10, 1968, 10, Medrano Papers, Box 2, Folder 2; Richard Medrano, "Pancho Medrano," leaflet, May 29, 1967, Medrano Papers, Box 2, Folder 2. Also see Castro, "The Medranos"; Cobler, "Unidad"; Sweets, "'Everyone Was Scared to Death'"; Ruiz, "A Lifetime Struggle for Rights"; "Medrano Was Force in Dallas"; *Medrano Post Office Building*, H1493; "Congresswoman Johnson to Unveil . . ."; Lantz, "Dallas, and I, Remember Pancho Medrano"; and the clippings files in Medrano Papers, Box 2, Folders 3–5.

On the participation of the Southern Christian Leadership Conference, see Behnken, "Fighting Their Own Battles," 224–25, citing reports from the *Texas Observer*, September 2 and 16, 1966.

The best secondary study of the United Farm Workers is Margaret Eleanor Rose, "Women in the United Farm Workers: A Study of Chicana and Mexicana Participation in a Labor Union, 1950–1980" (Ph.D. diss., UCLA, 1988). On the Texas campaign, see, for example, Mary Margaret McAllen Amberson, "'Better to Die on Our Feet Than to Live on Our Knees': United Farm Workers and Strikes in the Lower Rio Grande Valley," *Journal of South Texas* 20, no. 1 (2007): 56–103.

26. The characterization of Pancho as a "diplomat" comes from the author's interview with Gilbert Padilla, Fresno, California, October 12, 2009 (audio recording). Both Padilla and campaign co-coordinator Bill Chandler suggested that Pancho did not do much spadework in this campaign, but he always popped up when he was needed and offered his assistance, charisma, and UAW funds whenever he was in town. Author's interview with William Chandler, Jackson, Mississippi, February 15, 2010 (audio recording).

27. *Medrano v. Allee*, Case No. 67-B-36, 347 F. Supp. 605; *Allee v. Medrano*, 416 U.S. 802 (U.S. Supreme Court, 1974); U.S. Senate, Committee on Labor and Public Welfare, "Migratory Labor Legislation Hearings before the Subcommittee on Migratory Labor," Rio

Grande City, Texas, June 29, 1967 (Washington, D.C.: Government Printing Office, 1967), part 2 (pp. 337–700a). Chandler says that the UFWOC leaders asked Pancho to serve as lead plaintiff in order to ensure ongoing support from Reuther and the UAW (Chandler interview). Also see note 24; Robert M. Utley, *Lone Star Lawmen: The Second Century of the Texas Rangers* (New York: Oxford University Press, 2007), 242–47; "Pancho Walked and Talked Union"; Simnacher, "Francisco Medrano Sr."; and reports in the *Dallas Morning News*, May 28, 30, June 1, 9, 11, 30, August 13, 1967, and June 13, 14, 1968. Former attorney general and U.S. senator Robert F. "Bobby" Kennedy became an outspoken supporter of the farmworker cause during his 1968 presidential campaign, but he did not serve on the Labor Committee with his brother Ted, and I have not found any evidence that he came into contact with the UFWOC in Texas.

28. This spatial history is difficult to reconstruct, since urban renewal has destroyed much of the Medranos' neighborhood. The house at 2346 Douglas Street sits between Harry Hines Boulevard (a multi-lane expressway) and Interstate 35-E. See note 16 on Pancho's childhood and relocation to the edge of Oak Lawn. Contemporary newspaper reports confirm both the upward mobility that the move signified for the Medranos and the gradual transition of the neighborhood into barrio. See, for example, "Unionists' Reunion—25 Years Ago They Were Barefoot Buddies in Texas," unidentified newspaper, ca. 1968, in Medrano Papers, Box 1, Folder 8; and Castro, "The Medranos." Also see Robert Medrano, interview by author.

29. Ricardo Medrano, interview by author, Dallas, September 23, 2009 (audio recording); Pauline Medrano, interview by author, Dallas, September 25, 2009 (audio recording); Robert Medrano, interview by author. On Mrs. Medrano, also see Dallas Independent School District, "Esperanza 'Hope' Medrano Elementary School Dedication Ceremony" program, May 20, 2000, and "Esperanza Medrano," *Dallas Morning News*, May 8, 1983, clipping, both in author's possession, courtesy Ricardo Medrano. Landín printed numerous pamphlets for Medrano, including "Pancho's Qualifications" and the bulletin on the UFWOC: "Pancho Medrano," letter from Richard Medrano, Mission Texas, May 29, 1967, in Medrano Papers, Box 2, Folder 2; Ricardo Medrano interview.

30. Author's oral history interviews with Ricardo Medrano (September 23, 2009), Robert Medrano (September 24, 2009), and Pauline Medrano (September 25, 2009); Castro, "The Medranos"; Lantz, "Dallas, and I, Remember Pancho Medrano" and "Pancho Medrano Honored Again."

31. "Latins, Blacks Hold Vigil for Rodriguez," *Dallas Morning News*, March 7, 1971; Dave McNeely, "Rep. Moreno Visits Dallas to Ponder Rodriguez Case," *Dallas Morning News*, March 12, 1971; Marilyn Schwartz, "3,000 'Help' Rodriguezes," *Dallas Morning News*, March 15, 1971; Merikaye Presley, "Probe Asked for Lawmen in E. Dallas," *Dallas Morning News*, March 17, 1971; Terry Kliewer, "Rodriguez Rally: Protesters March in Shrine Parade," *Dallas Morning News*, March 21, 1971; Barta, "New Brown Leaders Emerge"; telegram from Rudolfo Corky Gonzales to Thomas y Berta Rodriguez, care Pancho Medrano, March 17, 1971, Medrano Papers, Box 1, Folder 2; U.S. Senator Birch Bayh to Medrano, March 16, 1971, Bayh to Attorney General John Mitchell, March 15, 1971, and Congressman Bob Eckhardt to Señor y Señora Tomas Rodriguez, March 12, 1971, all in Medrano Papers, Box 1, Folder 2. Also see the large files of clippings in Box 1, Folders 5–7, including Lupe Elizondo, "Black

Monday Slayings in Dallas," *Papel Chicano*, n.d. [February 1971], in Folder 6. Shirley Achor, *Mexican Americans in a Dallas Barrio* (Tucson: University of Arizona Press, 1978), 106–8.

32. See note 17 on Medrano's history of close contact with black civil rights organizations in Dallas; author's field notes on Ricardo Medrano, November 2, 2008; author's interview with Robert Medrano, September 24, 2009; voice memo on author's phone call with Al Lipscomb, September 23, 2009. On black grievances regarding police brutality, see, for example, the statements of Fred L. Bell in Pedro Vasquez, "Raza Rallies against Repression," *Papel Chicano*, n.d. [March–April, 1971], 8, copy in Medrano Papers, Box 1, Folder 7.

33. Ricardo Medrano, interview by author; Robert Medrano, interview by author; "Brown Berets," *Dallas–Fort Worth Chicano*, June 17–24, 1971, 5, copy in Medrano Papers, Box 1, Folder 7. Pancho also reached out to students, including white antiwar organizers at Southern Methodist University. See "Draft, Vietnam, Police Hit by Student Group at SMU," *Dallas Times Herald*, March 18, 1971, clipping in Medrano Papers, Box 1, Folder 6. Prodded by Medrano, Senator Birch Bayh of Indiana sent a letter of sympathy to the Rodríguez family immediately after the incident and asked Attorney General John Mitchell to launch a full investigation of police brutality in Dallas. Congressman Earle Cabell of Dallas responded by denouncing Bayh for seeking publicity in advance of his 1972 presidential campaign. See Bayh to Medrano, March 16, 1971, Bayh to Mitchell, March 15, 1971, and Eckhardt to Señor y Señora Tomas Rodriguez, March 12, 1971—all in Medrano Papers, Box 1, Folder 2; and McNeely, "Rep. Moreno Visits Dallas"; Presley, "Probe Asked for Lawmen in E. Dallas"; "El Senador Bayh Pide Investigacion: Sobre el Trato Policial Que Aterroriza a Mexicanos," *El Sol de Texas*, March 19, 1971, 1; and Margaret Mayer, "Cabell Says Bayh Seeking Publicity," *Dallas Morning News*, undated clipping—all in Medrano Papers, Box 1, Folder 6.

34. An exception to this trend was the reporting in *El Sol de Texas*, which highlighted the Medranos' role on the front page alongside its first reports of the shooting. Pancho and his family paid the $2,000 bond (an exorbitant sum at the time) to free Tomás from police custody. "La Familia Medrano Deposita Fianza," *El Sol de Texas*, February 26, 1971, 1, clipping in Medrano Papers, Box 1, Folder 6.

35. "Latins, Blacks Hold Vigil for Rodriguez" (first quotation); Vasquez, "Raza Rallies against Repression," 8. Frances Arredondo of the Mexican-American Progressive Association and Pete Martinez of Barrios Unidos (United Neighborhoods) are listed as co-organizers along with Pancho.

36. Vasquez, "Raza Rallies against Repression," 9.

37. "Mas de 3 Mil Chicanos en La Cena a Beneficio de la Familia Rodriguez," *El Sol de Texas*, March 19, 1971, 1, in Medrano Papers, Box 1, Folder 6; "They came from everywhere," the author in *El Sol* adds, "from poor families, from the middle class, and yes, even rich families, nearly 4,000 people." Blacks and whites also attended the dinner, but it was dominated by this cross-class ethnic Mexican mobilization. Organizers planned to set the minimum donation at $1.25 each. "MAPA Organiza Cena a Beneficio Flia. Rodriguez," *El Sol de Texas*, March 5, 1971, 1, in Medrano Papers, Box 1, Folder 6. Also see Schwartz, "3,000 'Help' Rodriguezes." All sources credit the Mexican-American Progressive Association and Robert Arredondo with organizing this dinner, though Pancho Medrano also spoke at the event.

38. Johnson led the local chapter of King's Southern Christian Leadership Conference. Quotation in Vasquez, "Raza Rallies against Repression," 9; Kliewer, "Rodriguez Rally."

39. "El 6 de Marzo: Chicanos, Anglos, Y Negros Protestaran" and photograph "Tres Colores de Piel Diferente en Defensa de Una Misma Causa . . . La Justicia," *El Sol de Texas*, March 5, 1971, 1, copy in Medrano Papers, Box 1, Folder 6.

40. "Lest We Forget . . . ," photo by Phil Garcia, *Dallas–Fort Worth Chicano*, June 17–24, 1971, 5, copy in Medrano Papers, Box 1, Folder 7.

41. "Chicanos y Negros Preparan Fuerte Boicot," *El Sol de Texas*, March 19, 1971, 1, copy in Medrano Papers, Box 1, Folder 6.

42. "Dallas y Ft. Worth Se Unen a Una Gran Marcha de Protesta Este Sábado," *El Sol de Texas*, March 26, 1971, 1, copy in Medrano Papers, Box 1, Folder 7; Vasquez, "Raza Rallies against Repression"; copy of clipping on "Rep. Moreno" with handwritten note reading "Ya Basta Vote 'No' to All C.C.A. Candidates. April 6 Tuesday. Vote Vote Vote," Medrano Papers, Box 1, Folder 5. The CCA is the Citizens Charter Association, a nominally nonpartisan slating body controlled by white elites that dominated city politics until the late 1970s. See Phillips, *White Metropolis*.

43. Outrage over police brutality against ethnic Mexicans reached a new peak when a police officer playing Russian roulette in a squad car shot and killed twelve-year-old Santos Rodríguez (no relation to Tomás) in 1973. The multiracial dimension of the protests in the wake of this episode have yet to be explored. See Achor, *Mexican Americans in a Dallas Barrio*. It is already clear from my preliminary research that Rev. Peter Johnson was intimately involved in the Santos protests as well. Author's interview with Rev. Peter Johnson, Dallas, February 23–24, 2010.

44. Author's field notes on Ricardo Medrano, November 2, 2008; author's oral history interviews in with Ricardo Medrano (September 23, 2009) and Robert Medrano (September 24, 2009).

45. Phillips, *White Metropolis*, 161; Ricardo Medrano interview with author, September 23, 2009, file 2, 23:30; Robert Medrano interview with author, September 24, 2009, file 3, 24:15; author's interview with Johnson.

46. Ricardo Medrano interview with author, September 23, 2009, file 2, 23:30; Robert Medrano interview with author, September 24, 2009, file 3, 24:15; voice memo on author's phone call with Al Lipscomb, September 23, 2009. NAACP youth organizer Juanita Craft, who had instructed the Medrano children in the youth group, was the first African American woman elected to the council when she won her seat in 1975. Phillips, *White Metropolis*, 168–69.

47. Castro, "The Medranos"; Barta, "New Brown Leaders Emerge"; Cobler, "Unidad"; Deener, "Hispanic Leaders Debate Ways of Solidifying Power"; Ruiz, "A Lifetime Struggle for Rights"; Sanders, "Activist's Life Was a Fight for Justice"; Simnacher, "Francisco Medrano Sr."; author's field notes on Ricardo Medrano, November 6, 2008.

48. Author's interview with Pauline Medrano, September 25, 2009. The one ethnic Mexican who was elected without the support of the Citizens' Charter Association was Pete Martinez (no relation to the El Fenix owner). On March 2, 2010, Adam's brother (and Pancho's grandson) Carlos Medrano won an election to serve as justice of the peace, marking the arrival of yet another Medrano to public office. In the late 1980s the Medranos lost a series of elections and were accused of widespread voter fraud. No charges were ever filed against the family, but nearly two decades passed before another Medrano ran for elected office. See, for example, Richard Connelly, "Medrano Says Loss Won't End

Activity—Family to Repair Political Machine," *Dallas Morning News*, April 20, 1987; Henry Tatum, "Fall of the Medrano Family," *Dallas Morning News*, June 1, 1988; and Mark Edgar and Carol Trujillo, "Vote Fraud Targeted in Medranos' District," *Dallas Morning News*, June 15, 1988; Gromer Jeffers Jr., "Medrano Political Tree," *Dallas Morning News*, March 28, 2006.

49. "Mexican Shirley Temple Turns Off Chicanos," *Dallas–Fort Worth Chicano*, June 17–24, 1971, 3, copy in Medrano Papers, Box 1, Folder 7; José Ángel Gutiérrez, "Oral History Interview with Anita Martinez," CMAS 129, *Tejano Voices*, TV-UTA, Dallas, June 10, 1999. Mexican American conservatism represented one branch of another, separate multiracial political coalition, one in which white elites offered various forms of patronage to black and brown "race leaders" in exchange for their electoral and cultural support. One type of patronage, used sparingly in Dallas but more frequently in San Antonio, was the symbolic and material benefits associated with inclusion on elite slates of candidates for local office. Martinez was nominated by the Citizens' Charter Association.

50. The same can be said of California activist Bert Corona. M. T. García, *Memories of Chicano History*.

51. Author's oral history interview with Arnold Flores, San Antonio, October 18, 2008, file 1, 0:00–17:35, and file 2, 11:05–15:45; author's oral history interview with Arnold Flores, San Antonio, March 11, 2010 (audio recording).

52. Flores interview, 2008, file 1, 30:20, 1:12:00; Flores interview, 2010; Rodolfo Rosales, *The Illusion of Inclusion: The Untold Political Story of San Antonio* (Austin: University of Texas Press, 2000).

53. Flores interview, 2008, file 2, 11:05–19:10.

54. Ibid., file 1, 19:10–21:45; "Discrimination Hearing of Mr. Arnold Flores," transcript, pp. 592–99, Boxes 91 and 92, Joe J. Bernal Papers, Benson Latin American Collection, University of Texas Libraries, University of Texas at Austin.

55. "Discrimination Hearing" transcript, 602–3.

56. Ibid., 603–6.

57. Ibid., 609–15, 945–46; Flores interview, 2008, file 1, 23:40; Howard G. Nickles, Special Grand Lodge Representative, International Association of Machinists and Aerospace Workers, and Arnold Flores to Grievance Examiner, December 13, 1966, appended to "Discrimination Hearing" transcript as Complainant's Exhibit 6.

58. "Discrimination Hearing" transcript, 629–32.

59. Flores interview, 2008, file 1, 33:00–36:55; author's interview with Arnold Flores, San Antonio, September 1, 2009, file 1, 2:10–6:05; FAMA advertisement in *Inferno*, October 5, 1967, copy in author's possession, courtesy Arnold Flores.

60. Flores interview, 2008, file 1, 23:40; Texas State Advisory Committee to the U.S. Commission on Civil Rights, "Employment Practices at Kelly Air Force Base, San Antonio, Texas," June 1968, reporting on hearings held November 7 and 8, 1967.

61. "Discrimination Hearing" transcript, 632–33, 950–51.

62. Flores interview, 2008, file 1, 21:45–24:20, 25:15–26:10; "Complaint of Discrimination in the Federal Government, as amended from original CSC Form 894," September 11, 1967, appended to "Discrimination Hearing" transcript as Examiner Exhibit 1. For a good summary of the myriad issues involved, see Garcia's closing argument, beginning on 945.

63. Texas State Advisory Committee, "Employment Practices at Kelly Air Force Base, San Antonio, Texas"; Flores interview, 2008, file 1, 26:10–29:30.

64. Flores interview, 2008, file 1, 30:20–32:20, 41:10, 50:15; Major General Frank E. Rouse, USAF, to Arnold Flores, December 18, 1967, Subject—Summary of Investigation–Complaint of Racial Discrimination, appended to "Discrimination Hearing" transcript as Examiner Exhibit 2.

65. Flores interview, 2008, file 1, quotation at 48:00, 29:30–30:20, 37:25–48:55, 51:25–54:50, and 1:09:20; Arnold Flores to Frank E. Rouse, December 26, 1967, RE: Request for Hearing, appended to "Discrimination Hearing" transcript as Examiners Exhibit 3.

66. Texas State Advisory Committee to the U.S. Commission on Civil Rights, *Civil Rights in Texas* (Washington, D.C.: U.S. Government Printing Office, 1970), 27–28.

67. Flores interview, 2008, file 1, 1:02:05–1:04:50, quotation at 1:03:45; author's interview with Arnold Flores, San Antonio, September 9, 2009, file 1, 30:15. I have not yet been able to verify all of Arnold's claims about his work in the union using SEIU records, but I have quizzed him on many of the details and cleared up murky areas through a series of four interviews over a period of nearly two years. His claims on other subjects (including the case, the Chicano movement, the "lunch bunch," and SACO) have all been corroborated in other oral and/or written sources, so I believe he is a reasonably credible source.

68. Flores interview, 2008, file 1, 1:19:25 to end, quotation at 1:21:50; Flores interview, September 1, 2009, file 2, 25:40–28:05.

69. Flores interview, 2008, file 2, 29:15–34:50, 44:30–49:50; author's interview with Robert de León, San Antonio, September 3, 2009.

70. Flores interview, 2008, file 2, 1:17:50 to end and file 3; copy of clipping, *Inferno*, October 5, 1967, featuring a photograph of Flores and Sutton at Kelly AFB with caption, in author's possession; author's interview with Rev. Claude William Black Jr., San Antonio, October 27, 2008; author's interview with Eugene Coleman, San Antonio, September 2, 2009; Rev. Claude W. Black Jr. with Taj I. Matthews, *Grandpa Was a Preacher: A Letter to My Grandson* (Bloomington, Ind.: Authorhouse, 2006). A vast but incomplete run of *SNAP News* can be found within the San Antonio Black History Collection, 1873–1996, MS 139, University of Texas at San Antonio Libraries Special Collections.

Sutton won a single term on the community college board in 1948, while his counterpart Gus Garcia won a term on the school board. See Leonard B. Murphy, "Sutton, Garlington Jerome," *Handbook of Texas Online*, http://www.tshaonline.org/handbook/online/articles/SS/fsu11.html; author's interview with Charles Andrews and Jeffrey Sutton, San Antonio, September 8, 2009; author's interview with Oliver Sutton Jr., Seguin, Texas, March 11, 2010. Charles Andrews and Oliver Sutton Jr. are two of G. J.'s nephews; Jeffrey Sutton is one of his daughters.

Robert A. Goldberg, "Racial Change on the Southern Periphery: The Case of San Antonio, Texas, 1960–1965," *Journal of Southern History* 49, no. 3 (1983): 349–74, still serves as the authoritative scholarly work on the poorly studied San Antonio black civil rights movement. He accurately divides the black community's leadership into "traditional" and activist camps, but he downplays the activities of the latter. Further, his concept of the "southern periphery" fails to explain the persistence of Jim Crow in the city as well as the militant resistance to it.

71. Flores interview, 2008, file 2, 25:30–29:15, 38:05–41:30, and especially 56:25; Flores interview, September 9, 2009, file 1, 57:45–1:03:35. Rev. Black did not speak specifically of

this incident in his 2008 interview with the author, and he has since passed away. Still, his reverence for Flores was obvious when we met. See author's interview with Black.

72. Flores interview, 2008, file 2, 25:30–28:20, 51:25. On the United Farm Workers generally, see Rose, "Women in the United Farm Workers." On Texas, see author's interviews with Gil Padilla and Bill Chandler.

73. Flores interview, 2008, file 2, 34:50–38:05; Flores interview, September 1, 2009, file 2, 19:40–21:40; "Sherrill Smith Returns to Help March," undated clipping, probably December 1970, in author's possession (courtesy of Arnold Flores).

74. Flores interview, 2008, file 1, 1:12:00–1:17:10; Flores interview, September 1, 2009, file 1, 1:23:10. Flores's friendship and collaboration with Peña as well as his service on various boards of directors can be verified in the correspondence and clipping files housed in the Albert A. Peña Jr. Papers, MS 37, University of Texas at San Antonio Libraries Special Collections. Also see José Ángel Gutiérrez's forthcoming biography, *Albert Peña, Jr.: Dean Emeritus of Chicano Politics* (Texas A&M University Press). On Crystal City and Del Rio, see I. M. García, *United We Win*; Navarro, *Mexican American Youth Organization*; and Navarro, *The Cristal Experiment*.

75. Flores interview, 2008, file 2, 23:30–25:30. For more on Velásquez, see Juan Sepulveda, *The Life and Times of Willie Velásquez: Su Voto es su Voz* (Houston: Arte Público Press, 2003).

76. Flores interview, 2008, file 2, 59:15; clippings in Peña Papers, Box 9, Folder 4; clippings in Bernal Papers, Box 98; author's interview with Coleman; Rosie Castro, interview by author, San Antonio, September 8, 2009. According to my 2010 Flores interview, the police initially detained many more people than the thirty-one who were officially booked. Arnold was surprised to learn recently that he was not officially booked and that therefore no record exists of his arrest in court or newspaper records.

77. Flores interview, 2008, file 2, 57:55–1:17:50, and file 3, 6:40; Flores interview, September 1, 2009, file 1, 38:40–46:35, 57:15, 1:10:05; Flores interview, September 9, 2009, 1:03:35; photograph of SACO members with Senator Ralph Yarborough, n.d., in author's possession; copy of open letter motion from SACO to San Antonio labor council, March 23, 1972, in author's possession; letter to Joe Hernandez signed by SACO members, n.d., p. 2 (in author's possession); author's interview with Paul Javior, San Antonio, September 4, 2009, esp. 37:15; author's interview with Roy Hernandez, San Antonio, September 8, 2009; author's interview with Jaime Martinez, San Antonio, March 10, 2010; author's interview with C. J. Littlefield, San Antonio, September 2, 2009. The informal group became the model for the national AFL-CIO when it created the Labor Council for Latin American Advancement, and Flores served on the national body's board. See "A New Awakening," n.d. [1975], and "Franklin Garcia (Left) Talks to LCLAA Committee," 1975, both in author's possession. On the Angela Davis rally, see Mario Marcel Salas Papers, 1968–2009, MS 142, University of Texas at San Antonio Libraries Special Collections, Box 15.

78. Author's interview with Bernal; Murphy, "Sutton, Garlington Jerome"; Goldberg, "Racial Change on the Southern Periphery"; author's interview with Black; Castro, interview by the author; Flores interview, file 2, 5:35 and 1:17:10 and file 3, 7:55; Office of the City Controller, "Office History Page," http://www.houstontx.gov/controller/section3.html.

79. For more information on these individuals, see Krochmal, "Labor, Civil Rights, and the Struggle for Democracy in Texas." The story of Moses and Erma LeRoy and other

black organizers also highlights the continued vibrancy of working-class African American activism in the postwar period, demonstrating that the rise of repression during the cold war and the subsequent decline of the Communist Party did not entirely destroy efforts to build "civil rights unionism" (author's conference paper on the LeRoys, "Black Texans and the Struggle for Jobs and Freedom, 1945–1970," Southern Historical Association, Charlotte, North Carolina, November 7, 2010). For the significance of this intervention and a summary of "civil rights unionism" during the Great Depression and World War II, see Hall, "Long Civil Rights Movement."

6

"Slaves of the State" Revolt

Southern Prison Labor and a Prison-Made Civil Rights Movement,
1945–1980

ROBERT T. CHASE

At daybreak on October 4, 1978, the inmates of the Ellis prison, situated in the heart of the cotton-growing region of East Texas, shuffled out of their prison cells for another grueling day of hard labor in which most prison guards expected fit inmates to pick between two hundred and three hundred pounds of cotton. As the inmates worked the field in racially segregated rows of African American, white, and Mexican American lines, a prison guard high rider, what inmates referred to as the "cap'ain," sat perched above them on his horse, with a .30 caliber rifle clutched in his hands and his face shaded from the sun by the broad rim of his Stetson. On this particular day, however, nine inmates refused to work and sat down in a coordinated work strike. Despite the guards' sharp barks and insistent demands that the inmates return to work, the inmates remained steadfast, and by midafternoon their example was followed by 408 other inmates. As news of the work strike spread across the prison system, the prisons at Coffield, Ellis, Clemens, Darrington, Eastham, and Ramsey I and II also erupted into disturbances and work strikes throughout the next week.

On Tuesday, October 10, the work strike escalated when fifteen hundred inmates at the Coffield prison barricaded themselves inside their cell blocks. They used blankets to tie their cell doors open and barricaded the openings to the cell blocks with mattresses, while also smashing benches, glass panes, mops, and brooms to make a series of lances with which they formed a defensive phalanx. In response, the Texas Department of Corrections (TDC) decided to storm the building, first using tear gas, then sending in corrections officers to quell the uprising. By the end of the week, the work stoppage and prison uprising occurred on six of the prison system's fifteen units and involved nearly fifteen hundred convicts, approximately 15 percent of the

Figure 6.1. Heavily guarded work details were an integral part of Texas's postwar incarceration regime. These inmates are picking cotton at the Ramsey Prison, Rosharon, Texas, October 1965. (Bruce Jackson photo.)

twenty-nine thousand total inmate population, leaving thirty-four prisoners and eighteen guards injured.[1]

In the 1970s, prison administrators became increasingly alarmed over a series of nationwide prison revolts that were inspired by the prisoners' rights movement, but seen by many in the press and cast by "law and order" politicians as examples of lawlessness and violent criminality. Parallel to the urban riots of the 1960s, a second wave of prison rebellions broke out in the late 1960s and early 1970s.[2] There were five prison riots in 1967; fifteen in 1968; twenty-seven in 1970; thirty-seven in 1971; and forty-eight in 1972, the most prison riots in any single year in American history. The September 1971 Attica, New York, prison riot, in particular, alarmed the nation's prison managers as nearly thirteen hundred of the prison's approximately twenty-two hundred prisoners revolted and seized control of the prison, taking thirty-nine correction officers hostage for over four days. The Attica affair ended in a bloody state police assault ordered by Governor Nelson Rockefeller that resulted in thirty-nine deaths, including those of twenty-nine inmates and ten correctional officers and civilians. As the state-appointed commission noted in 1972, the "state police assault which ended the four-day prison uprising was the bloodiest one-day encounter between Americans since the Civil War."[3] In Texas, the prison work strike of 1978 caused great consternation and concern, as the Texas prison system had never experienced a prison uprising on the scale of Attica. Robert DeLong, general counsel for TDC, admitted just that as he observed, with no small measure of trepidation, how the strike moved across the prison system. "Never before in the history of TDC has there been a work stoppage that spread to more than one unit," he warned. "We don't want to have another Attica or anything of that sort in Texas if it can be helped."[4]

The Texas work strike, however, drew upon the lessons and heartache of Attica by orchestrating a nonviolent and interracial sit-down strike to gain public attention and support for a class-action lawsuit against the Texas prison system. Butch Mendez, one of the first nine inmates who started the strike, wrote to state senator Chet Brooks and explained how the work strike unfolded: "On Oct 4th eight comrades and myself threw off our cotton sacks while out in the cotton fields and told the overseer that we refused to work. All of us nine quit at the same moment, for the same reason, which was to show our support for the brothers in court (David [Ruíz] vs. Estelle). . . . The following day (the 5th) as men were on their way to work some 148 just sat down and refused to go to work. Chicanos, blacks, whites! It was a united front to show support for the trial."[5]

First filed in 1972, *Ruíz v. Estelle* was the culmination of nearly a decade of struggle between keeper and kept. It was a massive omnibus lawsuit that demanded that Texas outlaw the practice of having inmates act as guards, and ordered the state to alleviate prison overcrowding, improve inmate health care, and grant inmates access to attorneys and legal representation. Central to the case, however, was the southern practice of dividing its prison labor between those inmates who worked in the field and a group of select inmates who served the prison administration as convict guards, known as trustees or building tenders. Texas followed a southern tradition of openly arming these "trustees" and allowing them almost total control of the prison. In Arkansas and Mississippi, such inmates were "trusty shooters" who oversaw field work and ensured that no inmate attempted escape.[6] In Texas, however, the official prison guards oversaw inmate field labor, and the building tenders maintained oversight of the cell block and the internal prison society, where they enforced a rigid racial hierarchy that privileged white inmates. This practice continued from the era of nineteenth-century convict leasing through the mid-1980s. The building tender system was a hierarchical labor regime that constituted a vicious sex trade in which building tenders were given the tacit approval from the prison administration to use their power to rape other inmates and engage in the buying and selling of inmate bodies as a sexual commodity that signified cultural standing and societal power. The *Ruíz* trial over the state use of such abusive convict guards subsequently became the largest and longest civil rights trial in the history of American jurisprudence, convening in October

1978 and adjourning in late-December 1980 when Judge William Wayne Justice ruled in favor of the prisoners and declared the Texas prison system unconstitutional. At the heart of the *Ruíz* case, then, was a struggle over how the prison system divided its prison labor between privileged enforcers and the regular inmates.

Those who have studied the legal implications of federal intervention into state prisons have done so largely from the vantage point of the judicial system, civil rights attorneys, and the prison administration, but rarely from the vantage point of the inmate activists. In this vein, Malcolm Feeley and Edwin Rubin's groundbreaking study on court-ordered prison reform concluded that the "prisoner petitions were probably no more of an influence on the pattern of decisions than the Supreme Court or Congress. It was the federal courts themselves that not only initiated the prison reform movement but established its specific contours."[7] Little attention is paid to the prisoners themselves or to their claim that a divided prison labor regime encouraged sexual violence and physical abuse. This absence mutes the voice of the prisoners and their claims against the prison labor regime even as these critics castigate federal court-ordered intervention as an unwanted and disastrous intrusion into state management. Historians, meanwhile, have shown how a massive wave of incarceration in the late nineteenth century ultimately recast the American South as it imperiled Reconstruction, contributed to the development of Jim Crow, assured the near-absolute control of the South by an all-white Democratic party, and served as a coerced catalyst of economic growth and modernization for the New South.[8] Yet historians of the twentieth century have only begun to uncover the historical development of prison systems and to explain how the nation's late-twentieth-century reliance on imprisonment has fundamentally reshaped the nation and turned the gains of the civil rights revolution into an age of racial disparity for a generation of African Americans who are imprisoned at historically unprecedented rates.[9] Recent and groundbreaking work on the first half of the twentieth century has begun to consider the relationship between the criminal justice system and persisting patterns of racial inequality, but the linkages between the prisoners' rights movement, the Black Power movement, and the civil rights legacy during the second half of the twentieth century are only beginning to come to light.[10] When historians have considered the prisoners' rights movement, they have dismissed it as a "naïve casting of prisoners as society's potential leaders" and as "one of the fatal mistakes leading to the demise of radical politics" in the world outside of prison.[11]

Returning the focus to the inmates themselves and chronicling the prisoners' rights movement through the lens of civil rights and labor protest situates the legal, political, and social struggle over prison in the broader framework of civil rights, black and brown power movements, and the labor movement. This essay, then, offers a two-part story of Texas prison labor that reveals the success of the labor regime, on the one hand, and mounting prisoner resistance, on the other. It considers how the Texas prison system managed to maintain its high external reputation for so long in the face of the internal reality, and how that reputation collapsed when inmates, inspired by the civil rights movement, revolted. In Texas, inmates housed in a racially segregated and antagonistic labor regime joined together to create an interracial alliance that drew important lessons from the violence of the 1971 Attica rebellion and the shooting of the "Soledad Brothers," particularly its leader, George Jackson, in California's Soledad prison. When seen in this light, the Texas court case and most other prisoner litigation cases reveal how inmates waged a public-relations campaign to challenge the model of southern prison order, efficiency, and cost-effectiveness by offering a counter narrative that southern prison labor and life was instead the living legacy of antebellum slavery and racial violence.

Crown Jewel of Corrections: The Rise of Texas Prisons and the Control Penology Labor Regime

The Texas prison system drew on a slave heritage where inmates labored on large agricultural prison farms that were once slave plantations. The prison administration divided and organized these prison farms through racial segregation. Only white prisoners were considered eligible for industrial jobs and for placement in the prison's flagship Huntsville institution, the "Walls." Black and Chicano prisoners, meanwhile, got the worst conditions, finding themselves posted to harsh cotton and sugar farms along the Gulf Coast. Throughout the postwar period, the TDC had twelve prisons dispersed around a two-hundred-mile radius of Huntsville, the prison system's headquarters, which was sixty-five miles north of Houston, where prisons lined the banks of the Brazos and Trinity Rivers. Agricultural work dominated the lives of inmates, as they toiled six days a week and ten-hour days in the fields of East Texas where they grew the area's produce, picked the cash crop of cotton, and cleared the land through logging.

In the aftermath of World War II, penologists and state politicians invariably dismissed the Texas prison farm system as backward and as the "worst prison system in the nation."[12] Wartime and the draft caused a precipitous drop in prison population, the number declining from 7,000 in 1939 to a wartime low of 3,394 inmates in 1944.[13] Although the prison population dropped to less than half its previous size, the wartime production demands remained high. War recruitment and the draw of wartime industries also resulted in a high turnover rate for guards and prison staff. Guards worked twelve-hour days for wages that were low in comparison with those for military and industrial work, usually between $100 and $130 a month.[14] A demoralized guard force increasingly brutalized inmates as the prison system demanded more labor out of fewer convicts. Throughout the 1940s, Texas prisons experienced an increase in escapes, inmate violence, work stoppages, and self-mutilations whereby inmates slashed their Achilles tendons in order to avoid harsh prison labor. This act of desperation and defiance was euphemistically known as "heel stringing."[15] Moreover, the prison system was inefficient and costly, so much so that its 1944 annual report showed a net loss of $1,500,675, amounting to a loss for the year of $436 for every inmate.[16]

Yet after the war, despite its prisons' national reputation as the "worst in the nation," Texas embarked on the nation's most ambitious reform program in an effort to replace its notorious plantation/prison farm system with an efficient, business-oriented agricultural enterprise system. The state's $4.2 million outlay in 1948 for a prison overhaul reform program was the nation's largest single appropriation for the reorganization of a prison system, with the exception of the reorganization of the Federal Prison System in 1930. When this new system was fully operational in the 1960s, Texas garnered plaudits as a pioneering, modern, efficient, and business-oriented Sun Belt state. Texas prisons went from what one newspaper termed the "worst in the nation" and "a modern version of the Black Hole of Calcutta" that was "the source of shame and disgrace to the Lone Star State," to what Austin MacCormick, the nation's leading post–World War II penologist, called "the best in the nation" and the "national prison yardstick."[17] The "national prison yardstick" that measured Texas prisons against other systems used a metric that considered work, order, control, productivity, economic self-sufficiency, and low-cost government as the indicators of good prison management. These were the key elements that comprised "control penology," the guiding philosophy of Texas prison management.

By emphasizing prison labor and work, Texas reenergized the southern tradition of prison labor, which convict leasing had stained.[18] Between the 1870s and World War II, contract labor came under increasing levels of legislative scrutiny, which culminated during the New Deal with the labor movement's successful lobbying effort to restrict the profitability of contract prison labor.[19] Congressional passage of the Hawes-Cooper Act of 1929, the Ashurst-Sumners Act of 1935, and the Sumners-Ashurst Act of 1940 made interstate commerce in prison-made goods illegal. Most states, including Texas, also prohibited the sale of prison-made goods. Where prison labor existed, it was largely focused on public works and was paid by state funds. Between 1932 and 1940 the implementation of these acts caused prison labor to decline nationwide, as the number of prisoners productively employed decreased from 52 percent of the nation's total prison population in 1932 to 44 percent in 1940. The value of that labor, moreover, experienced a precipitous decline of 25 percent, from $75 million in 1932 to $57 million in 1940, even as the total number of prisoners nationwide increased from 158,947 in 1932 to 191,776 in 1940.[20] Prisons outside the South, in particular, turned increasingly to therapeutic rehabilitation over labor, and adopted such practices as probation, parole, psychiatry, group therapy, secondary and college education, "bibliotherapy," and social work, and emphasized sports, television viewing, radio listening, and other pastimes. Indeed, during the postwar era, California even sought to encourage civic activity, employing inmates in forestry and firefighting duties.[21] But southern states were wedded to productive agricultural prison labor, and while state and federal laws forbade the sale of prison-made goods, there was no prohibition on prison labor geared toward the prison system's own self-sufficiency or for state use. Thus, by 1940 southern prisons still employed 60 percent of their total inmate population, while northeastern prison states employed only 31 percent of theirs.[22] In contrast, on Texas prison farms rehabilitative and recreational programs were virtually nonexistent as prison labor continued to order the lives of its prisoners.

There, prisoners labored under strict supervision and a tightly managed work regime that included using inmates to oversee and discipline their fellow prisoners. Inmates worked from "can see to can't see" or, as they ominously noted, from "can shoot to can't shoot." They rose at 5:00 to 5:30 a.m. for breakfast, which generally finished by 5:45 a.m., and assembled to work in the fields by 7:00 a.m. The workday was a full ten hours and lasted until late afternoon, when they returned to the building for supper. While in the field, inmates worked in squads, or "lines," that were segregated by race. The order, regimentation, and production demands of prison labor were shared by all prisoners, regardless of race. The prison administration selected a pair of veteran prisoners, known as the tail and lead row, to keep the line moving rapidly and maintain high production levels. The lead row, usually a man of some stamina who moved quickly through the field, would lead the line constantly forward by doing his work at a rapid pace. The tail row, meanwhile, would also be a fast worker and he would press the line from its rear so that those in the middle, known as "the swing," would never have a chance to fall behind or slow the line. An armed guard on horseback watched over the prisoners, while an inmate called the "striker," one of "the biggest and roughest guys in the squad," ensured that other prisoners continued working and did not fall behind.[23] When the line produced too little, it was the line leaders who would answer to the field major. These line leaders, in turn, exacted their own brand of inmate discipline when production quotas remained unmet. Inmate Lawrence Pope described the tail/lead row as "enforcers. Like in—under slavery, they had the drivers . . . and their job was to whip the other slaves into working harder and faster . . . the tail row and lead row out in the field . . . had no whips, but if you did not go fast enough to satisfy them, they had a perfect authority to go back and jump on you right in the field with the officer looking on, and it was condoned."[24]

Field labor was a particularly difficult and unfamiliar adjustment for the increasing number of inmates who hailed from urban areas. In 1940 the state population was 45 percent urban and 55 percent rural, but by 1980 the urban population had grown to 80 percent and rural population dwindled to 20 percent.[25] Convictions in the postwar period were therefore increasingly drawn from urban populations. By 1970, for instance, the inmate population of 14,000 was overwhelmingly composed of former urban dwellers, with the urban areas of Harris County (Houston) and Dallas County alone accounting for 2,536 of the total 3,904 of new inmates.[26] Most of these men were young, ill-educated, and lacked job skills.[27] Former Houston resident and African American inmate Arthur Johnson recalled with shock his first visit to Texas prison fields in 1962, at the age of nineteen, for a conviction of burglary: "You know, I had never seen no cotton in my life. . . . But if the officer told you he wanted two hundred pounds of cotton at the end of the day you had to get two hundred pounds of cotton, or they was going to whip you."[28]

A key tenet of the Texas prison system's labor regime and "control penology" was to work the newly arrived inmates in the field and use the system of "promotions" to building and indoor factory work as incentives for hard labor. From 1948 to 1978 more than half of the prison population labored in prison fields. But inmates who worked hard, remained obedient, and showed willingness to do the bidding of prison officers might earn a "promotion" to an inside job. Jack Kyle, warden of the Ferguson prison for youthful offenders, recalled that the promotion system was "absolutely foolproof" because "the men that came to prison, they're going to the field and go to work. And from outside, you're going to have the opportunity get a job inside." But, to do so, inmates had to "please the officers."[29] If an inmate disrespected the guards' authority, the prisoner could be kept in the field indefinitely. Bobby Mudd spent ten of his thirty years of incarceration working in the field, labor that he called "the purest form of slavery existing in this country today." Many inmates employed images of enslavement and coarse racial language and epithets to describe the field labor experience. "The [field] line is not considered a job," Mudd continued. "It has historically been used as a form of reprisal for misconduct or, for the newly arrived, it was used to condition you. Not physically, but mentally. Borrowing from slave terms, inmates working in the line are 'field niggers.' Once they feel they have you conditioned then you're given a job—many times in factories—and then you become a 'house nigger.'"[30] In the minds of many white inmates, the rigors of prison labor and the debasement of prison life made their experience one of enslavement that they viewed as decoupled from race. Their use of coarse racial language applied equally to all inmates, regardless of skin color, also shows how many Anglo inmates perceived their imprisonment as a loss of white privilege.[31]

Work also drove classification and an inmate's placement on one farm or the next. Displacement and reassignment therefore replaced the bat and the rubber hose as Texas's disciplinary tools. "A system of promotion and demotion could be cycled," explained O. B. Ellis, the prison system's director in the 1940s and 1950s. "In other words, if a prisoner is in Class 1, assigned to Huntsville with a good job and then made a mistake or was indifferent to his job assignment, he would be demoted to a farm unit and a boy on a farm unit who had built a good record could be promoted to his place. The same thing would be true at Central. A man who did not appreciate his job and who not do a good job would be demoted to Ramsey and a man from Ramsey promoted to take his place."[32] To implement his program, Ellis devised in 1948 a "point incentive program" (PIP), which graded all inmates on work, conduct, attitude, and participation in the various prison programs. Prison administrators required a score of 80 to qualify an inmate for parole or for a trustee position. In the 1960s and 1970s the PIP program proved a potent tool, and sometimes a weapon, in the prison system's struggle with rebellious inmates. Moreover, instead of relying on a formal parole board, Texas employed an early release classification system that was administered exclusively by prison officials. Under this "good time" law, inmates earned additional time taken away from their sentence for every day they labored on the basis of four levels of classification that prison officials could manipulate and change at will.[33] Indeed, Dr. George Beto, prison director of TDC from 1961 to 1971, admitted just how important the "liberal good time law" was in their effort to control the prisoners and ensure high production levels. "The most important commodity to a convict is time," Beto pointed out. "And he can build up this time—we can take it away from him and we can also restore it. It makes an excellent lever or motivation device for us."[34] Inmates who refused to work, participated in a work strike, or undertook any other form of collective action faced charges of "mutiny" or "aggravation to mutiny," which could result in a month or more in solitary confinement and the permanent loss of "good time." Thus, the price of collective organization was an inmate's potential freedom. Work performance therefore determined where inmates lived, how they were categorized, and whether or not they were favored.

As prison systems outside the South experienced cost overruns owing to expensive rehabilitative programs and the decline of prison labor, Texas prison administrators could point to a nearly self-sufficient and extremely low-cost record. In 1951 the average daily cost of maintaining a prisoner in forty-four states was $2.23 and $3.59 in federal prisons, while the cost per an inmate in Texas was a very low 49 cents.[35] Through the late 1970s, the low-cost prison remained a steady feature.[36] In 1978, the year of the Texas work strikes and *Ruíz* case, the state of Texas spent only $47 million to hold 23,614 prisoners, far less than what New York and California spent on 18,000 and 20,000 inmates, respectively. New York's prison system costs were $218 million and the California prison system spent $269 million, a sum five times that of Texas.[37] Moreover, Texas was one of only seven states that did not pay its inmates for their labor; it also maintained the nation's lowest inmate-to-guard ratio at twelve inmates to one guard, whereas the national average was three to one.[38]

In recognition of such cost-effectiveness and order, the penological establishment heralded Texas as a leader in prison management and a model for southern prison reform. E. R. Cass, general secretary of the American Prison Association, for instance, suggested in a letter dated July 6, 1953, to Alabama governor Gordon Persons that Texas was a model for prison improvement. Cass noted that the Texas system had gone from being "justly condemned" and a "vicious prison system" to a "very remarkable change for the better." Cass also wrote a congratulatory note to Texas governor Allan Shivers that the state prison system "had been raised from the gutter to a level of respectability." Cass saw such progress as occurring not just state-by-state but as a regional movement across the South in which Texas was the leader. "One by one the southern states are moving forward in prison affairs. Louisiana is on the march; so is Georgia; and I am sure you want Alabama to do likewise."[39] When Lewis Fudge, the senior planner for California's Department of Corrections, visited the Texas prison system in 1973 and 1976 as part of an effort to reduce California's mounting prison costs, he concluded that comparing Texas to other state systems was "like comparing the General Motors Corp with a local department of welfare."[40] Indeed, a 1978 *Corrections Magazine* featured article called the Texas prison system "the greatest system in the nation" and designated its sitting and past directors as "the crown prince and archduke of American corrections."[41]

The claims that Texas made for productive correctional management applied to a wider vision of a modernized and resurgent American South. In

1964, when George Beto addressed the members of the Southern States Prison Association, he articulated the role of the prison in the South's resurgence. Beto's ire had been provoked when a "distinguished and revered penologist" had claimed that "South of the Mason-Dixon line, there are no corrections." Beto countered, however, that "corrections in the South have entered a new day." He pleaded with southern prison administrators to "to hold your heads high, to rid yourselves of the feeling of inferiority which has in the past characterized Southern corrections and accept with pardonable pride the work you are doing—for the future of American corrections belongs to you and your colleagues." He closed with the rousing promise of southern redemption and that the South's vision for prison labor would ultimately shape the nation. "I have a college boy son who on occasion facetiously states, 'The South will rise again,'" Beto concluded. "As far as corrections are concerned, the boy is wrong; the South has risen."[42] The South had indeed risen, and its dominance of prison management set a standard of expansive and cost-efficient state power that the nation was soon to follow.

The Texas prison system, however, built its public reputation of economic success on an internal, informal, and hidden prison economy. While penologists, politicians, and much of the public heralded the state's prison system as a harbinger of modernity, the internal prison society bristled under the authoritarian grasp of a brutal and violent prison regime. The key to the Texas brand of "control penology" was thus not simply the prison system's economy but the way in which the prison administration ordered, controlled, disciplined, and worked the internal prison society and the hidden inmate economy. The Texas prison state depended on an internal government of prisoners who ruled over their fellow inmates. The prison system divided the inmate population between those who worked in the field and those who worked in the building. Those who worked in the building were known as building tenders. The building tender system was a hierarchical, almost feudal, regime of violence and domination in which inmates owed allegiances to other more powerful inmates who, in turn, owed fealty to prison guards and officers. The Texas prison system relied on a closely knit nearly all-white guard structure with kin networks drawn from the local community. Its wardens and guards divided inmate society by race and ruled it with inmate "snitches" and specially selected building tenders who served the prison administration as security forces. Building tenders acted as guards, enforcers, spies, and turnkeys. They engaged in routine beating and maiming of other inmates, practices known euphemistically as "tune-ups" or "head strumming." In return for their service, the prison administration gave building tenders almost total control of the prison wing, along with certain privileges. These included early release from their sentence; freedom of movement and keys to the various prison wings; being armed with knives, hammers, and bats; and private cells in vastly overcrowded facilities. Authorities allowed favored inmates to "run a store," which in prison argot meant that building tenders used their private cells to stock commissary items that they resold to other inmates at loan-shark barter prices. Perhaps most disturbing was a system of sexual domination, in which authorities looked the other way when building tenders raped other inmates or selected what they derisively called a "punk" for a longer-term relationship from the administrative wing where homosexual inmates were segregated.[43]

The comprehensive power and reach of the building tender system was central to the prison's productive labor regime. As prison director Beto explained, building tenders received as a reward far more "good time" than other inmates, which was the greatest privilege and labor motivation that incarceration could ever offer. "The law allows us to make certain men what is known as state approved trustees, which does not mean that we place confidence in them, it means because of their willingness to behave themselves in the type of work that they do—we can give them 30 extra days a month and they can knock off 60 days for every 30 they serve. And in an operation such as ours—where we are geared to production, this device is extremely important."[44]

Building tenders drew their ranks from a racially segregated prison society, in which members of any of the three major racial classifications—"Blacks," "Whites," "Mexicans"—could become a building tender. White inmates, however, ruled the hierarchical building tender system, as white inmates typically served as the prison's "head building tender," an inmate whose comprehensive power and influence within prison society was derived from his close working relationship with a prison administrator, usually a warden, assistant warden, or a prison major. Moreover, most inmate bookkeepers and office administrators, who in some instances were allowed to move inmates from one cell or wing to another, were white. At whatever prison warden Carl Luther "Beartracks" McAdams oversaw, for example, he always brought with him as the head building tender white inmate Robert Barber. Indeed, in 1971, when McAdams retired after thirty years of service to TDC, Barber was released from prison soon after. Lawrence Pope, an inmate activist who did his time under McAdams, reported that Barber "was Beartracks' right-hand man." Pope recalled that Barber "actually ran that unit" and that "he could himself fire just an ordinary officer . . . just tell 'em 'Pack your shit and git, I don't want you on this farm.' And this he had the authority to do, Bear Tracks backed him up 100%. And he was a psychotic killer type, and he had been into all kinds of brutality."[45] Carl Robbins, a white prisoner at Ellis who was housed across from Barber's cell, remembered how Barber's brutality was aimed against

African Americans in a kind of prison-made white terror: "He'd come in at night, bloody, I mean just bloody, he would change his clothes in the cell. 'What'dya been doin'?' [Robbins would ask and Barber responded] 'I been whipping niggers all night, All night!'"[46]

The external success of Texas prison management was rooted in a divided system of prison labor. Inmates acted as guards and maintained inmate control at low cost while also enforcing rigid racial hierarchies and white privilege behind prison bars. The price of this building tender system, however, was the welfare and humanity of the prisoners themselves. Exposing this system of hidden abuse began with the growing resistance of a group of inmates who taught themselves the law and confronted the Texas prison system in the courts.

Writ Writers and Jailhouse Attorneys: The Evolution of a Prison-Made Civil Rights Movement

The prisoners' rights movement in Texas started with a single inmate, Fred Cruz, who, during his eleven-year incarceration from 1961 to 1972, became an avid student of the law, mastering legal precedents, rules, and procedures. His reputation among other inmates, particularly among Mexican Americans and Black Muslims, became such that other inmates sought him out to help them work on appeals. Texas prisoners who acted as their own attorneys wrote appeals and writs of habeas corpus that sought court-ordered intervention to seek relief from what they argued was an unjust and illegal detention. Among fellow inmates Cruz was known as a "writ writer," but among the prison administrators he was simply called an "agitator."

Cruz's legal challenge to TDC was part of a major shift in American criminal law. Prior to the 1960s, the law considered inmates "slaves of the state," and courts at the state and federal level maintained a "hands-off" doctrine of nonintervention that denied inmates' right to turn to the courts to seek legal redress for their captivity or for the conditions of their confinement.[47] Extending civil rights to prisoners became a national issue in 1964 when the U.S. Supreme Court ruled that a Black Muslim prisoner in Illinois named Thomas X. Cooper could not be barred from having access to the Koran. The case, *Cooper v. Pate*, found that prisoners could challenge the practices of prison officials in federal court. The *Cooper* decision ignited a nationwide civil rights movement for prisoners, doing for prisoner rights what *Brown vs. Board of Education* had done ten years earlier for education and civil rights. Within a decade, Supreme Court Justice Bryon White had struck down the legal silence imposed on "slaves of the state" when he declared in the 1974 prisoners' rights case *Wolff v. McDonnell* that "there is no iron curtain drawn between the Constitution and the prisons of this country."[48] In the aftermath of *Cooper v. Pate* the number of prisoner rights suits dramatically increased, from 218 in 1966 to almost 18,500 in 1984.[49] Federal court intervention overwhelmingly occurred in southern state prison systems and elsewhere in the Sun Belt. From 1965 to 1995, federal courts found eight of the eleven states of the American South as having unconstitutional prison systems and ordered those state systems into federal receivership.[50] Only four of the thirty-nine states outside of the South, however, have been subject to a similar intervention from the federal courts.[51] On the heels of successful civil rights campaigns to end Jim Crow, the gaze of court intervention was thus fixed on prison abuse in the American South.

Inspired by the Supreme Court's recognition of prisoners' rights, Cruz concluded that Texas was ripe for a civil rights revolution of its own. He soon decided that making contact with people on the outside was essential if he was to have any hope of pressing his own claims against TDC. After repeated mailing attempts that were often thwarted by TDC's efforts to read and restrict inmate correspondence, in 1966 Cruz managed to contact Frances T. Freeman Jalet, a white attorney who worked for the federal Office of Economic Opportunity. After investigating the prison system, Jalet brought in William Bennett Turner of the NAACP's Legal Defense Fund, and together they challenged TDC in the court. From 1968 to 1974 a prison-made civil rights movement evolved in Texas prisons among a small cadre of "writ writers" who joined with Jalet and Turner to confront TDC in the courtroom. During this period, Jalet filed lawsuits in collaboration with these inmate "writ writers" centered on demands for religious freedom, complaints of physical and sexual abuse stemming from the divided prison labor system, denial of access to the courts, and the condition of solitary confinement.

TDC equated Cruz and Jalet's legal activities with what they saw as a dangerous lawlessness that was threatening the nation's prison system. The day of the 1971 state police assault at Attica prison, Texas prison director George Beto was speaking before the national governors' conference at San Juan, Puerto Rico. Calling the Attica revolt a "tragic and horrible example of the convict-run institution," Beto associated the New York uprising with his growing anxiety over Cruz's dissension and Jalet's legal efforts. Unlike other states, Texas experienced no prison riots and maintained near absolute control over its prison population. The occasional "work buck" in Texas was quickly put down, usually through enforced violence, and such work strikes never spread beyond any single prison and never included more than a handful of inmates during any given incident. Attica and the shooting and subsequent death of California inmate George Jackson on August 21, 1971, were foremost in the minds of Texas prison managers in the fall of 1971. Jackson had been incarcerated in California's prison system since 1961, where he developed a leftist political philosophy and advocated black political awakening behind prison bars. On January 16, 1970, the state of California charged that Jackson, along with fellow inmates Fleeta Drumgo and John Clutchette, had murdered guard John V. Mills in retaliation for guard O. G. Miller's alleged murder of three black inmates. The state held the trio of suspects in Soledad's maximum-security cell bock, and the case received nationwide attention as the press soon dubbed the three inmates the "Soledad Brothers." Confined in a solitary cell for twenty-three hours a day, Jackson used the time to write in 1971 the popular collection of his prison letters *Soledad Brother,* which earned him even greater notoriety. His death on August 21, 1971, during an alleged escape attempt brought further national attention to prison radicalism.[52] The state of California defended Jackson's killing by claiming that inmate Jackson's attorney, Stephen Bingham, had smuggled a pistol concealed in a tape recorder into the prison and gave it to Jackson. Bingham was later acquitted from having played any part in the San Quentin escape attempt. Administrators elsewhere, including Beto in Texas, used the Bingham case to warn the courts that "the seeds of unrest exist in every penal institution, and are being compounded by a few lawyers—some financed by federal anti-poverty funds—who make prison administration more difficult by stirring up malcontents behind the walls." Indeed, as Jalet pressed her inquiries into the prison violence, the prison system responded to the 1971 incidents of Attica and the "Soledad Brothers" by collecting her clients onto a single unit as a means to isolate them. The collection of "writ writers" was designated "Eight Hoe Squad" for their field line number, and it contained all twenty-seven of Jalet's inmate clients. They lived and worked together from November 1971 through October 1972, sowing the field in the day and sowing dissension at night.

"Eight Hoe" was unique in that it housed black, white, and Latino inmates together in an otherwise racially segregated prison system. The racial animosity that TDC hoped to foster within "Eight Hoe" never materialized. Instead the new living arrangement opened up previously closed avenues for interracial cooperation. Together these inmates made common cause with other prisoners across the Texas prison system, particularly with such African American activists as Eddie James Ward held at the Ramsey prison, the former defense minister of an Austin-based black power organization, and Ernest Marion McMillan, a former Morehouse student, civil rights veteran, and co-founder of the Student Nonviolent Coordinating Committee–Dallas (SNCC). With outside help from Jalet, these inmates taught themselves how to confront TDC in the courtroom, and they made it their goal to bring the internal prison economy to public attention. Beginning in the early 1970s, four major class-action lawsuits emanated from "Eight Hoe": *Lamar vs. Coffield*, challenging Texas's rigid system of racial segregation of inmates and charging that TDC practiced discriminatory hiring practices for its guards; *Guajardo v. McAdams*, challenging TDC's right to open an inmate's legal correspondence; *Corpus and Sellars v. Estelle*, demanding the right of prisoners to serve as their own legal counsel, thus eliminating the "jailhouse lawyer" prohibition; and, most importantly, *Ruíz vs. Estelle*.[53]

One of the prisoners who alerted the public to the ways in which the divided labor system resulted in savage treatment of inmates was civil rights veteran Ernest McMillan. Born in 1945 in one of Texas's oldest black communities in North Dallas, McMillan hailed from a middle-class home; his paternal grandfather, Dr. W. R. McMillan, was a well-known member of the local community. What captured Ernest McMillan's attention, however, was the racial inequality he saw all around him during his youth. In 1962, during his senior year at Booker T. Washington High School, McMillan joined the NAACP Youth Council and became active in local organizing. When he graduated from high school, he followed his father to Georgia and enrolled in Morehouse College. While there McMillan became increasingly disenchanted with the NAACP because he found its level of protest to be "mediocre," "lukewarm," and "ho-hum." He later complained that the NAACP idea of protest was to "dress up in your tie, go down to the movie theater, stand in line, ask for a ticket, they would refuse to give it to you, you'd go back to the end of the line and come back up again. That was the extent of protest for desegregating the movie theater, for example."[54]

McMillan found more direct and more vocal forms of protest in SNCC, which, he observed, "was about organizing grassroots people and helping them to build their own structures and being a part of the community with them, and helping them realize their goals which may be, you know, freedom schools or voter registration and elected officials." At the age of eighteen he became a SNCC field secretary and served as a community organizer for voter registration in Georgia, canvassing the more rural parts of the state. McMillan faced mounting racial violence and direct white resistance. "You had shootouts," he recalled, "people chasing you, running you off the road, shooting up houses, injuring people, beating people up in demonstrations, arresting you if you had your shirt tail out." When a friend and SNCC co-worker was killed in Mississippi, McMillan began to embrace Black Power as a more effective means to self-determination, because "there was no other adequate response to address murders and false imprisonment and bombings and Ku Klux Klan activities."[55]

In an effort to link civil rights to economic inequality, McMillan organized an economic boycott of the white-owned OK supermarket in Dallas. McMillan and SNCC charged that the white-owned store was "ghetto gouging" and that it routinely profiteered from the local black community by marking up prices and selling spoiled produce and meat. In response, McMillan and Matthew Johnson, another SNCC activist, held a demonstration against the store in which they told their fellow thirty to fifty demonstrators to fill their shopping chart with food and then walk out of the store. Some other items, such as eggs and a single milk bottle in McMillan's case, were intentionally smashed and broken, causing more than two hundred dollars' worth of damages to store merchandise. The state charged McMillan and Johnson as leaders of the demonstration and found them guilty of destruction of private property over the value of fifty dollars, which was a felony offense with a normal sentence of two to twenty years, for which the state gave McMillan a ten-year sentence.[56]

McMillan's conviction brought a veteran organizer and a political prisoner to the prison system. It did not take long before McMillan rose to challenge its harsh labor regime. On June 17, 1973, TDC ordered prisoners at the Retrieve prison to harvest a crop of nearly rotten sweet corn, even though it was Sunday and Father's Day. Retrieve was part of the alluvial swath of land outside of Houston where its majority African American prison population harvested the cash crops of corn and sugar. When McMillan and ten other inmates refused to work, they were told to file down a gauntlet of officers. McMillan recalled, "we started hearing them [TDC guards] start hollering and screaming, 'Getup out of there you sorry son of-a-bitch. Now get your ass out, get up nigger!'" McMillan and the other inmates were then "struck several times with a rubber hose and an ax handle" and told to run down a gauntlet of "twelve to fifteen guards within that hundred yards spread out evenly" who then beat each passing inmate. The beaten prisoners were then taken to the field, some without shoes and others just in their undershorts, and forced to labor in the hot summer sun. Once outdoors, the inmates were told to continue working and the other prisoners gathered around them "to observe us getting this retribution of justice from them [TDC guards]. They were beating us as we were picking up the corn."[57]

Although the prison administration hoped to keep the incident quiet, McMillan determined to bring what inmates called "the Father's Day massacre" to light. He and his mother managed to get a letter to Frances Jalet, and she helped McMillan contact sympathetic members of the newly formed Joint Committee on Prison Reform (JCPR), which included recently elected African American state legislators Mickey Leland and Eddie Bernice Johnson. While investigating McMillan's charges against the prison, Johnson and Leland found inmates who had "bruises on their bodies, shoulders, and backs." They reported to the press that "each prisoner was beaten severely, two were bleeding, and one 58-year man with a known record of hearing pathology [was beaten so badly he] was unable to perform the work. He blacked out, in fact, and attempts by another prisoner to aid this person were rewarded by further beatings to both."[58] Another inmate, the legislators reported, had a "tumor on his shoulder, the size of a baseball."[59] Leland was visibly angry. "It's just inhuman to use any kind of baseball bat or ax handle or rubber hose to force somebody to work and say that work is rehabilitation instead of punishment.... I think its absolutely horrible," he admonished.[60]

As McMillan made common cause with African American state legislators and roused African American inmates with the hope that civil rights protest would bring attention to the abuse of prisoners, the prison system faced its greatest legal challenge from David Ruíz, one of Jalet's clients and a student of Fred Cruz. Born to migrant workers on May 15, 1942, David Resendez Ruíz spent all but eleven of his sixty-four years in captivity. Ruíz experienced confinement at age eleven when the state consigned him in 1953 to the Gatesville Reformatory School for Boys for stealing from shoeshine and newspaper boys. Like many carceral institutions in Texas, Gatesville was a chronically violent place. Ruíz returned to the same reformatory three times before the state finally tried him as an adult in 1959 for burglary and car theft, a charge for which he was found guilty and sentenced to twelve years. He remained in the Texas prison system from 1960 until 1967, when he was released on parole. Ruíz thereafter met and married Rose Marie, but within the year he returned to prison for armed robbery, for which the state gave him a twenty-five-year sentence.[61]

In his unpublished memoir, "Tough with a Knife, Hell with a Writ," Ruíz reflected on his early prison experience in the East Texas cotton fields and how he decided upon a path of resistance. Ruíz recalled that the "the field work was brutal" and that he "barely made it day to day." Moreover, Ruíz bitterly recounted that he received "several tests of the club and reins" while working and that the "guards did not hesitate to knock a prisoner on the head with a club or reins if he could not stay up with the squad." Reflecting on how he came to be a writ writer, Ruíz wrote that by the late 1960s he had begun to focus his rage on the building tender system, which he saw as the root of all the evils in TDC: "I came to hate those prisoners who did the officers' dirty work mainly to receive extra privileges or a soft job."[62] When questioned by an Eastham guard as to why he engaged in such violent behavior toward building tenders, Ruíz responded with characteristic defiance: "I will take orders from officers and not building tenders; and if I am ever assaulted by a building tender, book keeper or turnkey, they better kill me because I ain't taking no more beating and I been ready to die since the first day I entered this shithole prison."[63] As Ruíz's reputation for rebellion grew, prison officials moved him from one prison farm to another, until finally he was assigned to Ellis, where he became one of Jalet's clients. He was also housed with the "Eight Hoe" group at Wynne, a maximum-security unit, and home to an entire wing of prison activists and "jailhouse attorneys." There Ruíz, who entered prison nearly illiterate, learned to turn his energies away from violence and toward legal redress. He subsequently became one of the prison system's most ardent and well-known writ writers.

In 1972 Ruíz wrote a twelve-page petition that came to the attention of federal judge William Wayne Justice for its explicit discussion of the building tender system and the lack of medical care, two issues that made TDC vulnerable to the charge that it operated an unconstitutional prison system. On April 12, 1974, Judge Justice consolidated six additional prisoner petitions with Ruíz's original petition as part of growing concern over the number of prisoner petitions, affidavits, and depositions he received regarding inmate allegations of prison abuse.[64] In the light of these petitions, Justice took an unusual step and ordered the U.S. Department of Justice to appear as amicus curiae, and six months later it joined the suit as co-plaintiffs. The filing of Ruíz's writ in 1972 now was a civil rights claim that represented the entire prison population of fifteen thousand against all of TDC and its thirteen prisons.

Slaves of the State Revolt: Prison Mobilization and Organization

From 1974 to 1978, as Ruíz and other remaining members of "Eight Hoe" prepared to testify in the coming trial, the prisoners' rights movement expanded to a mass movement that included prisoners across the system. It was no longer just a few activist writ writers and their attorneys. Chief among the mobilizers was inmate Johnny Swift, an active member of the Black Panthers and a veteran of the Black Power movement in California. Michael Jewell, a white inmate and writ writer, recalled that Swift served the prison community as a pioneer in political and labor organizing. "Johnny was much more than a writ writer. His forte was mentoring to other blacks. . . . He exhorted them not to lay up on their asses . . . but to study law and fight for their lives. And to write politicians and the media to tell their stories, and to complain of how they lived."[65]

While inmate "writ writers" compiled legal depositions and affidavits that they sent to federal judges and civil rights attorneys, inmates like Swift composed political tracts for the general inmate population with the aim of galvanizing widespread inmate unrest, collective activism, and organized resistance. The various tracts argued that prisoners of all races must "unite immediately" to "struggle for liberation and self determination that can only be carried out effectively by collective prisoners." The aim of this movement was to assist the "writ writers" and organize fellow inmates to resist actively the building tender system through self-defense and collective organization, and to organize a system-wide letter-writing campaign to state legislatures and the Civil Rights Division of the U.S. Justice Department. Its goal was to "raise at least 2,500 letters protesting these individuals [building tenders] and the use of administrative segregation."[66] One of the most daring and helpful aspects of the movement was naming the building tenders and those fellow endangered inmates whom TDC held in solitary confinement and administrative segregation. "We are all aware of snitches and the enormous power and influence they possess, but we continually display indifference and a dangerously self-defeating characteristic when we do nothing about them," Swift reminded his fellow inmates. "We must not cease our recognition of snitches, but actively censure, criticize, and condemn all snitches." In what had been an otherwise controlled prison environment, the listing of names of building tenders for all inmates to see was a bold and dangerous act. Their hundreds of letters, affidavits, and depositions became, in some cases, the material that the plaintiff attorneys used in making their argument against TDC in *Ruíz v. Estelle*.

The movement hoped to find educated inmates for leadership roles, but it also inspired the collective organizing of inmates who did not have the education or the inclination to become writ writers. Indeed, Swift's tracts and individual letters show his lingering fear that other prisoners might distance themselves from the fate of writ writers and that they might embrace instead the con colloquialism that each "man does his own time." In a population where few had more than a high school education and where self-esteem was often low, Swift attempted to instill confidence and inspire participation among all inmates. "Of course not everyone is destined for leadership, nor is everyone qualified to file a writ, write to the legislature, news media, Judges, or the Justice Department, but anyone can help by offering stamps, writing materials, or the loan of a typewriter or a signature to a petition.... Anybody can be a hero." Swift's aim was to broaden the movement beyond a few active writ writers and make it a system-wide effort at collective resistance. "We must intensify our efforts in recruiting additional members to the struggle by establishing communications, coordination, and rapport between the different wings and extending the spirit of awareness," he reminded his readers. "We must continue to actively support, in every way possible, the vanguard of the movement, the writ-writers, and all others who seek prison reform through protests, class-actions, affidavits, and letters to the legislature."[67]

Swift's movement was interracial and advocated self-defense. Swift was a frequent writer to state House representative Eddie Bernice Johnson, and he sought her advice as to how he might mobilize a racially segregated prison population with a long history of racial animosity. "By all the measurable indices," Swift wrote to Representative Johnson, "group consciousness among the Spanish-speaking minority is far below that of the Black community. The Panther Party has revealed that the Chicano community both admires and appreciates the heightened Black militance. But clearly, from an objective point of view, an alliance would be to the people's advantage."[68] His political tracts attempted to make common cause with Chicano inmates in particular. Swift, who had trained in the martial arts, was a proponent of collective self-defense, but he eschewed the idea of a prison riot and random violence that might only hurt the prisoner rights movement. In a February 1978 letter to Senator Chet Brooks, Swift wrote explicitly about self-defense and the less desirable choice of prison riot as a political option. "It is my opinion that *every* man has a *right to defend his life* when barbarically threatened." But, Swift acknowledged, he and his fellow inmates had "only two essential weapons to challenge and struggle against repressivism and racism in prisons: political letters and civil rights suits. There is an extended measure, of course, brutal confrontation, but such, in my opinion, is borne out of total desperation."[69]

Swift may not have embraced violent tactics, but he and other inmate revolutionaries did engage in revolutionary hopes to overthrow his keepers. His treatises were emphatic appeals to collective inmate resistance:

> He can no longer stand and say, that's HIS problem! "We" can NO LONGER say its NOT ME! Because everyday ITS "YOU" and "ME" who is and always has been subjected to trumped up charges, to the same, that has befallen "HIM: will befall you and me!! . . . Let us start now!! Be MEN!!! And FIGHT!! The Struggle!! Must be joined by ALL! Akeys! Comrades! Carnales! Brothers! N'dugus! Arise, arise, Strike! For your lives and liberties. Now is the day and the Hour. Let every SLAVE on the Ramsey 1 SLAVE CAMP do this and the days of the "Slave Holder" are numbered. . . . You cannot be more oppressed than you are. You cannot suffer greater cruelties that you have already. Let OUR motto be: Resistance! Resistance! Resistance![70]

These hopes caused those in TDC and many in state government to dismiss the movement and its aims. Within the prison community, however, revolutionary language and hopes helped to forge a united movement out of what had been a dispirited and internally divided prison population.

Swift was not alone, however. Other groups joined the movement, including such organizations as the Prisoner Solidarity Committee, Prisoners United, the JailHouse Lawyers Association, and Allied Prisoners Platform for Legal Equity. All adopted similar language, the purpose of which was to construct a counter-narrative to TDC's modernization success story by presenting their own narrative of a "backwards" prison system tied to slave practices, racial brutality, and plantation labor. The Prison Solidarity Committee, for instance, sent out a handbill titled "Texas Prisoners Resist Texas Slave System," which charged that the conditions of imprisonment in Texas "are the prison conditions of a century ago, of the pre–Civil War era. . . . It is scarcely what a reasonable person would expect to find in 1978 with a reputation for modern methods and proud structures." The handbill mocked TDC's claims of modernity, stating that "the distance from the prison farms of East Texas to the NASA Space Center is greater than the distance from the Earth to the Moon."[71] The words of Salvador Gonzales, leader of the Prison Solidarity Committee, speak to the urgency among prisoners that the public learn of the divided system of prison labor and its abuses. "What is really happening in this prison," Gonzalez charged, "society refuses to believe because they really believe in a humane world. . . . No one wants to be enslaved. To be powerless, to be subject to the arbitrary exercise of power, to not be recognized as a human being, is to be a slave . . . an object, a number, a thing, or worse a no-thing."[72]

Of course, prisoners were not literally slaves, and important historical distinctions marked each type of confinement as unique and different.[73] But by drawing analogies and comparisons between prison and slavery, activist inmates knowingly confronted TDC's modernization success story with a morality tale that equated modern-day prisons with the archaic memory of the brutality and inhumanity of nineteenth-century slavery.[74] As prisoners repeatedly reminded the courts and state legislators, they had been legally consigned as "slaves of the state," toiled daily in unfree prison labor on the grounds of nineteenth-century plantations, and experienced "civil death" as long as they remained prisoners. As one inmate put it, "Slavery, man, human slavery." Arnold Pontesso, Oklahoma's former director of corrections and an administrator of the Federal Bureau of Prisons, adopted the inmate's use of slave imagery and their language of dissent when his 1977 report declared: "On December 18, 1865, the 13th Amendment to the US Constitution was ratified to abolish slavery. . . . That vulnerable institution has continued, however, in penitentiaries throughout the country. Texas Department of Corrections is probably the best example of slavery remaining in the nation today . . . One gets a strong feeling that TDC exists not to punish offenders or deter others from committing crimes, not to rehabilitate criminals, but to perpetuate the plantation as the largest agribusiness operation in the state."[75]

A Peaceful Rebellion: The Work Strikes of 1978

The organizing and mobilizing effort came to full fruition on the week before the *Ruíz* trial's opening day of court, as organized inmates across the prison system prepared to make a public statement in support of the inmate litigants by staging the first-ever system-wide work strike in Texas prison history. The prison strike started at Ellis prison through interracial coordination and planning. Alvarro Luna Hernandez, one of the inmates involved in coordinating the strike, recalled that "we had been organizing months before that" and that "we had a little manifesto that we started distributing." "Attica was our model. We felt that we had to make a stand. The time was now because the publicity was there and we were tearing down the walls."[76] While Attica may have inspired the work strike, the Texas inmates hoped that they could avoid the bloodbath that New York inmates experienced. Inmate strike organizers planned a system-wide work strike that would attract the attention of the media, who, they hoped, would document any attempt by the prison administration to turn the inmate strike into another incident of prison violence similar to the state police assault at Attica or the 1971 killing of George Jackson during the "Soledad Brothers" incident. The planned work strike thus built on the lessons of Attica and the Soledad Brothers by drawing upon traditions of disruption from the labor movement and practices of militant nonviolence from the civil rights movement in an effort to gain the sympathy of the media, the public, and the federal court by avoiding violent riot. Inmates understood that prison labor stood at the heart of the Texas prison system and that a peaceful system-wide work strike would call attention to the hierarchical nature of the southern trusty system and its harsh labor regime.

The strikers hoped that the media would cover the "work buck" and that statewide media coverage would inspire inmates on other prisons to engage in a system-wide strike. "We'll use the media—their own media to spread the word to the other units," Hernandez recalled, "and the other units hopefully will follow suit, and that's exactly what happened."[77] As the strike entered its second day, the prison guards refused to feed the inmates and used hunger as a lure to get the prisoners back into the building. Undaunted, the inmates continued their strike for eight more days. Fellow striker white inmate Robert Mudd recalled the excitement of the media attention and yet also the strains of hunger: "a Channel 2 helicopter flew over at one point and we made signs with our black socks . . . and we put 'No water—no food.'"[78]

The unity of the prisoners spread even to those who were not striking. Prisoners who were not on strike inside the building broke the windows and passed food to the strikers.[79] Wilbur Collins, an African American inmate on Ellis's death row who was known as "Wolf" for his temperament and "Kojak" for his shaved skull, recalled how even the death-row inmates contributed their food to the strikers. "It was beautiful, really, the total unity that was behind this. Because the guys on H-18, which was directly across from J-23 [death row], they passed blankets and food out. And they would bring a food cart to death row. On death row we would eat every other meal. Everyone on death row agreed. If we eat breakfast, we wouldn't eat lunch. We'd place our food on fix up trays and pass them across the hallway to the turnkey and they would pass them to the guys on H-18 and they would then pass them out the window to the back slab" where the strike was taking place.[80]

Moreover, the strike mixed previously segregated inmate populations without incident and with peaceful racial solidarity. Throughout the strike, the press attempted to report on the interracial nature of the strike so that they could discern if Texas was undergoing a prison riot or a peaceful but militant civil rights and labor protest demonstration. "They had set up video cameras up on the roof, and they were filming us," Mudd recalled. "They had this long pole with a microphone on it, and they would stick this microphone out over the yard when we were having meetings. Each group had a representative—blacks had a representative, the whites had a representative, and the Mexicans had a representative."[81] During these meetings, inmates had the opportunity to stand before their fellow inmates to air grievances, maintain the strike's momentum, and pass the time. Hernandez conceived of these impromptu strike speeches as "an extension of the prison reform movement, an extension of the civil rights movement, an extension of the political consciousness of a certain segment of society that were just thrown in the slammer and forgotten."[82] "There was no love loss among the races back then," Mudd recalled "but at that point we were very unified in what we were doing as far as the strike. It was for the *Ruíz* trial, you know."[83] Hernandez had a similar memory: "During those two weeks, there was no racial tension whatsoever, and there was black inmates, Hispanic inmates, white inmates, and it was just like solidarity there." For Hernandez, the fact that the inmates remained nonviolent showed that victory for the prisoners' rights movement was finally in reach. "We felt that we had TDC on the run, and of course, remember one of the objectives was to show the public our humanity. To show the public that hey, we're not animals.... Should we tear this place down? Should we try to take it over? ... No, we'll just sit—we'll riot peacefully."[84]

The letter-writing, mass-mobilization campaign and the work strike pressed public opinion and caught the attention of the federal court. Prison activists thus influenced the discourse, debate, and final outcome of the trial. The trial began in October 1978 and included nearly two years of testimony from 349 witnesses, of whom more than 100 were TDC inmates, and lengthy expert testimony from activists, academics, psychiatrists, and penologists. In 1980 Judge Justice ruled in favor of the prisoners with a damning indictment of the TDC that described the divided labor system in Texas as "pernicious" and "sheer misery." It was dependent upon state-orchestrated "pain and degradation" that included "the gruesome experiences of youthful first offenders forcibly raped" and "bitter frustration of inmates prevented from petitioning the courts" to mediate the "cruel and justifiable fears of inmates."[85] With this verdict, the court thus declared the Texas prison system unconstitutional and demanded that it end the abusive labor practice known as the building tender system.

Although often overlooked, the prisoners themselves had brought attention to their cause and thrown the old prison order into crisis. A reassessment of *Ruíz* through the prism of inmate organization and mobilization reminds us that before the nation confronted the question of how to treat enemy combatants at Abu Ghraib and Guantánamo, there was a history of state-sanctioned violence against inmates and a struggle over prison labor and how to define the rights of domestic prisoners. Revealing the otherwise hidden history of inmate activism places the prisoners' rights movement as part of the broader civil rights struggle and extends the civil rights movement well into the 1970s.[86] Inmates who were veterans of the civil rights and Black Power movements felt that their struggle behind bars was intrinsically linked to their organizing experience out in the streets of free society. Inmates waged a public-relations struggle and labor protest campaign with TDC over the prison system's claim of progress by countering the prison modernization narrative and economic success story with what Heather Thompson has called sympathetic portrayals of a "barbaric" and racist South.[87]

The inmate outreach campaign to legislators and litigators required inmates to make a persistent, cogent, and persuasive case without resorting to a widespread prison riot and violent revolt. The work strike of 1978 remained nonviolent for ten days and did not result in the kind of violent uprising that so characterized the prison revolts of the late 1960s and 1970s. In the words of Alva Luna Hernandez, the Texas inmates "rioted peacefully," and their demands for "humanity" and to be treated humanely and not as objectified "convicts and criminals" were heard. Their victory in *Ruíz* resounded across the nation's courts and in its prisons. Indeed, the inmates' legal and labor protest strategy had implications beyond the South, particularly in the Sun Belt but also in the North, as prisoners' rights suits expanded in the mid-1980s beyond southern labor conditions and looked to the ways in which inmates across the nation were entitled to constitutional protection.[88] Civil rights had indeed come to the cell block and planted its legacy behind prison walls.

In the new, post-*Ruíz* prison system, inmates no longer toiled in fields of agricultural labor for ten-hour days, nor did they live under the threat of racial and sexual violence perpetrated by the building tenders' attempt to instill order and control. Instead, the prison system gave inmates makeshift garden work that barely resembled the field labor that created the state's agri-business empire of the 1950s, 1960s, and 1970s. Since the *Ruíz* decision of 1980, the prison administration has increasingly emphasized industrial labor, housed inmates in privatized prisons, and warehoused them in "super-maximum" security prisons with a largely idle prison population held in twenty-three-hour cell lockdown. Under the auspices of the 1977 *Lamar v. Coffield* consent decree, Texas prisons were no longer racially segregated, and the guard force was no longer exclusively white, largely rural, and entirely male.[89] The struggle for prisoners' rights also gave inmates the right to counsel, better medical care, and freedom from state-sanctioned racial hierarchies and institutionalized racial subordination. Gone were the prison's public images of slavery, plantation field labor, and inmate charges of brutal sexual and physical abuse at the hands of the southern trusty system. In short, nearly all the aspects that made the Texas prison system uniquely southern were dismantled after 1985. It did not, however, end violence between and among inmates, nor did it anticipate the degree of post-1980 growth that prisons would experience. Whereas no prison gangs other than building tenders existed prior to 1980, prison gangs proliferated across the prison system within only a few short years of the decision.[90] The prison system that Texas fashioned after the *Ruíz* case ended the "control penology" labor model, and from its ashes emerged neither the rehabilitative penitentiary of the Northeast nor the plantation prison farm model of the Old South. Instead, Texas was in the forefront of a new prison Sun Belt landscape that created a far more pervasive and much less remarked-upon form of racial oppression than the southern plantation prison labor model of the past.

Notes

1. "Three Inmates Injured by Warning Shots from Prison Guards," *Dallas Times Herald*, October 9, 1978; "TDC Head Refuses Comment on Prisoner Strike," *Dallas Times Herald*, October 10, 1978; "Convicts in Other Facilities Join Prison Work Stoppage," *Fort Worth Star Telegram*, October 11, 1978; "Texas Prisons: Overcrowded, Edgy, and Under Fire," *Dallas*

Times Herald, October 15, 1978; "Riot by 1,500 Inmates Acknowledged," *Houston Chronicle*, October 19, 1978.

2. For both analytical and narrative accounts of the prison revolts of the late 1960s and early 1970s, see Charles E. Silberman, *Criminal Violence, Criminal Justice* (New York: Random House, 1978); Tom Wicker, *A Time to Die* (New York: Quadrangle, 1975); Mark Colvin, *The Penitentiary in Crisis: From Accommodation to Riot in New Mexico* (Albany: State University of New York, 1992); Bert Useem and Peter Kimball, *States of Siege: U.S. Prison Riots, 1971–1986* (New York, Oxford: Oxford University Press, 1989); and James B. Jacobs, *Stateville: The Penitentiary in Mass Society* (Chicago: University of Chicago Press, 1977). See also Heather Ann Thompson, "Rethinking Working-Class Struggle through the Lens of the Carceral State: Toward a Labor History of Inmates and Guards," *Labor: Studies in Working-Class History of the Americas* 8:3 (Fall 2011): 15–46.

3. *Attica: The Official Report of the New York State Special Commission on Attica* (New York: Praeger, 1972).

4. Robert DeLong, Testimony of Julian Griego and In-Chambers Conference, October 16, 1978, David R. Ruíz et al. vs. W. J. *Estelle*, Jr., et al., Center for American History, University of Texas, Austin [hereafter CAH], MAI 8/J-92.

5. Butch Mendez, Ellis Unit, Inmate number 256311, to State Senator Chet Brooks, Chairman, Joint Committee on Prison Reform, December 15, 1978, Papers of Ron Chet Brooks, Texas State Library and Archives [hereafter TSLA], Box 1999/136.

6. On trustees overseeing field labor in Mississippi, see David Oshinsky, *"Worse Than Slavery": Parchman Farm and the Ordeal of Jim Crow Justice* (New York: Free Press, 1996), 140–50.

7. The literature on litigated Texas prison reform in the postwar period has approached the subject from a variety of valuable perspectives, but none of them tell the story of prison reform from the perspective of a social movement and in the context of interracial social and political organizing. On the litigation and its effects on the prison system from the perspective of the courts and attorneys involved in the cases, see Steve J. Martin and Sheldon Ekland-Olson, *Texas Prisons: The Walls Came Tumbling Down* (Austin: Texas Monthly Press, 1989); Malcolm Feeley and Edward L. Rubin, *Judicial Policy Making and the Modern State: How the Courts Reformed America's Prisons* (Cambridge: Cambridge University Press, 1998); and Frank R. Kermer, *William Wayne Justice: A Judicial Biography* (Austin: University of Texas Press, 1991). For a sociological account that offers the guard experience and the changing nature of inmate society from the perspective of criminologists, see Ben M. Crouch and James W. Marquart, *An Appeal to Justice: Litigated Reform of Texas Prisons* (Austin: University of Texas Press, 1989). For a critique of inmate disorder and a favorable account of Texas prison management from the perspective of political science, see John DiIulio, *Governing Prisons: A Comparative Study of Correctional Management* (New York: Free Press, 1987); and David M. Horton and George R. Nielson, *Walking George: The Life of George John Beto and the Rise of the Modern Texas Prison System* (Denton: University of North Texas Press, 2005). For the most comprehensive account of the case drawn largely from the perspective of David Ruíz and William Bennett Turner, see Robert Perkinson, *Texas Tough: The Rise of America's Prison Empire* (New York: Metropolitan Books, 2010), 251–85.

8. On the ways in which mass incarceration of American changed the political, social,

racial and economic dynamics of the South in the nineteenth century, see Edward L. Ayers, *Vengeance and Justice: Crime and Punishment in the 19th-Century American South* (New York: Oxford University Press, 1984); Alex Lichtenstein, *Twice the Work of Free Labor: The Political Economy of Convict Labor in the New South* (New York: Verso, 1996); Matthew J. Mancini, *One Dies, Get Another: Convict Leasing in the American South, 1866–1928* (Columbia: University of South Carolina Press, 1996); Martha A. Myers, *Race, Labor and Punishment in the New South* (Columbus: Ohio State University Press, 1998); Mary Ellen Curtin, *Black Prisoners and Their World: Alabama, 1865–1900* (Charlottesville: University Press of Virginia, 2000); Karen A. Shapiro, *A New South Rebellion: The Battle against Convict Labor in the Tennessee Coalfields, 1871–1896* (Chapel Hill: University of North Carolina Press, 1998); and Oshinsky, *"Worse Than Slavery."*

9. On the role that race and racial anxiety played in the creation of a post-1980s prison building boom, see Thomas Byrne Edsall with Mary D. Edsall, *Chain Reaction: The Impact of Race, Rights, and Taxes on American Politics* (New York: Norton, 1991); Michael W. Flamm, *Law and Order: Street Crime, Civil Unrest, and the Crisis of Liberalism in the 1960s* (New York: Columbia University Press, 2005); Tali Mendelberg, "Executing Hortons: Racial Crime in the 1988 Presidential Campaign," *Public Opinion Quarterly* 61, no. 1 (1997): 134–57; Loïc Wacquant, "From Slavery to Mass Incarceration: Rethinking the 'Race Question' in the U.S.," *New Left Review*, January–February 2002, 41–60; Michael Tonry, *Malign Neglect: Race, Crime, and Punishment in America* (New York: Oxford University Press, 1995); Jerome G. Miller, *Search and Destroy: African-American Males in the Criminal Justice System* (Cambridge: Cambridge University Press, 1996); and Marc Mauer, *Race to Incarcerate* (New York : New Press: Norton, 1999). For work that considers the current rates of racially disproportionate incarceration as extensions of slavery and a "new Jim Crow," see Michelle Alexander, *The New Jim Crow: Mass Incarceration in the Age of Colorblindness* (New York: New Press, 2010); and Douglas Blackmon, *Slavery by Another Name: The Re-enslavement of Black Americans from the Civil War to World War II* (New York: Anchor Books, 2009).

10. The work of Angela Davis, however, remains an important exception. On Davis and her own struggles with imprisonment, see Bettina Aptheker, *The Morning Breaks: The Trial of Angela Davis* (New York: International Publishers, 1975); Angela Y. Davis, *Angela Davis: An Autobiography* (New York: International Publishers, 1988); Angela Y. Davis (and other political prisoners), *If They Come in the Morning* (New Rochelle, N.Y.: Third Press, 1971); and Joy James, *The Angela Y. Davis Reader* (Malden, Mass.: Blackwell, 1998). On the linkages between the criminal justice system and racial inequality during the first half of the twentieth century, see Khalil Gibran Muhammad, *The Condemnation of Blackness: Ideas about Race and Crime in the Making of Modern Urban America* (Cambridge: Harvard University Press, 2010); Jeffery Adler, *First in Violence, Deepest in Dirt: Homicide in Chicago, 1875–1920* (Cambridge: Harvard University Press, 2006); Kali Gross, *Colored Amazons: Crime, Violence and Black Women in the City of Brotherly Love, 1880–1910* (Durham: Duke University Press, 2006); and Cheryl Hicks, *Talk With You Like a Woman: Urban Reform, Criminal Justice, and African American Women in New York, 1890–1935* (Chapel Hill: University of North Carolina Press, 2010). For recent historical work on prison unrest and the prisoners' rights movement, see Rebecca McLennan, *The Crisis of Imprisonment: Protest, Politics, and the Making of the American Penal State, 1776–1941* (Cambridge: Cambridge

University Press, 2008); Staughton Lynd, *Lucasville: The Untold Story of a Prison Uprising* (Philadelphia: Temple University Press, 2004); Perkinson, *Texas Tough*; Heather McCarty, "From Con-Boss to Gang Lord: The Transformation of Social Relations in California Prisons, 1943–1983" (Ph.D. diss., University of California, Berkeley, 2004); and Robert Chase, "Civil Rights on the Cellblock: Race, Reform, and Violence in Texas Prisons and the Nation, 1945–1990" (Ph.D. diss., University of Maryland, 2009). On the central importance of incarceration to the declension narratives of the late twentieth century, see Heather Ann Thompson, "Why Mass Incarceration Matters: Rethinking Crisis, Decline, and Transformation in American History," *Journal of American History* 97, no. 3 (2010): 703–34.

11. In his study of California's New Left and its alliance with the prisoners' rights movement, Eric Cummins criticized the New Left's embrace of prisoners as "authentic working-class heroes." Such an alliance, according to Cummins, naively tied radical political hopes to outlaws and violence, and thus doomed the New Left to political irrelevancy and revolutionary fantasy. Cummins, *The Rise and Fall of California's Radical Prison Movement* (Stanford: Stanford University Press, 1994), ix.

12. In his cover letter for an investigative report of the Texas penitentiary system, Representative Sam Sellar lamented that after reviewing "many penal institutions throughout the nation" he was forced to come to the sad conclusion that "we have the worst prison system of any State." State Representative Sam Sellars to Beauford Jester, Beauford Jester Papers, TSLA, Box 4-14/113.

13. In 1947, the year of Texas prison reforms, the total prison population numbered 5,700 in twelve prison units, which included one walled penitentiary and eleven prison farms encompassing a total acreage of 73,010. "Texas Prison System Runs Gamut of Bad and Best in Nation's Penal Institutions," *Tyler Courier-Times*, December 20, 1947; Annual Report of the Texas Prison Board to the Governor, Honorable Coke Stevenson, Texas Department of Corrections, 1945 and 1946; *Texas Department of Corrections: 20 Years of Progress, 1947–1967* (Texas Department of Corrections, 1967).

14. Crouch and Marquart, *An Appeal to Justice*, 24.

15. R. C. Koeninger, "What about Self-Mutilation?" *Prison World*, March–April 1951; Texas Prison Board, Annual Reports, 1940–1942; Paul Van Dyke, "An Investigation of Self-Mutilation at the Texas Prison System in Terms of Minnesota Multiphasic Personality Inventory and Other Measures" (master's thesis, University of Texas, 1953); and Dan Richard Beto and James L. Claghorn, "Factors Associated with Self-Mutilation within the Texas Department of Corrections, *American Journal of Correction* 30, no. 1 (1968): 25–27.

16. S. E. Barnett to M. Riley Wyatt, September 1947, Jester Papers, TSLA, 4-14/113.

17. "Texas Prison System Runs Gamut"; Austin MacCormick to O. B. Ellis, June 14, 1949, Jester Papers, TSLA, Box 4-14/113.

18. On the movement against convict lease in Texas, see Donald Walker, *Penology for Profit: A History of the Texas Prison System, 1867–1912* (College Station: Texas A&M University Press, 1988); and Perkinson, *Texas Tough*, 132–76.

19. The impetus behind the legislative effort to restrict convict labor came from two sources: the progressive movement to end the South's convict lease system, and northeastern labor organizations, which felt that profitable convict labor threatened free labor and collective organization. For the protest of organized labor, particularly in the Northeast, against convict labor, see Glen A. Gildemeister, *Prison Labor and Convict Competition*

with Free Workers in Industrializing America, 1840–1890 (New York: Garland, 1987) and Thompson, "Rethinking the Working-Class Struggle," 19–21.

20. Richard P. Jones Jr., *Prison Labor in the United States,* Bulletin No. 698, U.S. Department of Labor, Bureau of Labor Statistics (Washington, D.C.: Government Printing Office, 1941).

21. For the northern emphasis on the rehabilitative prison and reformatories, see David J. Rothman, *Conscience and Convenience: The Asylum and its Alternatives in Progressive America* (New York: Aldine de Gruyter, 1980); Alexander W. Pisciotta, *Benevolent Repression: Social Control and the American Reformatory-Prison Movement* (New York: New York University Press, 1994); Nicole Hahn Rafter, *Partial Justice: Women in State Prisons, 1800–1935* (Boston: Northeastern University Press, 1985); and David Garland, *Punishment and Welfare: A History of Penal Strategies* (Hants, England: Gower, 1985). On New York's adoption of the "new penology" during the progressive era, see McLennan, *The Crisis of Imprisonment*; and Rebecca McLennan, "Punishment's 'Square Deal': Prisoners and their Keepers in 1920s New York," *Journal of Urban History* 29, no. 5 (2003): 597–619. It is important to note that while Progressive and New Deal-era federal law constricted convict labor, it did not end prison work altogether. Some state systems, particularly California's, blended rehabilitative programs with a continuing emphasis on inmate labor through firefighting and forest camps. For California's emphasis on "bibliotherapy," group therapy, and education, see Cummins, *Rise and Fall*, 1–62. On its attempt to instill civic duty through forestry and firefighting camps for prisoners, see Volker Janssen, "When the 'Jungle' Met the Forest: Public Work, Civil Defense, and Prison Camps in Postwar California," *Journal of American History* 96, no. 3 (2009): 702–26.

22. In 1940 southern prisons employed 33,272 inmates out of a total inmate population (both male and female) of 53,804 prisoners. Prisons in the Northeast, however, employed only 9,886 prisoners out of a total prison population of 31,665 (both male and female). For the purposes of this essay, southern prison systems included the states of Alabama, Arkansas, Florida, Georgia, Kentucky, Louisiana, North Carolina, South Carolina, Tennessee, Texas, Virginia, and West Virginia. Northeastern states included Connecticut, Delaware, Maine, New Hampshire, New Jersey, New York, Pennsylvania, Rhode Island, and Vermont. Both male and female prisoners were included in the total number of inmates. See Jones, *Prison Labor in the United States*; Asatar P. Bair, *Prison Labor in the United States: An Economic Analysis* (New York: Routledge, 2008).

23. Jerry Quate, oral history conducted by the author, March 12, 2007, Institute of Oral History, Baylor University [hereafter IOH-Baylor].

24. Lawrence Pope, oral history conducted by John Wheat, Lawrence Pope Papers, CAH, 318. For the Texas tradition of slave punishment, particularly the use of the lash, see, Randolph B. Campbell, *An Empire for Slavery: The Peculiar Institution in Texas, 1821–1865* (Baton Rouge: Louisiana State University Press, 1989), 103–8, 145–53; on the use of enslaved African Americans who worked as "field drivers" in Texas cotton fields during the antebellum period, see p. 57.

25. U.S. Department of Commerce, *Sixteenth Census of the United States: 1940, Population, Vol. II, Part 6* (Washington, D.C.: Government Printing Office, 1943), 761; U.S. Department of Commerce, *Census Population: 1980* (Washington, D.C.: Government Printing Office, 1983), 45–51.

26. The number of new arrivals in 1971 for each county was as follows: Harris, 1,331; Dallas, 1,205; Tarrant, 407; Bexar, 379; Travis, 218; McLennan, 149; Nuece, 111; Jefferson, 104. See George Beto, "Outline of Address: The Complexion of the Texas Prison Population," 1970, Beto Collection, Sam Houston State University [hereafter SHSU], 1-4/38.

27. A 1971 survey of the inmate population found that "Of the total population of 16,500, 96 percent were school drop outs, 60 percent (using a strict definition) came from broken homes; 18 percent were illiterate; the average grade level of achievement being the 5th, with an average I.Q. of 80; 20 percent were mentally retarded, almost 1 percent actively psychotic, 40 percent with no sustained record of prior employment, 50 percent under the age of 25; 42 percent Black, 38 percent Anglo and 20 percent Mexican." Ibid.

28. Arthur Johnson, oral history conducted by author, March 20, 2008, IOH-Baylor.

29. Jack Kyle, interview with the author, June 25, 2005, IOH-Baylor.

30. Unpublished excerpt from Robert Lee Mudd's prison memoir, in the author's possession.

31. For the ways in which "white skin privilege" conferred racial identity and power, see David Roediger, *Wages of Whiteness: Race and the Making of the American Working Class* (New York: Verso, 1997); Noel Ignatiev, *How the Irish Became White* (New York: Routledge, 1995); Grace Elizabeth Hale, *Making Whiteness: The Culture of Segregation in the South, 1890-1940* (New York: Pantheon Books, 1998); George Lipsitz, *The Possessive Investment in Whiteness: How White People Profit from Identity Politics* (Philadelphia: Temple University Press, 1998); and Richard Delgado and Jean Stefancic, eds., *Critical White Studies: Looking behind the Mirror* (Philadelphia: Temple University Press, 1997).

For studies showing how the racial category of "whiteness" could change over time or even be lost for an individual or ethnic group, see Matthew Frye Jacobson, *Whiteness of a Different Color: European Immigrants and the Alchemy of Race* (Cambridge: Harvard University Press, 1998); and Neil Foley, *The White Scourge: Mexicans, Blacks, and Poor Whites in Texas Cotton Culture* (Berkeley: University of California Press, 1997). For a historical evaluation of white slavery, see Gunther Peck, "White Slavery and Whiteness: A Transnational View of the Sources of Working-Class Radicalism and Racism," *Labor* 1 (2004): 41–63.

32. "To Protect Society from the Criminal and the Criminals from Each Other: The Five-Point Prison Plan," O. B. Ellis memorandum, Texas Department of Correctional Justice [hereafter TDCJ], Prison Board Minutes, February 1948, TSLA.

33. At the behest of the prison administration, the state legislature established three classes of "good time." Class I provided that an inmate earns twenty extra days' time for each month served on his sentence, as long as that inmate maintained a clear conduct and work record. The prison administration immediately placed newly arrived inmates in Class I. Class II allowed an inmate to receive ten extra days' time for each month served. Class III required that an inmate serve his time day-for-day without any allowances. Texas Department of Corrections Rules and Regulations Chapter II, Sec. 2.52, cited in "Labor and Industry Working Paper," by Van Mendoza, Joint Committee on Prison Reform.

34. Beto, untitled speech, Beto Papers, SHSU.

35. "Texas Prison System Changes Afford New Hope for Inmates," *Houston Chronicle*, February 21, 1954.

36. George Beto, "The Case for Prisons," *Texas Police Journal*, August 1964, Beto Papers, 1-4/45, SHSU.

37. On the eve of the 1971 Attica riot and at the very height of New York's experiment with the rehabilitative prison, the state's Department of Correctional Services operated twenty-one correctional facilities, including prisons, hospitals, reformatories, work and environmental conservation camps, and a narcotics rehabilitation center, with a staff of over 7,650 people and an annual budget of more than $100 million. The cost of such a vast therapeutic network nearly bankrupted the New York prison system and did nothing to deter the 1971 Attica revolt, causing Governor Nelson Rockefeller, the very embodiment of New York liberalism, to abandon "scientific treatment" and the state's traditional rehabilitative approach. For statistics concerning the size of New York's prison system in 1971, see *Attica: The Official Report*.

38. In 1978, for instance, the states that did not pay inmates even a nominal wage included Texas, Arkansas, Mississippi, Georgia, and Maine. Within a few years of the survey, Mississippi and Maine started a pay program for their prisoners. By way of comparison, California paid inmates between 50 cents and $2.60 an hour; New York paid between 25 cents and $2.30; and Illinois paid the most, at 40 cents up to $7 an hour. See CURE Report, authorized by CURE member Gonzalo Barrientos and by Bruce Hupp, Chet Brooks Papers, 1991/068-29, CURE file, TSLA; "Shortage of Guards Is a Major Problem in State's Prison System," *Houston Chronicle*, September 9, 1978; *Houston Chronicle*, September 9, 1978.

39. E. R. Cass to Gordon Peters, April 17, 1953, and E. R. Cass to Allan Shivers, April 17, 1953, TDCJ, Prison Board Minutes, July 1953, TSLA.

40. "Former California Official Praises TDC as the 'General Motors' of Prisons," *Dallas Morning News*, August 2, 1979.

41. Kevin Krajick, "Profile Texas," *Corrections Magazine*, October 1978, 13.

42. Dr. George Beto, "Address to the Southern Prisons Association," keynote address, New Orleans, Louisiana, April 1964, Beto Papers, SHSU.

43. On the building tender's ability to have single cells and choice of cell assignment and cell partner, see David A. Christian at pp. 149, 288, Center for American History, University of Austin Texas, Papers of the Special Master Ruíz [hereafter CAH], MAI 8/J-93; William Forrest at p. 1, CAH, MAI 9/J-91; Hill at p. 12, CAH, MAI 8/J-92; James Lagermaier at pp. 41–42, CAH, MAI 8/J-98; Walter Harvey Ballard at pp. 32, 36, CAH, MAI 8/J-88; Francisco Guerra at pp. 21–22, CAH, MAI 8/J-91.

On the building tender's ability to have more personal property, including clothes, stereos and pets, see John Albach at pp. 118, 207, CAH, MAI 8/J-88; Arnold E. Pontesso at pp. 113–14, CAH, MAI 8/J-94; Jeters at 78–82, CHA, MAI 8/J-102; David A. Christian at p. 103, CAH, MAI 8/J-96; Francisco Guerra at pp. 51–52, CAH, MAI 8/J-91.

On the building tender's close relationship to top prison officials, particularly assistant wardens and majors, see John Albach at pp. 118, 207, CAH, MAI 8/J-88; Arnold E. Pontesso at pp. 113–14, CAH, MAI 8/J-94; Jeters at pp. 78–82, CAH, MAI 8/J-102; David A. Christian at p. 103, CAH, MAI 8/J-96; Francisco Guerra at pp. 51–52, CAH, MAI 8/J-91.

On the building tender's access to weapons, ability to "run a store," manage a sex trade, and freely engage in prison rape, see James Eckles at pp. 24–31, 42–44, 45–48, 234–35, 239–41, CAH, MAI 8/J-91; Guerrant at pp. 14, 50, 87, CAH, MAI 8/J-92; Francisco Guerra at pp. 18–19, 161–63, 165–70, CAH, MAI 8/J-91; Paul Crosson at pp. 28, 29, 72–73, CAH, MAI 8/J-96; Simonton at pp. 27–30, CAH, MAI 8/J-88; Gibson at pp. 46 and 134, CAH, MAI 8/J-92; Eddie James Ward at p. 143, CAH, MAI 8/J-95; Hubbard at pp. 150–53, CAH,

MAI 8/J-92; Lovelace at pp. 49–52, CAH, MAI 8/J-98; Robles at pp. 32, 97, 113–14, CAH, MAI 8/J-99; Oscar Turner at p. 35, CAH, MAI 8/J-99.

44. Building tenders were generally considered a State Approved Trusty (SAT), providing them even more "good time" than Class I inmates. There were three categories of State Approved Trusty Classifications, and all three categories of SAT earned thirty extra days for each month served, which was ten more "good time" days than inmates in Class I received. The principles and rules of "good time" can be found in Article 6184l, *The Revised Civil Statues of Texas*; and Wayne Oakes, Committee Staff, Joint Committee on Prison Reform, "Custody and Security Working Paper," Ruíz Special Master Collection, Center for American History, University of Texas, MAI 8/J-85; Beto, untitled speech, Beto Papers, SHSU.

45. Lawrence Pope, oral history conducted by John Wheat, Lawrence Pope Collection, Center for American History, University of Texas, Austin, Box 4C982.

46. Carl Robbins, interview in *Writ Writer: One Man's Journey for Justice*, a documentary film by Suzanne Mason.

47. On the U.S. Supreme Court's historic shift away from the notion of prisoners as "slaves of the state" and its rejection of the "hands off" doctrine and its embrace of prisoners as citizens with a right to be heard in court, see "Beyond the Ken of the Courts: A Critique of Judicial Refusal to Review the Complaints of Convict," *Yale Law Journal* 72, no. 3 (1963): 506–58; John A. Filter, *Prisoners' Rights: The Supreme Court and Evolving Standards of Decency* (Westport, Conn.: Greenwood Press, 2001); John DiIulio, ed., *Courts, Corrections, and the Constitution: The Impact of Judicial Intervention on Prisons and Jails* (New York: Oxford University Press, 1990); Alvin J. Bronstein, "Prison Reform Revisited: The Unfinished Agenda," *Pace Law Review* 24, no. 2 (2004): 839–46; Malcolm Feely and Edward L. Rubin, *Judicial Policy Making and the Modern State: How the Courts Reform America's Prisons* (Cambridge: Cambridge University Press, 1998); and Kim Gilmore, "States of Incarceration: Prisoners' Rights and US Prison Expansion after World War II" (Ph.D. diss., New York University, 2005).

48. *Wolff v. McDonnell*, 414 U.S. 539 (1974), 555–56.

49. Other important cases of the late 1960s include *Holt v. Sarver* in Arkansas and *Pugh v. Locke* in Alabama. In *Holt v. Sarver*, inmates challenged the practice of forced physical labor and corporal punishment in the form of whipping. In 1969, Judge J. Smith Henley ruled that the Arkansas prison system was unconstitutional. See, *Holt v. Sarver I*, 300 F. Supp. 825. In 1970 in *Holt v. Sarver II*, 309 F. Supp. 362, Judge Henley ruled the entire Arkansas prison system unconstitutional and ordered the State Correction Board to devise a plan of action. In that same case in 1971, Judge Henley enjoined the Arkansas prison from preventing the inmates' access to court and from inflicting cruel and unusual punishment upon them. On the Arkansas decision and its impact on prison management in that state, see Feeley and Rubin, *Judicial Policy Making*, 51–80. The Arkansas struggle for prisoners' rights differs from the Texas story because Arkansas prison administrators sought prison reform and court-ordered litigation, while Texas prison administrators fought tooth-and-nail the grassroots prisoners' rights movement and court-ordered intervention.

50. Alabama, Arkansas, Mississippi, South Carolina, Tennessee, and Texas were all declared as having unconstitutional prison systems. Georgia and Louisiana, meanwhile, had their principal maximum-security facility under similar federal court orders, and Florida had its entire system under court order. Virginia remains the only southern state that did

not either have its prison system declared unconstitutional or have its principal prison under federal court order.

51. Prisons of Alaska, Delaware, New Mexico, and Rhode Island were declared unconstitutional by a federal court, but New Mexico is a Sun Belt state and Rhode Island has but a single prison in the state. Those states with limited prison litigation cases are Maine, Massachusetts, Montana, Nebraska, Vermont, and Wyoming. States that had no prison litigation whatsoever include Minnesota, New Jersey, and North Dakota. Feeley and Rubin, *Judicial Policy Making*, 40–41.

52. For a critical assessment of how the New Left "constructed" George Jackson as a revolutionary hero, see Cummins, *Rise and Fall*, chapter 7, 151–86.

53. See *Lamar v. Coffield*, 951 F. Supp. 629 (S.D.Tex.); *Guajardo v. McAdams*, 349 F. Supp. 211 (1972) and *Guajardo v. Estelle*, 580 F. 2d 748 (1978); *Corpus v. Estelle*, 409 F. Supp. 1090 (1975) and *Corpus v. Estelle*, 551 F. 2d 68 (1977). For a sociological account of how racial desegregation unfolded in the 1980s and 1990s in Texas prisons, see and Chad R. Trulson and James W. Marquart, *First Available Cell: Desegregation of the Texas Prison System* (Austin: University of Texas Press, 2010).

54. Ernest McMillan, oral history with the author, April 4, 2007, IOH-Baylor.

55. Ibid.

56. For an analysis that considers McMillan's role in the OK supermarket demonstration as part of a local, Dallas trend that rejected SNCC and militant violence, see Brian D. Behnken, "The 'Dallas Way': Protest, Response and the Civil Rights Experience in Big D and Beyond," *Southwestern Historical Quarterly* 140, no. 1 (2007): 1–29. Behnken concludes that "clearly SNCC was unwelcome in Dallas" and that "the lack of violence in Dallas . . . suggests at the very least that scholars have overemphasized the role of violent behavior in racial change in the civil rights movement" (29). An analysis of the prisoner rights movement, however, shows the ways in which McMillan and former SNCC members continued to forge a vibrant interracial movement in Texas. For an account of the OK supermarket demonstration as "symbolic of how the civil rights movement in Dallas remained fractured," see W. Marvin Dulaney, "Whatever Happened to the Civil Rights Movement in Dallas, Texas?" in *Essays on the American Civil Rights Movement*, ed. W. Marvin Dulaney and Kathleen Underwood (College Station: Texas A&M University Press, 1993), 66–95.

57. McMillan, oral history with the author.

58. "Legislators Call for Probe into Alleged Prison Beating," *Dallas Morning News*, September 14, 1973.

59. Ibid.

60. Eddie Bernice Johnson, Ruíz Special Master, MAI 8/J-102.

61. Eric Hartman, "David Ruíz: Profile of a Writ Writer," *Texas Observer*, September 22, 1978, 6–7.

62. Ruíz unpublished memoir, "Tough with a Knife, Hell with a Writ," in author's possession, given with permission of Rose Marie Ruíz upon David Ruíz's death in 2006.

63. Ibid.

64. The other inmate complainants consolidated into the *Ruíz* civil suit included L. D. Hilliard, Ernesto Montana, Herman Randall, Leandro Pado, O. D. Johnson, and Arthur Winchester.

65. A seventeen-page letter to the author, Michael Jewell to Robert Chase, November 1, 2008, in author's possession.
66. TDCJ, Office General Counsel, Ruíz, "Inmate Writings and Correspondence," TSLA, 2004/016-55.
67. Ibid.
68. Ibid.
69. Johnny E. Swift to Chet Brooks, February 2, 1978, Papers of Chet Brooks, TSLA, 1999/136-20.
70. TDCJ, Office General Counsel, Ruíz, "Inmate Writings and Correspondence," TSLA, 2004/016-55.
71. Its sponsors included state representative Ben Reyes of Houston, state senator Carlos Traun of Corpus Christi, Ray Hill of the Human Rights League, Gargland Jaggers of the Black Secretariat of the Roman Catholic Archdiocese of Detroit, Diane Goldberg of AFSCME Local 140 (Houston), Demetrio Lucio AFSCME Local 1550 (Houston), Lorenzo Cano, Harris County Raza Unida Party (Houston), Antonio Orendain of the Texas Farmworkers Union, Rado Rosales of the Brown Berets (Houston), L. C. Dosey of the Southern Coalition on Jails and Prisons, Ron Welch of the Mississippi Prisoners Defense Committee, Eddie Sandifer of the Mississippi Alliance for Human Rights, Ruby Tobias of the Mississippi Council on Human Relations, Tom Soto of the Prisoner Solidarity Committee and a representative of Attica prisoners, Eduardo O. Canales of Centro Aztlan, and poet Allen Ginsberg.
72. Salvador Gonzales to Senator Chet Brooks, July 29, 1973, Papers of Senator Ron Cloward, TSLA, 1981/217-93.
73. In *Slavery and Social Death*, Orlando Patterson explicitly defined prisoners as having an entirely different restriction in their liberties than slaves. Patterson's trenchant definition argued that slavery was a "permanent, violent domination" of those born into slavery who subsequently were made the lifelong victims of white supremacy and a coerced labor system controlled by private ownership and sanctioned by the state. Prisoners, on the other hand, were not born into their condition and their confinement was due to their crime against society. Most prisoners could expect to return to society as full citizens, and no inmate, of course, was imprisoned from birth. Patterson, *Slavery and Social Death: A Comparative Study* (Cambridge: Harvard University Press, 1982), 13. For scholarship stressing the historical similarities between slavery and prison confinement, see Kim Gilmore, "Slavery and Prison: Understanding the Connections," *Social Justice* 27, no. 3 (2000): 195; and Wacquant, "From Slavery to Mass Incarceration."
74. "Prisoners Resist Texas Prison Slave System," handbill, Prisoner Solidarity Committee, in author's possession.
75. Expert Report Security, Arnold Pontesso, Prepared for U.S., Plaintiff-Intervenor, filed February 18, 1977.
76. Alvaro Luna Hernandez, oral history with the author, March 23, 2007, IOH-Baylor.
77. Ibid.
78. Robert Mudd, oral history with the author, March 30, 2007, IOH-Baylor.
79. Ibid.
80. Wilbur Collins, oral history with the author, March 21, 2007, IOH-Baylor.
81. Mudd, oral history with the author.

82. Hernandez, oral history with the author.

83. Mudd, oral history with the author.

84. Hernandez, oral history with the author.

85. Judge William Wayne Justice, memorandum opinion, Papers of Frances Jalet-Cruz, CAH, 94/042-16.

86. On the conceptualization of the "long civil rights movement" see Jacquelyn Dowd Hall, "The Long Civil Rights Movement and the Political Uses of the Past," *Journal of American History* 91 (March 2005): 1233–62; and Kevin Gaines, "The Historiography of the Struggle for Black Equality since 1945," in *A Companion to Post-1945 America*, edited by Jean-Christophe Agnew and Roy Rosenzweig (Malden, Mass.: Blackwell, 2002), 211–34; Peniel E. Joseph, "Waiting 'Till the Midnight Hour: Reconceptualizing the Heroic Period of the Civil Rights Movement, 1954–1965," *Souls* 2 (Spring 2000): 6–17. For work that considers the civil rights and black and brown power movements into the 1970s, see Peniel E. Joseph, ed., *The Black Power Movement: Rethinking the Civil Rights-Black Power Era* (New York: Routledge, 2006); Komozi Woodard, *A Nation within a Nation: Amiri Baraka (Le Roi Jones) & Black Power Politics* (Chapel Hill: University of North Carolina Press, 1999); Nikhil Pal Singh, *Black Is a Country: Race and the Unfinished Struggle for Democracy* (Cambridge: Harvard University Press, 2003); Ula Taylor, "Elijah Muhammad's Nation of Islam: Separatism, Regendering and a Secular Approach to Black Power after Malcolm X (1965–1975)," and Johanna Fernandez, "Between Social Service Reform and Revolutionary Politics: The Young Lords, Late Sixties Radicalism, and Community Organizing in New York City," in *Freedom North: Black Freedom Struggles Outside the South, 1940–1980*, ed. Jeanne F. Theoharis and Komozi Woodard (New York: Palgave McMillan, 2003), 177–98 and 225–86; and Scott Brown, *Fighting for US: Maulana Karenga, the US Organization, and Black Cultural Nationalism* (New York: New York University Press, 2003).

87. On the "irony" of the southern prisoners' rights movement, see Heather Thompson, "Blinded by a 'Barbaric' South: Prison Horrors, Inmate Abuse, and the Ironic History of American Penal Reform," in *The Myth of Southern Exceptionalism*, ed. Matthew Lassiter and Joseph Crespino (Oxford: Oxford University Press, 2010), 74–93.

88. In the wake of the "conservative revolution" of 1994, however, the conservative members of the new 104th Congress acknowledged the growing number of prisoners' rights suits and considered how it might curb "frivolous and abusive prison lawsuits," restrict the power of "liberal Federal judges," and return control of prisons to state legislatures. On the eve of his presidential bid of 1996, Republican Robert Dole led the response to the successes of the prisoners' rights movement by introducing and subsequently gaining passage of the Prison Litigation Reform Act (PLRA) of 1995, which made lawsuits like *Ruíz* nearly impossible in the future. What ultimately stifled the prisoners' rights movement, then, was a series of political calculations made by those who used the power of the national legislature to weaken judicial intervention and an otherwise effective legal strategy. On the Prison Litigation Reform Act, see S. 1279, 104th Congress (1995), The Prison Litigation Reform Act (PLRA); Prison Litigation Reform Act of 1995, Pub. L. No. 104-34, 110 Stat. 1321; Barbara Belbot, "Report on the Prison Litigation Reform Act: What Have the Courts Decided So Far?" *Prison Journal* 4, no. 3 (2004): 290–316. On the practical effect of PLRA on the filing of inmate lawsuits in federal court, see Matthew T. Clarke, "Barring the Federal Courthouse to Prisoners," in *Prison Nation: The Warehousing of America's Poor*, ed. Tara Herviel and Paul Wright (New York: Routledge, 2003), 301–14.

89. On the impact of racial integration on Texas prisons, see Trulson and Marquart, *First Available Cell*; Chad Trulson and James Marquart, "The Caged Melting Pot: Toward an Understanding of the Consequences of Desegregation in Prisons," *Law and Society Review* 36, no. 4 (2002): 743–82; and Chad Trulson and James W. Marquart, "Racial Desegregation and Violence in the Texas Prison System," *Criminal Justice System* 27, no. 2, (2002): 233–55.

90. On prison gangs in Texas during the mid-1980s, see Mary E. Pelz, James W. Marquart, and C. Terry Pelz, "Right-Wing Extremism in the Texas Prisons: The Rise and Fall of the Aryan Brotherhood of Texas," *Prison Journal* 71, no. 2 (1991): 23–37; Robert S. Fong, "A Comparative Study of the Organizational Aspects of Two Texas Prison Gangs: Texas Syndicate and Mexican Mafia" (Ph.D. diss., Sam Houston State University, 1987), 11–12; and Crouch and Marquart, *An Appeal to Justice*.

7

Obreros in the Peach State

The Growth of Georgia's Working-Class Mexican Immigrant
Communities from a Transnational Perspective

MICHAEL K. BESS

In 1994, fifteen-year-old Rigo Nuñez emigrated from central Mexico to the United States, crossing the border through the Sonoran desert as an undocumented immigrant. For more than a year, he worked ten-hour days as a migrant farm laborer living in Arizona, Pennsylvania, New York, and Florida. In 1996 he relocated to Dalton, Georgia, because he had learned of higher-paying jobs in the carpet mills and poultry-processing plants. With a fake ID, he took an entry-level position in one of the chicken factories, hoisting the birds onto passing hooks where they would claw at his arms and defecate on him. His fortunes changed when his mother, stepfather, and brothers moved to Dalton; this gave him the opportunity to return to high school, where he excelled in his studies. His plans to attend college and study engineering, however, were cut short due to his immigration status. As a result, Rigo returned to work after graduation, serving as a line cook in a fast-food restaurant.[1]

In many ways, Rigo's story illustrates the broader set of challenges and abuses faced by Mexican working-class immigrants. Economic pressures at home served as an impetus to move, while social networks spread news about job opportunities in various locations. Once the difficult crossing of the boarder was made, highways linked sojourners to the possibility of contact with Mexican immigrant communities stretching across the United States. In Georgia, Rigo became another point in the series of transnational social networks connecting immigrants with their families in North America. Like many others, his family relocated to Dalton because of his presence in the area. The legal barriers to advancement out of the factories, farms, restaurants, and construction sites that prevented Rigo from attending college also kept thousands of undocumented immigrants from Mexico in the position of a subordinated status in U.S. society.

Figure 7.1. By the turn of the twenty-first century, a substantial majority of the South's agricultural workers were Latinos. This migrant farmworker pauses while harvesting onions in Lyons, Georgia, in 2000. (Dr. Debra Sabia photo.)

As Mexicans considered relocating to Georgia, social networks composed of family and friends played a critical role in the decision-making process. In 1971, when Adolfo Morones opened the first Mexican restaurant in Dalton, he knew of few other Mexican families in the area. Over time, however, these circumstances began to change as people encouraged their relatives to move north. Drawn to Dalton because of nearby jobs in light industry, Morones observed: "Soon after more and more families came . . . more restaurants and businesses were opening."[2] In another example, Alonso Acosta's family moved to Dalton in 1973 after having lived for a time in New Mexico. At first his parents complained "you couldn't find a good tortilla," but that changed as more people arrived: "Everybody was missing tortillas. Now we have tortillas galore." Eventually, Acosta gained U.S. citizenship and later found work as a disc jockey for a local Spanish-language radio station and as a court interpreter.[3] Acosta's and Morones's stories speak to the cultural changes that have occurred with the formation of a Mexican immigrant community in Georgia that linked the state to other sending and receiving regions across the United States and Mexico. Furthermore, these linkages left their mark not only on places like Dalton but also on immigrants' hometowns and villages in Mexico as remittances flowed in from family members working abroad.

Since 1980, Georgia has emerged as an important destination for Mexican working-class immigrants. It has served as a land of opportunity for some and a place of frustrated dreams for others, where job discrimination and racial tensions remain palpable issues to this day. Beginning in the 1970s, individuals and families settled in the state to work in local industries, transforming places such as Gainesville and Dalton into new settlement areas. These pioneering immigrants established seed communities that supported subsequent arrivals and helped to grow the presence of a Spanish-speaking minority, while also facing the pressures of low wages, job-site abuse, and poor housing. By 2000, Mexican immigrants and others had effected a shift in Georgia's demographic composition as they contributed new cultural expressions to the broader society, opened businesses, and influenced the priorities of existing institutions. Transnational social networks played an integral role in this process as individuals shared information about living conditions and work opportunities in the state with newcomers. Aided by communal ties that stretched across political boundaries, Mexican working-class immigrants integrated Georgia into a complex framework of formal and informal relocations from Mexico to the United States. This migration trend was facilitated, in part, by a series of factors, including social networks, technology (in the form of modern highways and telecommunications), governmental policy, and the economy.

Studying these issues from a transnational perspective is necessary for an appreciation of the broad socioeconomic patterns that are connected by human migration. Changes in Mexico's economy and body politic have had a direct impact on the development of Mexican working-class communities in Georgia. Likewise, economic growth around Atlanta and other cities in the state has served as an impetus for the relocation of thousands of Mexican citizens to the region. As a result, it is important to examine not only the changes that have occurred in Georgia due to immigration but also to trace the journey and motivations that brought new migrants to the area. In doing so, it becomes possible to better understand how the state fits into the expansive immigrant social networks that reach across political, cultural, and economic borders. Moreover, by investigating social change and internal migration in Mexico, further linkages can be uncovered between that country and Georgia.

Individuals who identify as Mexican make up the largest subgroup represented in Georgia's Hispanic/Latino community.[4] Shared cultural and regional bonds among immigrants who gather in Georgia connect the state with specific places of origin in Mexico.[5] In Georgia, migrants from Guerrero, Michoacán, and Guanajuato make up 30 percent of the Mexican immigrant population; those from an additional five states, Hidalgo, Oaxaca, Estado de México, San Luis Potosí, and Veracruz, along with the Distrito Federal, make up another 30 percent.[6] The kinship and friendship bonds maintained between Mexico and the United States form an interpersonal web that distributes information among persons living across North America; the presence of individuals in one area provides another place within the social network that transmits news of job opportunities and economic conditions to family and friends living elsewhere.[7]

In order to understand the process of immigration to Georgia, it is important to examine a series of U.S. and Mexican economic and labor policies that emerged in the latter twentieth century. The Mexican government promoted industrialization of the border states following the cancellation of the bracero program, an important guest-worker agreement forged between Mexico and the United States that lasted from 1942 until 1964.[8] Likewise, civil infrastructure projects in the two countries, such as new highways, helped to mobilize workers. After 1917, with the end of the military phase of the Mexican Revolution, an ongoing road-building program made it easier for laborers to move from once-remote towns and villages to the country's major cities as well as to the rapidly industrializing northern sector.[9] The decreased cost in travel and availability of new highways crossing Mexico and linking it to population centers in the United States facilitated subsequent trends in human mobility. Once migrants decided to relocate, they could do so more easily and cover greater distances faster.

Changes in U.S. immigration law also contributed to the conditions that Rigo Nuñez and other immigrants encountered when they crossed the border. In 1965 the U.S. Congress passed the Hart-Celler amendment to federal immigration law, which eliminated the racially discriminatory National Origins Act of 1924. The new law made it easier for immigrants from India and other countries in the Eastern Hemisphere to gain visas to enter the United States. However, it also placed the first artificial cap on visa applications from Latin America. In a speech to Congress, President Lyndon Johnson declared, "the days of unlimited immigration are past."[10] As a result of this legislation, however, the number of undocumented entrants into the United States from Mexico increased markedly in subsequent years.

In response to this rise in undocumented immigration, Congress sought to address the issue. In 1986 it passed the Immigration Reform and Control Act (IRCA), which provided amnesty for 2.5 million undocumented immigrants already living in the United States. At the same time, however, it also increased funding for border patrol and deportation procedures, but did not address another one of the glaring problems with existing immigration law.[11]

It made available only 5,000 H-2A unskilled, non-farm-labor work visas at a time when contemporary studies estimated that roughly 400,000 unskilled workers crossed into the United States as undocumented immigrants from 1990 to 1996. Although Congress granted an amnesty to some immigrants living in the country in 1986, IRCA did not adequately address the issue of a continuing influx of this category of workers.[12]

Alongside immigration law, a combination of shortsighted energy and monetary policies led to disastrous consequences for Mexico's working class during this time. In 1982 the Mexican government experienced a severe credit crisis when the price of oil dropped precipitously. Previously, policy makers had used petroleum exports to finance public debt and underwrite social spending. In the 1970s, a relatively high oil price buttressed these plans. However, when prices dropped, the government did not act soon enough to prevent the need for a rescue from the International Monetary Fund and the World Bank. The crisis depressed workers' wages and limited the government's ability to provide an adequate social safety net. As a result, it led to an increase in trans-border crossings by workers seeking job opportunities in the United States. These problems were not limited to Mexico, however. Texas also suffered during this period as economic shocks related to oil affected the state's population. Atlanta now emerged as a popular destination for many Mexican immigrants, many of whom moved eastward from Houston. Experience in poultry processing and the service industry among these individuals contributed to their decision to relocate, as they were able to transfer these skills to new jobs in northern Georgia.[13]

In conjunction with this growth, however, came widespread reports of worker abuse. The Mexican consulate in Atlanta identified increasing problems across the state in many of the industries that relied heavily on Mexican workers, notably construction, poultry, and agriculture.[14] Farmworkers were particularly vulnerable, as Georgia did not require employers to pay for compensation insurance in case of injury or death. Companies operating outside the farming sector could be required to cover as much as $100,000 in benefits. In 1999, however, when sixteen-year-old migrant agricultural employee Oscar Patonza was killed by lightning while working near Vidalia, Georgia, his family and the local Mexican immigrant community were the ones who paid the $4,000 cost of his funeral and return to Mexico for burial.[15]

Networks of family and friends played an important role in how immigrant communities formed, shared information, and helped to grow the Mexican working-class population in Georgia. The transnational ties that existed across Mexico, the United States, and Georgia after 1970 complicated the conventional, binary categorization of migration sites across North America.[16] Typically, researchers designated locations as either "sending" or "receiving" on the basis of a general perception as to whether immigrants were leaving or entering the area in question. Such a categorization failed to take into consideration the role of intermediary locations in these processes. Internal migration in Mexico and the United States factored into the emergence of Georgia's Mexican immigrant working-class community as these trends became linked by international border crossings. Sites within Mexico attracted labor from other locations, as occurred in the 1960s with migration from the nation's core to its periphery along the northern border to work in the growing industrial sector. Similar trends occurred in the United States as Texas emerged as a major intermediary point in the migration process for individuals who ultimately relocated to Georgia. Simultaneously, regions could serve as "sending" and "receiving" sites for migrants; human mobility across North America exhibited greater complexity than the "sending/receiving" dichotomy suggests.

In 1999 the Universidad de Monterrey and local officials in Whitfield County (north of Atlanta) conducted area surveys to study the origins of the region's Spanish-speaking population from Mexico; researchers discovered that only 4 percent of these residents had lived in the Dalton area for more than twelve years, with the average duration being fewer than five years. Furthermore, the survey found only 25 percent of the population had relocated to Georgia directly from Mexico. Despite an already-established Spanish-speaking community in the county, most individuals reported a diverse migration experience; prior to Georgia, many of the respondents reported living in one or more of the following states: California, Texas, New York, Illinois, Colorado. The most common pattern was "a Mexico-Texas-Georgia course."[17]

These multiregional trends also occurred in southern Georgia. For example, in the 1990s, Bulloch and surrounding counties were destinations for seasonal migrant laborers who arrived in the area to participate in the harvest of onions and other crops. They came from Texas and other southern and western states that traditionally had a strong demand for unskilled farm laborers. Regional businessmen and farmers in Georgia actively sought out Mexican labor for a variety of reasons, including reliability, cost, and unwillingness of local residents to perform what they considered menial labor. Typically, these businesses contracted with Mexican American labor agents who traveled to other states and to Mexico to bring workers to the area. By 1999, as seasonal migrants had begun to relocate to Bulloch, Toombs, and other counties in southeast Georgia, a visible community had developed with new businesses, including ethnic grocery stores and restaurants, to serve these new migrants.

At the same time, local schools, alongside religious and civic organizations, developed programs to protect Spanish-speaking immigrants from exploitation, while helping them to integrate into the general community.[18]

While various regions of the state evolved along different time lines owing to local conditions, the earliest established Mexican working-class communities formed around metropolitan Atlanta in Whitfield and Hall Counties. Labor demand from carpeting mills and poultry-processing plants in Dalton and Gainesville opened space for Mexican workers from outside the state. As later occurred in southern Georgia, area businesses worked with labor agents to obtain new employees, many of whom came initially from Texas. Owing to the needs of plant managers in these industries, immigrants who arrived to work settled to become permanent or long-term residents rather than seasonal migrants who traveled between regions. In Gainesville in the 1980s, Hispanic/Latino-owned businesses, Spanish-language religious bodies, and financial services emerged along with cultural festivals and regular bus service with Mexico.[19]

Social aid organizations played important institutional roles in the city's growing network of Spanish-speaking immigrants. Founded in 1972, the Latin American Association provided legal advice and other services to immigrants focusing on issues related to residency and citizenship from offices across metropolitan Atlanta. In 1998 the group recorded helping more than 5,700 individuals.[20] Religious organizations also figured prominently within immigrant settlement areas. Like others from Latin America, many Mexicans identified with the cultural and religious practices of the Roman Catholic Church. By 2006, with 103 churches across northern Georgia, the Archdiocese of Atlanta represented one of the largest in the area. Sixty percent of its parishes operated Hispanic/Latino ministries, employed Spanish-speaking religious and social workers, and coordinated their efforts with the community through a central office in the state capital. In the same year, Leonardo Jaramillo, regional director of the archdiocesan Hispanic Youth Association, described the church's program in Atlanta as being "concerned with developing processes for culture integration, not assimilation." His organization sponsored socializing opportunities for Spanish-speaking youth and support for families. These activities complemented broader programs within the diocese that performed religious rituals common to Latin America and provided a network of parallel organizations within existing church communities across metropolitan Atlanta.[21]

Other Christian denominations also pursued active outreach programs in Georgia. Across the United States, the broader Hispanic/Latino population represented one of the fastest-growing groups for Protestant churches, with evangelical churches identified as the most popular organizations. In contrast to the Catholics, not only did Protestants provide parallel religious and social services at existing sites, but some enterprising ministers opened fully independent churches specifically to target emergent Spanish-speaking groups. Older mainline Protestant denominations and newer start-ups became alternative forms of religious expression for immigrants; in common with the Catholics, these groups provided a sense of belonging and support to new arrivals from Latin America.

In Warner Robins, Georgia, two hours south of the state capital, the First Hispanic Baptist Mission provided an annual mobile health fair for migrant workers. In 1981, when Daniel Carrazco first began working at a local peach orchard, the mission helped him to establish himself; he later relocated his family to the area and gained U.S. citizenship. In 1999, his daughter, Laura, described the role played by the church's medical and community outreach programs: "Some people come from places in Mexico where they don't have doctors. And sometimes they don't go to doctors here because they're afraid of immigration. They're afraid they'll be sent back." Migrant workers felt that they could trust the services provided by the mission, because of its religious character. Alongside medical support, the church also conducted food and clothing drives, English classes, and religious training.[22] The emergence of these autonomous Spanish-language entities within existing social and religious institutions, as well as independent Hispanic/Latino churches, reflected the growth of this community in the United States and Georgia.[23]

Innovations in communications and transportation facilitated socioeconomic linkages between regions in Georgia and Mexico. As the flow of ideas and people became easier and faster, cultural interaction increased. Once Mexican working-class immigrants arrived in Georgia, technology made it easier for them to maintain these broad, transnational social networks. The availability of affordable international phone cards helped to reduce the time information took to travel between regions, allowing immigrants to relay details of living conditions in one settlement area to those residing in another.[24]

Immigrants living in Georgia could send information and remittances to Mexico, thus transforming their home communities in Mexico into "receiving" regions for news and financial assistance. In turn, Mexican towns and cities participated in the traditional but imperfect definition of "sending" regions when additional residents relocated elsewhere within the country or to the United States in order to find work. While these relationships had existed in past migrations, modern telecommunications contributed to the formation of persistent, up-to-date bonds between regions. Immigrants in the latter twentieth century had a variety of new and old tools at their disposal, including landline and mobile phones and the Internet, in order to close the practicality gap and maintain relationships with family and friends in faraway locations.

Modern communications, however, represent only one aspect of how technology influenced human migration across North America and Georgia. A very old form of technology also affected these trends: road construction. In the mid-1920s and 1930s, Mexico embarked upon ambitious infrastructure projects that included the development of modern highway systems and the extension of these networks to rural communities. By the beginning of the 1940s, the state of Oaxaca (an important source of immigrants to Georgia) was linked to this national system. With it came new opportunities as inexpensive manufactures from the central and northern regions of Mexico began to replace local goods produced by the indigenous populations. Roads also linked Oaxaca to transnational labor markets, making participation in the U.S. bracero program easier. It initiated a preference for migration as a means of support among the working poor in Oaxaca that continued even after cancellation of the bracero program. Furthermore, tourism to Oaxaca increased, allowing for a rise in the production of some indigenous goods for sale to this market and heightening the importance of the regional capital at the expense of rural communities. By the mid-twentieth century the government's programs of infrastructural development had begun to change Oaxaca's population mix. Its residents increasingly saw migration as an option in their efforts to improve living standards and persue personal ambitions.[25]

Internal migration in Mexico intensified thanks to the construction of federal highways and local thoroughfares. Across the country, these roads helped decrease the costs of shipping and travel. They also meant that citizens could look beyond their local communities for economic opportunities. After 1964, when the federal government initiated policies for intensive industrialization of the border states, these new roads played pivotal roles in human mobility trends.

Likewise, Georgia became a more likely place to relocate to thanks to the convergence in Atlanta of highway networks serving the eastern United States. After the completion of I-85 and I-75 in 1964 and 1977, respectively, one could easily travel to Atlanta from major U.S. cities, including Houston, New York, and Miami. At the same time, as larger numbers of Mexican working-class immigrants settled around metropolitan Atlanta in the 1980s and 1990s, the city became an important hub for air travel, commerce, and financial services. Road building was crucial to the city's development and laid the foundation for further ongoing highway construction; moreover, innovations in transportation and communication technologies facilitated the transfer of people and information, becoming an important element for transnational social networks and international migration across North America in the late twentieth century. Mexican workers in Georgia used these technological and infrastructural developments to respond to the new economic opportunities that Georgia now offered.

The proliferation of new highways broadened and accelerated human migration processes occurring in Mexico. Oftentimes, the first move did not include an international relocation but rather an in-country rural-to-urban migration. The 1960s and 1970s marked an important era of internal mobility for Mexico as federal and state governments developed programs to stimulate economic development, while hundreds of thousands of the country's citizens relocated in response to emerging opportunities. In 1964, the end of the bracero program contributed to the modern era of U.S.-Mexico immigration trends.[26] The Mexican government responded to this program's cancellation with industrialization programs meant to bolster the economies of the border states.

In 1961 it instituted the Programa Nacional Fronterizo (PRONAF), which supported the construction of factories known as maquiladoras in northern Mexico. Mexican leaders encouraged the flow of direct foreign investment into this region, in part to provide jobs to Mexican workers, stimulate population growth, and further integrate the borderlands economy of the United States and Mexico. The program also brought new patterns of economic growth to Mexico and attracted workers from the nation's urban core, including Mexico City, Guadalajara, and the Estado de México, to its less-developed periphery along the U.S. border. These population flows represented a turning point in the relationship between Mexico and the United States while also providing the workers for continued industrial growth in Mexican border states.

Between 1961 and 1982, Mexico engineered dramatic economic and population growth at the border through its promotion of the maquiladora system. While workers from across the country relocated to the burgeoning manufacturing centers in the north, the Distrito Federal and the states of Guerrero, Guanajuato, Michoacán, Oaxaca, and Puebla recorded some of the highest rates of labor emigration. In Ciudad Juárez, Chihuahua, PRONAF provided federal funding for new roads and bridges and for an industrial park that attracted foreign-owned factories to the area. Infrastructure developments and new highway construction along the border expanded existing infrastructure programs begun after the Revolution. Between 1961 and 1965 the federal government invested more than $400 million in civil, commercial, and industrial projects in the largest borderlands cities, including Nogales, Tijuana, Nuevo

Laredo, and Ciudad Juárez.[27] In addition, from 1960 to 1980 the Mexican side of the border experienced rapid population growth thanks to internal migration trends as laborers relocated from Mexico's central and southern regions. The development of the maquiladora system facilitated this process, with workers moving to the borderlands in search of employment in the new factories. Likewise, as urbanization occurred in the area, Mexico's cities also grew faster than their U.S. counterparts.[28]

The ramifications of the 1982 collapse in world oil prices reverberated throughout Mexico. Since the government had relied on high petroleum prices to fund national spending, this change placed pressures on the ability to maintain its debt-repayment schedule. Subsequent restructuring of the government's budget forced deep cuts in social spending that severely affected working- and middle-class Mexican citizens. For example, in Oaxaca, the introduction of neoliberal economic strategies during the credit crisis cut subsidies to poor Oaxacans and increased economic inequality. Sixty-one percent of emigrating residents came from some of Oaxaca's poorest regions, a development that disproportionately affected the state's rural and indigenous population.[29] The credit crisis also severely affected the Mexican heartland and increased the importance of the maquiladora system to working-class citizens. During the 1980s, despite nationwide cuts in spending, foreign direct investment in the industrial sector at the border spurred the construction of new factories that attracted thousands of new Mexican workers from economically depressed areas.[30]

Meanwhile, particular states and local communities in the United States also suffered economic downturns in the 1980s as a result of the drop in global oil prices. Texas was an epicenter of the crisis. Between 1982 and 1987, with the collapse of the oil-dependent Houston economy, an estimated 210,000 jobs were lost in the city alone. This economic downturn in the state influenced the redirection of human migration coming from Mexico and opened up opportunities for the emergence of other settlement areas. One contemporary Mexican immigrant who emigrated from Houston to Atlanta at the time commented, "We thought the whole town of Houston had moved here [to Atlanta]. Since the collapse of the oil economy in Texas, people began to flock here and they haven't stopped."[31] This event served as one of the turning points that contributed to Georgia's integration into the long history of internal and transnational migrations occurring across Mexico and the United States. Migrants who had already experienced the journey from communities in the heart of Mexico and crossed the border turned their sights toward new settlement opportunities. In the early 1990s, a building boom in Georgia served as an impetus for the rapid growth of the Mexican immigrant community in the state.

The 1996 Olympics brought a series of important construction projects to Atlanta as state and private entities invested hundred of millions of dollars in the city for urban renewal and expansion. New projects included the building of a $63 million residential facility for athletes and staff, as well as creating a five-kilometer city renovation zone, known as the "Olympic Circle," to update Atlanta's appearance for the international media and for millions of expected visitors.[32] Labor demand was particularly pronounced in the construction and service industries as the city required thousands of low-wage workers to help prepare it for the Olympics. In 1994, as the city came under criticism for construction delays, employers turned to existing social networks within the Mexican immigrant and Hispanic/Latino communities in order to recruit new workers. Former consul general for the Mexican Consulate in Atlanta, María de los Remedios Gómez-Arnau, observed that "there was a need for workers, clearly during [preparations] for the Olympics games . . . at the same time people in other states and in Mexico knew of these job opportunities."[33]

These new economic options in Georgia occurred at a time when Mexico had experienced another serious economic setback. On December 20, 1994, the new finance minister under President Ernesto Zedillo announced a series of policy shifts to correct the overvalued currency. Fiscal mismanagement and politically motivated policy delays led to insufficient stabilization measures, which precipitated a dramatic collapse of the peso and high inflation. In the United States, the Clinton administration, in concert with the international community, sought to intervene in this chaotic situation, but the loss of foreign confidence and investment hurt Mexico's economy and its ability to provide for its people. Furthermore, the passage of the North American Free Trade Agreement earlier that year had also had a serious impact on Mexican workers' economic competitiveness. While some industries benefited, others lost trade protections formerly afforded to them by the federal government.[34] Both events had an unsettling effect in Mexico, as workers confronted with unemployment and inflation relocated to the United States. In 1994 and 1995 the U.S. Bureau of Labor Statistics calculated that the entry of undocumented Mexican immigrants into the country increased from 400,000 to over 600,000 people.[35]

With high demand for labor, Atlanta benefited from the increased emigration from Mexico. During this period, Georgia enjoyed one of the fastest-growing economies in the United States and attracted Mexican labor to assist in the preparations for the Olympics and later to remain in construction and services as the state went through a subsequent housing and population boom. The U.S. Census Bureau has reported that between 1990 and 2000 the Hispanic/Latino population increased from roughly 108,922 to 435,227 persons. Mexicans accounted for 60 percent of this emergent minority group.[36] In certain ways, the processes, which occurred in the metropolitan area in the 1990s, resembled those that had occurred in Gainesville and Dalton in the 1970s and 1980s. Local employers solicited the aid of labor agents and existing transnational social networks to attract Mexican workers to their areas. After 1996, however, the arrival of new Mexican working-class immigrants to Atlanta accelerated as the state's economy continued to outperform the national average. The emergent Hispanic/Latino minority followed similar gains in the general statewide population, which rose by 26 percent during this period. In 1990 the labor market in Georgia employed 47,000 Mexican immigrant workers; by 2000 this figure had risen to 193,321, with representation across a number of industries.[37]

With these gains in employment among Hispanic/Latino laborers, however, came continued reports of worker abuse. For example, in 1997, advocacy groups reported cases of maltreatment by employers against Mexican immigrant workers. One case in April 1997 found that laborers lost two weeks' worth of wages when their overseers decided not to pay them. Since many of the workers had come to the state without proper documentation, they feared that reporting the company to authorities could result in their deportation.[38] In 1999 the onion harvest in Vidalia County created employment for five thousand manual laborers, with a large percentage of these individuals originally from Mexico. Many of these workers were housed in unsafe and unclean living conditions while they worked during the harvest season.[39] These examples highlight the difficulty of life for undocumented laborers in the United States; the lack of legal protections increased their vulnerability to unscrupulous employers. Nevertheless, despite these recurring hardships, Georgia remained a popular new settlement area because it offered jobs and the opportunity to send money back home.

For immigrant workers' families who remained in Mexico, remittances served as an important economic benefit. Residents of San Andrés Tlalnelhuayoca, Veracruz, a rural town forty-five minutes outside of the state capital of Xalapa, have seen many young men and women follow relatives who had already immigrated to Georgia and other states across the U.S. South. The funds they have sent back home have helped to stimulate the local economy; family members have opened small businesses in the community and also built new homes. Since 2003, Oscar Romero has worked as the principal of the *telesecundaria* in San Andrés.[40] He described the impact that remittances have had on meeting some of his students' everyday needs: "The father sends money to buy clothes, to buy the uniform and also provides money for breakfast, because the students have to pay for their meals at school."[41]

Growth in remittances from Georgia's migrant laborers to Mexico attested to the state's importance as a source of economic funding for Mexican families. In 1994 the Bank of Mexico reported an 11.2 percent increase in the dollar amount of remittances (compared to the previous year), which totaled more than $4 billion transferred by immigrants in the United States to families in Mexico. This figure also marked the only positive area of growth for the nation's balance of trade in foreign exchange for that year.[42] Through the remainder of the 1990s and into the new century, the importance of remittances as a percentage of the economy in Mexico continued to grow; at its height in 2007, the level of remittances sent by Mexican immigrants living in the United States exceeded $26 billion. By 2004, Georgia ranked as the tenth most important state of origin for remittances to Latin America, and Mexico was a key recipient of these funds. Furthermore, more than 80 percent of Georgia's Hispanic/Latino community regularly transferred money to family members living abroad.[43]

These processes contributed to a complex economic network in which communities in Georgia, elsewhere in the United States, and Mexico benefited each other. An immigrant economy emerged that not only transferred remittances but also created individual demand for new products and services in U.S. settlement areas. Between 1980 and 1989 more than 32,000 Mexicans immigrated to Georgia; between 1990 and 2004 an additional 216,000 arrived. This demographic shift brought change with it.[44] Not only did Mexican immigrants predominantly come from the working class and fill low-wage jobs in construction, manufacturing, agriculture, and the services sector, but these individuals also forged a new immigrant economy in Georgia.

Local businesses responded to the emergent Spanish-speaking demographic by offering goods and services targeted at this group. During the 1990s and 2000s the University of Georgia recorded a dramatic increase in the economic weight of the state's Hispanic/Latino community, which by 2006 accounted for a considerable portion of consumption. During the 1990s, Dalton's consumer demographics were particularly affected by the rise in emigration from Mexico. In 1999, Rafael Sanhueza-Bazeas, director of the local Centro Latino observed, "If you go to Wal-Mart or a couple of strip centers, it is completely Latino. The number of businesses has grown to 75, and most of that is in the last two years. They are providing services from money transfers, insurance, banking, shoe stores, money management." Another local resident,

Homero Luna, noted that when he first arrived in 1993, he used to feel conspicuous when shopping. Six years later, he said, "Now when I go to Wal-Mart, I say, 'Did you notice those Anglos?'"[45]

This market presence also supported the opening of ethnic businesses that catered to Mexicans and other Latin Americans. Family-owned grocery stores stocked goods from home countries, restaurants catered to immigrants' tastes, and ethnic media provided print and broadcast outlets. Non-Spanish-speaking companies also adjusted their business models in Georgia (as elsewhere in the United States) to accommodate this burgeoning minority population. Banks and retail stores hired bilingual employees and offered goods and services targeted to immigrants' needs, while existing media evolved to incorporate new minorities into their target audiences. In November 2006, Clear Channel radio networks transferred one of its English-language rock stations in metropolitan Atlanta into a Spanish-language format, bringing the total number of the area's radio broadcasters serving Hispanic/Latino listeners to seven. Furthermore, across the state, authentic Mexican restaurants and stores became increasingly common and accessible.

By 2004, Mexicans and other Hispanic/Latinos wielded a combined total of more than $5 billion in buying power in the statewide economy. While still much smaller than total non-Hispanic/Latino figures, it nonetheless represented a growing market in the state that attracted existing companies and institutions while spawning its own businesses within the settlement community.[46] In Mexico, communities experienced the effects of this immigrant economy through remittances, which became a form of "foreign" direct investment by relatives living in the United States. Money from abroad helped families to build new homes, enlarge existing ones, and open businesses in Mexico; returning immigrants also contributed to the local economy with money saved working across the border. But access to remittances brought associated social costs, as children became estranged from parents who lived for many years in the United States and villages and towns lost access to labor that emigrated elsewhere for better pay.[47]

Despite economic gains, life in Georgia has also been marked by social challenges and alienation for Spanish-speaking communities. In 2006, six Mexican immigrants were killed during a series of home invasions at a trailer park in Tifton, a town of about fifteen thousand people located three hours south of Atlanta. With the arrest of four African Americans for the crimes, racial tensions were heightened considerably between the communities. In order to avert further violence, Hispanic/Latino, African American, and white leaders came together to condemn the robberies and call for greater understanding and cooperation among the town's citizens.[48]

This episode reflected a broader mood in the state that speaks to the difficulties accompanying major shifts in population demographics. Due to differences in language and culture, barriers formed between Spanish-speaking immigrant settlements and preexisting white and African American groups in Georgia. In Willacoochee (Atkinson County), the friendship between two spiritual leaders highlighted this divide. Reverends Harvey Williams and Atanasio Gaona have known one another since 1993, and they described their relationship as a "brotherhood" based on mutual beliefs in Pentecostalism. The men prayed together regularly and collaborated on local civic and religious issues, but also acknowledged that neither man had ever preached in the other's church, nor were their families friends. Gaona described the challenges facing their communities: "I remind them [Hispanic/Latinos] that we need to respect people, no matter how they look or their color. But mostly, we don't know them [African Americans], and they don't know us. There's no real communication going on."[49]

A lack of communication has seen emergent trends of hostility and alienation affect the lives of working-class Mexicans and other Spanish-speaking immigrants who have settled in Georgia. In Pearson, also a part of Atkinson County, Elton Corbitt, a seventy-six-year-old white business owner, blames immigration for threatening the quality of the town's public schools and way of life. He fears that "the way the Mexicans have children, they're going to have a majority here soon. . . . [Whites] are going to become second-class citizens." In contrast to Corbitt's sentiments, local Mexico-born residents express a mixture of pride and concern. Olga Contreras-Martinez immigrated to the area in 1993, and over time much of her immediate family and other relatives also relocated to Pearson. She described the subtle tensions that exist among the small town's inhabitants: "Because of my color, my last name, people always question me. I call it home, but I know I'm not welcome in my own home." In many ways, her words reflect the myriad social challenges faced by the Mexican immigrant community in the state. At the same time, her acknowledgment of Georgia as her home also speaks to the enduring changes that have continued to transform the region's demographic composition. Whereas a long-standing racial binary between whites and African Americans described the state's past, today, Mexican immigrants and other groups have transformed this dynamic into one that is more socially complex, multilingual, and multicultural.[50]

Conclusion

Between 1970 and 2000, Mexican immigrant workers became an important source of low-wage labor in Georgia, filling positions in poultry processing, carpet manufacturing, agriculture, construction, and the service industries.

The emergence of Mexican immigrant communities in the Peach State occurred within broader migration trends across North America that brought growing numbers of Mexicans to the United States. Transnational social networks linked settlement communities, allowing them to share information and resources.

Social conditions and economic policies within Mexico played a critical but often overlooked role in the formation of a Mexican immigrant working class in Georgia. The construction of highways across Mexico in the early and middle decades of the twentieth century lowered the cost of travel and facilitated individual labor relocation. Initially, these workers arrived in the country's sprawling core cities, notably Mexico City and Guadalajara, but later economic slowdown in these areas, combined with the rise of the Mexican border as an industrial engine, brought hundreds of thousands of individuals northward. The memory of earlier guest-worker programs, especially the Bracero Agreement of 1942, created a class of Mexican laborers who experienced life in the United States and informed future migrants about the costs and opportunities associated with immigration. In the 1960s and 1970s the borderlands experienced rapid population growth, thanks to the creation of PRONAF and federal support of the maquiladora system, which increased cross-border economic interaction and created a physical space where millions of Mexican citizens had contact with the United States on a regular basis. Economic opportunities in these regions and beyond, alongside the 1982 credit crisis and the 1994 peso devaluation, not only encouraged many Mexican workers to become international immigrants but also impelled immigrants in Texas to move out of the U.S. Southwest in search of jobs in nontraditional settlement areas, such as Georgia.

What began as internal migration in Mexico from the nation's central and southern states to the borderlands evolved into modern immigrant trajectories that brought new Mexican workers to the U.S. South. Like the earliest communities in Gainesville and Dalton, where laborers arrived from Texas to work in local industries, metropolitan Atlanta emerged as a prominent hub for this minority group. The need for labor prior to the 1996 Summer Olympics, followed by subsequent construction and population booms in the state, provided economic opportunities that attracted Mexican immigrant workers and thus affected the state's demographic makeup. The concurrent rise of an immigrant economy, which opened new retail outlets and produced its own media, also influenced existing businesses and institutions. It created a space where diverse social communities could exist, incorporating Mexican culture and the Spanish language into the broader social fabric in Georgia. Beyond the market, noncommercial entities such as churches, schools, and mutual-aid societies either incorporated services targeted to the state's growing Spanish-speaking minority or (particularly among evangelical Christian groups) started new entities that eschewed the existing non-Hispanic majority.

By the 1990s these interrelated developments helped to make Georgia a prominent new settlement area for Mexican immigrants. Each of the state's counties experienced some growth of this new minority, while existing communities, particularly around metropolitan Atlanta, matured into permanent settlement areas with their own cultural characteristics amid the non-Hispanic majority. Furthermore, while other Hispanic/Latino migrants also moved into the state, existing social networks dating to the 1970s, in conjunction with Georgia's established economic ties to the U.S. Southwest and Mexico, meant that within this broader Spanish-speaking demographic, Mexicans occupied a dominant position, accounting for nearly 60 percent of the Hispanic/Latino category.[51] These trends also complicated conventional notions of immigrant entry into the United States. They expanded beyond familiar sites for Mexican immigrants, such as California and the U.S. Southwest, to include Georgia in a growing number of nontraditional settlement areas that formed over the latter decades of the twentieth century. In large part, this demographic change occurred thanks to the arrival of working-class individuals from Mexico in search of economic opportunities and better lives.

Within the broader context of U.S. immigration history, Georgia's chapter occurred much later than other parts of the country and has been ongoing for only forty years. Its story, however, is connected to the larger framework of Mexican identity in the United States. Whereas California, New York, Chicago, and other parts of the country had experienced this process of community development before, these trends now extended to Georgia. Likewise, social conditions in the U.S. South brought new challenges for Spanish-speaking immigrants moving into the region. It has also engaged in the cultural question of what it means to be a Mexican and Mexican American living in a part of the United States where southern accents and identities have changed the way people view themselves and others. In many respects, this is an ongoing process that has had important implications not only for Georgia but also for the Mexican working-class immigrants who continue to call the state home.

Notes

1. Jim Dyer, "The Dreams of Rigo Nuñez," *Atlanta Journal and Constitution*, January 24, 1999, 01C.

2. Perla Trevizo, "East Dalton Bustles with Ethnicity," *Chattanooga Times Free Press*, May 28, 2008, NG1.

3. Shelia M. Poole, "How Latinos Have Settled into Three Southern Communities," *Atlanta Journal Constitution*, May 3, 1998, 04H.

4. It is important to recognize the differences inherent in the terms "Hispanic/Latino" and "Mexican" and resist the urge to use them interchangeably. The former refers to all individuals who self-identify with a Latin American cultural heritage; this broader cohort includes Guatemalans, Cubans, Colombians, and others, as well as U.S. citizens, and does not distinguish between documented and undocumented immigrants. Likewise, the latter term, which describes individuals who originated specifically from Mexico, is also complicated by sub-identities in culture and political status; Mexicans came to Georgia from various places and for diverse reasons, and they carried with them regional and social distinctions. At times, however, it is necessary to speak of these diverse cohorts in a variety of ways, and as such, there exist three tiers of commonly accepted identifiers: Hispanic/Latino, Mexican, and state identities (Oaxacan, for example). The more specific term "Mexican working-class immigrant" refers to individuals from Mexico who arrive in the United States with either documented or undocumented status and work in labor-intensive sectors. In Georgia these fields predominantly include construction, restaurant and hotel services, light industry, and agriculture. Beginning in the 1970s, members of the Mexican immigrant working class and other Hispanic/Latino groups became a key source of labor for local businesses such as poultry processing and the carpet-making industry.

5. Writing on the immigrant experience, cultural critic Homi K. Bhabha described the process as "a time of gathering. Gatherings of exiles and émigrés and refugees; gathering on the edge of 'foreign cultures'" (Homi K. Bhabha, *The Location of Culture* [London: Routledge, 1994], 199). Communities of working-class immigrants from Mexico grew around this process of gathering.

6. Instituto de los Mexicanos en el Exterior, *El Sistema de Información Origen-Destino de Comunidades Mexicanas*, http://www.ime.gob.mx/estados.html.

7. Tamar Jacoby, "Immigration Nation," *Foreign Affairs* 11 (2006): 2, http://www.foreignaffairs.org/20061101faessay85606-p10/tamar-jacoby/immigration-nation.html.

8. Edward J. Williams, "The Maquiladora Industry and Environmental Degradation in the United States–Mexican Borderlands," paper delivered at International Boundaries and Environmental Security Conference, University of Singapore (1995), http://www.natlaw.com/pubs/williams.htm.

9. Rafael Reyes Morales, Antonio Yúnes Naude, Alicia Sylvia Gijón Cruz, and Raúl Hinojosa Ojeda, "Características de la migración internacional en Oaxaca y sus impactos en el desarrollo regional," in *Nuevas tendencias y desafios de la migración internacional México–Estados Unidos*, ed. Raul Delgado Wise and Margarita Favela (Mexico City: Universidad Autonoma de Zacatecas, 2004), 197–207.

10. Lyndon Johnson, "Remarks at the Signing of the Immigration Bill," speech, Lyndon Johnson Presidential Library (October 3, 1965) http://www.lbjlib.utexas.edu/johnson/archives.hom/speeches.hom/651003.asp.

11. U.S. Congress, Immigration Reform and Control Act (1986) http://thomas.loc.gov/cgibin/bdquery/z?d099:SN01200:@@@L&summ2=m&|TOM:/bss/d099query.html|#summary.

12. Hans P. Johnson, *At Issue: Illegal Immigration* (San Francisco: Public Policy Institute of California, 2006), http://www.ppic.org/content/pubs/atissue/AI_406HJAI.pdf.

13. Maria Puente, "Newcomers Encounter Disparate Greetings," *USA Today*, July 3, 1995, Final Edition, 8A.

14. Elizabeth Kurylo, "Georgia Migrant Workers Face Harsh Reality," *Atlanta Journal Constitution*, July 22, 1997, State News, 02E.

15. "Migrants' Plight: Worker's Death Renews Debate," Associated Press State and Local Wire, May 20, 1999 (Lexis Nexis Academic).

16. The term *transnational social network* describes a collection of interpersonal relationships between individuals and groups that share information. These entities have predominantly appeared in two forms: personal and institutional. The first comprised those familial and friendship bonds human beings create throughout their lives; in transnational networks these became important interchanges that communicate between immigrants and potential immigrant communities about living conditions and job availability. They also provide for a support network once new individuals have arrived in a settlement area. Fernando Herrera-Lima, *Vidas Itinerantes en un Espacio Laboral Transnacional* (Mexico City: Universidad Autonoma Metropolitana, 2005), 265.

The second form describes businesses and organizations, such as mutual aid societies and religious groups. Networks of labor agents and employers exchange information with workers to direct them to particular locations. On the other hand, churches allow immigrants to express different aspects of their identity through regional organizations including the Archdiocese of Atlanta and the Southeastern Pastoral Institute, a Hispanic/Latino body based in Miami with offices across the South. These institutional networks played a crucial bridging function between established immigrant communities and emergent new settlement areas. In the 1970s and 1990s, in the case of the Mexican immigrant working class in Georgia, labor agents sought out these to fill positions in construction and other industries. Pew Research Center, *Changing Faiths: Latinos and the Transformation of American Religion,* http://pewhispanic.org/reports/report.php?ReportID=75.

Once a new community was established, the relative importance of labor agents diminished in relation to the rise of new entities based around family, religious, and mutual-aid networks. Sociologist Tamar Jacoby has noted the dynamism in these forms of associations, highlighting how immigrants in the United States spoke with relatives and friends about job projects and living conditions in various places across the country. If the market was flat in one area but growing in another, social networks improved the ability of individuals looking to relocate to make informed decisions, producing "a just-in-time delivery of workers wherever they are most needed." This process also occurred within internal migration trends in both countries as a mobile working class relocated from their homes in Mexico's central and southern regions to the assembly plants along the border and from economically depressed areas in the United States to places with growth opportunities. Jacoby, "Immigration Nation," 2.

17. Victor Zúñiga and Rubén Hernández-León, "A New Destination for an Old Migration: Origins, Trajectories, and Labor Market Incorporation of Latinos in Dalton, Georgia," in *Latino Workers in the Contemporary South*, edited by Arthur D. Murphy, Colleen Blanchard, and Jennifer A. Hall (Athens: University of Georgia Press, 2001), 126–36.

18. Debra Sabia, founding director of the Center for Hispanic Outreach, interview by author, April 21, 2009, Statesboro, Georgia, digital recording, author's collection.

19. Greg Guthey, "Mexican Places in Southern Spaces: Globalization, Work, and Daily

Life in and around the North Georgia Poultry Industry," in Murphy, Blanchard, and Hall, *Latino Workers in the Contemporary South*, 64.

20. Mark Bixler, "Immigrants Flood Clinics for Legal Aid," *Atlanta Journal and Constitution*, October 28, 1999, 14A.

21. Leonardo Jaramillo, director of Archdiocese of Atlanta Hispanic Youth Ministry, interview by author, March 2, 2007, Atlanta, tape recording, author's collection.

22. Elliot Minor, "Migrant Ministry Helps Workers in Peach Country," June 11, 1999, Associated Press State and Local Wire (Lexis Nexis Academic).

23. Pew Hispanic Center, *Changing Faiths*.

24. Jacoby, "Immigration Nation," 4.

25. Reyes Morales et al., "Características de la migración internacional."

26. Carlos Marentes, *Los Braceros, 1942–1964* (1997) http://www.farmworkers.org/benglish.html.

27. Wilebaldo Martinez-Toyes, "Programa Nacional Fronterizo: El caso de Ciudad Juárez" (Ciudad Juárez: Universidad Autónoma de Ciudad Juárez), 1, http://docentes2.uacj.mx/rquinter/cronicas/pronaf.htm.

28. David Lorey, *The U.S.-Mexican Border* (Wilmington, Del.: SR Books, 1999), 104–6.

29. Reyes Morales et al., "Características de la migración internacional."

30. Lorey, *U.S.-Mexican Border*, 108.

31. Puente, "Newcomers Encounter Disparate Greetings."

32. *Atlanta Journal Constitution*, September 16, 1990.

33. Maria de los Remedios Gómez-Arnau, interview by author, March 30, 2007, Atlanta, tape recording, author's collection.

34. Barbara Hogenboom, *Mexico and the NAFTA Debate: The Transnational Politics of Economic Integration* (Utrecht: International Books, 1998), 20.

35. Johnson, *At Issue*, 7.

36. University of Georgia Business Outreach Services, *Hispanics by the Numbers in Georgia*, 1–4, http://www.sbdc.ugo.edu/pdfs/hispanicfactsheet.pdf.

37. Beata Kochut and Jeffrey M. Humphreys, eds., *Going North: Mexican Immigrants in Georgia, Alabama, Mississippi, and Tennessee* (Atlanta: Selig Center, 2006), 8–12.

38. Kurylo, "Georgia Migrant Workers."

39. Jingle Davis, "Vidalia Country: Growing Pains," *Atlanta Journal and Constitution*, April 25, 1999, 4F.

40. *Telesecundarias* are built in rural communities that lack access to typical middle schools and high schools. Classrooms include an instructor but are also set up to provide distance learning via television and VCR.

41. Oscar Romero, interview by the author, December 15, 2008, San Andrés Tlalnelhuayoca, Veracruz, Mexico, digital recording, author's collection.

42. Bank of Mexico, *Informe Anual* (Mexico City, 1995), 134.

43. Federal Reserve Bank of Atlanta, *Banks and the Growing Remittance Market* (Atlanta, 2004) http://www.frbatlanta.org/invoke.cfm?objectid=6553F3D5-BF6E-C31B-B89F8C1231EDF320&method=display#table.

44. Kochut and Humphreys, *Going North*, 8–12.

45. Gil Klein, "Hispanic Population Grows Rapidly in South," *Tampa Tribune*, September 7, 1999, 1.

46. Kochut and Humphreys, *Going North*, 74.

47. Romero, interview by author.

48. "Minority Cooperation Lacking in South," *Grand Rapids Press*, November 5, 2006, A12.

49. Rachel Swarns, "Bridging the Racial Rift That Isn't Black and White," *New York Times*, October 3, 2006, 1.

50. Rachel Swarns, "In Georgia, Newest Immigrants Unsettle an Old Sense of Place," *New York Times*, August 4, 2006, 1.

51. University of Georgia, *Hispanics by the Numbers*, 4.

8

Race and Labor in Memphis since the King Assassination

MICHAEL K. HONEY AND DAVID H. CISCEL

In 1968, African Americans in Memphis had good reason to hope for a future of racial equality. The Civil Rights Act of 1964 promised equal treatment in public accommodations and employment, while the 1965 Voting Rights Act promised equal access to the ballot. Dr. Martin Luther King Jr. called these legislative victories "phase one" of the freedom struggle.[1] Speaking to thirteen hundred striking black sanitation strikers and about ten thousand of their supporters in Memphis on March 18, 1968, King called for a phase two "struggle for genuine equality, which means economic equality."[2]

Phase two did not happen. While the struggle for civil rights seemed to triumph in the election of President Barack Obama, the struggle for economic equality since King's death has continually moved backwards. The story of what has happened in Memphis over the past four decades parallels the story of economic inequality in the United States as a whole. After a few remarkable steps toward success, opportunities vanished in a series of social and economic policies that marginalized the economic power of working men and women. Most importantly, the power that comes from unionization declined dramatically.

First, corporate opposition to unions and union rights grew. Second, manufacturing, the heart of unions in the United States, fled to low-wage sanctuaries beyond U.S. borders. Third, new low-wage and non-union industries—logistics (delivery and storage of goods) and health care in Memphis—came to replace manufacturing.[3] These new industries often implemented 24/7 flexible labor policies where the workers had no job control. Finally, learning-by-doing was replaced by formal education, a shift that opened opportunities for many but closed the door to those without access to higher education.

The combined impact of these trends has perpetuated a society marked by economic inequality, the opposite of what Dr. King had envisioned. That story,

Figure 8.1. On April 8, 1968, in the aftermath of the murder of Martin Luther King Jr., thousands demonstrated in support of Memphis sanitation workers. Limited job opportunities, low wages, and poor working conditions have continued to plague the city's African American workers into the twenty-first century. (Mississippi Valley Collection, Ned McWherter Library, University of Memphis.)

seen through the lens of the Memphis region, is the story of a negative social transformation that followed the classic civil rights period and that calls for a renewed commitment to King's phase two.

King's Agenda for Economic Equality

Since the mid-1960s, King had been calling for a redistribution of wealth and power and a shift from military spending to economic development. In January 1968 he launched the Poor People's Campaign, a crusade asking Americans to build a multiracial national coalition to end poverty. He wanted Congress to shift its spending priorities to investing in housing, health care, jobs, and education. He thus sought to attack the roots of poverty and cut funding for the war machine at the same time. He said that civil rights laws were not enough to end racism and poverty. From 1964 to 1968, violent inner-city rebellions in Watts, Detroit, and other urban areas, usually sparked by police brutality and economic frustration, made this reality difficult to ignore.[4]

In Memphis, King added unionization and workers' rights to his demands for economic restructuring. In his March 18, 1968, speech at Mason Temple supporting sanitation workers striking for the right to union representation, he said "All labor has dignity" and called for "economic equality." He didn't mean that everyone should make the same income but rather that all people should be afforded full respect for their work and their personhood and be compensated with a family wage and benefits. King said union rights provided the best way to get respect as well as the best antidote to poverty wages and poor working conditions. He also called for a radical change in how America did business at home and in the world.

He summarized his phase two demand for economic justice by saying, "One day our society will come to respect the sanitation worker if it is to survive, for the person who picks up our garbage is just as significant as the physician." King told the cheering crowd, in probably the largest indoor gathering of the civil rights movement in the South, "You are reminding not only Memphis, but the nation that it is a crime too for people to live in this rich nation and receive starvation wages." In powerful cadences, he demanded economic justice in the same way he had demanded desegregation and voting rights: "Now is the time to make real the promises of democracy. Now is the time to make an adequate income a reality for all of God's children. Now is the time for City Hall to take a position for that which is just and honest. . . . *Now is the time.*"[5]

King had supported unions for many years, and he lost his life in the struggle for union rights to an assassin in Memphis on April 4, 1968.[6] Many believed the election of Barack Obama as president forty years later confirmed phase one's success. But what has become of phase two? Looking closely at Memphis as one important example of the urban economy, we see why a vast economic divide with clear racial characteristics continues in an America that has barely begun to address phase two of the freedom struggle. As social and political equality has become a day-to-day reality, economic equality has fallen by the wayside. That story can be told as part of the experiences of working men and women in the Memphis regional economy since King's death.

What Became of King's Dream of Union Rights?

As the result of the hard struggle of 1968, Memphis sanitation workers won union rights and some control over their work. The American Federation of State, County, and Municipal Employees (AFSCME) Local 1733 for a time became the largest union local in Memphis and the state of Tennessee. The success of the sanitation workers broke down barriers to public employee unions and led police officers, teachers, and other Memphis-area municipal workers to unionize and improve their wages and conditions dramatically.[7] The slow transformation of the Memphis region from an economy based on racial suppression and cotton/agricultural products toward a more modern industrial/service economy that accepted unions and equal rights seemed to have taken a tentative step forward.[8]

Despite union advances in the public sector, however, the economy of 1968 still left most black workers on the outside both economically and politically. Only very small numbers of blacks moved into white-collar, supervisory, and skilled-labor jobs. Better-paid industrial occupations employed very few black men and largely excluded black women. Memphis had only a few African American white-collar professionals—doctors, accountants, and lawyers. In addition to salespeople, secretaries and clerical workers, licensed black plumbers, pipe fitters, heating and air-conditioning workers, and electricians all remained scarce, frozen out by white employers and local craft unionists. Most African Americans still worked in personal services, as laborers, or as the perpetual assistant, doing the same hard labor for white craftsmen that they had done for generations.

Manufacturers and white-collar employers largely refused to hire black women except as cleaners and laborers. More than 80 percent of employed black women remained trapped in domestic work, while over 80 percent of employed black men still worked as laborers. A mechanizing cotton economy surrounding Memphis had largely eliminated black agricultural workers from a viable place on the land, and they remained desperate for any kind of work.[9]

Opportunities for African Americans remained circumscribed at almost every turn. A long history of black labor exploitation shaped these conditions. Slavery, segregation, and racial economic and gender oppression created generations of deep poverty in the African American community. In 1968 (and for many years after) black family income remained less than half of white family income, and most black workers made less than $2.00 an hour, just above a poverty minimum wage of $1.60 an hour. Nearly 35 percent of all African Americans lived below the poverty threshold, while some estimates suggested even higher rates of black poverty. At least one-quarter and probably more of the Memphis black community remained in poverty even before the Great Recession began in 2008.[10] The fate of black workers, used as a reservoir of cheap labor since the days of slavery, remained at the core of the problem of poverty in Memphis.[11]

The only relief came from a long history of community struggles, with women and workers at the center of them.[12] Title VII of the Civil Rights Act of 1964 prohibited employment discrimination, and African Americans in a few unionized factories and in some occupations did break down the barriers to advancement. As an example of this development, in 1966 blacks made up about 1 percent of factory officials and managers and less than 3 percent of technicians, office, and clerical workers; forty years later, they made up 11 and 30 percent of employees in these categories, respectively. They had nearly equal access in operative positions in manufacturing, after breaking down barriers that had long kept them out of upper-echelon factory jobs. Despite these long-term improvements, at another level conditions for black workers took a sharp turn for the worse in the decades after 1968.

In the 1970s, economic downturns and federal cutbacks to urban budgets held wages in check. In the 1980s a tidal wave of economic deregulation made it more difficult for workers to organize while also shifting tax burdens from the wealthy to the working class. In both decades (and after), factory closings and assaults on union rights undercut the wages and job control of workers everywhere. In Memphis, employer and government opposition largely stopped public employee unionism from expanding into the rapidly growing hospital and health-care sector. The 1968 victory for public employee unionism had occurred in one of the states of the anti-union South that took advantage of section 14(b) of the Taft-Hartley Act by outlawing the union shop. Anti-union employers called this a "right to work" law, but as King said, such a law "provides no 'rights' and no 'work.'" For lack of workplace prerogatives for unions or a clear legal framework for public employee unionization in Tennessee, even after 1968 worker demands for unions remained on shaky footing.[13]

Ultimately, in this debilitating economic and political climate, AFSCME and public employee unions did not continue to expand or to increase wages in tandem with the growth of government and the economy. After a nasty fight with the management of St. Joseph's Hospital (where King died) and in the midst of a mass community movement to open the school board to black participation in 1969, Local 1733 of AFSCME proved unable to break into the hospital system. In a critical blow to unions, the "health-care industry" expanded without unions that could fight for people at the bottom, in clerical, custodial, and nursing jobs.[14]

Particularly damaging to the black wage-earning working class, large industrial and unionized production facilities shut down just as black workers had finally achieved more or less equal opportunity in unionized factories. Manufacturing jobs that unionists (and economists) thought would now open up for African Americans instead nearly vanished from the region. Electronics, represented by a large RCA television plant, had employed a huge, racially diverse workforce, organized by the International Union of Electrical Workers. At its peak, four thousand workers there made good wages, enjoyed good benefits, and exercised job rights. But in 1970, the company moved to Taiwan. And that was only the beginning. International Harvester (organized by the United Auto Workers) and Firestone (United Rubber Workers) did not experience job growth in the 1970s. In the 1980s they closed, eliminating nearly ten thousand jobs between them and impoverishing the working-class suburbs of Frayser and Raleigh. Following these large factories, production operations for fans, pianos, and furniture—all staples of Memphis manufacturing—closed, often amid contentious labor battles.[15]

As multinational corporations such as RCA moved work to cheaper labor markets in Asia and Latin America, they devastated local working-class incomes. Workers couldn't win in this economic and political climate, even when they fought militantly to advance their interests. The city had long attracted outside investors by falsely characterizing black workers as "docile," but labor unrest in the aftermath of the sanitation strike made it difficult for RCA and other employers to maintain this supposedly subservient labor force. However, when black workers fought to maintain union rights, they experienced sharp defeats.[16]

In 1980, when the Memphis Furniture Company, employing hundreds of black women, waged a campaign to break their union, these militant and angry women struck. They gained support from Coretta Scott King and civil rights activists and defeated the company's union-busting attempt. Soon after, Memphis Furniture simply shut its doors, eliminating their jobs. Apparently, black workers pressing for their rights only speeded the process of deindustrialization in a "global economy" that encouraged plant migration to areas outside of the United States.[17] The process of union destruction accelerated when President Ronald Reagan fired eleven thousand striking professional air traffic controllers (PATCO) in 1981, giving a green light to other employers to do the same. Firestone worker Edward Lindsey said, "What happened to the PATCO workers was the turning point as far as labor was concerned . . . once President Reagan got rid of them, that was it." He felt union members should have mobilized resistance all over the country, but instead throughout the 1980s government and private employers picked off unions one by one.[18]

Economic downturns, out-migration of industry, and attacks against unions practically destroyed the income base for unskilled and factory workers, and not just in Memphis. As late as 1979, manufacturing remained one of the most common forms of employment in the United States, but in the 1980s and beyond it was far surpassed by trade and services. In Memphis, manufacturing probably never encompassed more than a third of the city's employment, even at the high point of the Congress of Industrial Organizations in the early 1950s, but unionized manufacturing brought up working-class wages in the city as a whole. Deindustrialization proved devastating to the unionized wage base. Table 8.1 illustrates this long-term trend in the Memphis economy. In 1966 manufacturing provided almost a quarter of all jobs, and unions represented workers in many of these jobs. Forty-one years later, the number of manufacturing jobs in Shelby County (the center of the Memphis Metropolitan Statistical Area) had fallen dramatically, and the percentage of all manufacturing jobs in the metropolitan area had collapsed to 7.6 percent. As industry disappeared, industrial unions also collapsed.[19] Black men disproportionately lost manufacturing jobs, and black women often remained the only breadwinner. For non-college-educated workers, gone with unionized factories was the dream of a good job providing a decent life based on jobs with fair wages.[20]

These developments had devastating effects on the black community in the Reagan era and after. Edward Lindsey recalled one Firestone worker who took his own life after layoffs. Many other Firestone workers lost their families and homes. Hillie Pride, another Firestone worker, surveying the situation in 1983, said deindustrialization had decimated the black community in Memphis. "There's nothing here anymore. We're just sitting here. You can't make a dime, no kind of way." At least during the Great Depression people grew some food crops, but those days had vanished. He said many young African Americans sold drugs or stole from their neighbors, and he saw no relief in sight. "They're all in a pile now, one can't help the other, because none of them have jobs."[21]

As manufacturing declined, so did unions, and that meant that remaining manufacturers paid less. According to one study, manufacturing jobs in the 1960s and 1970s had paid 25 percent more than average wages in Memphis. But after that, manufacturing wages declined across the board: by 2007, Memphis manufacturing wages averaged a mere $30,400 annually for full-time work—less than the per capita income in the region, and barely enough to provide a living wage for a family of three. The decline of unionized manufacturing undermined the wage base for many other jobs, and the result was more poverty. In 1969, 144,927 (20.1 percent) of all the people living in Shelby County lived in poverty. By 2004 that ratio had only fallen to 19.1 percent, but in absolute numbers there were 171,289 people living in poverty.[22]

The figures for African Americans in Memphis, though hard to verify and compare to the metropolitan and the Shelby County census, proved much worse. One way to view this is to compare white and black family income: in 1950, black family income in Memphis averaged 44 percent of white family income; by 1990 it was 48 percent, and by 2000 it was 45 percent. This trend represented modest improvement, and Memphis still has one of the country's worst ratios of black-to-white income. In 1990 the great majority of people in nine largely African American census tracts in the inner city lived in poverty, as did 40 percent of the city's children. By 2008, half or more of the city's

Table 8.1. Distribution of jobs by industry: Memphis MSA 1996 and Shelby County 2007

	1966	Percent Job Distribution	2007	Percent Job Distribution
Total	236,400	100.0%	507,335	100.0%
Construction	13,600	5.8%	20,149	4.0%
Manufacturing	54,200	22.9%	38,718	7.6%
Transportation and public utilities	17,700	7.5%	56,319	11.1%
Wholesale and retail trade	60,600	25.6%	90,040	17.7%
Finance, insurance, real estate	12,900	5.5%	27,468	5.4%
Services	36,100	15.3%	206,237	40.7%
Government	41,300	17.5%	67,889	13.4%

Note: The entire MSA for 2007 covers another 100,000 jobs, though most African Americans work in the core of the MSA, Shelby County. In Services, health care employment in 2007 was 57,778, and temporary staffing jobs numbered 48,853 in 2007 in Shelby County.
Sources: *Tennessee Statistical Abstract: 1969*. Center for Business and Economic Research, University of Tennessee, Knoxville, and Quarterly Census of Employment and Wages, Annual Averages, 2007, Shelby County, Tennessee Department of Labor and Workforce Development, http://www.tn.gov/labor-wfd/.

black children received their nutrition mainly through school lunches and food stamps.[23]

Memphis Joins the Service Economy

This was not how proponents of the "new economy" of service and "intellectual" jobs thought things would turn out. Future employment prospects at family-wage jobs for many African Americans evaporated. Like the rest of the country, Memphis reeled from the shock of the first energy crisis of 1973 along with deindustrialization and the globalization of work. The city also faced the impact of its poor reputation earned by the assassination of King and the city government's lack of response to its continuing racial crisis in the aftermath of his death, which caused business investors and tourists to turn away. As government began to enforce anti-discrimination laws and as some educational opportunities expanded, the regional economy did not expand in terms of well-paying working-class jobs.

The core reason was the decline of unionized manufacturing jobs, which were largely replaced with logistics (the integration of transportation and warehousing) and medical services. Globalization of industry required huge supply chains, as parts and products move slowly from the sweatshops of the Caribbean and Asia, through packing and reassembly in intermediate ports, to the final consumers in the United States. As these supply chains grew, the jobs created tended to be non-union transportation jobs. Deregulation of trucking and airlines in the 1980s led not only to massive numbers of bankruptcies and corporate turnovers but also to the creation of large numbers of non-union and hard-to-unionize low-wage, low-benefit jobs. Memphis experienced an almost complete turnover of trucking companies. In the 1980s the city developed a new airport, it already had excellent rail connections, and its relatively new Interstate highways connected Memphis east, west and north. Combined with a mild climate and an underemployed workforce, new trucking companies, railroads, the overnight-delivery company Federal Express (now FedEx) prospered. Memphis, once the hub of a regional agricultural economy, became the hub of a non-union global package- and freight-delivery system. Increased availability of poor whites and African Americans due to the decline in manufacturing employment and unions, along with increasing numbers of Mexican and Central American immigrants, made Memphis a cheap-wage logistics way station for the global economy.

By 2007 the change in employment patterns was complete. As table 8.1 reveals, as manufacturing employment collapsed, employment in transportation grew both absolutely and relatively. And the greatest growth occurred in services, which made up almost 41 percent of Shelby County employment. Within services, the two largest components are health-care employment, at 57,778 (11.4 percent of employment), and temporary staffing jobs, at 48,853 (9.6 percent).

Logistics and medical services industries came to define the conditions of work in Memphis for thousands of black, white, and Latino workers. Logistics requires fluidity and flexibility, with little emphasis on training. Work follows the material needs of the supply chain. Medical services are structured in a rigid, hierarchical fashion and use the educational system to organize a de facto racially segregated occupational structure. Both industries built employment conditions that emphasize 24/7 on-demand work, job control that is completely externalized from the worker, and use of contract/temporary labor as a key component of the labor market discipline.[24]

Memphis thus became a place where workers store products, repackage products from big boxes into little boxes, and ship products manufactured everywhere to be sold through mega-marketing outlets such as Target and Walmart. It also became a center of medical services. In these sectors, the work was hard and the pay was low. In addition, the Memphis–Shelby County economy featured two other defining characteristics: jobs are non-union, and working conditions are controlled totally by the employer.

Optimists had thought that in the "new economy," jobs—in particular, skilled, education-intensive jobs—would open up in enough numbers for African American workers who had wanted unionized manufacturing jobs. Instead, the job growth was in logistics and the service economy. And in Memphis, this new employment was even more interchangeable than the old factory assembly jobs. Training, except for enculturation in conservative managerial values, was not necessary for many of these jobs. In others, training was on-the-job or received in corporate-controlled educational facilities.

Most importantly, increasingly such work was temporary. The jobs only existed when a new rail/truck shipment arrived for storage, repacking, or reshipment. For warehouse workers, for transportation workers, for guards and security personnel, for "customer associates" in retail trade, and for an army of new medical personnel, training and education remains either on-the-job or tightly controlled by the employer. Furthermore, employer restructuring of working conditions meant the end of the nine-to-five, Monday-through-Friday, forty-hour workweek. The imposition of mandatory overtime alternated with mandatory short-time. Employers organized worker turnover into the new job structure, requiring company loyalty by workers but rarely returning loyalty to workers in the new economy.

The African American worker, who in 1968 might have anticipated joining the unionized manufacturing workforce as a step into the middle class, instead stepped into this new world of untrammeled employer prerogatives. Tables 8.2 and 8.3 illustrate the employment changes that took place for African Americans in key sectors of the regional economy.[25] Table 8.2 shows that in manufacturing overall, employment percentages for African American workers increased, most importantly among the two critical occupations of operatives and craft workers; their share of white-collar manufacturing jobs also increased. Blacks and women had often been excluded from such jobs in the past. But for black workers, the key factor is that their penetration into these higher-paid occupations over four decades occurred as the manufacturing sector and unions went into sharp decline. Black employment opportunities opened up as factories shut down.

Table 8.3 illustrates the 2007 occupational distribution of employment by race in logistics and health care. In both sectors, the large employment base is almost half African American (similar to their representation in the population of the region). Many black workers made their way through the regional community colleges and university systems into the managerial, professional, technical, and sales jobs associated with these two sectors. But most have ended up in the large non-union clerical and blue-collar workforce of these two sectors. In health care, the largest occupation category after professional workers is service workers (maids, janitors, and orderlies), and African Americans made up 81.8 percent of that category. Similarly, African Americans composed more than half of the large office and clerical occupational grouping.

In the dynamic logistics (transportation and warehousing) sector, operatives and laborers made up almost half the recorded employment in 2007. Black workers composed 73.2 percent of all laborers and 52 percent of all operatives. The logistics sector is noted for its large number of temporary contract workers, so the number of minority workers in these high-turnover jobs is probably understated by official statistics. Black and Latino workers played and continue to play key roles in this sector.

On the positive side, jobs and occupations completely segregated forty years earlier were open in 2007 to those African Americans who could find them and had the right credentials. The numbers of jobs available to everyone—minority and non-minority—expanded rapidly in health care and logistics. But the desegregation of these segments of the labor market did not bring the degree of affluence or stability for which many advocates of a new economy had hoped.

Incessant Labor and Loss of Worker Control

Memphis logistics involves a combination of transportation, warehousing, and computer scheduling that defines the way products move across the globe to retailers and consumers. FedEx is at the top of the logistics pyramid—moving high-value goods, organizing supply systems, and providing the link among far-flung producers, warehouses, and retailers. But beneath FedEx is a vast array of employers with jobs, many of them employed on temporary contracts, that fill out the growing logistics sector of warehousing and transportation services. In Memphis, beyond the employment directly at FedEx, logistics may employ as many as an additional 100,000 workers, many of them in temporary, flexible jobs.

Those who work in the modern supply chain—in the warehouses, airport hubs, in trucks and on airplanes—work when they are needed for as long as they are needed. Flexible, incessant work denies them the benefits of regular hours and wages. Sanitation workers would clearly recognize this never-ending workweek, one of the causes of their 1968 strike. The new distribution economy includes whites, blacks, and Latinos, many of them women, but it does not provide equality or prosperity for workers. It has facilitated the development a factory system of employment outside the factory.

The current job configuration is historically unique and still not fully understood by society or by workers themselves. There are four key aspects to the

Table 8.2. Occupational participation rates by race in manufacturing in the Memphis MSA: 1966 and 2007

	Black Worker Participation Rate		
	2007	1966	Change
Total	42.9%	33.9%	9.0%
Officials and managers	14.1%	1.1%	13.0%
Professionals	16.1%	0.3%	15.8%
Technicians	31.2%	2.5%	28.7%
Sales workers	11.1%	2.6%	8.5%
Office and clerical	33.8%	2.9%	30.8%
Craft workers	37.0%	13.1%	23.9%
Operatives	71.3%	40.7%	30.6%
Laborers	63.3%	70.3%	-7.0%
Service workers	59.8%	71.8%	-12.0%

Source: U.S. Equal Employment Opportunity Commission, *Job Patterns for Minorities and Women in Private Industry* (EEO-1 data), Washington, D.C., U.S. Government Printing Office. Results of surveys of private industry.

new workplace. First, time at work is defined by the needs of the management of the supply chain for goods and services. Second, hours may be short or long relative to the forty-hour week. Shifts disappear, because the time of day for work is defined by the movement of the product. In areas such as medical services, 24/7 availability for work is the norm. Third, workers are taught to understand that the needs of the global production/distribution system, not workers' needs, define their terms of employment, conditions of work, and the rhythm of the work experience. Fourth, workers become temporary employees. Staffing-agency workers come and go according to shipment demands and earn a sub-living wage without benefits. Most important, the employer of record (the legal employer) is not the actual daily workplace employer.

Black Workers and the New Economy

For the African American worker, compared to the sanitation, domestic work, and laboring jobs of years ago, these new jobs are better in terms of working conditions, although they remain dangerous to workers' health. But the key to understanding this new job world is its profound segregation, which encompasses race but is fundamentally tied to the educational system. In theory, success in today's world is based on merit, but the facade of educational advancement often hides a rigid structure of occupational segregation that traps African Americans in low-rung jobs while allowing those in the middle

Table 8.3. Occupational participation rates by race in medical services and logistics in the Memphis MSA 2007: Black participation rates by occupation

	Health care 2007	Transportation and warehousing 2007
Total	49.9%	49.2%
Officials and managers	27.5%	31.0%
Professionals	28.0%	9.6%
Technicians	49.4%	42.4%
Sales workers	15.2%	28.3%
Office and clerical	57.4%	55.3%
Craft workers	46.6%	25.9%
Operatives	61.8%	52.0%
Laborers	38.3%	73.2%
Service workers	81.8%	43.3%

Source: U.S. Equal Employment Opportunity Commission, *Job Patterns for Minorities and Women in Private Industry* (EEO-1 data), Washington, D.C., U.S. Government Printing Office. Results of surveys of private industry.

and upper classes, many of them whites, to pass on the best jobs to the next generation.[26]

Nowhere is this job model more clearly delineated than in medical services. Most learning usually takes place on the job, but the occupational segregation of medical services limits upward mobility to those workers who can afford to exit for extended periods to gain the education and training necessary for the top-paying occupations. It is an industry built on highly defined crafts, but in general, these are not crafts controlled or defined by the workers themselves.[27]

Three large hospital corporations plus a public hospital dominate the Memphis health-care market. Except for small portions of the public hospital, the entire system is non-union. Jobs in the medical services sector are large in number, and the numbers continue to grow (see table 8.3). Many of the workplaces are 24/7 operations. Work is very hierarchical, with authority concentrated at the top both professionally (physicians) and organizationally (managers).

Thousands of entry-level jobs exist in medical services. Cleaners, orderlies, and licensed vocational and practical nurses come from the vast supply of African Americans and, increasingly, from a large Latino working class whose numbers in the mid-South expanded dramatically in the twenty-first century.[28] Most working-class medical jobs pay poorly and carry few benefits. But while entry-level employees work next to and with nurses, therapists, physician's assistants, and physicians, rarely does anyone promote or train them on the job for higher-paying crafts. Managerial power to define occupations, to limit learning opportunities, and to set the conditions of daily work organization dominate the workplace.

Today, Memphis is the home of flexible, service-based jobs that often trace the employer of record to a staffing agency. Those jobs sometimes require twenty hours a week and sometimes demand sixty hours; those jobs come and go. Those jobs often are most compatible with the powerlessness of the undocumented worker. Thus, another aspect of working-class reality in Memphis is the rapidly growing population of immigrants from Mexico and Central America. They do household, yard, construction, service, and medical work. Blacks and whites and Latinos tend to work in different occupations and different industries and live in different neighborhoods.[29] The issues facing workers in trying to organize unions today focus not only on the long-standing division between blacks whose families had been enslaved and whites whose families had been free. They also include those cross-cutting schisms involving race, class, ethnicity, national origin, and gender emerging in the urban, suburban, and exurban zones of twenty-first-century America.[30]

The black worker in Memphis has moved through the entire cycle. Black workers moved out of personal service, agricultural day labor, and general laborer status in factories, but the result proved the opposite of King's dream. Statistics show that African Americans have moved up to managerial, supervisory, and white-collar jobs, and some have moved into higher education. But many others have experienced a downward trajectory with no end in sight. They are in free fall.

Labor, Race and Poverty

In 2011, Memphis residents can point to a city with powerful black political elites. Blacks are represented in the dual city and county mayor system, including the city and county council and agencies that control much of local and regional government. Dr. Willie Herenton, as mayor of Memphis, exercised considerable powers during his tenure from 1991 to 2009, while A. C. Wharton held the office of county mayor and beginning in 2009 the city mayor position. There are middle-class success stories. In addition to black political leaders, those African Americans with higher education have made their way into college and university teaching in the region. A suburban black professional class also serves the growing medical sector. It is a city of several large corporate headquarters, and the city derives special dynamism from the headquarters and operating centers of FedEx. And many of the local corporations have been honored for their commitment to a diversified workforce. A strong tourist industry now celebrates the National Civil Rights Museum and the legacy of King and black political power.

Yet Memphis remains a city with high poverty and inner-city crime rates, a weak educational system, high rates of mother and infant mortality, and a population still separated by race and class. As many whites and some blacks move out of the city to escape its taxes and underfunded school system, generations of slavery, job segregation, poor education, job and union loss, and government neglect have left behind a sub-proletariat of permanently poor people. Black political power has changed the tone of the city's politics. Yet in many respects, African Americans in Memphis won, as Sharon D. Wright explains, a "hollow prize" of political power with little economic clout. The current research of social scientists presents a sobering picture of racial-economic disparities and white business and corporate rule over economic resources. Blacks lead the city politically, but wealthy whites still own and run most of the corporate business sector.[31]

The lack of a powerful union movement and organized labor base in the region has undermined the possibilities that emerged from the civil rights movement. Even the unionized sanitation workers have barely kept up with the increasing cost of living, and their incomes do not allow for a middle-class lifestyle. Mechanization and privatization continue to thin the ranks of union workers in the region's garbage and trash collection. Statistics for wage workers as a whole reflect their plight. In 2005, African American workers in the metropolitan Memphis had median earnings of $20,833 per year—a median wage of about $10.00 per hour, hardly a living wage for a family of any size.

Overarching issues of black poverty in urban areas such as Memphis continue to compromise more than forty years of struggle for a better deal for black workers since King's death. In the 1990s, half of all black children in Memphis were born to single mothers who earned the family's income, and that percentage has increased since the economic collapse of 2008. Untold numbers of black male youths are victims of drugs and the prison-industrial complex.[32] Racial-economic inequality saps the ability of the city's public school system, with over 90 percent black students, three-fourths of whom lived in poverty in 2005, to prop up the declining standards of living of the black community.[33]

Black political success is not enough to reverse these trends. When the city first elected Mayor Herenton in 1991, at least 35 percent of blacks lived in poverty in Memphis (about 8 percent of whites did). While the figures have improved, blacks still remain in poverty in far greater numbers and percentages than whites.[34] In 2005, 29 percent of the black population in the metropolitan area remained in poverty, and the percentages were much higher in the inner city. Moreover, official poverty statistics vastly understate the income needed for a family living wage: a family requires about twice the poverty income to exist without food stamps and other social assistance.[35] While a full set of statistics is not available for the increasing number of Latino immigrants, their wages and incomes remain similarly far below those of whites.

Many years after King's death in 1968, the general trend toward less equality, fewer manufacturing jobs, and more expensive education has frustrated all workers, but especially workers of color. In the United States as a whole in 1950, black men's income was just 48 percent that of white men; by 2007 the ratio of their weekly full-time earnings had improved to 76 percent, while black women earned 85 percent of what white women earned (but only 68 percent of what white males earned). According to Robert H. Zieger, equal opportunity laws and affirmative action programs that opened up positions that African Americans had previously been excluded from led to some of this improvement. Yet, as he also documents, the disappearance of 3 million factory jobs between 1998 and 2004 (and more since then), along with the destruction of unions, has hit black workers especially hard, eliminating "the relatively well-paying entry-level jobs that had enabled an earlier generation to establish stable families and move into the economic and educational mainstream."[36]

Statistics vary, but it is clear that earnings for working-class black men and women almost everywhere remain at lower levels than for almost all other workers. And it was worse in Memphis than in the nation as a whole. In 2005, full-time black workers still earned only 64 percent as much as white full-time workers, and these disparities increased for part-time workers. Hence the long-term prospects for King's "economic equality" do not look good in hard-hit areas with a long history of white supremacy and black labor exploitation such as Memphis.[37] The loss of manufacturing jobs and unionized jobs has produced a generation of workers without health-care benefits and of families that can no longer afford to send their children to college. The shifting economic terrain has disadvantaged the black working poor and black communities the most, but Latinos coming into the Memphis economy suffer similar privations. All this happened even before the Great Recession of 2008 through 2010, after which things got much worse for the people at the bottom of the wage, gender, and racial hierarchy. The recession highlighted the economic vulnerability of the African American community. As unemployment rates rose, foreclosures in Memphis's communities of color increased the number of empty homes, the number of homeless families, and the extent of urban blight. The big banks, including local financial institutions, had used the housing and credit bubble to prey upon workers who desired to own their homes but who lacked the means to pay off high-risk inflated mortgages.[38] The low wages of Memphis non-union workers remained at the root of an economic crisis now out of control. The inequality of the past forty years became all the more visible as financial crisis and recession quickly sapped the finances of those workers whose lives had been neglected by an economy that deemphasized the "economic equality" sought by Martin Luther King.

A Return to Phase Two

The story of African Americans in Memphis illustrates the need to return to King's call for economic equality. Job control is the straightforward solution to today's work problems. Until workers can once again "own" their jobs, the path to equality will remain grown over with the briars of corporate power. A contingent or temporary job robs employees not only of compensation but of the right to be part of the production process. A job without advancement potential reduces on-the-job innovation, productivity, and pride. But these sorts of jobs are just what businesses have created since 1968. Not coincidentally, many African Americans and a growing number of Latino immigrants—two groups that have been historically disadvantaged by racial exploitation and discrimination—remain the most likely to be trapped in these jobs.

To set the United States on the path to economic equality, we need policies that return control to the workers rather than policies that increase inequality. Three basic changes would allow working men and women to hold the sign "I Am a Man," used in the sanitation strike of 1968, and have it signify the reality of their daily working lives.

First, the restoration and encouragement of unionization by governmental authorities is a basic necessity. Labor and immigration law reforms that more significantly penalize employers who cheat, intimidate, or in other ways exploit their labor force would help workers faced by powerful corporate employers to deliver a better future. In the modern 24/7 logistics, medical services, and retail economies, unions would balance the needs of the lives of workers against the constant downward corporate pressure on wages and benefits.

Second, occupational entrance rules in the mid-South region need to shift away from educational credentials, state licenses, or corporate educational facilities back toward direct worker control of occupational standards, either through apprenticeship programs or through union-controlled learning by doing. Third, and related, control of jobs by workers or their representatives would reduce the alienation that occurs in today's here-today, gone-tomorrow work environment. The union shop of yesterday allowed workers to be a real countervailing power to the corporate desire for profits and control over the work process. That countervailing force needs to be reestablished.

Memphis in the twenty-first century has as much or more potential than it did in 1968. African Americans have entered numerous occupations from which they had been excluded in 1968. Matriculation at the college level has soared; the University of Memphis, which before the 1960s denied African Americans entrance, now has one of the largest black college populations in the country. But while the facade of social equality is apparent everywhere, Memphis has also remained a highly segregated and unequal society, largely mirroring the American society around it.

The root of the problem is America's system of unbridled market capitalism. Without unions and the progressive labor–civil rights alliance that King envisioned in the political arena, workers have little power to shape their own lives. King's promise of a future of freedom and economic equality remains unfulfilled. It is time to think again about implementing his demand for equality, voiced to the mass meeting in Memphis on March 18: "Now is the time to make an adequate income a reality for all of God's children."[39]

There are practical steps that could bring about King's phase two. The problem is straightforward. There is less ability to struggle for economic equality in today's economy than in the economy of King's era. While social equality has risen between races and genders, job rights have vanished into the corporate structures of the global economy. Without control of the job in the clinic, at the warehouse, or on the showroom floor, modern workers may find that they work with men and women of other ethnic backgrounds, but almost none of them earn a living wage. If you don't quite believe this picture of the modern workplace, come to Memphis.

Notes

1. King's analysis of phases appears in "Civil Rights at the Crossroads," An address by Martin Luther King Jr. to the shop stewards of Local 815, Teamsters and the Allied Trades Council, New York City, May 2, 1967, Martin Luther King Papers, ser. III, box 15, Martin Luther King Jr. Center for Nonviolent Social Change, Atlanta, Georgia [hereafter MLK Papers].

2. Address of Rev. Martin Luther King Jr., March 18, 1968, at Mason Temple mass meeting in Memphis, MLK Papers. Reproduced in *"All Labor Has Dignity,"* Michael K. Honey, ed. (Boston: Beacon Press, 2011), 179–80.

3. Originally, the term *logistics* referred to the military supply train required to wage war. In recent decades the term has come to mean the integration or management of the delivery of goods from the point of production to the consumer. Logistics combines two traditional industries, transportation and warehousing, with information technology.

4. Thomas F. Jackson's *From Civil Rights to Human Rights: Martin Luther King Jr. and the Struggle for Economic Justice* (Philadelphia: University of Pennsylvania Press, 2007) traces King's development of an economic agenda from his youth. Jackson notes that King's emphasis on economic issues increased from 1964 forward. This interest intensified after the massive rebellion and bloodshed in the Watts neighborhood of Los Angeles just days after

President Lyndon Baines Johnson signed the Voting Rights Act. King's Poor People's Campaign speeches are located in series III of the MLK Papers. For the most recent treatment, see Gordon Mantler, "Black, Brown, and Poor: Martin Luther King Jr., the Poor People's Campaign, and Its Legacies" (Ph.D. diss., Duke University, 2008). Laurie B. Green's *Battling the Plantation Mentality: Memphis and the Black Freedom Struggle* (Chapel Hill: University of North Carolina Press, 2007) stresses the long-term legacy of black Memphians' struggles for civil rights and social justice.

5. King, *"All Labor Has Dignity,"* 176. For an overview of the speech, see Michael K. Honey, *Going Down Jericho Road: The Memphis Strike, Martin Luther King's Last Campaign* (New York: Norton, 2007), chapter 13.

6. King had supported union rights since his teenage years and had made his strongest appeals for economic justice speaking before unions. Honey, *Going Down Jericho Road*, 26-27, 47-49; King, *"All Labor Has Dignity."*

7. For a compressed account of the Memphis story, see Michael K. Honey, "Industrial Unionism and Racial Justice in Memphis," in *Organized Labor in the Twentieth-Century South*, ed. Robert H. Zieger (Knoxville: University of Tennessee Press, 1991), 135-57; and Honey, "Martin Luther King Jr., the Crisis of the Black Working Class, and the Memphis Sanitation Strike," in *Southern Labor in Transition, 1940-1995*, ed. Robert H. Zieger (Knoxville: University of Tennessee Press, 1997), 146-75. For an assessment of the significance of the strike, see Honey, "The Memphis Strike: Martin Luther King's Last Campaign," *Poverty and Race* 16, no. 2 (2007): 1, 4-6; and Honey and David Ciscel, "Memphis since King: Race and Labor in the City," *Poverty and Race* 18, no. 2 (2009): 8-11.

8. On the slow transformation, see Arthur M. Ford, *Political Economics of Rural Poverty in the South* (Cambridge: Ballinger, 1973); and Robert A. Sigafoos, *Cotton Row to Beale Street: A Business History of Memphis* (Memphis: Memphis State University Press, 1979).

9. Michael K. Honey, *Southern Labor and Black Civil Rights: Organizing Memphis Workers* (Urbana: University of Illinois Press, 1993), 280-82, and see sources in note 6 above.

10. In 1968 the poverty threshold for an urban family of four was $3,526. A full-time job at $2.00 per hour earned a family $4,160. The minimum wage was $1.60 per hour, but many of the jobs African Americans held in Memphis were probably exempt from minimum-wage enforcement. While 34.7 percent of all African Americans lived in poverty in 1968, today the number is close to 25 percent. However, Memphis clearly had a much poorer black population than the nation as a whole. See U.S. Census, Poverty, Income thresholds at the Poverty Level in 1968, http://www.census.gov/hhes/www/poverty. F. Ray Marshall and Arvil Van Adams estimated a poverty rate of 57 percent in the black community in "Negro Employment in Memphis," *Industrial Relations*, May 1970, 308-23. The official U.S. Census poverty figures are considerably lower than this. However, African Americans in 1968 lived so close to the poverty that any small change in definition results in very different estimates. Clearly, poverty in the black community was widespread and much higher than national averages. Marcus D. Pohlman cites the higher number used by Marshall and Van Adams. See *Opportunity Lost: Race and Poverty in the Memphis City Schools* (Knoxville: University of Tennessee Press, 2008), 30-33.

11. For chapter and verse on labor racial inequality in Memphis, see Michael K. Honey, *Black Workers Remember: An Oral History of Segregation, Unionism, and the Freedom Movement* (Berkeley: University of California Press, 1997).

12. On the long civil rights movement in Memphis, see Green, *Battling the Plantation*

Mentality; Honey, *Southern Labor and Black Civil Rights*. See Honey, *Black Workers Remember*, 86–88 and passim, on the plight of black women workers, who played a crucial role in resisting racial oppression and generating movements for change in Memphis and across the South. See also Jacqueline Jones, *Labor of Love, Labor of Sorrow: Black Women, Work and the Family, From Slavery to the Present* (New York: Random House, 1985, 1995).

13. King quoted in Honey, *Going Down Jericho Road*, 175. The plight of public workers in "right to work" states grew especially difficult as urban budgets went into crisis in the 1970s and even a civil-rights-oriented leader such as Mayor Maynard Jackson attacked AFSCME unions in Atlanta. See Joseph A. McCartin, "'Fire the Hell Out of Them': Sanitation Workers' Struggles and the Normalization of the Striker Replacement Strategy in the 1970s," *Labor* 2 (Fall 2005): 67–92.

14. See Honey, *Going Down Jericho Road*, epilogue.

15. The overseas flight of Memphis industry is documented in David Ciscel and Thomas Collins, "The Memphis Runaway Blues," *Southern Exposure* 4 (Spring/Summer 1976): 143–49. For a global treatment, see Jefferson Cowie, *Capital Moves: RCA's Seventy-Year Quest for Cheaper Labor* (New York: The New Press, 1999). The job loss statistics are from Pohlman, *Opportunity Lost*, 29.

16. Honey, *Black Workers Remember*, passim.

17. Green, *Battling the Plantation Mentality*, 265–68, 289–90. On the Memphis Furniture strike, see Honey, *Black Workers Remember*, 343–47, 366–67.

18. Lindsey quoted in Honey, *Black Workers Remember*, 331.

19. The statistics in the rest of this account come from the sources in the following note, but these statistics need some qualification. In 1966, the Memphis Metropolitan Statistical Area (MSA) was completely centered on the core county, Shelby County. Today the MSA is made up of eight surrounding counties, with approximately 100,000 jobs in the other counties. However, African Americans tend to live and work in Shelby County, which is still the population core of the region. Our descriptions and statistics in this section come from a series of studies undertaken by David H. Ciscel and created from the raw data from the census and related data, unless noted otherwise as coming from a secondary source.

20. Data on employment and wages in this article are largely taken from the Tennessee Department of Labor and Workforce Development, Labor Market Information, http://www.state.tn.us/labormarketinfo.html, and U.S. Census Bureau, Small Area Income and Poverty Estimates, http://www.census.gov.

21. Honey, *Black Workers Remember*, 332, 326–27.

22. Ibid. The 25 percent figure is from Pohlman, *Opportunity Lost*, 33.

23. Marshall and Van Adams estimated the poverty rate at 57 percent of the black community in "Negro Employment in Memphis," while other ways of measuring poverty suggest a poverty rate of about a third. But statistics do not convey the depth of poverty in certain areas of Memphis from 1970 to the present. Pohlman, *Opportunity Lost*, 30–33.

24. The transition to an incessant or flexible workplace is clearly documented in many research articles. See, for example, Deborah M. Figart and Lonnie Golden, "An Introduction to the Social Economics of Work Time," *Review of Social Economy* 56 (Winter 1998): 411–24; and Lonnie Golden, "Flexible Work Schedules: What Are We Trading Off to Get Them?" *Monthly Labor Review*, March 2001, 50–62. For an analysis that puts a largely posi-

tive spin on these work trends, see Daniel S. Hamermesh, *Workdays, Work Hours, and Work Schedules* (Kalamazoo, Mich.: W. E. Upjohn Institute for Labor Research, 1996).

25. EEO-1 data has its problems as a reliable data source: the data-collection techniques have changed over the years, the data are biased toward larger employers (more than fifty workers at an establishment), and it is not clear that metropolitan industry data are always accurate. However, it is the one source of establishment data that has a racial and gender breakdown by occupation. It also has a time span that reaches back into the period of almost compete racial and gender segregation. U.S. Equal Opportunity Commission, Job Patterns for Minorities and Women in Private Industry (EEO-1 data) Washington, D.C., U.S. Government Printing Office (various dates) and http://www.eeoc.gov/stats. The foundation for EEO-1 data is the seminal analysis of the Memphis occupational structure in the 1960s: Arvil Van Adams, *Negro Employment in the South*, vol. 2: *The Memphis Labor Market* (U.S. Department of Labor, Manpower Research Monograph No. 23, F. Ray Marshall, Project Director, 1971).

26. The rise of new working conditions in the postmodern service economy has been conceptually developed in David Harvey, *The Condition of Postmodernity* (Oxford: Blackwell, 1990). An empirical analysis of the impact of flexible labor on the entire industrial structure is available in Ian MacLachlan, *Kill and Chill: Restructuring Canada's Commodity Chain* (Toronto: University of Toronto Press, 2001).

27. The changes in the structure of work analyzed in this essay are described in David H. Ciscel and Barbara Ellen Smith, "The Impact of Supply Chain Management on Labor Standards: The Transition to Incessant Work," *Journal of Economic Issues* 39 (June 2005): 1–9.

28. The number of documented and undocumented Latinos residing in the Memphis area is the subject of considerable controversy. See David H. Ciscel, Marcela Mendoza, and Barbara Ellen Smith, *Latino Immigrants in Memphis, Tennessee: Their Economic Impact* (Working Paper 15, The Center for Research on Women, The University of Memphis, January 2001).

29. For a discussion of the impact and roles of Latinos in the regional economy, see David H. Ciscel, Barbara Ellen Smith, and Marcela Mendoza, "Ghosts in the Global Machine: New Immigrants and the Redefinition of Work," *Journal of Economic Issues* 27, no. 2 (2003): 333–41. See also Barbara Ellen Smith, Marcela Mendoza, and David H. Ciscel, "The World on Time: Flexible Labor, New and Global Logistics," in *The American South in a Global World*, ed. J. L. Peacock et al. (Chapel Hill: University of North Carolina Press, 2005), 23–38. This research highlights, through ethnographic interviews, the problems of Latino workers in the Memphis logistics sector.

30. Robert H. Zieger, *For Jobs and Freedom: Race and Labor in America since 1865* (Lexington: University Press of Kentucky, 2007), 218–33, paints a devastating picture of manufacturing and union job loss as a crucial ingredient in the crisis of labor and race in America's inner cities. Thomas J. Sugrue, *The Origins of the Urban Crisis: Race and Inequality in Postwar Detroit* (Princeton: Princeton University Press, 1996) and William Julius Wilson, *When Work Disappears: The World of the New Urban Poor* (New York: Knopf, 1997), document how the fate of inner-city African Americans was intimately tied to the decline of manufacturing and unions and the continuing effects of institutionalized racism. Sugrue's *Sweet Land of Liberty: The Forgotten Struggle for Civil Rights in the North* (New York: Random House, 2008) shows the many ways the freedom struggle is tied to the continuing

struggle for economic justice. Wilson's *More Than Just Race: Being Black and Poor in the Inner City* (New York: Norton, 2009) and an article by the same title in *Poverty and Race* (18, no. 3 [2009]: 1, 2, 10–11) argue that all of the issues affecting black workers and the inner-city poor are tied together and need to be solved together. These accounts back up the argument King made in 1968 for a mass coalition to solve the problems of racism, poverty, and war as all part of the same problem. See Nancy MacLean, *Freedom Is Not Enough: The Opening of the American Workplace* (Cambridge: Harvard University Press, 2006).

31. According to Wright, Herenton won initial election on the narrowest of margins and African Americans found that they could not govern on the sole basis of the black electorate. Black politicians turned to white business elites to accomplish goals and, over time, largely followed a corporate agenda for economic development. In the end, that process shortchanged the needs of the black working class and poor and left African Americans with a "hollow prize" of political power without accompanying significant economic clout. This is typical of what happened to many black communities that elected black mayors since the Voting Rights Act of 1965. In the 1980s, conditions became even more perilous as whites fled the inner cities, whose tax bases then shrank. Sharon D. Wright, *Race, Power, and Political Emergence in Memphis* (New York: Garland, 2000), 152–55.

32. Pohlman, *Opportunity Lost*, 30.

33. Michael K. Honey, "A Dream Deferred," *The Nation*, May 3, 2004, 36–38; Pohlman, *Opportunity Lost*, 22, 82. Wright documents that 35 percent of blacks remained in poverty in Memphis in 1993, while only about 8 percent of whites did (*Race, Power*, 153). Conflicting interpretations of poverty rates are addressed in endnotes 9 and 10 above.

34. Wright, *Race, Power*, 153.

35. David H. Ciscel, "What Is Living Wage for Memphis?" University of Memphis Center for Research on Women, newsletter, 2002 edition.

36. Zieger, *For Jobs and Freedom*, 216. Some estimates suggest even wider racial income gaps. Such estimates are subject to wide variation, based on how they are computed. Differences are significant for full- versus part-time employment, for different industries and occupations, and for different education levels, as well as whether the data is presented in median or mean form. But however the data is parsed, large income gaps exist between the races. The early 1950 data comes from the U.S. Bureau of the Census, General Population Statistics, and includes both part- and full-time employment. The black-white income gap changed very little over the following thirty years using Census income data. For recent data see the American Community Survey and Bureau of Labor Statistics on median weekly earnings of full-time workers. http://www.bls.gov.

37. The 2005 American Community Survey provides gendered data for full-time employees by race. See http://factfinder.census.gov.

38. Michael Powell, "Blacks in Memphis Lose Decades of Economic Gains," *New York Times*, May 30, 2010.

39. King, *"All Labor Has Dignity,"* 176.

9

Shutdowns in the Sun Belt

The Decline of the Textile and Apparel Industry and Deindustrialization in the South

TIMOTHY J. MINCHIN

The decline of the textile and apparel industry is one of the most striking features of recent southern history. Since the 1980s, hardly a week has gone by without mill closings in the region making headlines, and the southern piedmont is now home to more than its fair share of shuttered and decaying factories.[1] Although the industry has been losing jobs since the early 1970s, the pace of decline quickened in the 1990s. Between 1997 and 2001 alone, for example, nearly 200,000 textile and apparel jobs were lost in the Carolinas, the industry's heartland. As the authors of the landmark *Like a Family* have established, it was textile mills that "built the New South," and the industry's demise has therefore had enormous economic and cultural consequences for the region. Despite the industry's importance, southern historians have yet to study its decline in any detail, although they have explored the earlier years of growth and consolidation thoroughly. In particular, scholars have explored the distinctive nature of mill workers' culture and the relationship between this culture and organized labor's repeated failures in the region. An examination of the industry's decline complements this earlier scholarship, showing that textile workers' strong sense of attachment to their jobs ensured that deindustrialization was particularly painful for those involved. In addition, the demise of the textile industry reminds us that there were many southerners who did not prosper during the "Sun Belt" years.[2]

Examining the textile industry's decline contributes to important work in labor studies. Beginning with Barry Bluestone and Bennett Harrison's influential *The Deindustrialization of America* (1982), which introduced the term "deindustrialization" to a wide audience, many scholars have explored the decline of manufacturing industries and how it has affected workers. They have thrown much light on a major shift in the U.S. economy; in 1950, half

Figure 9.1. These Virginians were among thousands of textile and apparel workers who protested federal trade policies in the 1980s. They called on Washington to restrict imports and safeguard their jobs. (Amalgamated Clothing and Textile Workers Union (ACTWU) Papers, Kheel Center for Labor-Management Documentation and Archives, Cornell University.)

of the American workforce was employed in the manufacturing sector, but by 2006 the figure stood at just 10.4 percent.[3] Existing scholarship, however, has concentrated almost entirely on the Rust Belt, the band of states in the Northeast and Midwest that have been hit hard by job losses, especially in the steel and auto industries. Works by Ruth Milkman and Thomas Dublin have explored the fate of post-industrial communities in New Jersey and Pennsylvania, adding to existing studies of classic Rust Belt communities such as Flint, Michigan; Homestead, Pennsylvania; and Youngstown, Ohio.[4] This literature has established that most workers identified closely with their jobs and were usually deeply affected by plant closures, with many left feeling devastated and bitter.[5] The South has been overlooked, however, even though it had a range of manufacturing industries. Textiles and apparel was by far the biggest, but the region was also home to a significant number of tobacco, furniture, steel, paper, and chemical plants. Since 1980, all of these industries have shed significant numbers of jobs, and the textile experience is thus representative of broader trends. It is only since the late 1990s that some scholars have explored how deindustrialization has also affected southern workers, and the human impact of the demise of the textile industry remains understudied.[6]

The case for incorporating textiles and apparel into the literature of industrial decline is compelling. While the terms "textile industry" and "apparel industry" are often used interchangeably, the industries are distinct. They are inextricably linked, however, since most textile workers are involved in the manufacture of products that are used to make apparel. As a result, any discussion of deindustrialization has to consider both sectors together.[7] Since the early 1970s, textiles and apparel have declined simultaneously. According to the Bureau of Labor Statistics (BLS), in 1973 there were more than 2.4 million textile and apparel workers in the United States. In the years that followed this number fell steadily, and by June 2009 just 415,700 textile and apparel workers remained on the job. In little more than a generation, therefore, around 2 million jobs were lost in this industry, a truly dramatic development.[8]

Yet even as a declining industry, textiles and apparel have remained a crucial part of the U.S. economy. As late as 1995 there were about 1.6 million textile and apparel workers nationwide, more than the auto and aircraft industries combined. They represented one in ten of all manufacturing workers in the country. As the U.S. Congress's Office of Technology Assessment put it, textiles and apparel was "a critical part of the national economy," especially as many mills were defense contractors. The industry's importance to national security was recognized in the long-standing "Berry Amendment," which required the Department of Defense to give preference in procurement to domestically made products, particularly textile goods. In civilian life, textile and apparel companies also made everyday products that virtually all Americans were familiar with. Overall, the industry's size and the scale of its job losses mean that it deserves to be a central part of any study of deindustrialization.[9]

The South bore the brunt of the industry's decline. In the late nineteenth and early twentieth centuries, the industry grew at a rapid pace as enterprising mill owners constructed hundreds of mills across the piedmont. Successfully recruiting white workers from rural areas, the industry quickly became the region's largest employer, a position it retained for decades. In 1984, for example, textiles and apparel remained the major employer in terms of payroll in Alabama, Georgia, Mississippi, North Carolina, South Carolina, and Virginia. These six states were home to almost 75 percent of all textile and apparel jobs in the country. A decade later the region still contained the top five states for textile and apparel employment, and in the leading textile state of North Carolina the industry provided over 273,000 jobs.[10]

There are several reasons why textiles and apparel has been largely omitted from the deindustrialization literature. Because textile production was decentralized, the industry lacked the huge, defining plants that have generally attracted scholarly attention. Most mills were relatively small, and it was easy to overlook their closure. In 1981, for example, there were more than six thousand separate textile manufacturers in the United States, and even Burlington Industries, the industry's largest firm, controlled only 6 percent of the overall business. Because fewer than 15 percent of textile workers were unionized in 1981, workers lacked the lobbying power of their more organized counterparts in the steel and auto industries. The textile and apparel unions certainly tried to protect their members' jobs, but their efforts were unsuccessful. The textile industry was also a large employer of women, and most accounts of deindustrialization have focused on male workers. As historian Jefferson Cowie has written, it is important to "adjust the popular image of the unemployed male steel or auto worker as the quintessential victim of deindustrialization."[11]

While the industry's decline has occurred for decades, since the mid-1990s it has accelerated dramatically and this sudden falloff has meant that scholars have also had little time to write up-to-date accounts. In the 1980s and 1990s, historians wrote pioneering studies of southern textile workers, rescuing them from decades of scholarly neglect, yet the bulk of attention concentrated on the industry's emergence rather than its demise. Particular attention was focused on the development of a distinct and close-knit culture in the southern mill villages.[12] It is now important to take this scholarship forward, outlining the reasons for the industry's decline and the effect it had on displaced workers and their communities. Work by Jacquelyn Hall and others has demonstrated that southern textile workers took pride in their jobs and their communities, and this close attachment to the mills made their disappearance traumatic for both workers and other residents. As the *Charlotte Observer*'s Jim Wrinn noted in 1999, displaced textile workers usually felt like they had been hit by a "tidal wave."[13]

Above all, the industry's location in the South rather than the traditional Rust Belt has caused scholars of deindustrialization to overlook its decline. It is no coincidence that Youngstown, Ohio, rather than a southern community, has become the "national 'poster child' for deindustrialization."[14] While the Rust Belt states were experiencing massive plant shutdowns, the South was widely perceived as a booming "Sun Belt." Influenced by Kirkpatrick Sale's *Power Shift* (1975), which depicted the area below the thirty-seventh parallel as vibrant and emerging, the *New York Times* ran a series of front-page articles that popularized the theme or concept of the Sun Belt. According to the *Times*'s B. Drummond Ayers Jr., this region was "the new American frontier, a section gaining population and economic and political power so fast that it threatens the national hegemony of the old, established Northeast." After this publicity, almost every national magazine carried flattering articles that pictured the region as free of the economic woes that afflicted the more industrialized North. Although Sale's Sun Belt included a number of southwestern and western states, the term soon became interchangeable with the South. Not used as heavily after 1980, the Sun Belt trope nevertheless persisted as a generic term for the region. Most scholars of the modern South have also continued to emphasize the region's ongoing economic growth and its gradual movement toward national norms.[15]

Many of the changes that the original press articles described were real. Census data recorded that southward migration was occurring at an unprecedented pace, and by 1976 all but two of the country's thirteen fastest-growing metropolitan areas were in the Sun Belt. In describing the region's main cities, especially Atlanta, Houston, and Charlotte, the Sun Belt image was largely accurate, and it was on these cities that the bulk of press coverage concentrated. These centers had burgeoning economies that were heavily based around the energy, banking, and service sectors, and their leaders had proved adept at attracting a disproportionate share of federal funds. Most textile and apparel plants were located in small towns or rural areas, however, and the press failed to mention this other side of the region. As historian Bruce Schulman has pointed out, there were actually "two Souths" in this era, as grinding poverty coexisted alongside dramatic growth. Across the piedmont, the staple industry was already in decline when the media proclaimed the existence of the Sun Belt, and its ongoing problems only exacerbated the gap between the two Souths.[16]

In fact, the textile and apparel industry was at the forefront of the deindustrialization process, which has traditionally been associated with the "Manufacturing Belt" states in the Northeast and Midwest.[17] Between 1973 and 1996 the industry lost 39 percent of its workforce, or around 900,000 workers. Among manufacturing workers as a whole, the decline was 8 percent over the same period. The causes of textile-apparel job losses were similar to those affecting northern industries. In both the North and South, companies struggled to compete with cheap imports, and they tried to do so by increasing productivity and cutting jobs. The industry therefore offers an excellent opportunity to study two major causes of deindustrialization. "Every industry in the American economy has been affected in some way by increased globalization and new developments in technology," declared BLS economist Mark Mittelhauser in 1997. "Few, however, have felt the effects of these trends more acutely than the textiles and apparel industries."[18]

As economists have noted, both textiles and apparel are "import-sensitive" industries that for decades have faced increasing international competition. In the mid-1950s, 5 percent of women's and children's apparel sold in the United States was imported, but by the mid-1980s this figure had increased to 52 percent. Over the same time, textile imports rose 428 percent. This influx occurred because American politicians consistently embraced free-trade policies, believing that these would open new markets for U.S. exports and promote democratic change in the developing world. Imports, however, have also caused domestic job losses, especially in labor-intensive industries such as apparel, footwear, and electronic appliances. In one careful study, economist Lori G. Kletzer found that imports were responsible for "considerable displacement" of apparel workers in the 1980s and 1990s; losses in the textile sector, while not quite as great, were still substantial.[19]

The rise of cheap imports, and the failure of legislative efforts to contain them, is a key cause of the textile industry's decline. As early as the 1950s, a decade when even the steel and auto industries were doing well, textile manufacturers and union leaders were already worried about imports. In 1957, at a time when most of the labor movement supported free trade, the leaders of the Textile Workers Union of America (TWUA) were already calling in vain for strict import controls.[20] Above all, however, it was the two apparel unions—the International Ladies' Garment Workers' Union (ILGWU) and the Amalgamated Clothing Workers of America (ACWA)—that led the fight for tight import controls. In 1966 the ILGWU's research department complained that the rate of import growth was "excessive," especially as clothing was increasingly shipped from the lowest-wage countries in the world. In 1970 the union's executive board called for legislation to address the issue; that year, an omnibus bill on imports was reported out of the House Ways and Means Committee but it failed to secure adoption.[21] As a result, textile and apparel imports continued to increase, as did domestic job losses in the industry.[22]

In the 1960s and 1970s it was the Japanese textile industry that aroused most concern in the United States. Helped by American aid, the Japanese had quickly emerged as a major economic power. By 1977, for example, textile imports were blamed for America's $8.5 billion trade deficit with Japan. In 1978, following industry lobbying, South Carolina senator Ernest Hollings introduced a proposal that granted the textile industry automatic exclusion from scheduled tariff reductions. Building on widespread concern about foreign competition, especially from Japan, the bill passed the House and Senate but was vetoed by President Carter, who worried that it would invite retaliation from overseas trading partners.[23]

In the early 1980s the decline of the textile and apparel industry quickened, especially as the leading southern manufacturers were hit hard by the general economic downturn. In early 1983, for example, the jobless rate in North Carolina's textile industry was 15 to 16 percent, much higher than the state's Sun Belt image suggested. During and after the recession, southern textile executives argued that they could not compete with imports made by workers who were paid as little as 20 cents an hour. In late 1984, Springs Industries CEO Walter Y. Elisha asked Congress for urgent action, claiming that an "unwarranted deluge of imported textiles" was "drowning" the domestic industry.[24]

Because deindustrialization was causing union membership to decline sharply, the textile unions consistently backed manufacturers' calls for import controls. Formed by a 1976 merger between the TWUA and ACWA, the new Amalgamated Clothing and Textile Workers Union (ACTWU) was particularly affected. Between 1980 and 1985, plant closings resulted in 53,047 members' jobs being lost, around three-quarters of them in the apparel sector.[25] In both 1985 and 1987, ACTWU and the leading textile companies worked together to secure passage of legislation to protect their industry from further import increases. Both bills were sponsored by southern representatives and sought to contain rather than stop imports; the 1987 effort, for example, introduced global textile quotas with an allowance of 1 percent total import growth a year. As union leaders realized, much was at stake in this legislative battle. In 1986, ACTWU president Murray Finley told his executive board that winning strict import quotas was "vital for the survival of our members and industries."[26]

In working to secure passage of the bills, the unions forged unprecedented links with mill owners. The newly formed Fiber, Fabric, and Apparel Coalition for Trade (FFACT) lobbied members of Congress, staged grassroots rallies, and mobilized thousands of textile workers to write their political representatives. These efforts seemed to have paid off, as the bills passed the House and Senate on both occasions, with strong support coming from textile-state representatives regardless of their party affiliation. In response, powerful opposition came from exporters, retailers, and consumer groups, who argued that import controls would raise prices and antagonize foreign governments. Clearly influenced by this strident opposition, President Ronald Reagan vetoed both bills. According to the president, the 1985 legislation would cause "immediate retaliation against our exports resulting in a loss of American jobs in other areas." The president reaffirmed these concerns three years later.

Despite determined campaigns, efforts to override the vetoes fell short in the House by eight and eleven votes, respectively.[27]

As the bills were debated, the free traders had decisive advantages, especially as they were able to castigate their opponents as "protectionists," a term that quickly took on pejorative overtones. They also had a powerful support base of their own, and this was reflected in the regional breakdown of votes. Although the bills attracted strong support in the northeastern and southeastern states, free traders held the upper hand elsewhere. In the Midwest, farming groups generally supported trade liberalization because they wanted greater access to overseas markets, while the West Coast's economy was also heavily geared to exports. As the American Textile Manufacturers Institute's (ATMI) Board of Directors noted privately in 1987, a key obstacle to quota legislation was the lack of congressional support "from areas west of the Mississippi river."[28]

Even after these disappointments, FFACT's leaders declared that they were "undaunted" and pressed on with their campaign. In 1990 a third effort to pass textile quota legislation produced the same result, although on this occasion it was President George H. W. Bush who exercised the veto. Again, the failure of the legislation reflected strident opposition, especially from the prosperous export lobby, whose members wanted greater access to lucrative overseas markets. Importers and retailers also showed little sympathy for the plight of domestic manufacturers. "They're running at over 90 percent capacity," blasted Mary GiaQuinta from the American Association of Exporters and Importers, "and a lot of the job loss they blame on imports is a result of efforts to become more competitive through automation."[29]

Although imports were the central cause of the industry's decline, on balance they were certainly not the only problem confronting U.S. textile makers. The demise of apparel production was also related to broader shifts in consumer tastes, as customers eschewed formal clothes in favor of cheaper imports. The rise of giant, cost-driven retailers such as Walmart also allowed these firms to call the shots with both textile and apparel manufacturers, and they demanded ever-lower prices that American firms often could not deliver. Widely associated with low wages, tough working conditions, and labor strife, the industry also suffered an image problem. It was an image not helped by the movie *Norma Rae* (1979), in which Sally Field won an Oscar for Best Actress. Watched by millions, *Norma Rae* dramatized the long-standing dispute between organized labor and the J. P. Stevens Company and depicted southern mills as noisy and dirty. As journalist Sandra Salmans summarized, "Propagated by *Norma Rae*, the movie based on the Stevens labor dispute, the industry's reputation for backwardness has clung as persistently as cotton dust." Mill owners insisted that the film projected an outdated image, because most textile plants were now clean and heavily automated. Beginning in the 1970s, executives spent huge sums on capital expenditures to try to compete with imports, changes that entailed significant job losses. By the late 1980s the industry was investing about $1.5 billion per year in new plant and equipment, and its productivity growth regularly exceeded the average for manufacturing as a whole.[30]

By spotlighting the industry's problems, the fight for import quotas also encouraged observers to associate the textile industry with plant closings and decline. The campaign therefore had unintended consequences, some of which could be seen in dwindling enrollments at the South's textile training schools. The industry's low wages also hurt its campaign, especially when the national economy was doing well. In 1988, for example, a *New York Times* editorial argued that because textile jobs were low-paying, displaced workers could simply secure better posts in other industries. A consistent foe of the textile bills, the *Times* supported both of Reagan's vetoes. Heavily dependent on advertising revenue from retailers, much of the press took the same position.[31]

The failure of the textile bills was a turning point, paving the way for the passage of new free-trade initiatives. Mill owners now worried that policy makers would sacrifice their industry in return for improved access to foreign markets, primarily to benefit other manufacturers. Apparently validating their fears was the 1993 North American Free Trade Agreement (NAFTA), a controversial measure designed to eliminate trade barriers between the United States, Mexico, and Canada. Realizing that NAFTA posed a particular threat to their members, both ACTWU and the ILGWU enthusiastically supported the campaign to defeat the treaty, although many textile companies supported it in the hope that increased trade with Mexico could help shield them from Asian competition. In contrast, the more labor-intensive apparel industry generally opposed the agreement. Helped by these industry divisions, the effort to stop NAFTA failed. With solid Republican support and with President Bill Clinton swaying key Democrats, NAFTA easily passed the House by a vote of 234 to 200, with Clinton signing it into law on December 8, 1993.[32]

In the wake of NAFTA, the decline of the textile and apparel industry accelerated. Within nine years of the agreement's passage, North Carolina had lost half of its textile and apparel jobs, and the situation was similar in neighboring Virginia and South Carolina. It was easy to blame NAFTA for the closures, and many workers and community leaders in the South duly did so. In Martinsville, Virginia, which once proclaimed itself the "Sweatshirt Capital of the

World," officials claimed that the treaty was responsible for the loss of 9,500 local manufacturing jobs in seven years, leaving the area with double-digit unemployment. "You have found the poster child for NAFTA," declared Tom Harned, Martinsville's economic development director. "We're losing jobs by the thousands and replacing them by the hundreds."[33]

Led by labor and environmental groups, NAFTA's critics blamed the treaty for heavy job losses, yet the agreement also retained plenty of supporters. An economic think tank dedicated to helping working Americans, the Economic Policy Institute blamed NAFTA for at least 500,000 domestic job losses, but most business groups and retailers saw the situation differently. NAFTA, they stressed, had opened markets for U.S. exporters and had lowered prices for American consumers. "NAFTA has 'locked in' trade gains to the benefit of U.S. exporters," asserted the Business Roundtable in one detailed report. "On balance the 'winners' outweighed the 'losers.'"[34]

NAFTA's impact was certainly complex, and various parts of the vast textile-apparel complex were affected differently by it. The agreement hurt labor-intensive apparel plants the most, yet within the textile sector some domestic manufacturers were able to sell more fabrics and yarn to Mexican garment makers. The real problem, insisted Carlos Moore of the ATMI, which had backed NAFTA, was cheap Asian imports. Unlike Mexico, many Asian countries imposed high import tariffs, making it almost impossible for American goods to penetrate their markets. After the 1997 economic collapse devalued Asian currencies by around 40 percent, garment manufacturers in the Far East had a decisive advantage. Indeed, by the turn of the century, textile executives increasingly complained about unfair competition from Asia, and especially from China, rather than about NAFTA. "China is the 800-pound gorilla," declared industry lobbyist Jock Nash. "I don't know anybody who can compete with them—not in textiles, not in electronics, not in anything."[35]

In China, the state-run textile and apparel industry grew at a phenomenal rate. As was the case in other developing countries, China's politicians promoted the industry because of its labor-intensive nature and its ability to generate much-needed export revenue. As early as 1988 the industry was China's biggest foreign exchange earner, and further growth was to come. By 2000 China's garment exports were worth $36.1 billion, fifty times more than in 1978. At the start of the twenty-first century, Chinese mills employed an amazing 18 million workers, more than double the population of North Carolina.[36]

In the United States, the industry's decline was accelerated by China's accession to the World Trade Organization (WTO), which was formally approved in 2001 following lengthy negotiations. Pointing to China's "violations of human rights," the AFL-CIO mounted an intensive campaign against admission, but it was not enough to overcome the powerful free-trade lobby. Reassuring many doubters, the Clinton administration again played a crucial role in the buildup to China's admission. "China's accession to the World Trade Organization will help promote reform, accountability, and openness in China," promised the president's press secretary in 2000. Determined critics responded that China had a poor record of living up to its international obligations, and the Asian power's increasing dominance of global textile production certainly allowed it to brush off Western criticisms of its labor practices and human-rights record.[37]

In addition to trade developments, the events of 9/11 also contributed to the decline of the American textile industry. For some struggling firms, the economic downturn that followed the terrorist attacks was the final blow. In November 2001, Burlington Industries, once the largest textile producer in the world, was forced to declare bankruptcy. Cheap imports, claimed CEO George Henderson, were "devastating for the industry," and on top of this, consumer spending had slowed because of the recession. Eighteen months later, the collapse of debt-ridden Pillowtex Corporation led to the closure of sixteen plants and the loss of 6,450 jobs. Most of the affected plants were located in North Carolina, where the mass layoffs were the largest in the state's history. In Kannapolis, a historic mill town that was home to Pillowtex's main complex, the closures were particularly devastating. At the end of 2003, denim manufacturer Cone Mills similarly filed for bankruptcy, another high-profile victim of the prevailing economic conditions. Although financier Wilbur Ross bought both Cone and Burlington, he was soon slashing jobs and encouraging outsourcing. Moreover, the two firms no longer technically existed but were part of the anonymously named International Textile Group. The textile industry, concluded journalist Katherine Yung, was now "in tatters," its largest players either in bankruptcy or on the verge of it.[38]

The Pillowtex closures attracted national media attention and spurred visits to Kannapolis by Senators Elizabeth Dole and John Edwards, who both called for tougher trade policies. The high-profile case indeed prompted renewed demands for tight import restrictions. In October 2003, 165 members of Congress wrote President George W. Bush and urged him to help, while textile companies also stepped up their lobbying efforts. Keen to retain southern votes, in November Bush agreed to impose temporary restrictions on three categories of Chinese imports: bras, dressing gowns, and knit fabrics. While they were pleased with the move, industry executives stressed that it was of little long-term help, especially as most Chinese goods were unaffected. "Everybody knows the answer," fumed North Carolina mill owner Gerald Cauthen. "They don't have the guts to step up and turn the ships back to China."[39]

As the industry's campaign intensified, it was opposed by the same groups that had defeated the earlier legislation, including textile importers, retailers, and export-focused businesses. They all argued that imports had brought lower prices for consumers, claims that the shrinking textile lobby struggled to refute.[40] In addition to outside opposition, divisions within the textile and apparel manufacturers also remained a problem. By this time, for instance, some textile and apparel companies had embraced offshoring and consequently opposed quotas. Between 1994 and 2004, major player Vanity Fair increased its number of overseas workers from 6,000 to 35,000 while its number of American employees fell from 52,000 to 19,000. Seeing trade liberalization as inevitable, firms such as Vanity Fair and International Textile Group broke with other parts of the industry, which remained committed to domestic manufacturing.[41]

As the industry's contraction continued, some closures were particularly noteworthy. In 2003, WestPoint Stevens closed its towel-making complex in Roanoke Rapids, North Carolina, shuttering the mills that had inspired *Norma Rae*. In 1974 the TWUA's election victory at the plant had inspired hopes of unionizing southern mill workers, but now there were few workers left to organize. Other closures affected mills that had played a notable role in local and national history. A good example occurred in 2005, when Mount Vernon Mills closed its plant in Tallassee, Alabama. Operating continuously since 1844, and reputed to be the oldest cloth factory in the country, Tallassee Mills had once made fabric for both slave clothes and Confederate army uniforms. As journalist Jay Reeves wrote, although Tallassee now had other industries, the mill's closure represented "a psychological blow to a small town that is losing the very thing that made it a community."[42]

After January 1, 2005, beleaguered manufacturers also had to contend with the abolition of all global textile quotas. As part of an international trade deal reached in 1994, the newly formed WTO absorbed the earlier Multifiber Agreement (MFA), which for twenty years had regulated the international trade in textiles. Although the industry had complained about the inadequacy of the MFA, the agreement did contain some protections that were now to be phased out over the following ten years, with all quotas to be gone by the start of 2005.[43] After this, Chinese firms had the open access to the giant American market that they had been seeking for some time. The move indeed followed intensive lobbying from the Chinese; according to Sun Zhenyu, China's ambassador to the WTO, the abolition of quotas would bring "fair competition to the sector." The contrast with the reaction of American manufacturers could not have been greater. "We're exporting our middle-class jobs, the American dream for the next generation," declared mill owner Roger Chastain.[44]

The abolition of quotas devastated what remained of the domestic textile industry. The BLS recorded that between December 2004 and July 2009 the U.S. textile and apparel industry lost 256,300 jobs, or 38.2 percent of all remaining posts. Losses accelerated as soon as the quotas were removed. In the early months of 2005, for example, the rate of textile plant closings tripled when compared to that of the previous year. Although American mill owners claimed that Chinese imports were surging to unprecedented levels, the Chinese opposed American efforts to reimpose temporary safeguards on several major categories, as allowed under the terms of China's admission to the WTO. According to government spokesman Liu Jianchao, the Americans had "unreasonably" sheltered their textile industries for decades, and there was no point in turning back the clock. Responding to lobbying from the newly formed National Council of Textile Organizations, which was attempting to overcome the industry's divisions, the Bush administration was able to get some "sensitive" textile items put back under quota in May 2005, but overall the Chinese continued to make inroads. After January 1, 2009, moreover, all temporary safeguards were removed and the United States was not allowed to reimpose them. By June 2010 the U.S. Commerce Department recorded that China was responsible for 45.75 percent of all textile and apparel imports.[45]

Despite press claims that they could easily find better-paying jobs, southern textile workers were hit hard by the industry's demise. In 2003, one Organisation for Economic Cooperation and Development (OECD) study found that two-thirds of reemployed textile and apparel workers earned less on their new jobs than they had previously, while one-quarter experienced losses greater than 30 percent. Although textile jobs paid poorly by manufacturing standards, they still offered better pay than the retail and service sectors, where displaced mill workers often ended up, and came with a range of fringe benefits, including employer-sponsored health care, which service jobs often lacked. Testimony confirms that workers lost economically when the mills closed. Commenting on the Pillowtex closure in Kannapolis, former textile worker Robert Freeman noted, "I have friends who have lost their job and are now dealing with foreclosures, having their cars taken away, and telling their kids they can't pay for college this fall."[46]

Of course, not all workers suffered economically when the mills closed, and after a period of adjustment some ended up doing well. This was especially the case in the mid- to late 1990s, when the economy was particularly resilient. Apart from the standard twenty-six weeks of unemployment pay, many workers qualified for extra help under the Trade Adjustment Assistance (TAA) Program, which was designed to help those who had lost their jobs because of the pressures of foreign trade. Under the TAA, which dated back to the Trade

Act of 1974, certified workers received training, income support, and other reemployment services. A domestic measure separate from the international MFA, the Trade Act generally promoted free trade, but it also sought to help displaced workers phase into other industries. Using the TAA benefits to qualify for new careers, some seized the opportunity with enthusiasm. With more qualifications and education, white-collar workers fared better than most, often setting up businesses or retraining in service-oriented careers. Seeing retraining as the solution to the industry's problems, conservative leaders liked to stress these success stories. In 2003, when President George W. Bush visited North Carolina's textile belt, it was no accident that he talked with Scott Hiner, a former textile supervisor who was using the TAA program to retrain for a career in biotechnology. "In other words," commented Bush, "things are beginning to brighten up for people looking for work, which is positive. And, therefore, we must make sure that people are trained for jobs that exist."[47]

Overall, however, these workers were definitely the fortunate minority, as even retrained workers often struggled to find suitable positions. In 2001 the unemployment rate in Robeson County, North Carolina, was 12.3 percent, despite the fact that many former mill workers had attended the local community college. This figure was matched in several other textile-dependent counties.[48] By 2002, economic conditions in North Carolina's Gaston County were so bad that one regional daily termed it "ground zero when it comes to displaced textile workers." In that year, the governors of North Carolina, South Carolina, Georgia, and Virginia held a "textile summit" in the county to try and secure more aid for former mill workers. At the time, the official unemployment rate in the area exceeded 10 percent, well above the state average. All down Interstate 85, which ran through Gastonia and many other former textile communities, the situation was similar. "Along the asphalt artery that binds the economy from Charlotte, N.C., through South Carolina and Georgia to Montgomery, Ala., it is the workers, many laid off by electronics and textile plants, who are begging," wrote *New York Times* journalist Peter T. Kilborn. Rather than working in the showcase business parks that had been built along the highway, most displaced textile workers held menial posts in the fast-food restaurants, retail stores, and motels that clustered around the exit ramps. Overall, I-85 was a striking illustration of how the two Souths coexisted.[49]

Several characteristics of the southern textile workforce increased the impact of mill closures. For example, the industry contained large numbers of workers over the age of forty-five, many of whom lacked formal educational qualifications. Most had worked in the mills since high school and were poorly placed to start new careers. When the Pillowtex plant in Kannapolis shut, for example, the average worker was forty-six years old and had worked in the plant for seventeen years. In addition, 45.7 percent of employees did not have a high school diploma or a GED. Believing that the mills would always be there, these workers were shocked by their sudden disappearance. Even after the mills were gone, many displaced southern workers were unwilling (or unable) to relocate because they remained closely tied to their local communities, ties that free traders discounted or overlooked.[50]

In textiles and apparel, deindustrialization hit racial minorities especially hard. The textile and apparel sector was a major employer of racial minorities, and BLS economists have repeatedly shown that these groups fared particularly badly when they lost manufacturing jobs. Between 1984 and 1992, black men experienced rates of job displacement that were some 30 percent higher than white men, and their reemployment rates were also 30 percent lower. By 2003, the year that many large textile closures occurred, unemployment among blacks was rising twice as fast as it was for whites, and most of the jobs being lost were in manufacturing, where the pay for African Americans has historically been higher than in other fields.[51] Until the 1960s, blacks had been largely locked out of mill jobs, and change came only because of civil rights legislation and pressure from activists. By 1978, African Americans held a quarter of all production jobs in the southern textile industry, and they made further gains in subsequent decades. This was a significant breakthrough, as mill jobs paid higher wages and seemingly offered security to a generation of African American workers. In Lancaster, South Carolina, for example, the textile mill dominated the local economy, but for decades production jobs were reserved for whites. In the 1960s, however, workers such as Esterlean McGriff went from caring for the children of white women who worked in the weave rooms to working alongside her former employers. "It was a better job for us," she recalled, adding that her three sons had followed her into the mill. For McLean, as for many other African Americans, the mill closures were devastating. In the 1990s, Latino migrants also broke through into textile jobs in large numbers, and by 2002 they represented 16 percent of all workers. Many lost mill jobs only a short time after being hired, and because of language barriers these workers were often unable to complete retraining courses as easily as their English-speaking counterparts.[52]

Deindustrialization also hurt many women workers, particularly in apparel plants. In 1996, for example, nearly half of all textile workers were women, while in apparel the figure was close to three-quarters. In comparison, women made up only about one-third of workers in the manufacturing sector as a whole.[53] Striving to avoid competition from higher-wage industries, clothing manufacturers had often built plants in small towns, and generations of women workers had used these jobs to raise their families, especially since a fair number were heads of households. After NAFTA, however, scores of these plants disappeared, particularly in the Deep South. Between 1995 and 2001, for example, Vanity Fair closed plants in a series of small Alabama towns, including Atmore, Hanceville, Robertsdale, Demopolis, and Centreville. "Many of those losing the $8 to $10 an hour sewing or manufacturing jobs are single women with children," noted the *Mobile Register* after an investigation of the closings. Textile plants also tended to be located in small communities, and female breadwinners depended heavily on the mills. "You got married and raised families and you never worked for anyone else but the mills, because they always provided," explained Barbara Gauldin from Eden, North Carolina. "There is nowhere I can go to now. When you talk about your job, you're talking about your life. They're doing away with my job, they're more or less doing away with my life." Gauldin added that displaced textile workers had three things to keep them going: their churches, their families, and their pride.[54]

Most mill closures also had an enormous economic impact on the communities in which they were located. Because mills were typically built in small towns, their disappearance weakened the local tax base and forced cuts in municipal services. In Martinsville, Virginia, for instance, the shutdown of the large Vanity Fair plant forced the local board of education to close four schools. Even in Spartanburg County, South Carolina, which was often held up as a classic Sun Belt area, the closure of large textile mills hurt local services. Following eight mill closures in 2001 alone, cuts had to be made in the county's education and fire budgets.[55] These experiences were not unusual. In the same year, more than a dozen piedmont textile towns hired a lobbyist to try and recoup funds that had been lost owing to mill shutdowns. "The impact from the undoing of this once-vibrant industry will be more far-reaching than the empty pay envelopes of workers, the demolition of plants and the changes in landscape seen in most mill villages," summarized one piedmont journalist.[56]

Aside from the economic consequences, mill closures were a significant psychological blow for both workers and community members. As recently as the 1980s, textile mills had been the backbone of life across much of the region. In communities such as Fort Mill, located just south of Charlotte, residents recalled how tufts of cotton had often floated through the air and how traffic backed up through town when shift changes at the mill took place. As the *New York Times*'s William E. Schmidt explained in 1984, "The mills, with their aging brick factories, remain the dominant life force in many small towns, the source not only of paychecks but civic energy, fielding softball leagues as well as the labor and sometimes the cash to help rebuild churches and repair school gymnasiums." The decline of such a large industry had enormous cultural and psychological ramifications. "This is something historical," asserted textile union leader Harris Raynor in 1999. "The whole country is losing something here."[57]

Scores of southern communities had originated as mill towns, and in many cases the mill had been constructed before the community around it even existed. As a result, the closure of these defining facilities produced a strong sense of loss. Community leaders often expressed this sentiment well. In 1997, for example, when Johnston Industries announced the closure of its 131-year-old Langdale plant in Valley, Alabama, industrial development official Danny Games summarized what the move meant for local people: "There's a lot of pride in Langdale. It's too easy to underestimate the sentimental attachment and the community importance that mill played. You can't just sum that up. It hurts." For the town of St. Pauls, North Carolina, the closure of five textile mills even dictated a change to the municipal seal, which depicted a cone of yarn with the motto "The Textile Center of Robeson County." As Mayor Gordon Westbrook admitted, "We will have to change the seal because it's misleading."[58]

Following closures, southern mill buildings also faced an uncertain future. When they were located in growing urban centers, mills had a good chance of being converted into retail or residential spaces. In Columbia, South Carolina, for example, the former Springs Industries mill was converted successfully into desirable apartments.[59] In smaller towns, however, it was usually difficult to find new uses for the mills, which were often large, imposing structures. Some were used as storage facilities, but many others stood empty and abandoned. As the *Philadelphia Inquirer*'s Ken Moritsugu wrote in 2001, "Padlocked gates and knee-high grass surround many of the textile mills that were the lifeblood of this region for much of the last century. The scars—like the silent brick smokestacks—will remain for some time."[60]

Because renovation was usually costly, many mills were demolished, thus eradicating evidence of the South's textile past from the landscape. Some of the region's most famous mill buildings met this sad end. In 2005 the huge former Cannon Mills complex in Kannapolis, North Carolina, was pulled down to make way for a new research park, yet former workers harbored few hopes of reemployment in the high-tech complex. That same year, the 400,000-square-foot headquarters of Burlington Industries in Greensboro was bulldozed to make space for a new shopping center. Both jobs were so large that they were carried out by D. H. Griffin Wrecking Company, the firm that had cleaned up the Ground Zero site after the 9/11 attacks. The eradication of the Cannon Mills complex, which covered an area larger than either the Sears Tower or the

Pentagon, was reported to be the third-largest demolition project in American history.⁶¹

The same fate met Dan River Mills in Danville, Virginia, which at one time had been the largest single textile mill in the entire South. Following the mill's closure in 2006, local preservationists were only able to salvage the "Home of Dan River Fabrics" sign, which had stood on top of the White Mill building for almost sixty years. The rest of the vast complex was obliterated in a dramatic explosion that was recorded on local television. As they watched the mills literally disappear, local people were sad, yet some also recognized the inevitability of change. "It's hard," reflected Danville resident Lisa Reynolds, "but you have to let go of the past to let the future in."⁶² By 2005, efforts were afoot to try and preserve key sites; North Carolina's Textile Heritage Center, for example, aimed to turn 464 miles of I-85 into a "textile corridor for heritage tourism." Despite these good intentions, the scale of the task meant that mills were still being eradicated much faster than they could be saved or restored.⁶³

As the mills were razed, Walmart stores were being built in former textile communities, and they often used displaced mill workers to help sell the cheap imported clothes that lined their shelves. In Kannapolis, for example, the Walmart Supercenter opened in the summer of 2003, just at the time when Pillowtex collapsed. When the store opened, former Pillowtex worker Judy Hatley recalled that more than half of its staff were laid-off Pillowtex employees. In an interview with the local press, Hatley did not comment on how she felt about her new job but added that she missed the mill, which she described as "the life of the town." A few years later, former Pillowtex workers portrayed working at Walmart as a grim necessity. "Quite a few . . . work there, and work at all the Walmarts, because they've got to have income," recalled Ruth Crisco in 2010, adding that the pay was much lower than it had been in the mill.⁶⁴

Since the 1970s, textiles and apparel has not been the only industry to shed southern workers. Despite the growth of the service sector, many pockets of the region depended heavily on traditional manufacturing. By promising low wages and weak unions, southern politicians had lured these companies to the region, yet many firms would soon move offshore in search of even cheaper labor. In 1982, with the national economy in recession, five Deep South states had double-digit unemployment as a variety of manufacturing industries cut staff. Layoffs and closures were particularly common at garment and electronics factories, most of them located in non-metropolitan areas. "This is supposed to be the Sun Belt," commented small business owner Bill Markham in Fayetteville, Tennessee, where unemployment stood at over 11 percent in 1981.

"But industry's having a hard time, people don't have the money to spend." The demise of Alabama's steel industry was easier to spot than these small town closures, yet it has not attracted the attention that scholars have lavished on the demise of the large northern mills. In Birmingham, once dubbed the "Pittsburgh of the South," big steel employed about 25,000 workers at its peak, but by the early 1980s just 3,000 remained. "Birmingham, like the nation itself," reported the *Washington Post*, "is going through a rite of passage that is transforming the community," as manufacturing jobs were replaced by service and retail positions. Indicative of this shift, tobacco factories in North Carolina, Kentucky, and Virginia also shed workers on a steady basis.[65]

Even as the national economy picked up, BLS economists repeatedly challenged glib assumptions of a Rust Belt/Sun Belt dichotomy. In 1984 the bureau's "East South Central" division, which covered the states of Kentucky, Tennessee, Mississippi, and Alabama, had the highest unemployment rate in the country. Two years later, staffer Philip L. Rones pointed out that New England had the lowest unemployment rate of any region, partly because it had enjoyed more time to adjust to plant closings and attract new employers. In contrast, a "considerable majority" of states in the South and West had jobless rates above the national average, a trend that was clearly related to deindustrialization. Referring to Kirkpatrick Sale's influential work, Rones concluded that, "The economic 'Power Shift,' as it has been called, is clearly not as immutable as once thought."[66]

By the mid-1980s the national press was becoming more sensitive to the South's complexity, noting that booming cities were usually surrounded by rural areas that were losing their manufacturing base. It was in these non-metropolitan areas that most textile and apparel plants were located, yet they were also home to several other struggling industries. Charlotte provided a good example; the city grew rapidly, yet just beyond its suburbs lay decaying textile towns such as Gastonia, Kannapolis, and Shelby. As the *New York Times*'s Peter Applebome noted in 1989, the Sun Belt image concealed "a growing regional imbalance that is seeing metropolitan areas increasingly healthy while rural areas continue to decline." In 1986, for example, per capita income in the non-metropolitan South was less than three-quarters of that in urban areas, while unemployment was some 37 percent higher. Between 1980 and 1986, confirmed a study by the Southern Growth Policies Board, the South did grow faster than the national average, yet most of this growth was concentrated in the large cities; total civilian employment increased by 14.4 percent in twelve southern states (compared to a national average of 11.5 percent), yet in large southern cities the growth rate was 21.9 percent.[67]

In the 1990s the South suffered further job losses as a wide range of manufacturing industries hit hard times. Between 1995 and 2004, employment in the nation's paper industry, much of it located in the rural South, slumped from 639,000 to 499,000 as companies were hit by overseas competition and reduced earnings.[68] The electronics industry, which had moved south in search of cheaper labor, was now lured away by even lower wages in Latin America and Asia. There were also problems in the furniture industry, which had developed alongside textiles in the wake of the Civil War. Between 1990 and 2003, North Carolina lost almost 26,000 jobs in this important industry. American furniture makers faced rising competition from cheap Asian imports, and they were also hurt by a shift in consumer preferences toward cheap, utilitarian goods. Again, labor costs were crucial; at the start of the twenty-first century, furniture manufacturers in Asia could hire workers for $12 to $15 a day, compared to $12 to $15 an hour in the United States. The closures hurt a range of communities, especially piedmont towns that were already reeling from textile shutdowns.[69]

As the textile experience highlights, plant closures were just as painful for southern workers as they were for their northern counterparts. In many respects, the South's experience with deindustrialization was very similar to that outlined in classic studies of northern communities: workers were displaced and struggled to find comparable work, communities lost tax revenue, and there were heavy emotional costs for both workers and their family members. As a local official in Martinsville, Virginia, put it, "The human suffering in this community that has come from the textile industry, and directly related to the trade policy of the United States, is immeasurable."[70] Early case studies of plant closures in the North Carolina furniture industry and the Alabama paper industry have reached similar conclusions.[71]

The demise of the textile industry also suggests that deindustrialization in the South has had some defining characteristics. In some respects, the decline of the southern textile industry was more traumatic for those involved than it was for northern workers who lost their jobs. Interestingly, it was often the northern press that picked up on these differences. As early as 1986, the *Detroit Free Press* carried a special feature on job losses in the southern piedmont, noting that displaced autoworkers fared better than their textile counterparts because they were paid more and received better benefits. Further, most textile workers did not have strong unions to lobby their case; in contrast, the power of the United Automobile Workers ensured that laid-off autoworkers were usually given generous severance packages. In scores of small southern towns, the textile industry's economic dominance also left displaced workers with few options. The *Free Press* found that six out of twenty-six mills in the Eden, North Carolina, area had closed in the previous two years and that very few workers had landed comparable jobs. As Marcia Stepanek concluded, Eden may have proclaimed itself as "The Village of Bounty," but in reality it was "no paradise."[72] In subsequent years, northern writers retained an interest in the southern textile industry's demise, especially as it accelerated when many northern states began to do a little better. In 2001, for instance, the *St. Paul Pioneer Press* recorded that few areas of America were in as bad shape as the South's textile belt, where job losses were "the worst since the Great Depression."[73]

Above all, it was southern mill workers' strong attachment to their jobs and their communities that made the closures so painful. As the authors of *Like a Family* have demonstrated, southern textile communities were distinguished by "a distinctive mill village culture" that "provided comfort and reassurance in an often hostile world."[74] To be sure, after World War II this culture was buffeted by the sale of company-owned housing and the influx of new residents and industries. Despite these changes, many workers and residents remained proud of the mills, and they found it difficult to imagine a world without them. When Burlington Industries closed its plant in Mooresville, North Carolina, in July 1999, the community no longer depended on the mill, but most employees still found the shutdown "traumatic." They were proud of their jobs, which had provided a stable living to generations of local people. Many had worked at the plant since high school, and they often labored alongside family members. Although they were aware of the industry's problems, most reasoned that their jobs were safe. "I thought Mooresville Mills would be there forever," commented fifty-five-year-old George Abernathy. "The mill meant a whole lot to me. If it reopened tomorrow, I'd go back to work there."[75]

Locked out of the industry until the 1960s, African American workers, it is important to realize, had a somewhat different perspective from that of whites.' While very few sources identified racial difference in workers' reactions, some interviews suggest that blacks were less likely to express nostalgia or a sense of lost cultural identity, instead viewing the decline of the mills in more instrumental terms. These differences were evident, for example, in the reaction of Pillowtex workers to the closure in Kannapolis, as illustrated by interviews carried out by the local newspaper. Thus, while veteran white worker Agatha Overcash reminisced that "it was a family at the mill . . . that was tough to see go," black worker Leonard Chapman measured the closure primarily in economic terms. "The mill sustained the town for a long time," he commented. "The workers weren't well off, you may have lived from paycheck to paycheck but you were able to stay above water. . . . I think people will always remember what the mill did for the town." For Chapman and other non-white textile workers, the loss of the mills represented a serious economic setback, but they were much less likely to use the "family" metaphor.[76]

What blacks and whites shared was a dependence on the mills as a source of stable employment, and it was this reliance that made the industry's rapid demise so catastrophic. Senator John Edwards was among those who tried to help the devastated workers. The son of a mill worker from Robbins, North Carolina, Edwards frequently toured struggling textile communities as he ran for national political office in 2004 and 2008. "People don't understand, it's not just a paycheck for you," Edwards told one crowd of displaced workers in Columbus, Georgia. "It has some effect on your self-respect and dignity. I hear that and I see it in your face, and I hear the same thing over and over and over across this country." Edwards was one of several southern politicians to call for import safeguards and tax incentives to help the beleaguered industry, but to date there have been no major shifts in national policy. If textile and apparel job losses continue at their current pace, the industry will be virtually extinct, and so will the culture that it nurtured for over a century.[77]

Notes

Funding for this essay was provided by grants from the U.S. Studies Centre at the University of Sydney, Australia, and the Australian Research Council. The author would also like to thank Bronwyn Naismith, John Salmond, and Robert Zieger for their help in the preparation of this essay.

1. Since the 1980s, the decline of the textile and apparel industry has generated hundreds of articles in the southern press, creating a rich source that few scholars have yet to access in detail. In combination with archival and secondary sources, this press coverage is the main source used here. The limited existing scholarship on the decline of the southern textile industry is discussed further below (see especially note 6).

2. Tony Mecia, "Governors Want Federal Actions to Aid Textiles," *Charlotte Observer*, March 23, 2002, 1A; Jacquelyn Dowd Hall, James Leloudis, Robert Korstad, Mary Murphy, Lu Ann Jones, and Christopher B. Daly, *Like a Family: The Making of a Southern Cotton Mill World* (Chapel Hill: University of North Carolina Press, 1987), 1. For fine overviews of the recent scholarship on southern textile workers, including the debates about the distinctiveness of mill village culture and the reasons for the weakness of unions in the region, see Robert H. Zieger, "Textile Workers and Historians," in *Organized Labor in the Twentieth-Century South*, ed. Zieger (Knoxville: University of Tennessee Press, 1991), 35–59; and Robert H. Zieger, "From Primordial Folk to Redundant Workers: Southern Textile Workers and Social Observers, 1920–1990," in *Southern Labor in Transition, 1940–1995*, ed. Zieger (Knoxville: University of Tennessee Press, 1997), 273–94. Key textile studies are discussed in more detail in note 12 below.

3. Barry Bluestone and Bennett Harrison, *The Deindustrialization of America: Plant Closings, Community Abandonment, and the Dismantling of Basic Industry* (New York: Basic Books, 1982); Barry Bluestone, foreword, in *Beyond the Ruins: The Meanings of Deindustrialization*, ed. Jefferson Cowie and Joseph Heathcott (Ithaca: ILR Press, 2003), xii; Testimony of Betty McGrath, Labor Market Information Division, Employment Security Commission of North Carolina, September 6, 2007, available at www.uscc.gov/hearings/2007hearings/transcripts/sept_6/betty_mcgrath.pdf.

4. For a sample of studies of deindustrialization with a northern focus, see Thomas Dublin, *When the Mines Closed: Stories of Struggles in Hard Times* (Ithaca: Cornell University Press, 1998); Terry F. Buss and F. Stevens Redburn, *Shutdown at Youngstown: Public Policy for Mass Unemployment* (Albany: State University of New York Press, 1983); Steven P. Dandaneau, *A Town Abandoned: Flint, Michigan, Confronts Deindustrialization* (Albany: State University of New York Press, 1996); Ruth Milkman, *Farewell to the Factory: Auto Workers in the Late Twentieth Century* (Berkeley: University of California Press, 1997); Kathryn Marie Dudley, *The End of the Line: Lost Jobs, New Lives in Postindustrial America* (Chicago: University of Chicago Press, 1994); William Serrin, *Homestead: The Glory and Tragedy of an American Steel Town* (New York: Vintage Books, 1993); Mark Reutter, *Making Steel: The Rise and Ruin of American Industrial Might* (New York: Summit Books, 1988); John P. Hoerr, *And the Wolf Finally Came: The Decline of the American Steel Industry* (Pittsburgh: University of Pittsburgh Press, 1988); Sherry Lee Linkon and John Russo, *Steeltown USA: Work and Memory in Youngstown* (Lawrence: University Press of Kansas, 2002); Staughton Lynd, *The Fight against Shutdowns: Youngstown's Steel Mill Closings* (San Pedro: Singlejack Books, 1982). Apart from these case studies, Steven C. High has recently published a somewhat broader work on the entire North American Rust Belt, *Industrial Sunset: The Making of North America's Rust Belt, 1969–1984* (Toronto: University of Toronto Press, 2003).

5. For some representative conclusions, see Dudley, *The End of the Line*, esp. xi; David Bensman and Roberta Lynch, *Rusted Dreams: Hard Times in a Steel Community* (New York: McGraw Hill, 1987), esp. 2–9; Steve Mellon, *After the Smoke Clears: Struggling to Get By in Rustbelt America* (Pittsburgh: University of Pittsburgh Press, 2002), esp. 7. Dudley summarizes her study of the closure of a Chrysler plant in Kenosha, Wisconsin, by noting that "the loss of an industrial job can be so devastating. Friendships built up over twenty years on the shopfloor gradually fade away, and with them the sense of community that gives us all a meaningful place in the world" (xi). For a broader context in regard to these conclusions, see Richard Sennett and Jonathan Cobb, *The Hidden Injuries of Class* (New York: Knopf, 1972), 267–68; Bluestone and Harrison, *The Deindustrialization of America*, 11–12; John Russo and Sherry Lee Linkon, "The Social Costs of Deindustrialization," in *Manufacturing a Better Future for America*, ed. Richard McCormack (Washington, D.C.: Alliance for American Manufacturing, 2009), 187–98.

6. In their introduction to *Beyond the Ruins*, Cowie and Heathcott observe that northern cities have captured "the lion's share of scholarly attention" and more attention needs to be focused on the process of deindustrialization in the South (12). The bulk of the essays in *Beyond the Ruins* still concentrate on the North and fail to cover the South, with two notable exceptions: Steve May and Laura Morrison, "Making Sense of Restructuring: Narratives of Accommodation among Downsized Workers," and Joy L. Hart and Tracy K'Meyer, "Worker Memory and Narrative: Personal Stories of Deindustrialization in Louisville,

Kentucky," 259–83 and 284–304, respectively. For coverage of southern workers, see also Bill Bamberger and Cathy N. Davidson, *Closing: The Life and Death of an American Factory* (New York: Norton, 1998). None of these studies covers the textile industry, although economists and sociologists have written some work on the industry's decline. See, for example, Lauren A. Murray, "Unraveling Employment Trends in Textiles and Apparel," *Monthly Labor Review*, August 1995, 62–72; John Gaventa and Barbara Ellen Smith, "The Deindustrialization of the Textile South: A Case Study," and Rhonda Zingraff, "Facing Extinction?" both in *Hanging by a Thread: Social Change in Southern Textiles*, ed. Jeffrey Leiter, Michael D. Schulman, and Rhonda Zingraff (Ithaca: ILR Press, 1991), 181–96 and 199–216; Cynthia D. Anderson, Michael D. Schulman, and Phillip J. Wood, "Globalization and Uncertainty: The Restructuring of Southern Textiles," *Social Problems* 48, no. 4 (2001): 478–98; Grace I. Kunz and Myrna B. Garner, *Going Global: The Textile and Apparel Industry* (New York: Fairchild, 2007), 211–18. This work is largely quantitative, and the impact of deindustrialization upon workers and community members is not explored in detail. For case studies that give limited coverage to individual mill closings, see Beth English, *A Common Thread: Labor, Politics, and Capital Mobility in the Textile Industry* (Athens: University of Georgia Press, 2006), esp. 173–76; Douglas Flamming, *Creating the Modern South: Millhands and Managers in Dalton, Georgia, 1884–1984* (Chapel Hill: University of North Carolina Press, 1992), 307–27. The mill closures that English and Flamming explore occurred in 1959 and 1969, well before the industry's broader collapse.

7. Mark Mittelhauser, "Employment Trends in Textiles and Apparel, 1973–2005," *Monthly Labor Review*, August 1997, 24–25. Highlighting the links between these industries, the closure of apparel plants also hurt textile makers who could no longer supply these firms with the yarn and fabric they needed to make clothing. As the main textile union noted in 1978, "If imports of apparel increase, this will adversely affect textiles as well." Amalgamated Clothing and Textile Workers Union (ACTWU) General Executive Board Minutes, June 12, 1978, p. 5, untitled minutes folder, box 854, ACTWU Papers, held at the Kheel Center for Labor-Management Documentation and Archives, School of Industrial and Labor Relations, Cornell University, Ithaca, New York (hereafter ACTWU papers).

8. Mittelhauser, "Employment Trends," 24; BLS employment data at http://www.bls.gov/iag/tgs/iag_index_alpha.htm. Under the BLS's North American Industry Classification System (NAICS), data for the textile and apparel sector are divided into three codes: Apparel (NAICS 315), Textile Mills (NAICS 313), and Textile Product Mills (NAICS 314). See www.bls.gov/bls/naics.htm for more information about these classifications. The BLS is part of the Department of Labor, and its site provides a wealth of official employment data for all sectors of the American economy.

9. Murray, "Unraveling Employment Trends," 62; U.S. Congress, Office of Technology Assessment, *The U.S. Textile and Apparel Industry: A Revolution in Progress*—Special Report, OTA-TET-332 (Washington, D.C.: Government Printing Office, 1987), 3; "The Berry Amendment: Requiring Defense Procurement to Come from Domestic Sources," Congressional Research Service Paper, April 21, 2005, available at www.fas.org/sgp/crs/natsec/RL31236.pdf.

10. William E. Schmidt, "Future of 2 Southern Industries Raises Concern," *New York Times*, December 9, 1984; "Top Ten States—Total Textile and Apparel Employment (1994)," in "Textile Industry Employment, By State" folder, box 2, Research Department Files,

papers of the Union of Needletrades, Industrial, and Textile Employees (UNITE), held at the Kheel Center for Labor-Management Documentation and Archives, School of Industrial and Labor Relations, Cornell University [hereafter UNITE Papers].

11. Sandra Salmans, "The Textile Industry Shakes Itself Up," *New York Times*, May 10, 1981; Jefferson Cowie, *Capital Moves: RCA's Seventy-Year Quest for Cheap Labor* (Ithaca: Cornell University Press, 1999), 5. Cowie's study of the electronics industry, which employed large numbers of women, has helped to redress this imbalance.

12. Influential works in this vein include Hall et al., *Like a Family*; David L. Carlton, *Mill and Town in South Carolina, 1880-1920* (Baton Rouge: Louisiana State University Press, 1982); James A. Hodges, *New Deal Labor Policy and the Southern Cotton Textile Industry, 1933-1941* (Knoxville: University of Tennessee Press, 1986); I. A. Newby, *Plain Folk in the New South: Social Change and Cultural Persistence, 1880-1915* (Baton Rouge: Louisiana State University Press, 1989); Michelle Brattain, *The Politics of Whiteness: Race, Workers, and Culture in the Modern South* (Princeton: Princeton University Press, 2001).

13. For a helpful summary of the conclusions reached by the *Like a Family* collective, see Jacquelyn Dowd Hall, Robert Korstad, and James Leloudis, "Cotton Mill People: Work, Community, and Protest in the Textile South, 1880-1940," *American Historical Review* 91, no. 2 (1986): 245-86. The closing quotation is from Jim Wrinn, "Mill's Ex-Workers Weave New Life," *Charlotte Observer*, November 21, 1999, 41.

14. For an excellent exploration of why so much has been written about deindustrialization in Youngstown, see John Russo and Sherry Lee Linkon, "Collateral Damage: Deindustrialization and the Uses of Youngstown," in Cowie and Heathcott, *Beyond the Ruins*, 201-18, quote on 203.

15. Kirkpatrick Sale, *Power Shift: The Rise of the Southern Rim and Its Challenge to the Eastern Establishment* (New York: Random House, 1975); B. Drummond Ayers Jr., "Developing South Hopes to Avoid North's Mistakes," *New York Times*, February 12, 1976, 1; Numan V. Bartley, *The New South, 1945-1980: The Story of the South's Modernization* (Baton Rouge: Louisiana State University Press, 1995), 431-32, 470; James C. Cobb, *The Selling of the South: The Southern Crusade for Industrial Development, 1936-1980* (Baton Rouge: Louisiana State University Press, 1982), 187. The *Times*'s complete series of articles on the Sun Belt ran from February 8-13, 1976.

16. Robert Reinhold, "Sunbelt Region Leads Nation in Growth of Population," *New York Times*, February 8, 1976, 1; James P. Sterba, "Houston, as Energy Capital, Sets Pace in Sunbelt Boom," *New York Times*, February 9, 1976, 1; Bruce J. Schulman, *From Cotton Belt to Sunbelt: Federal Policy, Economic Development, and the Transformation of the South, 1938-1980* (New York: Oxford University Press, 1991), 175.

17. Cobb, *The Selling of the South*, 196. Cobb uses the term "Manufacturing Belt" repeatedly in his study in order to provide a contrast with the growing "Sun Belt."

18. Mittelhauser, "Employment Trends," 24.

19. Zingraff, "Facing Extinction?" 208; Lori G. Kletzer, *Job Loss from Imports: Measuring the Costs* (Washington, D.C.: Institute for International Economics, 2001), 16-19, quote on 17. For a fine study of how the move toward an open trading system has hurt the American apparel industry, see Ellen Israel Rosen, *Making Sweatshops: The Globalization of the U.S. Apparel Industry* (Berkeley: University of California Press, 2002).

20. "American Cotton Textile Industry and Foreign Trade Policy," November 8, 1957,

pp. 1, 27, in "ILGWU, TWUA and Other Union Statements on Imports, 1950" folder, box 532, ACTWU Papers.

21. "Conditions in the Women's Garment Industry," September 6, 1966, in "GEB 1966" folder, and "Import Curbs Essential to Save Garment Jobs," October 29, 1970, in "GEB October 1970" folder, both in box 1, Wilbur Daniels files, papers of the International Ladies' Garment Workers' Union, held at the Kheel Center for Labor-Management Documentation and Archives, School of Industrial and Labor Relations, Cornell University [hereafter ILGWU Papers].

22. "Imports of Tailored Clothing," in "Imports of Tailored Clothing" folder, box 456, ACTWU Papers; "Textile Plant Liquidations: Non-South and South, 1970–1979," in "Textile Plant Liquidations: Non-South and South" folder, box 2, Research Department files, UNITE Papers. These latter figures do not include the apparel sector.

23. Jack Anderson, "A Last-Minute Rescue for U.S.-Japanese Trade," *Washington Post*, January 15, 1978, B7; Jimmy Carter, "Memorandum of Disapproval," November 11, 1978, box 8, Ninety-fifth Congress files, Ernest F. Hollings Papers, held at South Carolina Political Collections, University of South Carolina, Columbia. For a useful summary of Hollings's efforts and the Carter veto, see Ernest F. "Fritz" Hollings (with Kirk Victor), *Making Government Work* (Columbia: University of South Carolina Press, 2008), 194–97.

24. Caroline Atkinson, "The Regions of America in the Grip of Recession," *Washington Post*, January 9, 1983, G19; "Table 1: Hourly Compensation (Wages and Fringes), Production Workers, Apparel Industry, U.S. and Major Apparel Exporters, 1984–1985," in "Wages, Textile and Apparel Industry: Compares U.S., Foreign Countries" folder, box 793, ACTWU Papers; Statement of Walter Y. Elisha to the Congressional Subcommittee on Commerce, Consumer and Monetary Affairs of the House Committee on Government Operations, November 28, 1984, box 10, 99th Congress files, Hollings Papers.

25. "ACTWU Apparel and Textile Plant Closings, 1980–September 1986," ACTWU Research Department report, December 1986, in "Plant Closings 1980–1986" folder, box 1019, ACTWU Papers.

26. ILGWU General Executive Board Minutes, March 17–20, 1987, in "ILGWU GEB Minutes 1986–89" folder, box 2, Carl Proper files, ILGWU Papers; ACTWU General Executive Board Minutes of January 13, 1986, in "GEB Minutes, January, March, July, October 1986" folder, box 1006, ACTWU Papers (Finley quote).

27. "Veto of H.R. 1562," December 17, 1985, in "Textile and Apparel Trade Enforcement Act 1985" folder, box 7, President's Office Files, ILGWU Papers.

28. Ed Jenkins interview with author, June 25, 2010, in Jasper, Georgia; ATMI Board of Directors Meeting Minutes, October 25–27, 1987, item 12, box 20, series 1998/18, Harmony Grove Mills Papers, 1898–1994, Richard B. Russell Library for Political Research and Studies, University of Georgia.

29. "Undaunted by Override Defeat, Union Vows Continued Fight," *Labor Unity*, November 1988, 2; "Will Textile Industry Loom Large in '90s?" *Virginian-Pilot*, April 29, 1990, E1 (GiaQuinta quote); G. Donald Jud and Nancy L. Cassill, "Local Textile Companies Can Survive with Long-Term Vision," *Greensboro News and Record*, February 21, 1999, F1.

30. Nelson Lichtenstein, *The Retail Revolution: How Wal-Mart Created a Brave New World of Business* (New York: Metropolitan Books, 2009), esp. 149–78; Salmans, "Textile Industry Shakes Itself Up" (quote); U.S. Congress, Office of Technology Assessment, *The*

U.S. Textile and Apparel Industry, iii, 3; Chris Burritt, "Textile Industry Trying to Stitch Up a Ragged Image," *Atlanta Journal-Constitution*, July 21, 1986, C1; Joel B. Obermayer, "Wake Forest Plant Closing Will Idle 730," *Raleigh News and Observer*, June 6, 1996, A1. For an excellent analysis of *Norma Rae* and its broader impact, see James A. Hodges, "The Real Norma Rae," in Zieger, *Southern Labor in Transition*, 251–72.

31. Burritt, "Textile Industry Trying to Stitch Up a Ragged Image"; "Twice Right on Trade," *New York Times*, October 3, 1988. For other examples of hostile press coverage, see "When Labor Owns the Mill," *New York Times*, January 16, 1984; "Why Rig the Rules against Imports?" *New York Times*, September 28, 1987; "Who'll Pay to Fatten Textile Profits?" *New York Times*, September 8, 1988; "For Freer Trade—and Better Jobs," *New York Times*, November 29, 1994; "Textile Bill Could Spur Trade Problems," *The State*, September 19, 1988, 12A.

32. Robert H. Zieger, *American Workers, American Unions*, 2nd ed. (Baltimore: Johns Hopkins University Press, 1994), 203; "Why NAFTA Should Be Rejected," untitled folder, box 798, ACTWU Papers.

33. Ariel Hart, "North Carolina: A Case against Free Trade," *New York Times*, October 18, 2003; "America's Textile Industry Is In Deep Crisis," *Charleston (W.V.) Daily Mail*, January 5, 2002, 5C (Martinsville quotes). For another example of local officials and workers blaming NAFTA for textile and apparel plant closings, see David Sinclair, "Whisper Knits Blames Closing on Free Trade," *Fayetteville (N.C.) Observer*, September 29, 1998.

34. Jeff Faux, "Viewpoints: NAFTA at 10," Economic Policy Institute document, http://www.epi.org/content.cfm/webfeatures_viewpoints_nafta_legacy_at10; "NAFTA: A Decade of Growth," 24, Business Roundtable Publication, http://www.businessroundtable.org/publications.

35. Dave Baity, "Cause of Lost Jobs Is Bigger Than NAFTA," *Charlotte Observer*, December 2, 2001, 1L; Nash quoted in Jim Nesbitt, "Textile Trouble: Imports Will Cut U.S. Jobs, Close Plants, Experts Say," *Augusta Chronicle*, August 10, 2003, D1.

36. P. T. Bangsberg, "China Urged to Boost Investment to Stay in Global Textile Race," *Journal of Commerce*, January 12, 1988, 4A; "China-Made Garments Said to Account for One-Fifth of Global Market," Xinhua News Agency Press Release, April 30, 2001, in "Trade: China WTO—107th Congress" folder, box 16, Legislative Department files, UNITE Papers; Stella M. Hopkins, "Tough Times Ahead for Home Textiles," *Charlotte Observer*, December 12, 2004, 1D; "Chinese Premier Praises 1999 Textile Industry Profits," *BBC Monitoring International Reports*, January 25, 2000. This last item is based on a report from the Xinhua News Agency.

37. John J. Sweeney to Senator, March 14, 2000, and "The U.S.-China WTO Agreement Will Help Promote Reform, Accountability, and Openness in China," White House Press Release, March 8, 2000, both in folder 2, box 11, President's Files, UNITE Papers.

38. "Burlington Forced to Wear Bankruptcy Label," *New York Daily News*, November 16, 2001, 93 (Henderson quote); Amy Martinez, "Pillowtex Goes Bust, Cuts 5500 Jobs," *Raleigh News and Observer*, July 31, 2003, A1; "Cone Mills' Closings Continue a Textiles Trend," *Winston-Salem Journal*, October 10, 2003, D1; Katherine Yung, "Trade Deal Hurts U.S. Textiles," *Dallas Morning News* column, reprinted in *The State*, October 19, 2003, F1.

39. Marilyn Geewax, "Textile Makers Press Bush," *Atlanta Journal-Constitution*,

November 16, 2003, H1; "Textile Quotas Will Ease Industry Decline," *Greensboro News and Record*, November 20, 2003, A14; Cauthen quoted in Julia Oliver, "Too Little, Too Late?" *Fayetteville (N.C.) Observer*, December 10, 2003. Under the terms of China's admission to the WTO, U.S. manufacturers could file "safeguard petitions" with the U.S. government seeking to limit Chinese imports if they could prove that these imports were causing trade "disruption." For further details of this mechanism, see Woody White, "Textiles Fight Back against Imports," *Greenville (S.C.) News*, July 12, 2005, 9A.

40. Donald W. Patterson, "Losses Mount for N.C. Workers," *Greensboro News and Record*, January 16, 2004, A1; Woody White, "Battling Back," *Greenville (S.C.) News*, April 10, 2005, 1, 6, 7.

41. Jeffrey Sparshott, "An Industry Unraveling: U.S. Textiles Threatened as Quotas Expire," *Washington Times*, December 26, 2004, A1.

42. Tony Mecia, "Plant Depicted in 'Norma Rae' to Close," *Charlotte Observer*, April 26, 2003; Jay Reeves, "Oldest Cloth Factory to Shutter Its Looms," *Akron Beacon Journal*, August 28, 2005, D1.

43. The MFA had been an exception to the 1947 General Agreement on Tariffs and Trade (GATT), an international trade framework primarily committed to reducing trade barriers. For a detailed explanation of GATT and the MFA phaseout, see Kunz and Garner, *Going Global*, 103–8.

44. Hopkins, "Tough Times Ahead for Home Textiles," 1D; Keir Jorgensen to Ann Hoffman, January 16, 1997, in "Trade: MFA Phaseout" folder, box 18, Legislative Department Files, UNITE Papers; Zhenyu quoted in "Chinese Trade Official Hails WTO's End to Textile Quotas from 2005," *World Sources Online*, September 29, 2004; Chastain quoted in Woody White, "Textile Industry Looking to Regain Quotas, But Will It Really Help?" *Greenville (S.C.)News*, April 10, 2005, 1. For an overview of the quota phaseout, see Rosen, *Making Sweatshops*, 202–3.

45. BLS data cited in "Plant Closings and Job Losses," available at http://www.ncto.org/ustextiles/joblosses.asp; "2005—The Quota Phaseout and NCTO Response," available at http://www.ncto.org/tradejobs/index.asp; Donald W. Patterson, "Calls Renew for Textile Curbs," *Greensboro News and Record*, April 1, 2005, B8; "China Not to Blame for Textile Trade Disputes, Official Says," *BBC Monitoring International Reports*, March 22, 2005 (Liu quote); Import data from the Office of Textiles and Apparel, International Trade Administration, U.S. Commerce Department, at http://otexa.ita.doc.gov/msrcty/a5700.htm.

46. Sparshott, "An Industry Unraveling"; "The U.S. Textile Industry," NCTO document available at http://www.ncto.org/ustextiles/index.asp; 2009); Paul Nowell, "N.C. Summit Focuses on Job Creation," *The State*, August 7, 2003, B7 (Freeman quote).

47. Diane Fuhrer, "Loss and Gain: Columbus after Textile Plunge," *Wilmington (N.C.) Star-News*, September 6, 1999, 1A; Rob Christensen, "Bush Upbeat on Economy," *Raleigh News and Observer*, November 8, 2003, A1. For more information on the TAA program, as well as other federal programs to help displaced textile and apparel workers, see U.S. Department of Labor, *The Past, Present and Future of Employment in the Textile and Apparel Industries: An Overview* (Washington, D.C.: Government Printing Office, 2004), 11–18, 29–32.

48. Al Greenwood, "Jobless Seek Employment," *Fayetteville (N.C.) Observer*, August 19, 2001. Located west of Charlotte, Cleveland County, North Carolina, also had double-digit

unemployment at this time; unemployment stood at 12.2 percent in July 2001, chiefly because of mill closings. See Ken Moritsugu, "Jobs Vanishing in the Textile Industry," *Philadelphia Inquirer*, September 8, 2001, C1.

49. "Textile Industry Topic of Summit," *The State*, March 21, 2002, B6. Although he had planned to attend this summit, Virginia governor Mark Warner ended up staying at home in order to monitor severe flooding in the southwestern part of his state; Tony Mecia, "Governors to Be Voice on Textiles," *Charlotte Observer*, March 22, 2002, 1D. For more on economic conditions along I-85, see Peter T. Kilborn, "Jobs Are Scarce in the Newest Economy," *New York Times*, October 9, 2001.

50. Myra Beatty, Douglas Longman, and Van Tran, "Community Response to the Pillowtex Textile Kannapolis Closing: The 'Rapid Response' Team as a Facilitative Device," April 2004, p. 5, University of North Carolina study available at www.unc.edu/depts/econ/PlantClosure/beatty_longman__tran.pdf; Barbara Hagenbaugh, "Lives Unraveled," *USA Today*, July 30, 2004. For insights into the difficulties that older workers face after job loss, see Philip L. Rones, "The Labor Market Problems of Older Workers," *Monthly Labor Review*, May 1983, 3–12. After a thorough examination of displacement data from workers over fifty-five, a group well represented among the southern textile workforce, Rones concludes that "when they become unemployed, they are less likely to find a job, and more likely to leave the labor force in discouragement" (3).

51. Robert W. Fairlie and Lori G. Kletzer, "Jobs Lost, Jobs Regained: An Analysis of Black/White Differences in Job Displacement in the 1980s," *Industrial Relations* 37, no. 4 (1998): 460–77 (statistics on 460); Louis Uchitelle, "Blacks Lose Better Jobs Faster As Middle-Class Work Drops," *New York Times*, July 12, 2003. For similar findings, see also Francis W. Horvath, "The Pulse of Economic Change: Displaced Workers of 1981–85," *Monthly Labor Review*, June 1987, 3–12; Diane E. Herz, "Worker Displacement in a Period of Rapid Job Expansion," *Monthly Labor Review*, May 1990, 21–33, esp. 23.

52. Jim Davenport, "As Mills Close, Lancaster Faces End of Era," *The State*, September 8, 2003; Jim Davenport, "Textile-Plant Closings Reshaping Life in South," *San Jose Mercury News*, September 22, 2003, 6E. For the broader significance of black entry into textiles, see Timothy J. Minchin, *Hiring the Black Worker: The Racial Integration of the Southern Textile Industry, 1960–1980* (Chapel Hill: University of North Carolina Press, 1999), esp. 1–6, 183–87 (statistic on 3). The information on Latino employment is drawn from U.S. Department of Labor, *Past, Present and Future of Employment*, 71–72.

53. Mittelhauser, "Employment Trends," 25.

54. "Bibb County Plant to Close, Lay Off 296," *Mobile Register*, July 4, 2001, B6; Marcia Stepanek, "For Laid-Off Textile Workers, Eden, N.C., Is No Paradise," *Detroit Free Press*, September 2, 1986, 17A (Gauldin quote).

55. "America's Textile Industry Is in Deep Crisis," *Charleston (W.V.) Daily Mail*, January 5, 2002, 5C; Jeffrey McMurray, "Southern Lawmakers Struggle to Get Help for Textile Industry," *Anderson (S.C.) Independent-Mail*, January 14, 2002.

56. Baity, "Cause of Lost Jobs Is Bigger Than NAFTA"; Gary Henderson, "Closings Take Jobs, Tax Dollars from County," *Spartanburg (S.C.) Herald-Journal*, January 28, 2002, A6 (quote).

57. Cory Engle et al., "Counties Brace for Closure," *Charlotte Observer*, July 11, 2003, 1Y; Schmidt, "Future of 2 Southern Industries Raises Concern"; Richard Lezin Jones, "N.C.

Plant Closing Indicative of Eroding Workforce in South," *Philadelphia Inquirer*, October 10, 1999, A20 (Raynor quote).

58. Eric Bruner, "Langdale Plant Set to Close This Year," *Columbus (Ga.) Ledger-Enquirer*, August 12, 1997, A1 (Games quote); Venita Jenkins, "Historic Ties Unravel," *Fayetteville (N.C.) Observer*, September 2, 2001 (Westbrook quote).

59. Tony Adams, "Apartments Planned for Abandoned Textile Mill," *Columbus (Ga.) Ledger-Enquirer*, March 27, 2001, C4. The information on the former Olympia Mills site is based on a visit to the location by the author in the summer of 2008.

60. Moritsugu, "Jobs Vanishing in the Textile Industry," C1. For an example of a former mill building being used for storage, see the Jackson Mills case as covered in McMurray, "Southern Lawmakers Struggle to Get Help."

61. Sharif Durhams, "Dropping Name That Made Kannapolis," *Charlotte Observer*, August 11, 2006; Paul Davis, "Starmount Plans to Redevelop Burlington Industries' HQ Site into Mixed-Use Area," *Greater Triad Business Journal*, March 8, 2004.

62. Denice Thibodeau, "Local Group Buys Dan River Sign," *Danville Register and Bee*, October 3, 2007; Denice Thibodeau, "Some Sad, Some Glad as Sign Fades Away," *Danville Register and Bee*, October 3, 2007 (Reynolds quote); "Textile Mill in Virginia Demolished," CBS News story, November 19, 2008, available at http://cbs5.com/watercooler/Danville.Virginia.implode.2.86828.html.

63. Anne Blythe, "Weaving Textiles into State's History," *Raleigh News and Observer*, July 26, 2005, B1. For an update on these ongoing plans to create a textile heritage corridor along I-85, see Donald W. Patterson, "Efforts to Save Pieces of Textile Past," *Greensboro News-Record*, May 18, 2009.

64. "Judy Hatley," profile available on the *Kannapolis Independent-Tribune's* "Pillowtex: Five Years Later" web site at http://independenttribune.net/index.php/pillowtex/article/judy-hatley; Ruth Crisco interview with author on June 22, 2010, in Concord, North Carolina.

65. Cobb, *The Selling of the South*, 64–95; Reginald Stuart, "Deep South's Economic Surge Found Slowing," *New York Times*, March 12, 1982; Reginald Stuart, "Boom in Sun Belt Bypasses Older Industrial Towns in South," *New York Times*, June 4, 1981 (Bill Markham quote); Thomas W. Lippman, "Twilight of the God of the Forge," *Washington Post*, July 25, 1982, A1 (closing quote). For classic accounts of deindustrialization in the northern steel industry, see Serrin, *Homestead*; Reutter, *Making Steel*; Hoerr, *And the Wolf Finally Came*; and Linkon and Russo, *Steeltown USA*. For one work that does give limited coverage to the decline of the steel industry in Alabama, see Judith Stein, *Running Steel, Running America: Race, Economic Policy, and the Decline of Liberalism* (Chapel Hill: University of North Carolina Press, 1998).

66. Susan Elizabeth Shank, "Changes in Regional Unemployment over the Last Decade," *Monthly Labor Review*, March 1985, 17; Philip L. Rones, "An Analysis of Regional Employment Growth, 1973–85," *Monthly Labor Review*, July 1986, 3 (quote), 6. "Power Shift" is a reference to Sale's *Power Shift*, a seminal work that propagated the idea of an increasingly ascendant "southern rim" (see note 15).

67. Peter Applebome, "Challenging Atlanta: The South Has Its Second Cities, and They Thrive," *New York Times*, April 23, 1989 (quote); William E. Schmidt, "Not All of the South Is in the Sunbelt," *New York Times*, January 19, 1986. The Southern Growth Policies Board study refers to cities with a population of 100,000 or more.

68. "Employment, Hours, and Earnings from the Current Employment Statistics Survey," October 13, 2004, U.S. Department of Labor, Bureau of Labor Statistics, http://data.bls.gov/PDQ/servlet/SurveyOutputServlet.

69. For an insight into "capital flight" in the electronics industry, see Cowie, *Capital Moves*, 1–11. Information on the decline of the furniture industry is drawn from Amy Martinez, "As Layoffs Mount, Import Relief Sought," *Raleigh News and Observer*, August 27, 2003, A1.

70. Barry Bluestone, "Deindustrialization and Unemployment in America," in *Deindustrialization and Plant Closure*, ed. Paul D. Staudohar and Holly E. Brown (Lexington, Mass.: D.C. Heath, 1987), 3–16; Daniel Nelson, *Farm and Factory: Workers in the Midwest, 1880–1990* (Bloomington: Indiana University Press, 1995), 191; "America's Textile Industry Is in Deep Crisis," *Charleston (W.V.) Daily Mail*, January 5, 2002, 5C (quote).

71. For similar conclusions in other southern industries, see Bamberger and Davidson, *Closing*; Timothy J. Minchin, "'Just Like a Death': The Closing of the International Paper Company Mill in Mobile, Alabama, and the Deindustrialization of the South, 2000–2005," *Alabama Review*, 59, no. 1 (2006): 44–77.

72. Stepanek, "For Laid-Off Textile Workers, Eden, N.C., Is No Paradise."

73. Ken Moritsugu, "A Frayed Economy," *St. Paul (Minn.) Pioneer Press*, September 1, 2001, C1. For a similar story, see Moritsugu, "Jobs Vanishing in the Textile Industry." For the more generous benefits available to displaced auto workers, see Sara Rimer, "Closing Willow Run," *New York Times*, October 29, 1992, D1. This article shows that laid-off workers from GM's Willow Run plant in Ypsilanti, Michigan, considered themselves "more fortunate than thousands of other American workers," because "with their union behind them," the company was obligated to offer workers' positions that become available at other plants. In addition, workers received nearly their full income, plus benefits, until the current union contract expired nearly a year later. For a similar article, see Doron P. Levin, "GM and Its Union Plan to Encourage Early Retirements," *New York Times*, December 15, 1992, A1.

74. Hall et al., *Like a Family*, 140, 180.

75. Wrinn, "Mill's Ex-Workers Weave New Life."

76. For the Pillowtex worker profiles, see http://independenttribune.net/index.php/pillowtex/profiles. As noted in the text, very few sources noted any racial differences in textile workers' reactions to losing their jobs, and articles accessed electronically had all images removed, making it very difficult to identify the race of those quoted in the text.

77. Rick Lyman, "Edwards Focuses His Efforts on 3 Promising Constituencies," *New York Times*, February 25, 2004 (quote); Tony Mecia, "Pillowtex Fall Puts Focus on China," *Charlotte Observer*, August 14, 2003, 1A.

10

A Different Kind of Union

SEIU Healthcare Florida from the Mid-1990s through 2009

BRUCE NISSEN

In the late twentieth century, the state of Florida did not provide a hospitable environment for unions, especially private-sector unions. The unionized percentage of the state's private sector declined from 7.1 percent in 1983 to 3.5 percent in 1995 and to 2.3 percent in 2008.[1] Private-sector workers attempting to form a union usually faced intense employer opposition and a dysfunctional labor law system that failed to protect the right to unionize. Yet, in the latter half of the 1990s through 2008, a healthcare union (SEIU Healthcare Florida, a local of the Service Employees International Union) grew from formative predecessor unions with fewer than fifteen hundred members to an organization with more than ten thousand members in 2010. This union faced the same strident employer opposition and ineffective legal protections as other private-sector unions in the state. But it was more successful than most other unions because of a number of unique factors: first, an unrelenting focus on organizing even against the toughest odds; second, a flexible tactical approach to how organizing is accomplished; third, a community focus involving the union in critical issues beyond the workplace; fourth, a heavy emphasis on rank-and-file involvement and leadership development; fifth, strong involvement in social movements related to the interests of its membership, such as the civil rights movement and the immigrant rights movement; sixth, strong emphasis on "public goods" such as quality of patient care; and seventh, grassroots-based political action focused on issues that simultaneously serve a broad public interest and the interests of health-care workers. This union's "social movement" orientation has proven successful even in a generally hostile environment.

Prehistory of SEIU Healthcare Florida

Prior to the 1970s, unions had little presence in the health-care sector in Florida, as was true in most sectors of the state's economy. Neither the state nor the

Figure 10.1. Workers from the Hillcrest nursing home in Hollywood, Florida, picket for a fair contract, October 29, 2009. Union successes in health-care facilities stemmed in part from the union's attention to the distinctive concerns of women and minority employees. (Photo by Kimberly Diehl, Communications Director, 1199 SEIU United Healthcare Workers East.)

industry provided much room for optimism regarding the prospects for union success. The state's public policies were generally hostile toward unions, and its workforce was quite transient, with newly arriving migrants (both from other U.S. states and from abroad) comprising a higher percentage of the overall workforce than in most other states. And, following national patterns, the health-care sector of the economy had very a low unionization rate.[2]

In the mid-1970s a New York–based nursing home union known as District 1115 established a very small presence within Florida nursing homes. The union had followed into the state a few New York nursing home employers who had Florida vacation homes and businesses; by 1997 District 1115 represented the employees of fifteen Florida nursing homes, ten in the Miami area and five in St. Petersburg.[3] But the vast majority of 1115's membership was in New York and New Jersey; only around a thousand of its fifteen thousand total members in 1999 were in Florida, the only state outside of New York and New Jersey in which it had membership.[4] The other potential claimant to health-care union representation, the Florida Nurses Association, was and is primarily a professional advocacy group that includes managerial nurses within its ranks. As of 2008 its small collective-bargaining (union) branch represented nurses primarily at a few Veterans Administration hospitals around the state.[5]

In 1996 a local of the garment workers union UNITE followed a number of laid-off garment workers out of its shrinking industry to their new employment as Certified Nursing Assistants (CNAs) in nursing homes. (UNITE is short for Union of Needletrades, Industrial and Textile Employees, newly created from a 1995 merger of the Amalgamated Clothing and Textile Workers Union and the International Ladies' Garment Workers' Union). In that year the union succeeded in unionizing four nursing homes in the Miami area with approximately 250 members.

In 1997 District 1115 (including the New York, New Jersey, and Florida branches) joined SEIU. Thus Florida in 1997 had two unions representing nursing home workers: SEIU Local 1115, with fifteen facilities and approximately 1,200 members, and the UNITE Local, with approximately 250 members. Twelve hundred of these union members lived in the Miami–Ft. Lauderdale area, while two hundred lived in the Tampa–St. Petersburg area. That year the two unions formed a joint organizing project titled "Unite for Dignity." The parent national unions, UNITE and SEIU, provided initial funding of $1 million per year, matched by a $1 million grant from the AFL-CIO.[6]

Unite for Dignity was not a labor organization for the purposes of collective bargaining or representation. Facilities were organized into one or the other of the two constituent unions in roughly equal proportions, reflecting the equal commitment of resources to the project. The staff structures were integrated, with UNITE's Monica Russo as the executive director and SEIU's Dale Ewart as the deputy director. Organizers were paid from three sources: UNITE, SEIU, and the independent funds of Unite for Dignity. Although they knew they were organized into one or the other of the parent unions, workers identified their overall organization as "Unite for Dignity." A council of elected representatives from all organized facilities was the basic governing body that made decisions on political program, organizing plans, and other matters.

In 2000, UNITE national union president Bruce Raynor decided to pull out of this arrangement so that he could organize in different jurisdictions. At that time, Unite for Dignity changed from an organizing project to a newly chartered Florida-based union local, SEIU 1199 Florida.[7] Between 2000 and 2004 the union steadily expanded geographically out of its main base in south Florida, spreading up the east coast to central Florida and into the Orlando area, complemented by expansion in the Tampa–St. Petersburg area on the west coast. In 2003 the union began to organize in acute-care hospitals, and in 2005 it changed its name to SEIU Florida Healthcare Union (SEIU FHU), which in 2008 was modified to SEIU Healthcare Florida. For reasons of simplicity and clarity, this union will be labeled simply "the union" or "SEIU Healthcare Florida" in the remainder of this chapter, even if a direct predecessor formation is being referred to.

Organizing Attempts, Employer Resistance, Legal Dysfunction, and Ultimate Union Success

From the late 1990s into the early 2000s, SEIU Healthcare Florida aggressively organized the workforces of Florida nursing homes. Managers at targeted nursing homes virtually always engaged in fierce "union busting" campaigns. The legal apparatus of the National Labor Relations Board (NLRB) failed to protect the workers' right to unionize, as lengthy delays and inadequate penalties for egregious employer behavior undermined the exercise of presumed legal protections. Despite these obstacles, the union succeeded in most instances and grew rapidly throughout this period.

The union originally employed young, energetic, and motivated organizers with backgrounds in student, community, and labor organizing. Later, virtually all organizers were rank-and-file nursing home workers recruited from the facilities themselves. The vast majority of organizing drives used the electoral procedure of the NLRB, even though the union leaders felt that this process was biased against employee free choice and encouraged anti-union coercion by the employer. They chose this route because the union lacked sufficient leverage over nursing home employers at the time to induce them to accept a fairer method of determining majority support, such as "majority sign-up" (also known as "card check"), which simply allows workers to unionize once a majority of them sign cards or petitions supporting the union.

Employer Reaction to Organizing Drives and Labor Law Inadequacy

Employer reactions to the organizing attempts were swift and often savage. In a typical situation, employees were threatened, intimidated, interrogated, and spied upon. Known union leaders and supporters within the workforce were harassed, discriminated against, disciplined, and often fired.[8] Over time the number of fired union "casualties" approached one hundred; employer repression was so extreme that this union attracted national attention. A 2000 report by Human Rights Watch concerning the violation of internationally recognized human rights via employer repression of labor organizing in the United States featured examples from this union to illustrate its claims.[9] *New York Times* reporter Steven Greenhouse's 2008 book *The Big Squeeze* also used this union's organizing attempt at a nursing home and the subsequent repression to highlight the anti-union attitudes of many employers.[10]

A 2003 report from the workers' rights organization American Rights at

Work (ARAW) further detailed the coercion and the extreme violations of the right of these workers to make a free choice for or against unionization.[11] That report found that employers engaged in a wide variety of legal and illegal tactics to thwart the will of their employees desiring to join together in a union. In addition, the law allowed lawyers representing employers to cause delays in everything from holding an election, to ratifying the results of the election if the union won, to actually beginning negotiations, to negotiating a first contract, so that the democratic will of the majority was thwarted almost indefinitely until almost all of the original participants in the vote were gone. Finally, it found that penalties for illegal employer behavior were so insubstantial that it was actually "profitable" for an employer to break the law in its attempts to defeat the union.

Typical examples contained in the ARAW report show that workers aiming to join together in the union of their choice had to be prepared for some of their most prominent leaders to be fired in the course of the organizing drive. As Marie Suprinat, a former Certified Nursing Assistant (CNA) at the Avante–Lake Worth nursing home who was fired for union organizing in 2001, stated, "If you are not brave, you cannot get a union. . . . Some of them are brave, some of them not."[12] Moreover, even if they braved a withering anti-union offensive and voted for the union in an NLRB-sponsored election, newly unionized employees likely faced a delay ranging from two to seven years or more before bargaining on a union contract commenced (in some cases, bargaining never would occur).[13]

In addition, workers who were illegally fired during or after an organizing drive in retaliation for their union activities were offered compensation for their loss so meager that it was usually meaningless. The case of Evanette Cyriac, a CNA at the Avante–Boca Raton nursing home, was typical: illegally fired in 1997 after being spotted at nearby Denny's restaurant speaking to an NLRB representative about illegal company behavior toward its workers, she was ordered reinstated almost two years later by an NLRB hearing officer. The company appealed, and almost two more years passed before the national NLRB upheld its hearing officer's recommendation and she was reinstated to her job. After almost four years after her illegal firing, the company was required to pay her less than $500 in back pay because she had been forced to get another job in the interim to survive, and all money she earned during that time was subtracted from the money owed her. Her reaction to this small amount of back pay: "That was nothing to me!"[14]

There were several reasons for the intense anti-union behaviors of the employers. First, virtually all private-sector employers in the state behaved similarly; used to a completely non-union workforce and state policies hostile to union rights, Florida employers generally acted aggressively to protect what they perceived as their own interests. Second, this particular industry operated on rather thin profit margins. Much of its revenue came from government sources that set reimbursement rates quite low. Bankruptcies and closure of facilities were not uncommon features. Third, as mentioned, the penalties for illegal behavior were so small that it actually paid to break the law through anti-union behavior. And finally, the vast majority of the unionizable workforce in nursing homes in south Florida was composed of traditionally vulnerable and relatively powerless demographic groups: heavily Haitian, supplemented by high representation of Hispanics and African Americans.

The cumulative impact of the strident anti-union employer behavior, incessant delays, and insignificant penalties that SEIU Healthcare Florida faced as it aggressively organized nursing homes in the 1997–2004 period is best illustrated by its experience at the King David nursing home in West Palm Beach. This facility, later renamed Greenwood Rehabilitation Center, had a predominantly Haitian workforce.[15] In July 1993 employees began meeting secretly to discuss forming a union. They contacted the union, formed an organizing committee, and slowly and deliberately prepared an organizing campaign. In January 1994 they openly began distributing union buttons and holding meetings to build an organizing campaign.

Reaction by managers at the facility was immediate. In late January, supervisors questioned employee Luders Esteril about his support for the union and forced from him an admission that he had signed a union petition. In late August, after repeated attempts to get him to change his mind, they fired him under the pretext that he had failed to call in when he was absent for work. The NLRB later found his firing to be illegal retaliation for his union support.

Outspoken union supporter (and undisputed leader of the union drive within the facility) Ernest Duval likewise faced retaliation. In late January, managers threatened him with disciplinary action for a manufactured incident and then exonerated him in a "good cop/bad cop" routine. In later months, when it became apparent that Duval would continue his union leadership activities, managers "set him up" for disciplinary action on several occasions and fired him shortly after the union won an election in early August. The NLRB subsequently found that the employer had illegally harassed and intimidated Duval and had falsely set up pretextual situations and a dismissal in retaliation for his union activities.

In early February 1994, management officials began a stealth campaign against union supporter Jean Aliza. Within weeks they fired him after a series of "phantom" disciplinary warnings written into his personnel file about which he was unaware, followed by a "set-up" incident wherein management claimed to find a sandwich in the drawer of one of his patients. The NLRB subsequently found the entire sequence of events to constitute illegal retaliation for Aliza's union support.

In early February the managers held a "captive audience" meeting during working hours where all employees on duty were forced to attend. Employees were told that they could vote for the union if they wanted to but that they could be fired at any time. The NLRB later determined this to be an illegal threat to intimidate workers into opposing the union.

In mid-February a supervisor threatened union supporter Marie LaRose with dismissal if she did not take off her union button. She refused to do so; shortly thereafter she was reduced to part-time status, and in late May she was fired. The NLRB later determined that this action constituted coercion and illegal dismissal.

At approximately the same time, management personnel questioned CNA Lude Duval about her husband Ernest's outspoken support for the union. (Both husband and wife were on the original organizing committee for the union drive.) In late April, Lude Duval was fired for lacking the proper credential to hold the CNA position. Meanwhile, an anti-union colleague who had testified against the union in NLRB hearings was allowed to temporarily hold a non-CNA position while she got her credentials in order. After Lude Duval had straightened out her credentials, she applied for reinstatement but was refused. The NLRB subsequently found that her discriminatory firing was due to her and her husband's support for the union.

In late May the employer issued a new rule forbidding Haitian workers from speaking Haitian Kreyol in the presence of patients. The new rule was subsequently used to harass and "set up" employees through falsely manufactured "incidents" even when no such event had occurred. Facility managers claimed to have conducted an "in-service" training for all personnel on the new rule, although the employee sign-in sheet for the training presented to the NLRB examining officer contained the signature of an employee who had been fired months before the alleged training was held, thus calling the company's documentation into question.

In July, pro-union CNA Quettelie Jean-Baptiste was threatened with dismissal if she supported the union and also was "set up" for an incident of not responding to a patient's "call light" even though the patient was not one for whom she was responsible. Continuing harassment of Jean-Baptiste eventuated in her having an "anxiety attack" in mid-August when she collapsed on the floor hyperventilating. After she was taken to the hospital and released, the director of nursing refused to let her return to work the next day until she had a "certification of fitness for work" from a doctor. It took her a week to get that certificate, thus costing her a week's pay. The NLRB later ruled that the company had in effect illegally suspended her for a week owing to her union support, and it ordered back pay for her.

In late July, just before a pending vote in an NLRB-sponsored election, pro-union CNA Pierre Exile was called into the supervisor's office and was grilled by three management persons as to his voting intentions. They intimidated him into promising to vote no even though he subsequently testified to an NLRB examiner that he actually ended up voting yes. After the union won the August 5 election, Exile, who was an assistant pastor at a church, was forced to work on Sundays, thus causing him to eventually leave his job in October. Again, the NLRB found the company's behavior to be illegal retaliation for union support.

On August 5 the NLRB election (which had been delayed months through employer objections about what was the proper "bargaining unit" for the union to represent) was held. Of the 78 valid ballots cast, the union won 48 votes; 29 voted for "no union," and 1 voted for an alternate "union" that the company had invited into the facility (and illegally favored, according to later NLRB ruling) in an effort to stop the original union-organizing drive. Company attorneys filed an appeal to overturn the election results, claiming union misconduct had tainted the results. The charges against the union were unsupported and often patently false, but owing to legal maneuvering and delays it was almost a year (August 3, 1995) before an NLRB officer ruled that the election was valid and that all the objections were without merit. Even then, legal maneuvering continued about other charges and counter-charges, further delaying any resolution of the employer's duty to bargain a first contract.

The anti-union intimidation campaign intensified after the union election victory. Union supporter and member of the union-organizing committee Carline Dorisca received punitive shift-change assignments, was cut back to part-time status, was denied a promised raise, and ultimately was fired in December 1994 in a "set-up" incident of alleged patient neglect. The NLRB subsequently found this series of events and the firing to be illegal retaliation for union support.

Visible union supporter and original organizing committee member Michelle Williams was next. Following earlier incidents of attempted intimidation, in November 1994 Williams was fired for excessive absenteeism. Although she had a somewhat problematic attendance record, it was better than that of an anti-union CNA who was not disciplined, and the NLRB later ruled that Williams's firing was illegal retaliation for union activities.

Marie Pierre Louis, another known union supporter, was the next victim of the firing campaign. In November she was fired, ostensibly for refusing to take a patient to the bathroom. Evidence for the alleged refusal was extremely flimsy. The lack of credible evidence, combined with previous employer conduct (including private warnings from lower-level supervisors that they were told that she had to be fired), led the NLRB to rule her dismissal to be illegal retaliation for union support.

By mid-November 1994 management had fired thirteen of the facility's CNAs, well over 15 percent of all the CNAs working there. All the union's strongest supporters were now gone. Working conditions for most employees had worsened; known union supporters were spied upon and constantly supervised. By the end of the year the intimidation had succeeded in ending any real union presence at the workplace, and further developments would depend on the ability of the slowly moving machinery of the NLRB to curb employer misbehavior and return union leaders to their jobs.

But speedy justice was not to be. In late February 1996, more than a year and a half after the union election, the NLRB hearing officer had waded through the 2,900 pages of testimony of the charges and counter-charges filed in the case. He ruled that the company had committed massive violations of labor law and ordered it to post a notice that it would not do so again, to reinstate the fired workers, and to commence bargaining with the union. In response, company attorneys filed legal objections to all of his findings, causing further delay.

Finally, on August 6, 1999, five years and one day after the union election, the NLRB issued its final ruling, upholding virtually all of its hearing officer's findings and ordering the company to comply. By this time, most of those employed at the time of the union election were gone from the facility, all but one of those fired did not want to return, and the union had been long crushed as a visible presence at the worksite. The one returnee, Ernest Duval, was soon hounded out of the facility. Union organizers never succeeded in helping employees overcome their fears enough to restart an organizing drive, despite repeated attempts to do so.[16]

Union Success Despite Employer and Legal Obstacles

While union-organizing drives were occasionally thwarted, as happened at the King David facility, in most cases organizing campaigns during this period succeeded despite anti-union employer behavior and lengthy delays. Between 1997 and 2004, union organizers and determined nursing home workers feverishly conducted organizing campaigns, faced strong employer resistance, frequently won union elections despite employer behavior, and then faced months or years of further resistance before being able to negotiate a first collective-bargaining agreement.[17]

After winning a union election and facing an employer unwilling to negotiate a meaningful first contract, union leaders realized that in most cases additional sources of power would be needed to force an employer to come to the bargaining table in good faith. Typically, they would ask local politicians friendly to the union to intervene to persuade a nursing home owner to accommodate the union rather than continue to fight it. Union leaders also asked community opinion makers, religious leaders, workers rights organizations, and racial/ethnic and immigrant group organizations to pressure employers to stop fighting the union. Workers also held spirited rallies during shift changes at facilities where they were struggling for a first contract and frequently drew press coverage for its public pressure activities during those years.

A highly publicized example illustrates the type of resistance workers faced when they attempted to establish a functioning union after an electoral victory.[18] In late February 2002 the employees of the Mt. Sinai–St. Francis (MSSF) Nursing and Rehabilitation Center in North Miami voted 49 to 37 in favor of unionization in an NLRB-supervised election. The facility's attorneys filed objections with the NLRB, claiming that pro-union workers and organizers had improperly used "voodoo" to intimidate the mostly Haitian-born workforce into voting in favor of the union. The complaint alleged that pennies left in the street around the facility and cups half full of water in the hallways indicated religious intimidation. Additional charges included the claim that a Haitian union organizer had worn intimidating perfume and had danced in delight while rubbing a set of beads after the union victory was announced (the beads turned out to be the rosary that this devoutly Catholic woman possessed).

On March 20 a group of community, political, and religious leaders held a press conference in front of the MSSF facility and asked management to drop what it termed frivolous and racist charges. At around this time managers began firing pro-union workers, one of whom ultimately ended up out of work for more than a year. NLRB hearings on March 25 and 26 provoked national news coverage, most of it depicting the "voodoo" charges as ridiculous. The *New York Times, Miami Herald, Seattle Times, Atlanta Journal-Constitution, USA Today*, and the National Public Radio program *All Things Considered* covered the story about "voodoo" union intimidation. Throughout the spring of 2002, union leaders and activists helped to orchestrate a series of candlelight vigils, rallies, and prayer sessions to keep the issue in the public eye. The public themes of all these activities were economic justice and opposition to racist stereotyping of Haitian immigrants.

On May 17 the NLRB hearing officer ruled that all the "voodoo" charges had no merit and recommended union certification. MSSF appealed to the national NLRB office, further delaying certification of the union. A June "emergency town hall meeting" and march called by Haitian pastors and community leaders drew a dozen local elected officials, all of whom pledged support for the workers' struggle. In July the South Florida Jobs with Justice chapter, of which the local was a founding member, held a Workers' Rights Board meeting in which prominent civic, religious, and political leaders listened to testimony from MSSF workers about their treatment. Actor Danny Glover served as an honorary member of the session and addressed a public meeting of more than four hundred people in support of the workers. Following the public testimony, those in attendance held a protest rally outside the MSSF facility.

These activities attracted an enormous amount of media attention, most of it conveying a highly unfavorable image of MSSF. The escalating set of tactics was probably the main factor that convinced MSSF officials that coming to terms with the union was critical to their public reputation and to their prospects for success. By the end of the year company officials agreed to negotiate a contract, and by February 2003, approximately one year after the workers voted to unionize, the members ratified their first union contract at MSSF.

Throughout the 1997–2003 period, amid almost monthly public demonstrations, considerable publicity, sustained political and community and religious intervention to curb management behavior, and steadfast worker determination, the union continued to grow steadily. Many of the struggles to actually establish a union and a first contract took longer than at MSSF; in most cases the union had to fight a resistant management. While other struggles lacked the celebrity intervention and laughable management missteps such as voodoo accusations, the union usually succeeded after protracted battles.[19]

Nursing Home Organizing Thwarted in 2004

However, in 2004 the union-organizing drive in nursing homes hit a plateau. The reason was quite unexpected. In early 2004, union organizers found that managers at nursing homes being targeted for organizing had already encouraged unionization by a different union, thus making every potential target either a facility already with a union or one with an organizing campaign already under way. This process spread so rapidly that by the end of 2004 SEIU was forced to abandon further mass organizing in the industry.

While there are numerous owners of nursing homes in Florida, a large percentage of them are owned or operated by "chains" with facilities in multiple locations. The two largest as of 2004 were the Delta and Sea Crest chains. Between 1996 and 2004 the union had organized twelve out of about forty-eight Sea Crest nursing homes in the state and six out of the approximately thirty-three in-state Delta facilities. Because these chains were "industry leaders" that set the standards for much of the rest of the industry in the state, the union had particularly targeted their operations for organization; if they could be organized at or close to 100 percent, a number of the smaller chains or individually owned nursing homes would be easier to organize.

In 2004 the person in charge of human resources for the Delta chain, trying to avoid the SEIU's aggressive organizing and strong worksite member representation, decided that while he could not avoid unionization altogether, he could ensure that many of his facilities would deal with a less assertive organization. The United Food and Commercial Workers (UFCW) Union Local 1625 already represented workers at some Delta facilities. Managers perceived this union as being less assertive. Therefore Delta management at the chain's non-union facilities notified UFCW 1625 officials that they would welcome the union, would recognize it on the basis of simple "majority sign-up" rather than holding a contentious election, and would not oppose union organizers entering the facilities to sign up members. Furthermore, management promised to employees that they would not harass any employees attempting to unionize through UFCW 1625.[20]

The Sea Crest chain followed suit. Smaller chains such as Senior Health soon did the same.[21] Thus, beginning in 2004 the nursing home division of UFCW 1625 exploded in size. By 2009, from just a few nursing home contracts, its representation had rapidly grown to approximately seventy sites. Thanks to aggressive organizing by SEIU and management fear of that union, the UFCW soon had a sizable presence in the state's nursing home sector, with management's blessing. SEIU organizers found that every time they approached a nursing home workforce about organizing a union, they would find the UFCW either already there or instantly invited in by management.[22] The presence of the UFCW at all of its organizing targets killed the momentum of SEIU's drive to become a dominant force in setting compensation and working standards in the nursing home sector; its "one at a time" organizing strategy was failing, and future growth seemed unlikely.

Management's cooperation with the UFCW to avoid the SEIU disappointed SEIU activists. SEIU members felt devastated; the dream of creating one unified voice for workers within the Florida nursing home industry that would be able to raise compensation standards and win affordable health-care and pension benefits was destroyed. But, realizing that SEIU Healthcare Florida would never reverse the "unionization through cooperation" that the UFCW was achieving, the SEIU leaders chose not to fight with its union competitor in the nursing home sector. Instead, almost immediately SEIU leaders began to work cooperatively with the other union, sharing contracts and information about employers and their behavior.

New Organizing Targets and Successes

Stymied on one organizing front, SEIU union leaders perceived other organizing opportunities if the union would reorganize to recruit all health-care workers, not simply those working in nursing homes. In 2005 the union renamed itself SEIU Florida Healthcare Union (in 2008 changed to SEIU Healthcare Florida). Under its new name the union put renewed energy into organizing in acute-care hospitals, a sector it had begun to organize in 2003.

At some hospitals it faced the same fierce resistance it had encountered in nursing homes. Thus, one hospital in the Miami area nearly destroyed itself in a lengthy battle against the will of its own workers to unionize. Bringing intense public exposure to bear on the hospital's anti-union activities, the SEIU was able to secure the replacement of the hospital's CEO with a more union-neutral executive, and the facility was successfully unionized.

However, the union also found it was able to leverage the strength of the national union over large hospital chain providers to facilitate organizing. HCA and Tenet are the two largest chain operators of hospitals throughout the United States. By 2005 the SEIU nationally had succeeded in unionizing a number of hospital facilities operated by each. Using its bargaining relationship with various hospitals owned by these chains as leverage, the national union negotiated "organizing agreements" that set up ground rules for behavior on both sides in future organizing drives. These agreements typically allowed for quick elections in various parts of the country. They allowed the union very little time to organize the workers, because the agreement expired in a matter of a few months, but they also promised that the employer would not engage in strident union-busting behavior within that short window of opportunity.

SEIU Florida Healthcare Union seized on this opportunity when HCA signed such an agreement for Florida.[23] HCA officials likely thought that the union would be unable to organize many workers within the agreement's six-month time period and the hundred-day "window of opportunity" within which an election must be held once the union began organizing at any particular hospital. But, with its own organizing capacity supplemented by national organizing staff brought in from around the country, the union successfully organized and won union elections in six (out of seven) HCA hospitals in the state. All six union victories were won in elections held within a ten-day period in October 2006. Thus, in short order, the union won representation rights for forty-five hundred hospital workers. The success of these drives can be attributed to the massive number of recruiters and organizers brought into the state by the well-resourced national union and to the absence of fear on the part of the employees because the ground rules for employer behavior prohibited the intimidating employer tactics frequently used during organizing drives.

The union was also able to win representation rights at three Tenet hospitals under similar circumstances. To be sure, the "organizing agreements" under which these victories were attained did not guarantee complete employer neutrality, but the most strident and egregious forms of union resistance were curbed, meaning that widespread firings and other forms of egregious harassment were absent.

Thus in the 2005–2008 period, the union made rapid progress in organizing large hospital units. It now represented Registered Nurses (RNs), Licensed Practical Nurses (LPNs), numerous categories of technicians, patient-care workers, secretaries, pharmacists, and the like, as well as the CNAs, of which there were many in its nursing home bargaining units. By 2009 it represented over more than fifteen thousand workers and had more than ten thousand of these signed up for the union in this "right-to-work" state, where union membership is optional for those covered by union contracts.

SEIU Healthcare Florida Activism beyond Its Organizing Work

The union's militant organizing is not its only unique attribute: SEIU Healthcare Florida has a record of social and political activism unmatched by any other union in the state. Community and political activism complement its organizing efforts. And because of its orientation in its community and political work, the union is able to develop a favorable image in communities that contain a large percentage of the types of workers it seeks to organize.

Community and "Social Justice" Orientation

Reflecting the broadly activist and progressive perspective of its leadership, this union has played a pivotal role in the creation and ongoing work of a number of community and labor-community organizations working for working-class, immigrant, and minority goals. In late 1999 it joined the local chapter of the National Association for the Advancement of Colored People (NAACP) and with others to form a south Florida chapter of the national labor-community organization Jobs with Justice.[24] South Florida Jobs with Justice played a major role in winning an organizing struggle at Mount Sinai–St. Francis nursing home; it has played a similar role in other labor struggles.

SEIU Healthcare Florida housed South Florida Jobs with Justice for its first few years and provided important resources until the group was able to sustain itself. In addition to supporting workers in unionization struggles, South Florida Jobs with Justice has engaged in "community benefits" work ensuring minority, community, and union gains when a new stadium was built for the Florida Marlins; it has also played a key role in immigrant rights' struggles, provided international support for flower workers in Colombia whose cut flowers are shipped into the United States through Miami, organized trailer-park residents, and been active in other working-class struggles.

In 2000, SEIU Healthcare Florida, together with South Florida Jobs with Justice, the NAACP, and others, organized a massive rally in the state's capital, Tallahassee, to protest the plan by then governor Jeb Bush to end affirmative action in the state's university system. Attendance was estimated at between ten thousand and fifty thousand, making this one of the largest demonstrations ever held in the capital. SEIU Healthcare Florida served as a south Florida staging ground for buses to the event and supplied hundreds of the attendees.

In 2001, SEIU Healthcare Florida created Unite for Dignity for Immigrant Workers Rights (UFD), a community appendage of the union that was designed to develop leadership among immigrant workers.[25] Its primary program is the Leadership Academy, which trains immigrant workers (primarily women) in leadership skills and in creating mobilizational capacity. The Leadership Academy had graduated more than one hundred emerging immigrant leaders as of the fall of 2009. Together with an immigrant voter registration group called Mi Familia Vota (later changed to Democracia USA), UFD extends the union's ties with immigrant communities. UFD also ran a popular Haitian radio program in the Kreyol language on issues concerning immigrant workers.

In the fall of 2003, SEIU Healthcare Florida and UFD played the leading role in organizing the Florida branch of a national caravan of immigrant workers to Washington, D.C., and New York called the Immigrant Workers Freedom Ride. This ride was intended to emulate the freedom rides of the African American civil rights era. It called for legalization of all immigrants in the United States, family reunification, and protection of the rights of immigrant workers in the workplace.

In November 2003, Miami hosted a summit of nations attempting to finalize the features of a proposed Free Trade Area of the Americas (FTAA) agreement between nations of the Western Hemisphere. The United States was pushing for an agreement to lower all tariff and other barriers to trade, while stiffening intellectual property rights regulations that would mostly benefit U.S. corporate patents and copyrights. The U.S. labor movement was strongly opposed to creation of an FTAA without strong labor and environmental rights, so it called for a march outside the hotel where talks were held. Although the direct impact of an FTAA on SEIU Healthcare Florida would likely be minimal, the union mobilized a large contingent to march at this demonstration in solidarity with other workers in the United States and in other countries whom the new law would harm. This and other instances of large-scale member mobilization to support broader working-class struggles demonstrate the essentially class-conscious approach to activism that the union has taken.

Class consciousness is supplemented by high sensitivity to, and activism around, discrimination on the basis of race or immigrant status. In the many demonstrations held in Miami in the late 1990s and early 2000s across the street from the Immigration and Naturalization Service (INS) building demanding better treatment and more favorable policies for Haitian immigrants, purple SEIU T-shirts in the crowd were ubiquitous. The union has been one of the foremost organizations in support of Haitian immigrants in south Florida; outside of Haitian-based organizations and an immigrant advocacy center, it is probably the leading advocate of Haitian rights in the area.[26] Owing to its ties with the NAACP and its strong stance on racial equality, it likewise enjoys an exceptionally positive reputation among African American activists in Florida, particularly in south Florida. Following its expansion into acute-care hospitals that contain a large number of Cuban workers, it also has embraced Cuban culture and held "José Martí" events in commemoration of a cultural hero and icon in the Cuban American community.[27]

SEIU Healthcare Florida has contributed to the growth of working-class and minority activism in other ways during this period also. Prior to the 1990s, community organizing in low-income and minority communities in the Miami area was rare. But such organizing grew rapidly in the late 1990s and early 2000s when former organizers for SEIU Healthcare Florida created a number of community-based organizing projects. In Miami in 1999, two former SEIU nursing home organizers created the Miami Workers Center, a political education and organizing project based in the African American community of Liberty City.[28] That same year, two other ex-SEIU organizers created Power U Center for Social Change in the black community of Overtown near downtown Miami.[29] In 2002 yet another former union staffer created a community organizing group composed primarily of Latino and Haitian immigrants and some African Americans in the Homestead area (southwest of Miami) named WeCount![30] In this way the union "seeded" the growth of what this author has elsewhere termed the "social justice infrastructure" of south Florida.[31]

Impact of the Union on Its Members and the Public

While SEIU Healthcare Florida has vigorously stimulated and supported activism in broader working-class and minority communities, it has also had a major impact on its own members and on their ability to provide high-quality patient care. A 2009 research report based on a random sample survey of the membership and more in-depth interviews and focus groups with leaders and activists revealed their perceptions of the union's impacts in these areas.[32] The report details numerous impacts perceived by its members.

That report found that the union had transformed the lives of a significant number of its members in a variety of ways, and that they also perceived it to be a force for bettering the quality of patient care. SEIU Healthcare Florida membership is overwhelmingly female (86 percent of survey respondents), almost half black (by self-identification), approximately half foreign-born, and over 20 percent Hispanic. The median wage in 2008 was $11.94/hour, below the median wage in Florida, which in 2007 was $14.70/hour. Likewise, median household income of $40,000 per year in 2008 was 16.2 percent below the state household median income of $47,452 in that year. The "median" SEIU Healthcare Florida respondent was fifty years old and had been in the union for approximately three years.[33]

A standard way to measure the effect of a union on its members is to investigate the degree to which it increases their wages and benefits. SEIU Healthcare Florida does indeed raise the compensation and benefit package of its members. Both the perceptions of the members (57 percent rate the union "good" or "very good" at raising wages, compared to less than 16 percent rating it "poor" or "very poor") and comparisons of union-contract wage rates and rate of increases with statewide wage rates and rates of increases in recent years show that the union does deliver on this front, albeit somewhat modestly. But members also emphasize the union's role in making wage increases fairer and less subject to management favoritism, whim, or arbitrary firing with the purpose of hiring newer and cheaper labor. Thus, one CNA noted, "As a union member, you have a legal binding agreement between you and the employer. Without that they can fire you and hire somebody and pay them less wages than you were [paid]."[34]

But the union affects workplace conditions in a manner that appears to have a larger impact than wage increases alone. Members use terms like "greater dignity," "more rights," "fairer treatment," "safer," and a "voice on the job" to characterize the ways the union has altered their experience of the workplace. On all of these dimensions, they rated the union "good" or "very good" over "poor" or "very poor" by margins between 2 to 1 to well over 3 to 1.[35]

It is clear that many union members feel empowered because of the union. "Workers are more empowered," declared one member. "They have a chance to stand up for their rights. They have more authority in expressing themselves and standing up for their rights.... SEIU has educated us and they have made us aware of our rights and what we need to do to enforce our contract." Another used the language of respect and dignity to make the same point: "Before we organized, we were beat down. We were disrespected! There was no dignity and respect for the workers, there was no just, say, common courtesy of that sort. Our workplace was fickle. Management would say, 'You do it or you can hit the door.' Well that got old and we brought the union to change this."[36]

Approximately 30 percent of the members reported that the union had changed the way they felt about work. Within that group, by an overwhelming 16-to-1 ratio they reported that it made them "feel better" rather than "feel worse" about their work lives. Clearly, for relatively low-wage workers who ordinarily have very little influence at work, the "voice" (and power) at the workplace provided by this union is extremely important.[37]

But the union's impact does not stop at the workplace. As noted earlier, it engages an unusually large number of its members in political and community affairs. In his best-selling book *Bowling Alone* (2000), Robert Putnam argues that Americans have become disconnected from friends, family, and neighbors, diminishing our lives. In particular, the country's democratic structures weaken when citizens withdraw into their private lives and disengage from their communities. This tendency impoverishes our lives in a variety of ways. Whatever we can do to reconnect individuals with their communities, neighbors, and democratic political structures should be attempted.[38]

SEIU Healthcare Florida has increased the civic engagement of its members on a very impressive scale. Almost one-third of its members claimed that the union had made them more attuned to politics and public affairs. Around 30 percent reported a greater interest in being active politically, in being likely to vote or register to vote, and in being interested in engaging state legislators on issues of interest to the members. And close to one-quarter stated that the union had stimulated them to become more active in some community organization.[39]

The active, grassroots political agenda of the union backs up these claims by the members. Known as the "purple people" because of their distinctive purple T-shirts when they descended on the state capital, the union's large delegations visiting state legislators were unmatched by any other union in the state during this period. The political presence of most unions has been limited to union officials or hired lobbyists, supplemented by much sparser activation of grassroots members. The union was also extremely active in Barack Obama's 2008 presidential campaign.

This grassroots political orientation has had its effect on the members. One member stated, "I just became involved in politics when I became a union member. It made me more interested and attentive to what's going on with senators and how it affects me and my workplace . . . and what can I do to help." A Haitian-born nursing assistant remarked on the extraordinary transformation it had brought about in her life: "Before the union, I don't know any politics. The union opened my eyes to see what is good for me. . . . I am proud of myself because of SEIU. It makes me so strong. I have never talked to people like that before. I was ashamed to talk to people. Now, I am willing to talk to people. My personality changed. My husband and family became active in politics, too."[40]

Voter registration is an important part of the union's repertoire for increasing member civic engagement. In a statement typifying the experience of many activists, one member related, "All my neighbors love me because I always talk to them about politics, go door to door to ask them, 'Do you have a voter registration card? If you don't have, please let me know. I am going to get the application.' At my church, I always ask them if they are a citizen, they should have the card. At my work, the families of patients, sometimes I talk to them, make sure they are voting. I started [doing] all of these things because I joined union. Without union, I don't know about politics."

The union addressed the broad public interest in one of its premier political campaigns: the struggle for a "safe staffing bill" requiring lower staffing-patient ratios for CNAs working in nursing homes. In the late 1990s and early 2000s, media exposures revealed the poor quality of working conditions and patient care in many Florida nursing homes.[41] Rates of health and safety violations well above the national average, coupled with a large and growing number of lawsuits from patient advocacy groups and families of patients, indicated that the state's nursing home industry was in crisis.

Prior to 2001, Florida regulations required nursing homes to provide only 1.7 hours of CNA time per patient for each 24-hour period. Following massive grassroots lobbying by the union and patient-care advocates, in 2001 the legislature raised the required level in increments over the years to a minimum of 2.9 hours per day. The new law also raised the required hours of Licensed Practical Nurse (LPN) time from .6 hours to 1.0 hours per patient per 24-hour day.[42]

Through the health-care union, workers have campaigned to improve patient care as well as their own working conditions. Besides the aforementioned staffing ratio legislation, which was first proposed in 1998 and fought for again and again in the early 2000s as industry lobbyists and lawmakers tried to repeal the 2.9 hours-per-day standard, union members also supported the Patient Right to Know Act in 2006. This measure would have required hospitals to make public and post on a state web site nursing staffing ratios for various departments, the rate of turnover, and staff vacancy rates.[43]

Both the perceptions of its members and objective evidence indicate that the union's efforts have improved the quality of patient care. The 70 percent of surveyed members who evaluated the union either positively or negatively rated its effectiveness in improving the quality of patient care "good" or "very good" over "poor" or "very poor" by a ration of more than 2 to 1. Asked to explain, one respondent stated, "We've [union] won improvements in staffing ratios, which result in fewer patients per staff." Another explained, "Before the union, the quality was not there. You had lawsuits on the rise because of poor nursing care. Before, residents weren't getting baths or being turned.... CNAs didn't have time to fulfill all the patient's needs. We don't have patients with bed sores anymore. Now I realize it's because of the union that we don't have so many feeding tubes in the nursing home. Oh! I feel much better about the care I'm giving; much better!"[44]

The members' positive assessment is backed up by hard evidence. The union was definitely the main force causing passage of the Florida law (SB 1202, otherwise known as the "2.9 law") in 2001. That law required at least 2.3 hours of direct patient care per patient in each 24-hour period as of 2002, rising to 2.6 hours in 2003 and 2.9 hours by 2004. The legislature repeatedly deferred the final 2.9-hour standard to future years, despite union opposition. It was not until 2007 that the 2.9-hour standard was implemented, albeit with some escape clauses. In 2009 it was implemented fully. A 2009 report by the state's Agency for Healthcare Administration found that passage of the 2.9 law led to clear and dramatic improvements in patient care. In 2002, following implementation, the percentage of facilities receiving citations for harm to patients dropped from 9.9 percent to 2.1 percent. Subsequent years showed further improvements.[45] The union improves patient care, an important plus for any who have loved ones or friends in a nursing home. It has been unable to win a similar law for nurses in hospitals, but it is working toward that end in those facilities as well.

Why the SEIU Florida Healthcare Union Has Been So Successful

The union's success has been closely related to the social vision it pursues, and the social movement orientation of its program. As related at the beginning of this chapter and documented throughout, the union combines seven features:

constant organizing of the unorganized; tactical flexibility in organizing methods; a community focus extending well beyond the workplace; rank-and-file leadership development; involvement in social movements of minorities and immigrants and the like; emphasis on "public goods" such as high-quality patient care; and grassroots-based political action. This combination sets the union apart from most others. It simultaneously pursues a broader social vision than most unions and employs a more grassroots approach than does a typical union.

Yet questions remain: Why does this union pursue such a different course than most others? What factors enable it to operate this way, and to be successful in a relatively hostile "right-to-work" environment like Florida's? One critical factor is definitely the ideology and vision of its leadership. Both President Monica Russo and Secretary-Treasurer Dale Ewart entered the labor movement from activist student- and/or community-organizing backgrounds. And certain grassroots leaders also bring to this union a vision of member empowerment and leadership development coupled with social justice for all. Stella Williams, who worked as a CNA in a nursing home for decades before joining the union's staff, provides just such clarity of vision. She is widely looked to within the union as the moral authority and visionary thinker to provide trustworthy guidance on difficult issues of union direction.

A second factor facilitating success is the nature of the industry and the workforce being organized. Health-care workers combine two characteristics that make them quite receptive to the social vision of progressive leaders: largely minority and/or immigrant and/or low-wage, and culturally focused on caring for others. Thus, the style of social movement unionism being practiced sits easily with much of the membership.

Third, the union has been fortunate to have a substantial initial commitment of resources from its national parent union. Fourth, the union operates in an industry with a lot of public funding that is widely seen as responsible for delivering a widely recognized public necessity (health care). All of these factors make SEIU Healthcare Florida's brand of social movement unionism easier to pursue than it might be under different circumstances.

Definitions of success for a union depend upon the standard being used to measure success. By almost any measure, this union has been a success. Numerical growth has been both enormous and unusual. The union has also transformed the lives of many of its members for the better in a variety of ways. And for those who desire and expect more from a union than simple economic improvement for its own members, the union has been a major force in the state for a broad, progressive social agenda for more fairness and justice in U.S. society. And it has incorporated marginalized populations in the civic and political institutions of the country—populations that ordinarily have very little influence over the major events affecting their lives.

Addendum

In July 2010, after this chapter was written, SEIU Healthcare Florida joined a "mega-local" of SEIU by merging into 1199 SEIU United Healthcare East, a 350,000-member local with members along the entire east coast of the United States from Massachusetts south.[46] A membership vote on the merger showed 97 percent in favor and 3 percent opposing. The Florida organization became a "region" within the larger local, with many of its internal operations unchanged.[47] The degree to which this new chapter in the organization's life will change it, and the manner of any change, remain to be seen.

Notes

1. Percentages taken from www.unionstats.com.
2. For previous literature on health-care unionization, the classic book is Leon Fink and Brian Greenberg, *Upheaval in the Quiet Zone: 1199 SEIU and the Politics of Health Care Unionism* (Urbana: University of Illinois Press, 2009). See also Karen Brodkin Sacks, *Caring by the Hour: Women, Work, and Organizing at Duke Medical Center* (Urbana: University of Illinois Press, 1988), an account of an unsuccessful fifteen-year attempt to unionize employees of the Duke Medical Center. Patricia Cayo Sexton's *The New Nightingales: Hospital Workers, Unions, New Women's Issues* (New York: Enquiry Press, 1982) focuses on hospital unionization from a feminist perspective. A contemporary firsthand account of unionization and union organizing in nursing homes is Steven Henry Lopez, *Reorganizing the Rustbelt: An Inside Study of the American Labor Movement* (Berkeley: University of California Press, 2004). For a study of health-care unionism attempting a "partnership" approach with management quite unlike the union portrayed in this chapter, see Thomas Kochan, Adrienne Eaton, Robert B. McKersie, and Paul S. Adler, *Healing Together: The Labor-Management Partnership at Kaiser Permanente* (Ithaca: Cornell University Press, 2009). For an example of historical scholarship on south Florida and immigrant organizing, see Melanie Shell-Weiss, "'I Dreamed I Went to Work': Southern Unionism in the Mid-Twentieth Century Lingerie Industry," in *Florida's Working-Class Past: Current Perspectives on Labor, Race, and Gender from Spanish Florida to the New Immigration*, ed. Robert Cassanello and Melanie Shell-Weiss (Gainesville: University Press of Florida, 2009), 227–56. For a more contemporary account of unions and immigrants in the context of union-unfriendly south Florida, see Bruce Nissen and Guillermo Grenier, "Local Union Relations with Immigrants: The Case of South Florida," *Labor Studies Journal* 26, no. 1 (2001): 76–97.
3. Dale Ewart interview by the author, June 10, 2009, Hialeah, Florida.
4. The membership figure of fifteen thousand is taken from Steven Greenhouse, "Growing Health Care Union Prepares to Show Its Muscle," *New York Times*, September 12, 1999, http://www.nytimes.com/1999/09/12/nyregion/growing-health-care-union-prepares-to-show-its-muscle.html?ref=stevengreenhouse.

5. In 1991 a strictly nurses unit in a Miami public-sector hospital that had been part of the Florida Nurses Association disaffiliated from that body and joined the Service Employees International Union (SEIU), forming a separate union local, SEIU 1991, which still exists as a separate union local.

6. Ewart interview, June 10, 2009; Monica Russo interview by the author, September 4, 2009, Hialeah, Florida.

7. The number "1199" came from a legendary union in New York formed by Leon Davis for drugstore pharmacists in the 1930s that expanded in the late 1950s and 1960s into a powerhouse health-care union among New York's nonprofit hospitals. The union later spread around the nation. Most of its units eventually joined SEIU after sojourns both as a unit of the Retail, Wholesale and Department Store Union and as an independent union. The story of 1199 is well told in Fink and Greenberg, *Upheaval in the Quite Zone*.

8. Due to the failure of U.S. labor law to protect workers' rights to organize or form a union and bargain collectively through that union, such behavior by employers is quite common. See Sheldon Friedman, Richard Hurd, Rudy Oswald, and Ronald Seeber, eds., *Restoring the Promise of American Labor Law* (Ithaca: ILR Press, 1994); John Logan, "Consultants, Lawyers, and the Union-Free Movement in the United States since the 1970s," *Industrial Relations Journal* 33, no. 3 (2002): 197–214; and John Logan, "The Union Avoidance Industry in the United States," *British Journal of Industrial Relations* 44, no. 4 (2006): 651–75. See also Gordon Lafer, *Neither Free Nor Fair: The Subversion of Democracy under NLRB Elections* (Washington, D.C.: American Rights at Work, 2007); and Kate Bronfenbrenner, *No Holds Barred: the Intensification of Employer Opposition to Organizing* (Washington, D.C.: American Rights at Work and Economic Policy Institute, May 2009). These final two publications are available at http://www.americanrightsatwork.org, under "Publications."

9. See Lance Compa, *Unfair Advantage: Workers' Freedom of Association in the United States under International Human Rights Standards* (New York: Human Rights Watch, 2000), available at http://www.hrw.org/reports/pdfs/u/us/uslbr008.pdf. It was reprinted in 2004 under the same title as a book by Cornell University Press.

10. See Steven Greenhouse, *The Big Squeeze: Tough Times for the American Worker* (New York: Knopf, 2008).

11. See Marybeth Maxwell and Bruce Nissen, *Some of Them Are Brave: The Unfulfilled Promise of American Labor Law* (Washington, D.C.: American Rights at Work, 2003), available at http://www.risep-fiu.org/wp-content/uploads/2009/04/arawbravefinal1.pdf.

12. Ibid., 2.

13. For a table outlining delays in the process after workers vote yes for a contract, see ibid., 7.

14. Ibid., 10.

15. In this and the following sixteen paragraphs, the account and quotations are drawn from Bruce Nissen, "Would the Employee Free Choice Act Effectively Protect the Right to Unionize? Evidence from a South Florida Nursing Home Case," *Labor Studies Journal* 34, no. 1 (2009): 65–90.

16. Ibid., 84.

17. According to Maxwell and Nissen, *Some of Them Are Brave*, between January 1996 and early 2003 the union participated in seventy-three NLRB elections, winning sixty of them. Not all those election victories resulted in a continuing union presence and a first contract, although most eventually did.

18. The particulars of the following case are taken from ibid., 11–12.

19. Although the legal delaying tactics of other employers did not draw the ridicule of the press and the public, they were often equally frivolous. An employer could have absolutely no reasonable basis for legally objecting yet would be free to do so, and to delay certification of the union for anywhere between two and ten or more years with repeated appeals and legal maneuvers. The only limitation was the size of the employer's legal budget and the cleverness of its lawyers in filing complaints and other legal motions.

20. This tactic is reminiscent of the behavior of a number of employers during the CIO upsurge in the 1930s. To avoid the more militant CIO unions, employers would cooperate to bring in AFL unions that were perceived to be more cooperative.

21. Information in this and the following paragraph was obtained from the Russo (September 4, 2009) and Ewart (June 10, 2009) interviews.

22. This history of management cooperation with UFCW 1625 raises the question of whether this union is merely a "company union" or something very close to it. Does it sign "sweetheart" deals with nursing home owners and fail to adequately represent its members? A comparison of union contracts negotiated by the two unions shows that the SEIU generally wins slightly superior compensation, but there is a lot of similar "standard" language in both. The greatest apparent difference between the two unions is not a vast difference in contract language but rather in the level of activism stimulated among the membership and (perhaps) how aggressively the contract is enforced. SEIU generates widespread political grassroots activism among its members, while the UFCW local does not. And although this assertion is not backed up by systematic research into the inner workings of UFCW Local 1625, it appears to an outsider that the SEIU local much more aggressively enforces its contract through rank-and-file actions and grievances. This is not to say that the UFCW local is a "company union"; it is not. It is simply a much more "typical" union that lacks the SEIU local's unusually activist "social movement" orientation.

23. Information in this and the following paragraph are taken from the Russo (September 4, 2009) and Ewart (June 9, 2009) interviews.

24. The following paragraphs on SEIU Healthcare Florida's community and political involvement are primarily based on Bruce Nissen and Monica Russo, "Strategies for Labor Revitalization: The Case of Miami," in *Labor in the New Urban Battlegrounds: Local Solidarity in a Global Economy*, ed. Lowell Turner and Daniel B. Cornfield (Ithaca: Cornell University Press, 2007), 147–62.

25. UFD's web site is http://www.unitefordignity.org.

26. With more than 26 percent of its membership born in Haiti, it also has the largest membership "base" in south Florida's Haitian immigrant community outside of perhaps the Roman Catholic Church.

27. The evaluations made in this paragraph are based on the author's personal observation of the union and its interactions with other elements of the south Florida communities in the period under study.

28. The Miami Workers Center's web site is http://www.miamiworkerscenter.org.

29. Power U Center's web site is http://www.poweru.org.

30. WeCount!'s web site is http://www.we-count.org.

31. For more on the south Florida social justice infrastructure and this union's contribution to it, see Bruce Nissen, "Social Justice Infrastructure Organizations as New Actors

from the Community: The Case of South Florida." *Journal of Community Practice* 17, nos. 1–2 (2009): 157–69.

32. See Bruce Nissen, Cynthia Hernandez, Marcos Feldman, and Yue Zhang, *Transforming Lives: The Impact of SEIU Healthcare Florida on Its Members* (Miami: Florida International University Research Institute on Social and Economic Policy [RISEP], December 2009), available at http://www.risep-fiu.org. Information in the following paragraphs is taken from that report.

33. Ibid.; State median household income figure taken from Census data obtained at http://www.census.gov/prod2010/acsbr09-2.pdf.

34. Nissen et al., *Transforming Lives*, 33.

35. Ibid., 7–14.

36. Ibid., 11, 12.

37. Ibid., 15.

38. Robert D. Putnam, *Bowling Alone: The Collapse and Revival of American Community* (New York: Simon & Schuster, 2000).

39. Nissen et al., *Transforming Lives*, 41–48.

40. Ibid., 42, 43.

41. Glenn Burkins, "Small Victories: Nursing Homes Are Labor's New Target in Its Promised Return," *Wall Street Journal*, July 8, 1997; Barbara DeLollis and Peggy Rogers, "Failed Nursing Homes: Company's Trail of Neglect, Financial Pain Spans Three States," *Miami Herald*, August 16, 1998, 1A, 18A; Colleen Dougher, "Where's the Care?" *City Link* (Broward and Palm Beach Counties), January 31–February 6, 2001, 17–24; Diane C. Lade, "'Overworked and Underpaid': Nursing Home Aides, Advocates Step Up Statewide Campaign to Win Better Pay," *South Florida Sun-Sentinel*, September 21, 2000, 1B; Joan Fitzgerald, "Better-Paid Caregivers, Better Care," *American Prospect*, May 21, 2001, 30–32.

42. Kathryn Hyer, Kali Thomas, Shabnam Mehra, Christopher Johnson, and Jeffrey S. Harman, *Preliminary Analyses on Outcomes of Increased Nurse Staffing Policies in Florida Nursing Homes: Staffing Levels, Quality and Costs* (2002–7), available at http://ahca.myflorida.com/Medicaid/quality_management/mrp/pdfs/preliminary_nursing_home_staffing_analyses_USF_final_031109.pdf.

43. Shana Gruskin, "Nurses Urge More Disclosure about Staffing to Patients," *South Florida Sun-Sentinel*, March 9, 2006; Ben Roussel, "Nurses Urge Florida Lawmakers to Increase Hospital Transparency and Pass the Patient-Right-to-Know Act," *Westside Gazette* (Broward County), April 12, 2006.

44. Nissen et al., *Transforming Lives*, 22, p. 23.

45. For more details see Hyer et al., *Preliminary Analyses*.

46. See http://www.seiuhealthcarefl.org/It_s_Official__.aspx.

47. For more information on the merger, see http://www.seiuhealthcarefl.org/Learn_more_about_our_merger_with_1199SEIU.aspx.

11

The Movement for Economic Democracy in the South

The Virginia Organizing Project, 1995–2004

MICHAEL DENNIS

In an era that celebrated the alleged virtues of the unfettered marketplace, progressive activists struggled to ameliorate the very real economic woes that afflicted average southerners. In the state that boosters described as the Silicon Dominion, the Virginia Organizing Project (VOP) spearheaded that effort. Launched by a group of longtime community activists in 1995, the VOP advanced a critique of free-market primacy that became the foundation for a wider social movement. While media lauded the era of entrepreneurial opportunity, the VOP highlighted the evidence of economic despair. The solution they proposed was collective social action. First, however, they sought to educate workers about the economic forces that governed their lives. In the process, they dismantled a set of interlocking assumptions nearly as pernicious as those that had supported Jim Crow.

Combining ideas and action, the VOP built the framework for a multiracial movement that made racial equality the essential precondition of economic democracy. The VOP fostered what could best be described as an "emergent oppositional discourse" that politicized the supposedly inevitable forces of global market integration. Central to that discourse was a critique the neo-social Darwinism of the late twentieth century. Through its publications and workshops, the VOP examined the impact of welfare reform, low wages, persistent racial inequality, discriminatory banking policies, and deindustrialization on working-class Virginians. Through rural and local organizing, campaigns of political pressure and education, public demonstrations, alternative journalism, and cooperation with organized labor, civil rights groups, and environmental activists, the VOP challenged the corporate dominance of public affairs. These efforts effectively countered the campaign to privatize

Figure 11.1. Living-wage rally at the University of Virginia, Charlottesville, in 1998. In Virginia and elsewhere in the South, the living-wage movement has brought together diverse coalitions of activists. (Rick Reinhard photo.)

and individualize social problems. In a state where labor organizers confront a multitude of political and ideological obstructions, the VOP's version of social-movement unionism presented a viable, albeit imperfect, alternative. Between 1995 and 2004 it crafted a discourse of racial and economic democracy that offered a starting point for the renewal of social-movement unionism in the South.[1]

In 1995, longtime community activist Joe Szakos set the wheels in motion for what would become the Virginia Organizing Project. A native of Pennsylvania and a graduate of the School of Social Service Administration in Chicago, Szakos cut his teeth as a community organizer in Kentucky. Joining the Kentucky Fair Tax Coalition in 1982, which developed into the Kentuckians for the Commonwealth in 1988, Szakos gained experience as a community organizer. The Kentucky Fair Tax Coalition tackled issues ranging from fair housing to progressive taxation. It was in Kentucky that Szakos confronted the challenges facing Appalachian-area social activists in the Reagan era. The question of focus for community organizers "took on a new urgency," Szakos and VOP activist Ladelle McWhorter recall, "as President Ronald Reagan engineered a massive 'devolution' in the United States. In accordance with

Reagan's neoliberal agenda, the national government was slated to diminish in size as 'states' rights' were emphasized and federal spending on domestic programs of all kinds was cut."[2] To address the knot of environmental, labor, and human rights issues facing the South, Szakos believed that community activists would have to apply political pressure at the state level.

After a year of grassroots organizing in Eastern Europe, this peripatetic activist returned to the United States in 1994, locating in Virginia, a state ravaged by deindustrialization. He logged some forty thousand miles in an effort to assess the damage and the prospects for progressive activism. According to Szakos, Virginia was a patchwork of desperately isolated community activists who lacked coordination. Statewide groups existed, but they were usually composed of two staff members who had little understanding of rural Virginia. Moreover, few community organizers understood that the Reagan administration's new federalism had made state governments the locus of power on a wide range of issues. Benefiting from the meager financial assistance of the Needmor Fund and the Unitarian Universalist Veatch Program, Szakos and a group of ten like-minded devotees launched the Virginia Organizing Project. Individual donations supplemented the project, but the financial state of the organization was anything but promising.[3]

What was promising was the VOP's commitment to racial justice. From its very inception, Szakos and collaborator Denise Smith of Wythe County insisted that any social reform movement must practice and promote racial equality. "When the first Organizing Committee for VOP met in August 1995," Szakos recalled, "the decision to build a political force composed of low- to moderate-income people, people of color, and others traditionally excluded from Virginia political life brought the young organization up against the difficult issue of racism."[4] Yet mobilizing a multiracial workforce required activists to confront the ideology of market dominance that now prevailed in the region. Racial justice could only be achieved by acknowledging the impact of economic restructuring on the South.

The Social Landscape of the South and Modern America

Workers may have felt the ground shifting underneath them, but proponents of the New Economy insisted that this was evidence of creative destruction at work. Business pundits, mainstream journalists, managerial experts, and conservative intellectuals heralded the arrival of a hypercompetitive economy in the 1990s. In part, this conviction reflected the growing influence of the anti-government, pro-free-market creed in national politics. Its most famous formulation appeared after the Republicans won a landslide victory in the 1994 midterm elections. Crafted by Dick Armey and Newt Gingrich, the Republicans' "Contract with America" manifesto articulated a vision of America redeemed from Big Government. "Government-imposed mandates and regulations suppress wages," argued Armey and Gingrich. It was "excessive taxation of capital" that was throttling "economic growth and job creation. Current federal policies threaten the competitiveness of American business, stifle entrepreneurial activity, and suppress economic growth and job creation."[5] Although the Republicans offered the most vociferous defense of this creed, they were not alone. By the 1990s, the Democrats had embraced a more palatable version of the free-market ideology. Nevertheless, it represented an unmistakable departure from the past. "We believe the Democratic Party's fundamental mission is to expand opportunity, not government," the Democratic Leadership Council (DLC) announced in 1990. According to the DLC, which would vault Bill Clinton to prominence and profoundly influence Democratic policies in the 1990s, "the free market regulated in the public interest is the best engine of general prosperity."[6] Liberated from the constraints of government regulation, a regenerated economy would thrive on technological innovation, employee productivity, and entrepreneurial risk.

The conservative insurgency was a key moment in the free-market revival movement. Yet business journalists and corporate reengineering experts were equally enthusiastic proponents of the New Economy. Acknowledging the challenges of deindustrialization, they advocated for a philosophy of "flexibility" in labor markets and corporate organization. Business reengineering would restore the corporate profitability that a combination of deregulation, intensifying competition, union wage gains, and chronic inflation had eroded in the 1970s. The rise of "shareholder activism" in the age of leveraged buyouts and massive mergers placed additional pressures on corporate managers to reduce labor costs.[7] As journalist Louis Uchitelle explains, "Raising shareholder value became the great justification for merger and acquisition activity, and out of this breeding ground came a new creature, the corporate raider, who multiplied the acquisitions and reorganizations—and the accompanying layoffs."[8] Where frontline workers sensed insecurity, New Economy advocates detected opportunity. Technology, they argued, would require greater workplace discipline and flexibility, but it would increase profitability. Corporate reengineering might require a leaner, "flattened" organization, but it also promised creative independence for employees. The elimination of workplace rules, union contracts, and government regulation would improve business profitability and global competitiveness, but it would simultaneously transform employees into intrepid entrepreneurs. In the wildest flights of New Economy fancy, practitioners of corporate reengineering became agents of democratic liberation. Even as late as 2000, news media extolled the benefits of unfettered capitalism. According to the consensus, increased productivity, low inflation, and widely distributed wage gains would flow from it.[9]

For all of the fanfare over silicon solutions for hidebound companies, the New Economy was ultimately a question of political power, not technology. Similarly, despite the enthusiasm over corporate reengineering, proponents were interested in restoring unrestricted capitalism, not unleashing the creative potential of their employees.[10] Editor James Bacon of *Virginia Business* made this calculation clear enough. Writing in 1991 about the shift of business to the South, which Virginia boosters interpreted as a sign of the coming economic order, Bacon concluded that, "in the final analysis, the problem is political. Rather than regarding business as a healthy element of society, Northeaster liberals blame it for all manners of ills from racism to sexual chauvinism, from the rape of the environment to the exploitation of the working class." More explicitly in the South than the rest of the nation, the New Economy promised to restore business dominance by curbing the influence of organized labor and government.[11]

The rhetoric of southern technological innovation also masked deeper uncertainties, which were particularly acute for black and Latino southerners. Despite the achievements of the post-civil-rights era, African Americans persistently lagged behind whites. This pattern of racialized economic disadvantage continued to mark the American landscape into the early twenty-first century. It was notably salient in the South following the economic miasma of 2008. Even in the alleged golden years of the 1990s, however, the legacy of racial discrimination was evident. In 1990 the per capita income of African Americans in North Carolina was 54.9 percent that of whites. More than 40 percent of black children lived in poverty in North Carolina. In Roanoke Rapids, the poverty rate for black children reached 68.2 percent in 1990.[12] As late as 1997, black unemployment still significantly outpaced white joblessness in Virginia. While white male unemployment stood at 2.7 percent that year, the figure for black males was 8.7 percent. The disparity for women was even more stark. In 1997, white female unemployment was 3.0 percent; for African American women it was 9.0 percent.[13] The economic collapse of 2008 amplified the pattern of African American disadvantage. In Virginia, Texas, and Louisiana the rates of unemployment for African Americans were more than twice those of their white counterparts. Just as Hispanics lost thousands of jobs in construction, African Americans found themselves dismissed from positions in manufacturing, the retail trade, wholesale distribution, transportation, utilities, finance, real estate, and insurance. The presence of blacks in those sectors did little to mitigate their historic vulnerability in periods of contraction.[14]

Despite the persistence of racial inequality, the most prominent motif of the late-twentieth-century South was the increasingly common experience of working-class insecurity. Global market integration, compounded by antiquated machinery, the waning demand for tobacco, and the inability of the region's manufacturers to compete against low-wage imports, cast tens of thousands of southerners into unemployment. According to a study by the Carsey Institute at the University New Hampshire, the rural South lost nearly 616,000 jobs between 1997 and 2003, the most of any region in the nation.[15] In Martinsville, Virginia, some 14,792 workers made a living in manufacturing in 1992. By 2004 this figure had been cut in half, sending Martinsville's unemployment rate to 16.2 percent.[16] By the time Tultex—one of Martinsville's major apparel manufacturers—closed its doors, African American employees were in the majority of what had once been a bastion of white privilege. Neither blacks nor whites were spared the downsizing deluge.[17]

The abandoned textile mill became the symbol of the South's manufacturing misfortunes. Yet even while the collapse of the textile industry had, according to historian Timothy Minchin, a "particularly cruel impact on African Americans who had struggled to secure good-paying jobs in manufacturing industries," the economic consequences were not limited to blacks.[18] White workers had never been shielded from market downturns. Nor, for that matter, did their comparatively privileged position in the textile mills, steel mills, and processing plants throughout the South win them the kind of security enjoyed by many of their northern counterparts in the postwar years.[19] That leads into a thicket of questions that are beyond the scope of this discussion. For our purposes, the relative convergence of the black and white working-class experience in the late twentieth century is pivotal. Job loss, the shift to low-wage service positions, long periods of unemployment, and the grinding sense of uncertainty that accompanied the New Economy crossed the racial divide of the modern South.

Of course, the historical record suggests that there is no automatic corollary between shared economic and interracial sympathy. If anything, the American past is littered with examples of job competition and widespread misfortune driving the racial wedge deeper. Yet the Populist Movement, the Popular Front, the "long civil rights movement," the example of the Highlander Folk School experiment, and sporadic episodes of interracial unionism in the South demonstrate the possibilities for racial cooperation, however tenuous.[20]

The Virginia Organizing Project echoed these movements. From its origins in the liberal enclave of Charlottesville, the VOP declared its determination to "shift the balance of power in the state." With a biracial leadership composed of men and women, the VOP signaled it would not repeat the mistakes of earlier labor union and civil rights ventures. Despite the organization's nonprofit status, its first newsletter read like a manifesto for social justice unionism. "An important target group for the project will be low-income and working-class people; we will focus on a multi-racial grassroots constituency." Endorsing participatory democracy, the central legacy of 1960s social activism, the VOP aimed at combining the disparate strands of Virginia progressivism into a coordinated movement.[21]

The VOP unequivocally endorsed liberal egalitarianism. It expressly embraced Virginians from across the spectrum of race, gender, and sexual orientation. At its founding convention on June 21, 1997, chairperson Anita B. Lawrence announced that, "Where there are racist programs, practices, and policies, VOP will work to dismantle racism." In words that recalled southern liberals like Virginia Foster Durr, Lawrence declared that she was "committed to being a white anti-racist ally." Joined by some 150 supporters, she challenged the prevailing conviction that America had absolved itself of racial and gender inequalities. "We have to learn about our racism," Lawrence announced, "our own sexism, our own homophobia, our own ageism and other oppressive systems and mechanisms in our society today."[22] Announcing the organization's egalitarian ethic, Lawrence also signaled the central place of education in its agenda. The VOP was determined to expose the racial elephant in the room of the modern South.

The VOP's determination to confront the legacy of segregation reflected the increasing racial friction in Virginia at the time. The Virginia Organizing Project was launched in 1995, the same year that a controversy over the placement of a statue of Arthur Ashe on Memorial Avenue rocked the capital of the former Confederacy. The idea of setting a black tennis star in contiguity to Stonewall Jackson and Robert E. Lee was enough to provoke an indignant protest at the monument's unveiling ceremony. While members of the Council of Conservative Citizens waved Confederate flags, unidentified white supremacists distributed racist literature to nearby houses. For their part, proponents of the monument believed it would promote racial harmony by visually "integrating" a public space dedicated to the memory of slavery's defenders. The inflammatory debate over Governor George Allen's proposal for a Confederate history month aggravated the racial climate in Virginia. Richmond may have been peculiarly sensitive to representations of its past, but Virginia was no exception in the region. The controversy over South Carolina's decision to continue to fly its Confederate battle flag at the state capitol as well as the NAACP's retaliatory boycott of the Palmetto State in 1999 illustrated the persistent tensions over historical memory. There was nothing trivial about the politicization of identity and history in the late-twentieth-century South.

"As has been true since the Civil War," writes historian W. Fitzhugh Brundage, "claims to material resources, political power, and moral high ground are at the center of contemporary debates over the South's history."[23] They also presented a consistent challenge to social progressives trying to establish common ground.

The mutual recrimination over the Arthur Ashe statue countered the claims of racial reconciliation in the South. Despite its tradition of genteel race relations, Virginia was as burdened by its past as the rest of the region. African American community activist Margaret Morton, a founding member of the VOP, recalled that she had never heard the question of racism discussed so directly as at the first VOP meeting she attended. "In Virginia, it's important for everyone to be polite, and racism is an impolite word. It upsets people, so people don't use it. When I found myself with a polite group of people talking about racism, I knew that VOP was going to be a different kind of organization."[24] The legacy of an unfinished civil rights revolution lingered. Surveying the racial landscape of the South in the 1990s, historian David Goldfield concluded that genuine racial integration remained a distant objective. Despite black economic advancement and high-profile political achievements, the racial archipelago had not changed. "The instances of racial contact that we see all around, in restaurants, businesses, and schools, are for the most part superficial." In Atlanta, a city often exalted as an example of racial harmony, blacks and whites lived in separate districts and carried on separate lives. The description fit Richmond, Petersburg, and several other Virginia cities just as well. In shopping malls, blacks and whites mixed equitably enough but drew sharp, invisible lines around their churches and homes. Voluntary or not, the separatism was pernicious. As Goldfield writes, it "reifies racial stereotypes that in turn enforce separateness and inequality." Southerners had apparently forgotten that separate never meant equal.[25]

Black southerners struggled against more than neo-Confederate nationalism and resegregation. They confronted a political climate permeated by the conviction that the problem of race had been solved in America. Emerging from the reaction against the Great Society, a new racial "narrative" coalesced during the years of the Reagan and Bush presidencies. According to this dominant view, the civil rights legislation of the 1960s had decisively solved the American problem of race. In fact, according to its proponents, the primary goal of the movement from the *Brown* decision through to the march on Selma was the achievement of a "color blind" America. According to conservative architects of this perspective, the lingering presence of racial inequality could only be explained by the failure of blacks to fulfill the promise of the movement. Convinced that the United States had become a color-blind society, proponents maintained that programs designed to ameliorate historical inequalities only violated the movement's ideals. "The American creed of free-market individualism," writes historian Jacquelyn Dowd Hall, "in combination with the ideological victories of the movement ... made the rhetoric of color blindness central to the 'war of ideas' initiated by the New Right in the 1970s." Using the words of Martin Luther King Jr. out of context and against his aspirations for economic justice, these "racial realists" claimed that race-oriented policies deny his vision of an egalitarian society.[26]

In the 1990s, conservative Virginians in both major parties endorsed this view. It was perfectly consistent with the strain of libertarian individualism in conservative thought. Frank Atkinson, a Richmond lawyer and adviser to Governor George Allen, encapsulated the racial views of conservative Virginians. "The race-based mantras employed for years to mobilize near-monolithic black support for Democratic candidates increasingly are ringing hollow," Atkinson announced in 1997, "not only among upwardly mobile middle-income blacks, but also among younger African-Americans with low incomes but high hopes." The evidence, according to Atkinson, was polling data suggesting that black voters supported Republican gubernatorial candidate James Gilmore's plan to eliminate a tax on car sales. Atkinson never seemed to consider that Virginia's regressive tax system and the low wages of working-class blacks would make them favorable to tax relief of any kind. Instead, he saw it as evidence that blacks supported the Republican anti-tax agenda. According to Atkinson, the Legislative Black Caucus was "hopelessly wedded to the old-style Democratic politics," presumably meaning the politics of affirmative action, labor rights, and modest assistance for Virginia's most needy. In its place, Atkinson detected "a new biracial conservative coalition ... now emerging. And where Virginia politics goes, national politics soon follows." Allen's counselor was confident that the Republican victories in the gubernatorial races of 1993 and 1997 could be explained by the development of a "biracial coalition centered on working family concerns."[27] Exaggerating black working-class support for the Republicans, Atkinson cast it in the framework of conservative populism. Even so, he had inadvertently identified the economic predicament facing black, white, and Hispanic workers.

Yet racial antipathies complicated ambitions for a united front. "By the beginning of the 1990s," writes journalist Godfrey Hodgson, "a witches' brew of stereotypes, some more or less remotely based on true facts, had poisoned the always-tense relations between working-class whites and blacks." Those would only be stoked by the media circuses surrounding the Rodney King beating incident and the O. J. Simpson trial.[28] Economic realities, such as the fact that the real median income for black males was 67.5 percent that of white males and the real median income of black families was 62 percent of the income of white families in 2001, were lost in the pseudo-debate over affirmative action.[29] Lacking a language of social democratic reform that could anchor a multiracial working-class movement, racial divisions deepened.

The Possibilities for a Social Democratic Movement

Despite smoldering racial tensions, whites were not prepared to repudiate the ideal of racial equality. Opinion polls consistently suggested that whites endorsed the principle of integration, even if skepticism about government involvement in achieving those ends had increased. Surveys also suggested that most whites and African Americans continued to support the central tenets of the New Deal order.[30] Abstract sympathy for racial equality and support for government responsibility offered a basis for advancement. The alteration of the economic landscape further enhanced the prospects for biracial working-class cooperation. Mounting job losses from the recession of 1991, military cutbacks, the decline of the apparel and textile industry, and relentless downsizing in the financial sector traumatized working-class Virginians across the racial spectrum. The worst hemorrhaging was in textiles. Between 1990 and 2000, Virginia textile mills shed 15,300 jobs, or 36 percent of the total industry in the state. During the same period, the apparel industry lost 15,400 jobs, an astonishing 54.3 percent of its positions.[31] The magnitude of the job loss was stunning, but equally significant was the shared experience of loss. Racial privilege did not protect white workers from protracted periods of unemployment. More often than not, displaced workers who found new jobs earned wages that were significantly lower than those they had earned in manufacturing. The entire manufacturing sector was in free fall, shedding a full 20 percent of its employees between 1990 and 2005.[32]

Hispanic and Asian immigrants further altered the system of racialized capitalism, producing a new and complicated reality. By the late twentieth century, Latinos and Asians constituted nearly 25 percent of the national population, producing nonwhite majorities in several areas of the country. Northern Virginia was a microcosm of the South's racial change. Drawn by the expansion of low-wage jobs and the impact of trade liberalization agreements, Latino workers flooded into the region. Between 1990 and 2000 the Hispanic population increased 105 percent in Virginia, from 160,228 to 329,540.[33] Latinos filtered into low-wage sectors such as poultry processing, janitorial work, agriculture, and the hotel service industry, gravitating to regions of economic expansion in the South. In Virginia, low-wage service work created a magnet for Hispanic immigration in Fairfax County and Arlington. By 2000, Hispanics made up almost 10 percent of the New Economy enclave of northern

Virginia.³⁴ In 2008, Michael Goldfield observed that these changes meant that "the system of racial domination is in turmoil." These economic and demographic changes produced "socially explosive tinder," Goldfield argued, "with occasional recognition by unions and workers that their formerly racially exclusive and anti-immigrant stances are counterproductive."³⁵ Although the racial character of the South was becoming more complex, the economic insecurities of the era pushed African American, Latino, and white workers onto a similar economic terrain.

Rediscovering the Vital Nexus

The return of political economy to American discourse generated the possibility for the renewal of social-movement unionism. The controversy over trade liberalization once again focused attention on business influence over social policy. The 1993–94 debate over the North American Free Trade Agreement (NAFTA) was critical. It raised questions about environmental protection, labor rights, and corporate prerogatives that had been effectively contained during the Reagan era. It produced an idiom of democratic opposition to corporate influence that profoundly influenced the era. Labor activists throughout the country challenged an agreement that seemed to expose the United States to cheap labor. For all of the rhetoric about emerging markets, labor and environmental activists considered Mexico a haven for companies seeking lower operating costs. At the same time, labor unions that had been reeling from the business campaign for concessions began to fight back. In places like Decatur, Illinois, organized labor challenged the aggressive corporate agenda through mass mobilization. In the A. E. Staley lockout, workers embraced the idea that grasping multinational corporations had launched "a war on the workers" that threatened entire communities.³⁶ Now, labor activists utilized a set of analytical tools based on the values of social democracy. Following the adoption of NAFTA, progressive labor activists turned their attention to global outsourcing. They explored the influence of the World Trade Organization (WTO) over social and environmental policy. Activists and labor intellectuals examined the corporate drive for privatization and the need for cooperation between American and foreign workers. According to historian John D. French, American workers sensed that "the world's peoples have collectively lost control of the world and the markets in which we live."³⁷ The growing demand by corporations such as Caterpillar for massive concessions and wage rollbacks sparked labor battles that engulfed entire cities such as Decatur.

The NAFTA debate was ultimately part of a larger struggle over the market triumphalism of the post-Soviet era. The rhetoric of capitalism ascendant had inadvertently injected the issue of labor standards and human rights into the public forum. The rhetoric flowed from an ideology of globalization that first emerged out of the economic morass of the 1970s. It assumed an almost messianic tone, however, in the years following the Soviet implosion. Proponents believed, according to commentator John Ralston Saul, that the expansion of international trade would "unleash an economic-social tide that would raise all ships" and that "prosperous markets would turn dictatorships into democracies." Furthermore, "all of this would discourage irresponsible nationalism, racism, and political violence" and create stability under the supervision of benevolent transnational corporations.[38]

However, the harmony implicit in this vision collided with the growing uncertainty of workers at the end of the century. In the heat of the NAFTA debate, southern labor leaders, social activists, and sympathetic journalists rejuvenated a language of progressive reform that acknowledged the resurgence of class divisions in American society. Local activists elaborated a vision of economic democracy that addressed the social impact of market liberalization. In effect, opponents of the trade deal turned the democratic rhetoric of NAFTA's champions against corporate-led globalization.

From its inception, the VOP clearly expresses this democratic ferment. As it contended in its "Statement of Beliefs," a living wage, adequate housing, health care, and a secure retirement were "entitlements" of the Commonwealth's citizens. The organization advocated the "elimination of the extremes of wealth and poverty" that had grown in spite of the much-heralded technological revolution of the 1990s.[39] Challenging the rhetoric of stockholder entitlement and entrepreneurial rebellion, the VOP championed the "rights of workers, consumers, shareholders, and taxpayers to democratic self-organization."[40] Szakos and his colleagues were early exponents of the post-NAFTA discourse of economic democracy. Yet they clearly understood that reform depended on a coalition of minorities and working-class whites. They persistently drew the connection between racial equality and economic justice. For them, any meaningful analysis of economic restructuring required an honest reckoning with race.

The VOP Engages the New Economy

In a sense, the VOP promised to revive the racial egalitarianism of Jesse Jackson's Rainbow Coalition in a program of economic democracy. In the pages of its magazine, *Virginia.Organizing*, the VOP critically investigated the social and economic policies of the era. Started in 1995 as a modest newsletter, by 2006 the magazine had grown into a thirty-two-page publication that circulated to more than eight thousand subscribers. The "Understanding the

Economy" column became an intellectual space for critiquing the notion of market dominance in the modern South. The column evolved out of workshops conducted in places hard hit by industrial decline. Martinsville in southwest Virginia was one of them. A community in the foothills of the Appalachians, Martinsville was emblematic of the textile-dependent southern town. Between 1998 and 2000 it lost two of its major textile employers. In December 1999, Tultex, the town's third-largest employer, declared bankruptcy, throwing forty-three hundred people out of work. Monumental unemployment claims, swamped local services, and the pending loss of $700,000 in annual revenue and $600,000 in water fees pushed the town of Martinsville to the brink. The town was reduced to offering "Free Land for Jobs" to any company that would fill the gap left by the collapse of the textile and apparels manufacturers. This was stunning evidence that in Virginia, the blessings of the new technology economy were, to put it mildly, unevenly distributed.[41]

The VOP targeted communities such as Martinsville because their experience stood in such stark contrast to the Pollyanna sermons of the New Economy boosters. "Press accounts say the economy is going great guns: low unemployment, low inflation, ample credit, record profits, a soaring stock market," Szakos and VOP organizer Ben Thacker-Gwaltney mused in 1998. "But are these good times producing prosperity and security for average Virginians?" The answer from Martinsville residents was a resounding no, and this was before the traumatic bankruptcy of Tultex, a major textile employer in Henry County.[42]

By educating their readers in the economic realities of the era, the VOP challenged the myth of market benevolence. They questioned what economist Ellen Frank has described as the "obscure and confusing economic arguments about finance" that prevent "discussion or even consideration of policies that might generate a more egalitarian distribution of the economy's output."[43] The VOP used its magazine to challenge the assumption that the economic rules were fixed and inflexible. By informing participants "about major economic trends—from the surge in income inequality to the growing power of financial investors over a broad range of economic decisions," the VOP questioned the basic axioms of the market ideology. For example, in January 1998, in the midst of the decade's high-tech hysteria, Thacker-Gwaltney and Szakos published a graph based on data in the Economic Report of the President showing that, in 1996 dollars, average hourly earnings had slid from $13.60 to $11.82. Equally compelling, they used Department of Commerce data to produce a bar graph illustrating a 64 percent increase in corporate profits between 1989 and 1995; in the same period, wages had increased by only 18 percent. From the analysis of state economic development programs to an assessment of the social impact of Federal Reserve Board policies to an examination of declining wages in the New Economy era, VOP activists sought to demystify the sources of working-class insecurity. At the same time, they offered concrete recommendations for resisting predatory capitalism at the community level.[44]

No less important, the organization addressed the moral and philosophical underpinnings of the New Economy. Ben Thacker-Gwaltney and Ellen Ryan, the principal authors of "Understanding the Economy," exposed the "values behind different approaches to organizing economic life." The economic system did not function according to immutable laws that only the chair of the Federal Reserve Board could discern. Cutting through the rhetoric of entrepreneurial liberation, the VOP cited a Department of Commerce report to document the disparity between rising profits and wages. That was distressing enough, considering the claims that turbo-capitalism was blazing a path to consumer utopia. Yet VOP editors cited the same report to show that prices had increased by 22 percent, leaving working people behind the cost-of-living curve. Beyond the pages of the magazine, the VOP encouraged participants in a Martinsville "Understanding the Economy" seminar to imagine that they were the founding mothers and fathers of a mythical "Free State of Henry." Coordinators asked them to draft economic guidelines for their community—in effect, an economic bill of rights. By critically investigating the current economic order, participants in the seminar broke free of the ideological straitjacket that bound average southerners.[45]

The authors of "Understanding the Economy" highlighted the discrepancy between the rhetoric of limitless economic opportunity and the lived experience of insecurity. When the Center of Budget and Policy Priorities reported an increasing income gap in Virginia in 1998, the VOP made it the focus of its July edition. Income disparities between the top fifth of families and those on the lower and middle end of the scale had grown in each state. In Virginia in the mid-1990s, the richest 20 percent of families with children enjoyed incomes eleven times larger than those of the poorest 20 percent. From the 1970s to the 1990s, the poorest fifth of Virginia families saw their incomes slide by 11 percent. Over the same period, the wealthiest fifth enjoyed a 23 percent income gain. Income disparities had increased despite the celebrated economic expansion of the Reagan era. According to Szakos and the VOP, however, pro-labor policies and government intervention could "influence the distribution of income" and change tax policies in a fashion that would "mitigate the effects on families of the pre-tax income distribution."[46]

While the VOP organized local communities, it tapped into dissident undercurrents at the national level. It supported progressive organizations such as United for a Fair Economy, ACORN, and the Center of Budget and Policy

Priorities, disseminating their ideas and applying them to local circumstances. It enjoyed particularly close relations with progressive intellectuals such as social critic Barbara Ehrenreich and novelist Barbara Kingsolver. Thacker-Gwaltney and Szakos expressly incorporated the discourse of political economy into their social commentary. Their analysis, like that of the critics of NAFTA and the WTO, reflected an understanding of the connection between the local experience of economic insecurity and the global functioning of finance capitalism. Exploring the "basics" of market liberalization, the editors examined how multinational corporations operated "subsidiaries in many countries," including the United States. They outlined the connection between foreign investment and the boom-and-bust cycle in the Southeast Asian market. They analyzed the social costs of corporate investment in the maquiladoras of northern Mexico, where companies operated factories that took "advantage of cheap labor and low costs." Financial speculation had wrought havoc in the form of currency devaluation in developing countries.[47]

According to the editors, the World Trade Organization and the International Monetary Fund were not abstract bogeymen. Instead, they had presided over the decline of very real American labor standards. The WTO functioned as a "watchdog making sure that the flow of cheap labor from poor countries continues." According to Thacker-Gwaltney, Federal Reserve Board policies and welfare reform seemed to be motivated by the desire to drive wages down in order to make American workers competitive. Workers had to respond by strengthening unions in Virginia and the United States. At the same time, they had to organize workers in export-oriented countries and forge citizens' coalitions that would advocate for national economic planning. The editors repeatedly stressed the global context of the state's growing uncertainties. "The connections between the WTO and the global economy flow right through our state, and Tultex is the proof." Even so, trade reform was not enough; workers needed a living wage to "fight against overcapacity and deflation in worker pay."[48] Nearly alone in Virginia, Szakos and the VOP explored heterodox economic territory by taking on inflation, the taboo of American monetary policy and the cornerstone of fiscal conservatism. Inflation was negligible, Thacker-Gwaltney argued, "since overcapacity creates the exact opposite, deflation. This will mean lower returns on investments, but stock prices on Wall Street could probably use a healthy dose of realism anyway."[49] Thacker-Gwaltney was anticipating the deflationary trend that would vex the American economy in the new century.

The VOP bolstered its call for labor rights by demanding tax reform and federal monetary policies that assisted working Americans. It advocated an end to corporate welfare that "subsidizes the rapid moves of multinational factories from place to place and country to country." Since profit motivated investment decisions, the VOP called for tax policies that discouraged corporate transience. The VOP also advocated a state-level Earned Income Tax Credit and the elimination of regressive sales taxes. More than this, it appealed for Federal Reserve policies that would benefit average working people. Szakos and the VOP argued that investment in community development projects would do more to help "low and moderate-income Virginians" than odes to personal responsibility. Challenging the economic orthodoxy that privileged investors over wage earners, the VOP insisted that the modest wage gains of the late 1990s should not become the pretext for imposing interest-rate hikes.[50]

The Long Reach of the Southern Past

Unlike many southern champions of the New Economy, the VOP drew the connection between globalization and the region's historical experience. In 1999, at the height of the free-market bonanza, Thacker-Gwaltney and Ryan wrote that "Thirty years ago, globalization in the American South occurred as domestic and international corporations moved in to take advantage of corporate welfare, cheap labor and cheap land." That pattern continued into the early 1990s, they argued, but the transitory character of external investment had become chronically apparent by then. Modern communications and distribution systems meant that corporations no longer cared "where they are located, as long as their costs are kept low. So many of the factories which the South gained from other areas have now moved on to other countries."[51] The experience of Martinsville and Danville seemed to support that conclusion.[52]

Placing social movement unionism at the centerpiece of its reform agenda, the VOP advocated for a collective response to market primacy. It called on "labor unions, citizens groups, non-profit agencies and religious institutions" to demand "labor rights, including decent wages and the right to organize."[53] The social-movement style of community organizing proved particularly appealing in the "right to work" South. Not only had unions calcified as vehicles of social reform, but they faced seemingly insurmountable obstacles in the notoriously anti-union region. Virginia Democrats may have endorsed the right-to-work mantra—in 1991, Governor Douglas Wilder told a Washington, D.C., current affairs magazine that "We are a right-to-work state, which means we are not slowed down by strikes and things of that nature"—but the VOP argued that organizing workers was vital to democratic reform.[54]

The VOP did not mechanically invoke race in every discussion of the economy. Instead, it tried to foster an atmosphere in which the evidence of persistent racial inequality became part of any analysis of political economy.

For example, the VOP worked relentlessly to convince the Federal Reserve Bank of Richmond to establish an advisory mechanism that would address "low-income and working class people." That effort proved successful. Yet the contemporary observer would have to have been willfully naive not to grasp that this was aimed principally at assisting Richmond's black working poor and unemployed. The announcement of a new United for a Fair Economy chapter in southwest Virginia in the January 1998 edition was notable enough on its own. Yet juxtaposed to a news item about the decision of the Charlottesville Labor Action Group to concentrate on a living wage campaign at UVA, it took on a more profound meaning. No less significant, it ran alongside a photograph of a VOP-sponsored "youth diversity workshop" in Charlottesville in which twenty young people learned "to work and live together across racial lines." Workplace justice and racial equality were inextricably connected. Similarly, a January 2002 article on the local economic benefits of a living wage was not explicitly racial. Even so, the accompanying photograph of "Unity," a chapter of the Tenants' and Workers' Support Committee holding an interfaith rally in Alexandria in support of child-care providers who were trying to obtain health benefits, spoke volumes about the organization's vision of economic democracy. Featuring African American, Hispanic, and white men in a brightly festooned church, the scene also captured the VOP's commitment to social-movement unionism. Living wages, a fair economy, racial reconciliation: these were the issues that bound the VOP together. It was a vision of grassroots organizing that few labor unions embraced.[55]

Reconciling with race meant examining southern history. The contributors to *Virginia.Organizing* consistently reminded their readership of Virginia's troubled past. Contemporary Virginia echoed a tradition of racial exploitation and working-class subordination. "The legacy of slavery, the plantation system, the Civil War and Reconstruction haunt the burgeoning new economy in which a few entrepreneurs and investors get wealthy at the expense of politically disenfranchised workers," wrote Ben Thacker-Gwaltney in a provocative article published in 2000. The state economy might have ranked twelfth out of fifty in "the rampaging new economy," he noted, but the evidence of continuity abounded. "While the economy appears to be booming, low wages in this historically low-wage state continue. Hostility to unions—even public employees are prohibited from collective bargaining by law—has long provided Virginia with a cheap labor force that benefits little from economic growth," he argued. However, Thacker-Gwaltney consistently juxtaposed race and labor, emphasizing how they were woven together in the southern experience. This binary relationship was the foundation for an economic system that preserved forms of racial exclusion while dividing the working class. Technology may have may leaped forward, but "politics has remained pretty much the same. Violence, poll taxes and literary tests for voter registration left a legacy of disenfranchised voters." That pattern had been perpetuated by "waiting periods for voter registration and voter identification cards." Virginia law prohibited thousands from exercising the franchise because of felony convictions. Prisons had become a growth industry as the war on drugs incarcerated more and more African American males. In a state that prohibited parole, imposed mandatory minimum sentencing, and executed prisoners on a monthly basis, Thacker-Gwaltney believed that the echoes of Virginia's racist past were very loud indeed.[56]

Privileging the Corporate Citizen

Szakos and his staff also trained a critical lens on the lavish incentives doled out to corporations seeking lower operating costs in Virginia. Corporate tax breaks, they argued in January 1999, reflected the assumption that "what is good for the corporations will also be good for the communities in which they are located." State and local governments make risky investments in a desperate effort to generate jobs. The beneficiaries of some of the largest payouts were often the same companies that had been "downsizing like mad for the last 10 years, cutting jobs, factories, and businesses in an effort to become more streamlined and efficient." Virginians were only beginning to realize that companies that received generous giveaways were "also perfectly willing to shut that factory down and move it somewhere with cheaper labor, lower operating costs or higher tax breaks." Here was a lesson in global capitalism that rarely appeared in mainstream newspapers.[57]

In a state largely bereft of progressive media, the VOP provided a vital forum for alternative journalism. Yet *Virginia.Organizing* ultimately flowed from the VOP's commitment to grassroots community activism. It was this investment in social-movement unionism that fueled its critique of the inimical consequences of free-market ideology. Through its community-level organizing, political lobbying, and critical journalism, the VOP helped to regenerate a social democratic movement that had withered since the 1970s.

From Ideas to Action

The group's commitment to racial amelioration was manifested in its "Dismantling Racism" workshops. The workshops rarely attracted more than twenty-five participants at a time, but for VOP board member Kathy Rowles, the diminutive numbers belied their significance. "Before we started meeting and having workshops, not many people were willing to talk about racism here," she observed. Harking back to the tradition of the Highlander Folk

School, the VOP tried to create a forum in which blacks and whites could discuss an issue distorted beyond recognition in the fun house of Virginia politics. The workshops directly challenged the dominant color-blind dogma of the 1990s. Participants were encouraged to confront "racism in the schools and in their workplaces," to become agents of reform rather than the objects of remote policy decisions.[58] They provided an opportunity for blacks and whites to move beyond the polemics of the Arthur Ashe statue debate.

By 1999 the VOP had established a presence on a range of social justice questions where race and labor intersected. That year, the Lee County chapter successfully challenged a jury-selection process that permitted "five white men to choose their friends for the jury pool, eliminating all people of color and effectively eliminating most low-income residents." It won a random selection process and the appointment of the first African American jury commissioner in Lee County. Collaborating with labor unions and citizen groups, the VOP pressured the Federal Reserve Bank of Richmond to establish a Community Development Advisory Council that would consult on matters relating to "low income and working-class people."[59] By 2002 the organization had conducted "Dismantling Racism," "Understanding the Economy," and community-organizer training workshops for 1,031 Virginians. More than this, it had launched a statewide affordable housing campaign. It participated in a coalition to halt legislation that would have prohibited localities from endorsing living-wage ordinances. It also waged a campaign to pressure the Courtyard Marriot in Charlottesville to pay a living wage, and decisively pressured the Charlottesville City Council to enact a living-wage ordinance. According to the VOP, the Charlottesville ordinance had effectively raised the wages of low-income workers by more than $9.3 million annually.[60]

By 2004 the VOP had become the leading vehicle of progressive reform in the state. It provided the linchpin for the Virginia Fair Wage Alliance, a coalition of religious, community, and labor organizations determined to raise Virginia's abysmally low minimum wage of $5.15 an hour. The VOP helped secure a state Earned Income Tax Credit for the working poor. The VOP mailed voting guides to nearly one hundred thousand citizens in 2004, and coordinated eighteen reform groups in a campaign to raise awareness about the negative impact of tax policy on local communities and the working poor. The VOP held tax/revenue workshops that attracted between six hundred and seven hundred participants over a two-year period. As organizer Ellen Ryan explains, the tax campaign reflected the organization's joint commitment to education and local democracy: "The aim was to make understanding taxes as simple as possible for as many people as possible so they could feel confident and well-informed in arguing the merits of tax reform, talking about it among themselves, with friends, neighbors, elected officials, and through letters to the editor in local papers, press conferences, and the like." Joe Szakos echoed these sentiments. The workshops on the economy "serve a strategic purpose in having more people understand the relationship between taxes/revenue and government expenditures. We deal with concepts of adequacy, equity and fairness in a practical way." These incremental victories underlined the potential for reviving a social democratic movement.[61]

While the organization examined issues ranging from tax law reform to environmental protection, it sought to develop a united front around the idea of working-class rights. That search for a coherent ideology and common political objectives was evident at its 1998 convention. There, Mandy Carter from Southerners on New Ground and Jim Leaman of the Virginia AFL-CIO raised the question of how the VOP could build a multiracial working-class movement that incorporated women, the poor, and citizens of alternative sexual orientation on an equal basis. "It's more than changing hearts and minds on cultural things," observed Carter. "It's also about changing policy. We need to look at the things that will get us to the common table." Leaman echoed Carter's views, advocating for more than "paid organizers." The movement needed "bridge builders, to get away from our safe space. . . . We need to organize across all spectrums. We need to band together." Although the VOP's nonprofit status hampered its ability to spearhead a direct challenge to the "right to work" law in Virginia, the 1998 convention signaled its determination to identify issues that "could be a unifying force among the various constituencies with which the organization works." It resolved to focus on living-wage campaigns, the Earned Income Tax Credit, the removal of the sales tax on food, and "accountability" from the banking industry and the Federal Reserve Bank of Richmond.[62]

Important as these initiatives were, it was the VOP's economic workshops that demonstrated its grasp of the connection between intellectual liberation and social reform. Through its "Understanding the Economy" initiative, the VOP sought to educate ordinary Virginians in the overarching economic realities of their era. The VOP borrowed the idea from United for a Fair Economy, a national nonprofit organization dedicated to economic democracy and community development. Titled "The Growing Divide: Inequality and the Roots of Economic Insecurity," the United for a Fair Economy workshops tried to dispel common economic myths and illuminate the local implications of financial policies. In 1999 the VOP sent a group of organizers to the workshop. Denise Smith, an African American founding member of the VOP who attended "The Growing Divide" session, found it transformative. "What I discovered through this workshop is that I know more than I thought about the growing divide in this country and what economic insecurity actually means by living through these times." The United for a Fair Economy workshop helped her to understand "the effects of what [was] happening in my own life and those of people around me . . . for once I can see how maybe we can make a difference just by sharing and identifying what is going on in this country." For Smith and probably most others, the workshops became a modern equivalent of the Populist sub-alliances, a vehicle for breaking out of the intellectual isolation of the New Economy era. Like the Populists, United for a Fair Economy and the VOP understood that only education in the rubrics of the economic system could persuade people that they were not the victims of incomprehensible and uncontrollable forces. It was in these workshops that the VOP most directly fostered an "emergent oppositional discourse," a "counter-hegemonic" analysis of the political and economic order. Education could become the catalyst for political action. Smith's recollections demonstrate that it could also convince people of the legitimacy of cooperative action.[63]

Although the workshops simulated the freedom schools of the civil rights movement and the community organizing projects of Students for a Democratic Society, they also extended the work of more recent southern ventures. In the 1980s the Black Workers for Justice started offering "workers' schools" in the predominantly black neighborhoods of North Carolina. In these sessions, students explored the connection between the civil rights movement and the labor movement. This dedication to "consciousness-raising and intellectual development," notes sociologist Vanessa Tait, characterizes the organizing strategies of the workers' centers, which have become vital to social justice unionism in the United States. Developing political awareness, a grasp of economic fundamentals, and a sense of political possibilities has been essential to campaigns ranging from shop-floor organizing to community-level mobilization. Workers' centers throughout the South have offered classes on labor history, gender inequities, legal issues, and environmental law as part of an effort to broaden the perspectives of the working poor. The VOP workshops mirrored these programs.[64]

What distinguished the VOP's campaign, however, was its determination to educate a multiracial coalition *and* challenge the economic orthodoxies of the New Economy era. The session held in Cape Charles on the Eastern Shore exemplified these impulses. With fifteen participants, the VOP and staff from an area housing reform group examined the economic power brokers in the area. They explicitly linked discriminatory bank lending, housing policies, seasonal unemployment, and low wages to a "local power structure that excludes low-income people and people of color." Race and labor were inextricably connected. The VOP also encouraged participants to examine the impact of the economic boom on the state. The group discovered that Richmond and Charlottesville had done quite well in the New Economy. By contrast, southwest Virginia, the Southside, the Northern Neck, and the Eastern Shore endured "near double-digit unemployment." (In fact, as *Virginia.Organizing* would later report, southwest Virginia endured the worst. In 1998, when the state unemployment rate stood at 2.9 percent, Buchanan County posted an unemployment rate of 14.1 percent; in Dickenson County it was 15.7 percent.)[65] The booming economy had lifted a few boats, but it had left many others utterly shipwrecked. Organizers repeatedly reinforced the idea that only a living wage could alleviate the economic insecurity of working-class Virginians. Group members agreed that wages would have to reach at least $7.50 an hour before workers could escape poverty. Organizers were probably not shocked to learn that food stamps, subsidized housing, and Medicaid were standard fare for those whose wages fell below the living wage.[66]

Workshop leaders provided an economic analysis that contested the orthodoxies of the mainstream media. Participants learned that interest rate decisions made in Washington directly influenced unemployment, wages, the country's debt, and inflation. Federal Reserve Board decisions to raise interest rates were designed to limit inflation and ensure high returns on stock portfolios. The same decisions, however, translated into unemployment, lower wages, and economic contraction. For Denise Wortham, the workshops provided "a lot of insight. I learned things which I didn't know before which I can take back to my community." More than any of the neoliberal proselytizing that appeared in the pages of *The Economist* or in the *Richmond Times-Dispatch*, the VOP educated black, Hispanic, and white activists in the intersection of politics and economics. Participants began to understand that decisions made at the highest levels of economic power affected them directly. Simultaneously, they began to grasp that many of those decisions were inimical to their most basic interests.[67]

Propelled by this kind of community organizing, African American, white, and Hispanic workers cooperated in a series of campaigns that illustrated the possibilities for social unionism. Working-class Latinos did not silently accept exploitation. In the most notable examples, Latino workers in Los Angeles and New York organized in the needle trades and joined the Justice for Janitors movement. It was the living-wage movement, however, that presented the most powerful demonstration of interracial solidarity. Beginning with the successful campaign for a living wage in Baltimore in 1994, the movement to require private businesses receiving public funds to pay their workers a decent wage took off. By 2001 as many as sixty-four living-wage campaigns were under way across the country. For most activists, the objective was to extract a wage that would lift a family of four above the poverty line. That meant a target of at least $8.50 an hour. For companies that failed to provide any health benefits, living-wage proponents demanded $10.00 an hour.[68] The VOP became directly involved in the Charlottesville campaign, both at the University of Virginia and at the Courtyard by Marriot Hotel in town.

In Virginia, the living-wage campaign evolved out of earlier efforts to achieve interracial solidarity and community control. In Alexandria, the Tenants' and Workers' Support Committee (TWSC, Comite de Apoyo de Inquilinos y Trabajadores), spearheaded the movement. A community action organization, the TWSC was established in 1986 when developers threatened to evict hundreds of low-income black and Salavadoran residents to accommodate upscale condominiums. They adopted a community-based form of direct action modeled on their experiences in El Salvador. The TWSC was able to protect approximately two thousand units of affordable housing. By 1996 some three hundred families from this low-wage community had established the Arlandria/Chirilagua Housing Cooperative. It was a limited-equity, affordable housing project that demonstrated the possibilities for interracial organizing.[69] The TWSC campaign created the momentum for a wider movement, including a campaign to organize two thousand poorly paid hotel workers in Alexandria and to promote a neighborhood planning project.

Most importantly, it propelled the TWSC into a living-wage campaign in northern Virginia. Alexandria offered an appropriate location for the campaign. Although the city became a showcase of New Economy, high-tech innovation, it simultaneously harbored the suburb of Arlandria/Chirilagua, where some ten thousand Latino and African American residents scraped together a meager existence. In 1997–98, the median income for a family of four was approximately $27,000, or 55 percent of the overall median of $50,100 for the city. That figure also represented only 40 percent of northern Virginia's median of $65,600.[70] Affiliating with the VOP, the TWSC's living-wage campaign became part of a growing reform coalition that synthesized the issues of race and class. The VOP lent its personnel, its resources, and the pages of *Virginia.Organizing* to the campaign. By printing almost half of its quarterly magazine in Spanish, reporting on the movement, and contributing personnel and resources to the effort, the VOP gave the movement an invaluable platform.

When the TWSC launched a living-wage rally on Labor Day in 1998, it was clear that the campaign had taken on the mantle of social-movement unionism. The demonstration exemplified the unification of organized labor, community organizations, local residents, and churches in a drive for basic social reform. In 1998 the TWSC and several other groups took to the streets in a protest against exploitive wages. Carrying signs reading "Salario Justo Ahora" and "End Poverty Wages," hundreds of Hispanic and African American workers disrupted the tranquility of corporate Alexandria in a militant show of strength. The Iron Workers Local no. 5 as well as the Communications Workers 2222, Grace Episcopal Church, the Beverly Hills United Church, and the VOP joined the TWSC. The TWSC reached out to the Teamsters, who were then organizing cleaning workers. They joined forces with the Iron Workers, who were struggling against non-unionized hires. They also demonstrated their support for striking flight attendants. Eventually, eighteen labor unions and seven churches joined the coalition. Although Hispanic workers dominated the movement, white labor unionists and liberal activists joined as mediators and organizers. Organized labor and organized religion both joined the movement, demonstrating the potential to restore not only the connection between racial equality and economic democracy but also the connection between social justice and spiritual faith.[71]

Living-wage activists took to the streets the following Labor Day while labor unionists, service workers, and liberal Christians descended on the offices of Arlington's local legislators. They sent more than six hundred postcards, signed by low-income residents during a door-to-door campaign, to city councilors. They delivered living-wage petitions that carried thousands of signatures. They conducted a mass telephone lobbying campaign, sometimes calling councilors directly from the shop floor. Legislative pressure supplemented the direct-action tactics. Movements for social reform had few victories to count in the 1990s, but this was one of them. On June 18, 2000, the city council voted 6-0 in favor of a living wage that paid workers a minimum of $9.84 an hour.[72]

It would be misleading to suggest that this was a VOP victory; it was the TWSC that spearheaded the campaign. Yet the Northern Virginia Living Wage Coalition had become the vehicle of this movement, and the VOP was its linchpin. Like the VOP, the TWSC advocated a set of values that offered a cooperative alternative to the competitive individualism of the New Economy era. The purpose of the organization was "to develop the collective power of Northern Virginia low-income tenants and workers—particularly immigrant and African American working-class women—and to fight institutional racism, develop collective ownership and control of community resources and build multi-racial understanding and collaboration."[73] The living-wage drive electrified the progressive alliance the VOP had built, extending it beyond workshops, training sessions, and newsletters. The VOP had established a network of communications and organizations that made it possible to forge a wider coalition.

Along with the TWSC and other community-based organizations, the VOP sliced through the rhetoric of market triumphalism that accompanied the drive for NAFTA. Instead of echoing the platitudes of risk-taking entrepreneurialism, movement organizers identified the human costs of the northern Virginia miracle. "Even though our economy is supposed to be doing better than ever," observed a representative of the Northern Virginia Living Wage Coalition, "too many workers are working longer hours, running between part-time jobs and still struggling to stay afloat. While paying poverty wages, companies benefited from "cities, counties, and states [that] doled out lucrative service contracts, industrial revenue bonds, tax breaks, and other forms of public subsidies."[74] The movement produced an interfaith rally on December 10, Human Rights Day. On Martin Luther King Jr. Day it launched a march to city hall that demonstrated a powerful fusion of social gospel Christianity, economic democracy, and interracial unity.[75]

Establishing something of a common ground, the coalition built a grassroots movement that fused the cause of organized labor and community mobilization. Gyula Nagy, organizer for the living-wage campaign, explained how important these relations of mutuality were. Sharing resources and expertise, building common membership lists, and developing a united communications front was critical for their success: "Our coalition-building committee met face-to-face with leaders of targeted groups. We pushed leaders to contribute: money, mobilizing members, printing flyers, or (for unions) lending us activists on lost-time pay. We visited leaders monthly, developing relationships, always asking what solidarity they needed from us." The AFL-CIO assisted by mobilizing its members to lobby the General Assembly to dismiss any bills that opposed the living wage. In the middle of this mix was the VOP, lending the pages of *Virginia.Organizing* and a coterie of activists to the movement.[76]

Emerging Discourses and the Origins of a Movement

The market-oriented ideology made enormous headway in the 1990s, but the Virginia Organizing Project demonstrated the possibilities for an emergent and oppositional discourse. The debate over multilateral trade deals injected a language of political economy into American public discourse that could be turned against the drive for corporate restructuring. Drawing a tactical and philosophical heritage rooted in the "long civil rights movement," the VOP established the outlines of a multiracial coalition committed to economic democracy. Through public advocacy, economic analysis, and grassroots organizing, it explored the possibilities of a biracial labor alliance. Interviewing labor unionists about the efficacy of workers' centers, Vanessa Tait highlighted the obstacles confronting any new workers' movement. "Sure, they organize the Chinese community, or low-wage Latino workers . . . but what about building unity with other workers, across ethnic and racial divisions?"[77] By organizing on a consistently multiracial basis around the question of working-class rights, the VOP moved toward bridging those gaps. Instead of focusing exclusively on cultural politics or identity, it made racial equality the sine qua non of the social justice movement.

For all of its accomplishments, the VOP continued to struggle against its own limitations as well as the considerable forces arrayed against it. Like the New Left of the 1960s, it excelled in the area of moral commitment but often lacked an overarching theoretical perspective or political strategy. Its relationship to organized labor, particularly mainstream unions, was hesitant and distant at best. Its multiple commitments sometimes diluted the organization's energies and communicated the notion that any and all social causes had equal merit. Its community-oriented focus often militated against the need to build alliances between local and national efforts. Its nonprofit status and ideological ambiguity prevented it from engaging in direct political or labor organizing.

Yet these limitations also reflect the fact that the VOP emerged in an era of militant market fundamentalism, in a region decidedly hospitable to the new religious conservatism, and in a state viscerally hostile to working-class activism, particularly of the multiracial variety. The VOP was developing an "emergent discourse" amid conflicting evidence of maverick hi-tech investment and steadily growing wage disparities. While the media highlighted the wonders of a wired universe and the benefits of multilateral trade deals, the VOP carved out a program that addressed the social consequences of relentless corporate downsizing and the shredding of the social safety net. At the same time, it had to situate itself in the tendentious racial politics of the era. Confronting the formidable cultural authority of southern conservatism, the VOP struggled to articulate a comprehensive program. But in its analysis of the impact of corporate-led globalization on working-class Virginians, it helped fashion a critical perspective anchored in the bedrock of economic justice. The VOP scrupulously avoided privileging class over race, economics over "identity." In addition, it offered more than a discourse. The VOP launched campaigns that made measurable improvements in the lives of black, white, and Hispanic workers. It demonstrated that building an interracial movement of the working poor was possible. That it did so in the very heartland of the conservative revival—the rural South—should not be overlooked.

In 2008, reflecting on his years as a community organizer, Joe Szakos explained how the political context of the period influenced the early VOP. "The strength of community-based organizing has long been understood by those in the conservative wing of American politics," he wrote in *Lessons from the Field*. "The Moral Majority, the Christian Coalition, even the Republican Party have used grassroots rural organizing to shift the balance of power in the country's heartland." It was in the 1990s that conservative Christians launched a massive drive to mobilize rural southerners "into a powerful force to support a right-wing agenda." From churches to radio programs to rural social networks, the conservative movement attacked not only the cultural manifestations of the 1960s rights revolution but the social and political reforms of the civil rights era.[78]

Szakos lamented the decline of the social contract in modern America. What distressed him most was the sense that rural Virginians had been sold a bill of goods. "Those in the right wing knew—and some progressives have known all along—that there is power in rural communities. The cynical organizing of the right, though, has exploited this power for its own agenda, convincing rural folks to support policies that were not in their own best interests." What did progressive organizers offer, by contrast? "True community organizing encourages people to work for positive change for the whole community, to reach solutions that benefit the largest number of people."[79] While the prescription for change was vague, the VOP had effectively challenged the New Economy maxim that entrepreneurial zeal would overcome the dislocations of corporate downsizing and outsourcing. Through its analysis of economic affairs, the VOP rekindled the notion that any economic system must be humane, that collective action is legitimate, and that government responsibility is the litmus test of political legitimacy. That was no small feat in a state where elites venerated privatization and the neo-states' rights agenda. Szakos and his supporters did more than foster an oppositional discourse; they educated working-class Virginians in the economic and racial realities of the era.

The VOP produced the foundations for a broader movement. Yet for all its accomplishments, the VOP provided the model, not the instrument, of wider working-class response. Only a militant, more expressly class-conscious, and explicitly political organization could generate the kind of countervailing force that Martin Luther King Jr. had hoped the Poor People's Movement would become. In the wake of the economic crisis, there was some evidence that just such a movement was emerging. In 2009, and again in January 2010, more than one hundred activists converged in downtown Richmond as part of the Virginia People's Assembly. African American, Latino, native white, and immigrant activists raised a banner demanding jobs, justice, and peace. Not only was the coalition multiracial, it was multi-organizational. Like the VOP, it incorporated labor, community groups, antiwar organizations, religious activists, and civil rights groups into a demonstration against cuts to state jobs and public services. Again, like the VOP, it drew participants from across Virginia, from Roanoke to Petersburg, Hampton Roads to northern Virginia. Most distinctively, and even more explicitly than the VOP, the People's Assembly emphasized the unifying experience of class. The online compendium *Truthout* captured the significance of the People's Assembly: "Multi-issue coalitions are not uncommon in the US, but what's unique about the VPA is its politics and organizational structure. While embracing a wide range of causes, the coalition emphasized the common issue of class, actively promoting the interests of working people and the poor."[80] The People's Assembly, however, was a short-lived affair. At the end of the first decade of the new century, the question still remained whether organized labor, or a group such as the tenants' and workers' committee, or the Virginia People's Assembly, or some other collection of committed Virginians could translate the VOP's achievements into a mass movement. If the dramatic uprising in Wisconsin has taught us anything, it is the necessity of moving beyond a politics of spectacle, of joyous demonstrations and inspiring speeches, to a politics of action. As the Tenants' and Workers' Support Committee understood, such a politics must originate in a shrewd and calculated appreciation of just how much power the working class really does possess, even in Virginia.

Notes

1. The notion of emergent and dominant discourses is ultimately drawn from Raymond Williams, but the current discussion is informed by historian Mary E. Triece's linking of "emergent oppositional" discourses to the community organizing of women in the housewives and industrial auxiliary movement of the 1930s. See her *On the Picket Line: Strategies of Working-Class Women during the Depression* (Urbana: University of Illinois Press, 2007), 3–6, 141–42.

2. Joe Szakos and Ladelle McWhorter, "Organizing for the Common Good: The Action Is at the State Level," 18, unpublished paper in author's possession.

3. Ibid., 1–5; Joe Szakos to author, e-mail, March 25, 2010.

4. Szakos and McWhorter, "Organizing for the Common Good," 1–5.

5. Ed Gillespie and Bob Schellhas, eds., *Contract with America: Gingrich, Armey, and the House Republicans* (New York: Random House, 1994), 128.

6. Quoted in Godfrey Hodgson, *More Equal Than Others: America from Nixon to the New Century* (Princeton: Princeton University Press, 2004), 50.

7. Doug Henwood, *After the New Economy* (New York: New Press, 2003), 214–15.

8. Louis Uchitelle, *The Disposable American: Layoffs and Their Consequences* (New York: Knopf, 2006), 139.

9. Robert Pollin, *Contours of Descent: U.S. Economic Fractures and the Landscape of Global Austerity*, 2nd ed. (New York: Verso Press, 2005), 77. The most famous expression

of the vision of New Economy emancipation appeared in Michael Hammer and Douglas Champy's *Reengineering the Corporation: A Manifesto for Business Revolution* (New York: Harper Collins, 1994).

10. On the connection between the New Economy rhetoric and the movement for an unregulated market economy, see David M. Kotz and Martin H. Wolfson, "Déjà Vu All Over Again: The 'New' Economy in Historical Perspective," *Labor Studies Journal* 28 (Winter 2004): 25–44; and Hodgson, *More Equal Than Others*, 108.

11. James Bacon, "Economic Exodus," *Virginia Business*, July 1991, 55.

12. David R. Goldfield, *Still Fighting the Civil War: The American South and Southern History* (Baton Rouge: Louisiana State University Press, 2002), 277–78.

13. Table VA-4, "Virginia Employment Status by Demographic Groups, 1997 and 2000," *State Profiles: The Population and Economy of Each U.S. State*, ed. Helmut F. Wendel, 2nd ed. (Lanham, Md.: Bernan, 2002), 494.

14. Algernon Austin, "Unequal Unemployment: Racial Disparities by State Will Worsen in 2010," Economic Policy Institute no. 257, July 21, 2009, available at http://epi.3cdn.net/57b.

15. Amy Glasmeier and Priscilla Salant, "Low Skill Workers in Rural America Face Permanent Job Loss," Carsey Institute Policy Brief no. 2, Spring 2006, 3, available at http://www.carseyinstitute.unh.edu/publications/PB_displacedworkers_06.pdf.

16. "Virginia City Seeks 'Something Else,'" *Washington Times*, April 20, 2004.

17. Jane L. Collins, "Deterritorialization and Workplace Culture," *American Ethnologist* 29 (February 2002): 159. Writing in 2000, geographers Amy Glasmeier and Robin Leichenko offered this cautious assessment of the impact of trade liberalization: "the South's industry structure will face serious challenges from lower-cost locations from around the world. The more capital-intensive industries, such as textiles and machinery, will be encouraged to change locations as markets mature in developing countries." Nothing in the intervening years has occurred to reverse that trend. "From Free-Market Rhetoric to Free-Market Reality: The Future of the U.S. South in an Era of Globalization," in *Poverty or Development: Global Restructuring and Regional Transformations in the U.S. South and the Mexican South*, ed. Richard Tardinico and Mark B. Rosenberg (New York: Routledge, 2000), 35.

18. Timothy J. Minchin, *Fighting against the Odds: A History of Southern Labor since World War II* (Gainesville: University Press of Florida, 2005), 164.

19. Minchin notes that southern manufacturers benefited from a regional wage differential that set pay at 40 to 50 percent discount for those operating below the Mason-Dixon Line throughout the twentieth century. Ibid., 184.

20. The example of the New Orleans General Strike of 1892, and the role that biracial unions played in it, stands out as one of the most prominent exceptions to the rule of white working-class racism. See Sharon Smith, *Subterranean Fire: A History of Working-Class Radicalism in the United States* (Chicago: Haymarket Books, 2006), 36–40.

21. Szakos and McWhorter, "Organizing for the Common Good," 4, 21; "What Is the Virginia Organizing Project?" *News from the Virginia Organizing Project* 1 (December 1995): 4, 5; "Building Public Relationships: The Cornerstone of Our Approach," *News from the Virginia Organizing Project* 1 (February 1996): 1.

22. "VOP Holds Successful Founding Convention," *News from the Virginia Organizing Project* 2 (August 1997): 1–2.

23. W. Fitzhugh Brundage, *The Southern Past: A Clash of Race and Memory* (Cambridge: Belknap Press of Harvard University Press, 2005), 316–18, 337–38, quote on 318.

24. "Leadership Development in a Statewide Multi-Constituency Multi-Issue Organization," *Virginia.Organizing* 5 (July 2000): 6.

25. Goldfield, *Still Fighting the Civil War*, 290.

26. Jacquelyn Dowd Hall, "The Long Civil Rights Movement and the Political Uses of the Past," *Journal of American History* 91 (March 2005): 1237–38, quote on 1238; Michael K. Brown et al., *Whitewashing Race: The Myth of a Color-Blind Society* (Berkeley: University of California Press, 2003), 1–9.

27. Frank Atkinson, "The Realignment: Virginia GOP Develops Populist Appeal, But with a Generational Divide," *Richmond Times-Dispatch*, November 14, 1997.

28. Hodgson, *More Equal Than Others*, 193.

29. Brown et al., *Whitewashing Race*, 13.

30. Hall, "Long Civil Rights Movement," 1262.

31. Christine Chmura, "Global Competition Results in Loss of State Textile and Apparel Jobs," *Richmond Times-Dispatch*, October 16, 2000.

32. Robert H. Zieger, *For Jobs and Freedom: Race and Labor in America since 1865* (Lexington: University Press of Kentucky, 2007), 218.

33. U.S. Bureau of the Census, 2000, quoted in Barbara Ellen Smith, "The New Latino South: An Introduction," 7, A Joint Project of the Center for Research on Women at the University of Memphis, the Highlander Research and Education Center, and the Southern Regional Council, available at www.highlandercenter.org/pdf-files/new_latino_south.

34. Ibid., 8.

35. Michael Goldfield, "The Racial Divide and the Class Struggle in the United States," *Working USA: The Journal of Labor and Society* 11 (September 2008): 324–25.

36. Steven K. Ashby and C. J. Hawking, *Staley: The Fight for a New American Labor Movement* (Urbana: University of Illinois Press, 2009), 99–111, 194–211.

37. John D. French, "From the Suites to the Streets: The Unexpected Re-emergence of the 'Labor Question,' 1994–1999," *Labor History* 43 (2002): 303.

38. John Ralston Saul, "The Collapse of Globalism and the Rebirth of Nationalism," *Harper's*, March 2004, 34.

39. "Statement of Beliefs," *Virginia Organizing Project Founding Convention*, June 21, 1997, in author's possession. As economist Robert Pollin notes in *Contours of Descent*, "both the average wages for non-supervisory workers and the earnings of those in the lowest 10 percent decile of the wage distribution not only remained well below those of the Nixon/Ford and Carter administrations, but were actually lower even than those of the Reagan/Bush years." In addition, Pollin observes, "wage inequality . . . increased sharply during Clinton's tenure in office, even relative to the Republican heyday of the eighties" (42–43).

40. "Statement of Beliefs."

41. "A Change of Fortune: Loss of Biggest Employer Unravels Lives in Textile Town," *Virginian-Pilot*, February 20, 2000; "We're Rebounding: Jobless Rate Helps Martinsville Area Attract Businesses," *Richmond Times-Dispatch*, June 18, 2000; "Tultex a Virginia Victim of Free Trade," *Virginia.Organizing* 5 (January 2000): 8; Collins, "Deterritorialization and Workplace Culture," 156.

42. "Understanding the Economy," *Virginia.Organizing* 3 (January 1998): 26.

43. Ellen Frank, *The Raw Deal: How Myths and Misinformation about the Deficit, Inflation, and Wealth Impoverish America* (Boston: Beacon Press, 2004), 6.

44. "Understanding the Economy," *Virginia.Organizing* 3 (January 1998): 26–27.

45. Ibid., 27.

46. "Report Finds Income Inequality Growing," *Virginia.Organizing* 3 (July 1998): 10–11.

47. "Some Basics of Economic Globalization," *Virginia.Organizing* 4 (April 1999): 6–7.

48. "Tultex a Victim of Free Trade," *Virginia.Organizing* 5 (January 2000): 8.

49. Ibid., 7–8.

50. Ibid.

51. "Some Basics of Economic Globalization," *Virginia.Organizing* 4 (April 1999): 6.

52. If anything, the experience of Virginia's manufacturing workers would confirm what Glasmeier and Leichenko argue, namely, that "Because the U.S. South contains a disproportionate number of the nation's unskilled workers, it may be especially vulnerable to the long-run negative effects of trade liberalization." "From Free-Market Rhetoric to Free-Market Reality," 33.

53. "Some Basics of Economic Globalization," 6.

54. "Interview: L. Douglas Wilder," *Europe* 310 (October 1991): 33. Wilder's opinion was anything but an aberration for Virginia Democrats. In 1996, Democratic House of Delegates Majority Leader Richard Cranwell told the *Virginian-Pilot* that "we are not a liberal party; we're a moderate centrist party, conservative with taxpayers but fair on social issues." According to Cranwell, this position was completely consistent with the "greater allegiance to a conservative mindset" in Virginia. See "Commonwealth Conversation: Richard Cranwell," *Norfolk Virginian-Pilot*, October 16, 1996.

55. "Richmond Federal Reserve Bank Sets Up Community Dev. Advisory Council," *Virginia.Organizing* 4 (January 1999): 1, 26; "A Living Wage Makes Good Economic Sense for Local Communities," *Virginia.Organizing* 7 (January 2002): 12–13; "News from Other Groups in Virginia," *Virginia.Organizing* 3 (January 1998): 28–29.

56. "Leadership Development in a Statewide Multi-Constituency Multi-Issue Organization," *Virginia.Organizing* 5 (July 2000): 6.

57. "Corporate Welfare: Who Benefits?" *Virginia.Organizing* 4 (January 1999): 9.

58. "Lee Co. Chapter Works on Racism," *Virginia.Organizing* 3 (January 1998): 4.

59. "VOP Accomplishments," *Virginia.Organizing* 4 (January 1999): 6.

60. "VOP Accomplishment List Grew in 2001," *Virginia.Organizing* 7 (January 2002): 8.

61. "History, Accomplishments, and Current Projects of the Virginia Organizing Project," 2–6, September 12, 2006, unpublished report in author's possession, courtesy of Julie Blust; Ellen Ryan to author, e-mail, April 17, 2010; Joe Szakos to author, e-mail, April 9, 2010.

62. "Carter and Leaman Address 1998 VOP Convention," *Virginia.Organizing* 3 (July 1998): 3.

63. Denise Smith, "The Growing Divide: Inequality and the Roots of Economic Insecurity," *Virginia.Organizing* 4 (July 1999): 26–27. Jack Beatty stresses the importance that the Southern Alliance and the Populists placed on education. "No other radical movement in American history set such store by education. Striking autoworkers sat down. Civil rights activists marched. Alliance farmers learned." The kind of learning they engaged in was "counter-hegemonic," writes Beatty quoting Gramsci; the "counter-hegemonic" quality of

the United for a Fair Economy and Virginia Organizing Project workshops was equally powerful. *The Age of Betrayal: The Triumph of Money in America, 1865–1900* (New York: Random House, 2007), 321–24.

64. Vanessa Tait, *Poor Workers' Unions: Rebuilding Labor from Below* (Cambridge, Mass.: South End Press,) 146–47.

65. "Virginia Wages: Are We All Better Off?" *Virginia.Organizing* 5 (October 2000): 7.

66. "Understanding the Economy Workshop Held on Eastern Shore," *Virginia.Organizing* 4 (July 1999): 18–19.

67. Ibid., 19.

68. David Reynolds and Jen Kern, "Labor and the Living-Wage Movement," *Working USA: The Journal of Labor and Society* 5 (Winter 2001–2): 17–18.

69. "New Chapter, Affiliate Join VOP," *News from the Virginia Organizing Project* 2 (August 1997): 6; Janice Fine, *Worker Centers: Organizing Communities at the Edge of the Dream* (Ithaca: Cornell University Press, 2006), 191–92.

70. Dan Moshenberg, "Occupied Territories: Occupational Health and Citizenship in the Fifteenth Department, USA," *Interventions: International Journal of Postcolonial Studies* 8 (July 2006): 320.

71. "Living Wage Campaign Rocks Northern Virginia," *Virginia.Organizing* 3 (October 1998): 1, 4.

72. "Living Wage Victory in Alexandria," *Virginia.Organizing* 5 (July 2000): 1, 10.

73. Quoted in Fine, *Worker Centers*, 191.

74. Ibid.

75. Gyula Nagy, "Winning a Living Wage Ordinance from the Grassroots," *Labor Notes* 274 (January 2002), available at http://labornotes.org/archives/2002/0102/0102d.html.

76. Ibid.

77. Tait, *Poor Workers' Unions*, 151.

78. Joe Szakos and Kristin Layng Szakos, *Lessons from the Field: Organizing in Rural Communities* (New Orleans: American Institute for Social Justice, 2008), 8.

79. Ibid., 8–9.

80. "Virginia People's Assembly Challenges State Budget Cuts and Layoffs, Demands 'Jobs! Peace! Justice!'" *Truthout*, January 17, 2010, available at http://www.truthout.org.

Contributors

Jane Berger teaches in the history department at Moravian College. She completed her Ph.D. at the Ohio State University. Her dissertation, "When Hard Work Doesn't Pay: Gender and the Origins of the Urban Crisis in Baltimore, 1945–1985," won the 2009 Lerner-Scott Prize awarded by the Organization of American Historians.

Michael K. Bess received his M.A. in history at Georgia Southern University. In 2009 he entered the history doctoral program at the University of Texas at El Paso. His current research project examines infrastructure development, state formation, and internal migration trends in modern Mexico.

Robert Bussel is associate professor of history and director of the Labor Education and Research Center at the University of Oregon. He is currently working on a book about Harold Gibbons, Ernest Calloway, and the St. Louis Teamsters.

Robert T. Chase is the Public Historian at the Avery Research Center for African American History and Culture at the College of Charleston. He was previously a postdoctoral fellow at the Center for Historical Analysis at Rutgers University, the postdoctoral fellow in African American Studies at Case Western Reserve University, and a postdoctoral fellow at the Clements Center for Southwest Studies at Southern Methodist University. His article in this volume draws upon his forthcoming book, *Civil Rights on the Cell Block: The Prisoners' Rights Movement and the Construction of the Carceral State, 1945–1990*.

David H. Ciscel is Professor Emeritus of Economics at the University of Memphis. His research specialties include labor issues and problems of the Memphis regional economy.

Michael Dennis teaches history at Acadia University in Nova Scotia, Canada. He is the author of *The New Economy and the Modern South* (2009) and *The Memorial Day Massacre: Chicago, Labor, and the Movement for Industrial Democracy* (2010). He is currently working on a study of Chicago and the Spanish Civil War.

Tami J. Friedman is associate professor of history at Brock University in St. Catharines, Ontario, specializing in twentieth-century U.S. history. Her publications include "Exploiting the North-South Differential: Corporate Power, Southern Politics, and the Decline of Organized Labor after World War II," which received the Binkley-Stephenson Award for the best scholarly article published in the *Journal of American History* in 2008.

Michael K. Honey is the Fred and Dorothy Haley Professor of Humanities at the University of Washington, Tacoma, Harry Bridges Chair of Labor Studies Emeritus at the University of Washington, and former president of the Labor and Working-Class History Association. He is the author of *Going Down Jericho Road: The Memphis Strike, Martin Luther King's Last Campaign* (2007) and has edited Martin Luther King Jr.'s *"All Labor Has Dignity": On Labor Rights and Economic Justice* (2011).

Max Krochmal is assistant professor of history at Texas Christian University. A former labor and community organizer, he earned his Ph.D. at Duke University in 2011. His article in this volume draws upon his book manuscript, "Black and Brown at Work: Labor, Civil Rights, and the Struggle for Democracy in Texas, 1935–1975." He is also the author of "An Unmistakably Working-Class Vision: Birmingham's Foot Soldiers and Their Civil Rights Movement" (2010).

Timothy J. Minchin is professor of North American history at La Trobe University in Melbourne, Australia. He has published widely in the field of southern labor history, including *Fighting against the Odds: A History of Southern Labor since World War II* (2005).

Bruce Nissen is a labor studies scholar and sociologist at Florida International University who also has served recently as a staff representative for the higher education union in the Florida public higher education system.

Michael Pierce is associate professor of history at the University of Arkansas and author of *Striking with the Ballot: Ohio Labor and the Populist Party* (2010).

Robert H. Zieger is Distinguished Professor of History Emeritus at the University of Florida. He is the editor of two previous collections of essays on southern labor history and has twice been recipient of the Philip A. Taft Prize for the best book in labor history. His most recent book, *For Jobs and Freedom: Race and Labor in America since 1865* (2007) earned an "Outstanding Academic Title" designation from Choice.

Index

A. & M. Karagheusian Company, 30
Abernathy, George, 278
ACORN (activist organization), 327
Adams, Leoulie, 115
A. E. Staley labor dispute, 324
Affirmative action, 303
African Americans: in Arkansas, 47, 48, 55–56, 57–58, 60, 61, 62, 63–64, 66–67, 75n68; in Baltimore, efforts to gain equal employment opportunity, 76–92; in Greenville, Miss., 32–33; in Florida, 294, 304; in health care industry, 294; in Maryland, 79; in Memphis, 236–53, 254n10,12; relations with Mexican Americans, 138–39, 140–41, 145, 146–47, 149. 150, 151, 157–58, 161, 162–63, 228–29; in North Carolina, 318, 334; in St. Louis, 113–14, 118, 119, 123; in South, 1, 3–4, 6, 7, 8, 20, 29–30; in Texas, 133, 137–41, 143, 145–47, 149–51, 157–58, 161, 175–76n79, 318; in Texas prisons, 177, 181, 188, 189, 191, 193, 194, 200; in textile industry, 272, 278–79; in Virginia, 318, 319, 322,–23, 330, 331, 332, 335, 336, 337, 340–41; women workers, 77–92, 254n12, 318
Afro-American (Baltimore newspaper), 76, 80, 82–83, 90
Agricultural and Industrial (A&I) Board, in Mississippi, 21, 24
Agricultural workers, 1, 3, 218, 229, 239, 249
Alabama, voting patterns in, 5
Albany, Ga., 30
Albertson's grocery chain, 10
Alexandria, Va., activism in, 330, 336, 337
Albuquerque, N.M., 139
Alexander Smith, Inc., 19, 26, 27, 31–32
Alinsky, Saul, 154
Aliza, Jean, 294–95
Allen, George, 320, 322
Allied Prisoners Platform for Legal Equity, 198
Amalgamated Clothing and Textile Workers Union (ACTWU), 264, 266. *See also* Textile Workers Union of America
Amalgamated Clothing Workers union, 160
Amalgamated Meat Cutters union, 160, 161
American Association of Exporters and Importers, 265
American Federation of Labor (AFL), 21–22, 24, 29, 60, 104, 124. *See also* individual unions
American Federation of Labor-Congress of Industrial Organizations (AFL-CIO), 45, 64–65, 83, 267–68, 291, 338; expels Teamsters union, 66, 67; merger, 30, 63
American Federation of State, County, and Municipal Employees: in Baltimore, 91; in Memphis, 238, 240
American Federation of Teachers, 104
American G. I. Forum, 137, 138, 141, 142, 149, 154
American Prison Association, 186
American Rights at Work (ARAW), 292–93
American Textile Manufacturers Institute (ATMI), 265, 267
Andrade, Erasmo, 153
Applebome, Peter, 276
Archer, George F., 26, 34
Arkansas, 50, 61, 65; and organized labor, 23, 45
Arkansas Democrat, 55
Arkansas Democratic Voters Association, 55
Arkansas Free Enterprise Association, 47, 49, 63
Arkansas Highway Commission, 52
Arkansas Industrial Union Council, 53–54, 55, 56, 59, 61, 63
Arkansas Power and Light, 57
Arkansas National Guard, 66
Arkansas State AFL-CIO, 67
Arkansas State Federated Labor Council, 46, 63
Arkansas State Federation of Labor, 53–54, 55, 56, 57, 60, 63

350 · Index

Arkansas State Press, 71n34; 75n68
Arlandria/Chirilagua Housing Cooperative, 336
Arlington, Va., 337
Armey, Dick, 316–17
Ashe, Arthur, statue, 320, 321, 332
Ashurst-Sumners Act, 182
Ashley County, Ark., 58
Ashmore, Harry S., 47, 59
Atkins Saw company, 33, 34
Atkinson County, Ga., 229
Atkinson, Frank, 322
Atlanta, Ga., 2–3, 262; Mexicans in, 218, 220, 222, 224, 225; postwar labor-liberalism in, 102–3; race relations in, 321
Atlanta Journal-Constitution, 298
Atmore, Ala., 273
Attica (N.Y. prison), 178, 190, 199, 208n37
Avante-Boca Raton nursing home, 293
Avante-Lake Worth nursing home, 293
Ayers, B. Drummond, Jr., 262

Bacon, James, 318
Baltimore City Council, 76, 81, 82, 85, 88
Baltimore Department of Education, employment patterns, 84, 86, 88
Baltimore Department of Housing and Community Development, 89
Baltimore Federation of Labor, 81
Baltimore living wage campaign, 335
Baltimore Teachers Union, 91
Bank of Mexico, 227
Barber, Robert, 188–89
Bartley, Numan, 1
Bass, Harry, 55
Bates, Daisy, 71n34, 75n68
Bates, L. C., 71n34, 75n68
Bayh, Birch, 171n33
Beck, Dave, 65, 117
Bell, Fred L., 146
Belue, Dora, 33
Benson, George, 50, 67
Bentonville, Ark., 10
Berger, Jane, 11
Bernal, Joe J., 153–54, 155, 157, 158, 161
Berry Amendment, 260
Bess, Michael K., 11
Beto, Dr. George, 185–86, 187, 190
Beverly Hills United Church, Va., 337
Bexar County Commissioners Court, 151

Bexar County Democratic Coalition, 157
Big Squeeze (book), 292
Bilbo, Theodore, 28, 58
Birmingham, Ala., 20, 276; postwar labor-liberalism in, 102–3
Black, Rev. Claude, Jr., 157, 158, 159, 161
Black Panthers, 146, 195
Black Power, 180, 192, 195
Black Muslims, 189
Black Workers for Justice, 334
Blanton, Carlos, 137
Bluestone, Barry, 258
Booker, J. R., 56; 71n34
Borg-Warner Corporation, 33
Boston, Will, 58
Botelho, Michael, 25
Bowling Alone (book), 306
Bracero program, 217, 223, 230
Brackett, Pearl Cole, 89
Brailey, Troy, 83
Branton, Wiley, 56
Brewer, Vivion, 54
Bridges, Harry, 61
Brigham, Stephen, 191
Brody, David, 123
Brooks, Chet, 179, 197
Brookwood Labor College, 104
Brotherhood of Locomotive Engineers, 50
Brotherhood of Railroad Trainmen, 30, 81
Brown Berets, 146
Brown v. Board of Education, 48, 58, 137, 189, 321
Brundage, W. Fitzhugh, 321
Buchanan County, Va., 335
Building tender system, in Texas prisons, 179, 187–89, 194
Bulloch County, Ga., 219
Burlington Industries, 268, 274, 278
Bush, George H. W., 265, 321
Bush, George W., 268, 270, 271
Bush, Jeb, 303
Business Roundtable, 267
Bussel, Robert, 11
Bussey, Charles, 55–56
Byrnes, James F., 26

Cabell, Earle, 171n33
California: 1968 election, 139; farmworkers in, 143, 158; Mexican immigrants

in, 219, 231; prisons in, 181, 183, 186, 190, 191, 195, 208n38
California Department of Corrections, 186
California State Federation of Labor, 105
Calloway, Deverne, 128n16
Calloway, Ernest: biography and background, 104–5; political activism of, 101, 105–6, 107, 119, 122, 123, 128, 128n16
Campbell, Marguerite, 89
Canada-U.S. trade relations, 266
Cannon Mills, 274–75
Cape Charles, Va., 334
Capitol Transit Company (Little Rock, Ark.), 62
Carrazco, Daniel, 221
Carrazco, Laura, 221
Carsey Institute, 319
Carson, Gordon, 21
Carter, Hodding, Jr., 26, 34, 35
Carter, Jimmy, 5, 161, 263
Carter, Mandy, 333
Cash, W. J., 1
Cass, E. R., 186
Casso, Fr. Henry, 154, 155
Castillo, Leonel, 161
Caterpillar manufacturing firm, 324
Cauthen, Gerald, 268
Center of Budget and Policy Priorities, 327–28
Central America, immigrants from, 3, 4, 249. *See also* Hispanics; Latinos
Central High School (Little Rock, Ark.), 54, 66
Centreville, Ala., 273
Centro Latino (Dalton, Ga.), 227
Chapman, Leonard, 278–79
Chase, Robert, 11
Charlotte, N.C., 2, 3, 262, 271, 273, 276
Charlotte Observer, 261
Charlottesville, Va., 319, 330, 332, 336
Charlottesville Labor Action Group, 330
Chastain, Roger, 269
Chávez, César, 143
Chen, Anthony S., 4
Cherry, Francis, 52–53, 57, 59, 60
Chicago, Mexican immigrants in, 231
Chicago Mill and Lumber Company, 21, 28, 29
Chicano Moratorium demonstrations, 139
Chicanos/Chicanas, militancy and activism, 133–63, 164n4; 181. *See also* Hispanics; Latinos; Mexicans, Mexican Americans
Chilhowie, Va., 19
China, textile and apparel industry, 267–68, 269–70
Chinese people, in Virginia, 339
Christian Coalition, 340
Ciscel, David H., 11
Citizens' Charter Association (Dallas, Tex.), 148
Citizens' Committee (Arkansas), 55, 56
Citizenship Training Conference (Arkansas), 62–63
Ciudad Juárez, Mexico, 224
Civic Progress (St. Louis civic organization), 118, 119–121, 122, 124
Civil Rights Act of 1964, 5, 85, 140, 236, 239; Title VII, 239
Civil rights movement, 5, 80–81, 238, 334, 340; and Mexican Americans, 137, 138, 174n70; in Texas prisons, 189–95
Classified Municipal Employees Association (Baltimore, Md.), 83, 91
Clemens (Texas prison), 177
Clinton, Bill, 5, 226, 266, 317
Clutchette, John, 191
Cobb, James, 1, 2
Coffield (Texas prison), 177
Coleman, Eugene, 157
Collins, Wilbur, 200
Columbia, S.C., 274
Columbus, Ga., 279
Commonwealth College, 59, 61
Communications Workers of America Local 2222, 337
Communists, Communist Party, 59, 61, 137, 176n79
Community Development Advisory Council (Virginia), 332
Community Relations Commission (Baltimore agency), 86, 87, 88–89. *See also* Equal Employment Opportunity Commission (EEOC)
Community Stewards Program (IBT Local 688), 101–25; and city charter controversy, 118–21; economic and political role, 107, 108; housing program, 114–15, 125; Labor Health Institute, 110; origins and development, 106–7, 108–9, 110–11, 111–12, 123–25; and racial issues, 113–14;

Community Stewards Program—*continued*
and rat control problem, 115–18; and tax issues, 121–22; and women workers, 112–13. *See also* Calloway, Ernest; Gibbons, Harold
Cone Mills, 268
Congress of Industrial Organizations (CIO), 24, 27, 28, 47, 51, 55, 56, 58, 60, 62, 81, 104, 124, 241; launches southern organizing drive ("Operation Dixie"), 21–22, 23; Political Action Committee (CIO–PAC), 52, 53, 55,56, 58, 60, 62. *See also* Organized labor; individual unions
Congress of Racial Equality, 87
Connally, John, 143
Construction industry, Mexican workers in, 218, 225–26, 229–30
"Contract with America," 317
Contreras-Martinez, Olga, 229
Cook, Kenneth, 25
Cooper, Thomas X., 189
Cooper v. Pate, 189, 190
Corbitt, Elton, 229
Cornejo, Juan, 142
Corno, Walter J., 30
Corpus and Sellars v. Estelle, 192
Corrections Magazine, 186
Cortés, Ernesto, 154
Council of Conservative Citizens, 320
Cowie, Jefferson, 261
Cox, Harold E., 29
Craft, Juanita, 145
Crisco, Ruth, 275
Cronk, John, 153
Cruz, Fred, 189, 190, 194
Crystal City, Tex., 142, 149, 159, 160
Cuban workers, in Florida, 304
Cyriac, Evanette, 293

D'Alesandro, Thomas, Jr., 82
D'Alesandro, Thomas, III, 87–88, 89
Daggett, John L., 49, 50
Daily Sentinel-Star (Grenada, Miss.), 22–23
Dallas, Tex., 133, 139–40, 144, 145, 146, 147, 148, 161, 162, 192–93
Dallas City Council, 148, 149
Dallas County, Tex., 184
Dallas Independent School District, 148
Dallas Morning News, 146
Dallas Police Department, 146

Dalton, Ga., Hispanics/Latinos in, 214, 215–16, 219, 220, 226, 227, 230
Daniel, Cletus, 137
Dan River Mills, 275
Danville, Va., 275, 329
Darrington (Texas prison), 177
Darst, Joseph, 110
Davis, Angela, 161
Davis, Leon, 311n7
Dawson, William, 56
Debs, Eugene V., 59
Decatur, Ill., 324
Deindustrialization, 6–7, 79, 91–92, 241–42, 258–79. *See also* Manufacturing
Deindustrialization of America (book), 258–59
Delano, Calif., 143
de León, Robert, 160
DeLong, Robert, 179
Del Rio, Tex., 159
"Del Rio Manifesto," 159
Delta Council (Mississippi), 30
Delta Democrat-Times (newspaper), 26, 28, 34
Delta Leader (newspaper), 32
Delta nursing home chain, 299–300
Democracia USA, 303
Democratic Leadership Council, 317
Democratic Party: in Arkansas, 47, 48, 49, 51, 56, 59–60, 61, 65, 67, 74n54; in Baltimore, 83, 85; in Bexar County, Tex., 151; in Missouri, 107; in 1990s, 317; in South, 5, 48–49, 51, 180; and trade legislation, 266. *See also* Carter, Jimmy; Clinton, Bill; Johnson, Lyndon; Kennedy, John F.; Kennedy, Robert F.; Roosevelt, Franklin D.; New Deal; Truman, Harry S.
Demopolis, Ala., 273
Dennis, Michael, 10–11
Detroit, urban disorder in, 237
Detroit Free Press, 277–78
D. H. Griffith Wrecking Company, 274
Dickenson County, Va., 335
District 1115 (labor union), 290
Distrito Federal, Mexico, 217, 223
Dixon, Walter, 82
Dole, Elizabeth, 268
Dole, Robert, 212n88
Dorisca, Carline, 296
Douglass, Robert L., 87

Drumgo, Fleeta, 191
Dublin, Thomas, 259
DuChessi, William, 30
Dunaway, Edwin, 59
Dunbar High School (Little Rock, Ark.), 56
Duval, Ernest, 294, 295, 297
Duval, Lude, 295

Earned Income Tax Credit (Virginia legislation), 329, 332, 333
Eastham (Texas prison), 177
East Side Civic League (Little Rock, Ark.), 55
Economic Policy Institute, 267
Economist, 335
Edelman, John W., 25
Eden, N.C., 273, 278
Edwards, John, 268, 279
Ehrenreich, Barbara, 328
"Eight Hoe Squad," 191, 192, 195
Eisenhower, Dwight D., 84
El Dorado Daily News, 51
El Fenix restaurant, 133, 138, 148
Elisha, Walter Y., 264
Ellis (Texas prison), 177, 188, 195, 199, 200
Ellis, O. B., 185
El Paso, Tex., 139
El Sol de Texas, 146, 147
Equal Employment Opportunity Commission (EEOC), 81, 82–83, 86
Estado de México, Mexican state, 217, 223
Esteril, Luders, 294
Estrada, Joe, 156
Evans, W. A., 24
Ewart, Dale, 291, 309
Ewing, William F. C. "Bill," 19, 26
Exile, Pierre, 296

Fairfax County, Va., 323
Fair Labor Standards Act, 57, 63
Fantus Factory Locating Service, 19, 21, 29
Farmworkers: activism among, 142–43, 160; United Farm Workers Organizing Committee (UFWOC), 143–44, 147, 153, 158
Faubus, Orval, 57, 59, 61, 62, 64–65, 66–67, 75n68,69
Fayetteville, Tenn., 275
Federal Reserve Bank of Richmond, 330, 332
Federation for the Advancement of Mexican Americans (FAMA), 153–54, 158, 159, 161
FedEx, 3, 10, 244, 246, 249

Feeley, Malcolm, 180
Ferguson (Texas prison), 184
Ferguson, F. Eulalian, 89
Fiber, Fabric, and Apparel Coalition for Trade (FFACT), 264–65
Field, Sally, 265
Fink, Leon, 4
Finley, Murray, 264
Firestone corporation, 241, 242
Fite, Gilbert, 1
Fleishman-Hillard public relations firm, 119
Flint, Mich., 259
Flores, Arnold, social-political views/activities, 149–61, 162–63
Flores, Gloria, 151, 155
Florida: health care industry in, 290ff.; and organized labor, 23, 291, 293–94; voting patterns in, 6
Florida Agency for Healthcare Administration, 308
Florida Marlins, 303
Florida Nurses Association, 290–91
Flowers, W. H., 58
Foley, Neil, 137
Food Stamp program, 84
Fordist production system, 10, 11
Fort Mill, N.C., 273
Fort Smith, Ark., 56, 57
Fort Worth, Tex., 147
Frank, Ellen, 326
Freeman, Joshua, 130–31n43
Freeman, Robert, 270
Free market ideology, 326–27, 328. *See also* Globalization; New Economy
Free Trade Area of the Americas (FTAA), 303–4
French, John D., 324
Friedman, Tami, 11
Fudge, Lewis, 186
Fulbright, J. William, 50

Gainesville, Ga., Hispanics-Latinos in, 220, 226, 230
Games, Danny, 274
Gaona, Atanasio, 229
García, Franklin, 161, 163
García, Gus, 136
García, Hector, 136
García, Ignacio, 136, 137
García, Mario T., 135, 136, 137

García, Matt, 154, 155, 158
Gaston County, N.C., 271
Gastonia, N.C., 271, 276
Gatesville Reformatory School for Boys (Texas), 194
Gauldin, Barbara, 273
General Motors Corporation, 186
Gentry, Tom, 57, 63
Georgia, Mexican migration to, 214–31
GiaQuinta, Mary, 265
Gibbons, Harold: biography and background, 104; role in IBT, 123, 125; social and political activism of, 101, 102, 105–6, 107–8, 111, 115, 121, 124
Gingrich, Newt, 316–17
Glasgow, Va., 27
Glisper, Floyd, 111
Globalization, 6, 11, 319, 325, 329
Glover, Danny, 299
Goldfield, David, 321
Goldfield, Michael, 324
Gómez-Arnau, María de los Remedios, 225
Gonzales, Henry B., 156
Gonzales, Salvador, 198
Good Government League (San Antonio, Tex.), 151, 157
Grace Episcopal Church (Alexandria, Va.), 337
Grand Prairie, Tex., 138
Great Society, 77, 78, 90, 321
Green, William, 21
Greenhouse, Steven, 292
Greensboro, N.C., 274
Greenville, Miss.: Chamber of Commerce, 21, 25, 26; efforts to attract industry, 19, 21, 26, 27–28, 31
Greenville Citizens Committee, 28
Greenville Mills, 27, 33
Greenwood Rehabilitation Center, 294
Grenada, Miss., efforts to attract industry, 22–23
Grenada County Weekly, 23
Grenada Industries, 22
Griffith, Barbara S., 22
Gross, Ariela, 137
Guadalajara, Mexico, 223, 230
Guajardo v. McAdams, 192
Guanajuato, Mexican state, 216–17, 223
Guerrero, Mexican state, 216–17
Guglielmo, Thomas, 137

Guthridge, Amis, 63
Gutiérrez, David, 136
Gutiérrez, José Ángel, 142, 159,160

H-2A program (immigration measure), 218
Hahn, John, 121
Haitian health care workers, 294, 295, 298, 299, 303, 304, 307, 312n26
Hall County, Ga., 220
Hall, Jacquelyn Dowd, 67, 261, 322
Hall, Rothchild, 115
Hampton Roads, Va., 341
Hanceville, Ala., 273
Harding College, 50
Harris County, Tex., 184
Harris, Ivy Logan, 89
Harrison, Bennett, 258
Hart-Celler amendment (U.S. immigration law), 217
Hatley, Judy, 275
Hawes-Cooper Act, 182
Hawkins, Jeffrey, 55
HCA hospital chain, 301–2
Health care industry: in Florida, 289–310; in Memphis, 236, 240, 245, 248, 252; and organized labor, 289–310
Henderson, George, 268
Henry County, Va., 326
Herenton, Dr. Willie, 249, 250, 257n31
Hernandez, Alvarro Luna, 199
Hidalgo, Mexican state, 217
Highlander Folk School, 331–32
Hill, Betty, 109
Hiner, Scott, 271
Hirsch, Arnold, 4
Hispanics: in Georgia, 216, 220, 225, 226, 227, 228, 229, 231; in health care industry, 294, 305; nomenclature regarding, 232n4; in Virginia, 323, 324, 330, 337; as voters, 6; as workers, 3, 4, 8, 318, 322
Hispanic Youth Association, 220
Hiss, Alger, 61
Hodcarriers' Local 490, 66
Hodgson, Godfrey, 322
Hoffa, James, 65, 67, 122–23
Hollings, Ernest, 263–64
Holt, Jack, 47, 48, 52
Homestead, Fla., 304
Homestead, Pa., 259
Honey, Michael, 4, 11

Hot Springs, Ark., 57
Hoxie, Ark., 63–64
Houston, Tex., 2, 3, 136, 156–57, 224, 262
Howard, Nova, 141
Hudson, A. C., 58
Hughes Tool Company, 156–57, 160
Human Rights Watch, 292
Humes, Rev. H. H., 32
Huntsville (Texas, prison), 181, 185

Immigrant Workers Freedom Ride, 303
Immigration Reform and Control Act, 217–18
Industrial Areas Foundation, 154
Inter-Agency Committee on Mexican American Affairs, 139
International Association of Firefighters (Baltimore local), 83
International Association of Machinists, 58, 153
International Brotherhood of Teamsters (IBT), 45, 54, 55, 104; in Arkansas, 54, 55, 57, 65–66, 67, 68; Central States Pension Fund, 54–55; in Missouri, 102–3, 105, 106, 122–23; reputation of, 45, 119–20; in Texas, 142, 151, 159; in Virginia, 337. *See also* Community Stewards Program
International Harvester corporation, 240–41
International Ladies' Garment Workers' Union (ILGWU), 263, 266
International Monetary Fund, 218, 328
International Textile Group, 268, 269
International Union of Electrical Workers, 160, 240
International Woodworkers Association (IWA), 27, 28, 58, 62
Iron Workers Local 5, 337

Jackson, George, 181, 190–91, 199
Jackson, Jesse, 325
Jackson, Lillie Mae, 80, 81
Jackson, Thomas Jonathan "Stonewall," 320
Jacoby, Tamar, 233n16
Jailhouse Lawyers Association, 198
Jalet, Frances T. Freeman, 190, 191, 193, 195
James Lees and Sons carpet company, 27
Japan, textile industry in, 263
Jaramillo, Leonardo, 220
Javior, Paul, 160
Jean-Baptiste, Quettelie, 295–96
Jefferson County, Ark., Voters Association, 62

Jewell, Michael, 195
Jim Crow (segregation), 20, 78, 79, 180. *See also* Segregation
Jobs with Justice, 299, 302–03
Johnson, Arthur, 184
Johnson, Eddie Bernice, 193, 197
Johnson, Jim, 57, 59, 60, 63, 64–65, 67
Johnson, Lyndon, 84, 86, 140, 217
Johnson, Rev. Peter, 146
Jones, C. H., 56, 58; 71n34
J. P. Stevens Company, 265–66
Justice for Janitors, 335
Justice, Judge William Wayne, 180, 195

Kannapolis, N.C., 268, 270, 271–72, 274, 275, 276, 278
Kelly Air Force Base, 150, 151, 152, 153, 154, 155, 156, 157, 158, 160
Kennedy, Edward "Ted," 143
Kennedy, John F., 84, 91, 151
Kennedy, Robert F., 139
Kentucky Fair Tax Coalition, 315
Kiko's store/community center (Dallas, Tex.), 144, 145, 148
Kilborn, Peter T., 271
King David nursing home, 294, 297
King, Coretta Scott, 241
King, Rev. Martin Luther, Jr., 236, 238, 249, 251, 252, 253, 253n4, 322
King, Rodney, 322
Kingsolver, Barbara, 328
Kletzer, Lori G., 263
Korean War, 25, 26
Korstad, Robert, 4
Krochmal, Max, 11
Kroll, Jack, 52, 55, 62
Kroeger grocery chain, 10
Ku Klux Klan, in Texas, 192
Kyle, Jack, 184

Labor Health Institute (Teamsters Local 688 program), 105
Labor's Joint Educational Committee (Arkansas), 60–61, 62, 63
Labor's League for Political Education, 52, 53, 58, 60–61
La Follette Committee, 105
Leland, Mickey, 193, 194
Lamar v. Coffield, 192
Lambert, George, 162

Lambert, Latane, 162
Lancaster, S.C., 272
Landín, Joe, 144
Landrum-Griffin Act, 123
Laney, Benjamin Travis, Jr., 47, 48, 49, 50, 51, 52, 58, 64
Langdale (Alabama factory), 274
Lanier High School (San Antonio, Tex.), 150
LaRose, Marie, 295
Latinos: in Florida, 304; in Georgia, 11, 216, 220, 225, 226, 227, 228, 229, 231; in Memphis, 244, 246, 249, 251, 252, 256n28; nomenclature regarding, 232n4; as prison inmates, 191; in South, 4, 6, 7, 248; in textile and apparel industries, 272; in Virginia, 323, 335, 336, 339, 340–41. *See also* Chicanos/Chicanas; Hispanics; Mexicans; Mexican Americans
Lawrence, Anita B., 320
League of United Latin American Citizens (LULAC), 136, 137, 141, 142, 154
Leaman, Jim, 333
Ledesma, Irene, 137
Lee County, Va., 332
Lee, Robert E., 320
Lehman, Herbert, 25
LeRoy, Erma, 162
LeRoy, Moses, 162
Letner, Russell, 116–17
Levingston, Sidney, 30
Liberty City (Miami), 304
Lichtenstein, Nelson, 10
Life magazine, 63
Like a Family (book), 278
Lindsey, Edward, 241, 242
Lipscomb, Al, 145, 147, 148
Littlefield, Clarence "C. J.," 160
Little Rock, Ark., 54, 55, 58, 62, 64
Living wage campaigns in Virginia, 315, 330, 332, 333, 335, 336–38
Logistics (economic sector), 236, 243–46, 248, 252, 253n3
"Long civil rights movement," 67, 161, 338
Louis, Marie Pierre, 296–97
Louisiana, elections/voting patterns in, 5, 50
Luna, Homero, 227–28

MacArthur Park (Little Rock, Ark.), 59
Maddox, C. D. "Charlie," 24
Mann, Woodrow Wilson, 62; 74n54

Manufacturing, in South, 1, 67, 16, 18, 239, 240, 241–42, 243, 244, 245, 251, 262–63, 319, 328. *See also* Deindustrialization; Textile and apparel industries
Maquiladoras, 223, 230
March for Jobs and Freedom, 139
Markham, Bill, 275–76
Marriot hotels, 332, 336
Marshall, Thurgood, 79
Martin, Lester, 25–26
Martinez family, 133
Martinez, Anita, 149
Martinez, Jaime, 162
Martinez, "Papa," 148
Martinsville, Va., 273, 277, 319, 326, 327, 329
Maryland, 2, 90
Maryland Commission on Interracial Problems and Relations, 90
Masonite Corporation, 28
"Massive resistance" (Arkansas), 64
Mayor's Task Force on Equal Rights (Baltimore), 87
McAdams, Carl Luther "Beartracks," 188
McAllister, William, 160
McCain, John, 5
McCarthy, Jake, 106
McCarthy, Margaret, 89
McCarthy, Joseph R., and McCarthyism, 59, 61, 102
McClellan Committee (United States Senate Select Committee on Improper Practices in the Labor or Management Field), 11, 45, 55, 65–66, 67, 123
McClellan, John: and African Americans, 57–58, 60, 63; and Arkansas politics, 48–49, 50, 51, 52–53, 57, 58–60, 63, 64, 65, 67–68; and organized labor, 45–46, 46–47, 55, 57, 60, 62, 63, 65–66, 67–68; in U.S. Senate, 11, 45, 55, 61–62, 65–66, 67
McClellan, W. H. "Pete," 51
McClinton, I. S., 55, 71n34
MacCormick, Austin, 182
McGriff, Esterlean, 272
McKeldin, Theodore, 85–86, 87
McMath, Sidney S.: and African Americans, 48, 51–52, 56, 57–58, 63; and Arkansas politics, 48, 49–50, 57, 59, 60, 61; and organized labor, 46, 47, 50–51, 52, 53–54, 55, 57, 58, 59, 60, 65, 66. *See also* Smith, Odell
McMillan, Ernest Marion, 191, 192–93

McMillan, Dr. W. R., 192
McWhorter, Ladelle, 315
Meany, George, 55
Medicaid, 84
Medicare, 84
Medrano, Adam, 148
Medrano, Carlos, 172n48
Medrano, Esperanza, 144, 148
Medrano, Francisco F. "Pancho," 138–49, 150, 151, 159, 161, 162–63
Medrano, Pancho, Jr., 144–45
Medrano, Pauline, 148
Medrano, Ricardo, 144, 145, 146, 148
Medrano, Robert, 145, 146, 148
Medrano v. Allee, 143
Memphis Furniture Company, 241
Memphis, Tenn.: postwar labor-liberalism in, 102–3; economic conditions in, post-1968, 236–53
Mendez, Butch, 179
Metropolitan Church Federation (St. Louis, Mo.), 114, 116
Mexican American Generation, 134–35, 136, 137–38, 139, 141, 142, 149, 150, 159
Mexican American Unity Council, 159
Mexican American Youth Organization (MAYO), 159
Mexican Revolution, 217
Mexicans and Mexican Americans, 134–35, 136, 137, 141, 188, 189, 200, 215, 223, 249; activism of, 136, 137, 138, 145–46, 149, 150–51; conservatism of, 173n49; discrimination against, 137, 140, 143, 144; in Georgia, 216, 217, 218–19, 225–26, 228–29; nomenclature regarding, 164n4; relations with African Americans, 141, 142–43, 145, 146–47, 153, 157–58, 159, 161, 162–63, 228–29; relationship to Chicano/Chicana movement, 147, 164n4. *See also* Chicanos/Chicanas; Hispanics; Latinos
Mexico, economic activities and conditions, 4, 136, 216, 217, 218–19, 222, 223, 224, 225, 227, 266, 267, 324, 328. *See also* Globalization
Mexico City, 223, 230
Mi Familia Vota, 303
Miami, Fla.: labor activism in, 290, 298, 303, 304; postwar labor-liberalism in, 102–3
Miami Workers Center, 304
Miami Herald, 298

Michoacán, Mexican state, 216–17
Milkman, Ruth, 259
Miller, O. G., 191
Mills, John V., 191
Minchin, Timothy, 7, 11
Mississippi: elections and voting patterns in, 5, 50; industry, efforts to attract, 16–36; organized labor in, 24, 25, 27, 28–29, 29–30, 31, 33–34, 35
Mississippi Balance Agriculture with Industry (BAWI) program, 20–21, 22–23, 24, 26, 33
Mississippi Farm Bureau Federation, 24
Mississippi Manufacturers Association, 27
Mississippi State AFL-CIO, 31
Mississippi State Employment Service, 19
Mississippi State Federation of Labor, 24
Mississippi State Industrial Union Council, 24
Missouri-Pacific Railroad, 50
Mitchell, Clarence, 80
Mitchell, Attorney General John, 171n33
Mitchell, Juanita Jackson, 80
Mobile Register, 273
Model Cities program, 84
Montgomery, Ala., 139, 271
Moore, Carlos (Teamsters representative), 142
Moore, Carlos (American Textile Manufacturers Institute official), 267
Mooresville Mills, 278
Moral Majority, 340
Moreton, Bethany, 8
Moritsugu, Ken, 274
Morones, Adolfo, 215
Morris, C. L., 19
Morton, Margaret, 321
Mosow, William A. "Bill," 34
Mount Sinai-St. Francis nursing home, 298–99, 302
Mount Vernon Mills, 269
Moynihan Report, 88–89
Mt. Zion First Baptist Church (San Antonio, Tex.), 157
Mudd, Robert "Bobby," 184–85, 199, 200
Multifiber Agreement (MFA), 269, 271
Muñoz, Carlos, 136
Murphy, Carl, 80
Murphy, Ike, 52
Murray, Philip, 21, 28, 51

Nagy, Gyula, 338
Nash, Jock, 267
Nashua, N.H., 25
National Association for the Advancement of Colored People (NAACP): in Arkansas, 58; Dallas Youth Council, 192; in Florida, 302–3, 304; Legal Defense Fund, 190; in Maryland, 79–80, 83; and Mexican Americans, 145; in Missouri, 101, 105, 119–20, 122, 123; national organization, 80; in South Carolina, 320; in Texas, 158, 192
National Civil Rights Museum, Memphis, 249
National Council of La Raza, 159
National Council of Textile Organizations, 270
National Labor Relations Act (Wagner Act), 46, 57, 63
National Labor Relations Board (NLRB), 9, 27–28; and health care industry, 292, 293, 294–97, 298–99, 311n8; ineffectiveness of, 292, 298–99
National Maritime Union, 19, 35
National Origins Act, 1924, 217
National Public Radio, 298
Needmor Fund, 316
Negro American Labor Council, 83
Nelson, Gene, 143
New Deal, 8, 10, 19–20, 67, 84, 138, 141, 182, 206n21
New Economy, 316, 317–18, 319, 323, 325, 326, 327, 329, 330, 334, 335, 336, 337, 340, 341n9, 342n10
New Left, 339; and prison issues, 205n11
Newman, Robert, 1
New Republic, 107
New Right, political movement, 322
New York Times, 21, 78–79, 262, 266, 271, 273, 276, 292, 298
Nichols, Fred, 82
9/11 attacks on World Trade Center and Pentagon, 268, 274
Nissen, Bruce, 8, 11
Nogales, Mexico, 223
Non-Partisan Political League (International Association of Machinists), 58
Norma Rae (film), 265–66, 269
Norris-LaGuardia Act, 47
North American Aviation Company, 138

North American Free Trade Agreement (NAFTA), 225, 266–67, 273, 328, 338
North Carolina, 2, 6, 334; textile industry in, 264, 264, 268; voting patterns, 6
Northern Virginia Living Wage Coalition, 337, 338
North Little Rock Civic League, 56
Nuevo Laredo, Mexico, 223–24
Nuñez, Rigo, 214, 217

Oak Lawn, Tex., 144
Oaxaca, Mexican state, 217, 222, 224
Obama, Barak, 6, 236, 238, 307
Olympic Games (Atlanta, Ga., 1966), 225–26, 230
"Operation Dixie," 28
Organisation for Economic Cooperation and Development (OECD), 270
Organized labor: and African Americans, 29–30, 91–92, 108, 141, 150, 151, 334; in Arkansas, 53, 56–57, 60–61, 64–65; employer opposition to, 16–36, 293–94; in Florida, 289, 291–92, 293–94, 304; in health care industry, 289– 310; historical development, 45, 102, 123–24, 242, 243; in Memphis, 236, 238; and Mexican Americans, 138, 160–161; in South, 4, 8–11, 18–19, 20–21; in St. Louis, 106; in textile and apparel industries, 264, 265–66, 267–68, 269; in Virginia, 314, 315, 320, 324, 325, 328, 333, 334, 338, 340–41; and Virginia Organizing Project (VOP), 314, 315, 320, 333, 337, 340–41; in Texas, 143; and women workers, 158. *See also* American Federation of Labor; American Federation of Labor-Congress of Industrial Organizations; Congress of Industrial Organizations; individual unions
Orlando, Fla., 291
Orozco, Cynthia, 136
Overcash, Agatha, 278

Pascagoula Star and Moss Point Advertiser, 31
Passano, William, 81
Patients Right to Know Act, 308
Patonza, Oscar, 218
Patterson, Orlando, 211n73
Pearson, Ga., 229
Pegler, Westbrook, 61–62, 67
Peña, Albert A., Jr., 151, 156, 157, 158, 160, 161

Pentland, Robert, 110
Pérez, Emma, 136–37
Persons, Gordon, 186
Petersburg, Va., 341
Pillowtex Corporation, 268, 270–71, 275, 278
Philadelphia anti-discrimination ordinance, 81
Philadelphia Inquirer, 274
Pierce, J. L., 30
Pierce, Michael, 11
Pine Bluff, Ark., 57
Pittsburgh, Pa., 276
Political Association of Spanish-Speaking Organizations (PASO), 139, 142, 149
Polk, Ed, 147
Polk, William, 2
Poll tax: Arkansas, 48, 56–57, 60, 63, 65, 75n68; Texas, 145; Virginia, 331
Pontesso, Arnold, 198–99
Poor People's Campaign, 237
Pope, Lawrence, 188
Populist movement (19th century), 334
Potts, Herbert J. "Jack," 27, 32
Poultry processing industry, Mexican workers in, 218, 220, 229
Poverty, in South, 3, 239, 242, 250, 254n10
Powell, Adam Clayton, 47
Power Shift (book), 261–62
Power U Center for Social Change, 304
Pride, Hillie, 242
Prison labor, 177–202
Prison Litigation Reform Act, 212n88
Prisoner Solidarity Committee, 198
Prisoners United, 198
Professional Air Traffic Controllers (PATCO), 241
Programa Nacional Fronterizo (PRONAF), 223, 230
Progressive Voters League, 138
Pruitt-Igoe housing project, 114
Publix grocery chain, 10
Puebla, Mexican state, 223
Pulaski County, Ark., 62
Putnam, Robert, 306

Rainbow Coalition, 325
Ramsay, Claude, 31
Ramsey I, Ramsey II (Texas prisons), 177, 185, 191
Randolph, A. Philip, 83

Rankin, John, 28
Ray, Victor, 54, 67
Raynor, Bruce, 291
Raynor, Harris, 274
RCA corporation, 240
Reagan, Ronald, 241, 264–65, 266, 315–16, 321, 324, 327
Reeves, Jay, 269
Remmel, Pratt, 62; 74n54
Republican Party: in Arkansas, 51, 67, 74n54; in Maryland, 85; in Texas, 151; and trade legislation, 266; in South, 4, 6; in Virginia, 317, 322, 340
Research Triangle (N.C.), 3
Retrieve (Texas prison), 193
Reuther, Walter, 55, 139, 141, 143
Reverchon Park (Dallas, Tex.), 146
Reynolds, Lisa, 275
Rhode Island Textile Association, 25
Richmond, Va., 320, 330
Richmond Times-Dispatch, 335
Riesel, Victor, 51
"Right to Work," 8, 11, 23, 24, 25, 28, 29–30, 31, 46, 47, 240, 302, 329
Rio Grande City, Tex., 143
Roanoke, Va., 341
Roanoke Rapids, N.C., 269, 318
Robbins, Carl, 188–89
Robbins, N.C., 279
Robertsdale, Ala., 273
Robeson County, N.C., 271, 274
Robinson, J. M., 56
Rockefeller, Nelson, 178
Rodríguez, Berta, 145
Rodríguez, Thomás, 145, 146, 147, 149
Romero, Oscar, 226–27
Rones, Philip L., 276
Roosevelt, Franklin D., 84, 105. *See also* New Deal
Ross, Fred, 143
Ross, Holt E., 24, 29
Ross, Wilbur, 268
Rowles, Kathy, 331
Rubin, Edwin, 180
Ruíz, David, 179
Ruíz, David Resendez, 194–95
Ruíz v. Estelle, 179–80, 186, 192, 196, 199, 200, 201–02
Ruíz, Rose Marie, 194
Ruiz, Vicki, 137

360 · Index

Ruskin College, 104
Russo, Monica, 291, 309
Rust Belt, 259, 261, 276
Ryan, Ellen, 327

Sachs, Leon, 87
Safeway grocery chain, 10
Salazar, Reuben, 139
Sale, Kirkpatrick, 261, 262, 276
Salinas, Mary, 162
Salisbury, Robert, 121
Salvadorans in Virginia, 336
San Andrés Tlalnelhuayoca, Mexico, 226–27
San Antonio, Tex., 149–50, 151, 153–54, 157–58, 159, 162
San Antonio Central Labor Council, 159, 160
San Antonio Chicano Organizers (SACO), 160
San Antonio City Council, 161
San Antonio Independent School District, 156
San Luis Potosí, Mexican state, 217
Sánchez, George I., 137
Sánchez, George J., 136
Sanhueza-Bazeas, Rafael, 227
Sanitation workers, Memphis, Tenn., 236, 238, 246, 247
Saul, John Ralston, 325
Schmidt, William E., 273
Schulman, Bruce, 1, 262
Sea Crest nursing home chain, 299–300
Seattle Times, 298
Segregation, 90, 113–14, 177, 181, 201, 321. *See also* Jim Crow
SEIU Healthcare Florida, 289, 291–92; 292–310; community activities, 302–4, 307; membership profile, 305–6, 308
Selby Shoe Company, 21
Self, Robert, 4
Selma, Ala., 139
Senior Health nursing home chain, 300
Service Employees International Union (SEIU), 150, 289; in health care industry, 291–312; Local 84, 155–56, 157–58, 159, 160, 161, 300
Service sector employment, in South, 7, 11, 218, 229, 241, 243–46, 248, 252, 275, 323
Shelby County, Tenn., 242, 244
Shelby, N.C., 276

Sherman, O. A., 56
Shivers, Allan, 186
Slavery, legacy of, 211n73, 239, 330
Smith, Alexander, 21
Smith, Fr. Sherrill, 159
Shropshire, Jackie, 56
Simpson, O. J., trial of, 322
Smith-Connally Act, 47
Smith, Denise, 333–34
Smith, J. Earl, 116
Smith, Odell, role in Arkansas politics, 46, 54–55, 60, 62, 65–66, 67
SNAP News, 157
Social Security, 58
Social Security Administration, 80–81, 90
Soledad (California prison), 181
Soledad Brother (book), 191
"Soledad Brothers," 181, 191
South: definition of, 2, 11, 12, 15n34; economic and demographic patterns, 1, 2, 4, 6–7, 16, 18, 20, 21, 231, 258–79, 318, 329; "exceptionalism" of 3–4; "New South," 11, 20, 180, 258; "New New South," 11; "Old South," 8; organized labor in, 7–11, 16–17, 18–19, 20–21, 21–22, 35–36; political patterns, 4–6, 20, 47; prison systems in, 180, 201. *See also* individual states
South Carolina textile industry, 25, 266
Southern Christian Leadership Conference, 143
Southern Cotton Oil Mill, 51
Southern Growth Policies Board, 276
Southern Mediator Journal (Little Rock, Ark.), 56, 58
Southern States Prison Association, 187
Southwest Council of La Raza, 159
Southwest Voter Registration and Education Project, 159
Spartanburg, S.C., 273
Springs Industries, 264
St. Louis, Archdiocese, 114
St. Louis, labor and community activism in, 101–25
St. Louis Argus, 122
St. Louis Board of Aldermen, 115, 117, 118
St. Louis Circuit Court, 112
St. Louis County, Mo., 122
St. Louis Department of Public Safety, 109
St. Louis Globe-Democrat, 112, 119–20, 121

St. Louis Housing Authority, 114
St. Louis Post-Dispatch, 101, 121, 125
St. Paul Pioneer Press, 278
St. Pauls, N.C., 274
St. Petersburg, Fla., 290, 291
Starnes, Robert W. "Bob," 28–29
Starr County, Tex., 144
States' Rights Democratic Party, "Dixiecrats," 29, 48–49, 49–50, 53, 57, 58, 63
Stein, Lana, 106
Stepanek, Marcia, 278
Stone, Thelma Lee, 110
Student Nonviolent Coordinating Committee (SNCC), 146, 157; Dallas chapter, 191, 192, 193
Sugrue, Thomas, 4
Sullivan, Patricia, 4
Sumners-Ashurst Act, 182
Sun Belt, 2, 258, 261–62, 273, 275, 276
Sun Zhenyu, 269
Suprinat, Marie, 293
Sutton, G. J., 157, 158, 159, 160, 161
Sutton, Ozell, 55
Swift, Johnny, 195–97, 198
Szakos, Joe, 315–16, 325, 326, 327, 328, 331, 339–40

Tackett, Boyd, 52
Taft, Robert A., 74n54
Taft-Hartley Act, 23, 24, 47, 50, 51, 54, 102, 105, 240
Tait, Vanessa, 334, 338–39
Tallassee, Ala., 269
Tampa, Fla., 291
Target retail company, 244
Tate, John, 9
Taunton, Mass., 26
Tenants' and Workers' Support Committee (TWSC), 330, 336–37, 338, 341
Tenet hospital chain, 301, 302
Tennessee Coal and Iron Company, 20
Terry Dairy strike, 62
Texarkana, Ark., 57
Texas: prison system, 177–202; migration to, 219
Texas Council of Voters, 145
Texas Department of Corrections (TDC), 177, 179, 181, 189, 190, 193, 194, 195, 196, 198–99, 200

Texas Employment Commission, 141
Texas Rangers (law enforcement body), 143, 144
Texas Southern University, 156–57, 160
Texas State AFL-CIO, 144
Textile and apparel industries: in China, 267–68, 269–70; in Japan, 263; in South, 3, 11, 16, 25–26, 30, 258–79, 323, 326
Textile Heritage Center (North Carolina), 275
Textile workers, 30, 258, 260, 261, 264, 270, 271–72, 273, 275–76, 277–78, 278–79, 279n4. *See also* Amalgamated Clothing and Textile Workers Union; Textile and apparel industries; Textile Workers Union of America
Textile Workers Organizing Committee, 104
Textile Workers Union of America (TWUA), 25, 27, 30, 33, 263, 264, 269. *See also* Amalgamated Clothing and Textile Workers Union; Textile and apparel industry; Textile workers
Textron, Inc., 25
Thacker-Gwaltney, Ben, 326, 327, 328, 330–31
Thurmond, Strom, 49, 50
Tidelands Oil controversy, 107
Tifton, Ga., 228
Tijuana, Mexico, 223
Toombs County, Ga., 219
"Tough with a Knife, Hell with a Writ" (prison memoir), 194
Trade Act of 1970, 270–71
Trade Adjustment Assistance Program (TAA), 270–71
Trades Union Congress (Britain), 104
Trask, Herbert, 121
Truman, Harry S., 23, 47, 48, 49, 50, 51, 53, 80
Truthout (nonprofit news organization), 341
Tucker, Raymond, 101, 114–15, 116, 118, 119, 130n37
Tultex apparel manufacturer, 319, 326

Uchitelle, Louis, 317
Unemployment: African American, 84–85; compensation, 270; Memphis, 251; postwar Maryland, 79; southern workers and, 319; in textile and apparel industries, 271, 276, 277–78; in Virginia, 326, 33
Unitarian Universalist Veatch Program, 316
UNITE (labor organization), 291

Unite for Dignity for Immigrant Workers Rights (UFD), 291, 303
United Automobile Workers (UAW), 53–54, 116–17, 124, 138, 139, 140, 141, 142, 143, 144, 160, 241, 277
United Brotherhood of Carpenters and Joiners, 21, 29
United for a Fair Economy (Virginia organization), 327, 330, 334
United Food and Commercial Workers (UFCW) Local 1625, 300–301
United Mine Workers of America, 19
United Retail, Wholesale, and Department Store Employees, 104
United Rubber Workers, 241
United States Army, 59
United States Bureau of Labor Statistics, 225, 260, 276
United States Census Bureau, 226
United States Civil Rights Commission, 90
United States Commission on Civil Rights, 154–55
United States Conference of Mayors, 86
United States, Congress, House, Committee on Ways and Means, 263
United States, Congress, Office of Technology Assessment, 260
United States, Congress, Senate, Committee on Labor and Public Welfare, 143
United States, Congress, Senate, Permanent Investigations Committee, 61–62
United States, Congress, Senate, Select Committee on Improper Practices in the Labor or Management Field. *See* McClellan Committee
United States Department of Commerce, 270
United States Department of Defense, 260
United States Department of Justice, 195, 196
United States Equal Employment Opportunity Commission, 76, 139, 247 (table), 248 (table)
United States Fair Employment Practice Committee (1941–1946), 141
United States Federal Bureau of Prisons, 198
United States Federal Reserve Board, 327, 328, 329, 335
United States Immigration and Naturalization Service, 161, 304
United States National War Labor Board, 105
United States Postal Service, employment in, 80–81
United States Veterans Administration, 291
United Steelworkers of America (USA), 33–34, 35, 58
United Transport Service Employees, 104
University of Arkansas School of Law, 56
University of Georgia, 227
University of Maryland, 80
University of Memphis, 253
University of New Hampshire, 319
University of Texas at Austin, 156
University of Virginia, 330
Urban League: Baltimore, 80, 81–82; Little Rock, 59; national, 79
USA Today, 298
U.S. Gypsum Company, 21, 27–28, 35
Utica, N.Y., 25
Utica and Mohawk Cotton Mills, 25

Valle, Francis, 82
Valley, Ala., 274
Valley Workers Assistance Committee (Texas), 153
Vanity Fair apparel manufacturer, 269, 273
Vargas, Zaragosa, 137
Velásquez, Willie, 159, 160
Veracruz, Mexican state, 217, 226
Veterans for Good Government (Arkansas), 56
Vickery, Harry, 35
Vidalia/Vidalia County, Ga., 218, 226
Vietnam War, 139
Vinyard, Vera, 111, 113
Virginia, 11–12; social activism in, 314–41; textile industry in, 266–67; voting patterns, 6
Virginia Business, 318
Virginia Fair Wage Alliance, 332
Virginia.Organizing, 325–26, 331, 335, 338
Virginia Organizing Project (VOP), 314–41
Virginia People's Assembly, 340–41
Virginia State AFL–CIO, 333
Viva Kennedy clubs, 138–39, 141, 149, 150, 159
Voting patterns: in Alabama, 5; in Florida; in Louisiana, 5, 50; in Mississippi, 5, 50; in North Carolina, 6; in Virginia, 6; in Wisconsin, 6
Voting Rights Act of 1965, 5, 148, 236, 257n31

Wages: in carpet industry, 19; in health care industry, 305; in Memphis, 236, 239, 240, 242, 250, 251–52; in Mississippi, 21, 30, 31, 32; in service sector, 323; in southern states, 1, 2, 21, 28–29; in textile industry, 25–26, 266; in Virginia, 326–27, 335
Wall Street Journal, 21
Walmart, 3, 8–10, 227, 244, 275
Walton, Sam, 8, 9
Ward, Eddie James, 191
Warner Robins, Ga., 221
War on Poverty, 78, 84, 86, 146
Washington, D.C., 2
Washington Post, 276
Washington University (St. Louis, Mo.), 114, 121
Watts (Los Angeles, Calif.), rebellion in, 237
Weber, Robert, 111, 112
Weightman, Philip, 55, 56, 62, 71n34
Westbrook, Gordon, 274
West Palm Beach, Fla., 294
WestPoint Stevens, textile manufacturer, 269
Wharram, Andrew, 152
Wharton, A. C., 249
White, Justice Byron, 189
White Citizens' Council (Arkansas), 64
White, Hugh L., 26
Whitfield County, Ga., 219, 220
Whittenton Manufacturing Company, 25–26
Wilder, Douglas, 329
Willacoochee, Ga., 229
Williams, Rev. Harvey, 229
Williams, Michelle, 296
Williams, Stella, 309
Wingate, N. E., 21
Winston-Salem, N.C., postwar labor-liberalism in, 102–3

Wisconsin: protests in, 201, 341; voting patterns in, 6
Witwer, David, 45
Wolfe, Walter, 30
Wolff v. McDonnell, 189–90
Women workers, 3, 7, 8, 32, 76–92, 112–13, 136–37, 158, 239, 245, 246, 261, 272–73
Wood, John, 51
Woods, Henry, 50, 53, 54, 55, 57, 58, 59, 60, 62, 65, 66
Woodward, C. Vann, 1, 2
World Bank, 218
World Trade Organization, 267–68, 269, 270, 324, 328
Wortham, Denise, 335
Wright, Fielding, 29, 49, 50
Wright, Gavin, 1
Wright, Sharon D., 250
Wrinn, Jim, 261
"Writ writers," 189, 190–91, 195, 195–96
Wynne (Texas prison), 195

Xalapa, Mexico, 226

Yonkers, N.Y., 19, 27 , 31
Young Communist League, 156
Youngstown, Ohio, 259, 261
Yung, Katherine, 268

Zagri, Sidney: biography and background, 105; community activism of, 108, 109–10, 111, 112, 114, 120, 121, 124; and International Brotherhood of Teamsters, 123. *See also* Community Stewards Program
Zalauf, Harold, 19
Zamora, Emilio, 137
Zedillo, Ernesto, 225
Zieger, Robert H., 251

WORKING IN THE AMERICAS

Edited by Richard Greenwald, Drew University, and Timothy J. Minchin, LaTrobe University

Working in the Americas is devoted to publishing important works in labor history and working-class studies in the Americas. This series seeks work that uses traditional as well as innovative, interdisciplinary, or transnational approaches. Its focus is the Americas and the lives of its workers.

Florida's Working-Class Past: Current Perspectives on Labor, Race, and Gender from Spanish Florida to the New Immigration, edited by Robert Cassanello and Melanie Shell-Weiss (2008)

The New Economy and the Modern South, by Michael Dennis (2009)

Film Noir, American Workers, and Postwar Hollywood, by Dennis Broe (2009)

Americanization in the States: Immigrant Social Welfare Policy, Citizenship, and National Identity in the United States, 1908–1929, by Christina A. Ziegler-McPherson (2009)

Black Labor Migration in Caribbean Guatemala, 1882–1923, by Frederick Douglass Opie (2009)

Migration and the Transformation of the Southern Workplace since 1945, edited by Robert Cassanello and Colin J. Davis (2009)

American Railroad Labor and the Genesis of the New Deal, 1919–1935, by Jon R. Huibregtse (2010)

Seated by the Sea: The Maritime History of Portland, Maine, and Its Irish Longshoremen, by Michael C. Connolly (2010; first paperback edition, 2011)

Strike! The Radical Insurrections of Ellen Dawson, by David Lee McMullen (2010)

New York Longshoremen: Class and Power on the Docks, by William J. Mello (2010)

Life and Labor in the New New South, edited by Robert H. Zieger (2012)